CARIBBEAN AND THE BAHAMAS

FODOR'S MODERN GUIDES

are compiled, researched, and edited by an international team of travel writers, field correspondents, and editors. The series, which now covers almost the entire globe, was founded by Eugene Fodor in 1936.

OFFICES
New York and London

Fodor's Caribbean and the Bahamas

Caribbean Area Editor: VIRGINIA PUZO

Editor: MARY ANN PALMER. Editorial Associate: JUDITH DE RUBINI. Maps & City Plans: DYNO LOWENSTEIN, XHARDEZ. Drawings: MICHAEL KAPLAN

CARIBBEAN AND THE BAHAMAS 1983

FODOR'S MODERN GUIDES
New York

ISBN 0-679-00904-3 (McKay, Traveltex edition)
ISBN 0-340-32177-6 (Hodder edition)

All the following Guides are current (most of them also in the Hodder and Stoughton British edition.)

CURRENT FODOR'S COUNTRY AND AREA TITLES:

AUSTRALIA, NEW ZEALAND AND SOUTH PACIFIC
AUSTRIA
BELGIUM AND LUXEMBOURG
BERMUDA
BRAZIL
CANADA
CARIBBEAN AND BAHAMAS
CENTRAL AMERICA
EASTERN EUROPE
EGYPT
EUROPE
FRANCE
GERMANY
GREAT BRITAIN
GREECE
HOLLAND
INDIA
IRELAND
ISRAEL
ITALY
JAPAN
JORDAN AND HOLY LAND
KENYA
MEXICO
NORTH AFRICA
PEOPLE'S REPUBLIC OF CHINA
PORTUGAL
SCANDINAVIA
SOUTH AMERICA
SOUTHEAST ASIA
SOVIET UNION
SPAIN
SWITZERLAND
TURKEY

CITY GUIDES:

BEIJING, GUANGZHOU, SHANGHAI
CHICAGO
LONDON
LOS ANGELES
MEXICO CITY AND ACAPULCO
NEW YORK CITY
PARIS
ROME
SAN DIEGO
SAN FRANCISCO
TOKYO
WASHINGTON, D.C.

FODOR'S BUDGET SERIES:

BUDGET BRITAIN
BUDGET CANADA
BUDGET CARIBBEAN
BUDGET EUROPE
BUDGET FRANCE
BUDGET GERMANY
BUDGET ITALY
BUDGET JAPAN
BUDGET MEXICO
BUDGET SPAIN
BUDGET TRAVEL IN AMERICA

USA GUIDES:

ALASKA
CAPE COD
COLORADO
FAR WEST
FLORIDA
HAWAII
NEW ENGLAND
PENNSYLVANIA
SOUTH
USA (in one volume)

MANUFACTURED IN THE UNITED STATES OF AMERICA
10 9 8 7 6 5 4 3 2 1

CONTENTS

EDITORS' FOREWORD

"I saw so many islands that I hardly knew to which I should go first." The year was 1492. The writer, Christopher Columbus. The place: the Caribbean Sea.

The problem of choice remains. So do the golden beaches, the crystal water, the sapphire bays, and blazing blue skies which dazzled Columbus along with "the soil, so beautiful and rich, the mountains, full of trees, so lofty that they seem to reach the sky, the singing nightingales, parrots, birds of a thousand sorts . . ." These marvels, noted in the admiral's journal, are still to be found throughout the Caribbean.

As the cradle of the New World, the Caribbean holds some impressive records. Spanish explorers replenished ships at the thriving port of Santo Domingo, to set out for discoveries to the west (Mexico and Panama) and the south (Venezuela and the coast of South America). Ponce de Leon touched Florida from his base in Puerto Rico; Alexander Hamilton came to the United States from Nevis, by way of St. Croix; tiny Sint Eustatius, known as Statia, was the first foreign power to acknowledge the independence of those United States, when its governor ordered a gun salute to the American flag flying from the "Andrew Doria" as she sailed into port on November 16, 1776. The list of Caribbean firsts is impressive.

The Caribbean is 1,700 miles wide, 700 long. Most of its islands are washed by the Atlantic on the windward side, with rollers pounding in with surf-riding force on the northeastern coasts of many areas, and placid seas (and the best beaches) on the protected western shores. All the islands are swept by the trade winds, that never failing air conditioner which keeps them comfortably cool even in summer. Together with the Bahamas, they share a year-round temperature which fluctuates between 65 and 89 degrees.

* * *

Fodor's Caribbean and the Bahamas has been prepared to help you choose wisely. We have combed the beaches, shopped the shops, checked the hotels, sampled the food and the rum, driven over the roads, and snorkeled and sailed the seas of the Caribbean to bring you the most complete and objective guide possible. If we have missed a good guest house, "a little place where they cook fabulous fish," or anything else between Anguilla and Trinidad, let us in on your discovery.

All comments in this guide, whether favorable or adverse, are based on the editors' personal experience. We feel that the first responsibility of a guide is to inform and protect the reader, rather than to praise indiscriminately. All comments are made in the spirit of constructive criticism and in the hope of stimulating improvements where they are needed.

Although we make a last-minute check just before going to press, much of the information herein is perishable. We cannot, therefore, be responsible for the sudden closing of a restaurant, bankruptcy of a hotel, or bad mood of an otherwise excellent chef, any (or all) of which can make one of our comments out-of-date. We welcome letters from readers whose opinions are at variance with ours (or who agree!), and are always ready to revise our opinions when the situation warrants. In the meantime, the editors assume responsibility for all the judgments in the book.

Send your letters to the editors at one of these addresses: **In the USA,** Fodor's Modern Guides, Two Park Avenue, New York, N.Y. 10016; **in Europe,** Fodor's Modern Guides, 9-10 Market Place, London WIN 7AG, England.

A CAPSULE VIEW OF THE ISLANDS

CHOOSING YOUR PLACE IN THE SUN. We know just how hard choosing a vacation island can be. People say, "What's your favorite place?" The answer has to be, "For what?" And even then, we're not sure that what we like (or are like) on vacation is perfect for you. All of the places covered in this guide have sun—and trade winds; many have mountains; some have deserts; all have plenty of deep blue sea. The Bahamas are included in this book, although they lie in the Atlantic and are not technically part of the Caribbean. However, in this era of independent island communities, there is a natural affiliation between the government of the Bahamas and the islands farther south.

For your preliminary planning, we present the area highlights as we see them, through the Atlantic and Caribbean communities. These highlights are culled from many memorable experiences during constant travels through the area over more than twenty years. We present them with the knowledge that even the best known and most cosmopolitan spots still have some place where you can hide.

Anguilla. Still so British and still so unspoiled. The name means "eel" and describes the eel-shaped small splinter of land just north of St. Martin, and easily reached by plane or boat from that island. Fresh-caught lobster is the "king-of-the-sea" here and the local chefs try to out-do each other in its preparation—not that there are dozens of restaurants, but the few there are, and those at the handful of hotels, more than add to the enjoyment of a visit here. Anguilla has lovely bays and long, quiet beaches, a few villas, and several cottages by the sea. The islanders go out of their way to prove that this is one of the best of the "away-from-it all" islands in the Caribbean. Local fishing boats can be hired for picnics, snorkeling, and even birdwatching on nearby uninhabited islands and cays. Even though cottage colonies and villas are abuilding, tranquility is still the name of the game on this English isle.

Antigua. Although this island achieved full independence in 1981, its British beginnings remain, and its 365 beaches never fail to please. But more than sandy shores, Antigua has been set down in history ever since Admiral Lord Nelson dropped anchor here 200 years ago and the island became headquarters for the British Royal Navy's Caribbean fleet. The restoration of Nelson's Dockyard at English Harbour is the island's major tourist attraction, and is guaranteed to take you back in time as you tour the old Sail Loft, the Paymaster's House, the Engineer's Workshop, and the simple home (now a museum) in which the Admiral lived. Large resort hotels, with full watersports programs, rim the shores around the island. There are two casinos and nightly entertainment at the major properties. In addition, there are dozens of tiny fishing villages to visit, and a rain forest ablaze in all shades of Caribbean greenery.

Aruba. Definitely Dutch, but with a tropical touch, this island is well known for its trade winds that keep their divi-divi trees bent to the prevailing breezes. Actually this island has three different faces–a calm western shore with a golden beach that stretches for seven miles; a rugged east coast where the waves of the Atlantic thunder in across the sands; and an arid interior marked with several varieties of cactus and a fair share of abandoned gold mines. High-rise hotels with gambling casinos and name entertainment hug each other on the Palm Beach strip. During the daytime, the action is on watersports; in the evening Aruba turns into a mini-Las Vegas seaside.

Bahamas. The appeal of these 700 islands ranges from the remote peace of the Out Islands to the frenetic gaming and gambling pleasures of Grand Bahama, Paradise Island and Nassau. There is something for just about any kind of tourist. Excellent fishing, sailing and diving, especially out of Nassau and off the small islands. For those in search of a bargain, there is shopping on Grand Bahama and New Providence. Beaches are best on the Out Islands and many small cays. Although most of the islands are uninhabited, there are more than a dozen that are ready and eager for tourists. And in addition to the islands, the cruising enthusiast can explore over 2000 cays and rocks in the gentle warm waters.

Barbados. This island has been British since the Crown took over in 1625, and in spite of its independence 15 years ago, it can still be called the "Little England of the Caribbean." High tea, cricket, horseguard parades, and police band concerts are as much a part of life here as the cane fields and flying fish. The luxury hotels along the Platinum Coast are among the finest and most expensive in the Caribbean, but there are dozens of other places to stay, with each of them offering their own version of Bajan hospitality. Barbados is also a hub of activity since it serves as the gateway to the islands of the Southern Caribbean.

Bonaire. The second largest, but least populated, of the Dutch "ABC" islands, Bonaire is a heaven, as well as a haven, for birdwatchers, scuba divers, and photographers. Flamingos hide out at the edge of the lake at Goto Meer to the north, and around the salt ponds at the island's southern tip, and more than 100 species of birds thrive at Washington/Slagbaii National Park, the island's huge wilderness preserve. The emphasis here is on relaxation, with long empty beaches and dramatic coves for sunning, swimming, and snorkeling. Divers come here in droves to explore the ocean floor and the undersea wrecks of ships left from centuries ago. Just four hotels, a few restaurants, and little in the way of nightlife other than one disco and a small casino.

British Virgin Islands. These islands, as small and scattered as they are, are *the* islands for sailing–by day, by evening, or by the week. They have been Crown property since 1666, and still fly the Union Jack above the palm trees. There are too many islands to count, but the major landfalls for day-trippers and visiting yachtsmen are Tortola, Virgin Gorda, Jost Van Dyke, and Peter Island. The action revolves around Road Town, Tortola, the capital and headquarters for most yacht rentals, boats for day sails, and excursions to smaller islands with such exotic names as Prickly Pear, Fallen Jerusalem, Scrub, Drake's Bay, and Ginger. There are caves to explore on Norman Island, said to be Robert Louis Stevenson's "Treasure Isle," and bathing pools to wade through amid giant, tumbled boulders on Virgin Gorda. Only 14 of the 60 odd islands, cays, and islets that make up the British Virgin Islands are uninhabited–the rest are sunswept treasures waiting to be found.

The Cayman Islands. These islands are small retreats that are fast becoming known as the top dive sites in the Caribbean. Essentially there are three–Grand Cayman, Cayman Brac, and Little Cayman–and there's more going on beneath the sea around them than on the landfalls above them. Snorkelers swim along with the fish and peer down at the sea gardens, while divers head for the sea floor to discover the black coral reefs and the wrecks of ships that ran aground decades ago. In fact, diving has become so popular here that divers have their own resorts, all of which have instructors on hand, and some of which offer courses in underwater photography. Swimming is ideal along the Seven Mile Beach on Grand Cayman; Cayman Brac is interesting for hiking to its bluff and exploring its caves; and Little Cayman's bonefish flats are a challenge for anglers. Those with an interest in Caribbean conservation will want to visit the Cayman Turtle Farm on Grand Cayman.

Curacao. Uniquely Dutch, right down to the pastel-colored, gabled houses and a pontoon bridge that swings back and forth over Willemstad's St. Anna Bay. One of the most interesting duty-free shopping ports in the Caribbean, with imported items from all over the world. Handsomely tiled pedestrian malls, which are closed to traffic and edged with small sidewalk cafés, make shopping for treasures a pleasure here. Not much in the way of beaches, but long on good restaurants and exciting casinos.

Dominica. Discovered by Columbus, invaded by the French, colonized by the British, and finally independent, the island of Dominica is a real beauty. Its waterfalls (officials claim there are 365 of them) run from fantastic cascades off the mountain peaks to silver strips down into the valleys, while its perennial rains turn its fruits and vegetables into plump treasures that are exported to several nearby islands. Banana plantations flourish, while the verdant lime groves have continued to supply a good part of the world with Rose's Lime Juice ever since that company began doing business here in the Nineteenth Century. Among the attractions on this island, which is always so green it sparkles like a newly cut emerald, are Trafalgar Falls with its extraordinary trio of waterfalls; Boiling Lake, with its volcanic bubbles; and the Botanical Gardens in Roseau, Dominica's capital city. Limited accommodations here, with no property larger than 50 rooms, and nothing at all in the way of nightlife–the accent on this island is its flora, which is magnificent.

Dominican Republic. Formerly called Hispaniola, this is the island where Columbus got his whole family involved. The explorer founded it in 1492; four years later his brother Bartholome became governor; and in 1509 his son Diego was appointed viceroy. Spanish by birth, the Dominican Republic continues to maintain its traditions and its heritage with ongoing restorations of historic buildings throughout the capital city of Santo Domingo. Highlights in the city include the Alcazar (a splendid palace built for Diego Columbus), the restored area called the Atarazana, and the Cathedral of Santa Maria la Menor (the oldest cathedral in the New World). Latest resort attractions are at Puerto Plata on the north coast; at La Romana on the south shore; and near Higuey on the east coast. Speaking Spanish adds to the enjoyment of a visit to this island.

Grenada. Called "The Spice Island of the Caribbean," and justly so, Grenada will make you heady with the aroma of nutmeg, ginger, and cinnamon. Beaches, especially the long white-sand stretch called Grade Anse, are lovely, and the mountain waterfalls are well worth the climb to the top. St. George's, the capital, is small and picturesque, with two harbors of the Carenage to explore and a bustling Market Square for browsing. With the exception of one condominium complex. accommodations are in small inns, either right on the beach, or within easy walking distance. Don't miss a visit to the spice plantation and the nutmeg factory at Gouyave on the northwest coast.

The Grenadines. Governed out of St. Vincent, these 100-plus islands and cays are the best cruising ground in the Caribbean. Resort islands are Bequia, with a few individual inns, Palm Island, Petit St. Vincent, and Mustique. Others of note are Cannouan, Mayreau, Union, and the Tobago Cays. These are still Robinson Crusoe-type places, reached via St. Vincent or Grenada.

Guadeloupe. As French today as it was when the French colonized it in 1635. The only change, and a fascinating one at that, is the language, which has a lilting Creole touch. Restaurants abound on the island, and they too offer a choice of French and Creole fare, or a combination of the two. Actually Guadeloupe is two islands in one, with Grand-Terre (high land) and Basse-Terre (low land) separated by the River Salee. The capital city of Pointe-a-Pitre, terrific restaurants, and the Gosier and St. Francois beach resorts are on Grande-Terre, while the 74,000-acre National Park, with its waterfalls, hiking paths, and cool and languid places to swim, is on Basse-Terre. A knowledge of French will add to your vacation pleasure.

Désirade. Off Guadeloupe and governed in her French family, this island is picturesque and perfect for a one-day excursion.

Marie-Galante. Also in the orbit of Guadeloupe. Boats make the two-hour crossing from the main island's Basse-Terre; small planes dart in from Guadeloupe's Raizet airport. The main attraction is Château Murat, 200 years old and still waiting for discovery.

Iles des Saintes. A cluster of eight small islands and a favorite of Jacques Cousteau for underwater work and with naturalists for their preserve on Terre-de-Haut. The boats from Guadeloupe take little more than an hour; the small planes come from the bigger island's airport. Peace and quiet with great beaches, but nothing fancy.

Haiti. The first Black Republic in the New World, Haiti today is a fascinating blend of Afro/French, complete with pulsating rhythms, voodoo, indigenous paintings, and foods that are French, Creole, and West Indian. Although English is spoken in the large hotels, French is the language of the land. Port-au-Prince, Haiti's capital, throbs with music and personality. Its old Iron Market is a landmark, with dozens of stalls displaying wares and echoing the sounds of the marketeers–it's a must for visitors who want to be in the heart of things and bargain for locally fashioned wood carvings, crafts and paintings. Cap Haitien's remarkable Citadelle in the north is a four-hour drive from Port-au-Prince, or just 40 minutes if you choose to fly. Accommodations range from small inns with lots of character to chic retreats with comparable prices. Good restaurants, nightly entertainment at the major resorts, and two casinos keep things swinging until the early hours.

Jamaica. This island/country is so large, so scenic, and so sophisticated that it is able to offer visitors everything but gambling casinos. Carved through its valleys and along its jagged coasts are lime-green 18-hole championship golf courses that dip and rise around the sea, and twist and turn through the hillsides. Kingston, Jamaica's capital, is a thriving metropolis on the southeast coast, a port city crowded with tourists, local people, and even donkeys vying for position on its narrow shopping streets. The art galleries and Royal Botanical Gardens are the attractions in this area. Montego Bay, to the west, hugs the shore in a series of high-rise hotels, shopping arcades, and steep hills that drop down to sea level and the harbor entrance. Or, if you prefer to cool off in exotic surroundings, climb the rocks to the top of Dunn's River Falls in Ocho Rios, or go rafting on the Rio Grand River in Port Antonio. Other island diversions are horseback riding through the woods into the back country, or trekking toward the top of Blue Mountain, Jamaica's highest point. Keep your eye on Negril as it emerges as the latest "in" spot and expands its "hedonism" concept.

Martinique. Truly French, from its language and cuisine to its pace-setting Club Mediterranee, modern hotels and Air France service, with beaches and watersports and a unique landscape shared only by its French affiliates. Fort-de-France, the capital, is reached by boat across the bay from most of the hotels. Among the tourist attractions here, in addition to watersports and a rousing nightlife, are visits to the birthplace of Napoleon's Josephine at La Pagerie, and hikes to Mt. Pelee, the infamous volcano that erupted in 1902 and destroyed the entire population of the once thriving town St. Pierre.

Montserrat. British-affiliated, but originally settled by the Irish in 1632, Montserrat is still referred to as the "Emerald Isle of the West." It is a green island indeed, and brings visitors to tee off at its Belham River golf course. It's only nine holes, but such a sparkle, that you'll be tempted to go round and round again. Swim at Carr's Bay on the north coast, or visit the volcano called Galway Soufriere. Among the other attractions are the Great Alps waterfall and the small capital city of Plymouth, an island port especially colorful on Saturday, which is market day. Accommodations are in comfortable small hotels and guest houses.

Nevis. St. Kitts' sister island, just 10 minutes away by air, or a one-hour ride across by ferry. A half-dozen plantation houses have been restored to accommodate tourists who come to see what Nevis was like in its heyday. The island became famous for its hot springs, mineral baths, and curative waters that drew European gentry to its Bath Hotel and health spa. The baths overlooked the capital city of Charlestown (just four blocks long), Alexander Hamilton's birthplace. Both the baths and the Hamilton house are in ruins, but plans are afoot to restore them. Black- and white-sand beaches for swimming, but little else to do on this quiet island.

Puerto Rico. Ever since 1508 when Ponce de Leon came through here in search of the Fountain of Youth, the Spanish influence has reigned in architecture, culture, language, and cuisine. San Juan is the hub of the northern Caribbean, with its international airport a beehive of activity, and its harbor usually crowded with cruise ships either steaming in or out. High-rise resort hotels provide the glitter with casinos and lively entertainment until the early hours along the city's northern strip, while a choice of almost 200 restaurants across the island make dining out a constant treat. Check on the Paradores Puertoriquenos, small and delightful country inns in the mountains, for a quiet and memorable look at the interior. There are also top-notch facilities for sports, expecially golf, at the Cerromar and Dorado resorts, and at Palmas del Mar on the southeast coast.

Saba. A tiny, lush and green volcanic Dutch island that rises regally from the sea, with a city called "The Bottom" sitting at the top of its cone-shaped peak. Saba has no beaches, just a few towns and country lanes to explore, and just a handful of spots for overnighting, so most people make a day-trip visit here from St. Martin.

Sint Maarten/St. Martin. Half-Dutch and half-French, this island offers the pleasures of both nations. Gingerbread houses in fretwork designs add a special Victorian touch to Philipsburg on the Dutch side, while the cafés and restaurants in French Marigot are reminiscent of Paris.There are 36 beaches to explore, close to 80 restaurants to sample, and a host of resorts with nightclubs and casinos. You'll find a complete range of watersports here, including jet-skiing, windsurfing, sailing, and scuba diving. Although Dutch and French are still spoken on this dual island, everyone speaks English.

St. Barthélemy. St. Barts, as it is affectionately called, measures just eight square miles, but comes complete with beaches, mountains, and an aura that is old-world French. This island was settled by Norman and Breton fishermen in 1645, and even though it was ceded to Sweden for a time, the only result of that move was naming the capital city Gustavia in honor of the King. The French flavor and language remained, and still does today. Just a half dozen hotels to choose from, but a score of fine restaurants for true Gallic dining. St. Barts is just a ten-minute flight from St. Martin; less than an hour by air from Guadeloupe.

St. Eustatius. Statia, as she is called, offers yet another look at the Caribbean's Netherlands Antilles. Its history is guaranteed to beguile American visitors, since Statia was the first foreign power to recognize the Stars and Stripes with a thunderous official salute from old Fort Oranje in 1776. An extinct volcano called "The Qill" is the island's focal point, with restorations of historic buildings in the works everywhere. This is one of the few islands where there are more donkeys available for touring than there are taxi cabs. Easily reached via a short flight from St. Martin. More places to eat than places to stay, but all small and special.

St. Kitts. A British colony since 1689, and now an Associated State of Great Britain, St. Kitts still boasts of ousting the French and building a fortress atop Brimstone Hill, which today is a bastion so tall, so thick, and so commanding that tourists stand below in awe. The massive fort, called the "Gibraltar of the

West Indies," is the island's major tourist attraction. Running second is its capital, Basseterre, which could be a mini-London, with its Old Court House on Pall Mall Square, its ornate version of "Big Ben," which sounds out the hours, and its "Circus," which is a small version of Piccadilly. The opening of the Royal St. Kitts Hotel and Casino really put this island on the map when it began to attract special "gaming-fun" charter flights. Otherwise, accommodations are in comfortable, small inns on the beach. Watersports are unlimited, with Frigate Bay and Cockelshell Bay top spots for swimming, snorkeling and scuba diving.

St. Lucia. Now independent, but for decades a battleground between the British and the French, St. Lucians speak English, but maintain their French heritage with a Gallic-Creole *patois* that can be almost unrecognizable. The island is shaped like a leaf, 27 miles long and 14 miles across at its widest point. Twin volcanic peaks called Petit Piton and Gros Piton rise dramatically above its coastline, and sulphur springs with supposed curative powers bubble nearby. The main attraction for tourists to this island is a chance to visit the world's only "walk in" volcano. There is fine selection of resort properties, with options that range from 18 rooms in a lovely West Indian home to 250 rooms in a busy and very active hotel. Most of the traditional action is in the middle and northern quarter, north of Castries, the capital, and noteworthy Marigot harbor, the gateway to spectacular sailing.

St. Vincent. This British-affiliated, 18-mile long island has long been a gracious host to visting yachtsmen who come through for provisions en route to the islands in the south. Kingstown, the capital, is a thriving little community, replete with 19th century houses, churches, and unusual gardens founded more than 200 years ago. St. Vincent is often referred to as the "Breadfruit Isle," since it was here that Captain Bligh, of "Mutiny on the Bounty" fame, introduced the tree to the Caribbean with the seeds he brought across from Tahiti. There's a volcano to climb, but the emphasis here is on watersports, with sailing the major attraction. Fine selection of small hotels and personality inns.

Tobago. Trinidad's sister island, just a short air-hop away. But as Trinidad sizzles, Tobago sleeps. History has it that this was the setting for Daniel Defoe's account of Robinson Crusoe's sojourn on a nameless Caribbean island "within sight of Trinidad." He referred to it as a tropic retreat "Bathed in the currents of the Orinoco." Tobago is green with cocoa and coconut plantations; its fishing villages dot the scallopped coastline, and steep horse trails run down to Man O' War Bay, one of the finest natural harbors in the Caribbean. Just off its northern tip is Bird of Paradise Island, the only place outside New Guinea where these beautiful birds exist in their natural state. Nice beaches, good snorkeling at Buccoo Reef offshore, golf at the 18-hole Mt. Irvine course. By way of contrast, Tobago is as quiet and as retiring as Trinidad is palpitating and electrifying.

Trinidad. The Land of Calypso teems with the rhythms of serveral lands, expecially during pre-Lenten Carnival, It's an island that is constantly in tune to the beat of the drums and resonant sounds of the steel pans that began here. Port-of-Spain, the capital city, is one of the most vibrant and busy ports in the Caribbean, and its residents come from at least a dozen different countries and ethnic backgrounds. English-speaking since the island was ceded to the British in 1802, but strictly Trinidadian otherwise. The beaches are an hour or more from the city, but worth the trip, especially for a swim at glorious Maracas Bay.

The Turks and Caicos Islands. Southeast of the Bahamas, these quiet islands form a tropical string through the Atlantic and along the fringes of the Caribbean. Although there are dozens of cays, there are just five islands equipped to handle tourists. Any of them (Grand Turk, North Caicos, South Caicos, Pine Cay, and Providenciales) are ideal for the traveler in search of beauty and seclusion. There are a few tennis courts, but the main attraction here is the water. Extensive beaches, exceptional underwater life, sport fishing, scuba diving, snorkeling, and simply sunbathing is about all there is here–but you couldn't ask for more. Accommodations are in small and special hotels and inns.

U.S. Virgin Islands. These islands are as different as a tropical trio can get, with St. Croix offering gracious island living and a fantastic underwater trail offshore; St. Thomas a busy port and the number one cruise ship destination, with a duty-free port offering the most varied selection of imported items in the Caribbean; and St. John a quiet respite for campers and nature lovers. But all three have a common denominator–watersports, which include everything from renting your own sailboat and finding a hidden cove for swimming and snorkeling to diving to the depths to explore the exotic technicolor coral reefs.

FACTS AT YOUR FINGERTIPS

WHAT'S WHERE. The myriad islands and countries in the vast expanse of the Atlantic-Caribbean region represent some of the most fascinating holiday opportunities available for the shopper, water sports enthusiast, gambler, golfer, beach-lover, and botanist. To make your island-hopping easier, our Caribbean coverage lists the islands that are within its confines alphabetically.

The islands follow an *S* curve from the United States to the shores of South America, with a final flourish from east to west along that shore. To see exactly where you'll be, consult our Caribbean map at the end of the book. To begin, curve southwest to the Bahamas, an independent country since July 1973, and a member of the British Commonwealth, firmly committed to maintaining and improving the vacation attractions of its many islands. We then head eastward to the four large islands that make up the Greater Antilles. These are Cuba, a Spanish-speaking independent republic gradually re-attracting the tourist trade; Jamaica, independent since 1962, with a tourist department that puts about $10 million per year into improving and presenting its vacation product; Hispaniola; and Puerto Rico. The large island of Hispaniola is shared by two independent countries: the Black, French-speaking Republic of Haiti, which occupies the western third of the island; and the Dominican Republic, whose official language is Spanish. These two countries, Johnnies-come-lately to the present tourism surge, offer some of the area's most attractive culture and accommodations. An hour's flight eastward across the Mona Channel will take you to Spanish-speaking Puerto Rico, the Commonwealth connected with the

U.S. that has pulled itself up by its "Operation Bootstrap" to become a vital vacation and business destination.

A short hop from Puerto Rico takes you to the Virgin Islands, three American ones (St. Thomas, St. John, and St. Croix) and a host of British Virgins (Tortola, Virgin Gorda, Peter Island among them) and the start of the Lesser Antilles.

This archipelago of the Lesser Antilles sweeps east and south in its own United Nations of Leeward and Windward Islands including Anguilla (British), St. Martin (French and Dutch), St. Barthélemy (French), Saba and St. Eustatius (Dutch), St. Kitts and Nevis (British), Antigua, Montserrat (British), Guadeloupe, Désirade, Marie-Galante, and Iles des Saintes (French), and Dominica. The British members of this group are known as the British Leewards; the Dutch islands are the Dutch Windwards (because they lie to windward of the main Dutch Caribbean possessions, the ABC islands of Aruba, Bonaire, and Curaçao).

Guadeloupe and her Gallic satellites speak and live French with a soft Creole accent as does Martinique, the "top" island of the Windwards, which now continue the Antillean arc southward. Guadeloupe and Martinique are full *départements* of France, with representatives in the French Parliament and all the benefits of French citizens in metropolitan France.

Continuing south of Martinique, you come to St. Lucia, once an Associated State of Great Britain and now independent, with a developing tourism infrastructure that awaits the birth of large-scale tourism; and St. Vincent and its Grenadines, havens for those of us who have island fever and like our islands friendly, beach-rimmed, and worthy of exploration. Grenada, at the southern end of the several small dots of the Grenadines, took the giant step to independence in February 1974, with full fireworks, flag raisings, and some local shenanigans that received big play in U.S. papers but were taken in West Indian stride in the new nation.

Barbados lies about 90 miles east of St. Vincent, out of the main current of Caribbean isles, but assuming the role of leader for the southern Caribbean islands. Most British of the islands in character and appearance, Barbados became independent in late 1966 and continues to build its tourism and its small industries within the British Commonwealth.

One hour southwest of Barbados by plane is Tobago, beach-rimmed resort part of the two-island nation of Trinidad-Tobago. Trinidad, rich in oil and asphalt, throbs with calypso and steel band music at carnival time and with the problems of a new (since 1962) nation for the rest of the year.

From here, the S swings to the coast of South America, to oil-rich Venezuela and refinery-rich Curaçao and Aruba, which, along with Bonaire and the three northern relatives (Sint Maarten, Saba, St. Eustatius) comprise the important group of the Netherlands Antilles. There can be no mistaking the European allegiance of these Dutch islands; they are Holland-in-the-sun, with food, language, architecture, and customs from the homeland.

WHAT WILL IT COST?

Since we are covering more than 35 islands and dozens of off-shore cays, we have studied each area individually and given a projected daily estimate for *two* persons within each island section. This daily rate includes hotel accommodations, 3 meals, tips, taxes, service charges, and a one-day tour of the island, either by taxi or rental car.

For an average Caribbean holiday, figure that you'll pay anywhere from $95 to $230 per day for *two* people in a double room, with all the above included, in season. The *most* expensive tropical landfalls are Aruba, Barbados, the Bahama Islands, St. Martin, and Curaçao. The *least* expensive are the smaller retreats, such as Saba, Montserrat, Anguilla, and Bonaire.

But bear in mind that once the *off-season* begins (from April 15 through Dec. 14), you can save anywhere from 20% to 40% per day. Also check out the all-year-round package/charter plans (see *Tour Operators* later in this section, or in individual chapters, and contact them for week-long holidays at substantial savings).

WHEN TO GO. The Caribbean "season" has traditionally been a winter one, usually extending from Dec. 15 to April 14. The winter months are the most fashionable, the most expensive, and the most popular for cruising or lazing on the beaches, far from the icy North, and most hotels are heavily booked at this time. You have to make your reservations two or three months in advance for the very best places. Hotel prices are at their highest during the winter months; the 20-40% drop in rates for "summer" (after April 15) is the chief advantage of "off season" summer travel.

There are others. The flamboyant flowering trees are at their height of glory in summer, and so are most of the flowers and shrubs of the West Indies. Many cruises operate year around—with special value rates in summer months. The water is clearer for snorkeling, smoother in May, June, and July for sailing in the Bahamas, the Virgin Islands, the Grenadines. In addition, you have a much wider choice of hotel accommodations, an atmosphere which is generally less "social," less dressy, more relaxed and, in some areas such as Barbados where there is a Crop-Over Festival in June and Antigua where Carnival takes place in Aug., special events.

The Caribbean climate, air-conditioned by the trade winds, approaches the ideal of perpetual June. Average year-round temperature for the region is 78-85°. The extremes of temperature are 65° low, 95° high, but as everyone knows, it isn't the heat, but the humidity that makes you suffer, especially when the two go hand in hand. You can count on downtown shopping areas being hot at midday any time of the year. Air-conditioning provides some respite; but from our years of Caribbean travels, we think it makes matters worse. You're cool while you stay inside—and smother when you step out into the sunshine! Stay near beaches, where water and trade winds can keep you cool, and shop early or late in the day.

High places can be cool, particularly when the Christmas winds hit Caribbean peaks (they come in late November and last through Jan.), but a sweater is sufficient for warmth from the trade winds (if not always from the air-conditioning).

Since most Caribbean islands are mountainous (notable exceptions being the Caymans, Aruba, Bonaire, and Curaçao), the altitude always offers an escape from the latitude. When it's 90° in the sun in Port-au-Prince, Haiti, it's a good 10° cooler on the heights of Kenscoff above the capital. Kingston (Jamaica), Port of Spain (Trinidad), and Fort-de-France (Martinique) are three cities which swelter in summer, but climb 1000 feet or so and everything is fine.

What about rainy seasons and hurricanes? You don't have to worry about either. Hurricanes can sweep through, but the warning service is now so highly developed that planes can change course in midflight to avoid any disturbances, and everything can be battened down ashore in plenty of time to ride out the storm. The rainy season, which usually refers to the fall months, consists mostly of brief showers interspersed with sunshine. You can watch the clouds come over, feel the rain, and remain on your lounge chair for the sun to dry you off. A spell of overcast days is "unusual weather," as everyone will gladly tell you.

Generally speaking, there's more planned entertainment in the winter months. The peak of local excitement on many islands, most notably Trinidad, St. Vincent, and the French West Indies, is Carnival. The Trinidad explosion ranks not far behind the gaiety of Rio, and most of the islands make a gala pageant of their pre-Lenten celebrations. Carnival in the U.S. Virgin Islands' St. Thomas is the last full week of April and has become somewhat subdued in recent seasons. Other special events are covered in complete lists available through the government tourist offices listed under "Events and Holidays" in each chapter.

HOW TO GO

All the fishnets of the Caribbean combined could hardly equal the intricate web of air and sea routes spread out over these islands. The sea routes that were the only links until 20 or so years ago have now been supplemented, and even superseded, by the speedier links by air. Almost every type of transportation is in the Caribbean, from the most modern 747 jets and L-1011 "wide-bodies" to single-engine props and sea planes and on to cruise ships and island-built sloops.

Below, we describe several package-tour programs and list regularly scheduled air and sea transportation along with a variety of cruise combinations by both air and sea. When you arrive at your island vacation "home," you'll soon find out about a lot more local air and sea links via small charter planes and interisland motor and sail boats. Many of them can make interesting day excursions, such as going to Saba, Anguilla, Statia or St. Barts from Sint Maarten; to St. Thomas, Tortola, or St. Croix from Puerto Rico; to Dominica from Guadeloupe or Martinique; to Isles des Saintes from Guadeloupe; to Bequia from St. Vincent; and so on through an endless list of get-away places to be reached from the place you've gotten to.

PACKAGE TOURS

First, what is a package tour, that term so freely used in travel parlance and in your hometown newspaper advertisements? Your travel agent has the responsibility for selling the world. Obviously, no one can be an expert on everywhere. Although he has probably been to the Caribbean, he probably does not know every nook and cranny, every palm-lined beach and West Indian inn. He therefore, may turn to a "wholesaler," or tour operator, for advice and information for *your* travel plans. The wholesaler does not sell to the public (although he may have a retail agency that operates under another name and shares office space), but he travels constantly through the Caribbean working on volume business for specific properties and destinations. Without further comments on those details, let's look at what that means to *you.*

Because of the "large group" rates the wholesaler is able to negotiate with hotels (usually the large hotels), he is able to sell to the travel agent at a rate that allows for the travel agent to add his commission and sell the room and holiday package to you at a rate lower than what you might pay for all the component parts individually. But watch out! Read the small print carefully. Contrary to some of the real "deals" on European airfare-hotel packages, those in the Caribbean often include "extras" you don't care about. Also, a specialty of the Caribbean area is small inns and guest houses. With a couple of exceptions, wholesalers do not use the small places. They get their best deals with the big chain hotels where there are a lot of rooms to fill.

Several airlines that service the Caribbean offer Tour Basing Fares (ITX), which means that when you pre-purchase an advertised air-tour package you qualify for the ITX fare, which is often the least expensive.

TOUR OPERATORS

Wholesale tour operators sell their product through retail travel agents. Several excellent firms specialize in the Caribbean, offering package holidays with special airfares, which put that considerable expense in its lowest possible range.

Those wholesalers who are authorized to operate on each of the islands are listed in the *Practical Information* section within each island chapter. Their addresses are given here and may be contacted through your local travel agent. For further information about wholesale tour operators, write to the Caribbean Tourism Association, 20 E. 46 St., New York, N.Y. 10017.

From the United States:

ADVENTURE TOURS
3653 Offutt Road
Randallstown, Md. 21133

A.O.T. TOURS
212-55 26th Ave.
Bayside, N.Y. 11360

AQUAVENTURE, INTERNATIONAL
P.O. Box 127
Gedney Station
White Plains, N.Y. 10605

ALKEN GROUP TOURS
1661 Nostrand Ave.
Brooklyn, N.Y. 11226

BAHAMA ISLAND TOURS
255 Alhambra Circle
Coral Gables, Fla. 33134

BONAIRE TOURS, INC.
P.O. Box 775
Morgan, N.J. 00879

BUTLER TRAVELS
32 First St.
St. Petersburg, Fla. 33731

CAREFREE/DAVID TRAVELS
49 West 57th St.
New York, N.Y. 10019

CARIBBEAN HOLIDAYS
711 Third Ave.
New York, N.Y. 10017

CARIBBEAN VACATION CENTER
77 West Washington Street
Chicago, Ill. 60602

CAVALCADE TOURS
254 West 31st St.
New York, N.Y. 10001

CLUB MEDITERRANEE, INC.
40 West 57th Street
New York, N.Y. 10019

FLYFAIRE, INC.
300 East 42nd St.
New York, N.Y. 10017

GOGO TOURS (LIB/GO)
P.O. Box 457
Paramus, N.J. 07652

GWV TRAVEL
1320 Centre Street
Newton Center, Mass. 02159

HALEY CORP.
711 Third Avenue
New York, N.Y. 10017

JAMAICA TRAVEL CENTER
5433 North Lincoln Ave.
Chicago, Ill. 60625

PATHFINDER TOURS
200 S.E. First Street
Miami, Fla. 33131

PLAYTIME VACATIONS
20950 Center Ridge Road
Cleveland, Ohio 44116

RED & BLUE TOURS
1518 Walnut St.
Philadelphia, Pa. 19102

SOJOURN TOURS
1220 Broadway
New York, N.Y. 10001

SUNBURST HOLIDAYS
4779 Broadway
New York, N.Y. 10034

THOMSON VACATIONS
401 North Michigan Ave.
Chicago, Ill. 60611

TOUR-TREC
49 Greenwich St.
Greenwich, Conn. 06830

TRANS NATIONAL TRAVEL
2 Charlesgate West
Boston, Mass. 02215

TRAVEL CENTER TOURS
5413 North Lincoln Ave.
Chicago, Ill. 60625

UNDERWATER ADVENTURE TO
5915 West Irving Park Road
Chicago, Ill. 60644

VALUE VACATIONS
151 Main St.
Winsted, Conn. 06831

From Canada

FAIRWAY HOLIDAYS
74 Victoria Street, Suite 708
Toronto, Ont. M5C 2N9

HOLIDAY HOUSE
25 Adelaide St. E., Suite 1313
Toronto, Ont. M5C 1H7

MIRABELLE TOURS ATLANTIC
Halifax Shopping Centre, Suite 103
Halifax, N.S. B3L 2H8, Canada

SKYLARK HOLIDAYS, LTD.
74 Victoria St.
Toronto, Ont. M4Y 2A7

SUNFLIGHT HOLIDAYS
1470 Don Mills Road
Don Mills, Ontario M3B 2X9

TOURS MONT ROYAL
6767 Cote des Neiges
Suite 505
Montreal, P.Q. H3S 2T6

UNITOURS, LTD.
3080 Yonge Street
Toronto, Ont. M4N 3N1

UTL HOLIDAY TOURS
22 College Street
Toronto, Ont. M5G 1Y6

WAYFARER HOLIDAYS, LTD.
235 Yorkland Blvd.
Suite 610
Willowdale, Ont. M2J 4W9

From Great Britain

ALTA HOLIDAYS
200 Buckingham Palace Rd.
London SW1

INGHAMS
329 Putney Bridge Rd.
London, SW15

KUONI TRAVEL
33 Maddox St.
London W1

RANKIN-KUHN & CO., LTD.
19 Queen St., Mayfair
London WLX 8AL

SOVEREIGN HOLIDAYS
P.O. Box 410, West London Terminal
Cromwell Rd.
London SW7

THOMAS COOK, LTD.
45 Berkeley Street
London W1A 1EB

THE AIRWAYS. The major air gateways from the U.S. to the Caribbean are New York, Washington-Baltimore, Philadelphia, Atlanta, Miami, New Orleans, Houston, Chicago, Los Angeles and San Francisco. From Canada, Montreal and Toronto are the points of departure. From Europe, the chief getaway points are London, Frankfurt and Lisbon.

American Airlines and *Eastern Airlines* are the primary carriers offering service from the northeastern U.S. to points in the Caribbean.

Air Canada offers direct flights from Toronto and Montreal to a number of Caribbean islands.

From Europe, *Iberia, British Airways* and *Air France* service the area.

In addition, a number of national airlines–*ALM (Dutch Antillean Airlines), Air Jamaica, British West Indian Airways,* and *Dominicana*–have flights from either North America or Europe.

This list is, of course, far from exhaustive. It is not only major airlines flying Boeing 707's and their like that service the Caribbean. There are also smaller companies with smaller jets and a host of single-engine small craft that dart like birds from landfall to landfall. *Leeward Islands Air Transport,* known as

LIAT, threads several islands together out of Antigua. *Prinair,* the national airline of Puerto Rico, ties San Juan to several islands; and *Windward Islands Airways* links St. Martin with Saba, Statia, St. Barts, St. Kitts, St. Thomas, Nevis, and Anguilla. The *Virgin Islands Seaplane Shuttle* planes dart across the water to link the U.S. Virgin Islands together.

Once you have decided where you want to go, ask your local travel agent or the appropriate tourist office for the best and least expensive way to get there. A qualified travel agent will know which airlines go where; he or she will also be able to explain the variations in rates for day and hour of departure and the ever-increasing array of excursion fares and group fares with land arrangements included.

CRUISING THE CARIBBEAN

The main reason to cruise the Caribbean is to visit a multiplicity of islands and sample the flavor of each with minimal effort. This book has been designed to accommodate visitors who come by ship as well as those who arrive by air (see "A Day On Your Own" in individual island chapters). The leisurely pace, the meals, the entertainment and activities, the elegance, the beauty of the powder-blue water combine to make a cruise a very special kind of vacation.

Having your floating "home" carry you in the dark of night from one Caribbean port to the next is certainly travel with maximum convenience and comfort.

Recent seasons have seen a crop of newer, smaller ships, many designed especially for Caribbean cruising–with less than the one-to-one staff to passenger ratio of the luxury cruising ships of the past. Most Caribbean cruises are aboard one-class ships, with more casual dress replacing the traditional black tie formality. (But check for attire on your cruise. The top of the lot still retain the traditional elegance.)

Ships have been sailing the Caribbean for more than 400 years. Today's fleet includes luxury ships, adding the Caribbean on round-the-world and other long cruises, as well as short and special cruises out of Caribbean ports, bargain cruises with luxuries (and cost) cut to the minimum, and the essential freighter services, where there are some berths for passengers. There are at least 300 passenger ships sailing the Caribbean all year round and a given month (January, for example) may see 40 cruises sailing from Florida. Because the trade winds limit the summer temperature rise to about 10°, summer cruises have become increasingly popular.

The number and variety of cruises grow each year. For a consolidated, complete list, write to the Caribbean Tourism Association, 20 East 46 St., Room 1201, New York, N.Y. 10017. If you are single, dieting, want to stop smoking, interested in theater, or would like to meet people living in the ports of call, special-interest cruises may be your choice. Cruise lines, like airlines, have group rates. And any group, large or small, may travel as a party on almost any scheduled cruise, arrange meeting rooms for seminars, screen special films, or set up whatever convention facility it needs.

After you've done some of your own research (the Sunday newspapers are one source, then the library, your friends, and the cruise lines listed below), see your travel agent for specific advice and booking. Remember that who your fellow passengers are will make a big difference in how you enjoy your holiday, and that while your travel agent cannot predict exactly who they will be he may be able to advise you about which lines and cruises are for what kinds of people.

Ship accommodations, all meals (maybe 5 a day!), the voyage itself, entertainment, cruise staff services, and landing and embarkation facilities such as tender service, are included in the price. Figure about $120 per day for a cruise. Not included in your fare are transportation to and from port of embarkation (unless it is a fly/cruise package); wines and liquors consumed on board; laundry, shore excursions, port taxes, personal services such as beauty shop or barber appointments, and tips. As to shore costs, excursions are optional. You can spend a whole day on almost any island, swim and have lunch ashore, for $25 or so, if you wish. Equally, you can have a good day and spend *nothing.*

How to Choose Cabins

If price is important, consider that you will spend very little time in your cabin and although the less expensive cabins are the smaller, inside ones, you have full run of the ship and all its facilities just as much as anyone staying in the most luxurious suites. (If you can afford it, there's nothing like the pampering in the luxury accommodations.) Almost every cabin available on every ship has a toilet and a shower. You pay extra for a bathtub. And note that many "single" cabins, especially on older ships, have an upper berth as well as the lower, available for a second person in the room, at *minimum* cost, so you can take a "better" cabin–i.e., a larger one–and pay minimum for the extra person, averaging out close to minimum rates for both. (Double cabins often have a similar possibility for a third and fourth person.) Aim for midship locations (less rolling and pitching) and remember that proximity to service areas such as kitchens or elevators may make for extra noise. Study the deck plan available for all ships, before you book. (Most ships have passenger elevators, if you are concerned about steps.)

Tipping

Most ship's personnel who serve you directly depend on tips for their livelihood. (Even the vaunted no-tipping policy of *Holland America* is misleading to a degree; their personnel do seem to depend on tips, however surreptitiously.) Tipping is not all that expensive or troublesome. The following rules of thumb are suggestions:

Cabin steward–$5.00 per person per day (he shares with cabin boy, etc.)

Dining room waiter–same (he shares with busboy).

Deck steward–$3 per person per trip.

Head dining room steward (maitre d'hotel)–$10, half on departure. Some may refuse a tip.

Wine steward–15% of the wine bill.

Bartender–tip as you would at home.

Most tips should be given on the last evening of your trip, with two exceptions: the bartender and the maitre d'. If you are concerned about a "good" table, the maitre d' can be of service to you only at the beginning of the trip.

Tipping on a ship is a little different from other places; you will be seeing your stewards each day and often develop a personal kind of relationship with them. As a matter of fact, you ought to, because you find out a lot that way.

If the cruise is longer than about 14 days, the daily tip average may be a little less, and half might be given after one week; the crew can use the money in port.

Seating Arrangements and People in General

Some lines accept table reservations and assign seats when you book passage; others want you to make arrangements when you are aboard. Table size varies from 2 to about 8 or 10. If you like to sit alone, say so right away. If you are traveling in a group, be sure that the maitre d'hotel or others making the assignments know your preference. If you don't like your table companions, with whom you will be eating at least two meals a day every day, let the maitre d' know right away so you can be moved–with a polite "I just found some old friends aboard" excuse. If you wait too long, it will be embarrassing.

One of the good reasons for cruising is to meet people. The ship is a very special kind of place, and all those stories about shipboard romances have a strong basis in fact. Beautiful clothes, dim lights, continuing dance music, soft air, champagne corks popping, the sound of water slipping past, work a kind of magic.

Even for less romantic souls, something happens. When you are with people on a ship for a week or two, their personalities become clear, and the shipboard characters emerge quickly. Everyone gets to know the best dancer, the clown, the seasoned traveler. And the usual social inhibitions which keep people apart, often unwillingly, in a hotel, dissolve in shipboard conviviality. After all, you're there in the middle of the great sea together–there is *possible* an unusual kind of closeness which no hotel, anchored as it is on solid land, can provide. But in communion with the sea there is also possible a quiet privacy, usually found on land only if you retreat behind a closed door. Shipboard life can provide as close, or as impersonal, an encounter as you like.

Weather and Health

If you are worried about seasickness, stop worrying. Most ships have excellent stabilizers, and medicines are available to stop the green death before it begins. The older remedies, such as *Dramamine,* often have side effects, such as making people sleepy, but the newer ones, chiefly meclizine, marketed over the counter under trade names like *Bonine,* don't do that. Check with your doctor. If you're really doubtful, take one (following directions) before you even board the ship, and continue during the cruise, *before* you feel anything. If you somehow wait too long and start to feel queasy, get to the ship's doctor right away; some of the newer shots are almost miraculous in their effectiveness.

One warning: when the weather is warmer than you're used to, you may lose a lot of body moisture. Be careful not to become dehydrated–drink plenty of liquids.

Departure Ports and Shore Excursions

More and more ships leave for Caribbean cruises from Port Everglades or Miami, San Juan and Los Angeles; fewer these days from New York. Shorter cruises usually leave from southern ports; long and/or special cruises tend to begin in New York. A number depart from Puerto Rico or other islands. The advantage is that you miss the 1½ days of cold weather you'd have in the winter if you left from New York.

If you choose to fly south to board the ship, investigate the variety of fly-cruise plans, whereby a portion of your airfare is absorbed by the cruise line or is completely free.

Almost all cruise ships maintain a shore excursion booking office on board. These are optional and are usually sold individually. If you are the kind of person who wants minimal responsibility for arrangements, but still wants to see the islands, consider such excursions. But if you like more freedom and want to explore on your own, or want to interact with the people on the island rather than the other passengers, write to car rental agencies and reserve a car (well in advance; at least a month) or ask your travel agent to book your car for the days you want. Or, hire a car and driver for the day, but be sure to fix the price, itinerary and hours *before* you enter the car. And don't believe a driver who tries to sell you his services and says that there are no rental cars available. Get that information only from a local tourist office (usually located near your landing point) or from a uniformed tourist guide.

If driving, be sure to read up on the island first (see our sections on "Exploring" and "A Day On Your Own" in individual chapter listings).

What to Wear

Clothing aboard ship is like that seen at any elegant landbound resort. Even with the trend toward informality, bring a dinner jacket or several long dresses. Dressing up is part of the fun of cruising especially for the Captain's Dinner and the Captain's Cocktail Party. Even on less formal evenings, passengers change for dinner. Suits or sports jackets (with shirts and ties) are expected on men, and while turtlenecks may be generally accepted, there is a tendency for maitre d's to grimace.

During the day, resortwear is fine. Sports shirts, shorts, slacks, sweaters, sandals and sneakers are all acceptable (but no bathing suits in the public rooms!). You will need comfortable clothes for shore visits. Very brief clothing worn on public streets is not considered proper, even though on beaches less-than-minimum may be acceptable.

Daily Schedule and Available Services

The daily activities are usually announced the night before, by a printed schedule; these include lectures by experts in such fields as law, psychology and finance; descriptive lectures about the islands by the cruise director; arts and crafts; scheduled and unscheduled bridge games; dance lessons (free daily); a library; games at poolside; shuffleboard; ping-pong; a gym; a sauna; language lessons (depending on the nationality of the ship's crew); movies (features, often first-run, sometimes non-English).

There is usually a photographer on board. The ship's drug store is stocked with such sundries as toothpaste, shoelaces, etc., but, of course, bring your own prescription medications. Usually there are facilities for religious observances. Ships' gift shops often can compete with land shops in price. Beauty and barber shops are on board. Make your appointments early in the cruise. Laundry and dry cleaning facilities are often available, but try to stick to wash-and-wear when you can.

FLY-AND-CRUISE

Fly-and-cruise tours are a varied lot and are sold under a baffling variety of names although all boil down to the same thing: flying to meet the cruise. We'll start by saying that almost every cruise line now has some version of the fly-cruise plan. You'll have to read the small print carefully to find out which is the best for you. As a general rule, the pattern is for cruise lines to offer a "deal" on your airfare from the major airport nearest to your hometown to the cruise departure point. The total price you will pay for the air-plus-cruise will be less than you would pay if *you* bought a round trip air ticket plus the cruise. And cruise lines frequently have representatives on hand to meet your in-bound flights and transport you to the pier.

NOTE: The more competitive the season, the better the air credits become. You'll have a choice of everything that floats in and stops around Caribbean ports, with the exception of the month of January when the Round-the-World cruises begin.

BAHAMA CRUISE LINE, INC. (61 Broadway, New York, N.Y. 10006) has the *Veracruz,* which sails from Tampa, Fla., on weekly cruises to the Mexican Riviera during fall through spring, with ports of call at Cancún, Cozumel, and Key West, continuing through April. The ship then makes New York its home base for Eastern Canada cruises through early fall.

CHANDRIS, INC. (666 Fifth Avenue, New York, N.Y. 10019) has the *Britanis* and the *Victoria* in winter and spring service out of San Juan to the Caribbean. Two different itineraries are featured. Weekly cruises are every Monday. The weekly trips may be combined for a two-week journey. This line is credited with originating the air/sea concept more than a decade ago.

CARNIVAL CRUISE LINES, INC. (3915 Biscayne Blvd., Miami, Fla. 33137). The *TSS Mardi Gras* and the *Carnivale* sail on 7-day cruises every Sunday from Miami. Departing Saturdays from Miami is the *Festivale* and the *Tropicale.* Fly-cruise programs are also available from more than 35 U.S. cities, and from Toronto and Montreal.

COMMODORE CRUISE LINE LTD. (1015 North America Way, Miami, Fla. 33132). The *Bohème* has 7-day cruises sailing Sat. year-round from Miami to Puerto Plata (D.R.), St. Thomas, San Juan, and Cap Haitien. New fly-cruise programs feature add-on fares from 59 U.S. cities.

COSTA CRUISES (733 Third Avenue, N.Y. 10017). The line has two ships operating out of South Florida and the *Carla C, World Renaissance* and *Danae* cruising for 7 days out of San Juan. The *Amerikanis* sails from Miami to the Bahamas on 3- and 4-day schedules.

CUNARD LINE LTD. (555 Fifth Ave., New York, N.Y. 10017). The line's *Countess* offers week-long cruises out of San Juan stopping at La Guaira (Caracas), Grenada, Barbados, St. Lucia, and St. Thomas. Passengers may take advantage of the line's La Toc Hotel in St. Lucia and the Paradise Beach in Barbados on air/land/sea holidays. For details of the many variations, contact the line's office. The line's *Queen Elizabeth 2* or *QE2* calls at Caribbean ports year round out of New York. The line's *Cunard Princess* sails every Saturday (except June–mid-September) from San Juan to Tortola, Martinique, Antigua, St. Maarten and St. Thomas.

HOLLAND AMERICA CRUISES (Two Pennsylvania Plaza, New York, N.Y. 10121). Dutch hospitality, fine food and service on all of this line's ships. The *Veendam* sails every Sat. from New York to Bermuda, late May to mid-Oct. Features 3½ days in Hamilton, Bermuda. Ship goes into Caribbean cruise service out of Tampa rest of year. The *Rotterdam* sails late April and late fall on 7-day Caribbean cruises from Ft. Lauderdale. The line has added the *Volendam* which makes weekly trips to St. George's and Hamilton in Bermuda. The *Rotterdam* sails on its annual 83-day world cruise from New York, Ft. Lauderdale, and Los Angeles in mid-January.

HOME LINES (One World Trade Center, Suite 3969, New York, N.Y. 10048). The *SS Oceanic* switches to Fort Lauderdale, Fla., late Dec. to mid-March to the Caribbean. The ship returns to New York in spring for trips to Nassau and Bermuda, continuing through early November. The *Atlantic* sails weekly from New York to Bermuda and will sail in winter from Florida to the Caribbean.

NORWEGIAN AMERICAN CRUISES (29 Broadway, New York, N.Y. 10006). Scandinavian hospitality is tops on this line's luxury ship, *Vistafjord,* on regular service out of Port Everglades, with Faresaver plans available from most U.S. cities. *Sagafjord,* sails to the Caribbean in winter, and to Alaska and Eastern Canada in summer.

NORWEGIAN CARIBBEAN LINES (One Biscayne Tower, Miami, Fla. 33131). The line's 4 ships, *MS Southward, MS Starward, MS Skyward* and the *Norway* (former *France*) sail from Miami. The line offers 7-day cruises. Air/sea packages offered to more than 21 major cities involve 7 airlines. The *Southward* makes 7-day cruises to Cozumel, Grand Cayman Island, Ocho Rios and the Bahama Out Islands. The *Starward* calls at Nassau, San Juan, St. Thomas, and the Bahama Out Islands. The *Norway* calls at St. Thomas and a Bahama Out Island. The line's fifth ship, the *Sunward II* (the former *Cunard Adventurer*), sails from Miami, Fridays, for a three-day trip to Nassau and Chub Cay/Berry Islands and Mondays for four days to George Town, Great Exuma, Nassau and Chub Cay/Berry Islands. The trips, "Bahamarama Cruises," will cruise year-round to the Out Islands.

PAQUET CRUISES (1370 Avenue of the Americas, New York, N.Y. 10019). Without peer, for perfection and innovative cruising, the line continues to be a popular cruise choice. The *MS Mermoz,* based in San Juan from December into April, is designed specifically for cruising, offering gourmet cuisine and maximum comfort. The line's *Dolphin* sails year-round fom Miami on 3- and 4-day cruises to Nassau and Freeport. The newly acquired *Rhapsody* has 7-day winter cruises from Miami to the western Caribbean.

PRINCESS CRUISES (2029 Century Park East, Los Angeles, Calif. 90067). Cruises to the Caribbean aboard the *Island Princess,* about 14 days, departing from Los Angeles with return trip from San Juan. Cruises are from early Oct. to early May. The *Sun Princess* joins the circuit from mid-Dec. to early May. The ship has alternating Caribbean itineraries. Out of Los Angeles, the ship visits Acapulco, transits the Panama Canal, calls at Cartagena, Aruba, Martinique and St. Thomas. Out of San Juan, ports include St. Thomas, La Guaira (Caracas), Curacao, transits Panama Canal, calls at Acapulco, Cabo San Lucas and ends in Los Angeles. The *Pacific Princess* will do the same cruises in the fall. A variety of air/sea programs are featured.

ROYAL CARIBBEAN CRUISE LINE, INC. (903 So. America Way, Miami, Fla. 33132). *MS Song of Norway* and the *Nordic Prince* were cut in half and new mid-sections added in a Finnish shipyard. The *Song of Norway* sails from Miami year-round on weekly cruises to Puerto Plata (D.R.), San Juan and St. Thomas. The *Sun Viking* also sails on weekly western Caribbean cruises with ports-of-call at Jamaica, Cozumel, and Grand Cayman Island. The *Nordic Prince* makes 14-day Caribbean trips, sailing every other Saturday from Miami. A new ship, *Song of America,* will be sailing weekly from Miami, bound for Nassau, San Juan, and St. Thomas.

ROYAL CRUISE LINE (One Maritime Plaza, San Francisco, Calif. 94111) has the *Golden Odyssey,* which sails on 12-day cruises during winter, alternating between San Juan and Acapulco, transiting the Panama Canal and stopping at several Caribbean ports westbound. Additionally, the ship sails from San Juan on 10-day Caribbean and South American cruises. The cost of the trips includes roundtrip airfare from Los Angeles, with add-on airfares from various other U.S. cities.

ROYAL VIKING LINE (One Embarcadero Center, San Francisco, Calif. 94111; 630 Fifth Ave., New York, N.Y. 10020). The line's luxury ship, the *Royal Viking Sea,* entered service in 1974, giving the line 3 top luxury ships. The others are the *Royal Viking Sky* and the *Royal Viking Star.* All 3 luxury ships sail from both San Francisco and Los Angeles. The line offers "Trans-Canal Cruises." East Coast passengers can join the cruises in Pt. Everglades. The ships cruise from West to East Coast and vice versa. Eastbound ports of call from California include Mazatlan, Puerto Vallarta, Canal Zone, Cartagena, Curaçao, Pt. Everglades.

SCANDINAVIAN WORLD CRUISES (1080 Port Blvd., Miami, Fla. 33132) has daily car-ferry service from Miami to Grand Bahama Island. The ferry is the *Scandinavian Sun* (formerly Commodore's *Caribe).* The *MS Scandinavian Sea,* which sails daily from Port Canaveral, has weekend cruises to Grand Bahama Island. A new ship, the *Scandinavia,* has car-ferry service between New York and Grand Bahama Island.

SITMAR CRUISES (10100 Santa Monica Blvd., Los Angeles, Calif. 90067). A European crew aboard the *TSS Fairwind,* cruising from Pt. Everglades, on trips, ranging from 7 to 14 days. Ports of call for the 10- and 11-day trips vary but include St. Maarten, Curaçao, Aruba, St. Lucia, Antigua, Martinique, St. Thomas and La Guaira (Caracas). The *Fairwind,* with some exceptions, cruises year-round from Port Everglades.

SUN LINE CRUISES (One Rockefeller Plaza, Suite 315, New York, N.Y. 10020). The luxury *TSS Stella Solaris* cruises from Galveston (Texas) on new 11- and 21-day trips. The *Stella Oceanis* sails from San Juan. The longer cruises reach as far as South America, in addition to the Caribbean and Mexico ports touched on the 10-day cruises from Curacao. Special air/sea programs are available from all points in the U.S.

Among cruises out of Europe to the Caribbean are:

P & O/PRINCESS CRUISES (2029 Century Park East, Los Angeles, Calif. 90067). In spring, the *Oriana* sails from Sydney, Australia to the West Coast, Mexico, through the Canal, calling at Nassau, Port Everglades (Fla.) and Bermuda and then to Southampton. The cruise is sold in segments as air/sea programs. The ship returns in fall from Southampton, calling at the same ports en route to Australia. The *Sea Princess* has a 90-day Round-the-World cruise sailing from Southampton with ports-of-call at Madeira, Bermuda, Port Everglades, Curaçao, Panama Canal, Acapulco, and San Francisco, among others.

YACHTING. For sailors, private yacht cruising is becoming more and more popular, with the accent on leisure, informality, and freedom of movement. A wide variety of sailing yachts and motor vessels of all types, sizes, and degrees of luxury are available.

We carry further information on yachting and island-by-island charter in our sailing section, A Sun-Swept Playground, and in individual chapters.

Among the larger operators are:

CARIBBEAN SAILING YACHTS, LTD. (P.O. Box 491, Tenafly, N.J. 07670 (800) 631-1593) has about 100 boats available for bareboat (without a crew) charter, based in Tortola in the British Virgin Islands, and St. Vincent. Fully equipped and provisioned (except for liquor, beer, and soft drinks). Summer bareboat rate for a party of 4, plus provisioning on Carib 34. Winter rates are higher, of course, but this firm makes a point of keeping its prices competitive. For the inexperienced, a Qualification Course is available and recommended. Also offering a Sail 'n' Learn cruise out of St. Vincent through the Grenadines for 10 days.

NICHOLSON YACHT CHARTERS (9 Chauncy St., Cambridge, Mass. 02138, (617) 661-8174. P.O. Box 103, St. John's, Antigua, W.I.). Handles about 80 charter yachts from Antigua to Grenada and the Virgin Islands. Winter rates are available upon request. There's a 20% discount in the spring and summer.

STEVENS YACHTS OF ANNAPOLIS (P.O. Box 129, Stevensville, Md. 21666; (800) 638-7044. Offers a variety of sailing ships, accommodating from 2 to 8 persons for one week or more. Includes ketch, sloop, North Sea Trawler, and cutters of varying sizes. Full provisions available. Crewed and bareboat charters with a fleet of 65 yachts. Departures are from Stevens' St. Lucia marina at Rodney Bay just North of Castries and from St. Martin.

TORTOLA YACHT CHARTERS (One Hale Lane, Darien, Conn. 06820, (800) 243-9936. With a base at Nanny Cay, Tortola, in the British Virgins, this firm sends its fleet of 30 sloops out on bare-boat charters. Boats featured are C&C 36s, C&C 39s, brand-new Endeavour 40s, and a tri-cabin C&C 49. Special week-long charter rates for summer include airfare from New York.

WINDJAMMER "BAREFOOT" CRUISES (P.O. Box 120, Miami Beach, Fla. 33139). 6-, 10-, 11-, or 13-day cruises with island stop excursions on a variety of air-conditioned ships through the Bahamas or the Caribbean. Ships range in size from 176 to 282 ft., and carry from 70 to 126 passengers, who may be asked to help with the sailing. Costs depend on cabin choice and length of trip. The *Yankee Trader,* a schooner, sails for Aruba and Curaçao. The 282-ft. barquentine *Fantome* cruises the Bahama Banks; the 208-ft. *Flying Cloud,* the British Virgin Islands; the 248-ft. *Polynesia,* the Leeward and Windward Islands; the 197-ft. schooner *Yankee Clipper,* the Grenadines and Antilles.

WORLD YACHT ENTERPRISES, LTD. (14 West 55th St., New York, N.Y. 10019; (212) 246-4811) offers fully-crewed charter yachts to the Virgin Islands. All sail from St. Thomas, U.S. Virgin Islands with recommended itineraries. However, passengers may plan their own routes. A sailboat for two, including crew, costs about $1,200 per week and covers all meals and an open bar. A charter for eight persons would cost $1,500 per person for a week, or a total of $12,000.

There are dozens of other firms offering yacht charters in the Caribbean and the Bahamas. Among them are:

ABACO BAHAMAS CHARTERS, LTD. Hope Town, Abaco. Fleet of 13 CSY 44s accommodates 2 or 3 couples. Also has 10 smaller boats from 28 to 35 feet. Reservations through Lynn Ruck, 10905 Cowgill Place, Middletown, Ky. 40243. (502) 245-9428.

ANN-WALLIS WHITE CHARTERS, 626 First St., Annapolis, Md. 21403. (301) 263-0399. Charters available in the British Virgin Islands, the Grenadines and Haiti.

"HARVEY GAMAGE"—the only U.S. registered 34-passenger schooner of its type cruising the Virgin Islands on weekly cruises. Also two schooners for up to 20 passengers each. Reservations and information from Dirigo Cruises, 39 Waterside Lane, Clinton, Ct. 06413. (203) 669-7068; or from Ocean Enterprises, St. Thomas, U.S.V.I. 00801.

SPICE ISLAND CHARTERS. Charters out of St. George's, Grenada, W.I. Contact them at 245 Queens Way West, Toronto, Ont. M5E 1M2. (416) 365-1950.

SPUR OF THE MOMENT CHARTERS. Crewed and bareboat fleets in the Caribbean. 1896 Leavenworth, San Francisco, Ca. 94108. (415) 885-0929.

THE MOORINGS, LTD. Sailing charters, bare-boat 39- to 50-foot, crewed 50- to 60-foot ketches and sloops. Dockside apartments. Road Town, Tortola, B.V.I., Marigot Bay, or Box 24459, New Orleans, La. 70184. (800) 535-7289.

WEST INDIES YACHTS. Sailing charters, 32 to 43 feet, plus bare-boats. Maya Cove, Tortola, B.V.I. Or 2190 S.E. 17th St., Fort Lauderdale, Fl. 33316. (800) 327-2290.

WHITNEY VIRGIN ISLANDS CHARTERS, INC. 120 crewed yachts in the Caribbean. Sail and power 37 feet to 120 feet. Write 2650 Lakeview Ave., Suite 3809 CWG, Chicago, Il. 60614. (312) 929-8989; 521 Fifth Ave., New York, N.Y. 10017; (212) 953-1111; (800) 223-1426.

European sources for charter opportunities on Caribbean yachts are:

CARIBBEAN SAILING YACHTS (c/o Weald House, Pluckley, Kent, TN27 OSN). Operating as the British base for the U.S. firm discussed above, this office can give full details on the CYS programs out of St. Vincent and the British Virgin Islands (Tortola).

HALSEY MARINE LTD. (22 Boston Place, London W1, England). Special airfare inclusive rates are available, in conjunction with some 100 yachts cruising the Caribbean, beginning and terminating at the most popular sailing ports (Antigua, St. Lucia, St. Vincent, Barbados, etc.).

HOLIDAY BOAT YACHTS (Berne, Switzerland). As agent for CSY, the firm has their listings as well as specific, larger yachts in several of the other islands such as Antigua, St. Lucia, and elsewhere. Holidays for European Yacht Clubs on a group basis are a feature.

VOILE VOYAGES (Paris, France). Operating as the agent for Caribbean Sailing Yachts in France, the firm has details on CSY programs, but also on listings out of Guadeloupe, Martinique, and the other islands of the French West Indies. Cost-saving holidays are worked out with Air France low Paris-F.W.I. airfares.

RENTING A HOME—A WAY TO KEEP THE COSTS DOWN. While Caribbean luxury hotel prices continue to skyrocket, thanks in part to the high costs of importing food and of labor union demands, many people are turning to apartment and villa rental, helped along by a number of reliable firms. Your basic cost is clearly defined, and the extras can include (but don't always have to) maid service, a cook, gardener, and babysitters. Buying food can be done by your cook, or you can go with her to the local markets and learn how it's done in the land of no supermarkets.

When you rent, be sure you know exactly what the bedrooms are. Often one may be a bed-sitting room, or a maid's room which may not be as luxurious as you expect. If possible, have a friend go see the property first, to make sure everything works and that the place and the location are what you expect. Or better yet, spend a day of your hotel vacation to look into the rapidly increasing list of apartments and villas for next year. Nothing can be more infuriating than to expect a quiet beach only to find that you can touch the cottage next door and that all the neighbors have their radios and TV on the patio, and cricket commentaries and steel bands ring out loudly through most of the day—and night.

As a general rule, your quietest, most Robinson Crusoe vacations can be found in the British Virgins, on St. John in the U.S.V.I., and through the Grenadines on such islands as Bequia, Mustique, and Union Island. Private homes on Nevis, Montserrat, and some of the other lesser knowns have a lot to offer in the way of island-quiet, and even a popular resort island like Jamaica has its out-of-the-way places.

Put yourself in the hands of a reliable firm—a listing is available through most of the government tourist offices—and spell out your specific wants to them: the ages of your children or the special demands of the couples you are vacationing with; your likes and dislikes. The more information you give to the agent, the better he/she can match you to the facilities.

One of the most active firms in the Caribbean is *Caribbean Home Rentals,* also known as *Villas International;* contact P.O. Box 710, Palm Beach, Fla. 33480.

Others to contact are *At Home Abroad,* 405 E. 56th St., New York, N.Y. 10022, with villas and houses in Europe and the Caribbean. The firm usually rents for a week or more and charges a $35 registration fee for photographs and information about properties.

Holiday Homes, St. John, U.S.V.I. has a selection of private homes which it oversees during the owner's absence. They range from hillside cottages to handsome clifftop dwellings with 3-bedroom suites. Rates run $50 daily for two guests; $20 daily for each additional guest during the winter season. Contact "Sis" Frank, Holiday Homes of St. John, P.O. Box 40, Cruz Bay, St. John, U.S.V.I. 00830.

For Jamaica, contact *Jamaica Association of Villas and Apartments,* 200 Park Ave. Room 229, New York, N.Y. 10017.

Jamaica has the best organized program insofar as governments are concerned, with its *Jamaica Association of Villas and Apartments* (JAVA), with printed brochures and full information about a host of places around the island, from luxury spots on the north shore to small apartments and condominiums. Special off-season and shoulder season rates are worth checking into; the places are the same, but the demand is less, and you can pick up a home for a couple of weeks at a bargain rate.

The Cayman Islands Department of Tourism, 250 Catalonia Ave., Suite 604, Coral Gables, Fla. 33134, publishes a catalogue of cottages, apartments and villas for rent, with maps, photographs and complete details.

The *Tobago Cottage Owners' Association* puts together a list, with complete details, of rental properties around that island. The list is available through the Tourist Board offices.

SOURCES OF INFORMATION. The fountainhead of information on the Caribbean is the Caribbean Tourism Association, 20 E. 46 St., New York, N.Y. 10017, and the Eastern Caribbean Tourist Association, 220 E. 42 St., New York, N.Y. 10017. They can supply you with news of the latest developments for places in the Caribbean, particularly for those areas that do not maintain their own offices in the U.S. Areas with offices in New York City and Florida (see individual island sections for others):

U.S. Addresses

Antigua Tourist Board, 610 Fifth Ave., Suite 311, New York N.Y. 10020.
Aruba Tourist Bureau, 1270 Avenue of the Americas, New York, N.Y. 10020.
Bahamas Tourist Offices, 30 Rockefeller Plaza, New York, N.Y. 10020.
Barbados Board of Tourism, 800 Second Ave., New York, N.Y. 10017.
Bonaire Information Office, 1466 Broadway, Suite 903, New York, N.Y. 10036
British Virgin Islands Tourist Board, c/o J. S. Fones, Inc., 515 Madison Ave., New York, N.Y. 10022.
Cayman Islands Department of Tourism, 250 Catalonia Ave., Suite 604, Coral Gables, Fla. 33134.
Curaçao Tourist Board, 685 Fifth Ave., New York, N.Y. 10022.
Dominican Republic Tourist Information Center, 485 Madison Ave., New York, N.Y. 10022.
French West Indies Tourist Board, 610 Fifth Ave., New York, N.Y. 10020.
Grenada Tourist Office, 141 East 44th St., New York, N.Y. 10017.
Haiti Govt. Tourist Bureau, Rockefeller Center, 1270 Avenue of the Americas, New York, N.Y. 10020.
Jamaica Tourist Board, 866 Second Ave., New York, N.Y. 10017.
Puerto Rico Tourism Development Co., 1290 Ave. of Americas, New York, N.Y. 10019.
St. Lucia Tourist Board, 41 East 42nd St., New York, N.Y. 10017.
St. Maarten, Saba and St. Eustatius Information Office, 25 West 39th St., New York, N.Y. 10018.
Trinidad & Tobago Tourist Board, 400 Madison Ave., New York, N.Y. 10017.
Turks and Caicos Islands Tourist Board, 4470 Northwest 79th Ave., Miami, Fla. 33166.
U.S. Virgin Islands Tourist Office, 1270 Avenue of the Americas, New York, N.Y. 10020.

Canada Addresses

Antigua Department of Tourism, 60 St. Clair St. E., Toronto, Ont. M4T 1N5.
Bahama Islands Tourist Office, 85 Richmond St. W., Toronto, Ont. M5H 2C9.
Barbados Board of Tourism, 11 King St. W., Toronto, Ont. M5H 1A3.
Bonaire Tourist Information, c/o Travel Representations, 67 Yonge St., Suite 828, Toronto, Ont. M5E 1J8.
British Virgin Islands Information Service, 801 York Mills Rd., Suite 201, Don Mills, Ont. M3B 1X7, Canada.
Cayman Islands Department of Tourism, 11 Adelaide St., W., Toronto, Ont. M5H 1L9.
Eastern Caribbean Tourist Association (Antigua, Montserrat, Nevis, St. Kitts, St. Lucia, St. Vincent & The Grenadines). Place de Ville, Suite 1701, 112 Kent St., Ottawa, Ont. K1P 5P2.

French Government Tourist Office (Guadeloupe, Martinique, St. Barthelmy, St. Martin), 1840 West Sherbrooke, Montreal, P.Q. H3H 1E4; 372 Bay St., Toronto, Ont. M5H 2W9.
Grenada High Commission, 280 Albert St., Ottawa, Ont., K1P 5G8, Canada.
Haitian Government Tourist Office, 44 Fundy, Place Bonaventure, Montreal, P.Q. H5A 1A9.
Jamaica Tourist Board, 2221 Yonge St., Suite 507, Toronto, Ont. M4S 2B4.
Puerto Rico Tourism Co., 10 King St. E., Toronto, Ont. M5C 1C3.
St. Lucia Tourist Board, 151 Bloor St. W., Toronto, Ont.
St. Martin, Saba and St. Eustatius Information Office, 243 Ellerslie Ave., Willowdale, Toronto, Ont. M2N 1Y5.
Trinidad & Tobago Tourist Board, 145 King St. W., Toronto, Ont. M5H 1J8.
Turks & Caicos Islands, 111 Queen St. E., Toronto, Ont. M5C 1F2.
U.S. Virgin Islands, c/o R.B. Smith Travel Marketing Consultants, 11 Adelaide St. W., Suite 406, Toronto, Ont. M5H 1L9.

U.K. Addresses

Antigua Tourist Board, 15 Thayer St., London SW1.
Bahama Islands Tourist Office, 23 Old Bond St., London W1X 4PQ.
Barbados Board of Tourism, 6 Upper Belgrave St., London SW1 X8AZ.
Cayman Islands Department of Tourism, 48 Albermarle St., London W1X 4AR.
Eastern Caribbean Tourist Association (Antigua, the Grenadines, Montserrat, St. Lucia, St. Vincent), 200 Buckingham Palace Rd., London SW1W 9TJ.
French Government Tourist Office (Guadeloupe, Martinique, St. Barthelmy, St. Martin), 178 Piccadilly, London W1V 0AL.
Jamaica Tourist Board, Jamaica House, 50 St. James St., London SW1A 1JT.
Trinidad and Tobago Tourist Board, 20 Lower Regent St., London SW1Y 4PH.
U.S. Virgin Islands, c/o Travel Services, Ltd., 70 High St., Epsom, Surrey KT19 8BD.
West India Committee (British Virgin Islands, Nevis, St. Kitts, Turks & Caicos), 48 Albermarle St., London W1.

SPECIAL BEFORE-YOU-GO NOTES

OFFICIAL ENTRY DOCUMENTATION. You will find specific entry requirements under "Passports, Visas" within each island section. However, in order to familiarize you with the legal requirements and exactly what they mean, read below and proceed accordingly.

Proof of Citizenship. The best form of proof of citizenship is a passport. Many Caribbean destinations will accept an expired passport, birth certificate or voter's registration card from U.S. and Canadian citizens, but require valid passports of all other visitors. (Note: Although some islands will permit entry with your U.S. driver's license if a photograph is attached, the U.S. government will not accept this as your proof of citizenship upon your return.)

Visas. Visas are only issued to holders of valid passports. They must be secured through an embassy or consulate of the country that requires them for entry.

Tourist Cards. Some countries require these in addition to proof of citizenship. The cards are issued by travel agencies and at airline ticket counters for a small fee.

Airline Tickets. All Caribbean islands require that you have a return or ongoing ticket.

Money. Some islands require that you have sufficient funds to sustain you during your visit.

Health Certificates. Some places require a vaccination certificate, so get that scratch as soon as possible and have it duly recorded by your doctor on the International Health Certificate which your agent, air, or ship carrier will procure for you. Stash this in your purse or wallet. It's a handy, in fact, a necessary, part of your travel baggage. You can, of course, have the smallpox vaccination certified on a doctor's letterhead or a plain piece of paper by Public Health Authorities. The date of inoculation must be within 3 years of the time the certificate is used or you have to submit to inoculation on the spot, a big waste of time. Specific travel document requirements are listed in the text of this guide under each country. Local conditions can change quickly, so inquire at your nearest U.S. Public Health Service clinic or your state's Department of Health as to the latest recommendations.

PACKING. The smart traveler usually packs light, anyway, even though airline baggage now goes by size rather than weight. You may check two pieces; the dimensions of the first piece must add up to no more than 62 inches (158 c.m.) and the second to no more than 55 inches (102 c.m.). You may carry on pieces totaling no more than 45 inches (115 c.m.) and no more than 9 x 14 x 22 inches so they can fit under the seats. Charges for extra pieces of baggage are based upon the price of your ticket (minimum of $7 per piece). Local, inter-island carriers still use the weight system and will charge overweight by the pound if you are carrying in excess of 44 pounds. When baggage exceeds the minimum allowance and includes sporting equipment, the articles will generally be subject to specified excess baggage charges, applicable to the particular airline involved. Drip dry summer clothes are a boon, but remember that nylon can be hot in the tropics. The dacron cotton dries just as fast and just as smooth and is pleasantly cool to wear. Cotton knits stay comparatively wrinkle-free. It can get cool in the hill towns of the tropics after the sun goes down especially in winter months. Better take along at least one sweater or medium warm jacket. If you are going to a posh resort, you may want tropical dinner clothes but few places insist upon them these days. The emphasis everywhere is on comfortable and casual. In general, it's safe to plan your wardrobe as you would for summer at home, with more bathing suits.

WHAT TO WEAR. The question to ask is "Why are you going?" If the answer is for a convention or business meeting, the clothing situation seems to turn into a kind of fashion parade. There is usually a game of "one up-manship" among women, who wear colorful, long dresses or flowing lounge wear in evening and as little as possible on the beach at daytime. Men sport colorful jackets and other resort wear, most appropriately seen in luxury spots in Florida.

However, the convention group is unique in the Caribbean these days. Without question, most of the hotels prefer comfortable, non-showy evening wear. As new nations are gaining independence, local clothing styles have emerged. They are usually chic (often elegant) understated-but-fashionable dresses for women and the *guyabera, kereba, shirt-jac,* or whatever it is called on the island you happen to be visiting, for men, Whatever it *is* called, it is a safari-jacket with short sleeves, often worn with matching pants. It is what your island hosts will probably wear when they go out for an evening. Most men will be comfortable in a plain-colored jacket, with tie: neat, but not too formal.

Exceptions to this are enclaves of resort life such as Caneel Bay on St. John, a few properties in Jamaica as well as some of the St. James' coast places on the protected west coast of Barbados and a handful of other spots where the resort life thrives.

The young nations–and the young people–have set the trend for Caribbean holiday wear: casual, comfortable and carefree. Jeans, when they are neat, can go almost anywhere, with a T-shirt or regular shirt. Very few places will require men to wear a jacket and tie, although both are appropriate for meetings with government officials–at least until they tell you to take both off.

Bare-back dresses and decolletage on women in day time are sometimes offensive to local folk in the villages and towns, especially in the Latin-oriented countries and in the less touristed islands. Nothing at all goes well on almost any beach in the French West Indies and an occasional nudist beach (or cruise) elsewhere. Topless sunbathing is the fashion at even the poshest resorts in the French West Indies, although it is not sanctioned (or encouraged) on other islands.

As a general rule for Caribbean travel, take much less than you think you will need. The trend these days is to concentrate on you as a person–not you as a clothes horse. And, should you need some special dress or jacket, chances are the local tailor can sew one up for you.

CUSTOMS REGULATIONS. *Arriving.* The islands and countries to which you are going welcome tourists, and customs formalities are simple. Unless otherwise specified under the individual countries, you can bring in anything for your personal use.

Returning. If you are a resident of the U.S. you can import $300 worth of purchases duty-free, providing you have been outside of the U.S. for 48 hours and not already used this exemption within 30 days. Every member of a family is entitled to this same exemption, regardless of age, and a family's exemptions may be pooled. Infants and children get the same exemptions as adults, except for alcoholic beverages and tobacco. Puerto Rico counts as American soil, so don't let a stopover there invalidate your 48-hour exemption privilege. The Virgin Islands' free-port status exempts them from this restriction. Your exemptions include 1 quart of liquor per adult 21 years of age or older (1 gallon, U.S. Virgin Islands) and 100 cigars (non-Cuban). According to the law, the allowance of $300 is based on retail valuation, not wholesale as in the past. In the case of articles brought back from the U.S. Virgin Islands, the allowance is $600, of which not more than $300 may be acquired outside those islands. Your purchases may either be declared and mailed ahead or carried with you.

Unsolicited gifts of less than $25 value ($40 from the U.S. Virgin Islands) may be sent into the U.S. duty-free. Not more than one gift may be sent to the same person on the same day, and liquor, perfumes, and tobacco are not included in this category. Packages should be marked: "Gift, value less than $25." These gifts do not reduce your $300 exemption.

Canadian residents who have been out of their country for at least one week may import $150 worth of purchases duty-free if they have not used this exemption within the previous year. Unsolicited gift parcels sent back to Canada may be worth up to $25.

Citizens of the U.K may import the following goods duty-free: 200 cigarettes or 100 cigarillos or 50 cigars or 250 grams of tobacco; plus one liter of alcohol of more than 38.8% proof, or 2 liters of alcohol not more than 38.8% proof, or 2 liters of fortified or sparkling wine and 2 liters of still table wine; plus 50 grams of perfume and ¼ liter of toilet water; plus other goods to the value of £28.

MONEY. As a general rule, you get more for your money if you change it to the local currency. A March 1976 "request" by the Jamaican Government, however, insists that visitors pay in U.S. or Canadian dollars (to shore up dwindling foreign reserves).

Warning! *Be sure* you ask, if the price is quoted in dollars, *whose* dollars. As of this writing, the E.C. (Eastern Caribbean) dollar is worth about half the U.S. and many Caribbean folk will happily (and silently) let you pay in the harder currency! *Because of the recent erratic fluctuations of the dollar and other currencies, we strongly recommend that you recheck rates prior to your departure.*

TIPPING. A number of Caribbean hotels have adopted that excellent European habit of adding a service charge to your bill. A few hotels are still on that wonderful, old-fashioned 10% arrangement too, something that Europe and America have long since forgotten. Throughout the West Indies, however, you tip 15% in most restaurants. In luxurious hotels, night clubs, and restaurants the expectation is 12 to 15% of the bill. Don't forget the maids. Give the maid $1 a day for a stay of 3 or 4 days, $5 if you stay a week.

The important thing to remember in tipping is the human relationship involved. Tip what you feel you can afford for services received and give the money as a friendly gesture with a "Thank you for your help." A tip given in this way does more for international good will and the human soul than any amount of money thrown down with a grumpy or disdainful attitude.

TIME. Most Caribbean countries are in the same time zone as the U.S. East Coast's Eastern Daylight Savings Time. For Barbados, add 1 hour; for Haiti, the Dominican Republic and the Cayman Islands, subtract 1 hour.

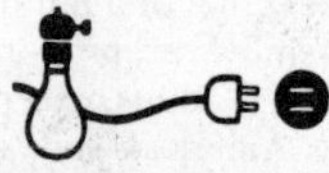

ELECTRIC CURRENT. 110 to 120 volts A.C. is the general rule throughout the Caribbean and the Bahamas. Here are the exceptions: St. Kitts, St. Lucia, St. Vincent, and Grenada, all of which have 230 volts A.C. Antigua has both 110 A.C. and 220 D.C. The French West Indies have 110 volt alternating current, but they use European plugs, so you will need a converter plug there for your razor, traveling iron, or other electric appliance.

AIRPORT DEPARTURE TAXES. Refer to "Taxes and Other Charges" in individual island chapters.

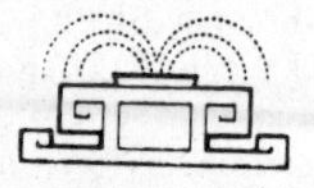

WATER AND MILK. Whenever there is a question about the local water, you will find bottled water in your hotel room and available in the dining room. Otherwise you can assume that the tap water, and certainly the water in the carafes in your room, is potable. If you are heading into remote regions, go armed with a supply of *Halazone,* a small pill available in most drugstores. It may make the water taste funny, but it renders it potable. The milk situation has improved as communications and nutrition campaigns have also. Fresh milk is available in the more developed Caribbean countries, but it may not be available everywhere and it is usually expensive. Certainly you will have no problem on Barbados, Puerto Rico, the U.S.V.I., major centers in Jamaica, and other places that have known tourists and affluence. It may be a problem in rural areas of Guadeloupe, Martinique and the other, smaller French islands, Haiti, rural Trinidad, Tobago, and Dominica. To be on the safe side, travel with powdered or canned milk if you are traveling with small children.

HEALTH. Hospital care has improved greatly in all the better known Caribbean destinations and, should you need a doctor, your hotel can easily direct you to the nearest clinic, hospital, and doctor. If you are staying somewhere else, the big tourist hotels are good sources for a doctor who speaks English. If you have a health problem, be sure to consult your hometown doctor about the possible effects of the sun, heat, and special foods. Take your records with you should you need them. The same precautions apply in the Caribbean as in other places: a second pair of prescription eye glasses, extra medicine if there is some you usually take, and any special potions and salves that you might not be likely to find "on location." Although it is possible to get doctors to some of the remote cays of the Grenadines, and the hinterland of Dominica, as well as to get yourself out, these are not the best places to head if you have a health problem.

The *I.A.M.A.T.* (Intern'l Assoc. for Medical Assistance to Travelers) provides a directory of approved English-speaking doctors who have had postgraduate training in the U.S., Canada, or Gt. Britain. Membership is free, and the scheme is world-wide, with several Caribbean countries participating. An office call is $15; house or hotel calls cost $20; Sundays and holidays the charge is $25. For information apply in the U.S. to IAMAT, Suite 5620, 350 Fifth Ave., New York, N.Y. 10001; in Canada, 123 Edward Street, Suite 725, Toronto, Ontario M5G 1E2; in Europe, 17 Gotthardstrasse, 6300 Zug, Switzerland. A similar service is provided by *Intermedic,* 777 Third Ave., New York, N.Y. 10017, but there is an initial charge of $6 per person, or $10 per family. *IAMAT* has the more extensive network of member physicians and clinics; *Intermedic* is affiliated with Carte Blanche.

Special shots are not required for most Caribbean travel. We have noted the exceptions when they occur in the individual chapters. It is wise to have your tetanus shot up-to-date, however, when you are traveling to areas where you will be barefoot much of the time. And during 1980 yellow fever inoculations were recommended particularly for Trinidad and Tobago, but equally for other islands that might require them of travelers coming from that country.

Watch out for the sun! Even tried and true Caribbeanists can (and do) get scorched after years of travel through the area. We can vouch for that. Even people who are not normally bothered by strong sun should head into this area with:

A long-sleeved shirt, a hat, and long pants or a beach wrap. These are essential for a day on a boat, but are also advisable for midday at the beach.

Some sun block lotion for nose, ears, and other sensitive areas such as eyelids, ankles, etc.

Plenty of sun lotion. Bring your supply from home if you are cost conscious. On-location prices are top dollar, responding to a captive audience. Bring also: plenty of after-sunning skin cream (even for the men). There's nothing worse than ruining your vacation because you've gotten too much sun the first day or two—and we see that happen all the time!

Food. Food preparation and facilities for storing have improved so much in recent years that there's little to think about with the local food, except whether you want to try some unknown dishes or not. Some items to avoid, however, are mayonnaise in the hot sun (check beachside buffets, and picnics you've taken from the hotel for your day excursion), less-than-fresh-fish (not a problem in many places where they catch it and cook it while you watch), and some of the fresh fruits that may be new to you and therefore hard on your system.

Local berries, herbs, etc., should be pursued with caution. Ask. The very attractive, shiny-leaved Manchineel tree, which lines many beaches and can be found on most islands, is highly poisonous. Even the water from its leaves after a rain can make you break out in a rash, its sap can cause blisters and temporary blindness, a nibble of the crabapple like fruit can cause throat contractions which can be fatal. Avoid it–and any other plant until you've checked with someone in the know. (Oleander, Poinsettia, and many other beautiful plants and trees are also highly poisonous.)

Bugs and snakes and the omnipresent "no see 'ums": The tropics are known for bugs. Our favorite lizards, the small ones that scamper over every inch of Caribbean landfall we've been on, are something to get used to. They far outnumber the tourists and must become friends if your holiday mood is important. They are harmless–and are everywhere. Snakes and other "uglies," mercifully, are not. The mongoose seems to have taken care of the snakes almost everywhere (and now seems to be taking care of the residents' chickens). You will see the muskrat-looking animals scurrying around the roadsides and in the countryside. Harmful snakes are hard to find, except in jungle terrain, and your guide will know what and where they are. "No see 'ums" are another matter. First of all, that's what the locals on some islands call the small sandflies that make their presence known after a rain, at beachside locations, near swamps, at twilight. They can make a sunset anchorage a nightmare and a beachside room a torture chamber. If little gnats get to you, then take along the best repellent you know, particularly to the Caymans, St. Lucia, and to humid warm spots. Even the experts cannot tell you when and if the sandflies appear, so be prepared.

BACKGROUND
TO
THE
CARIBBEAN
AND
THE BAHAMAS

CARIBBEAN CHRONOLOGY

From Arawaks to Independence

The New World became the focus of the Old on October 12, 1492, when the caravels of Columbus hove to in the Bahamas. That was his first voyage, and on succeeding ones he was to touch and name many of the isles of the Caribbees. There had been earlier civilizations, of course, riding in canoes that were faster than the caravels, gliding north from the coast of Venezuela to and through all of the islands, incising their cultural records on the walls of caves in Bonaire, Aruba, Antigua, St. John, and elsewhere, reaching heights of splendor in the Aztec kingdom of Mexico and the Inca empire of Peru and in the rich legacies that the Indian civilizations left in Colombia and Venezuela. In most of the islands, however, it was the peace-loving Arawaks, known also as Tainos, who left their mark on the early history. While the infamy of the Caribs made an indelible mark on the area, even to supplying its name, the quiet Arawaks "disappeared" from history. It is only in recent years that archeologists and other researchers have uncovered some remnants of that earlier civilization.

Crops and Conquests

Under the guiding hand of the Instituto Cultura Puertorriqueño, two Taino ballparks have now been painstakingly excavated in the midwestern mountains of Puerto Rico. From the fall of the stones and the life in the area, researchers have put together a life style that settles the Tainos in rounded homes built of palm trunks, lashed together with fibers, and covered with palm bark or leaf sheaves to be roofed with straw. These settlers of the 13th century (and before) cultivated cassava root–and bequeathed the sweet potato to future generations. They grew garlic, tobacco, and corn; they harvested papaya, guava, mamey apples, and higuera; and they developed the hammocks that were to impress Columbus and revolutionize the sleeping habits of sailors who abandoned the hard decks in their favor.

A peace-loving agricultural people, the Arawaks were no match for the fierce warrior Caribs, who swept northward from Paraguay like an Amerindian reincarnation of the Huns, conquering everything in their path. They added a word to the Indo-European vocabulary–their own tribal name, *caribe,* which is Spanish for cannibal. But the Caribs, too, would meet their match. The colonizing and Christianizing efforts of the steady stream of Spaniards, Dutch, French and British–often heady and heedless in their pursuit of gold–would take its toll in Caribs. Even with this onslaught, however, the near extermination of the tribe took almost three centuries. There are still a few pure Caribs today on the island of Dominica, where they live in a Carib village, making baskets, canoes, and cassava flour just as their ancestors did.

With this exception, there are no "pure" Carib communities in today's Caribbean.

The "modern" civilizations began within a decade of the first landfall, when Columbus went on to discover Hispaniola (now Haiti and the Dominican Republic), Cuba, Jamaica, all of the lesser Antilles, Trinidad, the coast of Venezuela, and Panama, claiming them all for their Catholic Majesties, Ferdinand and Isabella of Spain. In one of the ironies of history, Columbus would die in bitter disappointment and official disgrace in 1506, seven years before Balboa discovered the Pacific from a peak in Panama, the passage to the Indies which Columbus had sought in vain.

Columbus' discoveries led the way for the impressive events of the next few decades. Cortez would conquer Mexico, Francisco Pizarro would subdue Peru, and the gold of the Incas would be transported across Panama from the Pacific to the Caribbean and thence to the coffers of Spain. At this same time, Alonzo de Ojeda would explore the gulf coast of North America with its river delta–and the coast of South America with its Orinoco River. Governor Ponce de Leon of Puerto Rico would discover Florida in his unsuccessful search for the Fountain of Youth.

The Spaniards, with their zealous and often unwanted Christianizing, would wipe out a whole race of 2 million Amerindians within the space of a single century. They would find that sugar cane from the Canaries would grow in their new possessions, just as the Portuguese would find that it would grow in Brazil and the Dutch would eventually bring it from there to Barbados, and black slaves would be brought in to work the fields.

Columbus' Claim

Although many places claim the heart of Columbus, only the Dominican Republic truly has his heart–and bones. On December 5, 1492, he landed on *Hispaniola* (an island now shared by Haiti and the Dominican Republic) and built the first community from the wood of his shipwrecked *Santa Maria*. That was at Acul Bay, and the community of 38 men left to survive under the rule of Diego de Arana were destined to disappear.

A more lasting community, the result of the return voyage with 17 ships and more than 1000 colonists including doctors and priests, was started on January 6, 1494, at Isabela, inland on the Dominican Republic's north coast. It was here that Father Bonifacio celebrated the first Mass in the New World and Christian colonizing began in earnest.

Columbus returned to Spain in 1496, leaving his brother Bartolomé to bring peace between the colonists and the Caribs. He proved unequal to the task. It took a series of leaders, and the deportation of the Columbus family, to create the semblance of stability in the new colony. Indian wars and the Spanish thirst for gold kept life chaotic for the settlers until the arrival of Nicolas de Ovando, in 1502. He came with a new outlook–and more than 2000 settlers. It is Ovando who is hailed as the "founder of Spain's Empire in the New World," and, while he permitted the Columbus family to return to their favorite land, he maintained order with a gentler hand.

Ovando was succeeded by Diego Columbus, Christopher's son, who settled the community at today's Santo Domingo and proceeded to bring the good life to the New World with all the proper flourishes. During the first part of its history, Santo Domingo was the key to the New World. It was the port through which the riches of the Indies poured into Spain and from which the explorers set out, with restocked ships, to make their claim on South and Central America. It was here that the patterns were set for government of the New World. Queen Isabella kept strict controls through her customs house in Seville, Spain, and in 1511 set up a tribunal in Santo Domingo for appeals to the crown. This was to be the predecessor for the royal *audencia* established in 1526 to have authority over all the Antilles. It was also in these early years that the precedent for a municipal style of government, with a local mayor, was established.

The heyday continued–until richer treasures were found in Mexico when Cortez made his exploration in 1521. Sugar and livestock were no match for gold, and the control of power gradually slipped away from Santo Domingo, leaving the first settlements of the New World to become prey for pirates and temptations for the latecomers on the discovery scene: the English, French, and Dutch. The period of Spanish exploration and conquest was over. It was time for history to bring on the buccaneers.

Privateers, Buccaneers, Pirates

The first two freebooters to appear were gentlemanly prototypes of countless scoundrels to come. Their names were Drake and Hawkins. To the Spanish they were pirates out and out; to the English they were privateers on the business of Her Majesty the Queen. If they attacked the Spanish, it was an aggressive act of self-defense. Hawkins contented himself for the most part with slave-running, buying blacks on the Guinea coast, and selling them to Spanish colonists in defiance of the Spanish king. Drake's method was more direct. There was gold in the galleons of Spain, treasure piled high in the cities of the Spanish main, and he meant to get them for God, for Country, and for Queen, all three of whom were Protestant.

He attacked with religious zeal, with infinite audacity and courage. As red-haired as the Queen, he had the kind of personality that compelled faith, obedience, devotion. He was twenty-six years old, and the Caribbean was his. He lay in wait for Spanish galleons, striking at them from hidden bays. With each attack, another load of bullion was lost to Spain. Drake's most romantic coup was a night attack on a mule train plodding along the Camino Real of Panama, carrying the gold and jewels of Peru across the isthmus to Spanish ships waiting on the Caribbean shore. There were more than 200 mules in the caravan, each one with a fortune on its back. Drake got it all. The treasure went to England, not to Spain.

At a New Year's reception, Elizabeth wore part of the booty, a splendid brooch of Muzo emeralds. The Spanish ambassador simmered with rage. Two days later, he boiled over. Drake's name led the New Year's honors list. Thenceforth and forever more in history, this plundering pirate would be known as *Sir* Francis Drake.

Not only knighted, but equipped with thirty ships and more than 2000 armed men, Sir Francis attacked two of Spain's strongest Caribbean bastions, Santo Domingo and Cartagena. He took them both by the same stratagem, landing men at night and surprising the Spaniards. To add insult to injury, he captured Cartagena on Ash Wednesday. Both cities were plundered, their churches pillaged, their citizens forced to pay huge ransoms or see the towns go up in flames.

It was 1585. The Spanish, fed up with undeclared wars, began to build a great Armada. Like a bolt of lightning, Drake struck the harbor of Cadiz and set fire to the Spanish ships. Not until Pearl Harbor would there be such a stunning surprise again. Admiral Santa Cruz of the Spanish fleet had a heart attack. King Philip was almost paralyzed by the shock. It took him three years to get the Armada shipshape again. The rest is a simple historical statement, sung out in every British, American, and Canadian elementary school since the event itself: "1588: The English under Drake defeated the Spanish Armada."

Britannia Rules the Waves

The era of Rule Britannia was at hand. Drake was merely the first of a pack of English sea dogs who were to rule the Caribbean.

Among the more famous were Blackbeard the Pirate (real name: Edward Teach) and Sir Henry Morgan. The first operated out of New Providence in the Bahamas, that Cromwellian colony where pirates consorted with Puritans, and you could hardly tell one from another.

There was no mistaking Blackbeard, however. His coal-black beard was plaited into a series of braids. He swaggered about with three braces of pistols, his mad, febrile eyes shining in the glow of lighted tapers, which he stuck under his hat. He was fond of sticking splinters under the nails of his victims, and so was "gentleman" Henry Morgan.

Morgan's career was a 17th century parallel of Drake's. His name was anathema to the Spaniards. Operating out of Port Royal, the "Babylon of the West" on English-captured Jamaica, Morgan occupied and pillaged the colonial cities of Spain: Granada on Lake Nicaragua, Santa Maria de Puerto Principe of Cuba, Portobello, which he captured by forcing nuns and monks to precede his men up the scaling ladders of the fortress, and Panama City itself. Since England and Spain were ostensibly at peace, this was pure piracy. Madrid protested to London. Henry Morgan was summoned to England, put on trial, sentenced to imprisonment in the Tower, released, and knighted! He ended his days in Jamaica as Lieutenant Governor of that thriving colony. Uncrowned king of Port Royal, he sat in that doomed and wicked city, drinking rum and piously contributing portions of his pirate loot to the local church. There, in 1688, Sir Henry died in the odor of sanctity, four years before Port Royal with its unbearable burden of wickedness sank beneath the waves.

Blackbeard and Morgan were but two of the Caribbean's famous pirates. There were Newman and Jackman, preying on the Spaniards and planning to establish a Central American republic of buccaneers!

Piracy was by no means a British monopoly. There were the noble Frenchmen, Pierre Belain d'Esnambuc and Urban de Roissey. Their headquarters was the tiny island of Saba. In the neighboring waters they took so many prizes that Cardinal Richelieu got interested in the game. He bought $50,000 worth of stock in a new French company to exploit *Les Isles de l'Amerique,* commissioning Esnambuc to colonize, plunder, privateer–in short, make profits. France's hat was in the Caribbean ring. So was Holland's. The famous Dutch seaman Piet Heyn fell upon the Spanish fleet off the Cuban coast and took $5 million worth of booty home to Amsterdam. For this and other services to his country, Pirate Heyn became Admiral of the Netherlands.

All these, if you like, were national pirates, respected and rewarded citizens of their countries, which they were enriching at the expense of unhappy Spain. There were other buccaneers, freebooters whose only flag was the Jolly Roger, whose only loyalty was to captain and mates. Anything in the Caribbean was fair game for these cutthroats: any ship, any settlement, any woman. Tortuga, off Haiti, and the Virgin Islands swarmed with pirates. They lived on rum and smoked pig, *a la bucana,* whence the name buccaneers. Nothing in *Treasure Island* or the wildest fancies of fiction could equal the reality of this democracy of bandits, cutting a swath through the West Indies as they cut the throats of their victims. Epic binges, epic orgies were the order of the freebooter's day. They made the 17th century the most colorful of the Caribbean; call it the cycle of the corsairs.

Rum, Sugar, and Slaves

As the 17th century drew to a close, it was clear that the economic stakes in the Caribbean were high. The freebooters' days were numbered. It was time now for another kind of piracy, legalized, organized on a national scale. In other words, war. Exhausted Spain, plundered alike by English, Dutch, and French, now watched as her three principal tormentors began to torment each other. Between 1665 and 1702, there were at least eight separate wars among the three upstart powers which had challenged Spain's monopoly.

The stakes were sugar, rum, coffee, cocoa, and slaves. Europe had developed an insatiable hunger for the first four items. The West Indian plantations could not get enough of the last. The life blood of the plantations was black slave labor. Forty "factories" were operating on the coasts of Africa. These were actually camps where captured blacks were held pending transportation to the West Indies. The British owned about half the factories. The Dutch owned the rest. Native African chiefs cooperated by selling their prisoners of war to the enterprising slave traders. The British salved their conscience with this: by shipping blacks to the plantations of the West Indies, they were saving them from a far worse fate in Africa. At the end of the 17th century, about 75,000 slaves a year were being shipped from the gold coast of Africa to the cane fields of the Antilles. Slaves in good condition brought about £18 sterling a head, or the equivalent in sugar and rum, in the markets of the West Indies. So slavery itself was big business, to the tune of nearly $7 million a year.

It was on the slave trade and the plantation system that the economic prosperity of the West Indies was built. Never in the history of the world had there been a colonial economy as rich as this one based on slavery and sugar. This was the wealth over which the powers of Europe squabbled for 100 years. In the end, the whole structure was brought down by emancipation. The institution of slavery could not withstand the principles of the French Revolution or the humanitarian ideals that spread through Europe in the 19th century.

The Age of Revolt

The black slaves of Saint Domingue sounded the tocsin of revolt with their voodoo drums, and the fall of the fabulously rich French planter aristocracy was no less dramatic than that of the Bastille. The second republic in the New World came into being, a black one, Haiti, resuming its original Indian name, defying Napoleon, and, miraculously, surviving. By 1834, slavery was abolished everywhere in the West Indies. The plantations were in the doldrums. The beautiful islands of the Caribbean lay in abject poverty. There were the sun and the surf, the beaches, the splendid mountains, the climate. But, although all of Europe was stirred by a new romantic interest in Nature, the idea of exploiting its beauties for tourism still lay a century in the future.

The libertarian passions of the 19th century, however, spread like a brush fire through Latin America. Here the great leader was Simón Bolívar of Venezuela. Under his inspired direction, half the continent of South America was liberated from the Spanish yoke. He is the father of five countries: Venezuela, Colombia, Ecuador, Peru, Bolivia, the last one named in grateful memory of *El Libertador,* the Liberator.

President Pétion of the fledgling republic of Haiti had helped Bolívar with money and men during the early days when the liberating revolution had bogged down in what looked like hopeless defeat. And what of the other fledgling republic, prototype of them all, the United States of America? The Monroe Doctrine was promulgated, warning the powers of Europe and especially Spain that America would take the dimmest view of Old World interference in the affairs of the Western Hemisphere.

This famous and much-maligned doctrine was brought into play in 1898 when all America echoed with the cry, "Remember the *Maine!,*" the U.S. battleship which was blown up, some said at the instigation of William Randolph Hearst, in Havana Harbor. The dogs of the Spanish-American war were unleashed. It was Spain's expiring gasp in the golden world over which she had once ruled alone. Cuba became an independent republic. Spanish forces had abandoned Santo Domingo in 1865, and, although the country was theoretically independent, domestic turmoil caused the government to petition the U.S. for annexation. The U.S. Senate voted it down, only to agree to an "arrangement" in 1905. Ceded to America was Puerto Rico, the land of Ponce de Léon, an abject little island, an orphan, an "insoluble problem," the "stricken land." Within half a century it was to pull itself up by its bootstraps to the status of a thriving commonwealth.

The Present Day

It was a slow process, but each island began to realize its tourism potential and spruced up to await the visitors. After all, they had built-in attractions, such as year-round tropical sunshine, sandy beaches, a history to tell, and folklore to show.

Meanwhile, full independence became the quest on several islands, many of which were always rather lost together as "the British colonies in the Caribbean." As of this writing, those who had sought independence, and equal voting rights in the United Nations, have achieved it.

The Dutch and French islands have not been so inclined and probably won't be, as they continue to enjoy a casual autonomy, along with their allegiance to their "mother" countries.

THE LIVELY ARTS

Contributions to a Culture

The outstanding cultural contribution of the Caribbean has traditionally been in music and the dance. The West Indies throb with rhythm from the Bahamas to the Spanish Main. Although there is a good deal of Amerindian influence in that music, its essential beat was established centuries ago in the jungles of Africa, and it remains irrepressibly African.

Whatever their faults as colonists, the Spaniards loved music and adapted Indian and African tribal rhythms and melodies to their own uses. The British and the Dutch, however, responded as the puritanical Protestants most of them were. Music and dance thus thrived on Latin American soil, but languished in the Anglo and Dutch colonies, at least among the colonizers.

In the fields, hills, and living quarters, music proved to be a means of communication, racial identification, and cultural pride for the African slaves.

The most important musical developments on many Caribbean islands–calypso and steel bands–came late. Calypso, which is discussed at length in our chapter on Trinidad, flourishes in most of the Caribbean islands, sparked by its appeal to tourists. The resurgence of arts in the Caribbean–theater, dance, and song groups, and even in applied arts–has come about in conjunction with tourism and each island's attempt to show off its roots. Puerto Rico's *Le Lo Lai* Festival is a perfect example.

Afro-English Developments

The English suppression of African music and dancing may have done the art a favor. By going "underground," the African rhythms had a chance to survive in more or less pure form. Carnivals held throughout the Caribbean hint of the early tribal ecstasies. You'll be caught up in the excitement no matter which island you're on, but try not to miss the gala pre-Lenten Carnival in Trinidad, where events are at their spontaneous best. Shango, and voodoo, pagan religions officially repressed, are practiced in secret, with all the ceremonial dances and trances, in Haiti and the French Islands.

Waltzes, quadrilles, and even the minuet are still danced on all the islands with island variations. Tradition suggests that slaves, peering into the candlelit ballrooms of the great plantation Houses, saw these dances and adopted them. The Creole elite of the Republic of Haiti certainly danced every figure that Europe had to offer. The average ballroom dancer in Haiti is a natural genius of the dance. His African influence is strongest, of course, in the voodoo described in the chapter on Haiti, but try also to attend one of the Saturday night hoedowns called *bambouches.* Among the country dances performed at these fêtes are the conga and the *martinique.* These are variations of the stately quadrilles danced by the 19th century elite under crystal chandeliers and are some of the reasons why Haiti is the most fascinating of the Caribbean cultures from the point of view of dance and African folklore.

One of the dance legacies of the African slaves is the merengue, a graceful, rocking dance especially popular in Haiti, the French West Indies, and the Dominican Republic, where it is presumed to have originated and where there is an annual July Merengue Festival. The French merengue is smoother and more elegant than the Spanish variety, which is on the sultry side. The basic rhythm of the merengue recalls the rhumba and the *paso doble* (Spanish two-step) and has a rocking motion where hips move (plenty), but shoulders do not. One explanation of the metronomic motion derives from the limping of slaves who were forced to drag a ball and chain with one foot. This explanation is more romantic than scientific, and would be more accurately applied to the conga.

Martinique and Guadeloupe are fond of the merengue, but on these islands the *dance du pays* is the beguine, described in our chapter on Martinique. A striking contrast to the sultry weaving of the beguine is the Old World mazurka, which is danced here with a sort of clinging-vine Creole charm. Both these traditions and many more are poignantly performed by the Folkloric Group of Guadeloupe and Grand Ballets de la Martinique, a dance group of twenty, plus a singer, six musicians, and the ballet director, which has performed in the United States and Europe.

Calypso and steel bands (described in the chapter on Trinidad) became the rage, not only on this island but throughout the British-affiliated West Indies and beyond to America and Europe. "Jump-up," an Afro-Trinidadian invention that is now part of everyone's carnival, couldn't be more accurately named. The whole island jumps! And then there are the acrobatics of the limbo, in which the dancers writhe under a low horizontal bar, supine without touching the floor. For added effect, some performers light the bar aflame and slide under it, less than eight inches off the floor. This dance, part of every West Indian floor show, may have its origin in the motions used by slaves to writhe free from punishment cells.

Jamaica's reggae (pronounced reg-gay) deserves some mention as the only Caribbean music and beat to make an impact in recent years. Developed from the traditional rhythms of Jamaica's Rastafarians, a religious sect closely tied with Ethiopia, the music was called "ska" when Byron Lee and the Dragonaires brought the first ska star, Millie Small, to the New York World's Fair in 1964. It appeared in Britain as "blue beat" or "rock steady." No matter what its name, the beat–a combination of folk, rock, soul, blues and revival–has infected most of Jamaica and has spread through the United States and Europe. The words, if you can understand them, usually follow a protest theme, but the beat brings smiles to the faces of the traditional calypso bands and the authentic bands which are heavy with bass, percussion, and sometimes organ music.

Indian Dance Dramas

History tells us that the Indians on Santo Domingo (now the Dominican Republic) entertained the Spanish conquerors with graceful dances, performed to the accompaniment of drums and vocal music. These do not survive in pure form on the islands, where the Spanish all but exterminated the dancers, but you can find sufficient evidence that the Indians adapted the dance forms of the conquering Spaniards, absorbing them easily into their own highly developed dance tradition. When you watch certain dances of the Caribbean with that incredibly fast staccato stamping which the Spanish call *zapateos,* it's hard to tell where the Amerindian influence leaves off and flamenco takes over. To the insistent rhythms of jungle drums, the Spanish added the exotic Moorish wail of their own melodic tradition. Out of the plantation shacks and into the ballroom came the drums of Africa. The rhumba was born; the conga, the guaracha, the mambo. Half the world still thinks Ravel invented the bolero; it came from Cuba out of Africa and Spain.

Unlike the Cubans, who embraced African music *con mucho gusto,* the Puerto Ricans tend to look down their noses at hybrid dance forms. The country dance called *seis* remained uncorrupted by African rhythm, and it exists today both as a communal dance for six (hence the name) or as a ballroom exercise for two. It is charming to see this gay stamping dance, reminiscent of the *sardañas* or the *jotas,* danced by rural communities in Spain and miraculously saved from extinction by the efforts of the Instituto de Cultura Puertorriqueña. Even in the mid-1970s, when 20th century values seem to be stepping heavily onto Puerto Rico, the traditional dances can be seen at regularly scheduled performances of the Ballet Folklorico in Old San Juan and around the island.

In spite of Puerto Rico's "purity," an Afro-Puerto Rican song and dance routine did develop shortly after the turn of this century. This is the *plena.* It has a rhumba-like rhythm and amusing lyrics and offers the performer a chance to improvise and engage in a certain amount of pantomime. In many ways, the plena will remind you of a Spanish version of calypso, Subject matter for the plenas ranges from the pangs of unrequited love to current events and the high cost of living.

Dance Groups and Cultural Centers

The attention focused in recent years on the problem of identity has led to specific efforts in many Caribbean countries to delve into the traditions of the past. The Instituto de Cultura Puertorriqueña, the *Grand Ballets de la Martinique* and its Guadeloupian counterpart have all contributed greatly to the colorful traditions visitors witness today.

Probably the most impressive center for the performances of Caribbean artists is the National Theatre in the Dominican Republic, on the country's Plaza de la Cultura in Santo Domingo. Performances by artists from the Dominican Republic and by international stars are part of the cultural season in this country.

The Casals Festival, the inspiration of the late Pablo Casals, who adopted Puerto Rico as his home, is the height of the classical music season in Puerto Rico. It takes place annually in May and includes performances in many historic buildings in Old San Juan as well as around the island.

Another cultural center attempting to provide a forum for the arts in an outdoor setting is the Island Center on Peppertree Hill on St. Croix. Look into some of the special-interest cruises which feature concert groups and those which host folkloric groups at various ports-of-call.

Artifacts

Although less widely appreciated than the music and dance, Caribbean art makes its cultural contribution as well. The purest examples are, of course, those that existed in the area before the arrival of the Europeans–the pre-Colombian art found in Mexico and South America.

But there is no question that in the Dominican Republic, the Museum of Dominican Man on the impressive Plaza de la Cultura in Santo Domingo is the most noteworthy in the islands.

The early relics of the islands on the eastern rim of the Caribbean sea are a disappointing lot–mostly Arawak and Carib bones and beads with little of real artistic note. In recent years, archeologists working in the northeastern section of Martinique, have unearthed Arawak teeth, beads, and skeletons from the first Arawak period (A.D. 180-460) and the second. These have been displayed in a simple museum with the impressive name of Musée Départemental de la Martinique, with a small doorway on Rue de la Liberté in Fort-de-France.

The Taino Indians, as the Arawaks were also known, have been studied by officials from the Instituto de Cultura Puertorriqueña, and two Taino ballparks (one near Utuado in the central mountain area, and the other just a few minutes from Ponce) are well worth a visit for those interested in the early Caribbean cultures.

Other small Arawak and Carib museums have cropped up in Antigua, Dominica, and as a special exhibit in the Virgin Islands Museum in St. Thomas, but all have been largely the result of one or two enthusiasts who have turned over their private collections for the island's historic interest.

Painting

In the field of painting, Haiti has dominated the entire Caribbean area for well over a decade with the vigorous "primitive" art movement, which is described in our chapter on that country. While this movement breaks into splinter groups and diverges into what critics are fond of calling its "decadence," its original inspiration seems unimpaired. That inspiration, like the voodoo impulse behind Haitian music, is essentially African.

Almost without exception, the influences on original Caribbean art have been the influences of the conquered or the enslaved. In Central America and on the Spanish Main, where the Indians were not subjected to the ruthless genocide that characterized Spanish occupation of the islands, painting, architecture, and sculpture are indelibly marked with the Amerindian stamp.

Painting in Trinidad is, not too surprisingly, a cosmopolitan result of this island's racial richness. The African influence is seen here, too, but it is less primitive than the Haitian brand. Add to this the East Indian, Chinese, Hindu, French, English, and Spanish, and you have a creative spirit which is hard to parallel. It is this same spirit that gave birth to carnival and calypso, and while painting in Trinidad isn't as famous, it is definitely worth the trouble to try to see the work of some of the best artists. The Ministry of Culture is working toward development of the visual arts, encouraging talent which was dormant under British rule. So far, Trinidadian and Tobagan art has been exhibited in South America, Europe, and the United States, as well as throughout the West Indies. Of the more primitive school, or that which has its roots in black culture, Trinidad's leading artists are Leo Basso and Dominic Isaac. The Chinese influence is seen in paintings by Carlisle Chang, William Chen, and Patrick Chu Foon–but the results can only be called Trinidadian, and interesting. Both local scenes and international sophistication are displayed in the work of M.P. Alladin, who studied and taught both in the United States and abroad.

Old San Juan, in Puerto Rico, is an artists' quarter, with many galleries–some with interesting modern work–tucked into the honeycomb of boutiques. The famous *santos*–carved and decorated wooden figures representing the saints–are now mostly reproductions (no matter how old they look). The practice of trading new for old with the country folk has brought most of the old into the market or museums, and prices are high.

A special word on a recent development in Caribbean art should be said for the painting of Jamaica. Here, too, the dominant influence is African, specifically Afro-Haitian. Less vehement, less violent than the painting of Haiti, it is nevertheless deeply sincere and technically competent. Prices are more moderate than those for the works of the better-known Haitian painters, and you may very well make some personal discoveries among these young Jamaican artists. In his travels through the area, author-critic Selden Rodman, one of the initiators of the Haitian art movement, has noticed some promising trends among the country painters, notably the "op-like dynamism" of Donald Campbell and the "wiry style" of Wilfred Francis. The works of both men he first saw in a Kingston gallery. Other noted critics have been impressed with the work of Owen Marsh, a young Jamaican who paints in traditional style the country scenes of his childhood as well as Jamaica today. His work, and the work of other promising artists, is displayed at shows sponsored by the Jamaica Tourist Board and at Devon House in Kingston.

Handicrafts

Caribbean handicrafts came close to being buried in a sea of plastic substitutes. A few did succumb, but efforts by a special U.N. team and a few other interested groups have refocused the interests of many young Caribbean residents on their traditional arts. Many of these traditions have been kept intact (partly because not too many tourists have penetrated these areas), but recent seasons have seen handwork yield to sewing machines for mass production. It becomes harder and harder to find original pieces, and they're expensive when you do find them.

This is true also for the wood craft of the islands of Haiti, the Dominican Republic, St. Lucia, and other areas. Lathes have replaced hands for many pieces, but with perseverance and time it is sometimes possible to find interesting original work.

Rope, twine, pandanus grass, and palm fronds are woven into intricate baskets, mats, and hats. As the tourists swarm over a community, the quality usually decreases–and the prices go up. This has proved true in Jamaica, Puerto Rico, Barbados, and Trinidad and even in less traveled spots such as St. Lucia, St. Vincent, and Grenada, where someone seems to have taught the entire weaving population how to use colored raffia to spell out the island name on baskets. Far more interesting handwork can be found on Dominica and Montserrat, where school children learn the craft and where woven squares for rugs are sold at home industry shops. By far the best, at least as of this writing, is the intricate and delicate work done by the country women of St. Barts. Many of the baskets, mats, coasters, and hats are handsewn (a few, alas, are machine stitched), and all are original and individual. No mass production here, but then, there's no mass tourism either.

The most encouraging note struck by island artists is that inspired by silkscreen and batik studios, usually started by off-islanders but quickly incorporating local talents to the art-turned-trade. Jim Tillet's studio at Tutu has become an art colony, with classes for young people and a studio that prints yards of fabric to be mounted for wall hangings or stitched into clothing. Another studio is the Chandlers' operation, near Falmouth on the north coast of Jamaica, and a third is the Bagshaws of St. Lucia, American expatriates who have impressed their colorful interpretations of island flowers, birds, and motifs onto fabric that appears in dresses, shirts, place mats, and an assortment of other items eagerly acquired by visitors.

Batik studios also exist on Eleuthera, St. Martin and St. Croix, and small operations are in existence on other islands. While all those mentioned now look to the increasing horde of tourists to purchase the product, perhaps as this art becomes known to the island people some interesting "art for art's sake" may develop.

Architecture

Warm-weather adaptations of the architecture familiar in their home countries was what the earliest settlers brought to the New World. The initial style, something between that of the Middle Ages and the Renaissance in European capitals, set the tone for all subsequent architecture in Caribbean countries. The cathedral of Santo Domingo, in the Dominican Republic's capital, begun as early as 1496 and completed in the middle of the 16th century, is a fascinating mélange of Gothic and Renaissance elements. The interior has groined Gothic arches and heavy piers terminated by attenuated vaults. The exterior is pure plateresque, decorated with the fantasy of Renaissance Spain, a fantasy which was to burgeon into the baroque but which is here restrained by a certain classicism, reflected in Romanesque arches, Corinthian columns, and a frieze in the Roman manner. The Alcazar of Diego Columbus, built in the early 16th century and handsomely restored in the 20th, has the open loggias and other Italian features of Renaissance palaces in Florence or Barcelona. And the restoration at La Altarazana (The Arsenal), not far from the Alcazar, is now a living museum of the thriving culture of the Dominican Republic in those early days.

The oldest vestiges of Spain in the New World recall the Renaissance plus that special Hispanic addition, the exotic Moorish touch, which scholars call the *mudéjar* influence. If you want to see a superlative example of this, visit La Fortaleza, the Governor's Residence in Puerto Rico. Its Moorish dome, entrance gate, and Arabian Nights windows are designed harmoniously. The ambitious restorations of other "typically Spanish" architecture in Old San Juan, started by the Alegria family and a few others in the early 1950s and now absorbed into the plans of the comprehensive Instituto de Cultura Puertorriqueña, have set an impressive standard for the entire area.

About the middle of the 17th century, the baroque style, which was engulfing Europe as a reaction against the rigid "classicism" of the Renaissance, was brought to the New World. The Indians, many of whom were craftsmen employed by the Jesuit priests and other builders of the New World, embellished the curving lines wherever possible with motifs from their own civilization.

It was the neoclassical style which provided the Caribbean area with its domed capitols, its arcaded streets, its Roman porticos, its Greek façades, its general look of restrained elegance, which you will find in many plantation Great Houses, similar in style to those of the southern United States.

The Victorian obsession with gingerbread detail made its mark in the Caribbean, especially on the British islands and in Frederiksted, St. Croix (which burned down and was rebuilt in this period), but the taste for classicism persists in contemporary architecture, especially in the increasingly functional hotel architecture of Puerto Rico, St. Thomas, and Jamaica.

Since the former Danish West Indies–the U.S. Virgin Islands–are the only "possessions" for Hamlet's Denmark, there has been a strong bond forged with Danes and the Friends of Denmark in the U.S. Virgin Islands. That bond provided the impetus for a thorough study of Danish architecture in the Virgin Islands. To date most of St. Croix's Christiansted is now National Historic Site, with appropriate guided tours. Now a part of the National Park System, operated through the U.S. Department of the Interior, the area is subject to rigid building codes that will maintain the authentic Danish West Indian flavor.

A similar community, under Dutch domain, has been created in the Holland-in-the-sun town of Willemstad, Curaçao. Nowhere in the Caribbean are there more examples of warm-weather copies of the architecture of Holland, although Sint Maarten and Aruba have a few. On Dutch St. Eustatius, called Statia and most easily reached by plane from Sint Maarten, remnants of silt-covered town houses, blown to bits in reprisals for that island's recognition of the American flag in 1776, have been uncovered, and restoration of some of those early homes, built from ballast brick in an era of great prosperity for Statia is now underway.

Throughout the islands, loyal people interested in history have formed what are mostly volunteer groups, struggling to raise the necessary funds and interest to preserve the vestiges of the thriving 18th century life of the Caribbean.

CARIBBEAN COOKERY

Calypso Variations on National Themes

Caribbean cookery has not taken a place at the top of the list of international cuisines–or even in the top ten, but it may get there yet. The identity crisis that has made the area look hard at its own image in recent years has brought an awareness of customs, costumes, and cuisine. The Caribbean countries are concentrating on their own foods, acknowledging customs, and finally paying homage to recipes that have been "in the family" for generations.

It's been a tradition since the days of the planters to adapt French or Spanish or English recipes to island produce: to add the spices of warm climates to the preparation of local iguana, frogs, and fish; to cook breadfruit like the vegetables that the new Caribbean residents remembered from across the Atlantic; to brew mangoes into pies, and to "cook" fish in brine and spices. Traditional Indian foods–cassava, guava, and even garlic–were adapted by the invaders from Spain, France, and England to the recipes they remembered from home. Basics were brought from across the Atlantic to be cultivated in the West Indies. The African slaves contributed their okra, *calaloo,* and akee, and the *sofrito* the Spanish enjoyed made its transatlantic voyage into Caribbean kitchen pots.

Slowly through the years, a stew of Caribbean cookery has evolved. It was threatened with extinction when the Hilton/Holiday Inn invasion came from the north, claiming that all Americans must have steak (even if it was imported, expensive, not properly stored, and improperly cooked). But now that indigenous tourism has made sharing the local experience popular, Caribbean cuisine is simmering to a definable formula. Even charity cookbooks are coming to the fore on islands like St. Croix, Montserrat, and the Netherlands Antilles.

One of the most appealing books of Caribbean cookery is the Time-Life volume *The Cooking of the Caribbean Islands,* published first in 1970, but still readily available. The chief asset of this volume, in addition to its history and recipes (not always 100% authentic, but adapted for North American kitchens) is its pictures. Nowhere else can you get such a visual impression of the splashes of color that converge in Caribbean cooking.

Seafood

Fish is the expected staple of the Caribbean diet and, although too many hotels are now tucking the fresh fish brought in by local fishermen into their freezers, there are many places where it comes straight from the sea to me and thee. Try the flying fish of Barbados, the red fish in the French Islands, and lobster anywhere you can get it—usually fresh from the pot in the small islands, where you may be eating at the house of the fisherman. Conch, cooked as fritters and called *lambi,* is excellent wherever you find it, and turtle steaks appear on some menus, notably in the Caymans, where the turtle farm is working at cultivating the crop.

Pescado Santo Domingo is a Dominican Republic creation of sea bass, prepared and served cold as an hors d'oeuvre. The Dominican Republic has also contributed *sopa hamaca,* one of those Spanish stews in which lobster and cubed fish meet with rice, potatoes, tomatoes, onions, garlic, pimientos, shredded cabbage, and olive oil. The Jamaicans have a way of stuffing lobster with a concoction of chopped onions, mushrooms, breadcrumbs, and grated cheese, then baking the whole affair to a golden brown. Another Jamaica specialty is *stamp and go,* codfish fritters, which are served either with fried plantains or stewed green bananas.

In Haiti, basic cuisine is French with Creole additions. Try *huîtres marinées* (pickled oysters). The Haitians also turn out a superb shrimp and avocado salad, which will appear on menus as *crevettes et avocats vinaigrette.* Their greatest contribution, however, is *homard flambé,* flaming lobster, beautifully seasoned and set afire, not with cognac or armagnac, but with the local Barbancourt rum.

The waters around most of the islands teem with lobster, huge shrimp, and crab. Recent harvesting methods have reduced the easy-to-catch supply and have boosted the price, but it is still possible to find local fish on menus, particularly in smaller places. In Puerto Rico, order *pescado guisado,* the Puerto Rican fish stew, combining white fish with shrimp, conchmeat, onions, leeks, garlic, parsley, tomatoes, bay leaf, and seasoning to produce a rich and savory result that can stand the inevitable comparison with bouillabaisse. *Asopao,* the famous rice stew of Puerto Rico, is at its best when the chief ingredient is shrimp, crab, or lobster instead of the more conventional chicken.

Seafood is one of the greater joys of the Lesser Antilles, too. Here top honors go to Martinique and Guadeloupe, those creole outposts of *La cuisine française,* and to St. Lucia, now independent but keeping its French accent in the kitchen. If you are skeptical of the highly touted French touch, try *acra l'en mori* on Guadeloupe or Martinique. They're nothing but fish cakes, but they are good enough to rival the best *quenelles* of Paris or Lyon. They're often served as an appetizer. The tiny oysters of Trinidad and the flying fish of Barbados, which we mentioned earlier, are two obligatory items for any *fin bec* visiting these two islands. Turtle steaks in the Cayman Islands, where The Cayman Turtle Farm has cultivated them for increased yields, rank at the top of that local food list. Sint Maarten, Aruba, and Curaçao are famous for East Indian *rijsttafel.*

Specialties of the Islands

If you see *calaloo* on any menu in the West Indies, don't hesitate. This is the queen of Creole soups, the royal progenetrix of the famous crab gumbo of New Orleans. It's made with crab, okra, tomatoes, and onions, seasoned with thyme, bay leaf, and ground chili peppers. *Sans coche,* the king of Creole soups, takes us out of the fish and into the meat market. It is made with beef, pork, and pig tail and fifteen other ingredicnts (which you'll find listed in the chapter on Trinidad).

When it comes to soups that are meals in themselves, you have your choice of pepperpot (chicken, pork, and corn beef). Creole pea soup, and Puerto Rico's *sopa de cebolla* (a delicious cheese and onion concoction). Cuba's *sopa de judias coloradas,* a terrific black bean soup made with ham and garnished with sliced hard-boiled eggs and lemon, can now be found in Puerto Rico. *Soupe de poisson,* served in the French islands, can vary according to the chef, but at its best this fish soup is thick, filling, and topped off with croutons and a slice of breathtaking hot pepper.

A word to the wise here on Caribbean hot peppers: They are hot! Don't be disarmed by their tiny size or by the fact that they may be served to you as a pepper sauce. Try a speck before you commit yourself or your meal to the invisible flames of Caribbean pepper sauce. Most tourist places won't have it, but the local spots certainly will. A brand name, if you want to take a bottle home, is *Maktouk's,* made in Trinidad.

Wherever the Spanish go, *arroz con pollo* goes too, and so does roast suckling pig, a delicacy you may find on the menus of Puerto Rico or the Dominican Republic under its Spanish name, *léchon asado. Arroz con pollo* is chicken with rice and some fifteen other ingredients including saffron, that special seasoning that turns Spanish rice to gold. You'll find it in all the paellas of Puerto Rico. If you want Spanish-style chicken without rice, try *guisado de pollo,* a chicken stew made with potatoes, green peas, olives, pimientos, onions, olive oil, and white wine. *Aguacates rellenos* (stuffed avocados) are halved avocados, stuffed with a marinade of potatoes, carrots, peas, asparagus, and beets—or whatever else they happen to have in the kitchen. Since the avocados grow in abundance in this climate, they're on almost every menu, or can be if you ask.

The East Indian curries of Trinidad are hotter than any curry you ever had at home. There are some milder curries in Guadeloupe, Martinique (where its called *colombo),* and St. Lucia, a good island for crab back (cooked and restuffed in the shell), *calaloo,* and *chicken pelau,* a tender chicken and rice stew with typical Creole sauce. Try the *crabe farçi* in the French islands; it is stuffed land crab and good.

You'll hear references to "peas and rice" in calypso songs throughout the islands. The islanders really go for this combination which consists of pigeon peas, chopped onion, chopped tomatoes, olive oil, rice, salt, and pepper. There are many variations. It's a basic Creole dish, and it's very good. Pigeon peas are also combined with pork in Puerto Rico's *gandules.* Latin Americans love this dish and are also fond of *habichuelas* (red beans) and various kinds of tamale such as *hallacas* and *pasteles* combined with pork or chicken and steamed in banana leaves.

As for ice cream, try the coconut variety when you can find it. There were years when milk was a problem in many of the islands, and ice cream was way below par; that's not so on most islands today, and the variety of ice creams made from local fruits increases with each season. Most of the hotels offer island desserts like baked bananas with coconut cream, mango pie, and other local specialties—all very sweet and most of them delicious. All the exotic fruits are available for the plucking; you can eat all the mangoes and papayas you want. In the Spanish islands, try *yemo doble* (a Puerto Rican mixture of sherry, sugar, and six egg yolks) and *panatela* (coconut tarts).

Demon rum is the national drink of the Caribbean, an important factor in the region's past and present economy, and one good reason for going to the West Indies. There are many types of rum, and each island has its local brand, some not for export. In Barbados, there's *Mount Gay;* Jamaica has *Meyers;* the Dominican Republic has *Bermudez* and *Brugal;* Puerto Rico has *Bacardi;* Haiti has two offshoots from the *Barbancourt* family; the French islands have their very special and potent *Vieille Rhum;* and on some of the islands you can get the rum liqueur called *Rumona.*

When it comes to long, cool drinks, the most famous by far is the Planter's Punch. Here the heavy blackstrap type of rum comes into its full glory, mixed with native fruit juices, garnished with pineapple and other exotic items, served in a tall glass with plenty of ice, and sometimes lightly sprinkled with cinnamon, nutmeg, or some other magic dust of the spice islands. There are many variations from island to island on this classic drink.

For a selection of the foods available and where to find them, see our individual island listings under *Restaurants* in each chapter. And, for a chance to try your own Caribbean cookery, here are three special recipes which are island favorites (and our own).

CRUZAN CARROT CAKE

1 pound carrots finely sliced
1¾ cups sugar
2 teaspoons baking soda
2 teaspoons baking powder
2 teaspoons cinnamon
2 teaspoons nutmeg
4 eggs
2 cups flour
½ cup oil
1 tsp. vanilla

Blend all ingredients together and bake at 350° for one hour.

Annetta Joseph,
St. Croix

CHICKEN DOMINIQUE

2 pounds chicken parts
1 clove garlic, crushed
1 cup corn oil
Salt to taste
1 large onion, thinly sliced
1 cup vinegar
2 tablespoons flour
1 teaspoon black pepper

Spread chicken in dry frying pan. Place onion slices and garlic between them. Sprinkle the vinegar over the top. Cover and marinate for ½ hour. Then remove garlic and onion. Fry the chicken in the corn oil until golden brown. Drain off excess oil; add one cup water and the flour to thicken. Cover and simmer for ½ hour. Serves 4 to 6.

Dominique Jolly, Dominica

VIEUX FORT PUMPKIN SOUP

2½ pounds stew beef, cubed
1 onion, finely chopped
½ sweet green pepper
1 scallion, finely chopped
3 cloves of garlic, pounded
2 teaspoons butter
1 carrot, thinly sliced
2 pounds fresh pumpkin
3 stalks celery, finely sliced
1 fresh thyme leaf

Sprig of parsley
1 tablespoon tomato sauce
¼ teaspoon curry
1 potato, cut in quarters

Peel the pumpkin and remove seeds; cut into cubes. Combine with the meat. Add 4 quarts water, cover and simmer until the meat is tender (approx. 1½ hours). Combine all other ingredients, except the potato. Add enough water to cover, and cook over medium heat for ½ hour. Add the potato for thickening and cook for an additional 15 minutes. Serves 6.

Mary Clark,
St. Lucia

CARIBBEAN FLORAL EXOTICA

Perfumes in the Tropical Air

There's no place in the world that offers more color per square foot than the Caribbean and adjacent Atlantic areas covered in this guide. For gardeners and flower enthusiasts, the Caribbean is the Garden of Eden, full of exotic tropical flowers and trees and equally full of man's own handiwork in cultivating and landscaping.

Summer is the best time for flowers in the Caribbean—and the best time for bargain rates as well. From mid-April through mid-December, Caribbean rates are at their lowest, and in June, July, and August, the flowering trees are at their brightest and best.

Starting with the tropical trees whose flowering branches provide the colorful cover for the islands and countries of the West Indies, one of the most familiar is the flamboyant tree, or *flamboyán* if you prefer the Spanish version. Brought to the Caribbean by French Count de Poincy when he settled in St. Kitts in the 18th century, the brilliant flowers soon speckled the rest of the island group. In Jamaica, you'll hear the flamboyant referred to as the Royal poinciana. In Trinidad, it's called the flame tree. Even its official botanical name, *Delonix regia,* suggests the splendor of its scarlet blooms with their attenuated orchid-like petals capturing every ray of the tropic sun. Sometimes growing wild in solitary splendor, more often cultivated in a superb avenue of trees, the flamboyant sheds its leaves when it blossoms. New leaves appear almost at once, however, and the tender green foliage sets the scarlet flowers off to a maximum advantage for eight weeks and more in summer.

The sight of these flame-colored flowers against the brilliant blue of the Caribbean sky is one of the indelible memories of the West Indies. The tree blooms in Jamaica, Puerto Rico, and most of the northern Caribbean islands in May, June, and July. In Trinidad it reaches its height as early as April. The Royal poinciana sets the tone for the whole color scheme of summer in the Caribbean.

Next in popularity to the poinciana is the fragrant frangipani tree with its velvety star-shaped flowers, red, creamy white, sometimes pale pink, occasionally yellow. The strong sweet fragrance reminded the first European explorers of a popular Renaissance perfume called Frangipani after the chemist who produced it. Hence the name, imported from Italy, but appropriately exotic for this lovely flowering tree. Called plumeria in Hawaii, it has long been famous in the Pacific as an ideal flower for making leis. The frangipani flower fades quickly, however, once it is picked, and, as its edges darken, the sweet smell of the blossom becomes fetid. This may explain why its fragrance, so delightful on the tree, has never been successfully captured in a true frangipani perfume. Both leaves and clustering flowers of the frangipani grow at the extremity of the branch so that the interior boughs of the tree will remind you of Shakespeare's "bare ruined choirs." If you live in a tropical clime, a branch of the tree broken off and stuck in dry soil with good drainage immediately becomes another tree.

Cut the frangipani, even slightly, and a sticky, milky sap emerges. This milk has been used by natives as a poultice, but it should not be taken internally. As noted in our comment on "health" in the Facts section, avoid eating or licking this sap and any consumption in any form of the oleander, whose sap is so deadly that it has been known to poison people who ate chops that had been grilled over a fire of oleander wood.

The frangipani, to return to a less noxious beauty, blooms in Trinidad from November to January, but you will find it in full flower further north (in Jamaica, for example) from May through July. As a matter of fact, this fragrant tropical beauty seems to burst into flower whenever it feels like it. We have seen the same clump of frangipanis gaily blooming in the spring and again in the early winter of the same year!

The dazzling Shower of Gold, or *Cassia fistula* to use its academic name, often grows to a height of 40 feet. Its yellow buds and petals, cascading downward, really do look like a golden shower. The bark has long had a commercial use in the fabrication of dyes, and it has medicinal properties, which have produced various purgatives, astringents, and cough medicines wherever the tree is found. It's at its peak throughout the Caribbean from April to June.

Another flowering tree to watch for is the immortelle, known as *Erythrina cresta galli* or, more commonly, the coral tree. But immortelle is most appropriate, for these trees can put out their cock's comb blossoms even after they have been chopped down, sawed up, and burned in a fire! Haiti is one of the places to see this tree. It also thrives in Jamaica, Puerto Rico, Dominica, and everywhere that coffee is produced. The immortelle is a favorite tree for shading the smaller trees on which coffee, cocoa, and spices are grown, a fact which is reflected in popular names for the mountain immortelle in Trinidad: *coffee mama* and *cocoa mama.*

Two of the most outstanding plumed monarchs of the Caribbean are the jacaranda tree, a fabulous beauty from India and Ceylon with bell-shaped flowers and fern-like leaves, and the Pride of Burma, whose gold and vermilion inflorescence makes it one of the most prized ornamental trees in the world. You'll find it in Jamaica, Trinidad, and elsewhere in the Caribbean where it blooms from early winter right through to the following fall. Not as commonplace as the poinciana, the *Amherstia nobilis,* to use its botanical name, has to be sought for. But it is well worth the search. Almost as rare is the bombax, or silk cotton tree, whose silky red tassels appear in June and remain through July.

The commoners are as beautiful as the aristocrats in this part of the world, especially the African tulip tree with its cups of crimson and gold, and the ubiquitous *brassaia,* growing all over the islands with its gray bark, glossy green leaves, and stunning, deep red, spiky flowers. Two impressive towering African tulip trees stand sentinel at Josephine's childhood home on the island of Martinique. The brassaias bloom in early summer and are a flower-arranger's delight, since they last and last, long after they have been cut from the tree. Do not hesitate to cut them. The *brassaia* is another one of those indestructible tropical trees; like the banyan, it would take over your garden—and your house—if you didn't keep it under control.

Palms in Profusion

You will, of course, see every variety of palm tree in the islands. Perhaps the most majestic are the stately royal palms which line some of the handsomest avenues of the tropics. Two that come immediately to mind are the Royal Drive on the northern "wing" of Guadeloupe, not far from the capital of Pointe-à-Pitre, and the towering "avenue" that leads to the entrance of Codrington College on Barbados. As you fly over the islands, you'll see these trees everywhere, like millions of matchsticks stuck into the soil. When you're on the ground, these "matchsticks," soaring 50 and 60 feet in regal splendor, give the whole place an air of nobility and grandeur.

Less formal, equally appealing are the graceful coconut palms which fringe the beaches, their stiff fronds rustling in the breeze, their great clusters of fruit, green, golden, or brown, promising the pleasures of crisp white nut-meat, or if you prefer, gin and coconut water. Many Caribbean trees are as pleasing to the palate as they are to the eye. The avocado leads the lot; followed by the mango (pronounced with a broad *a),* queen of tropical fruits; the breadfruit, brought to the West Indies by Captain Bligh of the mutinous *Bounty* (St. Vincent claims credit for cultivating the only direct descendant from that original seed in its Botanical Garden near Kingstown); the sapodilla, the tamarind, the guava, the paw paw (maybe more familiar to you as papaya); the widespread banana trees with their great, ragged, fringed leaves, offering a delicious fruit which is one of the chief products of the area. The cashew nut tree, the macadamia, and the pomegranate are three more which offer special delights to the eye, the stomach, and the soul. Nor should the olfactory nerves be neglected. Remember the Spice Island, Grenada, with its nutmeg trees *(myristica fragrans),* its cinnamon, camphor, and clove trees, and that climbing orchid which produces vanilla beans both here and on rainy, aromatic Dominica.

The three c's, solace to the human race, grow profusely in the Caribbean too: coffee, cocoa, and cola. The coffee trees are beautiful: miniature affairs, not much higher than a bush, with glistening green leaves and the shiny red berry which will be burned by the sun to a dark brown bean. The cola nut tree is a tall evergreen, in the kernel of whose fruits is the narcotic essence of so many medicines and drinks. Still another tree with medicinal properties is the towering eucalyptus, splendid aromatic sentinel of the tropical forest.

Note: Perhaps this is as good a time as any to mention one of the terrors of Caribbean horticulture–the respected manchineel tree. While its waxy green leaves make it a favorite for beachside shade, its "little green apples" can fatally constrict and irritate your throat. Even the water off the leaves, when it spatters in a tropical rain storm, can cause a painful rash. While most places under development either mark or take out the manchineel trees, you will find them flourishing off the beaten path and along isolated beaches. Beware–and give them wide berth even though they look pretty.

Flowering Shrubs and Colorful Blossoms

The Caribbean's flowering trees cover the landscape with a mantle more varied than Joseph's coat of many colors. What they don't punctuate with color, the flowering vines and shrubs do: the begonia and orange trumpet vine; the popular bougainvillea, tumbling over walls in great splashes of vivid red, pinks, coral, purple, or white; hibiscus, king of all tropical shrubs, its large and showy flowers coming in many subtle shades of red, yellow, white, and pink; plumbago with its lovely blue blossoms; thunbergia, a wonderful aromatic yellow-flowered vine whose tender dark green stalks end up by becoming woody tree trunks; and crape myrtle, the blooming East Indian shrub which grows here as successfully as it does in Dixie.

Tourists from temperate climates will be fascinated to see the most expensive and exotic denizens of hot house and city florist shop growing in dazzling profusion in their native soil. On many islands, you will see orchids, not in constrained corsages, but in great sprays, literally dripping from the trees. The variety is staggering: cattleyas, vandas, dendrobiums, oncidiums, almost every kind of orchid that is known. The Orchid Society's regular meetings in Puerto Rico and the Virgin Islands are worth attending if you are fascinated by these plants.

Another great floral favorite is the anthurium, hardy but exotic perennial with its striking waxen spathe, blood red, sometimes pink or white, punctuated by its yellow priapic anther. You will also be tempted to "sport with Amaryllis in the shade," especially here where the red and tigerish blossoms of these bulbous plants are beautiful beyond compare.

Less exotic perhaps, but no less charming, are the African lilies *(Agapanthus africanus)* with their arresting blue flowers; the bright, showy cannas, bigger and more numerous here than they are at home; huge Shasta daisies; flaming poinsettias, which grow here not in pots but in fields or massed together on a scarlet ornamental band to set off a lawn; hydrangeas, those popular shrubs with the pink, white, or blue flowers that are called *hortensias* throughout Latin America; African violets, periwinkles, and brilliant, slightly wicked-looking zinnias. These last annuals, the alphabetical rear-guard of any floral check list, are among the most common glories of West Indian gardens.

Botanic Gardens

The gardens of the Caribbean, both private and public, and the magnificent rain forests of all the mountainous islands, will be pilgrimage goals for all tourists with horticultural and botanical interests. Some resorts, most notably the Rockresorts of the Virgin Islands (Caneel Bay and Little Dix), offer garden tours around their premises with full and fascinating commentary by specialists. And some specific islands are particular meccas for botanists—Dominica, for example, where the inner regions have never been fully explored and tropical growth has been totally undisturbed. These garden islands, areas, and resorts are places of beauty and tranquility which will also appeal to visitors whose knowledge of flowers is only rudimentary. Even if you don't know a dendrobium from a dandelion, it is doubtful if you'll be able to resist the charm of a place like Haiti's Kenscoff Gardens, where carnations, blue larkspur, snapdragons, gladioli, Shasta daisies, and Chinese asters spread out in mountain meadows as far as your eye can see. Even the shady staple Impatiens lines the interior mountain roads of Puerto Rico, rimming the roadbed with brilliant lines of scarlet, coral, or white.

One of the northern Caribbean's most spectacular projects is the Botanic Garden outside Santo Domingo in the Dominican Republic. Students from the Agricultural University work to plant every known shrub and plant in the area designated for that purpose near the zoo. The entire park area is an exhibition of the flora and fauna of the Caribbean.

Almost every British-affiliated island has its botanical garden, well organized and maintained, reflecting the traditional English love of flowers and shrubs adapted, by the earliest settlers, to tropical homes in the new world. Note especially the botanical gardens in Jamaica—many of which have been revamped recently to be included in new touring opportunities. The garden on the North Shore's Shaw Park estate is the locale for regular band concerts. Other botanical gardens to note are those at Kingstown, St. Vincent; in the hills of Grenada;

inland on Barbados (where Welchman Hall Gully preserves many plants now extinct in other areas); St. George's near Frederiksted on St. Croix; and at Trinidad, not far from Port of Spain.

The Asa Wright Nature Centre at the Spring Hill area in the northern mountain range of Trinidad offers one of the most fascinating stay-and-watch opportunities for those interested in Caribbean flora and fauna. It is possible to stay at the Centre and go on forays into the jungle area with experienced guides.

The gardens, usually providing qualified guides, are mentioned in more detail in the chapters that follow, as are the various experimental agricultural stations, rain forests, and other preserves where giant tree ferns, bamboos, mahogany trees and other floral glories of the tropics grow in settings that will remain among the most vivid memories of your Caribbean tour.

A SUN-SWEPT PLAYGROUND

From the Sea Depths to the Mountain Tops

The 2500 square miles of islands and sparkling blue water stretching southeast from Florida to the Spanish Main constitute the Elysian Fields of the Western Ocean as far as the sportsman is concerned. This happy hunting ground abounds with fighting fish and game and offers the tourist the best natural conditions for many sports, especially those practiced in, on, or under the sea. The great increase in Caribbean tourism has brought with it a corresponding development of sports and guide facilities. These are indicated under the separate country sections in this book. Here we present an overall picture of the Caribbean sports potential.

In different places, there are facilities for sports from horseback riding and snorkeling to surf riding and sky diving. Then there are many spectator sports, from baseball and horse racing to soccer and cockfighting, with opportunities to watch a good game of cricket.

Camping

Campsites are a part of the plan for the more sophisticated resorts like Jamaica, where a prime piece of shoreline has been set aside for campers. Called Strawberry Fields, the grounds are on the north coast, not far from Annotto Bay.

In the U.S. Virgin Islands, most of St. John is a National Park, with specific areas set up for tenting. The camping shelters at Cinnamon Bay can be rented through the park superintendent. At a privately leased bay in the Park area, Maho Bay Camps Ltd. offers about 50 wood-and-canvas "cottages" for campers.

In Dominica, which sits in the Caribbean sea between the French islands of Guadeloupe to the north and Martinique to the south, you can camp in jungle areas. (Since equipment is limited, bring your own.) And on St. Lucia, there has been talk of camping and climbing on the famed Pitons, the much-photographed twin peaks on the southwest shore.

Exploring is half the fun of camping, and half the islands of the Caribbean are still to be fully explored.

Cockfighting

Cockfights are held at Port-au-Prince, Haiti, and San Juan, Puerto Rico (Friday evenings, Saturday and Sunday afternoons). Fights are held in organized cockpits in Boca Chica and elsewhere in the Dominican Republic. St. Martin has an arena on the French Side. Guadeloupe and Martinique and the other smaller French islands also enjoy cockfights. Your hotel can fill you in on times, dates, and places.

The main interest lies in betting on the matches, but since the crowd that usually assembles is made up of avid enthusiasts, the action moves so fast that you may not even realize that your nod has placed a bet. Unless you have a guide, or are familiar with the ritual, it's best to stand in the background. You'll obviously be an outsider anyway.

Cricket

Cricket is a Caribbean ritual on all the British-affiliated islands from January through April. Jamaica, Barbados, Dominica, Trinidad, Tobago, Grenada, St. Vincent, Antigua have their most important matches–often with teams visiting from Britain, and/or Australia–toward the end of the season, but you'll see a game in progress (sometimes with the children beachside) at all times of the year. The "formal" cricket matches are well attended, with an enthusiastic and well-informed crowd.

Fishing

Big fish. Small fish. All colorful and sought from shore or from high sea. So organized has fishing become that there is a special Division of Fishing and Water Sports within the U.S. Virgin Islands Department of Commerce, so that those wishing to fish off St. Thomas, St. John, St. Croix, and even the British Virgins can get full and detailed information.

Record fish are commemorated with special certificates to the anglers, and tournaments are held, usually during the summer and fall, for islanders and visitors.

Grand Cayman boasts of bottom fishing and trolling for bonito, jack, and barracuda, or going farther out for the "big ones."

Fishing is also good 757 miles southeast of Miami off the Turks and Caicos Islands, where enthusiasts recently landed a 334-pound blue marlin.

In the Bahamas, Bimini is a tiny island devoted entirely to game fishing. Lying right on the edge of the Gulf Stream, it has already produced over three dozen world records. In Nassau, individually owned charter boats are available on a daily or weekly basis. Fishing grounds are along the north coast of the island of New Providence.

On Andros, there are charter boats available, as well as skiffs with outboards and guides for inshore work. There's good variety, with bonefishing on the flats and river fishing for tarpon.

Flying

The Caribbean has responded to the increase in private plane traffic with enthusiasm. The area is as perfect for small plane travel as it is for the sailing yachts that thread the islands by sea. The Bahama Islands are the leaders at the moment, with some fifty airports scattered over that area and special flying events held for those who are interested. The November Treasure Hunt by air has become a Bahamian tourist classic. The Tourist Board has details on the annual event.

In Jamaica, the several airports (Kingston, Ocho Rios area, Montego Bay, and Port Antonio) offer facilities for small planes—and flying lessons. Port Antonio is a favorite for many. The Civil Aeronautics Department in Kingston will give you an examination on the local regulations and endorse your flying license for use in Jamaica.

In San Juan, you can rent a Cessna or Piper Cub for about $30 an hour from the Isla Grande Flying School. It's a short flight from San Juan to St. Thomas, with the views making it well worthwhile, but there are plenty of interesting destinations right in Puerto Rico: Palmas del Mar on the southeast coast, Borinquen on the northwest coast (and a former U.S. military base now turned sports facility with golf, tennis, etc.), and Mayaguez, Ponce, and the islands off the east end, Vieques and Culebra.

The St. Thomas airport has a fleet of small craft available for charter or for flying lessons from experienced teachers. The same is true for St. Croix, 40 miles south.

Golf

The island-speckled seas of the Atlantic and the Caribbean offer courses for the pros and the duffers, ranging from the cluster of four Robert Trent Jones courses at the Cerromar-Dorado Beach complex in Puerto Rico to pitch-and-putt spots outside hotels where there's nothing but the sand and the sea. Rates vary, as do courses, but here's a selection:

For the Bahamas, a total of sixteen courses are scattered over the several islands. The heart of the matter (still) is New Providence, where there are four 18-hole championship courses, and one more across the bridge on Paradise Island.

On Grand Bahama, the casino island, the six courses are being put into golf packages, assuring their upkeep and play. As for the Out Islands, there are two courses on Eleuthera, one at Cotton Bay Club, and another at Cape Eleuthera Golf Club. Abaco has Treasure Cay, and the Berry Islands settle for Great Harbour's course.

In Jamaica, Tryall is tops, although there are seven other courses scattered over the island to lure vacationers away from the beach. Half Moon/Rose Hall course is considerably flatter and less exciting, and the Eden Country Club course is worth the play, but needs seasoning. Heading east along the shore, there are Runaway Bay and the Upton Country Club, just outside Ocho Rios. Constant Spring and Caymanas courses give you golf practice in the Kingston orbit, but not much.

The Dominican Republic's La Romana has been the pacesetter in recent seasons. Campo de Golf Cajuiles (Ka-wheel-ays) is on the Gulf and Western sugar and vacation estate about 45 minutes from the capital, along the southeast coast. It's a Pete Dye masterpiece, with seven of the holes running along, over, and through the Atlantic. It took two and a half years to mold by hand and is spectacular. So spectacular, in fact, that a second 18 was added. On the north coast at Puerto Plata, the new Jack Tar Village on Playa Dorado, has a fine 18-hole course that weaves its way along and around the sea.

Puerto Rico has a grand total of eight courses, most of them clustered on the north coast west of San Juan, where you can romp around four courses. The Dorado Beach and Cerromar combination of four 18-hole courses are all Trent Jones design. Save the South Course at Cerromar for your "final round." That's where the trade winds blow the hardest, and you should have a really good drive if you expect to score there. Dorado del Mar Golf Club has a seaside layout that abuts the other courses. Farther out, heading west, is the Borinquen course, formerly the U.S. military base course but, after a complete facelift, now part of an impressive recreation complex. At Puerto Rico's southeastern shore, the Palmas del Mar resort at Humacao not only has a spectacular course, but its own golf village.

As for the U.S. Virgin Islands, the Fountain Valley Course on St. Croix is one of the best in the Caribbean. It's in good shape with good facilities. One of the most convenient courses for vacation play is the Buccaneer Hotel's own course, meandering over shoreside, hillside acreage. There are golf carts for the 18 holes and a Pro Shop near one of the resort's beaches. There are 9 holes at the Reef, east of Christiansted. On St. Thomas, the brand new Mahogany Run 18-hole championship course is a real beauty, with each hole a challenge, as they run from oceanfront to hilltop.

St. Maarten's course at Mullet Bay has 18 holes, some with beachside views, but most over ponds and hills inland.

The islands in the "middle" Caribbean are light on golf. All have big plans, but as of this writing the only places with any kind of course are Nevis, where there are 9 holes at Zetlands Plantation; St. Kitts, where there is a full-scale course at Frigate Bay, at the "handle" of that cricket bat shaped island; Montserrat has its 9 abutting Vue

Pointe Hotel at the Belham Course, where the land crab holes vie with the planned ones for your ball.

St. Lucia's Cap Estate put the topper on that island. The North Point course is a few steps from the Cariblue Hotel and is entertaining, if not too challenging. La Toc provides golf facilities closer to Castries. On St. Vincent, the Aquaduct course is inland in a mountain setting, rambling along a Vincentian river valley. The first 9 offer a lot of challenges.

The French West Indies are talking a lot of golf, brought up by the big Méridien Hotel-Air France plans. At Martinique in the region of the Méridien at Pointe du Bout, across the bay from Fort-de-France there is a Robert Trent Jones 18-hole course; and another Jones beauty on Guadeloupe, adjacent to the Méridien, at Saint François, along the southeast coast.

Barbados has Durant's Championship Golf Course on a 216-acre development along the east coast. This is the home of the Barbados Golf and Country Club. In addition, there's the well-played Sandy Lane course in the heart of the luxury hotel area.

Trinidad has the Moka course in the Maraval Valley area, a few miles outside of Port of Spain. Tobago's Jack Harris course is on an old coconut plantation, along the sea at Mount Irvine. It's good.

Anyone who reads the golf magazines knows of the choices for golf tours, but check with your travel agent about special golfing vacations in the Caribbean. Many of the hotels with their own golf courses–or one nearby–give bargain rates at times other than height of season. It's worth checking, since the Caribbean weather seldom varies, and the low rates can give you golf and sunshine at good value.

No charge for golf equipment if it fits into free baggage allowance. If over, you pay 1% of one-way first class fare (even if traveling economy) to any destination.

Horse Racing

The principal track in the northern Caribbean is El Comandante in San Juan, Puerto Rico (racing three times a week all the year round). Other places offering horse racing are "Paso Fino" races at Salinas, Santa Cristo de la Salud Festival in old San Juan in August, Hobby Horse Hall in Nassau, Bahamas (Tuesdays and Saturdays, January to April), Cayman Race Track, Kingston, Jamaica (every Saturday). There are three big race meetings (Saturdays in February, August, and December) in Barbados. Occasional meetings are also held in Trinidad (January at Queen's Park), Tobago (March at Shirvars Park), St. Croix (Easter Monday and July), and at Perla de las Antillas track, Santo Domingo in the Dominican Republic. These, though smaller, are colorful and good for an afternoon's fun.

Horseback Riding

Horses are available for casual hacking in most of the islands. There are stables and good trails in Barbados; Port Antonio, Jamaica;

and Gulf & Western's Casa de Campo in the Dominican Republic. You can ride along the beach in Aruba and not far from Frederiksted on St. Croix. Nevis, Montserrat, and St. Martin also offer horses for rent.

Mountain Climbing

Most of the islands are high and mountainous, but little climbing has been done, and only in some places you can find guides. For the keen climber, the best is Soufrière village in St. Lucia, where the two bottle-shaped Pitons rise almost sheer out of the sea. Though not very high, the Petit Piton (2,461 feet) is very steep all the way, with a bare top from which you get a fine view, while the Grand Piton (2,619 feet and wooded) offers a slightly easier ascent and nearby Morne Gimme (3,145 feet) a very easy one.

Mt. Misery (3,792 feet) at St. Kitts presents a minor challenge, surpassed by Dominica's Mt. Diablotin.

In the northern part of St. Vincent, you can climb the Soufrière. A guide is recommended, since the paths are overgrown, and the most interesting way to climb is up one side and down the other, making it essential for you to negotiate with two cab drivers. One will drive you up the western shore of the island; the other will pick you up at a specified time on the eastern shore. There is no road around the island in the north.

Other volcanoes to climb are those on the French islands, with Mt. Pelée on Martinique the most famous. A guide is essential here, and arrangements can be made when you get to the starting point or through your hotel before you leave for the excursion. Guadeloupe's volcano, outside the town of Soufrière, is easy to conquer, with a road halfway up and paths clearly marked for the climb to the top.

Consider also Kingston, Jamaica, where the Blue Mountain (7,420 feet) offers a mild expedition. Saba and St. Eustatius, Netherlands Antilles, offer informal climbing.

Polo

Polo is played at Kingston, Ocho Rios, and Montego Bay in Jamaica on Sunday afternoons all through the winter and at several places in Barbados on Sundays, September to January.

In Santo Domingo, Dominican Republic, games can be had all year round on the grounds outside the capital, and an enthusiastic group of residents encourages vacationing polo players to participate in the games played at the field near Casa de Campo, the Gulf & Western luxury resort.

Sailing

The Caribbean has been known as a fog-free sailing area with good steady winds since the time of Columbus and the pirates—and even before. Almost every Caribbean inn is moored to the sea. If there's not at least a Sunfish or Sailfish with sails slapping in a beach-side breeze, then surely the management can put you in touch with some island resident with a boat. Sailing experiences can range from small boats to island fishing sloops and schooners to huge charter yachts with uniformed crew. Somewhere in the middle of that fleet are the bareboat business and the sail-and-learn programs that have become the features of recent seasons.

Literally thousands leave landlocked cities and towns in the north and head south for their first sail. Bill Stevens of Stevens Yachts reports that more than 80% of his clients are first-time sailors. Since his crewed yachts are manned by experts who often double as sailing instructors and gourmet cooks, the nonsailor need feel no handicap.

Although there may be more boats to charter than there are guest houses to stay in on some islands, Caribbean sailors beat to three "hearts." The Virgins–American and British–are the best areas for the small-boat sailor or the weekend lake sailor who knows the fundamentals, but has seldom handled a steady and stiff breeze. While the seas can kick up, landfalls are plentiful and easily reached if you're more comfortable riding out the stiff squalls in a protected cove.

The Grenadines, that spate of isles and cays running between St. Vincent and Grenada in the southern Caribbean, are the second cruising ground, regarded as the first by many experienced skippers. The first-time Grenadine sailor is best advised to hire a crewed yacht, even if he gradually takes over the sailing chores (and fun) as the cruise gets underway and courage increases. There's distance between each of the Grenadines and, until you learn to read the colors of the Caribbean (the shades of blue that indicate sandy bottom, reefs, and the cloud puffs) it's comforting to have an experienced hand on board. Reading Admiralty charts, with a buoy system that follows British custom in formerly British seas, and learning island lore also make a skipper worth his weight, space, and food and drink bill–which is your responsibility on most crewed yachts.

The third Caribbean area, in our oversimplified division, is the sea running west and south from Antigua, where Lord Nelson tucked into English Harbour. The Nicholsons established their chartering firm here when they dropped anchor of their *Mollihawk* after sailing from England. Antigua is at the elbow of the Caribbean just before the hand reaches to South America, embracing the Caribbean sea.

Although many private yachts head south for the winter to cruise through the Caribbean on more or less rigid itineraries, most report in to one of the five charter firms that have taken the lead in putting organized business practices behind the carefree matter of sailing.

For details, consult with *Caribbean Sailing Yachts, Nicholson's Yachts,* and *Stevens Yachts,* all discussed earlier in our *Facts at Your Fingertips* section under *Yachting.*

Firms like *Ocean Yacht Enterprises, Inc.,* in St. Thomas, V.I., act as booking offices for yachts in the area, and *World Yacht Enterprises,* with New York offices at 14 West 55th Street, includes Caribbean yachts.

For beginners, Stevens, and CSY have sailing schools, both in the

Grenadines. CSY's program is ten days on a Carib 41 out of St. Vincent.

Most skippers on crewed yachts will, of course, take the time to explain the rudiments of sailing and even give on-location lessons if you express the interest.

If you haven't gone this way before, head south with:

Guide to Bareboat Chartering, 72 pp. with charts and illustrations, from Caribbean Sailing Yachts, Ltd., Box 491, Tenafly, N.J. 07670.

Yachtsman's Guide to the Bahamas, 316 pp. 229 charts, from CSY.

Yachtsman's Guide to the Virgin Islands, 130 pp. 42 charts, from CSY.

Yachtsman's Guide to the Windward Islands, 248 pp. 122 charts and illustrations, from CSY.

No matter what your guest lists reads (and finding a compatible sailing six is more of a challenge than you may think), the most important sailing companions will be a hat, a long-sleeved shirt, and long pants. The sun is warm, but steady and hot, and until you've done it you cannot appreciate the effects of too much sun on the sea. Suntan lotions, preferably nongreasy, and a sun block are other musts. For the sake of your sailing companions and yourself, since space is at a premium even on the largest craft, soft suitcases which can be stuffed into spare nooks and a minimum of clothing become almost as important as your sailing companions.

Snorkeling and Scuba Diving

The underwater Caribbean is as exciting as the land, and every island has its links with the world below. Snorkeling is spectacular—even for the complete novice—at Buccoo Reef, off Tobago; at Sand Cay with its underwater reef not far from Haiti's Port-au-Prince; near Catalina Island, reached by boat from La Romana, Dominican Republic; along the trails with underwater signs near Buck Island, off St. Croix, or not far from Caneel Bay on St. John in the U.S. Virgin Islands.

For the diver, the challenges are endless—the most exciting yet to be discovered. The Cayman Islands boast of more than 365 wrecks off their shores, and frigates are still being found in waters off the British Virgin Islands—near reefs off Anegada or even at the area's main town on Tortola.

Scuba experts on Grand Turk can help you explore the little known Turks and Caicos, The reefs off Curaçao—and its relative Bonaire—are an easy distance from shore. On Bonaire, where conservationists urge looking, but not catching, road markers document interesting diving areas and enthusiasm for scuba holidays has burgeoned.

Tobago was early on the scuba and snorkeling bandwagon, and well she might be, because her underwater coral formations and schools of colorful tropical fish make these waters some of the most rewarding for skin-diving explorers.

Skin-diving in Jamaica is predominantly on the North Shore and off Negril. The Jamaica Hilton in Ocho Rios has a full scuba operation in its Aquatic Club.

The popularity of underwater exploration has resulted in professional instruction, equipment rentals, and guided excursions to offshore islands or reefs, where you'll see the most interesting fish, coral formations, and wrecks. For the most part, the people are experienced and highly competent; you can be sure of safety and getting your money's worth if you stick to recommended firms. Most will post their services and rates in your hotel, and some of the larger resorts have their own men on hand, with boats and diving equipment. In some cases, you have to bring your own equipment or rent it from a place in town.

There are a number of special holiday plans for experienced and for novice divers. Although all hotels on Bonaire are scuba oriented, the Hotel Habitat has a regular routine (and package weeks at good rates) for underwater enthusiasts.

The French West Indies has joined in the scuba enthusiasm, with one new scuba diving school on Guadeloupe and three on Martinique. And the new Club Mediterranee on Eleuthera in the Bahamas has chosen scuba as its emphasis for this particular property.

Each season brings new programs for this increasingly popular sport. Summer programs are usually less expensive and just as good as peak season winter excursions.

Surfing

From December through April, the trade winds send great rolling waves sweeping over the shallow sand bars in beautiful Maracas Bay, Trinidad, providing good conditions for surfing. An excellent surfing area is being developed in northern Eleuthera, near Gregory Town. The World Surfing Championships were held in 1968 at Punta Higuero, between Aguadilla and Rincon in Puerto Rico. One of the newer areas to come into focus is a beach outside of Port Antonio on Jamaica's eastern shore.

At Barbados, this sport can be enjoyed at North Point Surf Resort. Conareef Beach and Frigate Bay are the best in St. Kitts.

Swimming

The swimming is very good in all the islands, but the beaches do vary considerably in quality (from pure white sand to almost black) and also in accessibility. However, some are excellent, with white sand and crystal-clear water within easy reach of the hotels.

Antigua has several fine sandy beaches. Barbados has several along its western shore and an exceptional one at Crane Hotel on its eastern side. West Bay Beach on Grand Cayman runs for six miles without a break. The north shore of Jamaica is studded with well-known beaches such as Doctor's Cave, Discovery Bay, and Tower Isle. The island's most spectacular, Negril, is a seven-mile stretch of near deserted white sand beach, fifty miles west of Montego Bay.

At The Baths, on Virgin Gorda in the British Virgin Islands, swimmers wend their way in, around, and under the massive boulders tossed up on a stunning white sand beach. St. Thomas has several lovely strands, including big, deep Magen's Bay, its translucent sheltered waters framed by towering hills.

The Bahamas are made of sand, so there are beaches to spare. Sint Maarten's and St. John's are unsurpassed. Aruba's seven-mile-long white sand beach is excellent for all water sports. Tobago is studded with excellent beaches, including Pigeon Point, Store Bay, Bacolet Beach, and Great Courland Bay.

Puerto Rico has two sublime strands: Luquillo on the Atlantic, Boquerón on the Caribbean.

Soccer

In Port-au-Prince, Haiti, soccer is the most popular spectator sport, with regular night games throughout the year often drawing highly enthusiastic crowds of up to 25,000 people. It is also played in Trinidad, usually on Saturday afternoons from July to December (though they call it football).

In Jamaica, soccer is played year round all over the island, with school and amateur league matches during the October-January season at Kingston's National Stadium.

The Easter Sunday soccer game between Guadeloupe and Martinique is a classic sports event. Opening of the season in Aruba is April; in Trinidad, July.

Soccer is a fast, exciting game with simple, easily followed rules and well worth seeing when you have the chance. Dates, times, and locations of matches are listed in the local newspapers.

Tennis

Caribbean tennis has responded to the impact of stateside enthusiasts. New courts are cropping up throughout the islands, and interisland tennis teams compete. On most islands, there are some tennis courts available; on the largest islands there are many—usually at hotels, often as private tennis clubs—to which visitor introductions are easily arranged. If tennis is crucial for a happy holiday, check with the island tourist office and the hotel of your choice.

Here are some tennis highlights: On Puerto Rico, there are courts at most of the big hotels, with a grand array of almost a dozen at the Carib-Inn, which was built with tennis in mind. Cerromar Hotel has a summer tennis camp at its location on the north coast near Dorado, and the tennis area at Palmas del Mar on the southeast coast has spectacular courts.

The Rockresorts (Caneel Bay on St. John, U.S.V.I., and Little Dix on Virgin Gorda, B.V.I.) have tennis clinics. Check the hotels for details.

In Jamaica, you can challenge Jamaican talent on the courts. The Montego Bay Raquet Club arranges games between members and island visitors. More than fourteen hotels in the Montego Bay area have their own courts, with ten more sources outside the town and more at Ocho Rios and Kingston. In Ocho Rios, the Jamaica Hilton offers a tennis clinic program.

On St. Croix, there's a tennis Club and good courts with pro at Buccaneer, and other hotels.

On Antigua, the annual Antigua Open is a pro-am tournament in January, but Half Moon Hotel has special summer tennis clinics. Curtain Bluff also concentrates on tennis.

Water Skiing

Water skiing is spreading rapidly through the islands and there are dozens of places where regular schools with boats, equipment, and competent instructors are always available. Barbados has a "Competition" in February. Most hotels have their own facilities. If not, ask. As with the other water sports, rates vary from instructor to instructor, island to island. Don't hesitate to try; if you are in good health and a good swimmer, you'll find it easy to learn.

Parasailing

This soaring-into-the sky sport has just become an attraction in the Caribbean. The Bahama Islands started it all, with flights that last just five minutes, but provide a different thrill and certainly a different view of the tropics. The *Atlantik Beach Hotel* on Grand Bahama, and the *Nassau Beach* and *Ambassador Beach Hotels* on New Providence, provide the harness and the instructor who will have you aloft from a shoreside deck in no time. Other islands are experimenting with take-offs from their beaches to assure that you won't get wet enroute.

Windsurfing

Most of the islands that offer watersports now include this challenge. Be aware that strong arms and a great sense of balance are important (your instructors will make sure you're capable before they set you free from the "launching pad") and once you're on your own you'll sail free to explore the Caribbean waters in a new and exciting way.

THE ISLANDS

ANGUILLA

An Eel-shaped Eden

Take thirty-five square miles of arid, eel-shaped, beach-fringed land, add a combination of British and West Indian influences, and you have the island of Anguilla, which has long been a sleepy outpost just waiting for the nod from tourists. Until recently there wasn't much here other than peace, tranquility, and the opportunity to swim, explore the reefs, and take the sun. At last count there were thirty white coral sand beaches, some L-shaped, some a crescent, some shaded by coconut palms, others edged by undersea gardens.

St. Martin, its closest neighbor, lies ten miles to the south, and only when visitors began to make the excursion by small plane, sailboat or ferry did Anguilla realize its potential and take its first steps to reach out and beguile. Now villas and apartments are abuilding, and a health spa has opened out at Barnes Bay, but there's still plenty of room to "hideaway." Accommodations are all low-rise and so scattered on this island that wiggles along for sixteen miles that you'll still feel as if you're the only guest.

The principal port of entry, Road Bay, is a lovely little village where whoever is at hand will welcome you and make you feel at home. There are just 6,500 inhabitants, all of them friendly and eager to please.

The mainstay of the Anguillan is fishing and lobster pronging, a business which supplies the hotel kitchens on nearby islands. There is the salt industry at Sandy Ground, where salt is harvested and exported to several Caribbean islands. And, on their small farms, the islanders grow pigeon peas, sweet potatoes, Indian corn, beans, and sea island cotton.

History

Through the eye of Columbus's telescope, the long spindly landfall resembled an eel–*anguilla* in Spanish. But the explorer only named the island, and nothing much happened for almost 200 years. Then British settlers arrived in the seventeenth century. The French invaded in the eighteenth century. It was not until 1969 that America took note, when Anguilla ran notices in U.S. papers urging that tourists stay home but send donations. They needed funds, but not to be overrun by outsiders.

In their efforts to sever links with St. Kitts and Nevis, Anguillans made a stab at total independence by declaring their island a republic. In an escapade that had a bit of the "eel that squealed" aspect, British paratroopers landed in force at night. Cooler heads eventually prevailed. In 1976 Anguilla was given its own constitution as a separate British Dependent Territory. Today there is a British Commissioner to handle foreign affairs and an island-elected Legislative Assembly to handle internal ones.

EXPLORING ANGUILLA

The main attractions on Anguilla are its beaches and reefs, which make the island ideal for swimming, snorkeling, and scuba diving. The village of *Road Bay* on the northern shore is the focal point, with a spectacular bluff overlooking the salt ponds.

Heading east, *Crocus Bay* was the scene of an unsuccessful French invasion during the eighteenth century. Today it is a quiet spot and a favorite of local fishermen. Nearby *Shoal Bay* is an L-shaped beauty which also boasts glorious undersea gardens. *Island Harbour,* near the island's eastern tip, is a fishing village and the gateway to the offshore islands and cays.

Blowing Point, on Anguilla's southern shore, will probably be your introduction to the island if you arrive by boat. The ferries and sailboats from St. Martin dock here daily. *Forest Bay* to the east attracts the fishing boats; with its reefs, it is a favorite of divers.

Heading west, you reach beautiful *Rendezvous Bay*. It curves like a half moon, making it not only picturesque but perfect for sunbathing and for the best shelling on the island. For one of the few beaches fringed by coconut palms (a rare commodity on this scrub-oak island), visit *Cove Bay*. The reefs here have made it a popular spot with snorkelers. *Meads Bay* is a beauty with a long powdery beach and two luxurious villas, which are just the beginning of the new Mallouhana seaside resort. The new Anguilla Holiday Spa is nearby at *Barnes Bay*.

A DAY ON YOUR OWN

Anguilla is one of the few islands in the Caribbean where touring in a bathing suit and cover-up is a must. Make it a full day. The earlier you start out the better.

Whether you arrive by boat or plane, begin by driving north to *Road Bay*. As you approach you will see the shimmering salt ponds, and hills of salt crystals that have been harvested from them. This is the *South Hill* area, but plan to stop here as you return. Head east, passing *Crocus Bay*, to *Shoal Bay* for a swim and a snorkel view of the underwater garden trail. If you've packed a picnic lunch, this is the place to enjoy it. Otherwise, head back to *South Hill* for a leisurely seafood luncheon at the *Harbour View Restaurant*.

Drive south again to *Blowing Point* and west to *Rendezvous Bay*. This is "shell heaven," so you may want to spend some time ambling along the beach, taking another swim, and snorkeling if the spirit moves you. If you're really feeling energetic and have brought the proper attire, you can play a set of tennis at the Rendezvous Bay Hotel—or rent a sailfish or water skis. There's something for everybody, including a bar on the hotel's verandah.

PRACTICAL INFORMATION FOR ANGUILLA

HOW TO GET THERE. By air. *Windward Island Airways* (WINAIR) flies from Juliana Airport on St. Martin several times daily. The round-trip airfare is $24 per person. *LIAT* flies in from St. Kitts and Antigua.

By sea. There is daily ferry service, except on Thursday, between Blowing Point on Anguilla, and Marigot, the French port on St. Martin. Commercial boats from neighboring islands also are available.

FURTHER INFORMATION. Tourist information, including a list of hotel and villa accommodations, can be obtained from the Anguilla Tourist Office, c/o The Secretariat, The Valley, Anguilla, B.W.I.

ISLAND MEDIA. *Radio Anguilla* has news broadcasts several times throughout the day from 6:30–9:30 A.M., 12 noon–2:00 P.M., and from 5:00 P.M.–10:35 P.M.

PASSPORTS, VISAS. None required of citizens of the U.S., U.K. or Canada, but some proof of identity necessary, along with a return ticket. Visas required only for stays that exceed six months.

MONEY. The Eastern Caribbean (EC) dollar is the official currency, although U.S. and Canadian dollars are readily accepted. $1 US = $2.70 EC; £1 = $6 EC.

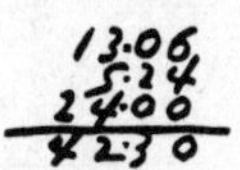

TAXES AND OTHER CHARGES. There is a 5% government tax on all accommodations. Some hotels charge an additional 10% for service. There is an island departure tax of $5 EC.

HOW TO GET ABOUT. Taxis are readily available and are inexpensive, with some drivers doubling as tour guides for the day, There are *Datsuns* and *Toyotas* for rent through *Connor's Car Rental* at South Hill. Rates run $30–35 per day, with reduced weekly rates; unlimited mileage, but gas is

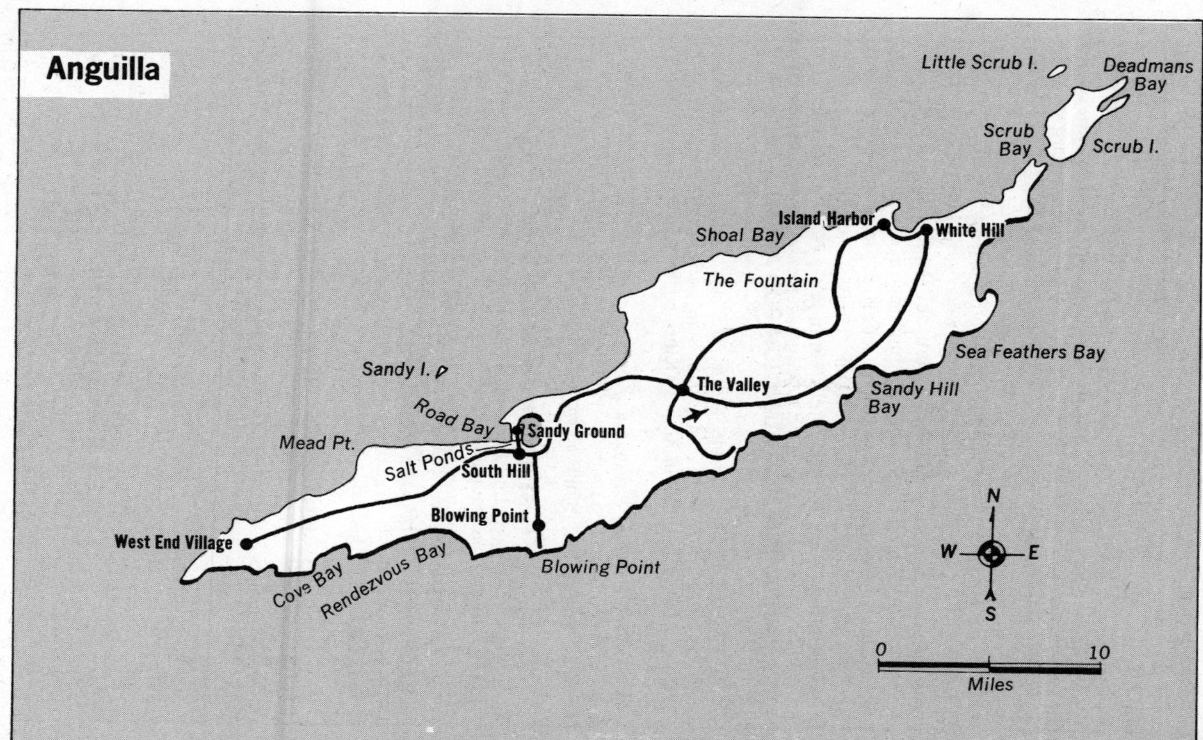
Anguilla
Little Scrub I.
Deadmans Bay
Scrub Bay
Scrub I.
Island Harbor
White Hill
Shoal Bay
The Fountain
Sea Feathers Bay
Sandy I.
The Valley
Sandy Hill Bay
Road Bay
Sandy Ground
Mead Pt.
Salt Ponds
South Hill
Blowing Point
West End Village
Cove Bay
Rendezvous Bay
Blowing Point
N
W
E
S
0
10
Miles

not included in the rates. You will need a local driver's license, which can be obtained at The Valley Police Headquarters or at the airport for $10 EC. Remember to drive on the LEFT!

EVENTS AND HOLIDAYS. The major events on Anguilla are the official parade to mark the Queen's birthday; Anguilla Day celebrations; and Carnival activities, which are held in August, but the boat races here seem to preclude costumes and parades at that time. The island's official holidays are *New Year's Day, Constitution Day* (Feb. 10), *Good Friday, Easter Monday, Whit Monday, Anguilla Day* (May 10), the *Queen's Official Birthday* (2nd Saturday in June), *August Monday* and *Thursday* (first week of the month), *Christmas Day,* and *Boxing Day* (Dec. 26).

WHAT WILL IT COST?

A typical day on Anguilla in season for *two* persons will run:

	US$	£
Hotel accommodations	70	38
Breakfast, lunch, and dinner, either at hotel or island restaurant	40	22
One-day sightseeing by rental car	30	16
	$140	£76

STAYING IN ANGUILLA

HOTELS. The hotels here are small, with the largest one offering 27 rooms. That number will change as building continues, but nothing will soar up into the sky. To date, all the accommodations available are "low-rise," whether they are in villas, cottages, apartments or hotels, and any and all new properties will conform.

Corito Beach Cottages. A pleasant bayside grouping of 11 cottages, some with two bedrooms and one bath; others with three bedrooms and two baths. Each is nicely furnished and fully equipped for couples or families to move right in. Strictly a "cater for yourself" spot since there's no restaurant on the premises. Seawater swimming pool, room to roam, and a nice view of off-shore islands. $80–100 double EP in winter; $60–80 double off-season.

Cul de-Sac. Six studio apartments at Blowing Point, out of the village. All rooms have a private patio, twin bedroom/living room with private bath. Guests can hide away here by preparing and serving meals in their kitchen/dining area, or dine on an à la carte basis at the gourmet restaurant on the premises. Swimming pool; small sandy cove and jetty; and a boutique for fashions and jewelry. $100 double EP in winter; $80 double off-season.

Lloyd's Hotel. This 14-room hotel in The Valley offers both single and double accommodations with bath. No frills, but clean and homey atmosphere. $45 double AP in winter; $40 double off-season.

Mallhouhana Hotel. A mouthful to pronounce (this is what the island was called when the Carib Indians were in residence), but a tropical wonderland for visitors in search of a gorgeous beach, villa living, and eventually, a full resort complex with all the sports and amenities required. It will take at least a year before additional villas, hotel rooms, tennis courts, swimming pools, and restaurant and bar are ready, but meanwhile two luxurious villas are available. They are two-story complexes that can be rented out in their entirety or in separate suites. Both are beautifully furnished, fully equipped, air-conditioned, and have terrace patios at the edge of the sand and private sun decks on the roof. From $110–450 EP all year, depending upon accommodations desired.

Rainbow Reef Villas. Four attractive self-catering two-bedroom villas quietly set on a three-acre site at Sea Feathers Bay. Their location on the beach is ideal and the "get-away-from-it-all" idea enhanced by the peace and quiet. Rates run $70 double EP in winter; $62 double off-season, including maid service.

Rendezvous Bay Hotel. The largest on the island, with 27 modern rooms and the beach at the doorstep. Watersports and tennis within arm's reach, and a popular restaurant that specializes in fresh-caught lobster and other local delights. $85 double in winter; $80 double off-season, with breakfast and dinner included.

Skiffles Villas. Another private spot, with six new villas available at Lowers Hill. Self-sufficient and attractively decorated two-bedroom units offer unique views from their galleries. Freshwater swimming pool; restaurant nearby. $125 double EP in winter; $80 double off-season.

HOME RENTALS. There are also cottages and fully furnished homes available on Anguilla. *Loblolly* is a two-apartment house with a single bath in each apartment. Also check the *Bayview Apartments* at Sandy Ground, and *Chinchary* or *Kolibri* at Sandy Hill for one- and two-bedroom apartments. Contact the Anguilla Tourist Office for rates and availability.

RESTAURANTS. Other than those at the hotels, we've found only two:

The Harbour View. Located on Back Street, South Hill. Owner/cook Lucy Halley serves fine fare at reasonable prices. One sample luncheon included salad, steamed grouper, broiled lobster, rice, and French bread. Open daily from 11 A.M. for lunch and dinner.

Riviera. A special spot for lunch or dinner, where the emphasis is on seafood with West Indian extras. A sample dinner can begin with highly seasoned fish soup, followed by broiled lobster with lime butter, sweet and sour conch, a salad, French bread and a choice of vegetables.

NIGHTLIFE. Other than an occasional local group, there is very little on this island in the way of evening entertainment.

SHOPPING. For tropical beachwear and other fashions, jewelry, and local handicrafts, try the *Sunshine Shop* at South Hill, or *Stephanie's Boutique* at Cul de Sac.

SPORTS AND OTHER ACTIVITIES. This is not a resort island yet, and as such concentrates on the sun, the sand, and the sea. On Anguilla snorkeling, scuba diving, and all watersports are naturals. To arrange for waterskiing and windsurfing, or for renting snorkeling equipment, check with *Anguilla Travel Services,* the island's local tour operator. They also offer snorkeling expeditions, boat trips to secluded Little Bay, picnics on uninhabited Sandy Island, or visits to the beaches and coral gardens of Prickly Pear Cays or to the caves on Little Scrub Island.

ANTIGUA

The Admiral's Dockyard and Other Pleasures

Antigua, the largest of the British Leeward Islands, lies 1,700 miles south of New York. Its 108 square miles are the limestone and volcanic remnants that have built beach-fringed, scrub-covered islands throughout the Caribbean. But Antigua is more than that. They say they have 365 beaches, one for every day of the year, and we don't doubt it.

Antigua is roughly circular in shape and ringed by jagged coves, silent bays, and small harbors, each with its sun-swept beach. In addition, there are off-shore islands such as Pelican, Crump, Guiana, and Long (uninhabited and not to be confused with New York's counterpart).

Hotels have been strategically placed around the island shores, which gives Antigua a resort look if you only take the coastal road. However, inland you'll see the island in all its glory, with a lush rain forest, pineapple groves and banana trees, and minute villages with open-air fruit and vegetable markets that give you the feeling that you're really on a tropical isle.

To add to it all, Antigua has a major attraction in its English Harbour. This is a well-done restoration of the eighteenth-century dockyard that was home for Admiral Lord Nelson and his British Navy fleet. More up to date, there are two gambling casinos that are aglitter until the early hours of the morning.

History

Discovered by Columbus in 1493, Antigua was named for Santa Maria la Antigua of Seville. The accepted pronunciation has always been English, however–An-*tee*-ga with a hard "g." The island was colonized by English planters from St. Kitts in 1623. After a brief period of French occupation in 1666, it was formally given to England by the Treaty of Breda in 1667, and it has remained British ever since, abandoning its Crown Colony government only when the committee system was introduced in 1951. In 1967, in the British government's first move to grant eventual independence to the former colonies, Antigua became an Associated State within the British Commonwealth. Then, finally, on November 1, 1981, Antigua achieved full independence.

Nelson's Dockyard was built in 1784 in landlocked English Harbour, so protected from the open sea that approaching yachtsmen rush to their charts, wondering if they've somehow missed the place. Horatio Nelson arrived here in 1784 and became Commander-in-Chief of the Leeward Islands Squadron. Under his command was the Captain of HMS *Pegasus,* Prince William Henry, Duke of Clarence, who was to ascend the throne of England as William IV, the "sailor king." He was Nelson's close friend and best man at his wedding to young Fannie Nisbet, which took place on the island of Nevis in 1787. A must on your exploring list is Clarence House, the handsome stone residence which was built for the prince on the heights opposite the Dockyard.

A twentieth-century counterpart of Lord Nelson came to his anchorage here in 1949 in the person of ex–Royal Navy Commander V.E.B. Nicholson, who sailed in with his family aboard his seventy-foot schooner *Mollihawk.* They anchored at Antigua on their round-the-world excursion from England and took up day chartering out of the Mill Reef Club. From that modest beginning, the Nicholson operation is now ably in the hands of son Desmond, who operates a fleet of yachts in all sizes and shapes, with radio contact and details for pick-up efficiently maintained.

EXPLORING ANTIGUA

You can circle the island in one day, or you can splinter your touring–including picnics on any number of beaches, and day trips to the offshore islands.

St. John's, the capital, has a population of about 35,000. The market place is still the focal point for local in-town activities. A few shops sell items for visitors, but the market is mostly for those who've come to buy and sell. It's fascinating to hear them bargain loudly for fruits, vegetables, fish, and spices that fill the trays of the market ladies. Most of the old-timers will smile and say "Good morning" and will expect you to do the same. If you want to take pictures, ask–and expect to part with a few coins. The open-air market is on Market

Street and at the pier at the foot of High Street, where the schooners come and go, carrying their island produce from place to place.

The Antiguan Post Office, at the waterfront, is the best place to buy the unusual stamps that the hotels never seem to have on hand. Nearby and upstairs is the Library, where the back room is full of books on island lore, and the front rooms often hold school classes making their regular library trips.

The Council Room in the Old Court House in town is worth a look, as is Ebenezer Methodist Church, built in 1839 to replace a smaller church. It is the Mother Church for Methodism in the West Indies.

St. John's Cathedral, the Anglican Cathedral, appears on postcards and in almost all visitors' photographs. The church was originally built on this site in 1683, but was replaced by a stone building in 1745. An earthquake destroyed the building almost 100 years later and, in 1845, the cornerstone of the present cathedral was laid. The figures of St. John the Baptist and St. John the Divine, erected at the south gate, were said to have been taken from one of Napoleon's ships and brought to Antigua by a British man-o'-war.

Still in town, but at the northwest tip of the harbor, on your right as you look toward the waterfront, is old Fort James, which guarded St. John's in the pirate days. Built in 1703, its ruined ramparts overlook small islands in the bay, and its cannons still point out to sea.

As you head out of town and round the island, the sights are mostly scenic—and, of course, there are the beaches. Antigua's heartland is dotted with churches. They tell the history. Each small village has its church, and some of the more famous include St. John's in town and St. Barnabas at the village of Liberta. Known in the area as the Chapel of Ease, the church was built over 100 years ago of Antiguan green stone. Green Bay was built by the Moravians in 1845 for the emancipated slaves, and the Spring Gardens Church, begun in 1755, was also for the slaves who, prior to that time, had worshipped under the old sandbox tree.

St. George's, the military church for the island's troops in the 19th century, has been restored and is used for regular Sunday worship. St. Paul's Church at Falmouth has been rebuilt on the site of the church used for the troops during Nelson's day. The Georgian church at Parham Village, St. Peter's, was built in 1840, following plans of Thomas Weekes, an English architect. It was considerably damaged by an earthquake in 1843, but the octagonal structure is still worth a visit.

If you plan on coming out this way, call ahead to make arrangements to visit Parham Hill and Mercer's Creek, two private plantation homes that are sometimes open to visitors who make special plans.

Seeing Nelson's Dockyard involves a 30-mile roundtrip from St. John's. You'll pass some small villages and mid-island homes which have been spruced up with the island's relatively recent prosperity, and many which have not. The waving fields of sugar cane have disappeared in recent years in favor of the more profitable fields of scruffy-looking sea island cotton and acre upon acre of pineapples.

Stone sugar mills still punctuate some of the most magnificent coastal scenery in the Caribbean.

The whole of Shirley Heights and English Harbour are fascinating to history buffs. The buildings have been reclaimed by the Dockyard and Shirley Heights restoration groups and the Society of Friends of English Harbour. The Dockyard, with its museum in the Admiral's House, with a display of Nelson mementos (Porter's Lodge, Guard House, Engineer's Workshop, its Sail Loft, Paymaster's House, capstans, bollards, etc.), is a vivid reminder of history, a living monument to the men and their commanders: Nelson, Rodney, Hood. While the historical part need not take you more than an hour at the most, the area is fun for the lore that comes from today's sailors and others who saunter around the boats tied up at the present active dockyard.

Clarence House is open to visitors when the Governor is not in residence. From its perch on the hillside overlooking English Harbour, the Duke of Clarence, once Prince William Henry and later King William IV, could look over the dockyard and his *Pegasus* as she rode at anchor in the harbor.

Shirley Heights, a short drive from the sea-level harbor, is a hillside fortification that is slowly being restored. It is historically interesting and dramatic, especially at sunset. The Admiral's Inn sometimes plans evening entertainments at Shirley Heights.

If you are interested in some of the archaeological finds of Antigua, track down Desmond Nicholson of *Nicholson Yacht Charters.* He has made a serious study of the island's history and early settlers. Professionals have come to Antigua from leading universities in the U.S. to assist with some of the dig.

Indian Town, one of Antigua's National Parks, is at the northeast point of the island. Breakers roaring in with all the force of the Atlantic have carved Devils' Bridge and have created blowholes with fuming surf. A newer sight, after all this history and religion, is the lake that now monopolizes the countryside in the "middle" of Antigua. The result of the Potworks Dam, the lake was created in the late '60s by rainfall and provides most of the island's water supply. For the small children who lived in this neighborhood prior to the lake, the accessibility of water was a new and mysterious thing. These people had not been fishermen; they had been inland farmers. A Sunfish sailboat race was held soon after the lake was created—and it was the first time many of these middle-country children had ever seen a boat!

A DAY ON YOUR OWN

Even though Antigua does have hundreds of beaches, your island tour, if you want to explore to the fullest, will probably not include any more than a quick look as you pass them at every bend in the road. If possible, allow a full day to drive the coastal roads; to travel inland to stop at the tiny villages with their even tinier open-air markets; and to spend time at the restoration of Nelson's Dockyard at English Harbour.

Begin your tour in St. John's,the capital city, early in the morning. This is market time and a colorful indoctrination to the island—be a part of it all, even if you only watch the bartering for fresh fish, fruits and vegetables. Afterward, walk around the city and make a special stop at the Anglican Cathedral, which was first built in the seventeenth century and has been rebuilt twice since. It is one of the loveliest monuments on the island. Then browse through the shops, but not for bargains in china, silver or crystal (they are on islands such as St. Thomas, St. Croix and Curaçao), but for indigenous items such as bolts of flour sacking. Either buy yardage or finished shirts and wrap skirts on the spot. They are inexpensive and make great mementoes.

In town you're bound to see groups of Antiguans bent low over a game that looks like backgammon from a distance, but is something very different close up. It's called *Warri,* a betting game where warri nuts are the men that move on a hand-grooved wooden board. It's fun to play and will provide you with a real conversation piece at home.

Drive south then to English Harbour, about one hour away but allow time for the villages and scenery. You'll pass the Castle Harbour Club & Casino almost immediately after leaving St. John's. Make a note of its location so that you'll know where the gaming tables are. A second casino, at the Halcyon Cove Beach Resort on Dickenson Bay opened last year.

Continue on the inland route to the town of All Saints and on to Liberta for a stop at St. Barnabas Church. The route will be lined with banana trees, usually just ripe for the picking.

Cruise into English Harbour and, as you approach the sea, head for The Inn, a lovely bluff-top retreat. A Planter's Punch on the terrace is definitely in order now, not only as a thirst quencher, but for relaxation and an opportunity to drink in the view. Nelson's Dockyard is spectacular from this height. For a different look at history, go on to Clarence House and see how royalty has been entertained for some 200 years.

Then come down to the water and the entrance to the dockyard. Lose another century or two as you tour the old shops, visit the museum and immerse yourself in the island's nautical history.

Have a late lunch at The Admiral's Inn in the dockyard, then head back to St. John's along Fig Tree Dive on the south coast. If time permits, turn inland and take the road through the rain forest to Fig Tree Hill. Then follow the coastal road and see the sunset from a perch at the Jolly Beach Hotel before returning to St. John's.

Antigua is an island with views, and they don't stop when the sun goes down. Plan to have dinner at Halycon Cove's terrace restaurant, which you reach by a Swiss-style Hillavator that propels you to the top. Either stay there for entertainment in the lounge or make the short trip south again to the casino and try your luck.

PRACTICAL INFORMATION FOR ANTIGUA

HOW TO GET THERE. By air. *American Airlines* and *British West Indian Airways* have direct service from New York; *Eastern Airlines* flies in from Miami. From San Juan, P.R., *BWIA, Prinair,* and other small airlines offer frequent service. *LIAT* flies out of home base Antigua for down-island destinations. *Air Canada* has flights from Montreal and Toronto; *BWIA* from Toronto; *British Airways* from London. Check the airline for special midweek excursion fares; they're lower than the weekend flights.

By sea. St. John's is an ever-changing port-of-call for cruise ships out of Miami, Port Everglades, and San Juan. There's a modern terminal building with some shops and plenty of taxis.

FURTHER INFORMATION. Contact the *Antigua Dept. of Tourism and Trade* at 610 Fifth Avenue, New York, N.Y. 10020. In Canada, the *Antigua Dept. of Tourism and Trade* is at 60 St. Clair St., East, Suite 205, Toronto, Ontario M4TIN5. In London, contact their office at 15 Thayer Street, London, W1. On the island itself, the Antigua Department of Tourism is located at High Street and Corn Alley in St. John's.

AUTHORIZED TOUR OPERATORS. Adventure Tours; Caribbean Holidays; Cavalcade Tours; Flyfaire; GoGo Tours; and Hill Tours from the U.S. From Canada, Fairway Tours; Holiday House; Sunflight Holidays; and UTL Holiday Tours.

PASSPORTS, VISAS. Antigua counts tourism as the No. 1 industry and makes getting in as easy as possible. Proof of citzenship is required, plus your return ticket.

MONEY. Antigua uses the Eastern Caribbean dollar, referred to in print as E.C., and about $2.70 E.C. to $1 U.S., $6 E.C. = £1. It's advisable to go straight to the local bank and get E.C. currency, since you'll do better if you pay in local cash. Be sure to ask when people quote you prices: a dollar is not the US dollar.

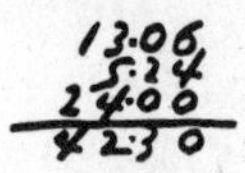

TAXES AND OTHER CHARGES. There is a 5% government tax on accommodations. In addition, hotels add a 10% service charge. The airport departure tax is $8 EC.

HOW TO GET ABOUT. There are plenty of taxis, and rates are standardized. Rates to all hotels are listed at the airport; it's advisable to check before you get into your cab. If you plan to stay at English Harbour, it's worthwhile to rent a car for a few days to sightsee and shop—and then stay put. There are some good roads, but many are one-car wide and full of bumps. The coastal scenery is worth the shake-up, whether you do it yourself or give someone else the pleasure. Driving is on the left. A local driver's permit can be obtained by showing your hometown license. The fee is $10 U.S.

Among the car rental firms are *Antigua Car Rentals* (Avis), *Ramco Car*

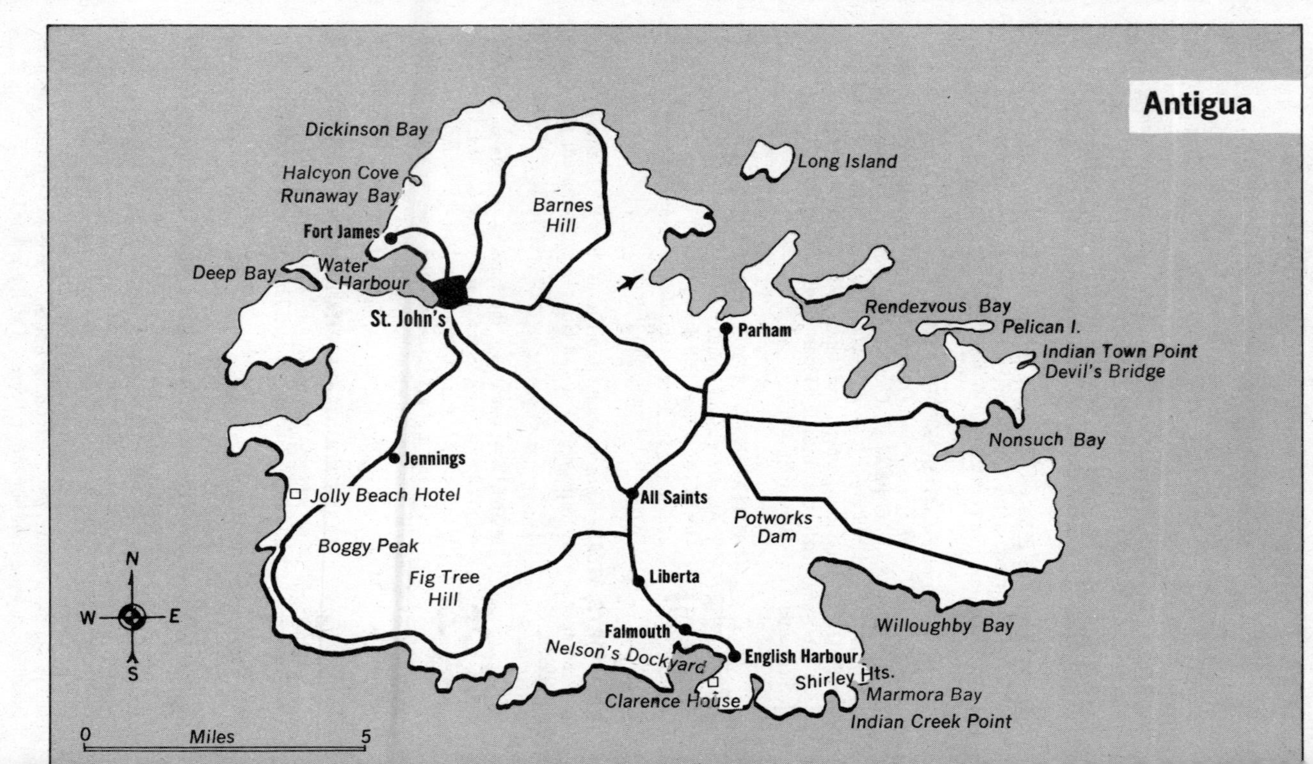
Antigua
Dickinson Bay
Halcyon Cove
Runaway Bay
Fort James
Deep Bay
Water Harbour
St. John's
Barnes Hill
Long Island
Rendezvous Bay
Pelican I.
Indian Town Point
Devil's Bridge
Parham
Nonsuch Bay
Jennings
Jolly Beach Hotel
All Saints
Potworks Dam
Boggy Peak
Fig Tree Hill
Liberta
Willoughby Bay
Falmouth
Nelson's Dockyard
English Harbour
Shirley Hts.
Marmora Bay
Clarence House
Indian Creek Point
N
W
E
S
0
Miles
5

Rental (Hertz) and *Silton's Car Rental* (National). Cars run from $20–30 per day, $130–160 per week, depending upon the season. Mileage is unlimited; insurance runs $4 per day.

Special sightseeing such as that from the water aboard the 100-foot *Tugboat Annie.* $15 U.S. per person for a 3-hour cruise; $25 U.S. per person for an all-day trip, including unlimited rum punches and a barbeque luncheon.

EVENTS AND HOLIDAYS. There are three *specials* here: Tennis Week in January; Sailing Week in April; and Carnival in late July–early August. The public holidays are New Year's Day, Good Friday, Easter Monday, Labor Day (May 1), Whit Monday, the Queen's Birthday (June 10), Independence Day (Nov. 1), Christmas Day, and Boxing Day (Dec. 26).

WHAT WILL IT COST?

A typical day on Antigua in season for *two* persons will run:

	US$	£
Hotel accommodations, with two meals	110	59
Luncheon in town or at another hotel	12	6
Tip or service charge; room tax	18	10
One-day sightseeing by rental car or taxi	25	14
	$165	£89

STAYING IN ANTIGUA

HOTELS. The resort hotels sit on Antigua's best beaches, leaving the inns and guest houses to the city and inland. You really can't go wrong with any of the seaside resorts. No matter where you roost, you'll be able to enjoy all that Antigua has to offer.

Admiral's Inn. This small, fourteen-room spot is another of our favorites. It's an enchanting establishment set within the confines of Nelson's Dockyard at English Harbour. Charming, simple rooms. The bar, cocktail lounge and dining room are in the lobby, and there is outdoor dining as well. The 200-year-old building, which has been skillfully renovated, is one of the most attractive in the West Indies. Fine food, personable management. Boat and auto transportation to the island beaches, but the short sea ride to the hotel's beach puts you on a remote, peaceful, powdery stretch of sand. $50–58 double EP in winter; $34–42 double EP off-season.

Anchorage Hotel. This is a sprawling ninety-nine-room beach resort at Dickenson Bay with three types of accommodations: the older rooms in cottages; the newer air-conditioned ones with patios; and unusual beach-front rondavels with airy and spacious rooms and patio. Beautifully maintained grounds and a fine beach. Dining terrace and indoor/outdoor bar; nightly entertainment. Three tennis courts; watersports available. $150–180 MAP double in winter, $64–80 EP double off-season, with breakfast and dinner included.

Antigua Beach Hotel. Older, more modest, but pleasant forty-four-room hostelry at Hodges Bay. Beautiful view from its bluff-top location. Tennis, horseback riding, golf of sorts on its own nine-hole course. Swimming pool; beach a short walk downhill. Popular with families. From $80 double EP in winter, from $60 double EP off-season.

Atlantic Beach Hotel. At Crosbies on the beach. Attractive twenty-four rooms–twelve are efficiencies–with patios facing the sea. Dining room, bar, a small freshwater pool, good snorkeling, watersports. Maids and babysitters available–some families settle in here. Pool, horseback riding, TV in the lounge, but the rates are too high for what you get. $70 double EP in winter; $45 double EP off-season.

Barrymore Hotel. Homey, Antiguan-run place with thirty-six rooms set on three acres of land. One mile from the beach and town. Informal and very friendly, with good West Indian food the dining room specialty. The new DuBarry's restaurant offers fine Continental cuisine. Swimming pool on premises; tennis and golf nearby. Rates run between $35–45 double EP throughout the year.

Blue Waters Beach Hotel. Located at Soldier Bay, four miles from St. John's. There are forty-nine beach-front rooms and two two-bedroom apartments set in a lovely tropical garden between the hotel and the sea. There is a freshwater swimming pool, with bar, a lighted tennis court, archery, and fishing right from the property. The dining room overlooks the pool and the beach. There are outdoor barbecues twice weekly and entertainment nightly. $94–132 double in winter, $47–80 double off-season.

Castle Harbour Club & Casino. On a hilltop near St. John's with a wonderful panoramic view of the harbor. Fifty rooms which attract guests in groups on good-value holidays, casino style. Not necessarily geared to Las Vegas high-rollers, this casino is appealing to less-sophisticated but equally enthusiastic gamblers. Swimming pool, pleasant dining with an interesting variety of entrees. $60 double EP in winter; $44 double EP off-season.

Catamaran Hotel. At Falmouth, on the shore of the harbor and adjacent to Nelson's Dockyard. Informal atmosphere for beachcomber enthusiasts. All watersports. Restaurant, cocktail bar. A congenial place to be. Accommodations in the eleven rooms are simply furnished. $54 double EP in winter; $44 double EP off-season.

Curtain Bluff Hotel. A special resort with fifty rooms on the southwest coast (the most tropical looking part of the island) at a point that separates the surf on one side from the calm seas on the other. Here you'll find an intimate atmosphere catering to compatible people. A resort aura is enhanced with four tennis courts, all watersports–including Sunfish sailboats–good food, and nightly entertainments. $230 double in winter, $155 double off-season, breakfast and dinner included. Closed mid-May to mid-October.

Galley Bay Surf Club. An exclusive spot, with thirty-two rooms and villas in a superb setting at Five Islands on the northwest coast. Gauguin-style, thatched-roof complexes on the lagoon consist of bedroom, sitting room, and bathroom/dressing room, connected by a breezeway and decorated with a fine artistic hand. Swim, sail, snorkel, fish, or go shelling. If the mood suits, there is also tennis and horseback riding. Dining is on the terrace overlooking the water; later on there is music and dancing. $114–124 double EP in winter; $70–80 double EP off-season.

Halcyon Cove Beach Resort and Casino. A gem of a place, with 145 rooms and six suites overlooking Dickenson Bay The view is spectacular, the accommodations handsome. The resort is spread out around a courtyard with a swimming pool in its center. There isn't much of a beach, but watersports are available. New casino here adds to the nightlife. Our favorite spot here is the casual restaurant that extends out over the pier. It's great for lunch, with a variety of entrees at reasonable prices. For high-in-the-sky dining, this spot has it all. You take a canopied bus up to the Panorama restaurant for memorable terrace dining. $112–140 double EP in winter; $74–81 double EP off-season.

Halcyon Reef Resort. One hundred rooms at Marmora Bay. What makes this hotel a little different is that it's stretched out on a peninsula on the southeast coast. Superb marina, swimming pool, tennis courts, and all the extras such as two double beds in each room, balcony or patio, dining room, cocktail lounge, coffee shop. $105 double EP in winter; $75 double EP off-season.

Half Moon Bay. This 100-room hotel is on a magnificent beach, with the surf directly in front and the calm Caribbean waters just a short walk farther along the sand. There is a freshwater swimming pool, a nine-hole golf course, and five tennis courts. All watersports are available. The food is excellent, the ambience unexcelled on Antigua. $180–210 double in winter, $120–175 double off-season, breakfast and dinner included.

Hawksbill Beach Hotel. There are fifty rooms, which open on to the beach. All facilities, including tennis, swimming on a choice of beaches, and all watersports. There is an open lounge, bar, dining room, and some entertainment in the evening. The cottage rooms come in couple and party size. Depending on accommodations, rates run from $120 double in winter, from $90 double off-season, with two meals included.

The Inn at English Harbour. A charming and delightful hotel across the bay from Nelson's Dockyard. Some of the thirty rooms are strung out on a hill, while others are right on the beach. Dining and dancing terrace with magnificent view. Its English pub bar has a warm atmosphere and is the place to stop for a superior rum punch. Breakfast, lunch, or tea can be served in the rooms, at the beach house, or at the main hilltop dining room. All watersports available. $110–200 double EP in winter; $60–80 double EP off-season.

Jolly Beach Hotel. New 475-room air-conditioned hotel with older wing, situated directly on a beautiful beach at Lignumvitae Bay. European, American, and local cuisine. Pool and "topless" beach. $160–180 double in winter MAP.

Long Bay. On the lovely bay of the same name. Informal, rambling, charmingly decorated. Each of the twenty rooms has a balcony overlooking the lagoon. Also four efficiency units. Huge stone lobby and bar. Beach house open to the public serves lunch at reasonable prices. Nice dining room; local entertainment in the evenings. All watersports; deep-sea fishing; picnics arranged to offshore islands. $140 double in winter, $110 double off-season, breakfast and dinner included.

New Antigua Horizons Hotel. On Long Bay, with a lovely crescent beach, in an out-of-the way location. Thirty-six delightful rooms, all with private terrace, are strung out in two-story buildings along the sea. You'll feel as if you're on a ship and long remember the view. Informal, unhurried atmosphere. Perfect for swimming or snorkeling in reef-protected waters, fishing, or just lazing around in a hammock. A new pool was added in 1981. Intimate dining room and bar. Breakfast on your own terrace. Imaginative menus, barbecues, steel band, dancing. Tennis court illuminated for night play. Rates run $142 double, with two meals, in winter; $84 double off-season.

White Sands Hotel. Island atmosphere in forty-room cottage-type hotel at Hodges Bay. Casual holiday living here, in simple but adequate accommodations. Swimming pool, watersports. $55–68 double in winter, $42–56 double off-season. Rates for air-conditioned rooms higher.

HOME RENTALS. The way to have a controlled-expense vacation in Antigua is to have your own cottage, apartment, or villa. There are a number of places available for rent on a week-or-longer basis. Some are within walking distance of the luxury properties, so that you can have all the activity of the hotel without the high prices. For cottage rentals, contact *Caribbean Home Rentals,* P.O. Box 710, Palm Beach, Fla. 33480. Summer rentals for a two-bedroom accommodation range from $210–350 per week; four-bedrooms from $400 per week. Winter rentals are about 40% higher. The *Antigua Tourist Board* lists several cottages and apartments. Contact them for rates and availability.

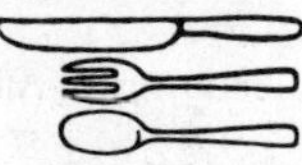

RESTAURANTS. The big specialty here is lobster, when it's available, and fresh fish. Locally grown pineapples, bananas, and other fresh fruits are choice; be sure to look for them on the menus. We call $5 per person *Inexpensive;* $6–11 *Moderate;* $12 and above *Expensive.*

In St. John's, most shoppers lunch at *Darcy's,* at Kensington Court on St. Mary's Street in the heart of town. Steel bands and calypso music fill the courtyard during the luncheon hours. Moderate. Also in town you can find lobster and local food at *Maurice's* on Market Street (moderate); *Brother's B's* on the corner of Soul and Long (inexpensive); the *Spanish Main Inn* on East Street in the two-story building that was once the Governor's mansion (moderate); and at the *Golden Peanut* (inexpensive). Around the island, try the *Catamaran* (moderate) at Falmouth, which has a following for its barbecues, fish and West Indian food. Another good spot is *The Admiral's Inn* (expensive) at English Harbour for its nautical, casual, West Indian atmosphere, and its food, which often features spectacular local recipes. For hilltop dining, try the *Panorama* at the Halcyon Cove. Make a reservation beforehand, and be prepared to get there (and enjoy the ride up) by canopied bus. A special retreat, with fine food and wines (expensive).

NIGHTLIFE. The Casinos at the Halcyon Cove Resort on Dickenson Bay and at Castle Harbour near St. John's make any evening lively and fun. You'll find the dancing and entertainment at your own or neighboring hotels.

SHOPPING. Cruise ship passengers don't have to go any farther than the collection of shops around the reflecting pool at the Deep Water Harbour's terminal. There are a lot of other items to be found, however, along High Street, St. Mary's Street, and some of the side streets in the capital of St. John's. With competition for luxury items at free-port prices as fierce as it is in the Caribbean, you'd do well to have hometown prices in mind before you pick up a lot of "bargains" that aren't.

The locally made items are the best purchases here, but even these take some shopping. In the straw line, count on paying from $2 to $4 for a hat, $2.50 to $6 for baskets, $2.50 to $4 for place mats. Warri boards, for that seed game you will see Antiguans playing at taxi stands and other gathering spots, cost from $10 to $20. *The Shipwreck Shop* has a good supply. Miniature steel drums are from $2 to $4. Locally printed fabric is fashioned into dresses, but the styles are fairly basic. We recommend buying the fabric by the yard or else bringing your own pattern for someone to put it together.

Imported English woolens and linens are very good buys, and there's cashmere and madras to choose from. English tobacco and pipes are at tempting prices; so is rum. *Darcy's Steel Band* record is a unique gift.

Coco Shop, on St. Mary's St. has Sea Island cottons and batiks. There is also a good selection of Irish linen, British tweeds, and Liberty fabrics. The shop's hand-screened prints on Sea Island cotton were above the ordinary run of this sort of stuff, and so were their hand-embroidered fabrics. They also have some stunning Siamese silks and a very wide selection of native crafts, like Antiguan pottery, steel band figurines, crystal, and some stainless steel. There are *Coco Shop* branches at the airport, Jolly Beach, Halcyon Cove, and other hotels.

Kensington Court is a collection of shops right in the center of town. There are a *beauty shop* and *barber shop,* an *art gallery* run by Pamela Wright, a *clothing shop* of fairly ordinary items, *Natasha's Shipwreck Shop,* intriguing things from Martinique, Guyana, Haiti, Grenada, and other southern lands. Also here are *Kel-Print* owned by George Kelsick, who designs the hand-screened prints which are used in the clothing offered, and a *straw goods* market. This is all part of a plan to make Kensington into a center for dining, shopping, afternoon tea, and late afternoon drinking. You can visit Kelsick's print shop to watch the actual printing; it's 3 blocks up from Kensington.

Handicraft Workshop on High St. has lots of local arts and crafts, sponsored by the government, at reasonable prices.

Coolidge Airport Shops. Interesting complex of shops near Departure Lounge selling liquor, locally-made items, steel band records. Branches of *Coco Shop, Kel-Print.*

The Ark on East St. sells native handicrafts including straw hats, shells and warri boards.

Bay Boutique, St. Mary's St., near Kensington Court. Ready-to-wear day and evening dresses, hostess and patio gowns, reversible bikinis. All done on premises by Heike Petersen of Montreal, of delightful fabrics imported from all over the world: Italy, Switzerland, India, Sea Island cottons (the fibre just may have been grown in Antigua). Prices are sensible, quality good to excellent.

SPORTS AND OTHER ACTIVITIES. *Swimming* is excellent on most of the beaches. You'll probably swim at your hotel, taxi fares being what they are, but if you're renting a car, remember that there is no such thing as a private beach in Antigua. Hotels can own property only as far as the beach; from there on it's public, so if you see an inviting, secluded cove, it's all yours.

For *golf,* you have a choice of three courses, not one of them up to the facilities in Puerto Rico, Jamaica, and a few of the other islands. The Cedar Valley Golf Club, about 3 miles from the airport, has an 18-hole course. Daily, weekly, and monthly memberships include *tennis* privileges as well as the golf. There's a modern club house with bar, restaurant, showers, and pro shop. Caddies, golf carts, and golf cars are available. Greens fees are about $10 per person, club rental $2.50, caddie fees for 9 holes about $1, cars $2 per person per 9 holes. Other courses are at Half Moon and Antigua Beach Hotel.

Horseback riding costs about $10 per hour. Horses are for rent at Antigua Beach Hotel, Half Moon Bay, as well as at some of the other hotels.

Deep-sea fishing off Antigua will cost about $90–100 for a half-day for 6 people; $145–160 for a full day. There's an annual Sportfishing Tournament at the end of April–early May. Check with Fisheries Division, St. John's, Antigua. Antigua has yet to prove that its waters can rival those of St. Thomas or Grenada for marlin and sailfish, but there's excellent year-round fishing for wahoo, kingfish, mackerel, dorado, tuna, and barracuda. The record fish for the tournament has been a 56-pound kingfish.

Tennis has become increasingly popular in recent seasons. In the hotel line-up we have noted courts when they exist and have pointed out those lighted for night play. (It's too hot to play midday.) If you're staying at a hotel without courts, arrangements can usually be made to use the nearest courts, sometimes at a small fee. First week in January is the annual Antigua Open Tennis Week with courts at Half Moon and Curtain Bluff for pro-am tournaments.

Water skiing, scuba diving, snorkeling, and Sunfish sailboating are all available from most of the larger resort hotels, especially Curtain Bluff, Half Moon, Halcyon Cove Beach Club, Hawksbill, and Anchorage.

Sailing has been a specialty of Antiguans since Admiral Nelson's day, but Caribbean yacht chartering owes its "big business" claim to *V.E.B. Nicholson & Sons,* the first of the Caribbean yacht-chartering agents. After World War II, Commander and Mrs. Nicholson and their two sons, Rodney and Desmond, bought a yacht with a plan to sail to Australia and a new life. In 1948, they headed west from England, with a cat and a few cherished possessions, on the 70-foot *Mollihawk.* On January 1, 1949, they arrived in English Harbour, now a handsome historic dockyard (largely thanks to the Nicholsons), but then a deserted shambles. When wealthy Americans, starting to build vacation homes at Mill Reef, asked for day charters aboard the *Mollihawk,* the Nicholson charter business began.

Today the firm lists almost 80 yachts, with rates from $430 to $535 per week per person, including food, fuel, and other costs of running a boat—everything, in fact, except liquor and soft drinks.

In addition, the Nicholson clan has a group of large, luxurious vessels with private sleeping cabins for parties of 4, 6, 8, and 10 people. These ships are operated by captain and full crew with a life comparable to that in a luxury hotel. Prices for sailing in this style are high, but the smaller, sportier boats are available on semi-bareboat, where you can help the sailing master with the operation of the cruise. Accommodations are much simpler, more informal, and—unless you've gone this way before—be prepared to be very cozy with your best friends (and maybe lose them in the bargain).

While all their yachts are not in Antigua, the main office is at English Harbour; or you can contact them in the States: *Nicholson Yacht Charters.* 9 Chauncy St., Cambridge, Mass. 02138.

ARUBA

Golden Hills and Golden Shores

Most of Aruba is stunningly stark, with dry open plains strewn with cactus, massive boulders seemingly tossed at will by a sea giant, and a seven-mile strip of uninterrupted dazzling beach that is its own Gold Coast. It lies 15 miles north of Venezuela, smack in the path of the trade winds, which keep the island cool and the divi divi trees forever bending in the breeze.

Aruba is the westernmost and smallest of the Netherlands Antilles' Leeward Islands. It and its sister islands of Bonaire and Curaçao have become known as the ABCs.

The basic attractions of Aruba are different from those of other Caribbean islands. Because of the light rainfall (drinking water is distilled from the sea), you'll find no lush, verdant-clad mountains here. You will find giant cacti, aloes, divi divi trees with branches flowing like hair in the wind, umbrella-like kwihi trees, kibra hacha trees with sunbursts of glorious yellow blossoms, and the late summer orange brilliance of the flamboyans.

You will also find monolithic rock formations, caves adorned with Indian inscriptions, green parakeets, golden beaches, and a pastel free-port shopping capital, *Oranjestad,* which is as neat as the Netherlands and as Dutch as Rotterdam, with a tropical touch.

Although Dutch is the official language, the "spoken" language here and in the other ABCs is *Papiamento,* which is a blend of Dutch, English, Spanish, Portuguese, Indian and African. It may sound difficult, but you'll be surprised how much of it you can understand, especially if you've studied a little Spanish. Try your hand at a few words: *bon dia* (good morning), *bon nochi* (good evening), *con ta bai* (how are you?). But don't be alarmed if you feel you're being misunderstood–everyone speaks English!

On this island, 20 miles long by 6 miles wide, nearly 64,000 people live under an autonomical arm of the Kingdom of the Netherlands. A large oil refinery spreads across the southern corner of the island, and a casino-dotted resort strip commands much of the calm leeward side. Wonders have been carved on shore by the thrashing of the sea on the windward coast, and long-abandoned gold mines stand as a symbol of forgotten dreams across the central plains.

History

No archives mention the exact date of Aruba's discovery, but Alonzo de Ojeda claimed the island for Spain in 1499. Potsherds and clay pottery collected from excavations, and hieroglyphics left in caves, are evidence that the island was inhabited by the Arawak Indians.

Aruba is one island where the Indian population was not exterminated. Although the Spanish deported the virile Indians to work the mines of Hispaniola (now the Dominican Republic/Haiti), the island enjoyed a special dispensation from the usual horrors of Spanish colonial policy. Charles V forbid further settlements of foreign colonists, with the result that the Indians remained free, sharing their island with a small Spanish garrison. Thus Spain gave the island its name–the Conquistadors called it *oro uba* for "there was gold."

More than half of today's Arubans are descendants of the indigenous Indians, so you'll notice a striking difference between the natives of Aruba, Bonaire and Curaçao. The Spanish remained on the island until 1636, near the end of their eighty-year war with Holland. The Dutch took over and have been overseers of Aruba ever since.

EXPLORING ARUBA

Taking a leisurely stroll around the capital of Oranjestad is the best way to see the sights. With its deep-water harbor and its traditional Dutch gabled houses, this town is a delight. Old blends with new in multi-colored, spotlessly clean houses. Fruits, vegetables, and fresh fish are displayed in stalls and on schooners tied up at the quay. A unique feature is that produce is sold directly from the sailboats, many of them from Venezuela.

Walking from the harbor along Lloyd Smith Boulevard, you'll pass government buildings on your left, an exotic Bali houseboat restaurant on your right, and come to rest at Wilhelmina Park, created in 1955 to celebrate the visit of Queen Juliana and Prince Bernhard of the Netherlands. The statue of Queen Mother Wilhelmina, unveiled by her daughter, was sculpted of white marble in Italy by Arnoldo Lualdi.

Another downtown highlight is old Fort Zoutman, built in 1796 as a bastion against buccaneers. An impressive clock tower, named for King Willem III, was added in 1868, and today it is a museum which is well worth a visit.

For a highlight of the beauties that line the Caribbean beaches, take the time to view *De Man's Shell Collection.* Be sure to call ahead for an appointment (phone: 24246).

You can drive the full 20-mile length of Aruba, from Seroe Colorado at the southern tip to the California Light at the northwestern end. One of the outstanding island features is 550-foot Hooiberg, or "haystack," mountain, rising strangely from the flat landscape and dominating the equally flat countryside which Arubans call the *cunucu.*

Another phenomenon of the *cunucu* is the presence of huge monoliths, of solid diorite, each weighing several thousand tons. Mammoth rocks, which furnish Arubans with interesting building material, are scattered about the area. Each is as different and fascinating as the next. The most impressive grouping is at Ayo, where boulders balance precariously on one edge or on each other as they have for generations. Geologists have not yet explained the origin and evolution of these rocks, nor the strange fact that many of them are hollowed out, with the cavity always on the side away from the prevailing wind. Even more interesting are the caves and grottoes, many of them, like Fontein Cave, decorated with drawings and symbols etched in red pigment by Indians long before Aruba was "discovered."

The scenery on Aruba's windward coast is the most spectacular, with the pounding surf sending gigantic walls of spray over huge jagged rocks. It is a desolate, windswept area, not unlike the coast of northern Maine. The pounding ocean has undercut the cliffs in one place and formed a natural bridge that arches over a small cove.

You can see the remains of one of the old gold smelters just north of the Natural Bridge, and there are more in the Frenchman's Pass area, where you will find the eerie ruins of a gold-mining ghost town, Balashi.

Aruba's leeward shore begins with the dunes surrounding the California Lighthouse. The beach is perfect for shelling, and calm waters offer the best snorkeling on the island. Travelling south, a glorious white-sand beach extends from Malmok all the way to Oranjestad. In between are Palm Beach with its high-rise hotels and Eagle Beach with its thatched umbrellas and picnic areas, all open to the public.

A DAY ON YOUR OWN

Whether you are staying on the island, or debarking for the day from a cruise ship, your island tour will begin in *Oranjestad,* the capital city. Allow at least six hours for the tour, or a full eight hours if you'd like to include swimming and/or snorkeling and a beach picnic.

Head south from *Oranjestad,* pass the airport and continue on the inland road until it joins with the coastal route and marks the beginning of the *Spanish Lagoon.* Turn left on the winding, narrow road that parallels the lagoon, until you reach the gold-mill ruins at *Frenchman's Pass.* Enough remains to give you a good idea of the full-scale operation that was located here more than 150 years ago.

Return to the coast road and follow the signs to *San Nicolas,* the island's second city and the site of the Lago Oil Refinery. Stop on the way at Brisas del Mar restaurant in *Savaneta* for a cooling bottle of Amstel beer; if time permits, stay for an excellent seafood luncheon served simply and inexpensively on the small beachside terrace.

Guided tours of the refinery are given every Tuesday and Thursday. You must be at the starting point, the Aruba Exxon Club in *Seroe Colorado,* no later than 1:15 P.M. Be prepared to spend a few hours and forego some of the island's natural wonders.

Other than the refinery, there is little to see on the southern tip of the island. If your schedule allows, have lunch at the Astoria Hotel Restaurant in San Nicholas. There you'll find the best Oriental food on the island. It's worth wending your way through town and the small hotel lobby to find a built-in tropical terrace and an exotic menu that is almost as long as your arm. The prices are right, the atmosphere soothing, and each course unhurried and delicious.

An unnamed road with hand-painted signpost will lead you directly north from *San Nicolas* to *Boca Prins,* a desolate and wildly beautiful windwardside area. Driving along the rugged, circuitious route to reach the sea is well worth the effort, especially when you spy the sand dunes that rise like mountains of soft snow at the edge of the sea.

Here, if you're game, you can try dune sliding! Conjure up thoughts of riding a sled without the sled. You will need a sturdier outfit than a bathing suit and cover-up, plus rubber-sole shoes to create your own stop-and-start tropical snowplow. The sea crashes against boulders at the shore's edge, but your ride will begin and end in the sand.

Head inland and follow the signs to *Santa Cruz,* then on to *Andicouri* and its spectacular *Natural Bridge,* carved by the sea.

If you've allowed extra time for a seaside picnic, this is the spot, but NOT if you want to swim and snorkel. The sea is much too rough and the undertow totally unpredictable. Save your swimming for the island's northern tip, your next destination.

Drive inland again from *Andicouri,* past *Ayo* and *Casibari,* where the strewn boulders are most impressive, and pass through tiny *Paradera,* north to the village of *Noord.* Take time for a brief stop to visit the Church of Santa Anna and see its altar, which was carved more than a century ago.

Afterward, head directly north to the California Light, the island's beacon and its northern tip. You'll find another desolate spot with sand dunes, but these gentle mini-mounds are strictly for strolling. The Malmok area here is perfect for shelling along the beach, floating on the gentle sea, or snorkeling at *the* best spot on Aruba.

Follow the shore road south along the gold coast, where sparkling high-rise hotels almost touch each other. If a late afternoon drink is in order, cool off at the Divi Divi Beach Hotel pool. Climb into a hanging wicker basket chair and swing to the sounds of the stereo, the surf and the sea.

Plan your evening to include two different island flavors. First have a drink at the Bamboo Bar on the dock of the *Bali* floating houseboat restaurant and watch the sunset. Then have dinner at *De Olde Molen,* an authentic windmill that was built in 1804 and brought to Aruba from Holland in 1964. If the spirit still stirs, cross the street and casino-hop along Palm Beach.

PRACTICAL INFORMATION FOR ARUBA

HOW TO GET THERE. By air. A $4-million airport terminal makes arrivals and departures exciting. The only place with an airport even comparable is Curaçao. *American Airlines* flies non-stop from New York; *Eastern* from Miami; *ALM,* the Dutch Antillean Airline, flies in from Miami and San Juan, and also links Aruba with Bonaire, Curaçao and St. Martin. There are special excursion fares, and Aruba is included in a Curaçao or Bonaire roundtrip if you make your plans in advance.

By sea. Several cruise ships out of Miami, Port Everglades and San Juan call at Aruba all year-round. Among them are the ships of the *Chandris Line,* the *Costa Line, Holland America Cruises, Home Lines, Norwegian American Line, Royal Caribbean Cruise Line,* and *Sitmar Cruises.*

FURTHER INFORMATION. The *Aruba Tourist Bureau* has its head office on L. G. Smith Blvd. in Oranjestad, with representatives providing information out of 1270 Avenue of the Americas, Suite 2212, New York, N.Y. 10020; and from 399 N. E. 15th Street, Miami, Fla. 33132.

ISLAND MEDIA. For further reading, the *Aruba Holiday* green sheet is a 24-page giveaway that is crammed with all the latest information and island attractions. Aruba's English daily, *The News,* is a good source for local and some international news. *Radio Antilliana, Radio Victoria,* and *Trans World Radio* have daily newscasts in English. Consult the green sheet for specific times.

AUTHORIZED TOUR OPERATORS. Adventure Tours; Alken Group Tours, Inc.; Butler Travels; Carefree/David Travels; Caribbean Holidays; Cavalcade Tours; Flyfaire, Inc.; GoGo Tours; GWV Travel; Hill Tours; Red & Blue Tours; Thomson Vacations; Tour Trec; Trans National Travel; and Value Vacations from the *U.S.* From *Canada:* Sunflight Holidays.

PASSPORTS, VISAS. U.S. and Canadian citizens need only proof of identity, such as a passport, birth certificate or voter's registration card. Passports are required of all other visitors. In addition, all visitors to the island must hold a return or ongoing ticket.

MONEY. The guilder or florin (both names are used interchangeably, although prices are marked with *fl.)* is the Netherlands Antilles' unit of money, subdivided into 100 cents. It is issued in all denominations, including a square nickel, which makes a nice souvenir. The official rate of exchange is US $1 = 1.77 NAf; £1 = 3.96 NAf.

TAXES AND OTHER CHARGES. All room rates are subject to a 5% government tax. Hotels also add either a 10% or 15% service charge. The airport departure tax is $5.75 per person.

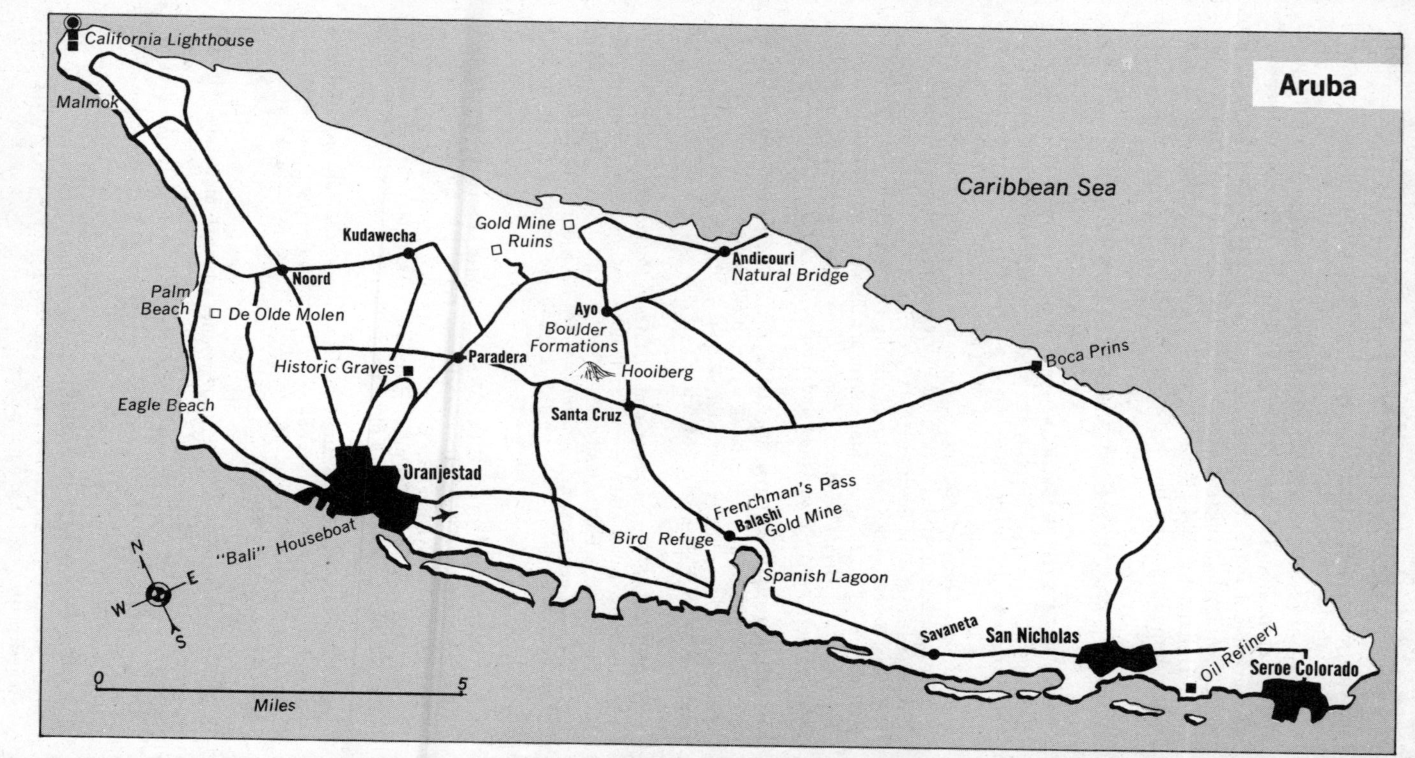
Aruba
Caribbean Sea
California Lighthouse
Malmok
Kudawecha
Noord
Gold Mine
Ruins
Andicouri
Natural Bridge
Palm
Beach
De Olde Molen
Ayo
Boulder
Formations
Paradera
Historic Graves
Hooiberg
Boca Prins
Eagle Beach
Santa Cruz
Oranjestad
Frenchman's Pass
Balashi
Gold Mine
"Bali" Houseboat
Bird Refuge
Spanish Lagoon
N
E
W
S
Savaneta
San Nicholas
Oil Refinery
Seroe Colorado
0
5
Miles

HOW TO GET ABOUT. Taxis are always available at your hotel or in Oranjestad, but they are expensive. Figure $5 at most for short trips in the capital city area, more from the airport to the Palm Beach hotel strip. All taxi drivers speak English, and many can be excellent guides. Discuss flat rates and tour possibilities with them, because they are congenial, as are all Arubans, and anxious to show you their island. For quick service from anywhere, telephone the dispatcher for the Central Taxi Association.

Rental cars are available from *Avis, Budget, Hertz* and *National,* as well as from a local firm, *Jansen's Car Rental.* Rates range from $20–48 per day, from $102–308 per week. There is no mileage charge, but gasoline is extra. For quick and inexpensive trips from Palm Beach into Oranjestad, bus service is frequent and inexpensive (40¢) and runs from 7 A.M. until 6 P.M.

For tours of the oil refinery, contact *Bruno Tours* to arrange pickup at your hotel. For tours of the island and all watersports arrangements, contact *De-Palm Tours,* either through your hotel or at their office at 142 L.G. Smith Blvd. in Oranjestad.

EVENTS AND HOLIDAYS. *Carnival* is the highlight. As on other islands, the colorful costumes and floats seen in the Great Parade on the Sunday before Ash Wednesday have been in preparation for a full year. Steel bands, the election of the Carnival Queen, and a *tumba* contest add to the festivities and the fun.

The *Watapana Festival* is celebrated during the off-season (April–December). The name was chosen from the old Indian word for the divi divi trees and the festival is celebrated every Tuesday evening from 7 until 10 P.M., presenting the island's heritage to Arubans and visitors alike. Stalls are set side by side offering local dishes; folkloric entertainment; and interesting displays of handcrafted items that are for sale. It's lively, fun, and a chance to really meet the people.

Carnival Monday is an island-wide holiday. Other Aruban holidays are *New Year's Day, Good Friday, Easter Monday,* the *Queen's Birthday* (April 30), *Labor Day* (May 1), *Ascension Day, Kingdom Day* (Dec. 15), *Christmas Day,* and *Boxing Day* (Dec. 26).

WHAT WILL IT COST?

For all its sun, sand and sea, Aruba can be an expensive place. The lavish hotels have casinos, nightclubs, restaurants and cocktail lounges. Therefore, this mini-Las Vegas that sprouted out of the desert sands over the last twenty years can command high prices during the winter season (Dec. 15–Apr. 14).

A typical day on Aruba in season for *two* persons will run:

	US$	£
Accommodations at one of the Palm Beach hotels	115	62
Full breakfast at the hotel	15	8
Lunch at a moderate restaurant in town	15	8
Dinner at one of the island's popular spots	40	22
Tips or service charges at restaurants; taxes and service charges at hotels	20	11
One-day sightseeing by rental car	25	14
	$230	£125

STAYING IN ARUBA

HOTELS. The big hotel strip is Palm Beach, as gorgeous a strand of powdery sand as you'll ever find. You can walk down the beach from one high-rise hotel to the next and be constantly amazed at the brilliant white/sparkling blue combination, with no greenery casting shadows across it.

Americana Aruba Hotel & Casino. This high-rise Palm Beach property has 200 air-conditioned rooms and is set dramatically on its own spacious section of sandy beachfront. Swimming pool; two lighted tennis courts; in-house casino and a selection of shops. Dine informally on charcoal-grilled specialties at their *Las Mañanitas Terrace Restaurant,* or at *Villa Fiorita,* well-known for its international cuisine. *Le Club Lounge* offers dancing and late-night entertainment. From $115 double EP in winter; $50–85 double EP off-season.

Americana Caribbean Hotel & Casino. This was the first of the luxury hotels here and it is still attractive. Handsome Delft-tiled lobby leads to the 200 rooms, most with terraces that wrap around them. Four lighted tennis courts; spacious Olympic-size pool; sauna and solarium. Full dining facilities include *Fisherman's Terrace* for seafood al fresco; the *Divi Divi Coffee Shop* and the *Cactus Needle Snack Bar* for fast foods; and *Le Petit Bistro,* their elegant French restaurant, which has made a name for itself on the island. At night drinks are served at *The Galaxy,* where there is a combo. The *Klompen Klub* offers dinner and entertainment in a supper club setting. A full-fledged casino adds to the fun. From $115 double EP in winter; $50–85 double EP off-season.

Aruba Beach Club. Attractive and modern low-lying complex of suites spread out on Druif Beach. The decor is Spanish, the atmosphere pleasant and unhurried. Swimming pool, tennis courts, terrace restaurant, supper club, entertainment. A small market on the premises for those who choose rooms with kitchenettes. From $115 double EP in winter; from $55 double EP off-season.

Aruba Concorde Hotel-Casino. The last hotel in a row of side-by-side high risers on Palm Beach, the Concorde opened in the summer of 1978 with 490 rooms soaring skyward for 15 floors. The largest on the strip, the hotel offers six different places to sip and/or sup, four lighted tennis courts, a swimming pool, private beach and all watersports. Small selection of shops includes a delicatessen. Color TV, refrigerator with mini-bar and private balcony with all rooms. $120 double EP in winter; $65–85 double EP off-season.

Aruba-Sheraton Hotel & Casino. Another Palm Beach beauty, this hotel is a typical Sheraton property with a tropical touch. Swimming pool, poolside coffee shop and bar, night club, and the superb *Rembrandt Room* for elegant dining. The cool Delft blue of the buildings blends into the Caribbean sky, emphasizing its white Moorish arches. Beautifully furnished. 200 rooms, some lanai suites. Facilities also include the *Club Galáctica* cocktail lounge; the Casino with special baccarat and chemin de fer rooms; the *Open-Hearth Steak Pub* and an outdoor bar. Children's playground, beauty parlor, tennis and shuffleboard courts, shopping arcade. From $125 double EP in winter; $70–90 double EP off-season.

Astoria Hotel. A small, ten-room commercial hotel in the heart of San Nicolas on the island's southern shore. The rooms all have private bath and are air-conditioned, but are more for businessmen who stay overnight for business at the nearby refinery than for those in search of sun and sand. Clean and inexpensive, but really not for tourists. The highlight here is the hotel's restaurant, which specializes in Oriental cuisine. $30 double EP, year-round.

Best Western Manchebo Beach Resort Hotel. Close to Oranjestad, with bus service to *Talk of the Town,* its sister hotel, and all the special facilities there, make these two properties a special twosome. Manchebo is a modern, two-story inn, with 72 rooms, a lovely beach; freshwater swimming pool; tennis courts; horseback riding and watersports options. Their *French Steak House* is famous for its elegance and special cuisine. $100 double EP in winter; $55 double EP off-season.

Best Western Talk of the Town Resort Hotel. Just slightly smaller than Manchebo Beach, this hotel operates on the same share principle. Its 62 rooms are attractively furnished, with some of them offering kitchenettes. Over-sized swimming pool; watersports, including windsurfing. Dine here by candlelight at one of the island's most popular gourmet restaurants. Feast on fresh lobster and fine wines, then stay on to enjoy their *Contempo Disco* that swings until 3 A.M. From $90 double EP in winter; from $50 double EP off-season.

Divi Divi Beach Hotel. Named for that odd-looking tree that is permanently bent by the prevailing winds. It's a ten-minute drive from Palm Beach in one direction and Oranjestad in the other. Even though there are now 152 rooms, the Divi Divi still has the atmosphere of a small, hospitable inn. Private beach. Rooms in main buildings, casitas or lanais, all air-conditioned. Fresh-water swimming pool, dining terrace, restaurant and bar. Shares everything with the *Tamarijn Beach,* its sister hotel. $110–150 double EP in winter; $60–80 double EP off-season.

Holiday Inn. This seven-story, 400-room hotel smacks of Holiday Inn U.S. motif, but it is much more than that. Although the hotel is geared for the tropics, you'll feel at home. The bulletin board heralds at least a half-dozen different activities each day. Children under twelve sharing a room with parents are free, and a variety of special package plans make looking into this hotel worthwhile. Olympic-size swimming pool and patio; four tennis courts; a selection of restaurants including the especially fine *Salon Internacional,* where there are three staggered dinner sittings to enhance quiet dining comfort. Its casual and friendly casino adds to the fun. Ideal for families. From $110 double EP in winter; from $73 double EP off-season.

Tamarijn Beach Hotel. A cluster of white stucco buildings done in cool Mediterranean style with 204 rooms stretched out along a 1,000-foot private beach. The Tamarijn is the Divi Divi Beach's mate and offers the same casual atmosphere. Barefoot is beautiful here, although the hotel advises that "ties and coats are reluctantly permitted!" Swimming pool, tennis courts, entertainment every evening. From $100 double EP in winter; $60–70 double EP off-season.

HOME RENTALS. While cottage and apartment possibilities are not extensive, there are large homes available for rental at rates that range from $350–550 per month. For a full listing, including apartments with kitchenettes and rooms in private homes, contact the Aruba Tourist Bureau at 1270 Avenue of the Americas, Suite 2212, New York, N.Y. 10020.

RESTAURANTS. There are dishes to suit every taste here, where the variety includes Indonesian, Chinese, French, Dutch, Italian and Creole, as well as extensive Continental selections. We call $6 per person and under *Inexpensive;* $7–15 *Moderate;* $16 and above *Expensive.*

Astoria Hotel. Well worth the trip to San Nicolas for the best Chinese food on the island. Standard dishes such as moo goo gai pan, subgum wonton and sweet and sour pork are available, but their highlight is lobster a la Astoria, a delectable dish with chunks of lobster sauteed with roast pork, vegetables and mushrooms, then pan broiled and served in its own shell. You can get an *inexpensive* meal by using the column A/column B method, while house specialties fall into the *moderate* range.

Bali Floating Houseboat. Beforehand have drinks under the stars at the Bamboo Bar on the pier, then climb aboard the oversize houseboat for a real treat. This is the place for *Rijsttafel,* the wonderful Indonesian concoction that means "rice table." And there is an art to eating it. Fill the center of your plate with rice and then choose from among twenty-one dishes–including beef with toasted coconut, curried veal, pork in soy sauce, pickled pineapple, and shrimp biscuits–and surround the rice with your choices. *Moderate* and marvelous.

Brisas Del Mar. Unpretentious and informal little restaurant in Savanetta, a village between Oranjestad and San Nicolas. Dine on a tiny terrace at the edge of the sea. Sandwiches, homemade soups and fresh fish served in a homey setting. *Inexpensive.*

Buccaneer. New in 1981 and delightful in that you feel as if you're dining at sea. They call it "the only saltwater aquarium restaurant in the Caribbean," and provide a ship's cabin atmosphere along with portholes at every table for viewing the fish as they float by. Emphasis on seafood naturally, but meat dishes also served. Find it at Gasparito, near the high-rise hotels on Palm Beach. *Moderate.*

The Cattle Baron. Shades of the Old West to be found here and U.S. Prime steaks are the specialty. Also fresh fish and seafood specialties, along with an extensive salad bar. This spot is in the Dakota Shopping Paradise, just a few minutes from town. *Moderate.*

De Olde Molen. This old mill, an Aruban landmark, was originally built in Holland in 1804. In 1964 it was dismantled, shipped to Aruba and reconstructed piece by piece on the sand across from Palm Beach. Inside it is small and full of atmosphere, but the Dutch touch ends with the mill itself. The menu is Continental, with the emphasis on steaks and seafood. Reservations are a must and jackets are required. Open for dinner only. *Expensive.*

Dragon Phoenix. Oriental decor that leans toward the exotic, and a Cantonese menu to please any palate. In the heart of town. *Moderate.*

Fisherman's Terrace. One of the Americana Caribbean Hotel's variety of restaurants. This one is informal, has tables set up in a terrace garden just off the pool and offers interesting new twists on usual seafood fare. Open for dinner only. *Moderate.*

French Steak House. A true French bistro with a tropical air at the Manchebo Beach Resort Hotel. The atmosphere is more casual than at *Le Petit Bistro,* but the Gallic flair is really there. Escargots and Chateaubriand are their specialties. *Moderate.*

Gatsby's. Roaring Twenties motif that would have made F. Scott Fitzgerald proud. Steaks, prime ribs, and seafood served. Open seven days a week for lunch and dinner. In town and *Moderate.*

Kowloon. They call this restaurant, which is on Emmastraat in Oranjestad, the "Happy Talk Chinese Restaurant," and it is just that with a variety of curried dishes and a special Chinese Rice Table Deluxe, served in an informal and cozy setting. *Inexpensive.*

La Dolce Vita. Fine Italian dining in an old Aruban home on Nassaustraat in Oranjestad. The menu is lengthy and creative; the food deliciously prepared according to time-honored family tradition. Rooms under the arches add to the atmosphere. Open for dinner only. *Expensive.*

Le Petit Bistro. An elegant French restaurant that exudes formality (jackets required) and takes the time to serve each course properly. Downstairs in the Americana Caribbean Hotel, it seats sixty people in candlelight and mahogany panels. One of the highlights is the hors d'oeuvres cart, which features salmon, shrimp and dozens of other delectables. The menu is price-fixed; hotel guests on the MAP plan pay a surcharge. Open only for dinner. *Expensive.*

Mido Restaurant. Another Aruban in-town spot where the emphasis is on Chinese. However, they do offer a mini-Rijsttafel for four and a few other Indonesian dishes. Open for lunch and dinner. Strictly informal. *Inexpensive.*

Talk of the Town Restaurant. Located in the hotel of the same name, and Aruba's most famous because of the international culinary awards it has received over the years. Gourmet entrees that range from subtle French to flambé fare by candlelight. *Expensive.*

Trocadero. Now in a new location on Nassaustraat, this restaurant is one of our favorites. They specialize in seafood, with at least a dozen different specialties each week, but also offer U.S. steaks and Oriental dishes. Open for lunch and dinner. *Moderate.*

NIGHTLIFE. Each hotel has its own, and plenty of it. Floorshows and cafe entertainment in the cocktail lounges and lively action in the casinos. You can easily walk along Palm Beach from one to the other, to find top stars performing at each. Casinos at the Americana hotels, the Aruba Concorde, Aruba Sheraton and the Holiday Inn. The smaller hotels have local entertainment, and the Talk of the Town Hotel has the Contempo Disco that swings until the small hours of the morning. To really electrify your experience on this island, head for the *Club Scaramouche,* which is still the "in" place for Arubans and tourists alike. They call it "trendy," but warn that proper attire is mandatory. Try it for fun and the experience to dance until dawn under a cascade of technicolor lights.

SHOPPING. Nassaustraat is the main shopping street of Oranjestad, with the best bargains in table linens, crystal, jewelry, china, perfume and liquor. (Check your hometown prices so you have some idea of the savings, since some items are not the bargains they once were.)

A unique item from Aruba is the kwihi table, cut from a slab of local wood and honed to a fine sheen. The legs are from another tree, and you can pick and choose the grain you want. If you think that you'd like to have one, measure the spot you plan to put it in before you leave home. Then go to one of the stores carrying tables ready-made. Leaving a special order to be shipped to you is a chancy proposition.

There's good shopping for last-minute purchases at the airport, but try to arrange at least a half day in town to get the feeling of the shops and all they have to offer. There are large department stores, such as the *Aruba Trading Company,* the *New Amsterdam Store* and the *Bon Bini Bazar,* but by far the largest complex is *Spritzer & Fuhrmann's* four stores that command the corners where Hendrikstraat crosses Nassaustraat. This four leaf clover of shops has jewelry, crystal, watches, fine china, Danish, Dutch and English silver, clocks of every description, leather goods, gold coins and charms, and even precious stones.

Other specialty shops in this line are *Kan* and *Raghunath* for exquisite jewelry; the *Aruba Peasant Shop* and *De Wit Stores* for Dutch pewter and Delft; *Photo El Globo* for cameras and electronic equipment.

Find the latest "in" fashions at Aquarius, a jet-set boutique; designer fashions at *Viva;* and imported cashmeres at *Fanny's.* For a complete selection of French perfumes, visit *Penha* or *El Louvre.* For native and imported handicraft, the *Aruba Peasant Shop* is the answer. The shops in town are open from 8–12 noon and from 2–6 P.M. Monday through Saturday. However, the hours vary in the hotel shopping arcades, even though many shops are branches of ones in Oranjestad.

SPORTS AND OTHER ACTIVITIES. *Swimming* on the southwest coast beaches is excellent. Palm Beach, with its gradual slope, is perfect for children and beginners. Andicouri, an old plantation with a beautiful cove, is excellent for *picnics.* Admission $1 per car. Eagle Beach, a lovely two-mile stretch of white sand just south of Palm Beach, is a public park with thatched roof shelters for picnickers. No charge.

Aruba's Caribbean waters are a natural playground for sports, and the island has them all. *De Palm Watersports,* located in town and on the hotel beaches, can make all arrangements for you. *Water skiing* costs $10 for two runs. *Sunfish* rent for $20 per hour, *pedal boats* for $8.75 per hour. There are *snorkeling* trips ($10 per person) and *scuba diving* trips ($28 per person) to the coral reefs and to the wrecks of the German freighter *Antilia* and the oil tanker *Pedernales.* The *Aquaventure* trimaran offers two-hour sails along the coast, during the day and at sunset, for $15 per person including snacks and complimentary drinks. Trips on the glass-bottom boat cost $8.50 for adults, $6 for children. The *Ali Kai* 42-foot catamaran sails out on four-hour ocean trips for fishing and snorkeling ($25 per person); two-hour snorkeling excursions ($12 per person); and also offers a sunset cocktail cruise ($12 per person); and even one by moonlight ($15 per person).

The newest addition to Aruba's fleet is the motored, multi-decked *Dreamboat,* offering all the ocean options such as a moonlight/dance cruise that departs nightly at 10:30 P.M. ($10 per person); a dinner cruise ($29 per person); and an elaborate brunch cruise ($15 per person) that departs daily at 1 P.M.

Deep-sea fishing trips, in pursuit of dolphin, marlin, wahoo, kingfish and yellow fin tuna, run $200 per half day for five persons. Tackle, bait and drinks are included. Visitors may also play *golf* on the nine-hole course at Lago's Aruba Golf Club. Clubs rent for $4 per day; greens fees run $5 per day for as many rounds as you'd like to play.

The local tourist bureau or your hotel can arrange for you to play *tennis* at any of the hotel courts. Country tours on *horseback* can be arranged through *Rancho El Paso.* Contact them by calling 23310, or check with the activities desk at your hotel.

BAHAMA ISLANDS

Seven Hundred Pieces of Paradise

Any set of 700 sun-baked islands scattered across 90,000 square miles of the Atlantic is bound to be bait for the traveler for at least 700 separate reasons. The casinos notwithstanding, the knowledgeable tourist can't lose in the Bahamas.

The islands can and do accommodate every sort of traveler–the diver in search of undersea coral reefs; the fisherman after white marlin or bluefin tuna; the yachtsman in search of uninhabited beaches; the day sailor who yearns to skim the waters toward a secluded cove; the scuba diver lured by exotic sea gardens on the ocean floor; the hunter eager to join a wild boar safari; the collector in search of odd shells that have been drenched pink by the coral; the sun worshipper in pursuit of a golden tan; the shopper after bargain items–even the gambler in search of an often elusive way to pay for it all.

The island chain starts east of Stuart, Florida and reaches 750 miles in a southeasterly direction to within fifty miles of Haiti. Any navigator who sets out today will find not only the 700 islands, but more than 2000 cays (pronounced "keys") and rocks en route, all of them washed by the gentle Gulf Stream.

Although most of the islands are uninhabited, there are more than a dozen that are eager and ready for tourists. Nassau, by far the most popular, is not an island, but the capital of the Bahamas, and is situated on the northern shores of the island of New Providence. It is also the gateway to the Out Islands (or Family Islands), all of which can be reached within an hour and a half from the Nassau International Airport.

Grand Bahama is another story–far too large to embrace the romance and far too busy and built-up to be called lush or unspoiled, it almost seems out of place in the 700 "pieces of paradise."

The Out Islands, on the other hand, have something for everybody. The Biminis, for example, boast the best game fishing in the world. Marlin, sailfish, dolphin, and swordfish are all found there. Fishing, incidentally, is magnificent all over the Bahamas. As of 1979, the International Game Fish Association listed over 30 world record fish caught here, among them a 633-lb. marlin and an 880-lb. shark, both caught by women anglers.

The Exuma islands are well known for their cruising grounds–and for the April "Out Island Regatta" when native sloops compete in a colorful series of races. Eleuthera, another of the islands, was the first one to be colonized by white settlers. Today, its way of life has not radically altered from those times, except that a dozen hotels have been developed along its 100 miles or so.

Other romantically named islands–the Abacos, Andros, Crooked Island, Ragged Island, San Salvador, Inagua, the Berries, Long Island–have their particular personalities, but what they have in common is a peace and tranquility unequalled elsewhere in the Bahamas–no crowds, no screaming headlines, no traffic jams. The people are friendly and the islands have an informal type of beauty giving the impression that man has never set foot on them before.

History

No other islands in the Atlantic or the Caribbean have a history so rich–everything from sunken treasure on one island to an ex-king for governor on another.

It all started in 1492, when Christopher Columbus came ashore on the first of the islands, then called Guanahani. He was greeted by the peaceful Arawak Indians, renamed their island San Salvador, and claimed the islands for Spain.

History has it that Columbus then wrote home: "The beauty of these islands surpasses that of any other land as much as the day surpasses the night in splendor." However, the Spanish made no attempt to establish a permanent settlement.

Spanish raiders did, though, and within the next fifteen years depopulated the islands by shipping the Arawaks to slavery in the mines and sugar mills of Cuba and Hispaniola (now the Republic of Haiti and the Dominican Republic).

Apart from a visit in 1513 by Ponce de León, who was commissioned by King Ferdinand to find the Fountain of Youth on the island of Bimini, and who instead found Florida, the Bahamas lay dormant for more than a century.

The first organized attempt to settle the islands came in 1647, when Captain William Sayle, former Governor of Bermuda, set sail with a group called the Society of Eleutherian Adventurers. In pursuit of religious freedom, they were shipwrecked off Eleuthera and stayed. It is believed that the first settlements were at Harbour Island and Spanish Wells, two islands near the coast of North Eleuthera.

Another group of Bermudians sailed south in 1656 to become the first settlers of New Providence, calling it "New" to distinguish it from the already settled British possession, Providence, Rhode Island.

In 1670, King Charles II of England put the Bahamas in the hands of the Lords Proprietors of the Carolinas, a distinguished group which did little to improve the island lot. Less than a decade passed before the islands were discovered by, and then infested with, pirates. These buccaneers, Blackbeard and Henry Morgan among them, terrorized the seas and plundered the merchant ships that plied the sea lanes between Europe and South America. Reprisal raids by the warships of the countries involved worsened the situation, one which lasted nearly 35 years.

Finally, King George I stepped in and appointed one Captain Woodes Rogers the Colony's first royal governor. He began to restore order by hanging many of the pirates, pardoning close to 1000 who surrendered, and forcing the rest to flee.

As a result, the coat of arms of the colony soon carried the motto *"Expulsis Piratis, Restituta Commercia"* (Pirates expelled, commerce restored), a motto which held until a few years ago, when it was changed to read "Forward, Upward, Onward, Together."

It was through Governor Rogers that a parliamentary government was established in the Bahamas, and its constitution, drawn up in 1728, remained unchanged for more than 200 years.

All was quiet until 1776, when a U.S. naval squadron captured Nassau, flew the American flag over the city for one day, and then withdrew. Five years later, the Spanish came back, only to be ousted again by the British. The Treaty of Versailles in 1783 finally confirmed the Bahamas as a British possession.

After the American Revolution, thousands of Loyalists from the Carolinas, intrigued by generous land grants from the crown, left the United States to settle in the Bahamas. They brought their slaves with them, even their animals, forebears of the wild boar and wild horses that roam the Abacos today.

It was about this time that a small village called Adelaide Settlement was established in the southwestern corner of New Providence. It still exists, but is a forgotten town, a place where some 15 or 20 families live life as it was 100 years ago. Their cottages are made of stone, with roofs of heavy thatch.

Years ago, they grew pumpkins, sweet potatoes, and melons there and fished in handmade boats. Not so today in the tiny settlement, where time has stopped. Adelaide is a place where chickens seem to have the right of way; where tourists come only if they've lost their way; but where the people wait in hope that a visitor will stop so they can spin their tales of life decades ago.

Prosperity began to come to the Bahamas during the American Civil War, when the islands served as transfer points for munitions and medical supplies that could be run through the northern ships

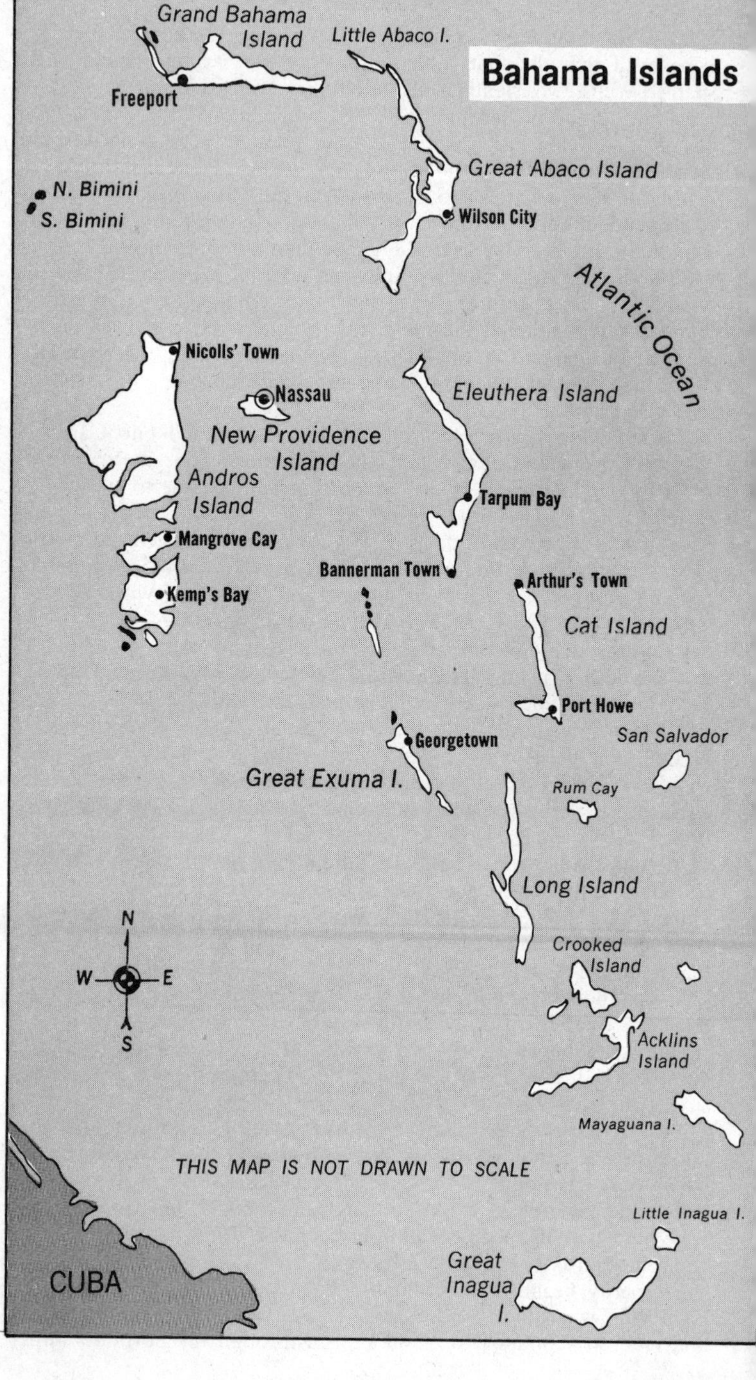
Bahama Islands
Grand Bahama Island
Freeport
Little Abaco I.
Great Abaco Island
Wilson City
N. Bimini
S. Bimini
Atlantic Ocean
Nicolls' Town
Nassau
New Providence Island
Eleuthera Island
Andros Island
Tarpum Bay
Mangrove Cay
Bannerman Town
Kemp's Bay
Arthur's Town
Cat Island
Port Howe
San Salvador
Georgetown
Great Exuma I.
Rum Cay
Long Island
N
W
E
S
Crooked Island
Acklins Island
Mayaguana I.
THIS MAP IS NOT DRAWN TO SCALE
Little Inagua I.
Great Inagua I.
CUBA

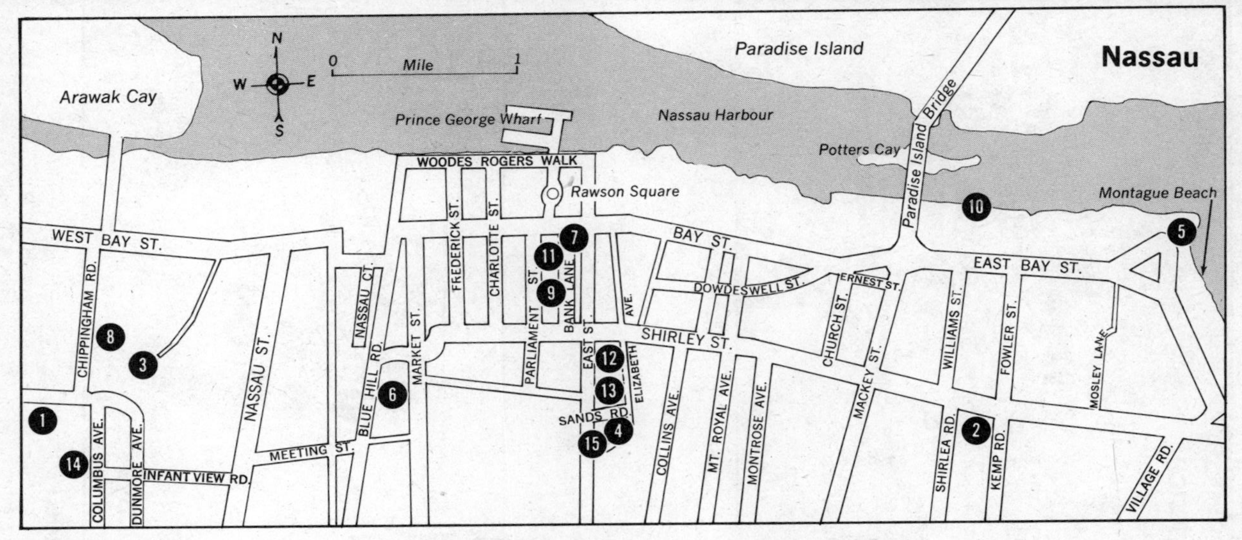

Points of Interest

1) Ardastra Gardens
2) Bahamas Antiquities Museum
3) Fort Charlotte
4) Fort Fincastle
5) Fort Montague
6) Government House
7) Ministry of Tourism
8) Nassau Botanic Gardens
9) Nassau Public Library
10) Nassau Yacht Club
11) Parliament Square
12) Princess Margaret Hospital
13) Queen's Staircase
14) Seafloor Aquarium
15) Water Tower

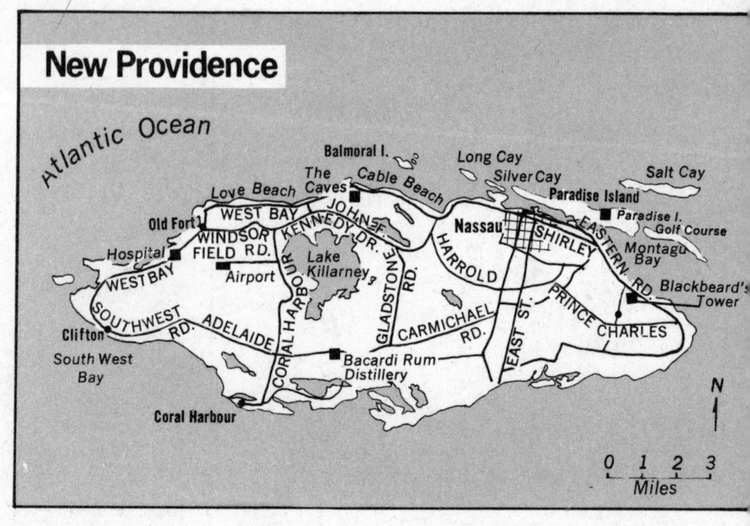

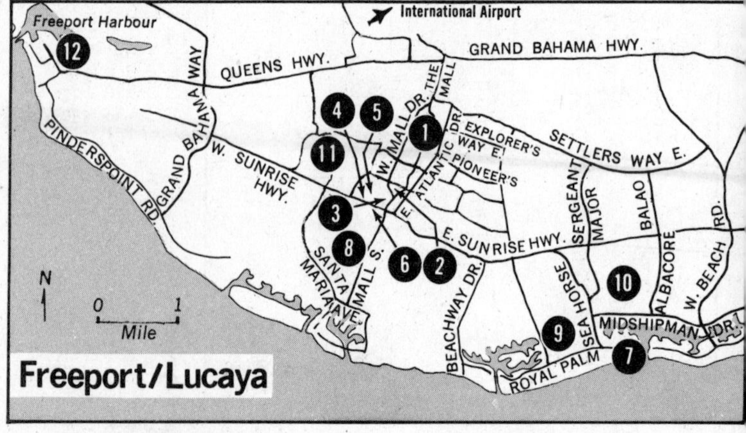

Points of Interest

1) Churchill Square
2) Castaways Hotel
3) International Bazaar
4) Bahamas Princess
5) El Casino
6) Princess Hotel
7) Holiday Inn
8) Emerald Golf Course
9) Bahama Reef Golf Course
10) Lucayan Park Golf Course
11) Ruby Golf Course
12) Customs

that were blockading Confederate ports. England wanted cotton from the South and the South needed arms: the result was a profitable four years for the colony.

They were to profit again when the United States established Prohibition. Gun-running was replaced by rum-running, a lucrative, if chancy, business which lasted for 13 years.

Two events brought the Bahamas before the public eye again in the early forties—an RAF training base was established to ferry U.S. and British aircraft to combat zones in Africa, Europe, and the Far East, and the Duke of Windsor, who had abdicated in 1936, was appointed governor of the colony, a post he held from 1940 to 1945.

Since 1946, the Bahamas have seen their real boom—in tourism, in real estate and, for a while, in finance. It is on tourism that the Commonwealth depends for its livelihood, and a solid recognition of that fact soon after the Independence celebrations in 1973 helped to refocus the wandering eyes of many Bahamians on improving their product in an increasingly competitive market.

Before World War II, the tourism on which the islands basically depended had been a matter only for the rich, and that for only three or four months every winter. In 1949, however, a group of businessmen determined to put tourism on a more popular footing and to provide all-year-round employment for the local people. They injected new life into the Development Board (now the Ministry of Tourism), voting large sums to promote the islands as an all-year resort. Their cause was helped in the early years by reports of sunken treasure off the southwest tip of Great Abaco Island. Two Nassau businessmen, who had spent 15 years searching, succeeded in bringing up several 17th century Spanish coins and a 72-pound silver bar that was identified as the personal property of King Philip IV of Spain. The worth of the silver bar was estimated at $20,000, bringing divers in droves to put the spurs to the slow-starting tourist industry.

Independence came to the Bahamas in July 1973, but did not end monarchial ties as the government decided to remain in the Commonwealth of Nations, with Queen Elizabeth II continuing as Head of State. Self-governing since 1964, the Bahamas since 1973 has had a Bahamian Governor General who serves as the Queen's Representative.

EXPLORING THE BAHAMAS

Although only 21 miles long and 7 miles wide, New Providence is the most important island in the Bahamas group because it contains the capital city of Nassau, named after William III of England, who was Prince of Orange-Nassau before occupying the throne.

If, like the majority of visitors to the Bahamas, your vacation starts at Nassau, you will reach it by sea at Prince George Wharf or by air at Nassau International Airport.

Your first impression of the Bahamas will be one of flower-scented breezes. Bahamian flowers are brilliant—purple and red bougainvillea; yellow and red hibiscus; pink, white, and red oleander; and royal purple passion flower–all their many mingling perfumes give a subtle fragrance to the southeast trade winds.

Next you will notice the characteristic architecture. Bahamian houses all have a traditional look. The old ones were built of the island limestone and have upper porches that hang out over the street. To protect the home from the sun, wide verandas were built in graceful wooden construction, and louvers were used to permit cooling breezes to enter. Georgian and Federal styles are the keynotes, and the best way to see it all is just to stroll Nassau's streets or go leisurely in a surrey.

Nassau is grouped around Bay Street, the bustling shopping center of the island. The focal point of Bay Street is Rawson Square, in which are located the Government administrative and legislative buildings. The House of Assembly is here, too, and the Supreme Court. If the House is in session, you can attend its sitting, when it meets with all the pomp and tradition of the Mother of Parliaments. Proper decorum in dress is required and you must apply in advance through the Clerk of the Courts. His office, at the House, is open Monday through Friday, from 9 to 5.

Admission can also be gained to the Law Courts, where standards of British justice prevail. Behind the statue of Queen Victoria is a fine garden containing the Public Library and museum. This octagonal building dates back to 1797 and was originally built as a prison. It now contains 20,000 volumes and relics of several centuries of Bahamas history.

There are three old forts well worth seeing in and around Nassau. The largest is Fort Charlotte. Named after the wife of King George III, it was built in or about 1790. Despite the fact that it mounted some 42 guns, plus a battery on the waterfront, it has to be reported that the fort never repulsed an invader nor fired a shot in anger. Built by Lord Dunmore, last royal governor of New York and Virginia, it has many grim dungeons and underground chambers. For those who want flowers in profusion, a visit to the Nassau Botanical Gardens, behind historic Fort Charlotte on Chippingham Road, will be worth a wander. Paths lead to a cactus garden, and then to a grotto of local quarry stone, with an area of tropical flowers nearby. There's a playground for children and a refreshment area. The 18-acre area is open from 9 A.M. to 4 P.M. daily.

Visit Fort Montagu, which was built in 1741 to guard the Eastern entrance to Nassau Harbour. It was captured by the Americans in 1776 during the War of Independence and captured again in 1782 by the Spaniards, only to be recaptured by the British soon after.

Finally, there is Fort Fincastle, also built by Lord Dunmore, who named it after his second title, Viscount Fincastle. It suffered the same fate as Fort Charlotte, in that it was never used in earnest. All three forts are easy to reach from Bay Street.

Most of the Bahamas are relatively low-lying, but Nassau itself is built on a hill. Surmounting this hill, close to Fort Fincastle, is a large water tower, 216 feet above sea level. It has been equipped with an elevator and makes a fine vantage point for viewing the city and its surroundings. Also close to Fort Fincastle is the Queen's Staircase, a flight of 66 steps cut in the solid rock of a deep limestone canyon. It was built by slave labor about the same time as the Fort and designed as an escape route for the troops garrisoned there.

A 12-foot statue of Christopher Columbus stands in front of Government House, also worth seeing. It was there that the Duke of Windsor lived during World War II, as well as all royal governors thereafter. One of the most impressive ceremonies here is the Changing of the Guard at Government House (alternate Saturdays, 10 A.M.).

Several miles to the east of Bay Street is Blackbeard's Tower, whose crumbling structure is said to be the remains of a watchtower used by the notorious pirate.

Ardastra Gardens, outside Nassau, are among the loveliest on the island. Here, every day at 11 A.M. and 4 P.M., you can watch the famous parade of the flamingos. It is impressive to watch the squad of close to 50 birds go through a drill routine. The flamingo is the national bird of the Bahamas and comes from Inagua Island, about 300 miles from Nassau. Dolphins perform in Nassau as well–at the Seafloor Aquarium four times a day.

The waterfront at Nassau is always worth a visit. Fishing boats tie alongside every day, and you can watch them unloading giant turtles, enormous lobsters, tropical fish, and a colorful assortment of conch shells, which will be polished and later sold to visitors.

If you choose to tour the island by sea, there are half-day catamaran cruises, complete with calypso band on board, that make stops along the way for swimming and diving. Glass-bottom boat cruises to the island's Sea Gardens are very popular and run about 1½ hours, at a charge of $5 per person. The *Nautilus,* a glass bottom submarine, also has a cruise (2 hours long, $15 per person).

Catamaran trips, deep-sea fishing excursions, all-day island tours, and night club visits can all be arranged very easily at every hotel desk on the island. The latest rage here is Parasailing. Take off from the Ambassador Beach Hotel, or the Nassau Beach Hotel.

Paradise Island, just across from Nassau Harbour, used to be famous enough for its magnificent beach alone, which can be visited for a day's swimming and sunning. All it cost then, and still costs now, is $2 for the day. Paradise Beach curves like a crescent moon and is the end of an island trail through a grove of casuarina trees that sweep down to form a tropical arcade. Brilliant red hibiscus provides added color to the soft green trail.

Thatched huts around the horseshoe beach look as if they had been planted to edge the shore. Sit inside if the tropical sun is too much, lean against a giant coconut palm, or stretch out on a straw mat and watch the water change color.

If time permits, take a day to go exploring–on a horse, on a Honda or bicycle, or in a metered taxi. Rent a peddleboat to skim Paradise Lake, or simply walk. Of course, the glittering casino is here to beckon the traveler, but see the island by day first.

Particularly lovely are the seven terraces of formal gardens, near the Ocean Club, that lead up to The Cloister, which was built in the

14th century by Augustinian monks. These gardens, which can rival Versailles, stretch as far as the eye can see and from their plateau provide an enchanting view of Nassau Harbor and the Paradise surroundings.

Grand Bahama

For many years, Grand Bahama Island was the sleeping giant of the Bahamian group, but 19 years ago it awoke with a roar. At the moment, it's difficult to decide whether the sudden awakening was a good or a bad thing.

In 1963, there were only 30 hotel rooms in Freeport; today there are more than 4,000, in addition to more than 2,000 apartments. Private land development, mostly in the form of the sale of small homesites, caused roads to be built, golf courses to be constructed, and land salesmen to proliferate.

There is little on the island that is more than twenty years old, and only the hotel at West End predates the current boom. It stands as a solitary development at that end of the island, with Freeport now the unquestioned center of things. In Freeport, virtually all the hotels are high-rise and huge, bustling with frenzied activity. Despite exteriors that seem to be vying for an unannounced "most garish façade" award, they are comfortable, air conditioned, and reasonably well run.

There are six superb golf courses, and, as a group, they are unequalled in the Caribbean for quantity-with-quality. The Underwater Explorers Club provides instruction and equipment for those who want to take to the sea. In just two days, a novice can have "checked out" in scuba gear and be exploring the nearby reefs.

Gambling draws thousands with dollar signs in their eyes. The two lavish casinos that opened some years ago have now been boiled into one, but the survivor, *El Casino,* claims to be one of the largest in the Western Hemisphere. And, if you want more return for your money (or at least an assured one), the International Bazaar allows you to shop and dine in an assortment of "countries."

Grand Bahama has chosen to fill its rooms (or try to) with a variety of Miami-style summer and winter specials and package holidays programmed to several interests: golf, honeymoon, tennis, gambling, and so on. However, they do offer value for the prices charged . . . and that's something these days.

Much of the exploring on Grand Bahama centers around the mammouth International Bazaar and the Casino in Freeport, a city that was just a village on a slab of sand less than 20 years ago. The International Bazaar, a 10-acre, $3-million shopping and dining complex, mixes and mingles foods and products from Europe, Asia, and the Near East. Designed by a Hollywood scenic effects expert, the bazaar is probably one of the most photographed spots in Freeport! Adjoining it is El Casino, which is an extravaganza. Even if you're not a gambler, this place must be seen to be believed.

Glass-bottom boat cruises, deep-sea fishing trips, and a 3-hour sail on a catamaran are typical ways to see the surrounding areas. A three-hour land tour by bus is the least expensive ($10 per person) way to see the island itself. Taxis are metered and the fare from the airport to the International Bazaar is about $4; from the airport to the Lucaya resorts it is about $6. Volkswagen buses run from Lucaya and other outlying areas to downtown Freeport for 65¢.

Golf is one of the island's main selling points, but tennis is running a close second, with more than 50 courts, most of them all-weather layouts and many of them illuminated for night play.

One of the loveliest sights in Freeport is the Garden of the Groves, a man-made floral and plantlife wonderland a 15-minute taxi ride from the bazaar. There is no entrance fee. You can wander among a countless number of exotic blooms, overhanging vines and waist-high shrubs, massive century plants, four man-made waterfalls that are lighted by color lamps at night, and rest alongside a lagoon in the center of this jewel-like setting.

Other than the beaches out at Lucaya, the small villages that line the route from Freeport to West End, and the Garden of the Groves, there is little for the sightseer to record on Grand Bahama–no old forts, no ancient buildings, no legends.

The Out Islands

These islands compose most of the Bahamas, but because they are not on the beaten path and are a short flight or boat trip from the capital, they have retained the naiveté of the oldtime Bahamas and have taken only halting steps into the hectic life of the 1980s (with phones, lights, water and the like).

As they come into vacation view, new hotels are appearing on the horizon, but the theme of an Out Island holiday is low key, low pressure, water and sun oriented, do-what-you-will.

Many of the small islands are private and you are welcome only by invitation, but there are plenty of public places with a Robinson Crusoe atmosphere, and in the following pages we'll look at some of them. We've continued our listing alphabetically by the name of the major island (usually the one with the airport), followed by the small cays in its orbit.

Sightseeing on the Out Islands is minimal–which is as it should be. Who could ask for a national art gallery, a governor's palace, or a wax museum on a small tropical island? Indian caves here and there, ancient settlements much as they were hundreds of years ago, thousands of pink flamingos at rest should be enough to whet the appetite.

Travelers to the Out Islands must be content to pull bananas or mangoes from the trees and to enjoy the best swimming, scuba diving, sailing, and fishing this side of the Pacific.

But by all means take the island tours. The villages and scenery are never the same, nor are the people.

The Abacos

This northernmost group in the Bahamas embraces about 775 square miles. The major islands are Great and Little Abaco, fringed by a colorful assortment of offshore cays that form a natural barrier reef against the Atlantic.

Similar to a boomerang in shape, Great Abaco is 100 miles long, but in some sections it is so narrow you can almost pole-vault across. Wonderful names like Tea Table Cay, Little Pigeon Cay, and Umbrella Cay are well-known to yachtsmen, while fishermen have their own favorite haunts.

The Abacos were first settled in 1785 by refugees from the American Revolution. Many of these Loyalists settled on the offshore cays, and their descendants still live there, in small villages reminiscent of 18th century America.

Abaco's 6,500 residents are engaged in the export of pulpwood, fashioned at Snake Cay after being brought in from the island's endless forest. Or they oversee the growing of cucumbers and tomatoes, or set out toward the deep waters in search of the daily catch.

Man-O'-War Cay, a 10-minute ferry ride from Marsh Harbour, the island's capital, has long been known as the boat-building capital of the Bahamas. Amid the hammering, visitors can still marvel at the art of shipbuilding, a craft that has been handed down from father to son for generations, and visitors will want to visit the sailmaker's loft of the Alburys, who have been making sails for decades.

This is the Abaco of the islanders, but the Abaco of the tourist means sailing, bonefishing, or even wild boar hunting.

There is little to see at Marsh Harbour, but it does have one of the island's international airports (the other at Treasure Cay) and serves as the gateway to the cays. It is also homeport to the sailing and cruising fleet of Bahamas Yachting Service, Ltd. A 20-minute ferry ride will take you to Elbow Cay, an island where its peppermint-striped lighthouse has become one of the most photographed landmarks in the Bahamas. The little village of Hope Town built around the harbor is quaint and colorful, and resembles a Massachusetts village seaport.

Wild boar country lies to the north, between Marsh Harbour and Treasure Cay. Without the aid of an experienced hunter, you'll rarely see a boar crossing the island road, or even in the forest for that matter. They are available here, and if a wild hog safari is your cup of tea, it can be easily arranged.

There is a multi-million-dollar development at Treasure Cay, including a fine hotel and beach. Green Turtle Cay, as its name implies, was famous in bygone days for the excellent turtle caught in surrounding waters and shipped abroad. It is a charming island, just three miles long, with hills that soar up to eighty feet. A water taxi makes the two-mile run from Treasure Cay, a worthwhile trip if only to see the township of New Plymouth, which offers a touch of New England in the tropics.

Andros

The largest of the Bahama Islands, Andros is actually a series of islands, most of them unexplored, but all of them bordered on the eastern shore by a barrier reef that is second in size only to Australia's Great Barrier Reef.

This is not only mangrove country, but Indian country. The first Andros settlers were Seminole Indians, who fled Florida in 1790, when Spanish slavery was at its peak. They brought their superstitions with them. Even though it's now called native folklore, the legend of the "Chickcharnies" is still going strong. Elsewhere, one might call them gremlins or even leprechauns, but on Andros they are tiny, red-eyed, tree-dwelling elves. The Chickcharnie has great influence for either good or evil, and is said to nest in pine trees. If that isn't enough, Andros also speaks of the elusive Lusca, a mythical half-dragon, half-octopus that lives in caves and devours anyone who comes close enough.

Diving and underwater photography, both around the barrier reef, are the main attractions of this island, which is still fairly undeveloped, although there are four airports.

The Berry Islands

These islands have remained in the "you can't get there from here" category for so long that they still qualify as unspoiled and serene. There is air service from Nassau but only two of the 30 cays are really developed. The others remain the haunts of millionaires and beachcombers.

Chub Cay, at the southern end of the chain, is a mecca for fishermen, and there are a dozen or so rooms available for tourists. Great Harbour Cay, on the northern tier, is far more developed, and may just be the "in-est" of all the Out Islands. It has a fashionable resort complex surrounding a championship golf course, and townhouses that have boat slips in their "basements."

The main attraction of the Berry Islands is the surrounding water and what you can do with, on, or under it. One of the beaches is seven miles long, and all are ideal for shelling, peace and tranquility.

Bimini

Ponce de León, the legendary Fountain of Youth, and Ernest Hemingway put Bimini on the map, but the fantastic fishing here and in its surrounding waters created for it the title "The Big Game Fishing Capital of the World."

Actually, there are two islands: South Bimini, which has frequent air service, and North Bimini, which is accessible only by seaplane or boat.

Accommodations for the airborne tourist are fine on both islands, but unless you fish or at least have a working knowledge of the sport, you would be better off on another Bahamian island.

Ernest Hemingway penned *The Old Man and the Sea* after a few experiences in the Bimini waters, and Ponce de León, who set out for the Fountain of Youth more than 350 years ago, missed the island completely and landed in Florida.

In any case, the Biminis are superior for the angler. The waters are filled with marlin and tuna and world records are set here regularly. But not the best spot for the first-time tourist to the Bahamas who wants to island-hop and get caught up in the history.

Cat Island

Cat Island is one of the loveliest in the Bahamas, with untouched beaches and verdant hills that soar up over the sea.

It was settled and abandoned by the Spaniards, then resettled by Loyalists from America, who established plantations there in 1783.

Explore the Indian caves along the island, particularly the one at Columbus Point on the southern tip and the thatched-roof farming village called The Bight to the north. From here it is possible to climb to the top of Mt. Alvernia, the island's highest point. At the peak is "The Hermitage," a small monastery built by the hermit, Father Jerome, an Anglican missionary who later became a Roman Catholic convert.

Eleuthera

A long (110 miles) skinny green island with three airports is the easiest Out Island to reach—in 20 minutes by air from Nassau. It is the oldest settlement in the Bahamas and one of the most developed of the Out Islands.

If you can imagine yourself an adventurer on a tropical island with nothing to do all day but swim or walk along the beach collecting shells, the lovely island of Eleuthera has your name on it.

That's how it all began when 70 pioneers from Bermuda and England, who had set out in search of religious freedom, were shipwrecked here in 1647. Known as the Eleutherian (after the Greek word for freedom) Adventurers, they settled the island to make Eleuthera the first republic in the New World.

One narrow road runs the length of the island, which is about 100 miles long and 3 miles wide, and from the air looks like a long crooked twig. Tiny villages, with houses painted in pastel colors, keep cropping up as you drive, but are so small the map makers have left them unnamed.

Most of the island's 6000 inhabitants are involved in farming the pineapple tomato crop or are employed at Hatchet Bay Plantation, the largest dairy and poultry farm in the Bahamas.

Long, pink uninhabited beaches, edged by casurina trees, run the length of the island. There is little or no night life and few shops to speak of, but the visitor will find horses to ride on the hard sand road or along the empty beaches.

Other pastimes include golf (Cape Eleuthera's course designed by Bruce Devlin and Bob von Hagge has a 4th hole rimmed by the ocean and often compared to the fabled 18th at California's Pebble Beach), scuba diving, and deep sea fishing–or simple lazing in the sun. Touring means visiting Rock Sound, the largest town on the island and the most exclusive area. Also in the southeastern corner of the island is Cape Eleuthera, which has traditionally been the locale of world records and near records for marlin, sailfish, wahoo, and dolphin. Charter boats and guides, available at the resort's docks, leave daily for excursions to the gamefish areas. Heading north, you'll see the sleepy fishing village of Tarpum Bay, followed by Governor's Harbour, a tiny town that curves around the bay, but is now coming into its own as Club Med's latest Bahamian destination.

The island twig then curves west to the sprawling Hatchet Bay Plantation, with more than 2000 acres of farmland, and then begins to narrow, so much so that it is no more than a few long strides from one side to the other.

Years ago, a small land bridge joined the island together here and formed a window in the rock, giving passing seamen a perfect view of the waters on the other side. The phenomenon was called the Glass Window. Although a much sturdier bridge has long since replaced the original, the name stuck, and it is the island's major attraction.

The largest village at the northern point is Current, one of the first settlements on the island and a place where even today the crowing of a rooster, the rustling of palm tree fronds in a breeze, and the shuffling about of native fishermen as they prepare to set out for a day's fishing are the only sounds to break the peace of early morning.

One exception is Thursday, when the weekly mail boat chugs into the harbor, making the five-hour trip back to Nassau on Sunday loaded with cargo and the few hardy people who want to make the crossing by sea. Three other mail boats make the weekly trip, landing at Spanish Wells, Tarpum Bay, Rock Sound and Governor's Harbour.

Most travelers these days arrive by air aboard daily flights.

Surrounding North Eleuthera's shores are two picturesque spots–Harbour Island and Spanish Wells on St. George's Cay.

Harbour Island

Just 1½ square miles of pink sand and history, this island is separated from the North Eleuthera mainland by a narrow channel.

Harbour Island was also settled by the Eleutherian Adventurers, and many of its residents still speak with traces of Elizbethan English. They call themselves "Brilanders," (short for Harbour Islanders) and are a hardy group whose forebears helped recapture Nassau from the Spaniards.

Dunmore Town, one of the oldest settlements in the Bahamas, is named for the Earl of Dunmore, who spent his summers here while he was governor of the Bahamas from 1786 to 1797.

Harbour Island has traditionally been popular with yachtsmen, fishermen, and those after the peaceful island life.

Spanish Wells

On a sandy little island called St. George's Cay lies Spanish Wells, a colorful little community with fewer than 1000 residents. The miniature houses are painted in a variety of pastels, creating an especially pretty scene, enhanced by the pine and palm trees that surround them.

Spanish Wells is another of the islands originally settled by the Eleutherian Adventurers. Their descendants are industrious people, excellent farmers and fishermen, who transport much of their produce to the Nassau market.

St. George's Cay lies off the coast of north Eleuthera. It is a short ride by ferry or water taxi and well worth the trip.

The Exumas

The Exuma chain, which begins just 35 miles southeast of Nassau, is made up of 365 cays and 2 islands that drift south for more than 100 miles. Great Exuma, the largest of the islands, opens its doors to thousands during the annual Out Island Regatta every April and then closes them just as quickly, to return to a way of life that hasn't changed much since the American Loyalists built sweeping plantations here two centuries ago.

Some of the plantations are in ruins today and offer ideal areas to explore for a day's picnic outing. One of the former plantations, Cotton House on Little Exuma, is still inhabited and, with special arrangements, is sometimes open to visitors.

The best known hotels are in the George Town orbit, all within walking distance of town. Watersports are the focus for activities at most of the cottages and hotels. The main excursion, once you've done the "around the Exumas" route by car and driver, is the 5-minute motor boat ride to Stocking Island. You can spend a delightful day on this completely unspoiled sandy strand where a small snack shop/bar is available for food and a mystery cave that goes from 12 to 80 feet deep and is unexplored beyond 50 feet inside. After swimming and sunning, the main activity will be to climb one of the steep hills that overlook the sandy beaches on the island's harbor side, perhaps to the obelisk that served as a landmark to identify the salt pans inside Elizabeth Harbour at George Town across the way.

The island of Little Exuma, just ten miles from George Town, is easily accessible via a one-lane drawbridge at a border town called The Ferry. Williams Town, the island's capital, is a three-block community surrounding the ancient plantation, Cotton House. There is a long shore where hundreds of brilliant conch shells have been abandoned, and a small group of farms.

One of the highlights of a visit to Little Exuma is a walk along the beach at a spot called Pretty Molly Bay. Not just because of the raw beauty of it all, but because of its legend: It seems that back in the days of slavery a tired laundress, by the name of Pretty Molly, simply set her iron down and walked off into the bay between the two boulders of coral rock. She was never heard from again, but legend has it that she still walks the beach on any moonlit night.

When you add the legends to the history, and then precede it with the fact that the Exumas were once the domain of the fearless pirates, the chain still has a lot going for it.

The Inaguas

This island grouping is made up of two islands—Great Inagua, the southernmost of the Bahamas chain, and Little Inagua, five miles above it.

Wildlife is in profusion on both, with wild donkeys and goats on Little Inagua and more than 30,000 flamingos on the larger island.

Most Inaguans work in the salt fields, an industry that has flourished here since 1800. Today, close to 1 million tons of salt is shipped each year from Matthew Town, the principal settlement on Great Inagua.

So far, there is little for the tourist here; accommodations are few, and much of the island is still undeveloped. However, there is raw beauty, particularly around Windsor Lake, which is twelve miles long. The entire area is a Wildlife Park maintained by the government for the preservation of the thousands of pink flamingos that nest there.

Long Island

Not to be confused with that 100-mile land mass at the southern tip of the State of New York, the Long Island of the Bahamas is one of Columbus' early landfalls.

The island was originally populated by Lucayan Indians and, if history is correct, they impressed the explorer when he came ashore on October 16, 1492.

As the story goes, he found them living in tent-shaped dwellings and sleeping in nets that were stretched between the posts. The Indians called them *"hamacs,"* and so awed was Columbus by the idea that he immediately arranged similar quarters for his crew.

He also changed the island's name (a habit he acquired early on) from Yuma and then left it for the Loyalists, who came 400 years later, to bring it into its own.

Cotton plantations flourished until the abolition of slavery, and now all that is left is fishing and farming. For the sightseer, there is Clarence Town, a pretty village to the south, where the Reverend Father Jerome built two churches, Deadman's Cay, with its fascinating caves, and an assortment of tiny hamlets that run the full length of the 57-mile island.

San Salvador

History has it that the New World was discovered here. On October 12, 1492, it is recorded, Columbus arrived at this small island, then called Guanahani by the Arawak Indians who were its inhabitants, and renamed it San Salvador in the name of Spain.

The island is only 14 miles long and 6 miles wide, yet no one is sure just where Columbus made that historic landfall, so there are three different monuments to the explorer at "exact spots" on the island.

It is also said that Blackbeard, Watling, and other buccaneers roosted here, which could be so, since the island was known as Watling's Island for years. Groups of Loyalists from the United States came next to build their plantations, a few of which still remain.

Other than the monuments and the largest settlement, called Cockburn Town, there is little to see here. But there are the usual empty white sand beaches and fine fishing in the surrounding waters.

A DAY ON YOUR OWN

Pack your camera, shine up your sun-glasses, and be prepared to bargain at the market for a straw hat to shade the sun. Then plan to spend a full day on your walking tour of Nassau.

Begin at Rawson Square, the hub of the city and the center of Nassau's straw market activity. Here you'll want to stop to look, listen and photograph the sounds and sights of Nassau at work. You'll find tourist-laden horse-drawn surreys creating traffic jams; smartly dressed policemen keeping motorists on their toes; blaring sirens from cruise ships to warn wayfarers that sailing time is nigh; and happy sidewalk vendors to convince you that you really need that large straw bonnet before you set out in mid-day.

From the Square, take a short walk down to the waterfront named after royalty–Prince George, where passenger liners are berthed, and where Out Island fleets arrive daily to unload their cargo of fresh produce and fish. Here you can purchase fresh pineapples, bananas, coconuts and sample other native fruit with strange sounding names like soursop, hog plums, and sugar apples. You can also buy those raspberry-tinted conch shells and listen to the sounds of the sea.

From the waterfront, retrace your steps back to Rawson Square and head south to Parliament Square. The three imposing Georgian structures house the Senate, the House of Assembly and the Supreme Court. A statue of Queen Victoria, in all her glory, stands guard at the entrance.

It will be time for lunch and something tall and cool. Cross Parliament Square to the Green Shutters Inn for lunch. Here, in a relaxing English countryside pub atmosphere, you can sip draft beer and order anything from a cheeseburger to fresh fish with local sidedishes.

Afterward, resume your walking tour by leaving the pub and turning east along Shirley Street. Walk for a block past the Zion Baptist Church and turn south into a street known as "East." Head south for a block to Sands Road, a street that takes you past a section of the sprawling compound of the Princess Margaret Hospital, and at its end, take a right turn to the 102-foot high Queens Staircase. This is one of Nassau's major attractions. Its well-worn 66 steps were hewn out of solid rock by slaves during the reign of Queen Victoria.

Climb the staircase to reach Fort Fincastle at its top. This bastion dates back to 1793 , but like most of the island's forts, it never saw action. Then, for the most spectacular view of the island, walk from the fort to the Water Tower. Located atop Bennett's Hill, this 126-foot tower rises 216 feet above sea level, the highest point on the island. The entrance fee to the tower is 50 cents and well worth it. Soar to the top in the elevator where a guide will be on hand to pinpoint every historic building in view.

From the base of the tower you can walk into town for last-minute shopping, or grab a cab or surrey back to your hotel.

PRACTICAL INFORMATION FOR THE BAHAMAS

HOW TO GET THERE. By air. Nassau's International Airport on New Providence Island is the hub of activity, with flights splintering out of here for most of the Out Islands and for Grand Bahama. There are also direct flights out of the United States and Canada to Grand Bahama and out of Miami to the Exumas and other Out Island areas as well as to the major airports at Grand Bahama and Nassau. Nassau is less than an hour by air from Florida and less than 1½ hours from any of the Out Islands.

Carriers serving Nassau (New Providence) from major cities include *Air Canada, Air Florida, Air Jamaica, American Airlines, Bahamasair, British Airways, Chalk's (International Airlines* from Miami with four sea planes), *Delta Air Lines,* and *Eastern Airlines.*

Grand Bahama's Freeport is reached from U.S. cities via flights of *Air Florida, Bahamasair, Eastern, Delta.* From Canada, *Air Canada* makes the connection.

If you don't have your private plane, air service to the Out Islands is provided by the following commercial carriers, always out of Nassau and sometimes from Miami:

The Abacos: Bahamasair to Treasure Cay and Marsh Harbour.

Andros: Bahamasair to San Andros, Andros Town, Mangrove Cay, South Andros.

Berry Islands: Bahamasair to Chub Cay.

The Biminis: Chalk's to North Bimini and South Bimini.

Cat Island: Bahamasair to Arthur's Town.

Crooked Island: Bahamasair.

Eleuthera: Bahamasair to North Eleuthera Governor's Harbour and Rock Sound; *Air Florida* to Rock Sound.

The Exumas: Air Florida and Bahamasair to George Town.

Inagua: Bahamasair.

Long Island: Bahamasair to Deadman's Cay and Stella Maris.

San Salvador: Bahamasair.

BY SEA. Several cruise lines feature Nassau and Freeport as ports-of-call from Miami and Port Everglades. Among them are the ships of *Carnivale Cruise Lines, Norwegian Caribbean, Royal Caribbean,* and *Sitmar.*

FURTHER INFORMATION. The Ministry of Tourism maintains several tourist offices overseas. For information other than the usual distributed by airline offices and travel agents, contact the closest *Bahamas Tourist Office.* Their locations: 3450 Wilshire Blvd., Los Angeles, Calif. 90004; 209 Post St., San Francisco, Calif. 94108; 1730 Rhode Island Ave., N.W., Washington, D.C. 20036; 255 Alhambra Circle, Coral Gables, Fla. 33134; 1950 Century Boulevard, N.E., Atlanta, Ga. 30345; 875 North Michigan Ave., Chicago, Ill. 60611; 1027 Statler Office Building, Boston, Mass. 02116; 30 Rockefeller Plaza, New York, N.Y. 10020; 42 South 15th St., Philadelphia, Pa., 19102; 2825 Southland Center, Dallas, Texas 75201; and 5177 Richmond Ave., Houston, Texas 77056. In Canada: 1255 Phillips Square, Montreal, P.Q. H3B3G1, Canada; 85 Richmond Street West, Toronto, Ont. M5H 2C9, Canada; and in England, 23 Old Bond Street, London WIX 4PQ, U.K.;

Headquarters of the Ministry of Tourism in the Bahamas is at Nassau Court, Nassau. Cable address: BAHMINTOUR, NASSAU. Mail address: P.O. Box N 3701, Nassau, New Providence, Bahamas.

ISLAND MEDIA. You'll never be without something to read in the Bahamas. The two daily newspapers are the *Nassau Guardian* and the *Nassau Tribune* (the *New York Times* is also flown in daily). Their *Bahamian Review,* a slick magazine, much like our Time, will give an interesting overview of all the islands. There are also special tourist publications, such as *Best Buys in the Bahamas; What to Do* in the islands (one with the emphasis on Nassau; the other on Grand Bahama); and *The Pocket Guide to the Bahamas.*

AUTHORIZED TOUR OPERATORS: Adventure Tours; Bahama Island Tours; Butler Travels; Caribbean Holidays; Caribbean Vacation Center; Cavalcade Tours; Flyfaire; Lib/Go; Playtime Vacations; Red & Blue Tours; and Travel Center Tours from the U.S. From Canada: Fairway Tours; Holiday House. From London: Kuoni Travel.

PASSPORTS, VISAS. U.S. citizens do not need a passport or a visa to enter the Bahamas, provided their visit does not exceed 8 months. Proof of citizenship is required (a birth certificate or voter's registration card will do), but if you do bring your passport, they will be delighted to stamp it for you. Canadians and citizens of the United Kingdom may enter the Bahamas without a passport, provided they have proof of citizenship, but only for visits of up to 3 weeks.

All visitors must have return or onward tickets and can obtain the necessary customs clearance forms from hotels and airline counters. Customs declarations (written) must be completed before passing beyond the ticket counter on U.S.-bound flights.

The health requirements in the Bahamas are minimal: smallpox vaccination and cholera inoculation certificates may be required only in cases where a person is arriving directly from an area that is reported to have an incidence of these diseases.

MONEY. It is advisable to check the latest quotations, but at the time of publication the Bahamian dollar was worth U.S. $1. This is equivalent to Canadian $1.02; £1.85. Foreign currency can be converted to Bahamian currency at the International Airport's Foreign Exchange Booth or at most of the local banks, which are open from 9:30-3:00 Mon.-Thurs; 9:30-5:00 Fri. Watch prices here. Extras (taxes, etc.) add up on an already high price for most food and drink.

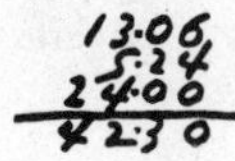

TAXES AND OTHER CHARGES. There is a 6% government tax on hotel rooms. Many add a 10-15% service charge." The airport departure tax is $4 US per person.

BAHAMIAN SPECIALS. The celebrated *fire dance* can often be seen in local night clubs. It is done to the famous goombay music—a delightful concoction from ancestral times. Usually, it is a simple couplet sung to a complicated rhythm beaten out of maracas, drums, and as many guitars as are available. Occasionally, it gets mixed up with the calypso strains, and a sort of hodgepodge but exciting goombay-rhythm-calypso emerges.

At many of the clubs you'll see the famous *limbo* dance, which consists of a kind of high jump in reverse. To the frenzied beating of bongo drums, performers wriggle underneath a bar or pole, which gets lower and lower. You have to see it to believe it, and our advice is to decline if you're asked to participate.

One of the most colorful local celebrations, either to watch or join in, is the *Junkanoo Parade,* held on Boxing Day (the day after Christmas) and again on New Year's Day. A kind of Bahamian Mardi Gras, it starts at 4 A.M. and goes on for hours. Wearing fantastically colored costumes and headdresses made of crepe paper, the merrymakers weave up and down Bay Street to the music of goombay drums, cow bells, and horns.

HOW TO GET ABOUT. On New Providence. Horse-drawn surreys, with fringe on top, can add a special flavor to a tour of Nassau and its environs. ($8 per hour for up to 3 people.) They can be found, forming a colorful parade at rest, at Rawson Square just off Bay Street. Rental cars are available through *Avis* and *Hertz,* as well as through local concerns. Rates range from $40 per day, $250 weekly, plus gas. Remember to drive on the left and observe the speed limit, which is 25 mph in the city, 30 mph out of town.

Bicycles can be rented for $5 per day; motor scooters for $16 per day. Or you can hire a taxi at the rate of $15 per hour for a 7-passenger cab, $12 per hour for a 5-passenger cab. Taxi rates are fixed by law, and cabs are metered. The fare from the airport to downtown Nassau will run about $10; $18 for hotels on Paradise Island, which includes the $2 bridge toll. Many of the hotels offer bus service at slight charge to hotel guests to take them to and from downtown Nassau throughout the day. Another way of getting between Nassau's Rawson Square and Paradise Island is via water-taxi shuttle service. ($2 round trip.)

On Grand Bahama. Taxis are the primary means of tourist conveyance here. Rates, which are identical to those in Nassau, are fixed by law, and the cabs are metered.

Rental cars through *Hertz, Avis,* and *Budget* are also available here, with prices similar to those in Nassau. A Honda goes for $6 per hour or $22 per day plus $2 insurance.

Nine passenger buses will take you anywhere on the island for 65¢; double-decker buses from London are on hand for touring, and many of the hotels in Freeport provide free transportation to the beaches for guests.

On the Out Islands. Once you leave New Providence or Grand Bahama, there are few cars or motor scooters for hire. You can rent your own horse to ride the uninhabited beaches, your own Sailfish to explore island coves, or your own bicycle to pedal the hard sand roads. But the best way to see as much of each island as you can is by private taxi. Taxi drivers are congenial, negotiations are easy, and prices are reasonable, particularly on half-day tours. What's more, the legends of each island, and there are many, are part of the narration at no extra charge.

EVENTS AND HOLIDAYS. In addition to the Junkanoo celebrations and those on Independence Day (July 10), you can find special, special events on these islands all year round. There is always a fishing or sporting tournament going on somewhere, and here, where the emphasis is "on the water," you'll find interesting events to be a part of as: The Annual Bahamas International Tuna Tournament, which is the highlight of the angling year; the White and Blue Marlin Tournaments in Bimini; the Bahamas Billfish Championship (Apr.-July); the Bahamas Bonefish Bonanza (in the Exumas in Sept.) and the annual Wahoo Round-Up in December.

The Miami-Nassau ocean yacht race (Feb.); the Out-Island Regatta (commercial sailing boats in a very colorful display at George Town, Great Exuma in April); the Bahamas "500" Ocean Power Boat Race from Freeport in June; and the Miami-Nassau Power Boat Cup Race in December are annual highlights.

In addition, there are golf tournaments, including the Pro-Am for the Bahamas Ryder Cup; and the spectacular Bahamas Flying Treasure Hunt in November, where enthusiasts search for and identify treasure clues from the air.

WHAT WILL IT COST?

The average rate on New Providence, Paradise Island, and Grand Bahama for *two* persons during the winter season will run:

	US$	£
Accommodations at one of the top hotels, including breakfast and dinner	150	81
Luncheon at a moderate restaurant	15	8
Taxes, tips & service charges	20	11
Car rental or one-day island tour	40	22
	$225	£122

ON THE OUT ISLANDS: The average range for all these islands runs from $55 double without meals to $100 double with breakfast, lunch, and dinner included, for *two* persons during the height of the season.

STAYING IN THE BAHAMAS

HOTELS. For those who insist on a lot of action, Nassau—with its Paradise Island—and Freeport on Grand Bahama are the liveliest places to be. They are also the most expensive, except for a couple of exclusive and high-priced spots on the Out Islands. But Bahamian bargains can still be found in special holiday rates for off-season travel, honeymoon, golf and tennis packages, as well as in apartment and cottage rentals.

To simplify the hotel picture, we've dealt first with the New Providence hotels, and then with those on Grand Bahama. The Out Islands and their properties, which are listed alphabetically, follow.

NEW PROVIDENCE

Ambassador Beach Hotel, Golf and Tennis Club. A real resort complex with 400 rooms on Cable Beach. The beach is gorgeous; the pool is huge; there are 4 all-weather tennis courts; and an 18-hole championship golf course. All watersports; deep-sea fishing and parasailing. Six dining rooms and lounge upon lounge–among them, the *Silk Cotton Tree* for dining and dancing; the *Sugar Mill* pub for island entertainment; and the *Garrison Bar,* the swinging nightspot. $105–115 double EP in winter; $80–90 double EP off-season.

Balmoral Beach Hotel. 220 rooms, several in villa settings. Swimming pool; seawall beach; own island with private beach, barbecue, and bar. Tennis courts, water sports. From $82–98 double EP in winter; from $65 double EP off-season.

Buena Vista Hotel. Only 7 rooms, but each charming, in this 175-year-old Bahamian Great House. The dining is superior (see our section on Restaurants) here, to add another nice touch to the old-world elegance of the place. $55 EP double in winter; $44 double EP off-season.

Club Mediterranee. The first of this vacation village organization's facilities to open in the Bahamas, the Paradise Island Club Med focuses on Tennis. There are 20 courts–8 lighted for night play–and 5 full-time instructors. As usual, the club's particular cost program is in effect. You pay one rate for all, which includes an air-conditioned room, all meals (with wine), and use of all sports and recreational equipment and facilities. In addition to tennis, there is sailing, snorkeling, swimming (both pool and ocean), boat trips, day-long sailing picnics and wind-surfing. (The only extras are costs for deep-sea fishing trips or greens fees on Paradise Island's 2 golf courses.) Nightly entertainment and a disco that begins at midnight and remains open until the last dancer has gone. From $520–700 per person, per week, depending upon the time of year. Definitely one of the best values here.

Graycliff Hotel. At Blue Hill Road and West Hill St., just across from the Governor's official residence and a few minutes' walk from Bay Street. This former home-turned-inn has 7 large and airy bedroom suites, 1 cottage, a swimming pool, patio and full house staff, a few of whom were in residence when the Duke and Duchess of Windsor stayed here as guests of former owners, the Earl and Countess of Dudley. Food is fantastic and beautifully served. $125 double in winter; $95 double off-season, full breakfast included.

Holiday Inn on Paradise Island. 18 stories of 535 rooms, all of them air-conditioned. No surprises here–it's HI all the way, with tennis, free-form pool, long beach and all water sports. A choice of places to dine, and nightly entertainment. From $88–126 double EP all year.

Loew's Harbour Cove. Multistoried, 250-room hotel on Paradise Island. Luxury living here, with a broad beach, swimming pool, unique "sip-in-dip" bar, and tennis court. Nice dining; free transportation to and from Nassau. $120 double EP in winter; $100 double off-season.

Nassau Beach Hotel. 425 luxurious, air-conditioned rooms, private balconies,

4 miles from town. Long, white sand beach; swimming pool; outdoor bar for drinks, snacks, and calypso music throughout the day (but watch the prices—exceptionally high for franks and hamburgers!). Attractive shopping mall; excellent food in a choice of restaurants; and the best "in-hotel" nightly entertainment on the island. $94–145 double EP in winter; $85–105 double EP off-season.

Nassau Harbour Club. This spot has been around for a long time, and its 50 rooms have always been a favorite of yachtsmen. The *Commodore Room,* for nice dining, overlooks the harbor; there is a small swimming pool; but the major attraction is the marina with its 65 slips. Its *Eight Bells* pub is still a gathering place for the nautically-minded. From $69 double EP in winter; from $59 double EP off-season.

Ocean Club. Our choice on Paradise Island, this 70-room club/hotel is a quiet and exclusive retreat. The architecture is Palladian; the breathtaking Cloister, a Versailles-type series of gardens, memorable. The long swimming pool is cross-shaped; the beach, which is down a series of wooden steps, is long and usually empty. Dining, either indoors or outside is always a treat. $150–175 double EP in winter; $118–250 double EP off-season.

Paradise Beach Inn. An especially cozy and casual property with 100 rooms on the beach on Paradise Island. Emphasis here is on water sports. Although you're close to "the action" on this island strip, you can also be "away-from-it-all." $80–100 double EP in winter; $65–85 double EP off-season.

The Paradise Island Resort and Casino. Composed of the Britannia Beach Hotel, the Paradise Island Hotel and the Paradise Island Casino, all interconnected under one roof. This beach-side property features 1,100 luxury rooms, 11 entertainment lounges and bars, 13 restaurants offering six culinary experiences from French and Continental to Italian and Polynesian. Pool with swim-up bar, beach deck, and 12 tennis courts. *Britania Beach:* $115–205 double EP in winter; $85–165 double EP off-season. *Paradise Island Hotel:* $110–180 double EP in winter; $75–130 double EP off-season.

Pilot House Club. Another Bahamian property that has been a favorite of not only yachtsmen, but sportscar racers, during the years when the Bahamas Speed Weeks rivaled the International Grand Prix. Still oriented for sports enthusiasts, the Pilot House Club has 125 rooms, all with either a balcony or patio. The Club overlooks Nassau's Yacht Haven, and its pool is within the palm gardens. Good food, and good value here, where rates run $75–85 double EP in winter; $65–70 double EP off-season.

Sheraton British Colonial. As pink as the Bahamian sands, and almost as old, this 255-room hotel has had its ups and downs over the years, but has always occupied a prominent position at the end of Bay Street in Nassau. We've never given up hope that it will emerge again in all its historic glory, and it has—adding a shopping arcade on one edge of its beach, and refurbishing its restaurant on the wharf for an added touch. The rooms have all been redone; the swimming pool and its poolside buffets back as an added treasure; along with 4 tennis courts. $82–102 double EP in winter; from $67–88 double EP off-season.

South Ocean Beach Hotel & Golf Club. Another special place, this 120-room resort swings low around a swimming pool and within the confines of a private beach and an 18-hole championship golf course. It's in the Lyford Cay section of New Providence (the west end) and offers all the privacy you might like, along with fine dining, nightly entertainment, and four tennis courts. $80–110 double EP in winter; $60–70 double EP off-season.

HOME RENTALS. This is the way to save, and still savor the Bahamian lifestyle. Consider *Cable Beach Manor,* a 44-unit efficiency complex, and the *Casuarinas,* also on the Cable Beach strip, 5 miles from Nassau. You'll have a swimming pool, maid service, beach facilities, and still be close to "the action." There are literally dozens of homes for rent here as well, and for full information and prices, contact the *Bahamas Real Estate Association,* P.O. Box N-837, Nassau, New Providence, Bahamas.

GRAND BAHAMA

Atlantik Beach Hotel. Originally built as a condominium, now 140 rooms and 35 apartments. 3 dining rooms, bar, 5 tennis courts, swimming pool, and parasailing options. $62–84 double EP in winter; from $44 double EP off-season.

Bahamas Princess Hotel. 800 rooms, 8 villas on a luxury property. Private beach, swimming pool, all water sports. 6 tennis courts and two 18-hole championship golf courses. A wide choice of restaurants from informal to gourmet. $69–99 double EP in winter; $49–69 double off-season.

Castaways Resort. 135 rooms. Exotic Polynesian decor throughout. Dining room, bar, swimming pool. Beach privileges. $46–67 double EP in winter; $34–59 double off-season.

Freeport Inn. Comfortable inn with 170 rooms and a superior steak house. Swimming pool. Golf privileges; water sports arranged. $49–79 double EP in winter; $34–64 double EP off-season.

Grand Bahama Hotel & Country Club. At the West End of the island. There's everything here and all of it geared to the resort life. The sprawling hotel has 580 rooms, a shopping plaza, an 18-hole golf course, champion skeet and trap range, 16 tennis courts, its own marina, and a fleet for chartering. Three large dining rooms (the *Hibiscus;* the *Out Island;* and the *Turtle Walk Supper Club).* International airport for charter flights from the U.S. and Canada. Freeport is 25 miles away. $80 double EP in winter; $55 double EP off-season.

Grand Lucaya Inn & Scuba Club. This spot, with only 40 rooms, is a special favorite for divers seeking all there is "beneath the sea." Their swimming pool and dining room are nice extras at the low rate of $52 double EP in winter; $36 double off-season.

Holiday Inn. A huge luxury hotel of 490 rooms on Lucayan Beach. Swimming pool, 5 tennis courts, boating, scuba equipment available, deep-sea fishing. The *Marine Lounge* is tops for evening entertainment. $72–89 double EP in winter; $48–59 double EP off-season.

Lucayan Harbour Inn. This 150-room hotel on Lucaya's south shore gives good value for its adequate accommodations and easy access to the big names and action. $50–60 double EP in winter; $31 double EP off-season.

Princess Towers. 400 room deluxe hotel with 20 suites. Designed to resemble a sultan's palace and it works. Ocean Beach Club, swimming pool, 3 all-weather lighted tennis courts. Moorish theme followed throughout. Selection of restaurants; nightly entertainment at the Sultan's Tent. $79–109 double EP in winter; $54–74 double EP off-season.

Shalimar Hotel. 150 rooms in the heart of Freeport. Dine at *Les Capade* at the top of the hotel for French and Continental cuisine. Bar, swimming pool, tennis. $60 double EP in winter; $37 double EP off-season.

Xanadu Beach Hotel. Luxurious with 113 rooms, 58 apartments and 3 villas. Howard Hughes' former suites on the 13th floor (4 suites, 11 bedrooms) can be rented. Ocean beach, swimming pool, marina, 3 tennis courts. French cuisine. From $100 double EP in winter; $76 double EP off-season.

RENTALS. There are hundreds of apartments available, such as the *Silver Sands Hotel* with 164 apartments, swimming pool, dining room, beach nearby.

Two major realtors preside here and have full listings of houses, apartments and condominiums for rent. Contact *MacPherson & Brown Real Estate Co.,* or *Tennant & Cooper Real Estate,* both in Freeport.

HOTELS ON THE OUT ISLANDS

We have dealt with the following areas as groups, listing hotels alphabetically within the group, according to the cay on which they are located: Abaco Islands, Andros Islands, the Berry Islands, Bimini, Cat Island, Eleuthera (Harbour Island, Spanish Wells), Great Exuma, Inagua, Long Island, and San Salvador. Self-sufficient travelers should contact the Ministry of Tourism for the apartment and villa listing in their *Travel Guide.* Additional (and often special) listings are carried at Bahamas Real Estate Association, Box N-837, Nassau, N.P., Bahamas. Specific contacts on the islands are mentioned when we look at each place.

THE ABACOS

Elbow Cay

Elbow Cay Club. 24 rooms on a private beach, with a great selection of watersports, including windsurfing. A place to arrange for deep-sea fishing in the Abaco waters. Restaurants and bar on the premises. $48 double EP all year.

Hope Town Harbour Lodge. Informal atmosphere for guests in seaside rooms and cottages. The lodge is located in a former Out Island commissioner's residence in Hope Town. There's a private beach, swimming pool, dining room, two bars, and options for all watersports. $62–82 double in winter: $55 double off-season, with breakfast included in the rate.

Great Guana Cay

Guana Harbour Club. This small property offers 16 air-conditioned rooms for guests who enjoy a private beach, out of the way atmosphere, and the boats that come and go at the dock. $50–60 double EP all year.

Green Turtle Cay

Green Turtle Yacht Club & Marina. Easily reached by water taxi from Treasure Cay Airport, this is a nice tropical colony with 32 rooms in villas and cottages, most of them at the water's edge. Activities here focus on the sea, with all watersports available. Dining room, bar, and swimming pool add to the pleasures along with meeting all the yachts-people who tie up at the marina. $87 double EP in winter; $68 double off-season.

Three dining-out spots in this area are *The Blue Bar Restaurant;* the *Plymouth Rock* (both inexpensive and well known for home-cooked local specialties) at New Plymouth, and the *Sea View,* which is a local bar/restaurant in a small village residential area.

Marsh Harbour

Conch Inn. 14 rooms either at the inn or in their cottages. Complete marina facilities and a restaurant that does spectacular things with fresh-caught fish. Swimming pool on the premises; beach not far away. $55 double EP all year.

Lofty Fig Villas. This small property, just across the road from the Conch Inn, provides good value in their handful of housekeeping units, which come complete with separate dining area, patio and a central pool. Easy access to fishing, boating, and the sea. From $62 double EP all year.

Treasure Cay

Treasure Cay Beach Hotel & Villas. An ideal place for an Abaco vacation. 35 hotel rooms; 178 more in apartments and villas; and a complete resort atmosphere. Four swimming pools; five miles of beach; 10 tennis courts; two restaurants; lively entertainment; and a superb 18-hole championship golf course. This resort is a special hideaway and one of our favorites. $91 double EP in winter; $78 double off-season. Their spacious villas run from $95–195 all year and accommodate from two to six people.

RENTALS. For apartments at the Treasure Cay complex, contact their offices, c/o P.O. Box 3941, Miami, Fla. 33101; for holiday homes (which range from $185-475 per week), write C. P. Gates, President, Hopetown Agencies, Ltd., Hopetown.

ANDROS

Andros Town

Chickcharnie Hotel. Casual and comfortable spot with 8 air-conditioned rooms. Boating and bicycling available. $59 double EP all year.

Small Hope Bay Lodge. 20 rooms in cottages right on the beach. Informal, with diving the house specialty. Andros Barrier Reef 1 mile offshore. Rates run $128 double in winter; $96 double off-season and include all meals.

Nicholl's Town

Tradewind Villas. 44 villas, each with 2 bedrooms. Located on private beach.

Freshwater swimming pool, scuba diving, fishing. The villas are available for $65–80 EP and accommodate up to six persons.

San Andros

San Andros Inn & Tennis Club. 22 rooms, fresh-water swimming pool, free transportation to beach a few miles away. Rates are $89 double all year and include three meals daily.

South Andros

Las Palmas. 20 nice rooms, each with private patio. Dining room, bar, and disco. Large swimming pool, watersports, putting green, and tennis. $40–50 double EP in winter; $30–40 double off-season.

BERRY ISLANDS

Chub Cay: *Chub Cay Marina Hotel.* The public is invited to rent privately owned condominiums when the owners are not in residence. 38 rooms, 6 villas, and a 4-bedroom houseboat. Complete marina, fishing, boating, tennis, swimming pool, private beach. An apartment where you do your own cooking can keep costs reasonable. Villas are comfortable for 4 or a larger family with small children. The houseboat rental provides a unique (and mobile) holiday. $80–90 double EP for rooms in winter; $60–70 double off-season; villas run from $160; the houseboat $230 per day.

BIMINI

North Bimini

Bimini Big Game Fishing Club. 51 rooms, 6 cottages, largest on the island. Swimming pool, tennis courts, beach within walking distance. Dining room, 2 bars, entertainment. $70 double EP all year.

The Compleat Angler Hotel. Very small, with only 13 rooms and one cottage, but a haven for fishermen. $40–50 double EP.

CAT ISLAND

Cutlass Bay Yacht Club. Unusual facility built on stilts for an instant command of the surrounding view. 12 rooms, 3 cottages. Private beach, swimming pool, all water sports. $80 double all year, including all three meals.

ELEUTHERA

Cape Eleuthera

Cape Eleuthera Resort and Yacht Club. Complete resort at southern end of island with 18-hole golf course and championship tennis courts. 128 spacious villa bedrooms. Private beach, free-form swimming pool, all water sports, including scuba, and a marina that can accommodate vessels up to 200 ft. $172–182 double in winter, $114 double off-season, including two meals.

Governor's Harbour

Club Mediterranee. The second Club Med in the Bahamas (the other is on Paradise Island), this $12 million resort opened in Spring '79 on an idyllic stretch of mid-island property that was once the luxury French Leave hideaway. The emphasis here is on water sports, with a special Aquatic Center providing separate facilities for sailing and water skiing. On the property itself, there are 8 tennis courts, a large swimming pool (including free group instruction); and endless activities that run almost 24 hours a day. As in all Club Med's, you pay for your drinks in beads–everything else is included in the rate. The meals are buffet-style and the variety at each is unbelievable; entertainment is "live" until midnight, then the "disco" takes over until the small hours. All 300 rooms are twin-bedded, air-conditioned and have private bath and shower. From $525–700 per week, per person, depending upon the time of the year.

Hatchet Bay

Rainbow Inn. Efficiencies and cottages, located mid-island. Dining room, bar, boating, fishing. Rates are lowest for rooms, but still low for apartments and the cottages. They range from $30–38 double all year, without meals.

Rock Sound

Cotton Bay Resort. 78 rooms, in cottages or clubhouse wing, and a magnificent 18-hole Robert Trent Jones golf course. Situated on a perfect white sand beach. Pool, tennis, sailing, fishing. $175 double all year with breakfast and dinner included.

Winding Bay Beach Resort. Ocean-front hotel with 36 rooms in 11 different cottage areas; situated on a beautiful beach. Horseback riding, water sports, 2 tennis courts lighted for night play, swimming pool, golf privileges at Cotton Bay Club. $145 double in winter; $108 double off-season, including two meals.

For home rentals, contact George Thompson, Gregory Town, Eleuthera or Errol Symonette, c/o Sea Raiders Cottages, Current, Eleuthera.

HARBOUR ISLAND

Coral Sands Hotel. 33 rooms on the ocean in two units, overlooking 3 miles of pink beach. Dining room, congenial, casual cocktail bar. Good food. Water sports, tennis. $80–90 double EP in winter; $50–60 double EP off-season.

Pink Sands Lodge. 53 rooms, suites in cottages. Dining room, but no bar. Tennis on 3 courts. Shares 3 miles of perfect pink sand beach with other hotels. Meals included in rates even though cottages have kitchenettes. Privacy assured by cottage arrangement. $80 double, with all meals, all year.

Romora Bay Club. 25 rooms, 3 cottages. On a secluded cove with fine dock, and short walk "across island" (about 300 yards) to beach. Tennis, entertainment, dancing. Club specializes in underwater activities–half-day scuba diving, snorkel trips arranged. Ideal for families. From $95–126 double EP all year.

Valentine's Yacht Club. On the water side of the main street of the small village, 21 rooms with a freshwater pool and informal atmosphere. Good beach a pleasant stroll away. $91 double EP in winter; $58 double off-season.

For home rentals, contact M. Rich & Sons, Real Estate, Harbour Island.

SPANISH WELLS

Sawyer's Marina. Informal. 9 units on the waterfront. Swimming pool, boating, fishing, dining room. From $35 double EP in winter; from $32 double EP off-season.

GREAT EXUMA

Hotel Peace & Plenty. A 32-room waterside inn that curves around the palms to form a half moon on Elizabeth Bay. Short walk into George Town. Faces uninhabited Stocking Island a short boat ride across the way. Fresh-water pool on the patio; al fresco dining; entertainment on weekends; free transportation to Stocking Island, the sandy strand that serves as the hotel's beach. $94–98 double in winter; $70 double off-season, breakfast and dinner included.

Out Island Inn. 80 air-conditioned rooms on a long stretch of beach in George Town. Restaurant and lounge with entertainment. Swimming pool, two tennis courts, watersports. $85–95 double EP in winter; $60 double off-season

Pieces of Eight. Small and casual with 33 rooms with balconies. Swimming pool, dining room, entertainment. $70 double EP in winter; $42 double off-season.

INAGUA

Ford's Inagua Inn. 6 rooms, some without private bath. Dining room serves local food. $20 double EP all year.

Main House. 11 air-conditioned rooms, bar, dining room. $40 double EP all year.

LONG ISLAND

Cape Santa Maria Club. Small, but the first accommodations to be built especially for tourists. Right on the beach. 5 cottages with 10 air-conditioned rooms, tennis, dining room, bar. Bone and deep-sea fishing. $110–125 double all year, including all meals.

Stella Maris Inn. 40 air-conditioned rooms, suites, and cottages. Newest on the island. Continental and Bahamian cuisine. 3 swimming pools, tennis courts, horseback riding, all water sports with complete diving program. $97–127 double, including all meals; apartments slightly higher; cottages highest.

SAN SALVADOR

The Riding Rock Inn. 45 rooms in cottages and villas. Swimming pool, private beach, scuba equipment on hand. Fishing and boating can be arranged. The inn is close to the airport and Cockburn Town. Rates for two, three meals daily, are $115 double at the inn; cottages usually rent with no meals and are available at good value on a weekly basis.

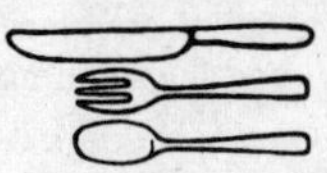

RESTAURANTS. All the leading hotels on New Providence and Grand Bahama have first-class restaurants, many of them offering international cuisine. There are also a number of excellent independent restaurants on both islands, offering everything from pancakes to gourmet dinners.

By all means try the local Bahamian dishes, particularly the conch, which is served in at least a dozen varieties. Conch chowder with a dash of sherry is delectable as are conch salad, a tangy dish spiked with hot peppers and lime juice, and fried conch, done in a light batter. Grouper cutlets, Bahamian baked crab, and red snapper fillets in anchovy sauce are other island specialties.

Try the fresh fruit from the Out Islands–the sweet pineapple, mango, breadfruit, and papaya–and the exotic Bahamian desserts, many of them with a rum base.

Nassau Royal, the Bahamas liqueur, is especially good. In some restaurants, it's served straight and set afire to create a lovely glow; in others, it's used with hot coffee and topped with whipped cream.

Special drinks run the gamut from Planter's Punch to an exotic island concoction called the "Bahama Mama." Even though liquor is less expensive by the bottle here, drinks in hotels, restaurants, and night clubs are not. Figure $2.50 for whisky–and barely one shot at that.

On New Providence, Paradise Island, and Grand Bahama, we call $20 and up *expensive;* $8–19 *moderate;* $7 and below, *inexpensive.*

NEW PROVIDENCE

Nassau

Beef Cellar. Choose and cook your own steak right at your table in this intimate restaurant at the Nassau Beach Hotel. *Moderate.*

The Bridge Inn. Ideal location opposite the harbor and the Paradise Island Bridge for a spectacular evening view. The inn specializes in Bahamian cuisine, but has a wide variety of other dishes as well. *Moderate.*

Buena Vista. One of Nassau's finest, if not the best, restaurant. Continues to please year after year, with Continental or Bahamian cuisine, excellent service, and extensive wine list. Dining on the palm-fringed patio or inside the manor house. Reservations required. *Expensive.* Less so in the new *La Taverna* late night supper club downstairs.

Europe Restaurant. Small but ideal restaurant for those after Bahamian or Continental specialties at moderate prices. Menu runs the gamut–*Sauerbraten,* Swiss cheese fondue, Bavarian *Knackwurst,* spaghetti Milanese, *Entrecôte,* Bahamian rock lobster, Irish coffee, peach melba. *Inexpensive.*

Graycliff Manor. This former home of Lord and Lady Dudley was opened as a restaurant in late 1975. 36 tables set up in different alcoves and sitting rooms. Antiques galore; excellent food and service; *expensive,* but well worth it.

Green Shutters Inn. A favorite luncheon rendezvous in the center of town. Full menu from Bahamian seafood to prime ribs. *Moderate.*

Moana Loa. Exotic spot in the Nassau Beach Hotel. Fine Polynesian cuisine in South Seas atmosphere. *Expensive.*

Pilot House Hotel. (The Admiral's Dining Room). International menu with emphasis on seafood dishes. Dining indoors or outdoors around the swimming pool. Very popular with sportsmen. *Moderate.*

Ristorante da Vinci. Three dining rooms. French and Italian gourmet cuisine. Elegant and expensive.

PARADISE ISLAND

Bahamian Club. Elegant restaurant with gourmet fare. Specialties are anything Bahamian, plus Continental dishes. *Expensive.*

Café Martinique. One of the most popular restaurants in the Bahamas so reservations are essential. Lovely setting on the edge of Paradise Lake, with indoor or terrace dining. French-style décor reminiscent of the Moulin Rouge in Paris. French-tinged Continental dishes. *Expensive.*

Coyaba Cantonese. Pleasant Oriental atmosphere in the only true Cantonese restaurant in the Bahamas. *Expensive.*

Villa d'Este. The décor here is of the Old World, with the emphasis on Florence and Rome. Italian murals cover the walls, and Italian dishes are a true treat for the gourmet. Fine service with an elegant flair. Reservations a must. *Expensive.*

There are many other less expensive restaurants in Nassau, most of them listed in the island publication entitled *What to Do.* It is published twice a year and is available free of charge at hotels or the Ministry of Tourism offices. For that stateside touch in Nassau, you'll find *Burger King, Howard Johnson's, Kentucky Fried Chicken* and *McDonald's.*

GRAND BAHAMA

Cafe Michel. In the French section of Freeport's International Bazaar. Authentic French cellar restaurant and bar, outdoor café. *Fondue bourguignonne* and other specialties to set the Parisian mood. *Inexpensive.*

Cafe India. Eastern cooking here at a small restaurant in the Coral Beach Hotel. *Inexpensive.*

Captain's Charthouse. Nautical atmosphere with Polynesian overtones. Steaks and lobster the house specialties; dancing after 8 P.M. *Moderate.*

China Temple. Fittingly located in the Oriental section of the International Bazaar. Tea house and restaurant open daily; also takeout orders. *Moderate.*

Cotillion Room. Lovely, elegant, and expensive spot in the Bahamas Princess Tower. *Expensive.*

El Morocco. Situated in El Casino, this restaurant offers superb food and service. Wide variety of international specialties. *Expensive.*

Freeport Inn Steak House. Fine steaks grilled in a casual atmosphere in their intimate Scotch & Sirloin Room. *Moderate.*

Island Lobster House. One of Freeport's restaurants for dining and dancing. Feature is the "early bird lobster dinner" served 5:30-6:30. *Inexpensive.*

Japanese Steak House. For a touch of the Orient in the tropics. Waitresses are kimono-clad, sake is on hand, and Kobe beef steak is the house specialty. Properly set in the Japanese section of the International Bazaar. *Moderate.*

Marcella's. Fine on-the-mall spot for Italian cuisine in Freeport's center. *Moderate.*

Pub on the Mall. Real British flavor here with ale on tap, steak and kidney pie, fish and chips, as well as steaks and prime ribs. King-size sandwiches always available. *Inexpensive.*

Sir Winston Churchill Pub. Another pub that offers all the British specialties. Has a comfortable beer garden out back; a Sunday smorgasbord and a 5 to 7 P.M. Happy Hour nightly. *Moderate.*

The Stoned Crab. Pleasant ocean-front restaurant overlooking Taino Beach. It is bright and airy, somewhat like a Swiss chalet. Everything from cheese-burgers to grouper, kingfish, and wahoo. Hickory-charbroiled steaks also one of the house specialties. *Moderate.*

NIGHT LIFE. New Providence. The *Playboy Casino* at Cable Beach is *the* spot on the Nassau side; The casino on Paradise Island is the major drawing card in the evening, as well as *Le Cabaret* night club, which is conveniently located next door. They feature Las Vegas-type revues twice a night and serve dinner during the early show. A 32-page program given to patrons has full list of activities around the Bahamas and rules for games of chance. All the major hotels on Paradise Island and in Nassau have cocktail lounges that stay open until the small hours, many with entertainment. A special favorite is the *Rum Keg* at the Nassau Beach Hotel.

Open seven nights a week, music and snacks until 4 A.M. *Dirty Dick's:* This place has been around for so long it's become an institution. Bahamian show every evening.

Among other nightspots are *The King & Knight Club,* where King Eric & His Knights perform twice nightly; and the Gatsby-like discotheque at Cumberland House that swings until the early hours.

There are dozens of other night spots, many of them situated "Over the Hill," the native part of the city. Cab drivers know them all and can outline their respective merits to you.

Grand Bahama. First and foremost there is *El Casino,* that giant Moroccan palace that is the hub of activity on the island. All roads seem to lead to the casino, where the gaming tables and slot machines are in full swing 24 hours a day.

Their *Kasbah Lounge* offers additional evening glitter with two shows nightly.

Other top spots are: *Bahamia Club:* At the Bahamas Princess Hotel has continuous shows and dancing from 9:30 P.M. until the early hours. *Coral Cove,* also at the Bahamas Princess, has island music nightly. Disco at *Lights* at the Castaways Hotel. *The Tipsy Turtle Lounge:* At the Holiday Inn has back-to-back shows and dancing from 4 P.M. until 3 A.M. *Pub on the Mall:* Freeport's original pub and a popular gathering place. Island calypso music nightly; sing-along on Wednesdays at 8:30 P.M. *Sandpiper Lounge:* Located in the Coral Beach Hotel, a short drive from the casino. Dining and dancing until 5, yes 5 A.M.! *Sir Winston Churchill:* A delightful pub any time of day. Watney's on tap plus dozens of other authentic pub features. Open every day of the week until

4 A.M. *Sultan's Tent:* Nightly entertainment here at another exotic Princess Hotel property, itself a replica of a Sultan's palace. Across the street from their Bahamia Club. *Xanadu Lounge:* Sophisticated spot at the Xanadu Beach Hotel. Nightly entertainment.

SHOPPING. Nassau and Freeport are the shopping centers of the Bahamas. You will find boutiques at some hotels in the Out Islands, but the only real places to buy imported items are in or near Bay Street in Nassau and Freeport's International Bazaar. Also, the Paradise Village Shopping Center just off the bridge on Paradise Island contains about 14 shops offering everything from perfume and jewelry to island souvenirs.

On Nassau's Bay Street, you will be greeted with traditional Bahamian politeness in many stores that have been owned by the same families for generations. Fine merchandise from around the world is available at prices usually below those you would pay in the States.

The goods are imported mainly from Europe: china, cutlery, leather, fabrics, and liquor from Britain; Scandinavian glass and silver; Swiss watches; German and Japanese cameras; French perfumes.

And for native craft, the selection is extensive. At Rawson Square, just off Bay Street, the open market sells straw goods and other native craftwork. Straw bags, hats—the big ones, admittedly difficult to pack—dolls, and a variety of things you would never dream of seeing made in straw. Seashell jewelry and decorative pieces are made and sold by native craftsmen. The shells, gathered in the Out Islands, are pierced with thin wires and arranged into floral patterns, earrings, necklaces, and bracelets. Wood carvers from New Providence and the Out Islands offer intricate carvings and sculpture fashioned from local materials.

Buy coconut, not for the protein value, but for the jewelry. Bracelets, earrings, and pendants come in shell shades that vary from soft white to dark brown. It's all inexpensive. Another local craft is tortoise-shell jewelry, created from the outer shell of the hawksbill turtle, a species found in Bahamian waters. Unfortunately, since the U.S. put them on the endangered species list, tortoise-shell products cannot be imported into the States. Look for the new jewelry made from conch shells instead.

Here is a selection of some shops we know and like. Many more are listed in the *What To Do* guide, available free at hotels and shops all over the island.

Ambrosine. Nassau's leading boutique, with a beautiful collection of Emilio Pucci designs for men and women, as well as Bleyle and Mirsa imports.

Brass & Leather. For all high-quality English leather goods—handbags, suitcases, and a good selection of gift items, including antique brass.

Bernard's China Shop. Exclusive agents for Wedgwood, Spode, and Ernest Borel Swiss watches.

Commonwealth Antique Shop & Art Gallery. On corner of Shirley and Parliament Streets, 200 year old mansion for browsing and buying local art and family antiques.

Greenfire Emeralds, Ltd. This spectacular shop, which is located on Paradise Island, offers a dazzling array of emeralds from Colombia at substantial savings.

Island Shop. Wide selection of men's and women's fashions, cashmeres, lambswool, and other imported sportswear.

Island Treasure Chest. Features a "Royal Worcester Room," with one of the largest selections of English bone china in the world. Also Royal Doulton.

John Bull. The best selection of cameras and equipment in Nassau, plus Rolex and Seiko watches.

The Linen Shop. On Parliament St., just off Bay, you'll find a complete line of Irish-imports at good prices.

The Nassau Shop. Largest on Bay St. with fine departments for men's wear and women's fashions. Also cameras, French perfume, and watches, including Piaget's ultrathin automatic timepieces.

Pipe of Peace. Astonishing collection of pipes, cigars, cigarettes, tobacco, and everything the smoker needs from ashtrays to imported lighters.

The Sand Dollar. A small shop in the Prince George Arcade, their specialty is sand dollars, which have been dipped in silver or gold. Also good buys on black coral and other jewelry.

Solomon's Mines. Fine china, figurines from Copenhagen and Germany, Swedish and Waterford crystal, cutlery, and jewelry.

Vanite. Tiny shop off Bay St., specializing in children's fashions. Also exclusive agent for Hummel figurines.

French perfume is available "everywhere" along Bay Street. Prices are lower than those in the United States and do not vary from shop to shop.

Records of Bahamian entertainers are also available at most shops. Don't expect to bargain with the sales people in Nassau's stores, as you can at the stalls in the straw market. Stores are open from 9 A.M. to 5 P.M. except on Friday, when many close at noon.

Go "around the world in eighty minutes" at the International Bazaar in Freeport, where 78 fascinating shops represent countless areas. The main entrance to the bazaar is through a huge Mandarin Gate, which opens onto Hong Kong Street. From there your international shopping trip takes you down alleys, through arcades and into small corners of the world, all set up on authentic streets. The aroma from each International cafe completes the "other country" aura.

Try *The Midnight Sun* for Scandinavian glassware and figurines; *Azteca de Oro* for Mexican jewelry; *Dynasty* for exotic clothing from the Orient; *Sabra* for Israeli items; *The Old Curiosity Shop* for European antiques. Most of the shops here are now open until 10 P.M. on Tuesdays and Thursdays.

Unique items worth looking for when you make your day trip or longer excursion to the Out Islands are the sandals that Wendell Cooper makes in George Town on Great Exuma and the canvas sailing and catch-all bags made at *Uncle Norman's Sail Loft* on Man-O-War Cay off Abaco. Cooper learned his craft from a Floridian craftsman who took him in tow after a visit to the island. The small shop on Queen's Highway in the center of the small town carries a variety of sandals and purses, belts and other small leather items, many of which are made to order if you allow some time. The Alburys have been making sails and other canvas items for the local boat building industry for almost a century. They also have a small stock of the canvas draw-string bags that are a part of any boatman's life and now double for holiday purses.

SPORTS AND OTHER ACTIVITIES. The *golf* enthusiast is in luck! There are fine 18-hole championship courses on **New Providence** at Coral Harbour, Lyford Cay, the Ambassador Beach Hotel, and the South Ocean Beach Hotel and Golf Club. The Paradise Island Golf Club, across the bridge, has a championship course as well. On **Grand Bahama** there are 6 courses: the Bahama Reef Club, Lucayan Golf and Country Club, Shannon Golf Club, Grand Bahama Club (West End), at the Bahamas Princess Hotel, as well as at the Fortune Hills Club in Freeport.

The Out Islands have only 4 courses at this time. They are Treasure Cay **(Abaco),** Great Harbour Club **(Berry Islands),** Cape Eleuthera Golf Club, and Cotton Bay Club, both on **Eleuthera.** Greens fees run $20 per person in winter; $15 off-season.

It makes no difference what time of the year the angler chooses to take a vacation; every month is a fishing month in the Bahamas. There is no better way to enjoy the wide variety of fish and fishing provided by this island area than to cruise the Out Islands aboard a charter boat, living on the craft throughout the trip. The fishing in these areas is so varied that no two days need be alike. Over the reefs are amberjack, grouper, mutton snapper, mackerel, jack, yellowtail, and the ubiquitous barracuda waiting to take a trolled bait, a drifted live bait, or any of the many artificial lures cast with plug, fly, or spin-tackle. Farther out in the deep water are wahoo, kingfish, dolphin, bonito, blackfin tuna, and marlin. On the flats are bonefish; up winding creeks in the deep holes of creek or bay or under overhanging ledges of mangrove cays there are wily grey snapper, all to be caught on light tackle and natural or artificial lures.

Grand Bahama's offshore waters are renowned for great sport fishing. Grouper, snapper, yellowtail, and kingfish abound on the nearby reefs. In the deeper offshore waters, sailfish, marlin, tuna, and dolphin are plentiful. Fully equipped cruisers for charter average $210 for a half-day, $420 for a full day. Charter rates become more reasonable when a party of 4 divides the cost of a charter boat for an Out Island cruise of a week or 10 days, living and eating on the boat.

Walker's Cay, a sport fishing resort on the northernmost of the populated islands in the Abaco chain, boasts one of the largest and best-equipped marinas in the Bahamas, with 75 berths for yachts. There's an annual bill fish tournament in April.

The Bahamas Ministry of Tourism maintains a Fishing Information Bureau, which will provide full details of all island facilities and fishing spots. Address inquiries c/o P.O. Box N3701, Nassau, Bahamas.

Some of the best *sailing and cruising* in the world can be found in and around the Bahama Islands. Almost everything the cruising visitor will need to know about sailing in these waters is gathered in the covers of the *Yachtsman's Guide,* available at Bahamian bookstores or from the Florida publisher, Tropic Isle, Box 340866, Coral Gables, Fla. 33134.

Charter firms operate in the Bahamas as follows:

In **Nassau:** *Bayshore Marina Ltd.,* East Bay Street; *East Bay Yacht Basin,* East Bay Street; *Nassau Harbour Club* and the *Nassau Yacht Haven* on East Bay Street.

On **Grand Bahama:** *Lucayan Beach Marina* at Bell Channel in Freeport; *Running Mon Fishing Fleet* at Oceanus Bay Dock in Freeport; *Grand Bahama*

Hotel and Country Club at West End; and *Xanadu Marina* in Freeport; *The Deep Water Cay Club* on Deep Water Cay can also be reached through Box 1145, Palm Beach, Florida 33480.

In the **Abacos:** *Abaco Bahamas Charters Ltd.* and *Lighthouse Marina, Ltd.* in Hope Town; *Green Turtle Club and Marina* on Green Turtle Cay; *Bahamas Yachting Service, Ltd.,* Marsh Harbour; *Treasure Cay Marina* on Treasure Cay; and *Walker's Cay Club* on Walker's Cay.

For charters on other islands, contact the *Andros Beach Hotel & Marina* at Nichol's Town; the *Chub Cay Marina Hotel* at Chub Cay in the Berry Islands, and Bimini's *Blue Water Ltd., Brown's Marina,* and *Weche's Marina* on North Bimini; on Eleuthera, *Davis Harbour Yacht Basin* at Rock Sound, the *Hatchet Bay Yacht Club,* the *Current Club,* and the *Cape Eleuthera Resort & Yacht Club* can arrange for boats. *Hotel Peace & Plenty* in George Town and *Staniel Cay Yacht Club* on Staniel Cay arrange for charters in the Exumas. On Harbour Island, turn to *Briland Yacht Club* at Dunmore Town and the *Romora Bay Club. Stella Maris Marina & Yacht Dock* on Long Island and *Sawyer's Marina* at Spanish Wells on St. George's Cay round out the official list.

Almost every hotel, even on the small Out Islands, has fine facilities for *spearfishing, skin diving, scuba,* and other water sports. Or contact *Underwater Tours, Ltd.,* at Nassau Yacht Haven, on East Bay St. Their slogan is "Learn today, dive tomorrow." They offer everything from aqua-lung pool lessons to weekly reef trips. Grand Bahama is also the world headquarters for the *Underwater Explorers Society,* an esteemed group of devotees of the submarine life. They offer group and private instruction, scuba trips to shallow and deep reefs, snorkeling near deserted cays, deep diving, night diving, and day trips to spectacular locations. In addition, the society holds workshops in diving technology and underwater photography.

Tennis is popular everywhere, and there are dozens of all-weather composition courts on New Providence and Grand Bahama. Many are lighted for night play. On the Out Islands, you'll find that even the smallest island has at least one well-surfaced tennis court.

Horseback riding has become popular as well. Check with the San Andros Hotel, Andros; Pinetree Stables, Freeport, Grand Bahama; or the Paradise Island Riding Stables, New Providence. Riding fees range from $10-15 per hour, depending on the tourist emphasis of the area. Big names equal big prices.

Parasailing is becoming more and more popular here. Take off from the *Ambassador Beach* or *Nassau Beach Hotels* on New Providence, or the *Atlantik Beach Hotel* on Grand Bahama.

BARBADOS

Fields of Cane and Corn

Easternmost of the Caribbees, Barbados remains one of the loveliest islands. Powdery beaches line the waters of the calm Caribbean Sea on the west coast, while the waves of the Atlantic thunder in on the eastern shore. Luxury hotels and fine restaurants, along with a lush terrain and dozens of natural and historic attractions, make it one of the most expensive, yet desirable islands in the Caribbean.

Since Barbados lies outside the gentle curve of the Caribbean Islands, it was spared the flashes of interest that pirates and explorers showed in its neighbors. Barbados remained British from its first British settlement in 1625 until independence in 1966, when it peacefully chose to be a nation within the British Commonwealth. Today, its government is one of the oldest democracies in the western hemisphere. (The United States Constitution borrowed wording from the Barbados declaration of 1635.) And Bajans, as Barbadians are familiarly called, proudly proclaim that their elections and changes of political parties are no more fearsome than switches between Republican and Democrat in the United States.

To make the expected visual comparison between Britain and Barbados seems to be stretching a point. The one obvious difference is the weather, the drawing card for the British visitors since the 17th century. To be sure, many British traditions are integral parts of life in sunny Barbados. Tea is a daily ritual in many hotels; tennis is played on grass courts at the established tennis club; cricket is an obsession that has the man in the street clutching a transistor radio to his ear, if he's unable to stand at the sideline of the matches that dot his countryside–and most of the Eastern Caribbean–during the cricket season; uniforms on policemen, bands, and Horse Guards are all reminiscent of those in Britain; judges are bewigged, and their court system is the British one; the emotional links are strong, and the heritage has provided the firm foundation for the stability we witness today.

Almost every inch of the island's 166 square miles of fertile soil is being cultivated. The placid countryside provides endless touring possibilities, with its pounding surf on the eastern (windward) coast contrasting with the quiet calm of the western shores, the leeward coast, where a diamond necklace of luxury hotels enhances the shoreline.

English place names–Yorkshire, Windsor, Hastings–strengthen the illusion, but the name Barbados is thought to be Iberian, a logical transition from *"los barbudos,"* meaning "the bearded ones" and probably referring to the beardlike hanging roots of the banyan trees which covered the island in profusion. Other less popular theories claim that the beards were on the Indians (Arawak and Carib descendants) or that, since 16th century Spanish charts designate the island as St. Barbado, Barbudoso, Bernardo, and similar variations, the island is really named for St. Bernard. Whatever the reason, the island is called Barbados–not *the* Barbados, as many people think.

Bridgetown, the island capital, with 98,000 inhabitants, is a hive of activity–except for Sunday morning, when the entire population of the country seems to go to church. The main shopping street is Broad Street, which is adjacent to the waterfront, but the real action is at the Careenage, where boats are careened to be repainted and refurbished. The waterfront is also usually alive with interisland schooners sharing their off-island wares with the local purchasers. A chief site in town is the statue of Admiral Lord Nelson in Trafalgar Square, antedating its counterpart in London by some 27 years. The planters of 19th century Barbados put it up in 1813 in grateful recognition of the hero who saved their sugar profits from the French. The town is replete with reminders of Nelson. The harbor police, difficult to find, but certainly there, wear the Jack Tar uniforms of his sailors: white middies, bell-bottom trousers, and those flat, round, wide-brimmed straw boaters–everything but the pigtails.

History

The Portuguese were the first to sight Barbados and to come ashore in 1536. They sailed away without making formal claim to the area, leaving that honor to a small group of Englishmen who landed at Holetown, which they named Jamestown, in 1625. It was not until February 1627 that the first permanent settlers arrived aboard the *William and John,* and the 350-plus years of British traditions began.

From the tourist point of view, Barbados offers everything: a trade wind-cooled climate, averaging to 80°; health and pure water standards so elevated that the place had a heyday as the sanitarium of the West Indies; an atmosphere that ranges from ultrasophistication (mainly on the western St. James coast) to barefoot hospitality on the Atlantic side; miles of powdered coral beaches, both pink and white; and thousands of quick-smiling Bajans.

Bajans are the descendants, for the most part, of slaves brought in to work the plantations after the sugar cane was introduced from Brazil in the 1630s. The Barbados planters seem to have had a more enlightened attitude toward their slaves than the French and Danes exhibited on their islands. There are records of masters supplying plantation hands with wives and rum "to cure and refresh the poor Negroes whom we ought to have a special care of, by the labour of whose hands, our profit is brought in." As a result of relatively humane plantation conditions, Barbados was spared the horrors and brutal recriminations of a slave uprising.

Among the earliest colonizers, as in our own country, were inmates of English prisons, transported overseas to do forced labor on the plantations. Their number was augmented by Royalist captives of Cromwell and indentured political prisoners who supported the bastard Duke of Monmouth's abortive rebellion against James II. Barbados, in short, became the outpost to which the rulers of England summarily sent unruly Scots and Irishmen, Presbyterians, Quakers, and other dissenters and free thinkers.

EXPLORING BARBADOS

Bridgetown, capital of Barbados, is best explored on foot, but you will need a taxi to get there. Many of the St. James coastal hotels provide transportation; all can arrange for taxis. Despite the cooling trade winds that sweep over Barbados before they reach the rest of the West Indies, Bridgetown is a leeward pocket and can be very warm. Plan your in-town trip for early morning, late afternoon–or make it leisurely with lunch outdoors at the Pelican Restaurant.

Watching the activity of the inner harbor known as the Careenage is as good a way as any to start your Bridgetown rambles. The bridges over this Caribbean inlet make it look like a canal. In actual fact, it has been the place for big sailing ships to be careened, caulked, and painted since the days of the clipper ships. Even with the modernization that has seen stucco rectangles replace the older wooden, fretworked buildings, the charm of this part of Bridgetown remains. You may occasionally see a woman selling her spicey mauby-bark brew to the stevedores from the cauldron she balances on her head, or an occasional donkey cart of the type that used to fill the streets of Bridgetown not even 15 years ago. Most often today, however, it's cars you dodge, and the mauby, if it is sold at all, comes from carts.

In this bubbling capital, established when the Indians still roamed Manhattan Island, history sometimes comes up with some odd juxtapositions of style. Look up, down and around–particularly along the waterfront, where the island schooners tie up to deliver and collect produce and gossip.

St. Michael's Cathedral in Bridgetown, symbol of the Church of England transplanted, was first built in 1665. The present structure, constructed of coral rock, dates from 1831, the original church having been smashed up by hurricanes in that year and in 1780. The church's original memorial tablets go back to the 17th century, stone histories of colonial days. The verger says that George Washington came here to worship in 1751.

One of the "official sights" of Bridgetown is the "George Washington House" on Upper Bay Street. It's an 18th century house, where he is supposed to have stayed. In any case, there is evidence that he did rent a house in Barbados for £15 a month "exclusive of liquors and washings."

Washington was enchanted by Barbados and described it accordingly: "We were perfectly enraptured with the beautiful prospects, which every side presented to our view the fields of cane, corn and fruit trees in a delightful green."

Aside from the cathedral and "Washington's House," there are no special sights to see in Bridgetown. If you want to spend a fascinating hour or more briefing yourself on Barbados history and lore, take a cab to Garrison, a suburb just a mile and a half out of Bridgetown, and visit the Barbados Museum. There's a great collection of miscellany here: old maps, sailors' Valentines, prints, coins, Indian relics, domestic arts and crafts, exhibits of Bajan fish, birds, and other fauna. Or make a night of it, and participate in *"1627 And All That Sort Of Thing,"* the newest tourist attraction on the island. It's an exciting cultural, dining, and entertainment experience, which is held in the museum's courtyard every Thursday and Sunday from 6:30 to 10 P.M. A tour of the museum, a colorful folkloric show and an elaborate Bajan buffet are included for $25 US per person.

The roads of Barbados are good, though narrow, and progress can be slowed down by donkey carts and other aspects of Bajan life and transport. Signposting is not all it might be, unless you are familiar with Lower Grays, Yorkshire, St. Patricks, Brighton via Windsor, or St. Georges Church via Bulkeley. You should know that the country is sectioned into parishes, each with its own church and name. That may help with map reading and signposting. Allow a full day to swing around the island's perimeter and explore the interior, even though the whole place measures only 21 by 14 miles. The variety of scenery is extraordinary, and there are more than 688 miles of well-paved roads from which to choose.

Driving south out of Bridgetown, you go through middle-class beach resorts like those of the New Jersey shore or the English Sussex coast: Hastings, Worthing, St. Lawrence. Visit Christ Church, scene of the famous 19th century "Barbados Coffin Mystery," in which coffins were switched around, stood on their ends, and disturbed in other ways inside a vault to which no one, presumably, had access. These ghoulish goings on caused such an uproar that the coffins were buried elsewhere on the orders of the Governor.

The Wild Atlantic Coast

The first part of your drive is through flat corridors of sugar cane. Beyond Crane, on the southeast coast, the scenery is beautiful, getting more and more so as you drive southeast along the wildly spectacular

Atlantic coast, which, with its cliffs, plunging headlands, and sometimes turbulent surf, reminds many travelers of the coasts of Brittany and Cornwall. One of the show places here is Sam Lord's Castle, an early 19th century mansion in the midst of an estate which overlooks the sea. Sam Lord's Castle now stands tall in the center of a Marriott Hotel development, fortunately low profile in the area of the castle-house.

Sam Lord was a kind of landlubber buccaneer whose chief pastime was luring ships to the reef by anging lanterns in the palm trees so that mariners, seeing them at night, thought they were the lights of ships anchored in a safe harbor. It was an old trick, practiced successfully in Cornwall and by the Nags Head bankers on the treacherous Hatteras reef. When the ships ran aground on the shoals, Sam Lord and slaves took possession of the cargoes, dispatching any sailors who had not drowned.

It must have been a lucrative business. Sam Lord imported Italian artisans to make his castle a thing of beauty; the plaster ceilings are their work. The present owners have kept it up in the style to which Sam Lord was accustomed. The place is furnished with splendid antiques, not the least of which are Sam Lord's mahogany four-poster bed and a wardrobe in whose lavishly-carved doors we detect the fine Italian hand of the imported artisan. Visitors are welcome at a nominal fee.

Next stop is Codrington College, which, despite its splendid avenue of towering palms, will remind you of Oxford. The flora may be tropical, but this is an English school in spirit and appearance, the oldest (1716) in the British West Indies. Just to the north is St. John's Church 800 feet above the sea, and affording a sweeping view of the spectacular windward coast. The church dates from the 17th century. Its rosy stone exterior has the patina of age.

Vacationers interested in seeing what life in a West Indian plantation Great House might have been like can visit Villa Nova, built from coral limestone in 1834 and reopened in early 1976 for visitors. Furnishings are mostly Barbadian antiques, made from local mahogany. Located in St. John parish, the Great House sits on a hilltop, amid six acres. Prince Philip and Queen Elizabeth have been guests at the Great House. It is open Monday through Friday, from 10 to 4.

Heading North

At Bathsheba the Atlantic booms against the cliffs, dashing high on "a stern and rockbound coast," which is obligingly modified here and there to form stretches of beach where the swimming is marvelous. Nonswimmers may want to visit the interesting pottery works at Chalky Mount, about 3½ miles away, heading north along the east coast road, and watch the native potters at work, or wander through the lovely gardens at Andromeda, a private home which opens its gates for a small fee.

Overlooking Bathsheba, the views get even more spectacular. That from Hackleton's Cliff, 1100 feet high, is hard to beat, even by the panorama from Cherry Tree Hill. Below on the coast, Belleplaine looks like a toy village from this height. Mahogany trees clothe the landscape, and a surrealist touch is added by a score of old windmills, once used to grind the sugar cane.

Near Farley Hill stretches the Scotland District, one of the most scenic on the island. To the east is the huge windmill at Morgan Lewis. It remains complete today, with arms and machinery intact.

Further south and almost in the center of the island (you may have to make a separate trip for this one), is Welchman Hall Gully. It is a valley rimmed by cliffs, inhabited by wild monkeys and planted and preserved as a botanical garden. The bearded fig trees grow here, the island's sole clove tree survives, and there are nutmeg, cocoa, citrus, banana, coffee, and bamboo trees, and other tropical flora. The cliffs themselves are studded with stalactite and stalagmite-filled caves.

From Farley Hill you can cut straight west across the island to Speightstown, the second "city" of Barbados, or you can make a loop to North Point at the top of the island and visit the fascinating Animal-Flower Cave. This is actually a series of sea grottos which can be visited only at low tide. The animal-flowers (local name for sea anemones) live in shallow pools left by the receding tide. One of the newest attractions in the area is St. Nicholas Abbey, a 300-year-old plantations great house now open to the public. The Abbey, which is located in the Parish of St. Peter, is open from Monday through Friday from 10 A.M.–3 P.M. The entrance fee is $5 BDS per person.

Speightstown, on the leeward coast, is your next destination. If you drive directly from Farley Hill, take the road to Six Men's Bay just north of Speightstown. It passes through the cane fields, dotted with the ruins of sugar mills and old plantation houses. At Six Men's Bay (you'll pass through here if you're coming south from the Animal-Flower Cave), there are other nostalgic reminders of a different past—old cannons and an anchor lie by the water as if no one has bothered to pick them up for the past 100 years. Here, too, are ruins of a few buildings which they used to dry whale blubber in the old days. At Speightstown, there are more guns pointed out to sea, and many old buildings.

The Platinum Coast

When you leave Speightstown you are officially on Barbados' celebrated "Platinum Coast." This is the protected western shore, gently laved by a limpid Caribbean. The road follows the coast south from St. Peter into St. James Parish. The contrast between this and the eastern shore could not be greater. If the latter was Brittany, this is the Mediterranean, calm, brilliant, luxurious. Britons, Americans, Canadians who have built and are building here are making a conscious effort to keep their haven of refuge tranquil and uncluttered. They are succeeding for the main part. Hotels like the Sandy Lane, Eastry House, Colony Club, and Coral Reef Club have done their part to preserve harmony with tropical gardens and landscaped grounds surrounding the precincts of beach resorts.

The center of the Platinum Coast is Holetown, taking its name from the town of Hole on the River Thames. Its church, one of the oldest in the West Indies, is as fashionable as the Abbey. Its font is dated 1684; its bell commands that "God bless King William, 1696." In the town an obelisk marks the spot where Captain Catlin of the *Olive Blossom* is presumed to have landed in 1625, although the monument decrees it, mistakenly, as 1605. This first Englishman to set foot on the island did so, they say, because he had been driven off his course; not so with the 350,000 or so tourists who come here each year.

A DAY ON YOUR OWN

Barbados is a large island as Caribbean islands go, and so you should devote at least one full day exploring it. The windward, or wild surf side, is glorious; the leeward (or calm) shores are perfect for a walk along powdery sands; and the interior is chock full of lush hills and special attractions.

Start your day in *Bridgetown* and drive north along the west coast toward *Holetown* in the Parish of St. James. This is the "Platinum Coast," site of chic and expensive hotels, and worth a stop, especially at *Sandy Lane,* where the elegance of a bygone era remains unchanged.

Head further north to the old fishing village of *Speightstown,* and then inland toward the east coast. The narrow highway that runs across the island is a special bonus in that its scenery changes at every bend in the road. As you get further into the thick forest here, don't be surprised to see wild monkeys leaping from limb to limb.

Climb high to the top of *Cherry Tree Hill* for a spectacular view of the island. White cliffs blend perfectly into rolling hills and small farms, giving the entire area the look of a patchwork quilt. Then drive south for a stop at the *Morgan Lewis Mill,* the only windmill left intact on the island.

Visit *The Potteries,* a small village at the top of *Chalky Mount,* and watch islanders work the ancient potters' wheels. Continue south along the East Coast Road to *Cattlewash Beach,* which is a real beauty. Low-lying sea-grape trees edge the shore, and the surf pounds against massive and exotic boulders called sea sculpts.

From there head for nearby *Andromeda Gardens* and plan to spend at least an hour among thousands of plants in bloom on the terraced hillside. The orchids are especially lovely.

You'll be ready for a rest on the terrace of the *Atlantis Hotel.* Sip a long rum punch and watch the fishing fleet at work below. Barbados is called the "Land of the Flying Fish," so what better choice for your luncheon entree. The *Atlantis* also offers a variety of local dishes that whet the appetite but not deplete the pocketbook.

Follow the coast road further south to *St. John's Church,* one of Barbados' treasures. It is as old as the cliffs it sits on, and has an historical cemetery and a beautiful coastal view. The next stop is *Codrington College,* which was founded in 1702.

Finally, pass the *Ragged Point Lighthouse* at the island's widest

Courtesy of U.S. Virgin Islands

The Caribbean is known for its beaches, bays and gentle trade winds. Magen's Bay, St. Thomas, is one of the most beautiful for swimming, while Aruba's waters are perfect for sailing a sunfish or maneuvering a windsurfer.

Courtesy of Aruba Tourist Bureau

Courtesy of Antigua Dept. of Tourism and Trade

Freshwater or saltwater swimming within minutes is the norm at Caribbean resorts where the pool is just a few feet from the sea; and while the tourists play, Saturday is market day for the local people.

Courtesy of Caribbean Tourism Association

Courtesy of Caribbean Tourism Association

Getting to know the people of the Caribbean is always an enticement to stay longer; many visitors choose apartment living–some in historical spots such as restored Nelson's Dockyard in Antigua.

Courtesy of Antigua Dept. of Tourism and Trade

Photo by V. Puzo

Contrasting islands, contrasting harbors: St. Thomas, where dozens of cruise ships anchor, and St. Croix, where hobiecats, sailboats and windsurfers ply the waterfront.

Courtesy of Caribbean Tourism Association

point and follow the signs to *Sam Lord's Castle.* For a small fee you can tour the castle and see the grandeur attained by privateer Sam Lord. Have a late afternoon drink at the pool bar, try your hand at the slot machines in a small room off the patio, and stroll the mile-long beach at sunset before heading back to Bridgetown.

PRACTICAL INFORMATION FOR BARBADOS

HOW TO GET THERE. By air. Barbados' facilities at Grantley Adams Airport have made it the hub of the southern Caribbean, with flights fanning out to Trinidad, St. Vincent, St. Lucia, and the islands to the north. Daily nonstop flights touch down **from New York** via *BWIA* and *American Airlines. Eastern Airlines* has daily nonstop flights from Miami.

From Miami, *BWIA; Eastern.*

From Montreal and Toronto, *Air Canada* has nonstop and direct flights, and *BWIA* flies from Toronto. Check *WARDAIR* for charters and special tours from Canada to Barbados for real bargains.

From Europe, there is frequent *British Airways* and *BWIA* service from London.

Best bets for direct inter-island air connections are *LIAT* and *BWIA,* which link Barbados and all the neighboring islands.

BY SEA. Barbados is a cruise port for ships making the longer cruises, including *Cunard, Norwegian American Lines, Royal Caribbean Cruise Lines, Royal Viking Lines,* and *Sitmar Cruises.*

FURTHER INFORMATION. In addition to head office on Harbour Road, Hastings, Barbados, W.I., the *Barbados Board of Tourism* has offices at 800 Second Ave., New York, N.Y. 10017; on Knowlbourne Square, 199 South Knowles Ave., Winter Park, Fla. 32789; at 666 Sherbrooke St. W., Montreal, P.Q. and 11 King St. W., Suite 1108, Toronto, Ont. Canada, and at the *Barbados High Commission,* 6 Upper Belgrave St., London S.W.I.

ISLAND MEDIA. Two very fine publications, the *Official Guide to Barbados,* and the *Free Guide to Shopping and Entertainment,* are available without charge at hotels and shops. In addition, there is *The Advocate-News,* the daily newspaper, which lists all current island activities. For further reading, pick up a copy of *The Bajan,* a slick magazine not unlike *Time,* which comes out monthly.

AUTHORIZED TOUR OPERATORS: *Adventure Tours, Caribbean Holidays, Flyfaire, Butler Travels,* and *Travel Center Tours* in the U.S.

From Canada: *Fairway Tours* and *Holiday House.*

From London: *Alta Holidays, Kuoni Travel, Rankin-Kuhn Tours, Sovereign Holidays,* and *Thomas Cook & Son.*

PASSPORTS, VISAS. Persons entering the island must be in possession of a valid passport or some other document satisfactorily establishing their nationality and identity and a ticket to leave. No visa is required of British, U.S., or Canadian citizens unless they plan to stay in Barbados for more than 6 months.

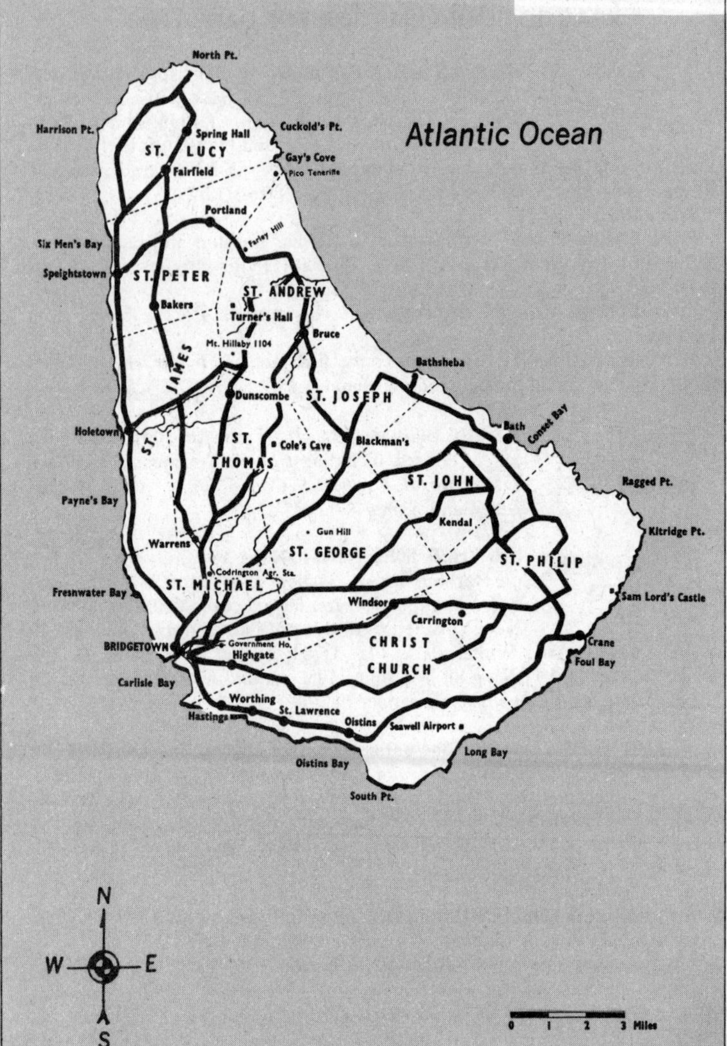

Barbados
Atlantic Ocean
North Pt.
Harrison Pt.
Spring Hall
Cuckold's Pt.
ST. LUCY
Gay's Cove
Fairfield
Pico Teneriffe
Portland
Farley Hill
Six Men's Bay
Speightstown
ST. PETER
ST. ANDREW
Bakers
Turner's Hall
Bruce
Mt. Hillaby 1104
ST. JAMES
Bathsheba
Dunscombe
ST. JOSEPH
Bath
Conset Bay
Holetown
ST. THOMAS
Cole's Cave
Blackman's
ST. JOHN
Ragged Pt.
Payne's Bay
Kendal
Gun Hill
Kitridge Pt.
Warrens
ST. GEORGE
ST. PHILIP
Codrington Agr. Sta.
ST. MICHAEL
Fresnwater Bay
Sam Lord's Castle
Windsor
Carrington
BRIDGETOWN
Government Ho.
CHRIST CHURCH
Crane
Highgate
Foul Bay
Carlisle Bay
Worthing
Hastings
St. Lawrence
Oistins
Seawell Airport
Long Bay
Oistins Bay
South Pt.
N
W
E
S
0
1
2
3 Miles

MONEY. Barbados has its own currency, the Barbadian dollar, which equals about 50¢ US; or one £ = $4 Bajan dollars. American and Canadian dollars are accepted at most hotels and restaurants, but you'll get a better rate if you stop at a bank and deal in local currency. Sterling is certainly familiar enough in Barbados, but U.K. travelers should check beforehand on the latest restrictions for importing pounds into Barbados.

TAXES AND OTHER CHARGES. There is an 8% government tax on all hotel accommodations, plus a service charge of 10%. The airport departure tax is US $5.

HOW TO GET ABOUT. The older gentlemen who drive taxis are a special group here, as on other islands. Their patience and tales of childhood can add immeasurably to your holiday. For sightseeing out of Bridgetown, a day tour to include the west coast up to the north point and a swing down the east coast past Bathsheba and Marriott's Sam Lord's Castle will take 5 hours minimum. You can arrange such island sightseeing with the cab drivers and negotiate the rate, or through *Paul Foster Travel* or *Dear's Garage,* who are on-island tour operators. Figure about $20 minimum for the taxi tour, which can include up to four people.

If you choose the island buses, you'll pay 45¢ for the full route or part thereof–in other words, return fare from the last scheduled stop to Bridgetown is 90¢. Cars are available for rental through *Avis, International Car Rental* (Hertz), and several local firms. Rates run $25–30 per day; $125–150 per week.

Sightseeing offshore is a great way to spend a day in the sun. The *Jolly Roger* costs about $30 US per person, with lunch and beverages included.

EVENTS AND HOLIDAYS. The biggest yearly event on Barbados is the *Crop Over Festival,* a month-long celebration that begins with a parade through the streets and continues with folk dancing, calypso and steel band concerts, Festival Queen contests and fancy dress balls. Everyone participates at one time or another from mid-June to mid-July.

Barbados' official holidays are *New Year's Day, Good Friday, Easter Monday, Whit Monday, May Day* (May 1), *Emancipation Day* (1st Monday in August), *United Nations Day* (1st Monday in October), *Independence Day* (Nov. 30), *Christmas Day,* and *Boxing Day.*

WHAT WILL IT COST?

A typical day on Barbados in season for *two* persons will run:

	US$	£
Accommodations at one of the large beachfront hotels	100	54
Breakfast at the hotel	10	5
Lunch at a moderate restaurant	15	8
Dinner at a moderate restaurant	30	16
Tip or service charge at the restaurants; tax and service charge at hotel	20	11
One-day sightseeing by rental car	25	14
	$200	£108

STAYING IN BARBADOS

HOTELS. Variety is the spice of life in Barbados. There is a place to suit every pocketbook and every mood. Hotels line the west (leeward, calmer) shore in profusion and most of them offer luxury living. The Hastings-Worthing area, southwest to east from Bridgetown, was the site of the first hotels in the country, during its turn-of-the-century popularity with British on holiday. Many of the properties are still in operation, although the once famous Marine Hotel is now headquarters for the Barbados Board of Tourism. Beyond the St. Lawrence area, on the south coast, the island bubbles north, with only a few properties on that eastern (windward) coast. Marriott's Sam Lord's Castle and the Crane Hotel are here.

Service in Barbados is generally a notch or two higher than on other islands, mainly due to the innate courtesy of the Bajans and the fact that there is "pride in industry." Most hotels provide some kind of transportation into town (and taxis are always available). In addition, a special feature for those interested is the "Meet the Bajan" program, where your hotel manager can put you in touch with residents whose interests parallel your own.

Accra Beach Hotel. On Rockley Beach. Wing of twenty-one housekeeping suites, with wall-to-wall carpeting and other luxuries. Fifty-three rooms in all. Dining room, cocktail lounge, and beach bar. $55–60 double EP in winter; $35–50 double EP off-season.

Arawak Inn. At Inch Marlow Point, on Long Bay Beach, ten miles from Bridgetown, this twenty-two-unit property is out of the tourist mainstream. Handsomely decorated luxury apartment suites, each with covered patio overlooking the sea. Freshwater pool; tennis on premises. Cozy, informal dining room. No children permitted. $80 double EP in winter; $40 double EP off-season. Add $20 per person for breakfast and dinner.

Atlantis Hotel. A very nice location away from it all on the Bathsheba coast. Warm, pleasant atmosphere in any of twelve rooms on a bluff overlooking the sea. Dining room is especially good, particularly for Bajan dishes. Nothing fancy, but plenty of peace and quiet. From $40 double all year, with all three meals included.

Bagshot House. On the beach at St. Lawrence, about three miles east of Bridgetown. A well-run hotel with good, plain English-style food, or West Indian dishes on request. Just sixteen rooms, with a club atmosphere because most guests are repeaters. $85 double in winter; $68 double off-season, with breakfast and dinner included.

Barbados Beach Village. One of the "sleepers" in the Parish of St. James on the west coast. Twin-bedded rooms, studios, apartments and duplexes included in its eighty-four units. Terrace bar, seaside restaurant, swimming pool and pool bar, disco nightclub. Nice beach, with water sports available. $160 double MAP in winter; $54 double EP off-season. Suites are slightly higher.

Barbados Hilton. On twenty-one acres at Needhams Point overlooking Carlisle Bay, about five minutes from the center of Bridgetown. There are 192 rooms and suites, all with balconies. Five-storied building has New Orleans–style courtyard with tropical foliage. Nice atmosphere. Elegant dining room with island and international food. Coffee shop, tennis courts, water sports. All facing a 1,000-foot beach that is unusually quiet. Swimming pool, health club, shops around porte cochere at entrance. $117–150 double EP in winter; $55–65 double EP off-season.

Buccaneer Bay. A perfect place for beachfront, do-what-you-like living, with thirty-eight housekeeping apartments facing the sea. Central bar and dining area for steel band and manager's welcome parties. Full maid service; complimentary bus service to town. Its beach is part of the fine St. James western strip. $93–108 double EP in winter; from $46 double EP off-season.

Cobblers Cove. In the Parish of St. Peter, about eleven miles up the coast from the capital city. Thirty-eight luxurious efficiency units with kitchenettes and balconies or patios. Private white-sand beach, dining terrace, swimming pool, and tropical bar. Comfortable and unpretentious, but one of the best small hotels on the island. $195 double in winter; from $75 double off-season, breakfast and dinner included.

Coconut Creek Club. Luxury cottage colony at St. James, with 48 housekeeping units set out on beautifully landscaped grounds. Private beach, freshwater swimming pool, dining room, pub, bar pavilion for entertainment and dancing. Breakfast and dinner are included in their rates, which run $148–176 double in winter, $78–92 off-season.

Colony Club. On the beach at St. James, this seven-acre cottage colony is one of the most attractive of the Bajan "residential clubs." There are seventy-five luxuriously appointed rooms, some with dressing rooms, all with private patios. Dining room (exchange dining if you like), cocktail terrace, swimming pool, water sports on the beach, and brilliant gardens to stroll. $180–225 double in winter; $105–130 off-season, with breakfast and dinner included.

Coral Reef Club. Next door to the Colony Club, this property has seventy-five rooms, many in cottages scattered around the grounds, with names such as Guava, Frangipani, Bamboo, and Jasmin. You'll enjoy luncheon on the terrace, gracious evening wining and dining. Entertainment includes dinner dances and beach barbecues. Freshwater swimming pool; water sports available. A sophisticated St. James spot. Highest rates are during the winter season, when they run $210–294 double, with all three meals included (AP).

Crane Beach. On a clifftop perch at St. Philip, twelve wiggly miles from Bridgetown, this remote twenty-five-room hotel has changed hands and personality often since it was built in 1790. Today its accommodations are in suites or one-bedroom apartments in the main building. Air-conditioned bedrooms are available at its Beach Club next door. Two swimming pools, two bars, pleasant restaurant with an interesting wine cellar. $75–95 double EP in winter; $55 double off-season.

Discovery Bay Inn. Nicely situated on four tropical acres on the St. James coast. Guests in the seventy-five rooms facing the sea are left on their own for diversion. Small pool, open lounge and dining room, dancing and entertainment. Also exchange dining with nearby resorts. From $120 double in winter; from $75 off-season, with breakfast and dinner included.

Eastry House. Perched on a hillside in St. Peter's Parish, just north of St.

James, Eastry has use of a beach across the way. Olympic pool on premises. Elegant atmosphere, exceptional food. Some suites available. Rates, including Continental breakfast, run $100–150 double in winter; $70 off-season.

Edgewater Hotel. Not for everyone, this hotel at St. Joseph on the Bathsheba coast is far from everything. The ten rooms here are popular with residents for weekends in the country and for those who like an informal fishing-and-outdoors kind of life. Freshwater swimming pool, tennis court. Food is local and usually good. This place is worth a lunchtime visit when you tour the island. $50 double EP in winter; $40 double EP off-seasons.

Glitter Bay. A lovely brand-new property on the calm western shore, which opened for the 1981–82 winter season. The accommodations are in 21 units surrounded by tropical gardens at the edge of the sea. The units vary, with six of them in three-bedroom penthouses; twelve in two-bedroom suites; and three in one-bedroom suites. The rooms are plush, large, and airy. Fine dining at their *Piperade Restaurant;* dancing; nightly entertainment. Swimming pool; all water sports; golf nearby. Rates run from $150–370 double EP in winter; from $100–240 double off-season, depending upon suites desired.

Holiday Inn. Lots of action here, with 138 rooms in the seven-story main building and in smaller garden cottages. Most rooms have two double beds with bath, private balcony and radio. Freshwater swimming pool and patio, busy beach with water sports available. Two restaurants, three bars, entertainment nightly. $114–134 double EP in winter; $60–66 double EP off-season.

Island Inn. If you want an indigenous inn, here's one. Guests in the twenty-two rooms enjoy a local, informal atmosphere. Across the street from Holiday Inn and down the road from Hilton, you have all the action within paces. Restaurant serves local specialties; popular night club swings until the early hours. $46 double EP in winter; $33 double EP off-season.

Marriott's Sam Lord's Castle. On the sea at St. Philip, about fourteen miles east of Bridgetown. It isn't really a castle with a tower and moat, but an impressive mansion surrounded by seventy-one acres of beautiful grounds, gardens and a fine beach. The nine rooms in the main house have canopied beds. Downstairs the furniture is Sheraton, Hepplewhite, and Chippendale, the china is Spode, and some of the paintings are by Reynolds. The rest of the property's 172 rooms are in surrounding cottages. Two swimming pools, a mile-long beach, and tennis courts lighted for night play. *Wanderer Restaurant* for Continental dining. Nightly entertainment, and even a few slot machines to add to the fun. $132–142 double EP in winter; $77–85 double EP off-season.

Miramar Beach. At St. James on the beach, eight miles north of Bridgetown, this charming hotel with tropical gardens is quiet, elegant, a bit on the formal side. Freshwater pool, tennis courts, water sports. Its one hundred rooms include garden suites with patios and beach suites with patio terraces. Open-air restaurant for fine dining, and beach barbecues weekly. From $105–130 EP in winter, depending on accommodations.

Ocean View. An ocean-front hotel at Hastings, sandwiched between road and sea at the heart of the coast. Convenient to town, it's popular with businessmen. Forty air-conditioned rooms, excellent food, traditional atmosphere and antiques, plus impressive flower arrangements in entryway which add to your warm welcome. From $35–49 double EP in winter, $30 double off-season.

Paradise Beach Hotel. On the beach at Black Rock, St. Michael, three miles north of Bridgetown. This 150-room holiday resort has a St. James aura but with lower prices. Large, attractive rooms, some beachfront suites. Beach-side bar, terrace dining area. Swimming pool, lighted tennis courts, all watersports. $140–160 double EP in winter. Off-season rates run $45–65.

St. James Beach Club. Opened in the fall of 1981 on the fashionable, uncrowded west coast, this 131-room rambling resort offers a variety of accommodations. There are 54 hotel rooms, 55 one-bedroom suites, 14 two-bedroom suites, and 8 penthouses. All units have terraces; suites and penthouses offer kitchen and dining facilities. Freshwater pool with swim-up bar, watersports facilities, air-conditioned squash court. Excellent *Sand Dollar* restaurant; coffeeshop; nightly entertainment. Rates for the hotel rooms run $120–135 double EP in winter; $50–65 double off-season. Suites and penthouses range from $160–360 in winter; from $75–175 off-season.

Sandpiper Inn. Thirty-four rooms in West Indian–style on St. James coast. Rooms are clustered around pool. A good beach is just steps away. Open-air bar and restaurant. Options for snorkeling, tennis, fishing and horseback riding nearby. High rates ($184–242 in winter) include breakfast and dinner.

Sandy Beach Resort. A new and delightful hotel on the south shore. 139 attractive rooms in 89 suites, all with patios or balconies facing the sea. Large swimming pool; all watersports, with options for fishing trips or harbor cruises. Drinks and entertainment at their *Sand Bar* poolside; excellent food at their *Green House* restaurant. Rates run $145 double EP in winter; $70 double off-season. The two-bedroom suites are $215 in winter; $95 off-season.

Sandy Lane. One of the Caribbean's most famous, this St. James beachfront resort combines 18th-century elegance with 20th-century luxury in 115 contemporary rooms and suites. The building itself is a lovely, wide affair of neo-Palladian architecture, with rooms arranged for sea view. Everything is airy and very plush, with such striking effects as ornate mirrors and crystal chandeliers against a background of pale coral-stone walls. The 1,000-foot beach offers all watersports. Five tennis courts, freeform swimming pool, 18-hole golf course. Two restaurants, two cocktail lounges, nightly entertainment. From $250 double in winter; from $150 double off-season, two meals included.

Tamarind Cove. Very attractive beachfront resort on the sands along the St. James coast. The architecture is Spanish; the rooms are one- and two-bedroom suites. Dining on the terrace, swimming in the pool or sea. All watersports. $115 double in winter, $70 and up off-season, with breakfast and dinner included.

HOME RENTALS. Cottages, villas and apartments have long been a part of the vacation life of Barbados, and now the rental of private homes is running a close second. Many are in the Hastings-Worthing area; some are scattered along the St. James coast, and others in the Parish of St. Peter.

British and Canadian visitors have long known that apartment hotels make a holiday economically attractive and pleasant, especially when there are children. They get complete hotel service, meals, swimming pool and beach, and save money by doing their own cooking (units are equipped with stove, refrigerator, and all necessary crockery and cooking utensils). A listing of sixty available apartments can be obtained through the *Barbados Board of Tourism.*

Private homes for rent range from five-servant, four-bedroom, three-bath estates with swimming pools, to comfortable seaside cottages that are fully equipped. Rates can be as low as $600 per week in season for a cottage that accommodates four people, to $3,000 per week for a well-staffed home that can easily accommodate eight. Contact *Caribbean Holidays, Inc.*, 711 Third Ave., New York, N.Y. 10017, for their full-color brochure entitled "Barbados Apartment, Cottage & Luxury House Holidays," which has photographs of the available properties and all they have to offer.

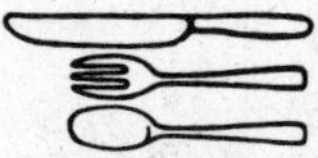

RESTAURANTS. This is rum country, and Barbados' Mount Gay Rum is one of the best to come out of the Caribbean. There are other local brands, along with a light, island-distilled beer called *Banks.* In the food line, among local specialties flying fish is the handsdown winner. The fish is moist and succulent, and the Bajans transform it into a gastronomic delight by boiling, baking, frying, stuffing, or serving it in a stew. If you like "hot" foods, ask for the locally made pepper sauce–but use it sparingly.

Dolphin, saltfish cakes and "crab-in-the-back" are other Bajan specialties. You may find roast suckling pig, which is sometimes served at hotel barbecue nights. As for island fruits and vegetables, papaya (pawpaw) is popular, and mangoes and limes are used freely.

We call $6 and under *Inexpensive;* $7–15 *Moderate;* $16 and above *Expensive.*

Atlantis Hotel. On the windward coast at Bathsheba, this is one of the most delightful luncheon spots on the island. Outdoor dining at the edge of the sea, with island specialties and fresh fish done in a variety of ways. *Inexpensive.*

Bagatelle Great House. Hidden in the hills of St. Thomas Parish, this converted plantation house puts you into the colonial life of Barbados. The restaurant is encased in thick stone walls. Dinner is a combination of Continental and local cuisine and served by candlelight. Wine list is extensive and expensive. So is the food. *Expensive.*

Bonanza Steak House. At Sunset Crest in St. James, this is a typical steak house with good food and hearty portions. *Moderate.*

Brown Sugar. A special restaurant in Bridgetown where traditional Bajan foods are served in a colonial setting. *Expensive.*

Chateau Creole. Great spot in the Parish of St. James, where fine Continental and local fare is served nicely. *Moderate.*

Da Luciano. Traditional Italian cuisine set out pleasantly in an old Victorian-era home. *Moderate.*

Dinner Bell. Friendly spot at St. Lawrence Gap in Christ Church. Steaks, seafood and other à la carte choices. *Inexpensive.*

Green House. Delectable dining here in an ideal setting–candlelight, soft music, sea breezes. Specialties always include Bajan bouillabaisse, delicately poached fillet of sole, and a seafood combo. Located on the edge of the beach at the Sandy Beach resort. *Expensive.*

Le Bistro. A tiny, second-floor restaurant on Prince William Henry Street in the heart of Bridgetown. The emphasis here is on the British, with steak and kidney pie the specialty. But they also serve slices of quiche, hamburgers, and chicken platters as part of their luncheon fare. *Inexpensive.*

Luigi's. On the south coast at Dover in Christ Church, this is the place for Italian food and lots of it, plus a variety of seafood dishes, all of it served in a Neapolitan setting. Open for dinner only. *Moderate.*

The Hide-Away. On the other side of the mini-moat from Bagatelle Great House, this open-air restaurant is informal and fun. Everything from fondues to lobster dishes for dinner. Snacks and sandwiches are served much later when Nick's becomes a disco that swings until 3 A.M. *Moderate.*

The Pelican. Good for a quick lunch during a visit to the crafts center at Pelican Village. *Inexpensive.*

Pisces. Located at St. Lawrence Gap, Christ Church, this is one of the island's best for seafood dinners. The atmosphere is homey, the fare really delectable. Open for dinner only; reservations a must. *Expensive.*

Sand Dollar. Excellent new restaurant at the St. James Beach Club. The menu is extensive, including broiled dolphin with almonds, roast duckling in a rum and pineapple sauce, and filet of red snapper. *Expensive.*

NIGHTLIFE. There's dancing most evenings in season at the big west coast hotels and at many of the other island hotels. Out of season, things taper off a bit, but the discos seem to swing year-round. The *Rendezvous Disco* at the Rockley Resort rocks until the early hours. So does the *Hippo Disco,* where, in addition to the beat, a dancer does her number while suspended overhead in a cage. On Maxwell Coast Road in Christ Church, you'll find another large "with-it" disco, the *Banana Boat,* which is open air. But the best of all is the *Caribbean Pepperpot,* where the well-known Merrymen perform. All four charge an entry fee that runs from $2.50–$3.50 US.

SHOPPING. Most Bridgetown shopping is department-store style, with *Cave Shepherd, Y. DeLima, Da Costa & Musson* and others on Broad St., the island's Fifth Avenue. Always ask if there is an in-bond department. It may take you longer, but the prices will be better. Among the several reliable jewelry shops are *Y. DeLima* (both the Broad St. shop and the branch in Hastings); *Louis I. Bayley* on Broad St. for Rolex watches; *J. Baldini* on Broad St. for Eterna and Longines watches, Brazilian jewelry, and Danish silver; *Correia's* on Prince William Henry St. for diamonds, semi-precious stones, cultured pearls, and other items.

Local tailors can make items on the spot. Your hotel can suggest some names or, if their list is short at the time of your visit, contact the Barbados Board of Tourism at Marine House for names.

Among the items made with the visitor in mind are place mats, rugs, handbags, dresses, dolls, and the usual shell jewelry. At *Pelican Village,* the outlet for the local handicraft and home industry, you can watch some of the items in the making. The Village is on the outskirts of town and, in addition to the cluster of conical shops, there is the *Government Handicraft Center.* The shop on the main floor carries items made from pandanus grass–rugs, place mats, bags, etc. Khus khus place mats are popular too. You can also visit the *West Indies Handicrafts* at Pierhead Lane, famous for 1-foot-square fiber mats made into floor coverings.

For fashion, the styling of most of the locally made items is not the most current. If you have a favorite pattern, bring it with you. The best resortwear shops are those in the luxury hotels along the St. James coast. We noted items in the shops at Sandy Lane and at Holetown, where there are several boutiques (men's and women's). Prices are not cheap, but items are often unique. There's a ring of shops at the entrance of the Hilton, and the peddlers along the beach will sell the *dashikis* that seem to be everywhere (for about $15, but a bargain) and some straw bags that looked better than usual.

The best island-designed fabric that we've seen is that sold at *Caribatik Island Fabrics* at the Crane Beach Hotel, a 10-minute drive east of the airport in the direction of Sam Lord's Castle. The fabric is batik-dyed in a studio at Falmouth, Jamaica, under the watchful eye of the Chandlers. Items for sale in the Barbados shop include wall hangings at about $35, caftans for $45, halter dresses at $22, neckties (made from leftovers) at $9, and fabric by the yard, the cotton selling at about $7 per yard. Designs are interesting and colorful.

For calypso and steel band records go to *Mannings Music City.* If you don't have a chance to hear The Merrymen in person, be sure to buy their record. They're still the best.

If you enjoy "typical" paintings as a reminder of your holiday (or for gifts), the prints by *Jill Walker* are engaging renditions of Bajan sights and customs.

SPORTS AND OTHER ACTIVITIES. Since Barbados is girdled with pink and white "granulated sugar" beaches with calm water on the west side, surf on the east, the island's *swimming* possibilities are hard to beat. Don't let the rim of hotels and other buildings that separate the beach from the roadside in the Hastings-Worthing area deter you. Good beaches dash along most of that coast.

For peaceful swimming near Bridgetown, the Hilton's facilities are the best. There's a small charge for towels, lounge chairs, etc., but it's convenient, pleasant, and the beach bar serves sandwiches, salads, and drinks. (You can also do your shopping from peddlers at this beach.) There's a concession for *snorkel* and *scuba* equipment at moderate rates.

North of Bridgetown, up the St. James coast, the luxury resorts discourage day visitors, but you may stop in for lunch and a swim. Paradise Beach Club, nearest Bridgetown, offers every activity imaginable: *scuba, snorkel, small boats for charter, diving trips,* etc. Willie's Water Sports is in charge. Les Wotton operates a scuba center at Coral Reef. Sandy Beach Watersports, headquartered at that hotel, has a complete program, including Sunfish sailing, windsurfing, snorkeling, scuba diving, and deep-sea fishing. Fishing rates aboard their *Scotch 'n Soda* run $150 per half-day; $300 for a full day.

The beaches at Crane and Bathsheba on the east coast are in the path of trade winds. For those who like to ride Atlantic breakers or duck under them, this shore offers good *surfing.*

Often a landfall for yachts sailing trans-Atlantic, Barbados government requires all yachts to remain in Carlisle Bay. The sight is a pretty one. Headquarters for *sailing* are at the Barbados Cruising Club and the Barbados Yacht Club (more formal). The local racing season lasts through May, with small craft races in the bay and some longer cruises offshore. Most of the beach-front hotels have Sailfish and Sunfish free or at small charge; some hotels even have their own yachts. For information on *day cruises,* contact the front desk at your hotel. The *Jolly Roger,* used in the filming of *Dr. Dolittle,* provides luncheon and cocktail cruises. Also check with *Cap'n Patch Cruises,* which are similar. Your hotel will be able to provide all particulars.

There are tennis facilities at many of the hotels, as well as at the Paragon Tennis Club and the Summer Hayes Club. Most are lighted for nightplay.

Golf is played on the course at Sandy Lane. Make reservations for play on the 18 holes. Durant's Championship Golf Course opened in early 1974 with 18 holes. It's the centerpiece of a 216-acre development on the south coast which will include private homes, apartments, a convention hotel, and shops.

The Barbados Game Fishing Club sponsors an annual fishing contest during March-April. The *game fishing* is first rate. Barracuda, dolphin, sailfish, marlin, tuna, and wahoo are the principal catches. Boats and guides can be hired at reasonable prices; your hotel desk will arrange it, or you can get in touch with the Game Fishing Club. There seems to be an island shortage of rods and tackle, although they can be had. If you're a serious fisherman, bring your own. Even if you shrink from baiting a hook, you'll be excited by the flying fish skimming the waters, sailing about, almost leaping into the boat. If fishing for them doesn't tempt you, enjoy it vicariously by watching the flying-fish fleet come in at Oistins or Tent Bay, near Bathsheba up on the breezy east coast. It's one of the sights of Barbados, although the boats have now been equipped with motors, subtracting from the picturesque while adding to the efficiency.

There are stables and good trails for *horseback riding* at Sharon Hill in St. Thomas Parish, Little Bentley in Christ Church, and the Brighton Stables in St. Michael's.

The popular spectator sports are *cricket, soccer, motor rallies, horse racing, horse shows,* and *polo.* There are two racing seasons a year (Jan.–April; July–Nov.) with horses running every other Saturday during that time on the Garrison Savannah. If you've never seen an island jump, this is your chance. The air vibrates to the rhythms of steel bands and hawkers' cries; the grounds are full of decorated food booths sizzling with fried flying fish, and the whole place swarms.

If you know and like *cricket,* you'll be impressed by the skill of the Bajans. Having adopted the sport from their British brothers, they now surpass them at it. The cricket season is June to Jan.

Polo is becoming increasingly popular. The season starts in July and runs to Feb. The games are played at Holder's, St. James.

An island event of special interest to those who want to learn something more about the country they're visiting is the annual *house tours.* The Barbados Board of Tourism can give you specific details on dates and houses open for visiting. Usually there are three or four on Wed. afternoons from Jan. through April. Besides providing an interesting day out of the sun, it's often interesting to see how island residents live. The cost is in the vicinity of $4 Bds; the money goes to the Barbados National Trust.

BONAIRE

Shades of Pink

As placid and quiet as it is, Bonaire exudes an unforgettable pink glow–from its thousands of prancing flamingos to its miles of raspberry-hued coral reefs. As islands in the Caribbean go, it can be considered large (24 miles long by 7 miles wide), but it is small in population, with just about 10,000 residents.

Bonaire lies 50 miles north of Venezuela and is within easy flying distance of Aruba and Curacao, its Netherlands Antilles' Leeward Island counterparts. *Papiamento,* which is a mixture of several languages, is spoken here and the first words you'll hear will be *bon bini,* meaning welcome. The last word will be *ayo,* or goodbye, but be assured that in between everyone speaks English.

Bonaire's terrain ranges from the flatlands in the south, where salt beds simmer and flamingos flourish, to the mountainous tropical forest in the north. The island is rimmed by beaches, both pink and white, and by exotic coral reefs which are visible to a depth of 100 feet in clear crystal water.

Early morning is the time for bird watching, which is rewarding on Bonaire because of flamingos and thousands of herons, snipes, tern, pelicans, green parrots, parakeets, and other birds of brilliant hue. The flamingos play hide and seek with the tourists, so be quiet, patient, and at the ready with binoculars or a camera with telephoto lens. Late afternoon is the best time to explore the cactus-strewn plains that surround the southern salt beds. And any time of day is ideal for a cool dip, snorkeling or scuba diving.

The island's capital is *Kralendijk,* a tiny town of 1,200 with a harbor large enough for cruise ships, and a fish market. An uninhabited offshore island, *Klein Bonaire,* is rocky, fringed by fine white sand, and a favorite with those who really want a day's retreat. Check with the watersports desk at your hotel to make arrangements for the trip. The boats usually set out at 10 A.M. and return at 4 P.M. to bring you back. Either pack your own picnic or have one prepared by your hotel.

History

The Indians were well settled when a landing party under Amerigo Vespucci discovered the island in 1499. Little is recorded of the next twenty-five years, until the Spaniards began their colonization, but what little there is can be found in the caves and grottoes where the walls are lined with Indian petroglyphs, some reputed to be more than 500 years old.

A century later, the enterprising Dutch took over, planting corn, raising stock and producing salt. French and British privateers discovered the island in the early 19th century, but it took the tourists another 150 years. Growth has been minimal and changes few. There are just four hotels, a handful of restaurants, and an ever-present Dutch ambiance in the small, pastel-painted houses that are neatly set side by side over the plains and along the sea.

Bonaire, along with the other five islands that make up the Netherlands Antilles, is an autonomous part of the Kingdom of the Netherlands, with its own Island Council and its own representative of the Crown.

EXPLORING BONAIRE

Kralendijk, the island's capital city, is smack in the center of the island, and is the focal point for hotels. There are just a few streets, and here, as on the other small Dutch islands, the names are almost as long as the avenues. Activity begins early in the morning at the fish market on Bernhardweg. There, at the edge of the bay, you'll find an impressive and colorful array of all that's caught fresh that day.

Some shops and restaurants are one block away on Breedestraat, while along Kerweg, which cuts through the two, you'll find the largest supermarket on the island, a movie theatre, and an ice cream parlor. There really isn't much more to see in town, but what there is is worth a short stroll, especially to visit the Arts and Crafts Center.

Don't miss the International Salt Company on Bonaire's southern tip. The salt beds appear like shimmering lakes and turn varying shades of pink as the water evaporates. It is here that flamingos nest, adding to the color, and over the scene towering stacks of salt crystals rise like snow-covered mountains.

Miniscule whitewashed slave huts have been restored; they housed the slaves who worked the salt pans. History has it that they lived here during the week but walked halfway across the island on weekends to their homes in Rincon, Bonaire's oldest village.

See the caves at Fontein or Boca Onima to ponder the ancient writings of the Indians, then visit Washington/Slagbaii National Park, a wilderness sanctuary that occupies the northwest corner of the island. This 13,500-acre preserve is open daily until 5 P.M. and is ideal for hiking, picnicking, birdwatching (more than 100 different species) or simply communing with nature. In order to keep it a natural preserve, no fishing, hunting or camping is permitted.

A DAY ON YOUR OWN

(Although commercial island tours include two hours in the north and two in the south, the time estimate for covering it all yourself would be 8 A.M. until 5 P.M.)

Start out as early in the morning as possible, not only because bird-watching is best then, but because it is cooler and there is so much to cover. Pack a bathing suit, snorkel equipment (mask, fins and snorkel can be rented through the dive shop at your hotel) and a picnic lunch which your hotel will prepare for you.

From *Kralendijk* head north along the Scenic Road to *Goto Meer* and the breathtaking view of the lake and the flamingo sanctuary. As you drive further north, *Brandaris Hill,* the island's highest point, will loom ahead as you approach *Washington/Slagbaii National Park.* Arrows mark the twenty-two mile route through the park. Drive slowly and watch out for birds and animals, as they roam free in the wilderness sanctuary. Enjoy a leisurely picnic here in the cool of the forest and then head back to *Goto Meer* and over to the west coast for a swim. The ideal spot here is called *Nukove* and is one of the best snorkeling areas.

Wend your way inland to *Rincon,* the island's oldest village, and on to *Fontein* to stop awhile and form your own interpretations of the Indian writings in the caves. Follow the inland road south to *Seroe Largu* and the marked observation point that offers another special view of the island.

Bypass the capital city in favor of the village of *Nikiboko* and stop at the *Nadia Snack Bar* for ice cream or a soft drink. You might consider stocking up for the drive around the south coast.

Just a few miles further on you'll come to a mini-forest of mangrove trees that form an arc around *Lac Bay.* The beach is long and powdery and the water crystal clear, just perfect for another swim. Then walk and inspect the piles of conch shells that have been brought from the sea by the local fishermen. Once they remove the succulent meat from the shells they either polish them up for in-town sales or toss them ashore for the taking. You're bound to find one pink-hued beauty that will make the perfect souvenir.

Follow the east coast road to the *Willemstoren Lighthouse* at the end of the island. As you curve around its base you'll see the sparkling white mountains of crystals at the salt works, the irridescent salt ponds, and the flamingos at play in their southern habitat. The restored *slave huts* nearby give a picture of life on Bonaire a century ago.

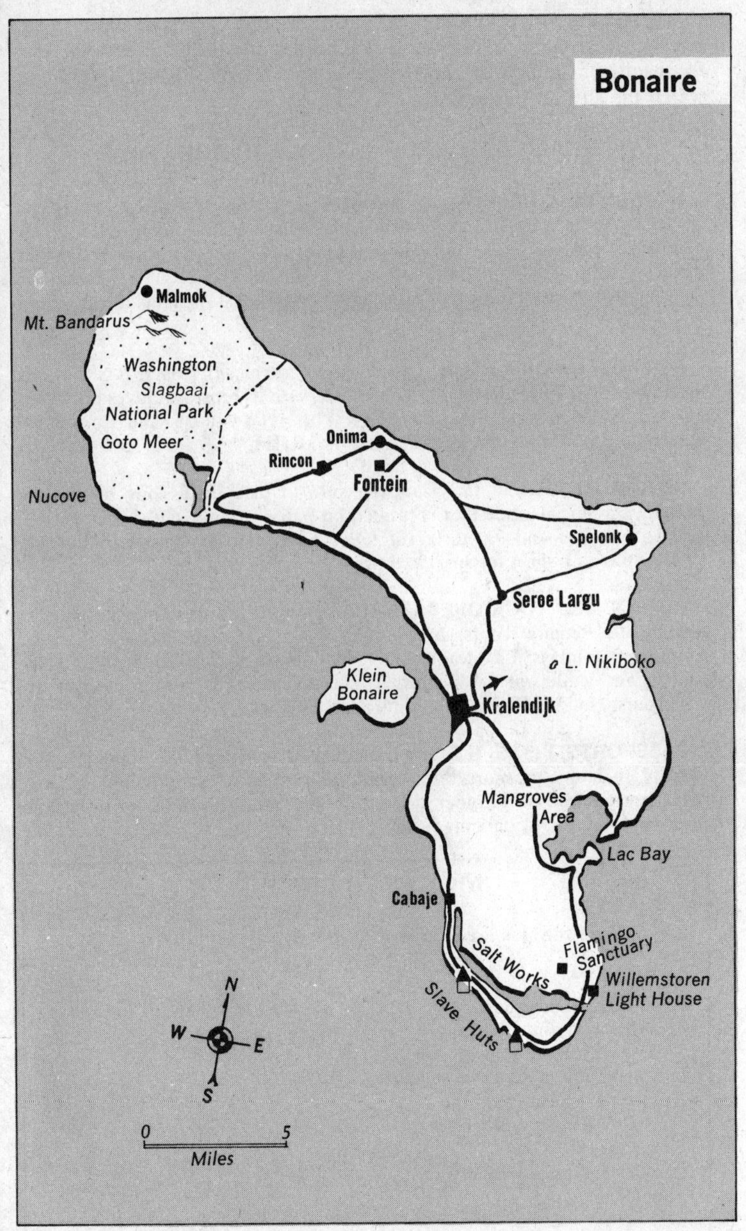
Bonaire
Malmok
Mt. Bandarus
Washington
Slagbaai
National Park
Goto Meer
Nucove
Onima
Rincon
Fontein
Spelonk
Seroe Largu
L. Nikiboko
Klein
Bonaire
Kralendijk
Mangroves
Area
Lac Bay
Cabaje
Salt Works
Flamingo
Sanctuary
Willemstoren
Light House
Slave Huts
N
W
E
S
0
5
Miles

After seeing the pounding surf on the island's western shore, head back to *Kralendijk.* You should reach the capital at the correct time for a tall rum punch on the terrace at the *Zeezicht* restaurant as you watch the sun set in the harbor.

PRACTICAL INFORMATION FOR BONAIRE

HOW TO GET THERE. By air. *American Airlines* has daily flights from New York to Curaçao and Aruba; *Eastern Airlines* flies nonstop from Miami. *ALM* handles the onward service to Bonaire with several flights daily. *ALM* also has direct service from Miami, San Juan, and St. Martin. The recent lengthening of the Flamingo Airport runway is expected to bring nonstop flights directly from major U.S. gateways.

FURTHER INFORMATION. The *Bonaire Government Tourist Board* has its head office at #1 Breedestraat in Kralendijk, with its representatives providing information from 1466 Broadway, New York, N.Y. 10036, and from 815A Queen St. E., Toronto, Ontario, Canada M4M 1H8.

ISLAND MEDIA. On the island be sure to pick up a copy of *Bonaire Holiday,* an official guide that is printed on paper as pink as the island itself. *Radio Nederland* and *Trans World Radio* have daily newscasts in English. Consult the pink sheet for specific times.

AUTHORIZED TOUR OPERATORS. Adventure Tours; Aquaventure, International; Bonaire Tours, Inc.; Butler Travels; Carefree/David Travels; Caribbean Holidays; Cavalcade Tours; Flyfaire, Inc.; Lib/Go; Thomson Vacations; and Underwater Adventure Tours from the *U.S.* From *Canada:* Fairway Tours, Holiday House and Sunflight Holidays.

PASSPORTS, VISAS. U.S. and Canadian citizens need only some proof of identity, such as a passport, birth certificate or voter's registration card. Passports are required of all other visitors. In addition, all visitors to the island must hold a return or ongoing ticket.

WHAT WILL IT COST?

A typical day on Bonaire in season for *two* persons will run:

	US$	£
Hotel accommodations	65	35
Breakfast and dinner at hotel or in-town restaurant	20	11
Luncheon at a moderate restaurant	8	4
Tips or service charge at the restaurants; tax and service charge at the hotel	12	6
One-day sightseeing by taxi or rental car	20	11
	$125	£67

MONEY. The guilder or florin (both names are used interchangeably, although prices are marked with fl.) is the Netherlands Antilles' unit of money, subdivided into 100 cents. It is issued in all denominations, including a square nickel, a nice souvenir that has been worked into key rings and the like. The official rate of exchange is US $1 = 1.77 NAf; £1 = 3.96 NAf.

TAXES AND OTHER CHARGES. You'll pay a straight 15% on your hotel bill, but this can be confusing. Three of the island's four hotels add a 10% service charge in lieu of gratuities, plus a 5% government room tax. The other one adds 15% across the board, which includes the government tax. There is an airport departure tax of $5.75 U.S.

HOW TO GET ABOUT. Walk in town and take a taxi elsewhere. Or rent a car through *ABC Car Rental, Avis,* and *Budget.* Rates begin at $20 per day. There are island tours by bus. You can choose the two-hour Northern Tour for $8.50, the Southern Tour for the same amount, or combine the two for $16. Contact *Bonaire Sightseeing Tours.*

EVENTS AND HOLIDAYS. The biggest events on Bonaire are its February Carnival celebrations, with dancing and parades in the streets, the *Annual International Sailing Regatta* in October, and the *Queen's Birthday* on April 30. In celebration of Her Majesty's day, the Lieutenant Governor hosts a cocktail reception at his home and everyone (tourists, too) is invited.

Other holidays are *New Year's Day, Good Friday, Easter Monday, Labor Day* (May 1), *Ascension Day, St. John's Day* (June 24), *St. Peter's Day* (June 29), *Kingdom Day* (Dec. 15), and *Christmas* (Dec. 25 and 26).

STAYING IN BONAIRE

HOTELS. There are just a handful of hotels on Bonaire, all with an emphasis on the sea. Watersports centers and dive shops can be found at each property, with choices of everything from boating to snorkeling and scuba.

Bonaire Hotel & Casino. Large, modern hotel spread along a 600-foot white sand beach, called *playa lechi,* or Milk Beach. 145 air-conditioned rooms. Dining room, cozy cocktail lounge, coffee shop and evening entertainment. The casino is small but busy–it is the only one on the island–and stays open until the early hours. Swimming pool, two tennis courts, miniature golf, and a watersports center. Their large beachside bar is an added bonus. $69–79 double EP in winter, $42–52 off-season. Add $28 per person per day for MAP.

Flamingo Beach Hotel. All that a small resort hotel should be. Right on the beach with accommodations in sea-front rooms or in individual cottages. This was the first hotel on the island and has expanded slowly, so that none of the informal inn atmosphere was lost along the way. Now has 110 rooms, freshwater swimming pool, Jacuzzi, a beach bar, a small boutique, and large area for terrace dining overlooking the sea. *Dive Bonaire,* headed by Peter Hughes, is headquartered here. Rates run from $60 for a standard double to $90 for an ocean deluxe room EP in winter; $40–60 off-season. MAP available for an extra $26 per person per day.

Habitat. The perfect place for snorkelers and scuba divers, this property has 9 two-bedroom cottages with kitchenettes and patios. There is also a limited number of economy rooms with bath. Large bar with open-air terrace for music and dancing. Scuba shop has all the equipment you'll need. Winter rates run $60 per cottage for two to $80 per cottage for four people per day. This is headquarters for *Aquaventure,* under the direction of Capt. Don Stewart. Good food available at reasonable prices.

Rochaline Hotel. In the center of Kralendijk, this twenty-two room hotel offers small air-conditioned rooms with a sea view. Neat, clean and fine for businessmen, students, and those to whom price is crucial. From $26–40 double EP all year-round.

RESTAURANTS. The hotels offer the most imaginative cuisine, with the *Hotel Bonaire* specializing in Continental and West Indian, and the *Flamingo Beach* in something different every night (Indonesian Rijsttafel on Tuesday, French specialties with wine on Wednesday, an old-fashioned barbecue with a calypso band for dancing on Saturday).

Other places to try in Kralendijk are the *China Garden* on Breedestraat, where curried dishes and Chinese specialties are served in an old Bonaire mansion that has been completely restored; *Great China* for Cantonese and local seafood dishes; the *Bonaire Yachtclub* for steaks and "seafaring" specialties; *Zeezicht* (Seaview) *Restaurant* for dining on fresh fish on the waterfront; and the *Beefeater,* opposite the Bonaire Tourist Office, for steaks and chops. Most are moderately priced, with $12 per person more than covering the meal, drinks, and service charge. The *Super Corner,* also in town, has its eye on the U.S. visitor, as it dispenses hot dogs, ice cream sodas, sundaes and shakes at reasonable prices throughout the day, every day.

NIGHTLIFE. For games of chance and one-armed bandit fun the Hotel Bonaire is it. For listening and dancing, local combos perform at the Flamingo Beach and also at the Hotel Bonaire. The "action" lasts until early morning at the *Diver's Bar* at Habitat. Although the music is piped-in stereo, you can rock to your heart's content in the lounge or on the terrace as the swinging sounds literally cover the waterfront. An in-town Disco called *E Wowo* rocks until the early hours.

SHOPPING. Chances are you won't be doing a lot of shopping here, but there is a limited selection available. There are small branches of *Spritzer and Fuhrmann* downtown and at the Hotel Bonaire. *Boutique Bonaire,* also in that hotel, has a selection of island fashions; while the *Ki Bo Ke Pakus* (What do you want shop) at the Flamingo Beach Hotel has interesting Batik, Dashikis, and island-made jewelry.

In town, handcrafted products in wood, leather and sterling can be found at *Bonaire Craftsmen;* delicate shell work at *Heit's. Fundashon Arte Industria Bonairiano,* an arts and crafts center on J.A. Abraham Boulevard, offers locally made items fashioned of black coral, goat-skin leather and wood.

SPORTS AND OTHER ACTIVITIES. *Watersports* enthusiasts will be in heaven. Visibility from the surface is nowhere less than sixty-five feet and can reach a depth of 125 feet. Over forty scuba diving locations are marked for snorkelers and skin divers, with more than half accessible from the road. Dive masters are Captains Don Stewart (Habitat), Eddie Statia (Hotel Bonaire) and Peter Hughes (Flamingo Beach Hotel); each operates extensive *diving* programs. They can also arrange *snorkeling* trips and *deep-sea fishing* excursions in pursuit of marlin, tuna and bonito. Also check with them for tours by glass-bottom boat, sailing, water skiing, and the rental of underwater cameras.

For *tennis* buffs, there are asphalt courts at the Hotel Bonaire. For *bird-watching* enthusiasts, Washington/Slagbaii National Park has it all.

THE BRITISH VIRGIN ISLANDS

Royal Sails in the Sunset

Ginger, Salt, Prickly Pear, West Dog, Mosquito—no, not the makings of a salad or a description of wildlife, but a few of the sixty landfalls that make up the British Virgin Islands. Along with larger Tortola, Virgin Gorda and Jost Van Dyke, this chain is a glorious collection of sun-swept and, in most cases, untouched islands just waiting to be discovered. Visiting yachtsmen chart their courses accordingly; day-trippers find something new on each visit.

The fourteen islands that are inhabited offer small inns and unpretentious cottages along the beaches. The area welcomed some 175,000 visitors in 1981 and put them in the small hotels or aboard the yachts that fan out from Tortola and the marinas at Little Dix Bay and Biras Creek on Virgin Gorda. Even if and when there is future hotel development, accommodations will be small and it seems certain that almost half the area's visitors will continue to be seafarers who stay aboard their chartered yachts. These islands are special in that you can sail from one to other in no time and find caves to explore, uninhabited beaches to roam, hidden coves, and other glorious wonders created by nature.

History

Columbus found the islands and named them for St. Ursula and her 11,000 martyred virgins, but for the first 150 years Spain did little about them. The copper on Virgin Gorda drew their attention for a while, but they soon sailed on to the richer lands of Central America.

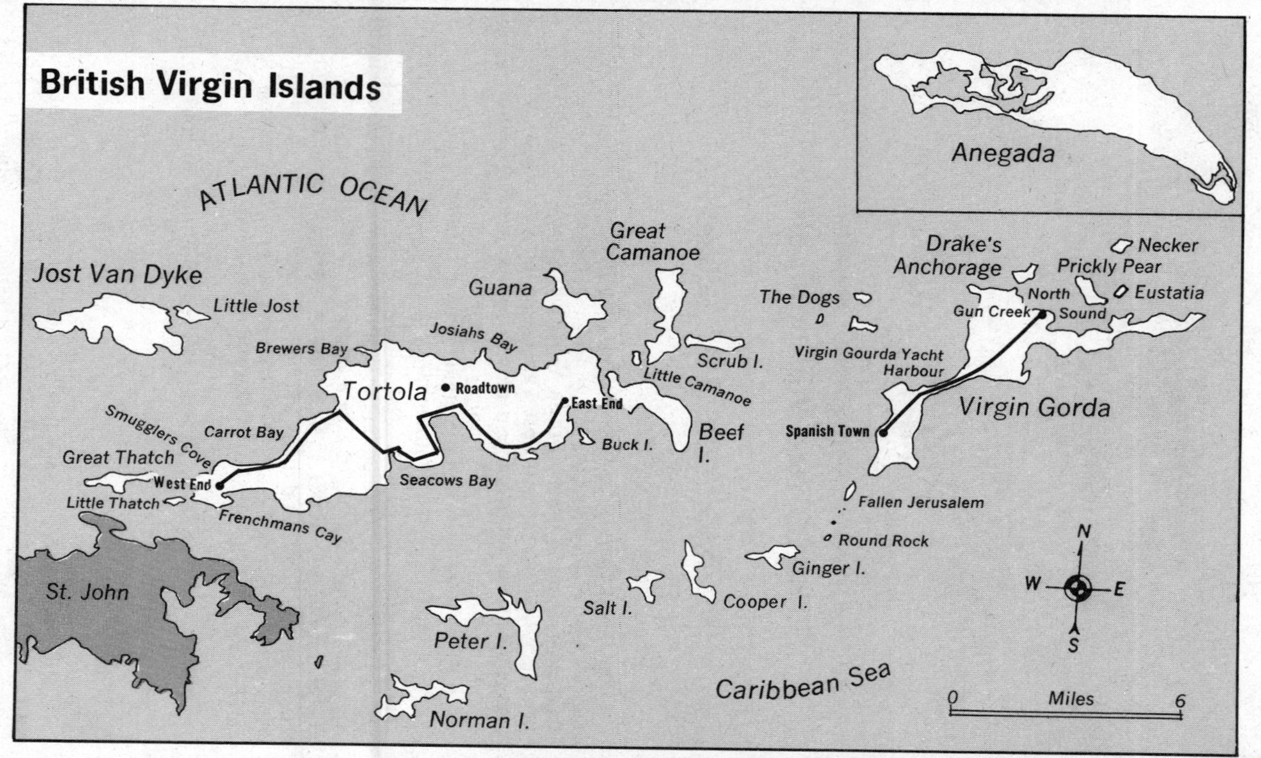
British Virgin Islands
ATLANTIC OCEAN
Jost Van Dyke
Little Jost
Brewers Bay
Josiahs Bay
Guana
Great Camanoe
Tortola
Roadtown
East End
Smugglers Cove
Carrot Bay
Great Thatch
West End
Little Thatch
Frenchmans Cay
Seacows Bay
Buck I.
Beef I.
Little Camanoe
Scrub I.
The Dogs
Virgin Gourda Yacht Harbour
Drake's Anchorage
Gun Creek
North Sound
Prickly Pear
Necker
Eustatia
Virgin Gorda
Spanish Town
Anegada
Fallen Jerusalem
Round Rock
Ginger I.
Cooper I.
Salt I.
Peter I.
Norman I.
St. John
Caribbean Sea
N
W
E
S
0
Miles
6

It wasn't until 1628 that the English made their claim on these islands. Not long after the Earl of Carlisle acquired Tortola from Charles I, the Dutch from nearby Sint Maarten moved in with little regard for the title, and began the lucrative sugar production that was to make them famous in the Caribbean.

Thus, the sugar crops, and later cotton, made the islands part of the rich rum-sugar-slave triangle trade. The British Virgins, commanding the Anegada Passage, were a favorite rendezvous for pirates lying in wait for the treasure-laden ships that passed between the New World and the Old. It wasn't long, therefore (1648), before the privateers moved into the settlement that the Dutch had established near Road Town, Tortola. By 1666, that community belonged to the pirates. The French made their claim several years later, yielding to the firm hand of the English in 1672. For the next several years, the English used these ports to launch repeated attacks on the nearby Danish Virgin Islands (now the U.S.V.I.). However, their prize location on the shipping lanes from Europe also made them attractive to the Spanish, Dutch, French and Danes, all of whom attacked regularly.

Throughout the eighteenth century trade with the American Colonies in New England was a mainstay of the economy of the British Virgin Islands. A planter class evolved in the small community, and slavery came into the islands, which were granted a charter in 1773 and have been British ever since.

The fragmented nature of the area made it difficult to defend, an ideal hideaway for assorted renegades. Quakers who came to save wayward souls were mainstays of the government of the British Virgins for a short but poignant period. Joshua Fielding set up his colony on Tortola and Virgin Gorda in 1727, and John Pickering, a governor of the islands, converted to the Quaker faith soon after.

John Lettsom, born on Jost Van Dyke in 1774, went on to England to found the London Medical Society and the Royal Humane Society; William Thornton, his contemporary and another British Virgin Islander, designed the Capitol building in Washington, D.C. By the 1780s, Quaker activity in this area, renowned among slave traders and pirates, began to disappear.

After the emancipation of the slaves in 1834, this area, like all others dependent on slaves to tend the sugar plantations, fell into a bleak period, and it wasn't until the 1960's, when Laurance Rockefeller built Little Dix Bay on Virgin Gorda and began to promote it, that tourism came to be looked upon as the mainstay of the islands.

EXPLORING THE BRITISH VIRGIN ISLANDS

Tortola, the capital, is best explored by car (see "A Day on Your Own"), while the other islands are best seen and reached from the sea. The ideal way is aboard a yacht charter from Tortola or St. Thomas, which passes dozens of them and anchors off four or five for meals, bathing and exploring.

A DAY ON YOUR OWN

With the islands as scattered and as small as they are, your all-day excursion by car will be on Tortola, the largest and most easily accessible by plane.

This is the island to explore in a bathing suit and a cover-up. Bring a towel and a camera; don't bother with a picnic lunch; but start out early in the morning so that you'll be able to sunbathe when the sun is at its peak.

Head out from Road Town, the capital city, and travel southwest along the shore, curving around Sea Cows Bay and along the coast road to West End, which is literally the end of the island. Make a note here–this might be your entry point on your next visit–the *Bomba Charger* and the *Native Son* come across several times daily from St. Thomas.

At West End you'll find a tiny main street, a grocery store for something cooling, and a small post office. Make a stop, not only to buy a few of the attractive stamps the B.V.I. are famous for, but to chat with visiting yachtsmen who must clear customs here. Then backtrack for a few miles and take the main road north to the other side of the island.

The coves and bays here are among the most beautiful in these islands. Take a look at Long Bay, with its cottages on the seaside; Little Apple Bay, where *Sebastian's on the Beach* offers open-terrace dining (consider this for an evening spot). For a special luncheon, continue on to the Sugar Mill Estate Hotel, where you can enjoy crab cakes, chef's salad, or even a hamburger at very reasonable prices. The atmosphere is terrific, including the Union Jack flying above the sands to add to the aura of being on foreign tropical soil.

As you travel further north, you'll see Mt. Sage, the highest point on the island, and beneath it Carrot Bay Mountain, a lush farmland where they grow sweet potatoes, avocadoes, bananas and sugar cane. The terrain is such that the farmers still use donkeys to go up and down.

From Great Carrot Bay and Little Carrot Bay on the coast, you'll climb another narrow road up to Windy Hill, a gorgeous overlook and perfect photo spot. From there, go downhill again to Cane Garden Bay and *your* swimming beach. You'll see sailboats at anchor, meet the cruising people, and enjoy luncheon or a snack at *Stanley's* or at *Jill's Beach Bar* next door. Stanley himself is a delight to talk to, and the hamburgers are perfect; but the most fun here is the old tire suspended from a giant palm tree so that you can swing back and forth over the crystal sands. The beach itself is gorgeous and the waters calm and lovely.

Then drive further north to Soldier's Hill, where you'll find mango and breadfruit trees and brilliant hibiscus, all overlooking Brewer's Bay (if you're a potential camper, take a look at their grounds). Then turn right and head back toward Road Town, but don't miss the Tropic Isle Shopping Center at the Village Cay Marina. It's ideal for browsing and has a restaurant called the *Upstairs/Downstairs* which appeals to everyone. Chances are that when you take a look at the gourmet dining facilities upstairs, you'll make a reservation for dinner; and chances are that if you plan to be in town the next day, you'll want to come out here for ice cream cones or large mugs of coffee served in their casual open-air Downstairs overlooking the marina.

In the shopping center itself, you can browse for souvenirs, jewelry or china. And don't miss *The Ample Hamper,* a gourmet shop, where they sell everything from mint toffee and anchovy sauce from London's Fortnum and Mason's to rum pepper sauce and BVI Native Seasoning, both of which are made in Tortola from native recipes.

PRACTICAL INFORMATION FOR THE BRITISH VIRGIN ISLANDS

HOW TO GET THERE. By air. From the United States, major airlines service San Juan, St. Croix and Antigua nearby. But be sure to know just where you're going in the B.V.I. since every dot has its "direct" route and what's good for one does not always mean that it's the best route to another. Most routes are combinations of air and sea. For example, to go to Road Town, Tortola, from St. Thomas, fly *AIR BVI* or *Prinair* to Beef Island airport and a taxi for the ½-hour ride into town.

Coral Air flies from St. Croix to Road Town, Tortola; *AIR BVI* from Antigua, San Juan and St. Thomas to Beef Island, Tortola. They also fly inter-island, operating shuttle services to Anegada and Virgin Gorda. *Crown Air* flies to Virgin Gorda from San Juan and St. Thomas; *Prinair* from San Juan.

By sea. From St. Thomas, the *Bomba Charger* and the *Native Son* ferry passengers across to West End, Tortola, in one hour. The *Bomba Charger* then continues on to Road Town. They also run from St. Thomas to Virgin Gorda twice a week. There is local ferry service daily except Sunday between Road Town and Virgin Gorda. Places like Peter Island, Biras Creek and other out-of-the-way spots have their own boats to fetch you upon arrival if you've planned ahead and given them advance notice.

One of the best ways to visit the British Virgin Islands is by sailboat. You can charter from *Caribbean Sailing Yachts* and *The Moorings* out of Tortola, but there are many others (see the listing in the Facts at Your Fingertips section).

FURTHER INFORMATION. The *British Virgin Islands Tourist Board* has an office in Road Town at the Palm Shopping Centre. For information in the U.S., contact John Scott Fones, Inc., 515 Madison Ave., New York, N.Y. 10022. In Canada: British Virgin Islands Information Service, 801 York Mills Road, Don Mills, Ontario, M3B 1X7. In the U.K.: The West India Committee, 48 Albermarle St., London W1X 4AR.

ISLAND MEDIA. The bi-monthly tourist news magazine, *The Welcome,* is chock full of information and is available free throughout the islands. Overseas subscriptions run $9 for one year (write Island Publishing Services Ltd., P.O. Box 133, Road Town, Tortola, B.V.I.). Another magazine, also printed in Tortola and called the *Virgin Islander,* comes out monthly and will be of interest to anyone with an addiction to this part of the Caribbean. For local and some international news, *The Island Sun* newspaper comes out weekly.

AUTHORIZED TOUR OPERATORS. *Caribbean Holidays; Flyfaire;* and *GoGo Tours* from the U.S.

PASSPORTS, VISAS. All visitors must have a valid passport, as well as onward or return air tickets.

MONEY. U.S. currency is used, even though the British Virgin Islands issued their own currency in 1973, in honor of the island's 300 years of constitutional rule. $1.85 U.S. = 1 £.

TAXES AND OTHER CHARGES. All room rates are subject to a 5% government tax. There is a departure tax of $5 per person for those departing by air, $3 per person for those departing by sea.

HOW TO GET ABOUT. Taxis are readily available on Tortola, and the drivers can also arrange for island tours. You can rent a car through *Avis, Budget, National* and *International Car Rentals* on Tortola or the *Virgin Gorda Tours Association* on that island. You'll need a temporary driver's license, which is available for $5 at Police Headquarters or through the car rental firms. Rates begin at $20 per day. Remember to drive on the *left!*

EVENTS AND HOLIDAYS. Carnival (the first weekend in August) and the Spring Regatta are the special highlights throughout the B.V.I. Other holidays are *New Year's Day,* Commemoration of the Visit of the Queen (Feb. 23), Good Friday, Easter Monday, Commonwealth Day, Whit Monday, Territory Day (July 1), St. Ursula's Day (Oct. 21), the Prince of Wales' Birthday (Nov. 14), *Christmas Day* and *Boxing Day* (Dec. 26).

WHAT WILL IT COST?

Since most of the properties on these islands are so scattered, accommodations range from small inns with all three meals, to large resorts that offer meal options at additional charge. The prices are just as varied, but as a guideline, figure on $65 double per day without meals; $90 double with breakfast and dinner; $100 double per day, all three meals included. Add $25 to each to include car rental for one day, plus hotel tax and service.

HOTELS. The inns and cottage colonies of the British Virgins are scattered over several islands, with the greatest concentration on Tortola and Virgin Gorda. Rates here seem high, and they are, but realize that all foodstuffs (except seafood) must be imported. For the big-name places, such as Little Dix, Peter Island and Biras Creek, the high prices reach the top, but so do service and ambience.

ANEGADA

The Reefs Hotel. Reached by air from Beef Island airport, this tiny 12-room inn is the only place to stay on this island. It's on the beach; has a beach bar there and a restaurant at the hotel. $100 double in winter, $89 double off-season, including all three meals. Sport fishing and scuba diving are the main attractions here.

BEEF ISLAND

The Last Resort. A 6-room yachting resort on tiny Bellamy Cay, across the bridge from Tortola. It's run family-style; has a restaurant, bar and nightly entertainment. $50 double all year, including 3 meals.

JOST VAN DYKE

Sandy Ground. The 8 homes-for-rent give you a base for a Robinson Crusoe holiday at reasonable rates. You're strictly on your own, beachside, with food you bring from home or from a provision stop in St. Thomas, U.S.V.I., or Tortola. The property's boat will pick you up at West End, Tortola, which you reach by boat from St. Thomas. $600 per week in winter, $450 per week in the off-season.

White Bay Sandcastle. These 4 octagonal, prefab housekeeping cottages are nestled among the palms and bougainvillea to provide an ideal away-from-it-all atmosphere. Informal housekeeping arrangements just perfect for families or self-sufficient couples. Beautiful beach, which is a favorite for visiting yachtsmen and guests; great restaurant. Your hosts will arrange to pick you up from Red Hook, St. Thomas. $140 double per day in winter, $125 double off-season, all 3 meals included.

MARINA CAY

Marina Cay Hotel. 16 rooms in 8 cottages, each with twin beds, in A-frame buildings on a six-acre treasure isle off Beef Island. Informal, and an ideal atmosphere for water sports (full scuba equipment available). Special shore-side dining area for yachtsmen who've anchored here in season, when guests who have anchored in the rooms for longer get priority at the hilltop *al fresco* restaurant. $210 double in winter, $125 double off-season, all 3 meals included.

PETER ISLAND

Peter Island Hotel and Yacht Harbour. A special resort that is spread out on the only 500 acres that have been developed on this island. The resort was the dream of a Norwegian ship owner who had its prefab units sent over from Norway. 32 rooms in 8 units, furnished in Scandinavian modern; central clubhouse with reception area; lounge, grill room, bar, game rooms and a huge saltwater swimming pool. The beach facilities are at palm-fringed Deadman's Bay. Fine dining with a variety of dishes served in the beachside area or in the more formal dining room. 3 tennis courts, and all marine facilities. Getting there is half the fun–a special launch brings you across from Tortola. From $200 double in winter, $180 double off-season, all 3 meals included.

TORTOLA

Brewers Bay Campground. Started by former employees of the U.S. National Park campground at Cinnamon Bay, St. John, who decided to bring the good idea home and put it into practice. 15 prepared sites and 10 bare sites, with grills and picnic tables. Included with the tents are propane gas stove, ice chest, water container, cooking utensils, picnic table and charcoal grill. Commissary on the premises, as well as cafeteria and bar. Tent sites run $14 per day for 2 persons, $2.50 for each extra person. Bare sites are $5 per day, $1 for each extra person.

CSY Yacht Club. The 8 rooms here are primarily for yachtsmen before or after a CSY charter through B.V.I. waters, but when available they can be rented by others. Waterside, on second floor of modern building, rooms are near the informal bar/restaurant that is a popular gathering spot for people waiting for the Peter Island ferry. All things nautical within arms' reach. $50 double in winter, $35 double off-season, including continental breakfast.

Long Bay Hotel. At West End, the 7 two-bedroom cottages, 20 suites and 6 new villas with 2 beach cabanas each are near a surf beach. All accommodations have kitchenettes; guests convene at central dining/recreation area. Good restaurant. Breakfast and lunch served at beach house, if you choose not to do your own cooking. Commissary for food and liquor. Salt water pool. Rates during the winter run $60 double EP for suites, $84 double for beach cabanas, $94 per day for cottages which accommodate 4 persons. Off-season rates are about half.

Moorings-Mariner Inn. On Wickhams Cay, one mile from Road Town center. 40 lanai-variety rooms with kitchenettes at this modern yachting resort which was built on reclaimed land in 1977. Very pleasant open-air restaurant, informal and popular bar, freshwater pool, tennis court. Marina with slips for 70 boats. Home base for Moorings Yacht Charters. $80 double EP in winter, $44 double EP off-season.

Prospect Reef. 131-room resort complex overlooking Sir Francis Drake Channel. These luxury units are built as condominiums, with suites, cottages and villas, most with kitchenettes. Villas have 2 bedrooms, courtyard, living area; all have modern, colorful appointments and cluster around the shore, with a small harbor and other yachting facilities. Restaurants, bars, choice of swimming pools, 6 tennis courts, water sports. Rates run $95–130 double EP for a cottage, $250 for a villa suitable for 4 persons in season. Inquire about their special package plans to cut costs.

Sebastians on the Beach. An informal spot, located on its own private sands at Little Apple Bay. 29 rooms, most in a two-story unit on the beach; meals served in the main house. Good food and pleasant open-terrace dining. $40–50 double EP in winter, $30 double EP off-season.

Smuggler's Cove. At West End. Rooms are in cottages, with 4 of them beachside and others on the hillside. Restaurant, beach with beach bar, selection of water sports. $53–58 double EP in winter, $43–48 double EP off-season. Special rates for their two- and three-bedroom houses. Informal atmosphere and a place to be on your own if you choose to be.

Sugar Mill Estate Hotel. Great location on the north shore. 13 studios, 4 suites, 3 efficiencies and 1 honeymoon cottage. The kitchens in the units make housekeeping easy. Beach and swimming pool. Babysitters available. Excellent restaurant which draws islanders and visitors for lunch and dinner. From $62 double EP in winter, from $38 double EP off-season.

Treasure Isle. One of the first hotels on this island, the place is a convenient, edge-of-town stopping place. 40 rooms in a tropical setting with sea view from private verandas overlooking Road Harbour. There are a freshwater swimming pool, 3 tennis courts, a squash court. Beach club on nearby Cooper Island. $83 double EP in winter, $48 double EP off-season.

Village Cay Marina. One of the better things to come out of the extensive landfill project at the waterfront in Road Town, the overnighting here has a nautical emphasis since facilities are used by Tortola Yacht Charters before or after sailing. 13 air-conditioned rooms with all modern comforts, 2 restaurants and shopping center surrounding. You can walk into Road Town's center from here. $55 double EP in winter, $34 double EP off-season.

VIRGIN GORDA

Biras Creek. A spectacular 15-cottage resort on a 150-acre chunk of land-with-beach on Gorda Sound. Saltwater pool amid the two-suite cottages (each with twin bedroom, bath, sitting room, patio); 2 tennis courts; superb food. Guests use the beach at Deep Bay and enjoy picnic-lunch stroll to it from rooms. Marina for 30 boats; fuel, ice, water, electricity. Slipway, marine shop, laundry, shower facilities. Taxis meet guests at Virgin Gorda airport and take them to marina jetty for short motor launch trip to hotel. $245 double in winter, $180 double off-season, including all 3 meals.

Bitter End Yacht Club. On Gorda Sound, just south of Prickly Pear Island and near Biras Creek. Popular with yachtsmen and sea-loving types in search of the informal barefoot life. 18 twin-bedded rooms in hillside cottages above the beach. Excellent open-air restaurant; lively clubhouse bar. Nice beach, plus perfect snorkel and scuba areas. Owners make arrangements for day charters (motor or sail) if you haven't sailed in on your own. Guests are met at Virgin Gorda airport, so be specific about your arrival time and flight number. $225 double in winter, $180 double off-season, including all 3 meals.

Fishers Cove Beach Hotel. 8 fully equipped holiday cottages and a new 12-room, two-story hotel on the beach at St. Thomas Bay. Restaurant is famous for its seafood, but there's also a commissary for do-it-yourselfers. Small boats for rent; horseback riding; great snorkeling. $90 double EP per day ($375 per week) in winter, $70 double EP per day ($275 per week) off-season.

Little Dix Bay. 84 lovely rooms in cone-topped cottages stretched around 400 lush acres. Sparkling beach front, all water sports, 5 tennis courts, full marina, commissary, shopping center. Delightful restaurant in the central pavilion serves Caribbean seafood buffets and continental cuisine. A typical *Rockresort* in that Little Dix offers an elegant hideaway with a very rich atmosphere. $285 double per day in winter, $160 double per day off-season, including all meals. But check on special vacation plans for tennis, honeymoons, scuba diving and special combination packages with its Rockresort sister, Caneel Bay Plantation on St. John.

Ocean View Hotel. 12 rooms operated in friendly guest-house atmosphere at the Little Dix marina area. Meals are served at the O'Neal family's seafood restaurant. Casual and comfortable spot. From $70–80 double all year, including breakfast and dinner.

Olde Yard Inn. 10 rooms, each with private bath, in a nice, small hideaway. A large welcoming bar-dining area overlooks the sea. Its restaurant is well known for its French specialties and its extensive wine cellar. Good beaches nearby (drive); fine library, the owner's own collection, now in a breeze-swept gazebo on the premises. Water sports and horseback riding can be arranged. Hiking any of the five trails up to Gorda Peak, or exploring the island by bicycle. $125–145 double in winter, $105 double off-season, including two meals.

HOME RENTALS. There are several homes, apartments and cottages available for rent on a weekly, monthly or longer basis. Contact the British Virgin Islands Tourist Board, P.O. Box 134, Road Town, Tortola, B.V.I., for information.

Among the properties to consider are *Nanny Cay Apartments,* a small condominium development on Tortola with apartments available for rental. Between Road Town and West End, the complex overlooks a yacht marina. Two-bedroom, two-bathroom apartments have kitchens and maid service included. Monthly rates ($700 in winter, $490 off-season) are the best deal.

On Virgin Gorda, the *Guavaberry Spring Bay Vacation Homes* are ideal, with 10 unique vacation sites, 5 of them hexagonal, 3 round and 1 oblong. They're located on a beautiful beach, adjacent to the tumble of giant boulders known as "The Baths," a real wonderland for explorers. Each home has either one or two bedrooms; all have kitchens and dining areas; maid service is included, and supplies can be provided upon request. Commissary on the premises. During the winter one-bedroom homes run $420 per week; $660 per week for two bedrooms. Off-season, $300 per week for one bedroom; $450 for two-bedroom homes.

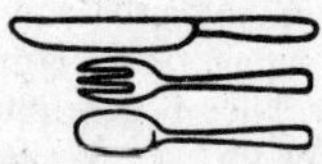

RESTAURANTS. In the B.V.I. dining is always the specialty of the house, usually based on seafood, since almost everything else has to be imported. Owners use their favorite recipes; and reservations are essential everywhere, since the chef cooks to the house count.

BEEF ISLAND: *The Last Resort* serves complete dinners from $10.50. The bar opens at 6:30 P.M. for cocktails; dinner is served at 8 P.M. Among the house specialties are home-made pumpkin soup, roast beef and Yorkshire pudding, roast duckling in brandy sauce.

JOST VAN DYKE: *Abe's at Little Harbour.* Open for lunch and dinner, with choices of chicken, fresh-caught fish or lobster. Lunch from $6, dinners from $7. *Foxy's* place is a legend in these waters, where lobster lunches and dinners are served family-style, from $7.50. Foxy is always on hand; the place is informal, the activity unpredictable and Foxy's calypso songs memorable.

PETER ISLAND: For a special evening, make reservations at the *Yacht Harbour* for dinner and dancing. It's elegant and expensive, but well worth the trip by launch from Tortola.

TORTOLA: *Carib Casseroles.* Basically a take-out place on Main St., but nice for luncheon on its tiny patio. Interesting selection of entrees that include beef and green banana curry ($7.50), sweet and sour pork ($7.75) and chicken in white wine ($6.75). Great selection of hot and cold soups and rich and delectable desserts. *Jill's Beach Bar* is just that, at Cane Garden Bay. Informal, with an atmosphere all its own, and home cooking. Also try *Stanley's* next door for super hamburgers.

Moorings-Mariner Inn: Delightful open-air waterside spot on Wickham's

Cay II. Nautical decor and great food, beginning with full breakfast or Eggs Benedict, the house specialty. Nice selection of omelets, crêpes and sandwiches for luncheon ($5 tops) and lobster, steak and veal dishes for dinner ($10 range). *Pavilion Restaurant/Prospect Restaurant,* both at the Prospect Reef Hotel. Have breakfast or lunch at the *Pavilion* poolside (moderate prices) or dinner at the *Prospect,* where special evenings include steak and lobster specialties (expensive). *Sir Francis Drake Pub* is on the water's edge. Everyone stops here for "elevenses" and to share the local gossip. Lunch and dinner served. Limited menu, which is usually chicken and/or scampi, with $6 top for all. *Sugar Mill Estate Hotel:* Outstanding place for lunch or dinner. Dinners are served in the mill, with American and native dishes featured. Atmosphere is seaside perfect and so is the food (approximately $10 per person) in the evening. Lunch runs $3–4 and can be anything from a terrific hamburger to a tempting chef's salad with crab cakes on the side. *Upstairs-Downstairs:* a very popular place at Village Cay Marina. "Upstairs" is an elegant dining room, for long luncheons and quiet dinners, where the entrees are special and the wine list extensive. "Downstairs" is open-air for breakfast, lunch, dinner. High prices upstairs; moderate below.

VIRGIN GORDA: *Bitter End Yacht Club.* A rendezvous for cruising yachtsmen; they start early here with a full champagne breakfast ($6), offer a club lunch (antipasto buffet, lobster crêpe or club hamburger and dessert ($9), or complete dinners ($14–20) including lobster, fresh fish or steak entrees. Lunch at the *Fishers Cove Beach Hotel* runs about $4 and dinner in the $10 range with wine. Conch dinners are the specialty. *The Bath & Turtle* offers a nice tavern-type atmosphere in the Virgin Gorda Yacht Harbour Shopping Centre. Their "Pub Fare" is served from noon until 9 P.M. and ranges from hamburgers and sandwiches ($1.50–2.75) to steak platters ($8) and broiled local lobster ($9). *The Wheelhouse* is the restaurant at the Ocean View Hotel. Popular with lunchtime wanderers; also open for dinner. Inexpensive; no reservations required. More expensive dining at *Biras Creek* (dinners from $20) and at *Little Dix Bay,* where dinners range from $25 (jackets and reservations required). And, for something different, try the *Olde Yard Inn,* a friendly spot located at The Valley. Good food, with French specialties and wines available. Dinners run from $9–12.

NIGHTLIFE. There is very little on these small islands that concentrate on sun-packed days. Local entertainment by steel and scratch bands and occasional music for dancing at the larger hotels.

SHOPPING. Except for the shops in Road Town on Tortola and those at the Little Dix Marina on Virgin Gorda, there's little to buy here. But chances are, if you sail from one island to another, you'll want to come away with a T-shirt as a memento of each.

SPORTS AND OTHER ACTIVITIES. *Sailing* in the British Virgin Islands is among the best in the Caribbean. Modern marinas have full supplies: Virgin Gorda Yacht Harbour, Leverick Bay Estates and Biras Creek on North Sound at Virgin Gorda, Peter Island Hotel and Yacht Harbour, Drakes Anchorage at Mosquito Island, The Moorings, Village Cay Marina, Nanny Cay Marine Center and Tortola Yacht Services at Road Town, and Indigo Landing opposite the West End Entry Port on Tortola.

Yachts may be chartered through Caribbean Sailing Yachts at Baughers

Bay; The Moorings at Road Harbour; West Indies Yacht Charters at Maya Cove; Tortola Yacht Charters and BVI Bareboats in Road Town; and Latitude 18°25′ at the Nanny Cay Marine Centre.

Tennis is also available, with courts at Long Bay Hotel; Treasure Isle; Prospect Reef; Moorings-Mariner Inn on Tortola; at the Hotel and Yacht Harbour on Peter Island; and at Biras Creek and Little Dix Bay on Virgin Gorda.

CAYMAN ISLANDS

Coral Reefs and Tortoise Shells

The Cayman Islands lie about 180 miles northwest of Jamaica and 480 miles (1 jet hour) south of Miami. They're only slightly closer to Jamaica's west coast than to the southwest of Cuba, which sits in the Caribbean between the Caymans and the Bahamas.

The Islands are essentially three: Grand Cayman, the largest at 22 miles by 8 at its widest; Cayman Brac, named for the Bluff that dominates its skyline; and Little Cayman, across a 7-mile channel from Cayman Brac, with 30 full-time residents. All three splinters occupy slightly more than 100 square miles, so it's no surprise that so little has been heard from this area until recently. The terrain and sights are interesting enough, but it is the Cayman beaches (especially Grand Cayman's Seven Mile Beach, which is a beauty) and the offshore reefs and wrecks which have begun to intrigue a rapidly increasing number of tourists.

History

Although Columbus discovered them on his fourth voyage in May 1503, and named them Las Tortugas, for the turtles that roamed the shores, he didn't linger, but left the colonizing to an assortment of Scottish farmers and shipwrecked buccaneers who followed his lead. The year 1586 brought Sir Francis Drake, fresh from an assault on the Dominican Republic. Caymanas he called these islands, for the crocodiles he found when he landed. The crocodiles have gone; only the iguanas and the turtles remain–and even today's turtles are "tourists." Although they were plentiful during past decades and provided a livelihood for Caymanian fishermen who stalked their prey and sold them for food and fortune, uncontrolled harvesting depleted the supply. It took the combined efforts of a group of British and American enthusiasts to create Cayman Turtle Farm, one of the island's few points of interest—an experimental laboratory where turtle eggs from far-off shores are hatched and cultivated under controlled conditions. Success with the plan, which involves returning some of the young turtles to their shores of origin, has put turtle steak back on the menus of local hotels and has saved a sea animal from possible extinction.

Seafarers have been another of the Cayman Islands "crops." A family tradition of the sea and honesty and integrity from Scottish forebears combine to make the Caymanians some of the most dependable seamen of the world. They can be found on ships in far-off ports of the world; the results of their paychecks can be found in the neat, carefully tended houses that dot the Caymans, home for their wives and families.

The small capital of George Town was named for George II, and an oft-repeated legend gives George III credit for the islands' tax-free status. So impressed was he with the bravery of the Caymanians as they rushed to the rescue of survivors from ten British ships which were wrecked offshore that he is said to have granted permanent tax holidays to all residents.

The Cayman Islands seem oblivious to the movements for independence of nearby neighbors. Sharing none of the enthusiasm for going it alone, they are a British Crown Colony with a governor appointed by the Queen, an Executive Council, and an elected Legislative Assembly.

Grand Cayman, with its 17,000 residents, is the hub of Caymanian activity, most of which is centered on water sports and banking. International finance makes its mark in the crop of banks appearing around George Town, and tax-free investment by foreigners may yet create a new Monaco-in-the-Caribbean here. To be sure, Seven Mile Beach, as West Bay is commonly called, is as grand a strand of sand as we've seen anywhere.

There are now almost two dozen hotels, with a total room capacity of close to 1,500, plus nearly 32 apartments-and-cottages resort complexes. A Department of Tourism is charged with controlling tourism development, avoiding overbuilding, keeping casinos and other forms of gambling out of the islands, encouraging more restaurants, tennis, golf, and other tourist-oriented ventures, increasing flights to the Caymans and training Caymanians, who have proved to be able seamen, to be effective in the tourism complex.

As for Cayman Brac, legend has it that an agreement was reached some years ago that the Presbyterians would not invade that island if the Baptists would stay off Grand Cayman. It's been that way ever since. The huge limestone spine that runs the 12-mile length of the island rises to a peak at the end and drops sharply into the sea. The caves that wind and water have pushed into the limestone were supposedly filled with pirate treasure in that lively era and are now

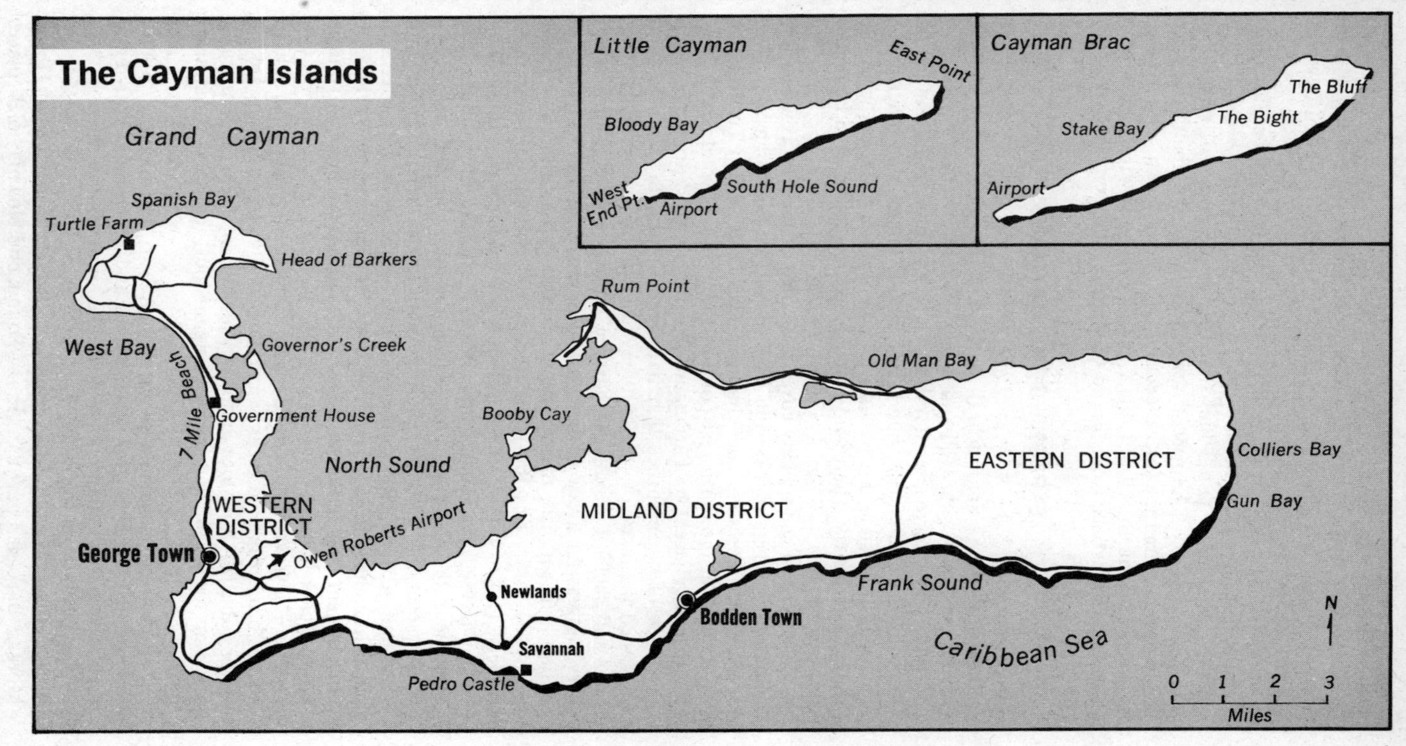
The Cayman Islands
Grand Cayman
Spanish Bay
Turtle Farm
Head of Barkers
West Bay
Governor's Creek
7 Mile Beach
Government House
North Sound
WESTERN DISTRICT
George Town
Owen Roberts Airport
Booby Cay
Rum Point
Old Man Bay
MIDLAND DISTRICT
EASTERN DISTRICT
Colliers Bay
Gun Bay
Frank Sound
Bodden Town
Newlands
Savannah
Pedro Castle
Caribbean Sea
N
0 1 2 3
Miles
Little Cayman
East Point
Bloody Bay
South Hole Sound
West End Pt.
Airport
Cayman Brac
The Bluff
The Bight
Stake Bay
Airport

diversion for treasure hunters who occasionally pluck a few hidden coins from the recesses. It's more usual to find the iguana, which now calls that hole home.

Finally, there is Little Cayman, which is just that, not because of its size–it measures ten miles long by two miles wide–but because of its sparse population. You'll find that the people here will regale you with their history. The special favorite is the bloody battle between island soldiers and the buccaneers.

Both Cayman Brac and Little Cayman can be day trips because of expanded air service from Grand Cayman.

EXPLORING THE CAYMANS

On shore there's not much. It can be done in a day and a half–less if you don't care about Hell and Roger's Wreck. The real exploring is offshore, where there are a number of wrecks jammed into and on the reefs that enclose North Sound, East End Channel, and other areas. Diving instruction is easy to come by (see Sports), and even beginners should give it a try. There's no better place. Equipment can be rented (see below).

On land, you can quickly cover the sights of George Town–a few trim houses, several banks, and a couple of free-port shops.

The most interesting and unique sight is the Cayman Turtle Farm on 10 acres at the northwest point of the island, beyond Seven Mile Beach and adjacent to Turtleland, its sister tourist attraction. When the stock of green turtles that had been natural to this area (and suggested the name of Las Tortugas to Columbus) was depleted for food and shells, the native fishermen turned to other waters, often harvesting as far away as the coast of South America. At one point during a recent visit, the farm had 100,000 green turtles of various ages. The turtle, like the palm tree, is 100% useful. In addition to turtle steak and *calipee,* the fleshy part is used for soups, the hide or leather is used for shoes, bags and so forth, the fat produces the cosmetic turtle oil, a *pâté* is made from the liver, the shells are sold as whole pieces or for jewelry, and the rest of the turtle finds its way into stews and pet food. (Remember, you can't come away with what you see. Turtles have been designated an endangered species by the U.S. Government and it is illegal for U.S. citizens to bring *any* turtle product back home.)

After you've visited Cayman Turtle Farm, go to Hell, that abused area of black, rumpled rocks where the Post Office and stamps are the major industry. Other local industries include rope making (you pay a few coins for the privilege of watching the local folk weave) and hammocks.

Leisurely day excursions might include a trip across North Sound by boat to Rum Point for water sports and lunch and a car-rental roam around the island to look at the ruins of two forts, one at Prospect Point and the other, Fort George, on the outskirts of town. And go on to Pedro Castle, reputed to be the former lair of Henry Morgan. Bat caves, parrots at Frank Sound, and blowing holes (places in the shoreline rock where the sea pushes the water into spouts) are other island sights to enjoy.

PRACTICAL INFORMATION FOR THE CAYMANS

HOW TO GET THERE. The islands are served by *Cayman Airways* with 40 weekly flights from Miami to Grand Cayman and between Grand Cayman, Little Cayman and Cayman Brac. *Republic Airlines* has daily service from Miami to Grand Cayman, and weekly service from Fort Lauderdale. *Cayman Airways* provides the link between Grand Cayman and Kingston, Jamaica, and also flies non-stop from Houston. *Red Carpet Flying Service* has flights between Tampa and Cayman Brac. Charter flights also are available. Inquire about special mid-week day tours and excursion rates within the islands.

By Sea. Ships of *Carnival Cruise Lines, Royal Caribbean Line,* and *Norwegian Caribbean Line* call at Grand Cayman.

TOURIST INFORMATION. The *Cayman Islands Department of Tourism* has offices in Florida at 250 Catalonia Avenue, Suite 604, Coral Gables 33134, in New York at 420 Lexington Ave., Suite 2312, New York, N.Y. 10017; in Texas at 9999 Richmond Ave., Suite 131, Houston, Tex. 77042; in California at 3440 Wilshire Blvd., Los Angeles, CA 90010; in Chicago at 333 North Michigan Ave., Chicago, Ill. 60601; in Canada at 11 Adelaide St. W., Suite 406, Toronto, Ontario M5H 1L9; in London at 48 Albermarle St., London W1, England W1X4AR. The mail address is Box 67, George Town, Grand Cayman, B.W.I.

ISLAND MEDIA. Ask for the *Cayman Islands Holiday Guide,* an excellent booklet full of facts, before you go. On the island, the publications include *The Cayman Times,* published twice a week; the *Caymanian Compass,* the weekly newspaper; and a monthly magazine called *The Northwester.*

AUTHORIZED TOUR OPERATORS. *Butler Travels, Caribbean Holidays,* and *Pathfinder* from the U.S.; *Fairway Tours,* and *Holiday House* from Canada.

PASSPORTS, VISAS. Not required for U.S. or Canadian visitors. However, you will need some proof of citizenship as well as your return ticket.

MONEY. The Cayman Islands dollar is based on the U.S. dollar, but not at par. $1 U.S. equals about 80¢ Caymanian, but check exchange rates when you go. It's advisable to exchange U.S. dollars at the bank to get the best rate, and be sure, when prices are quoted, which dollar you are discussing.

TAXES AND OTHER CHARGES. Hotels add a 5% government tax on rooms and usually a service charge of 10–15%. The airport departure tax is $4 US.

HOW TO GET ABOUT. A taxi and driver cost about $60 for an 8-hour day and, frankly, there's not that much to see on Grand Cayman or either of the other islands. The Cayman Islands Taxi Association meets all planes arriving at Owen Roberts Airport. Your fare to town will be about $5 and to most hotels on Seven Mile Beach between $8 and $10. From the airport to *Tortuga Club* the taxi fare runs $30, but they will meet you if they know when you're coming.

If you plan to stay out that far and want mobility, you'd do better to rent a car. *Ace Hertz, Cico-Avis, Coconut Car Rentals* and *National Car Rentals* have similar rates, which run from $16–30 per day depending upon the time of year. On Cayman Brac, *S&H Rentals* rents cars. Bicycles may be rented from *Cayman Bicycles* in George Town. They have tandems in addition to their regular bikes, and this island is flat enough to make bike riding fun. Hondas from *Caribbean Motors* are about $9 per day. There are some 80 miles of motorable roads on Grand Cayman and 21 on Cayman Brac. About 30 miles of road on Grand Cayman are surfaced with macadam. Driving permits are issued by the rental agencies when you show your hometown license. Remember to drive on the left. For those who'd rather ride than drive, there is inexpensive, frequent bus service along Seven Mile Beach, between George Town and West End, stopping at all hotels.

EVENTS AND HOLIDAYS. The outstanding special events here are *Discovery Day* (third Monday in May), which is celebrated with a sailboat regatta; the parades which herald the *Queen's Birthday* (June 12); and *Pirates' Week* (late October), which is now an annual event and includes parades, mini-festivals, land and underwater treasure hunts and a grand costume ball. Other island holidays are *New Year's Day, Ash Wednesday, Good Friday, Easter Monday, Constitution Day* (first Monday in July), *Christmas Day,* and *Boxing Day* (Dec. 26).

WHAT WILL IT COST?

Hotel rates vary so in the Cayman Islands, with many places on Grand Cayman and Cayman Brac including two meals in the winter rate, and so many apartments and cottages available, that it is possible to keep costs to a minimum. However, an average day in season for *two* persons will run:

	US$	£
Hotel with breakfast and dinner included	100	54
Light luncheon at hotel or in town	15	8
Tip or service charge at the restaurant; tax and service charge at the hotel	15	8
Car or boat rental for one full day	20	11
	$150	£81

STAYING IN THE CAYMAN ISLANDS

HOTELS. Know before you go that most of the hotels are on Seven Mile Beach, also called West Bay, an uncrowded stretch of powdery sand that makes sunglasses essential. Whether you stay on Grand Cayman or on Cayman Brac, you can be assured of a variety of watersports and a feeling of isolation that makes these islands unique.

GRAND CAYMAN

Beach Club Colony. On Seven Mile Beach, forty-one hotel units with two rooms per cottage, all air-conditioned, with private patios and a choice of ocean or garden view. The *Sea Grape Room* is set up for dinner, the outdoor, beachfront *Patio Veranda* serves breakfast, lunch and dinner. The *Canoe Disco* has music until 1 A.M. Tennis court, all watersports, beach barbecues with calypso music. New beachfront condo units are scheduled to open in the late fall of 1982. $93–143 double EP in winter; $69–82 double EP off-season. MAP available at $33 per person in season.

Caribbean Club. On Seven Mile Beach, with eighteen one- and two-bedroom villas, each fully equipped. Nice dining room and lounge, *The Green Turtle Bar,* which draws a congenial crowd. Rates run from $155 EP for a one-bedroom villa to $220 EP for two bedrooms in winter.

Casa Bertmar. A small property with 25 rooms located one mile south of George Town. Facilities are simple, but all rooms have private bath. Bar, restaurant on premises. Also a dive shop and a dive boat at the ready. $95 double in winter, $82 double off-season, with two meals.

Cayman Kai Resort. On the north side of Grand Cayman, near Rum Point. Seventy units include twenty-six one- and two-bedroom sea lodges and twenty deluxe villas with kitchenettes and maid service. The sea lodges rent for $70 EP for one bedroom, $168 EP for two in winter; $45 for one and $85 for two EP off-season.

Galleon Beach Hotel. A tennis court lighted for night play provides diversion after a day of swimming and/or strolling Seven Mile Beach or parasailing over it. Thirty-three rooms, all air-conditioned, and with balcony or patio. Restaurant and cocktail lounge, entertainment on some evenings. $85–105 double EP in winter; $75 double EP off-season.

Grand Caymanian Holiday Inn. 215 rooms that rise up or along Seven Mile Beach. This hotel put the island into the big time when it opened all its doors in 1972. Here you have a free-form swimming pool; three bars, including one *in* the pool; restaurant, nightclub and floodlit tennis courts. All watersports available on its beach, including instruction and equipment rental. From $98 double EP in winter; and from $78 double EP off-season.

Royal Palms. Another Seven Mile Beach enclave, this hotel has sixty-two round-the-pool rooms and forty one- and two-bedroom suites. It also has two restaurants, a nightclub, and a freshwater swimming pool. From $80 double EP in winter; from $60 double EP off-season. For MAP, add $24 per person per day.

Tortuga Club. A fourteen-room hideaway about an hour's drive from town. The atmosphere is informal; the emphasis is on watersports. Sunfish are free for guests and so are the hammocks tied to trees. The bar is at the beach, and so is most of the conviviality. $159 double per day in winter, $95 double off-season, with breakfast and dinner included.

CAYMAN BRAC

Brac Reef. This thirty-one-room hotel sits on the unspoiled island's south shore, and each room has an ocean view. Also two oceanfront suites available. Guests have an option of swimming in the Caribbean or in the saltwater swimming pool. Large dining room, cocktail lounge, tennis courts. $75 double EP in winter, $59 double EP off-season.

Buccaneer's Inn. With thirty-four rooms on this relatively isolated island, this place offers solitude. The inn specializes in seafood and native cooking. The open-air bar faces the road from the airport. Exploring the island and the waters offshore is the main reason for coming here. Pool on premises; beaches nearby. Scuba diving and fishing can be arranged. $115 double in winter, $97–112 double off-season, including all three meals.

LITTLE CAYMAN

Kingston Bight Lodge. Small resort property with 8 units and more abuilding. Popular with divers and fishermen. Bar, dining room. $90 double per day year-round, with all three meals included.

HOME RENTALS. Two apartment hotels with facilities that leave you independent (and on Seven Mile Beach) are *Harbour Heights,* with air-conditioned suites with two double bedrooms, living room, dinette kitchen, also a swimming pool and game room. And *Victoria House,* with studios, one- and two-bedroom apartments and a penthouse that can accommodate up to six people.

The Cayman Islands are probably the leaders in the do-it-yourself holidays. There's an awesome list of apartments, cottages, and villas. On the island, *Cayman Rent-A-Villas,* c/o P.O. Box 681, Grand Cayman, has a complete listing of one-, two- and three-bedroom apartments. There are more than two dozen places, some on Cayman Brac and Little Cayman, where good-size cottages that can house four people run about $250 per week.

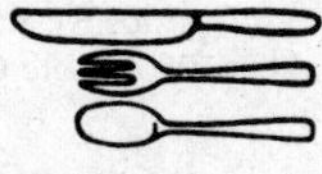

RESTAURANTS. Unless you've rented an apartment or a cottage, you'll probably find the hotel dining rooms serving varied enough menus so that you'll stay put. Otherwise, venture out and try a few of Grand Cayman's special spots; most are in George Town.

We call $6 and under *Inexpensive;* $7–15 *Moderate;* $16 and above *Expensive.* And don't forget you're on *Las Tortugas,* named for the turtles, so that those turtle steaks, soups, etc. are definitely the Cayman's "King of the Sea."

Almond Tree. The only thatched-roof restaurant on the island, this one puts the emphasis on seafood served with a South Pacific flair, and exotic rum drinks that are bound to please. *Moderate.*

Cayman Arms. Casual and convivial spot on the waterfront, which is especially nice for lunch. *Inexpensive.*

Grand Old House. Nice dining here, either on the terrace or indoors, with dinner by candlelight served by barefoot waitresses in costumes of a bygone era. What they are re-creating is the old plantation Great House atmosphere, and they succeed. The menu has a special French flair, and the wine list seems to put it all together. The place to have reservations beforehand, and to linger afterward. *Expensive.*

Lobster Pot. Very pleasant dining at the water's edge in George Town. You'll find the seafood delectable. *Moderate.*

NIGHTLIFE. While the hotels offer some form of entertainment, be it disco or a local steel band, there aren't any "in spots" late at night. The emphasis in the Cayman Islands is watersports, so they aren't the place for you if you are a Night owl!

SHOPPING. It's not reason for a Cayman vacation. There is duty-free shopping, but the prices are not always that much lower than in hometown discount stores. *Soto's Freeport Limited,* which has three shops, and *Far Away Places, Ltd.,* which is located in the Olde Fort Building in George Town, are especially popular for duty-free imports.

Try the *Kirk Freeport Gallery* for china and crystal; *Treasure Cove* for jewelry and watches; *Cayman Camera* for the latest photographic equipment.

For Caymanian crafts (mostly seashell jewelry and thatch products), contact the *Craft Market, Camandicraft,* or the *Cayman Curio Shop,* all in George Town. If you have a place for it, one of the most interesting items is a hammock you watch them weave for you. (Don't set your heart on it, though; they're not always in the mood.) For paintings by local artists (all of varying quality, mostly Sunday painters), stop in *Cayman Art Ventures* and the *Viking Gallery.*

SPORTS. The Caymans excel in all the water sports. *Swimming, water skiing, skin diving,* and *fishing* are all superb. There are many places to dive for wrecks around the islands.

Deep-sea fishing costs from $80 to $140 for a party of four for a full day, depending on your guide, and you'll track wahoo (Nov.-March), blue marlin, dolphin (all year), bonita, barracuda, and albacore. *Bottom fishing* costs about $40 for a half-day. There's challenging *spear-fishing* near the reefs. Scuba divers are not allowed to spear-fish, but free-divers can bring up 3 fish or 3 lobsters during season per day. No lobsters can be taken from Feb. 1 through July 31.

Recommended sources for water sports are *Cayman Kai* near Rum Point; *Tortuga Club, Cayman Shores, Harbour House Marina, Surfside Water Sports* at *Galleon Beach Hotel* and *Royal Palms Hotel F.L.A.G. Underwater Services, Spanish Bay Reef* and the *Cayman Diving Lodge.* On Cayman Brac, *Buccaneer's Inn* has equipment and services.

There are several Sunfish sailboats for use from hotel beaches. Big-time sailing hasn't hit there in full force, perhaps because there are few places to sail to without hitting rough seas and crinkly reefs.

Several hotels and apartments have *tennis* courts, some lighted for night-play. *Parasailing* is the latest sport to come to the Caymans. Available through *Surfside Water Sports* at the Galleon Beach Hotel.

CURAÇAO

A Dutch Gambol

It's all very Dutch in Curaçao, from the language to the three-masted schooners at anchor in St. Anna Bay. The largest of the six islands that form the Netherlands Antilles, Curaçao measures 173 square miles and is home for almost 160,000 people.

Although the island lies less than forty miles north of South America, the influence is strictly Dutch colonial. The homes are scrubbed and gleaming and, painted as they are in a variety of pastel colors, give the island a sparkling storybook look.

While Curaçao has its share of beaches, they can't compare with those of its sister islands, Aruba and Bonaire. The emphasis on this island is its shopping, fine dining, and enchanting capital city of Willemstad. The official language is Dutch, but the dialect of the people is a mixture of Dutch, English, Spanish, Portuguese, Indian and African. It's called *Papiamento.* Sounds difficult, but you'll be surprised at how much of it you can understand, especially if you know a little Spanish. Do you have to know Papiamento to get along? Not at all. As one Curaçao businessman put it: "We are Dutch, so we all speak English."

History

Curaçao was discovered, not by Columbus, but by Alonzo de Ojeda in 1499, and was first occupied by the Spaniards in 1527. In 1634, the Dutch arrived under the auspices of the Netherlands West India Company, banished the Spanish Governor and 400 assorted Spaniards and Indians to Venezuela, and set up a colony. Peter Stuyvesant became its governor in 1642, a post he held for three years before heading north to New York. Over the years the British and the French made stabs at capturing the island until the Dutch claim was firmly sealed by the Treaty of Paris in 1815. In 1954 Curaçao became an autonomous part of the Kingdom of the Netherlands, with its own parliament, Island Council, and a governor who is appointed by the Queen to represent the Crown.

EXPLORING CURAÇAO

The best place to begin is Willemstad, where St. Anna Bay cuts right through the capital city like an Amsterdam canal. A pontoon bridge connects the shopping area, the Punda, with the Otrabanda, which is easily translated as "the other side." One of the chief diversions in Willemstad is watching the Koningin Emma Brug, or Queen Emma Bridge, swing open to let ships pass into and out of the harbor, which it does on an average of thirty times a day. It is amusing to watch people scrambling to get across this floating bridge in order to avoid the fifteen- to twenty-minute wait or the trip by ferry. The bridge, which moves under your feet, was built in 1888 and used to be a toll bridge. The fare was two cents if you wore shoes, free if you were barefoot. The economic principle of this graduated toll was to tax each according to his ability to pay, but the authorities forgot the foibles of human nature. The proud poor begged, borrowed, or bought sandals for the "privilege" of paying two cents, while wealthy American tourists gaily kicked off their shoes and crossed the bridge barefoot as a lark. The toll eventually was abandoned. Although a multi-million-dollar wide-span bridge, the Queen Juliana, was opened in 1974, the historic Queen Emma pontoon remains.

Just as colorful an attraction is the native schooner market on the small canal leading to Waaigat, a yacht basin on the Punda side. Dozens of sailboats from different islands tie up at the Ruyterkade. Bartering still goes on here, but there is also a modern, air-conditioned market for those who prefer it. The produce is about the same at both markets, but clearly the one that "floats" is the most colorful. You will find fruit, vegetables, fresh fish, and even fabric to entice you—to buy, or just to photograph all the excitement of the morning scene.

In Willemstad, nearly everything is within short walking distance of the center of town. One highlight is Fort Amsterdam, no longer a fort but the dignified seat of government. Here is the handsome Governor's Palace and the beautiful old Dutch Reformed Church, built in 1769. A cannon ball fired by the English in 1804 is still embedded in its walls. The Mikve Israel Synagogue, perhaps the oldest in the Western hemisphere, was built in 1732 and is an outstanding example of eighteenth-century Dutch architecture. The interior is dignified and rich, with white sand, symbol of the Jews wandering in the desert before they reached the Promised Land, covering the floor like a thick carpet. The twenty-four-candle brass chandeliers which hang from the mahogany ceiling are replicas of those in the Portuguese Synagogue in Amsterdam.

Some of Curaçao's loveliest homes are in the Scharloo residential district on the Punda side. Here the Franklin D. Roosevelt House, splendidly situated on top of Ararat Hill, overlooks the city and the sea on the approach road to the new Queen Juliana bridge. It is a rare example of a gift to the United States by a local population, instead of vice-versa.

North of the Scharloo section is Fort Nassau, an impressive bastion built in 1792 on a 220-foot-high hill overlooking the city. In those days it housed the military. Today it welcomes visitors who come to explore and then to dine at its fine restaurant.

On the Otrabanda side of the pontoon bridge, see the statue of Pedro Luis Brión, which dominates the square called Brionplein. Another point of interest on the Otrabanda, but farther out on Leeuwenhoekstraat, is the Curaçao Museum, a former military hospital which was carefully restored as a fine example of Dutch architecture. Its gardens, containing specimens of all the island's plants and trees, are worth a visit. The museum is furnished with antiques, paintings and *objets d'art.* There are art exhibitions, as well as relics of the primitive Indian tribes which once lived on these islands.

At Chobolobo you'll find the Senior Liqueur Factory, distillers of the original Curaçao Liqueur, made from oranges grown locally. Close by, in the Gaito residential district, is the Centro Pro Arte, where concerts, ballets and plays are presented. Exhibits of paintings, sculpture, and other arts are held on a regular basis.

A DAY ON YOUR OWN

Since shopping is *the* highlight of a visit to Curaçao, allow a half-day (morning preferably) for Willemstad and a full afternoon for a drive to the island's northern tip.

Begin your walking tour in town at De Ruyterkade on the Punda side to see the Floating Market at its best. Then turn right on Columbusstraat to the Mikve Israel Synagogue and Jewish Museum. Then walk toward St. Anna Bay and the Plaza Piar where the Curaçao Plaza Hotel commands the waterfront. The hotel is built within the "Waterfort," a bastion completed in 1634. It's just as dramatic today as it must have been then, with cannons still set on the battlements to ward off invaders. Cross the square then and visit old Fort Amsterdam, which was also built in the seventeenth century. Today it is Curaçao's historic center and seat of government. See the old Fort Church and the Governor's Palace.

Now have a spree in one of the best shopping centers in the Caribbean. Within its five square blocks you'll find dozens of shops offering everything from island-made straw hats to emerald-and-diamond tiaras (see our section on *Shopping* for full details).

Head out of town for a pleasant lunch at Fort Nassau's Cafe Restaurant. Enjoy the view from the hilltop while you sample the Dutch specialties of the day. Then swing westward from Willemstad toward Piscadera Bay to the main road leading northwest. If you follow that road, you'll reach Landhuis Jan Kock, a seventeenth-century estate that is filled with antiques. It is worth a stop. There are several other country houses in this area, where the architecture is basically Dutch, with a Spanish touch of color and scroll work.

You'll find the landscape arid and cactus-spiked. Some cacti rise more than twenty feet in the air, and the divi-divi trees bend to the will of the trade winds. Flaming flamboyant trees punctuate the dry countryside from time to time, and you'll see a few picturesque thatched native huts that have not yet succumbed to the new and modern. It is in this countryside, or *cunucu,* that you may hear the happy rhythm of the *tumba,* Curaçao's "national" dance, with its traces of everything from the Latin American rumba to an Irish jig. Throughout the *cunucu* you'll see families weaving straw, women pounding cornmeal, and native fishermen casting their nets, occupations that are as old as time.

Follow the main road toward the coast, through the village of Soto and on up to Westpunt, or West Point, near the island's northern point. This is the perfect spot for a swim and then a wonderful seafood snack high above the beach at the Playa Forti Restaurant. If time permits, visit Boca Tabla nearby. The grotto here has been carved by the sea. If you plan to explore it, bring sturdy shoes.

Then it's back to your hotel for a well-earned rest before seeing Curacao by night, which means dining, dancing and casino-hopping until 4 A.M.!

PRACTICAL INFORMATION FOR CURAÇAO

HOW TO GET THERE. By air. *American Airlines* flies non-stop from New York; *Eastern Airlines* non-stop from Miami; *ALM,* the Dutch Antillean Airline, flies in from Miami and San Juan, and also links Curaçao with Bonaire, Aruba and St. Martin. There are special excursion fares, and Curaçao is included in an Aruba or Bonaire roundtrip if you make your plans in advance.

By sea. Over 200 cruises from Miami and Port Everglades, in addition to those from San Juan, stop in Curaçao. Among them are the ships of *Chandris Cruises, Costa Line, Cunard Line, Holland America Cruises, Home Lines, Norwegian American Line, Royal Caribbean Cruise Line, Royal Viking,* and *Sitmar Cruises.*

FURTHER INFORMATION. The *Curaçao Tourist Board* has its Tourist Information Office on Plaza Pier, near old Fort Amsterdam, at the edge of St. Anna Bay. For information in New York, contact their office at 685 Fifth Ave., New York, N.Y. 10022.

ISLAND MEDIA. For further reading, the *Curaçao Holiday* yellow sheet is a twenty-page giveway that is crammed with all the latest news on shopping, sports, and other island attractions. *Radio Korsow, Radio Victoria,* and *Trans World Radio* have daily newscasts in English. Consult the yellow sheet for specific times.

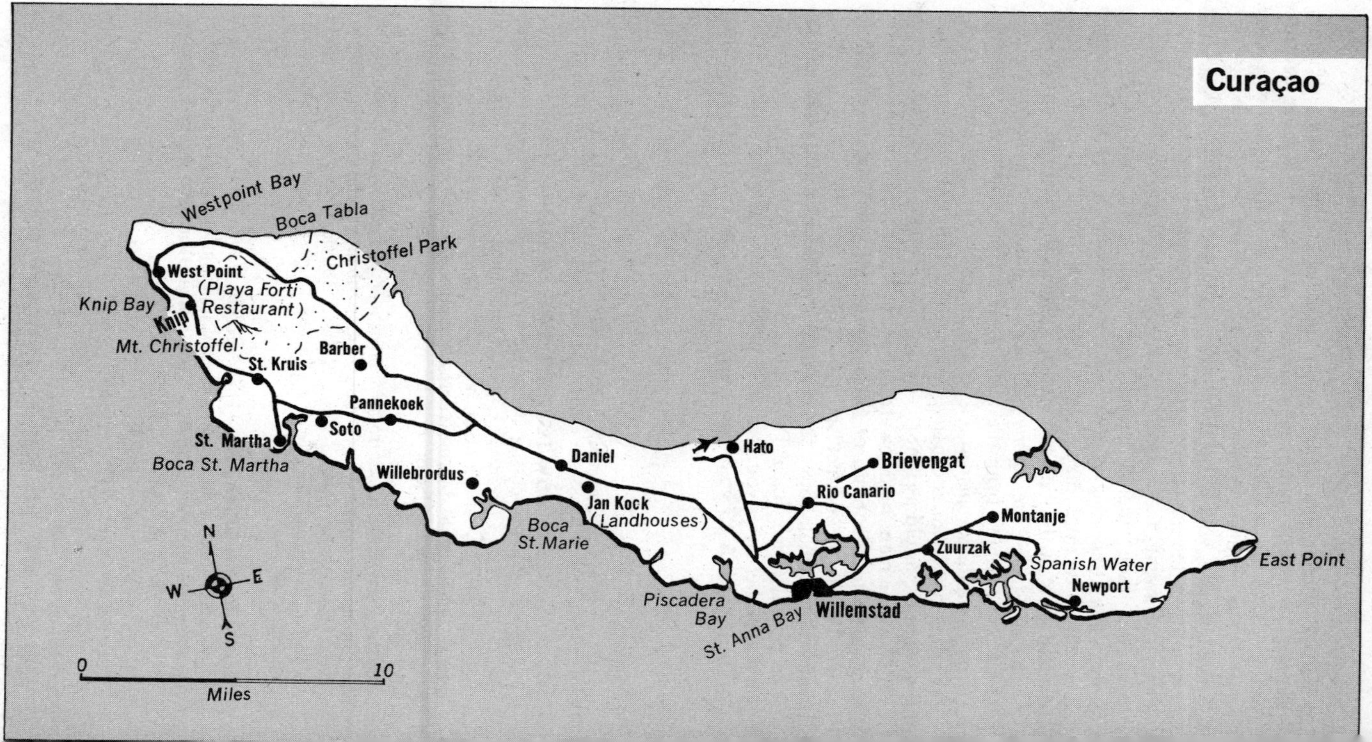

Curaçao
Westpoint Bay
Boca Tabla
Christoffel Park
West Point
(Playa Forti
Restaurant)
Knip Bay
Knip
Mt. Christoffel
Barber
St. Kruis
Pannekoek
Soto
St. Martha
Boca St. Martha
Willebrordus
Daniel
Jan Kock
(Landhouses)
Boca
St. Marie
Hato
Brievengat
Rio Canario
Montanje
Zuurzak
Spanish Water
Newport
East Point
Piscadera
Bay
St. Anna Bay
Willemstad
N
E
W
S
0
10
Miles

AUTHORIZED TOUR OPERATORS. *Adventure Tours, Butler Travels, Caribbean Holidays, Cavalcade Tours, Flyfaire, Go Go Tours,* and *Red & Blue Tours* from the U.S.

PASSPORTS, VISAS. United States and Canadian citizens need only some proof of identity, such as a passport, birth certificate or voter's registration card. Passports are required of all other visitors. In addition, all visitors to the island must hold a return or ongoing ticket.

MONEY. The guilder or florin (both names are used interchangeably, although prices are marked with fl.) is the Netherlands Antilles' unit of money, subdivided into 100 cents. It is issued in all denominations, including a square nickel, a good souvenir that has been worked into key rings and the like. The official rate of exchange is US $1 = 1.77 NAf; 1 £ = 3.96 NAf.

TAXES AND OTHER CHARGES. All room rates are subject to a 5% government tax. Hotels also add a 10% service charge to your bill. The airport departure tax is $5.75 per person.

WHAT WILL IT COST?

A typical day on Curaçao in season for *two* persons will run:

	US$	£
Hotel accommodations	80	44
Full breakfast at the hotel	10	5
Lunch at a moderate restaurant	15	8
Dinner at one of the island's finest restaurants	40	22
Tip or service charge at the restaurants; tax and service charge at hotels	20	11
One-day sightseeing by rental car	20	11
	$185	£101

HOW TO GET ABOUT. Walk through Willemstad, which is divided into two sections–the Punda (shopping area) and the Otrabanda (the "other side," with a few good shops of its own). Motorists can cross over the Queen Juliana Bridge, while pedestrians still use the famous Queen Emma pontoon bridge, one of the major tourist sights in Willemstad.

There are public buses for trips to the airport, suburbs, or out into the country; terminals are at Wilhelmina Square on the Punda side and at Brion Square on Otrabanda. Most visitors use either the complimentary bus service provided by the hotels, or the taxis, with rates of $8 per hour or part thereof. All fares are 50% higher for night drives. The drivers have an official tariff chart. Ask to see it. Fare from the airport to Willemstad is $7 for a cab, up to four people. Free ferry service is available for pedestrians and cyclists between Punda and Otrabanda when the pontoon bridge is closed to traffic.

Sightseeing on Curaçao can be done in one day, with extra time spent in Willemstad. Tours are offered by *Gray Line, Mike's Tours,* and *Taber Tours,* ranging from $7 per person for a 2½-hour city and suburbs tour, to $17 per person for an island tour, which includes luncheon and swimming. You can rent a car from *Avis, Budget, National,* or *Hertz,* among others, but unless you have business reasons for wanting a car, you can make do with the free transportation services from your hotel and an occasional taxi. A temporary driver's permit is available at Police Headquarters–just show your own driver's licence. Cars rent from $18 per day; from $115 per week. Gasoline and mileage charges are extra.

EVENTS AND HOLIDAYS. *Carnival* is king here, and is heralded by parades and dancing in the streets. In addition, on this "international" island there are special celebrations to mark Chinese New Year, India Republic Day, U.S. Independence Day, Bastille Day, Rosh Hashana, and St. Nicholas Day.

The official holidays are *New Year's Day, Carnival Monday, Good Friday, Easter Monday,* the *Queen's Birthday* (April 30), *Labor Day* (May 1), *Ascension Day, Kingdom Day* (Dec. 15), *Christmas Day,* and *Boxing Day* (Dec. 26).

STAYING IN CURAÇAO

HOTELS. Oddly enough, for an island that is thirty-eight miles long, there are just seven large hotels, all in the Willemstad area except for one on the coast near the island's northern tip.

Arthur Frommer Hotel. Built primarily with groups and budget travel in mind, the hotel offers one of the best beachside values, especially if you share one of the ninety-five two-bedroom villas. There are also 100 rooms in the main building, with restaurant, coffee shop, pub, and other facilities. Swimming pool, tennis courts, watersports. Shuttle bus service into Willemstad. Not for those who insist on top luxury, but ideal for fun-loving visitors in search of casual comforts. Rooms run $79–83 double EP in winter, $52–56 double EP off-season. The two-bedroom villas are $113 in winter, $85 in off-season.

Avila Beach Hotel. In Willemstad's residential section, on the ocean, and with a private beach. The forty-five air-conditioned rooms have spread out from what was once a Governor's mansion. Outdoor bar in the form of the bow of sailing vessel is called the *Schooner Bar.* Open-air dining on a terrace overlooking the sea. $44–62 double EP in winter, $41–59 double EP off-season.

Coral Cliff Hotel. Thirty-five attractive rooms in cottages in the secluded Santa Martha Bay area. Patio restaurant for oceanfront dining, tennis courts, sports fishing, snorkeling. Ideal for families and those who want luxury at reasonable prices. $85 double in winter, $75 double off-season, including Continental breakfast.

Curaçao Hilton Hotel. Dutch archways have been adapted and incorporated into this member of the chain, but otherwise you'll recognize all the typical Hiltoniana. There's a small beach with a netted area to assure fish-free swimming, and a fresh-water pool that's popular with the guests. Poolside eating and drinking areas. Sauna, tennis courts, coffee shop and elegant dining area. Octagonal casino and nightclub with professional entertainment that makes the circuit. $96–121 double EP in winter, $73–96 double EP off-season.

Curaçao Plaza Hotel. Seldom has there been such a happy combination of site and architecture as in this hostelry built right into the massive walls of a seventeenth-century water fort at the entrance to Willemstad's beautiful harbor. The ramparts rising from the sea have been left intact and now serve as a promenade for guests. A dramatic fourteen-story tower, which was added on some years after the hotel was built, has spectacular rooms with balconies overlooking the water. No beach here, but a swimming pool with shaded patio, two restaurants, night club and discotheque, a casino and a congenial bar with specialty drinks. $75–99 double EP in winter, $55–79 off-season.

Holiday Beach Hotel & Casino. 200 rooms, all with private balconies, on Coconut Beach. Freshwater swimming pool, all watersports, tennis courts. Restaurant, bar, coffee shop, and nightclub, with the casino an added bonus. $78–99 double EP in winter, $60–66 off-season.

Princess Beach Hotel and Casino. There are 140 rooms on a small beach that is one of the best in the Willemstad area. Swimming pool with sundeck, lounge chairs and poolside bar. Coffee shop and elegant dining room. Nightclub for dancing and entertainment, popular casino, tennis on premises, golf nearby. $69–79 double EP in winter, $53–65 off-season.

HOME RENTALS. There aren't many homes for rent on Curaçao. Your best source of information is either the Curaçao Tourist Board, or *Caribbean Home Rentals,* P.O. Box 710, Palm Beach, Fla. 33480.

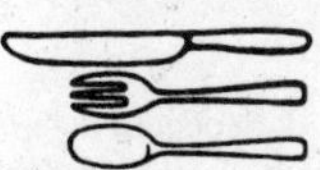

RESTAURANTS. The basic cuisine of Curaçao is Dutch with Latin American, Indonesian, and Chinese complements. Sometimes it tends to be on the heavy side, especially for the tropics. Nevertheless, try *Java honden povtie* (a hound's portion), which is an Indonesian dish consisting of a central mound of rice topped by two fried eggs and surrounded by steak, potatoes, and a variety of vegetables. The seasonings include curry powder, soy sauce, and a pimento paste, all of it guaranteed to make you breathe fire.

Perhaps the most famous Indonesian dish set before the tourists here is *Rijsttafel,* or rice table. A mountainous portion of rice is accompanied by a choice of at least twenty side dishes. *Erwtensoep* is a famous Dutch pea soup which is thickened with fat pork and sausage. Don't plan to eat anything else with it—it's two meals in itself. Then there's *Keshi Yena,* cheese, usually of the Edam variety, stuffed with meat or fish and baked.

The cosmopolitan character of Curaçao is reflected in its food. You can find French, Italian, Argentinian, and Swiss cuisine, Chinese, Indonesian, and typical American meals. Seafood is always good, with wahoo, dolphin, and red snapper most in demand.

As for drink, there's imported beer from Holland and locally brewed *Amstel,* the only beer in the world that is distilled from sea water; the Holland Gin, or *Jenever,* which the Dutch down neat like schnapps; and there's *Curaçao,* the liqueur that is made from island-grown bitter oranges.

We call $6 and under *Inexpensive,* $7–15 *Moderate,* $16 and above *Expensive.*

Bellevue Bar/Restaurant. Located outside the Punda, this place specializes in seafood and Creole dishes. Their waitresses wear folkloric dress to add to the atmosphere. *Moderate.*

Bistro Le Clochard. Dine by candlelight in what was once a prison in Curaçao's harbor fort. French and Swiss specialties carefully prepared and served in an intimate and charming atmosphere. *Expensive.*

Fort Nassau Restaurant. Have drinks on the battery terrace, meals within the old bastion itself and linger awhile to watch the old pontoon bridge below open and close. Savor the fresh lobster, the typically Dutch dishes, or the tried-

and-true American fare. Open for lunch and dinner, with the bar and snack bar open from 10:30 A.M. until 1:00 A.M. *Moderate.*

Fort Waakzaamheid Tavern. Dine on steaks or seafood in this rustic-style pub on Seru Domi on the Otrabanda side of the city. A pleasant place to be with *Inexpensive* prices for lunch and *Moderate* for full dinners.

Golden Star. *The* spot for local food, which might be *carco stoba* (conch stew), *bakijaw* (salted cod), or fresh fish with *funchi* (Curaçao's corn-meal patty). *Inexpensive.*

King Arthur's Pub & Restaurant. Steaks and seafood served in an atmosphere that would please the knights of old. Located in the Arthur Frommer Hotel, this spot is informal and delightful, especially on Saturday night when they present an island folkloric show. *Moderate.*

La Bistroelle. You'll have to take a taxi to find it, almost hidden behind the Promenade shopping center outside of town, but the trip is worth it. Escargots, salmon mousse and other French fare, with many of the delectable entrees served *en flambé.* Open for lunch and dinner. *Expensive.*

La Hacienda. Another very nice spot for Dutch fare, with the specialty *Keshi Yena,* which is cheese stuffed with meat or fish. Once a lovely country house, this place has been completely restored to show off its century-old architecture. *Moderate.*

Playa Forti. On the island's northern tip, overlooking West Point beach. Authentic local dishes such as goat stew, fish soup and fried plantains with funchi. *Inexpensive.*

Rijsttafel Restaurant Indonesia. This is *the* place to sample that wonderful feast that, with close to 25 dishes, seemingly goes on forever. Go there for dinner and the full Indonesian array; open for lunch but not nearly as elaborate as in the evening. *Moderate.*

San Marco. This air-conditioned second-floor restaurant is on Columbustraat in the shopping district. Extensive Italian menu, all of it excellent. *Inexpensive.*

The Wine Cellar. Very French ambience in authentic Dutch atmosphere. A small and special spot for the best Parisian appetizers and entrees, and for vintage wines. *Expensive.*

Victoria Station. Good steak and seafood dishes served in an interesting railroad depot atmosphere just a short walk from Wilhelmina Plaza. *Moderate.*

NIGHTLIFE. The smartest places in town for dining, dancing, and gambling are the *Curaçao Hilton* and the *Curaçao Plaza.* At both you will enjoy the floor show and the casino, with slot machines galore and gaming tables for the sophisticated international crowd. There also are casinos at the *Holiday Beach* and *Princess Beach* hotels.

The Curaçao Plaza's *Cave de Neptune* has entertainment and usually swings until 2 A.M., as does the Hilton's *Tambu.* There is a disco at the *Princess Beach* hotel, which also has folkloric shows at least once a week. Don't miss the

Discoconut, which swings once the diners finish at the Bellevue Restaurant, and *Plaza Simon,* a small disco at the Fort Waakzaamheid Tavern.

The *Centro Pro Arte,* Curaçao's Cultural Center, offers year-round programs of concerts, ballet, opera, drama and musical comedy. The concert hall seats 800. Consult the Tourist Bureau for weekly programs.

SHOPPING. Curaçao is a haven for shoppers, not only because it is a free port, but because the cosmopolitan character of the city is reflected in a staggering array of merchandise displayed in a wide variety of shops, ranging from those with a sleek, streamlined Fifth Avenue atmosphere to some which will remind you of a bazaar in old Baghdad. Most of the shops are concentrated in the Punda, the oldest quarter of Willemstad, a section that seems to have been invented for happy tourist browsing.

The chief shopping streets are Heerenstraat, Breedestraat, and Madurostraat. Caution: You can't walk two yards down any of them without seeing something you've just got to have. Heerenstraat is a pedestrian mall, as is Gomezplein. Both are closed to traffic, and their roadbeds have been raised to sidewalk level and covered with pink inlaid tiles. These promenades are delightful, with cafe tables and chairs set up for you to sit, sip and people watch.

The range of bargains here extends alphabetically from Antiques to Zulu sculpture, and includes Swiss watches, French perfume, gems, silver, crystal, cameras, Oriental silks, ivories, china, Indian brass, Dutch tiles and Delftware. If you don't see it, keep looking. It is a place where you will want to browse for hours. But remember that although the Netherlands Antilles are a GSP area, this type of exemption from U.S. Customs duties applies only to some local products. Pick up a copy of the *Curaçao Holiday* yellow sheet for a full listing of shops and specifics on current good buys. Among the best shops in Willemstad are:

Boolchand's. Located on Heerenstraat, behind a facade of red and white checked tiles. French perfumes, British cashmere sweaters, Italian silk ties, Dutch dolls, Swiss watches and Japanese cameras.

Cosmopolitan. Four floors of treasures from around the world. The best of Dior, Givenchy, Cardin, and other designers, at reasonable duty-free prices.

El Continental. Fine gold jewelry mounted with precious and semi-precious stones; Swiss watches; Hummel figurines; British woolens and cashmere sweaters.

El Louvre. Distributors for Caron, Balenciaga, Chanel and other haute couture scents and cosmetics. Also liquor, Dutch cigars, Kodak film and equipment.

Gandelman Jewelers. This fine shop at #35 Breedestraat offers a sparkling selection of diamonds, gold and gemstones, with settings unlike those you'll find anywhere.

Julius L. Penha & Sons. On the corner of Breedestraat and Heerenstraat, in front of the pontoon bridge. For French perfumes, Hummel figurines, linens from Madeira, Delftware, and handbags from Argentina, Italy and Spain.

Kan Jewelers. Swiss watches, semi-precious stones, and Rosenthal china, crystal and flatware.

New Amsterdam Store. Not just one, but three different shops that are so busy they don't even close down for the noon siesta. Designer fashions, imported linens, gold and silver jewelry, watches, and Delft pottery are among their items.

Spritzer & Fuhrmann. With fine shops in town and a boutique at the airport, they are the leading jewelers in the Netherlands Antilles. Swiss watches, Danish silver, Delftware, Limoges and other porcelains, gold coins, diamonds and emeralds, and Bing & Grondahl and Lladro figurines.

Windmill. Located on Heerenstraat, this shop is the place for Majorca pearls, Japanese cultured pearls, gold jewelry and Delftware.

The Yellow House. *La Casa Amarilla* has a complete line of French perfumes and cosmetics. Also leather goods, Hummel figurines and designer fashions from Europe.

If you are looking for recorded island and Caribbean music, there are several shops selling records both in Punda and in Otrabanda.

SPORTS AND OTHER ACTIVITIES. There's *swimming* at all major tourist hotels. Some charge a small guest fee, and some charge for towels, lounge chairs, and other equipment. You can drive out to Knip Bay, the Santa Cruz beaches, West Point, Santa Barbara, and several other bays, but we've never seen any beach on Curaçao that we think compares with those on Aruba and Bonaire.

Fishing is good at Spanish Water, but more challenging *deep-sea charters* can be arranged through Piscadera Watersports at the Hilton. They can also arrange *water skiing, snorkeling, scuba diving* and glass-bottom boat excursions.

You can play *golf* with sandy greens and powerful trade winds at the Shell Golf Club. Greens fees for the nine holes are $10, caddies $2. Clubs can be rented for $3 per day.

The Shell Country Club also has *tennis* courts (call ahead to make arrangements), as do many of the hotels, including the Hilton, Princess Beach and Holiday Beach hotel.

Hiking and *birdwatching* are just part of the pleasures to enjoy at St. Christoffel Reserve Park on the northwestern corner of the island. 4,000 acres surrounding Curaçao's highest point, which rises up 1,250 feet. Open daily from 8 A.M.–3 P.M. Perfect spot for a picnic as well.

DOMINICA

An Eternal Rainforest

Twenty-nine miles long by sixteen wide, Dominica lies at the top of the British Windward Islands. It is one of the most ruggedly beautiful islands in the West Indies, and those who have swept into her small airstrip (which ends in the sea) like a bird on the wing can appreciate the rough terrain, towering mountains, and forests so thick that you can't separate the trees. Morne Diablotin (4,747 feet) is the highest peak and is one of the several that cause Dominica to be called the Switzerland of the Caribbean.

This is an island where the country people still meander to market with mammoth parcels balanced on their heads; where the jarring and pot-holed roads lead eventually to a native boatman carving out his own *gomier*–a canoe whittled and burned and hacked from what was once a 150-foot-tall gomier tree.

Dominica is laced with rivers fed by an annual rainfall of 300 inches in the interior. They cascade into pools that speckle the countryside. The dry season (and even then it rains late at night or early in the morning) is from February to July. Traditionally, the wet season is July to November, and the evenings in the mountains are cool enough for blankets and sweaters all year. A 55° evening is not uncommon.

There are about 85,000 people on Dominica, cultivating bananas, limes, oranges, grapefruits, mangoes, avocados, copra, and cocoa. It would seem that, with well-planned cultivation and distribution, this island could feed fresh fruit and vegetables to the rest of the Caribbean. It already supplies many of its neighbors. Lime groves have traditionally been owned and leased by Rose's Lime Juice, one of the big employers on the island. Since the nineteenth century, when it was discovered that lime juice in kegs (for sailor's scurvy) would outlast the fresh limes, Rose's has been in business.

History

Dominica received its name from Columbus, who came in 1493 and christened it in honor of the Sabbath day. History has it that the ship's doctor reported that "On the first Sunday after All Saints, namely the third of November, about dawn, a pilot of the ship *Capitana* cried out: 'The reward, I see land.' All that part of the island which we could observe appeared mountainous, very beautiful and green, even up to the water, which was delightful to see, for at that season, there is scarcely anything green in our own country."

Although English is the official language, most of the Dominicans speak a French patois. Their place names of Pointe à Peine, Petit Savane, and Marigot mingle with St. Joseph, Douglas Bay, and Prince Rupert Bay. After several exchanges over the years, the island was officially ceded to the British in 1783. The French tried to invade in 1795, burned Roseau to the ground in 1805, and finally had to be bribed to leave the island for the hefty sum of £12,000.

Dominica became an Associated State of the British Commonwealth in 1967, but was eager to gain full independence. Finally, on November 3, 1978, exactly 485 years to the day after Columbus sighted it, Dominica became an independent nation. Princess Margaret officiated at the ceremonies.

One of the few things the French and English had in common during all those tumultuous years was their enmity with the Caribs. On Dominica, the Indians fought with such fury that, in 1784, both the French and English agreed to call the island a no-man's land, let the Caribs have it, and turn their attention elsewhere. As a result, Dominica has a settlement of pure Caribs which has withstood the trials of time. Their community is not too far from the airport and Salibia.

EXPLORING DOMINICA

The capital of Dominica is Roseau (pronounced Rose-oh), with a population of about 20,000 and threaded to the island's Melville Hall Airport by a serpentine drive that is not for the faint-hearted. The drive takes an hour or more and wiggles interminably through the mountains and valleys, crossing diagonally from northeast to southwest on the almond-shaped island. The best port is, not surprisingly, Portsmouth, with a population of just about 10,000. It's about five-sixths of the way up the west coast, at the northern point of the island, reached by a road that seems to withstand the torrential rains and other exigencies of tropical life.

For sheer unadulterated green, lush, plantation tropics, the island is tops. Botanists love to wander through the 5,000-acre National Park that is still in its primitive state, with many acres never penetrated.

You've never seen such a mass of bamboo, mahogany, cedar, tree ferns, and palm. The landscape is almost vertical in spots, with waterfalls plunging into swimming pools all around the island.

A DAY ON YOUR OWN

On Dominica, as opposed to many other Caribbean islands, we don't recommend that you rent a car and set out on your own. The roads for the most part are terrible, and even if you feel you can maneuver them, it will have to be by jeep or Land Rover. Therefore, on your day away from your hotel, leave the driving to the Dominicans. Jeep tours operated by local companies can run anywhere from three hours to a full day, depending on your stamina. You'll tour a plantation, swim in a thermal pool, visit Emerald Pool (formed by a waterfall), tour the Atlantic and Caribbean coasts, stop at the Trafalgar triple waterfalls, and see the fresh-water lake that is 3,500 feet up in the mountains. Lunch, refreshments (and raincoats when necessary) are furnished on the all-day tours.

An alternate tour takes you up the slopes of Morne Diablotin, the island's highest peak, and into the thick forests where the rare Sisserou parrot makes his home. If you're so inclined, you can also set out on overnight camping safaris. (These can be arranged at the Anchorage Hotel.)

PRACTICAL INFORMATION FOR DOMINICA

HOW TO GET THERE. By air. *LIAT*, with head offices in Antigua, flies south from Antigua and north from Barbados. *Air Martinique* flies nonstop from Fort-de-France; *Air Guadeloupe* from Pointe-à-Pitre. There are also daily flights between Dominica and St. Lucia.

By Sea. *Geest Lines* banana boats stop here on their pickup and delivery service. While it is primarily freighter service, there are comfortable cabins that are very much in demand for the inter-island routes.

FURTHER INFORMATION. For U.S. information, contact the Caribbean Tourism Association, 20 East 46th St., New York, N.Y. 10017. The Dominica Tourist Board operates out of offices in Roseau. Their mailing address is Box 73, Roseau, Dominica, W.I.

AUTHORIZED TOUR OPERATORS. Caribbean Holidays and the Haley Corp. are the U.S. tour operators for Dominica.

PASSPORTS, VISAS. All visitors need some proof of citizenship (US and Canadian citizens can use a voter's registration card, birth certificate, etc.; all others need passports) and a return or ongoing ticket.

MONEY. The Eastern Caribbean dollar (EC) is the official currency. Figure $1 US = $2.70 EC; $6 EC = 1£.

TAXES AND OTHER CHARGES. There is a 10% government tax on hotel

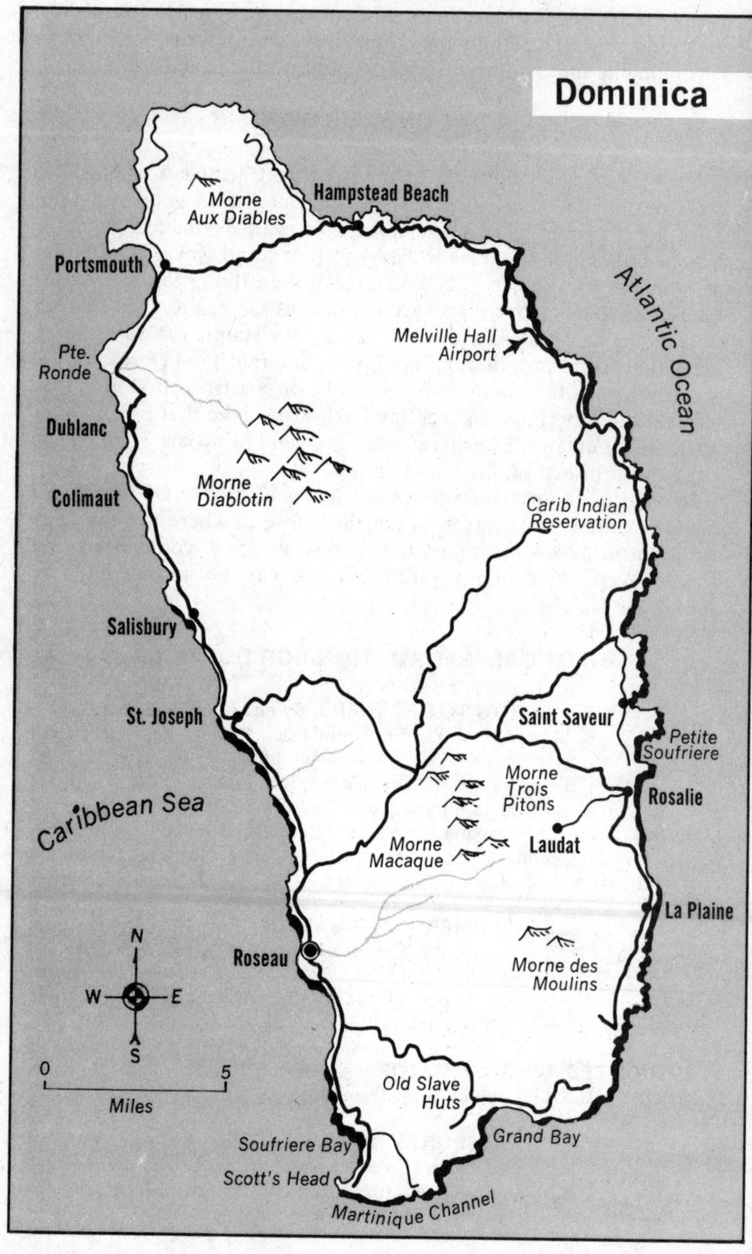
Dominica
Morne Aux Diables
Hampstead Beach
Portsmouth
Atlantic Ocean
Melville Hall Airport
Pte. Ronde
Dublanc
Morne Diablotin
Colimaut
Carib Indian Reservation
Salisbury
St. Joseph
Saint Saveur
Petite Soufriere
Morne Trois Pitons
Rosalie
Caribbean Sea
Laudat
Morne Macaque
La Plaine
N
W
E
S
Roseau
Morne des Moulins
0
5
Miles
Old Slave Huts
Grand Bay
Soufriere Bay
Scott's Head
Martinique Channel

rooms in addition to the 10% service charge. The airport departure tax is $8 EC per person.

HOW TO GET ABOUT. There are taxis at Melville Hall Airport and in Roseau. All operate at fixed rates. For the long trip (about an hour and a half) from the airport to Roseau, check the rate schedule posted at the airport. If you do want to rent a car, which we don't really recommend, contact the Dominica Taxi Association. They charge $20 US per day; you'll also need a temporary driver's permit ($5 US) which can be obtained at the Traffic Department in Roseau.

WHAT WILL IT COST?

Figure $90 a day for *two* persons on Dominica during the winter season. This includes all meals, taxes and service charges, plus a one-day sightseeing tour. (It's not that the hotels are so expensive–it's the hefty additional 20% for government tax and service that brings it up.)

STAYING IN DOMINICA

HOTELS. There isn't a big hotel on the island–the largest has just thirty rooms–but Dominican inns are personality places, with congenial hosts and typical island food.

Anchorage. The thirty rooms at Castle Comfort are in two wings, one three-storied with sea-view balconies, the other along the shore motel-style, all on the outskirts of Roseau. There is a restaurant and cocktail bar, swimming pool, and moorings off-shore for a dozen yachts. It is informal, a popular place for business travellers, and headquarters for tropical safari tours. $40–45 double EP in winter; $25–30 double EP off-season.

Emerald Resort. Situated in the center of the island, just one mile from Emerald Pool. Their restaurant serves local dishes as well as international cuisine. Bar for a chance to meet the local people; swimming pool. $40–50 double EP all year.

Papillote. An exclusive place in the rainforest, and just a short walk to Trafalgar Fall. Well-known for their hot mineral baths. From $50 double EP all year.

Reigate Hall. Just 12 rooms in a quiet and peaceful setting one mile from Roseau. Nothing fancy, but good food and a lovely view. $60 double all year, including two meals.

Sisserou Hotel. A nice spot with 20 air-conditioned rooms; swimming pool; options for watersports; dining room and bar with entertainment. $48 double all year.

Springfield Plantation Hotel. Formerly an old plantation house, this one has been modernized and enlarged. 15 rooms, some in cottages; West Indian cuisine. A real hideaway, 3 miles from the beach and 6 miles from Roseau. $60–80 double in winter; $40–50 double off-season, with two meals included.

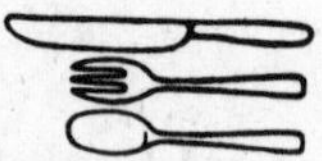

RESTAURANTS/NIGHTLIFE. The food is good and always nicely served. Local specialties include "mountain chicken"—succulent giant frogs' legs—stuffed land crab, local crayfish, fried titire (a tiny local fish that may remind you of English whitebait), and heart of palm salad. The Dominican version of *calaloo*, a West Indian crab stew, is wonderful. And so is the "real" chicken (see our section on Caribbean Cookery for a sample Dominican way of cooking it). Try dining at the *Anchorage,* and the other hotels, but make reservations in advance. The favorite in-town spot is *La Robe Creole.* As for nightlife, there really isn't any to speak of. Most visitors stay put in the evenings.

SHOPPING. Shopping is not the reason to come to Dominica, nature is, but there are a few things to buy. The grass rugs that are woven by the island girls are famous, and they are beautiful and inexpensive. Carib baskets, some of them ingeniously waterproofed, come in many shapes and sizes up to suitcase proportions. Local shell work is also good. See and buy these items in Roseau at *Tropicrafts* (where the fibre rugs are made), the *Workshop for the Blind,* and the Saturday morning market which is occasionally attended by Carib Indians.

SPORTS AND OTHER ACTIVITIES. Walking, hiking, and mountain climbing are the chief drawing cards for sports in Dominica. The island is a favorite for botanists, since portions of the interior have plants that have grown for decades. Among the destinations that lure hikers into the rugged terrain of Dominica are the Carib Reservation, Boiling Lake, Fresh Water Lake, Boeri Lake, and the Emerald Pool. The four-hour ascent of Morne Diablotin should be undertaken only with a local guide, since the paths are overgrown and sometimes treacherous.

This is not a swimming island, although there are some good black sand beaches at hard-to-get-to coves and some ice-cold river pools. The sandy beaches are in the north. Fresh-water swimming in the thirty or more rivers is the big thing. There is good deep-sea fishing, as well as lake and river fishing. Dominicans are expert at lobster progging, crayfish plucking, and hunting the giant frogs which are known locally as "mountain chicken" or *crapauds.*

You can sail in a dugout canoe (inquire at Portsmouth or at the tourist board in Roseau), or take a tropical safari tour, which can be arranged at the Anchorage Hotel. For spectators, cricket, soccer and basketball are played in season.

the seesaw of power that was to be a familiar tale on many of the Windward Islands. In 1779, the French took control, until the Treaty of Versailles in 1783 returned the island to the British. There was a French-instigated uprising in 1795, in which the Lieutenant Governor and 47 of his Majesty's subjects were massacred and, although this rebellion was put down with proper reprisals, trouble persisted until the abolition of slavery in 1834.

Grenada became a Crown Colony in 1877 and, with nine other islands, was involved in the plans for the West Indies Federation that occupied the later years of the 1950s. Not long after these plans were abandoned, Grenada became an Associated State (in 1967) with full internal self-government and plans for independence that was realized in February 1974.

While Grenada speaks for itself, it also controls the destinies of three of the dots of the Grenadines: Carriacou, Petit Martinique, and Isle de Ronde, and a handful of uninhabited specks where most of the action is the lowering of sails by charter yachts that anchor in the harbors. Carriacou's history had paralleled that of Grenada, although its minute size (13 square miles) and distance from Grenada (23 miles) make it of much lesser significance. A chain of hills runs through the center of the island, from Gun Point in the north to the favorite, protected harbor of Tyrrel Bay in the south. Mangrove oysters, lobsters, and a few turtles have fed the population and now interest the few visitors who make their way to Carriacou. There's an airstrip to receive the daily flights of *Inter-Island Air Transport* (and charter flights) and inter-island schooners that operate on a weekly basis for passengers and mail. Hillsborough is the main town, and August, when the Carriacou Regatta brings workboats from Grenada and surrounding islands, as well as international yachts from other Caribbean areas, is the main social season.

Five miles to the northeast of Carriacou, Petit Martinique's 486 acres hold about 600 year-round inhabitants, most of whom join their Carriacou colleagues in the vocations of boat building and seamanship. Like Carriacou, Petit Martinique was settled by the French.

EXPLORING GRENADA

St. George's, on its protected harbor and blue inner lagoon, is the most delightful little capital and one of the cities in the Caribbean; Willemstad can compare with it in European atmosphere and color, but St. George's has the advantage of being even smaller, quainter, and more "unspoiled" than the capital of Curaçao. Pastel warehouses cling to the curving shore of the Carenage; gabled houses, red, white and rainbow, rise above it, kaleidoscope of form and color against the hills. One of these is so steep that it cuts the capital in half. But old world charm can hide marvels of engineering: there's a tunnel connecting the two sections. Stroll through the town with its neat houses, gardens, flamboyant and frangipani trees. Explore the Carenage, both the inner and outer harbors, old Fort Rupert (built by the French, now used as Army Headquarters), the Market Place and Marryshow

House, home of the Grenada branch of the University of the West Indies, and a gallery with exhibits of works by local artists. Also well worth a visit is the Yellow Poui Art Gallery on Melville Street with interesting exhibits of local art sculpture. You can "do" St. George's on foot in about two hours. Before you start, drop in at the office of the Grenada Tourist Board on the Carenage. Don't miss the Botanical Gardens and the zoo. They're at the southern edge of town.

Among the most popular tours are an afternoon tour of St. George's and environs, including Grand Anse beach, and an all-day round-the-island trip, which hits the high spots. The island buses are more a sight in themselves than a recommended means of transport. They are brightly colored wooden affairs, and each has been christened with a whimsical name painted on its backside.

From the Yacht Basin at the harbor, you can take a two-hour glass-bottom boat cruise ($18 US) over the reefs and coral. For another look at Grenada, sign aboard the 36-foot trimaran *Sand Dollar* and enjoy a full afternoon of sailing, swimming, and snorkeling over the reefs. They provide the equipment, along with complimentary rum punches, in their low rate.

Grand Anse Beach, a two-mile stretch of gleaming sand and transparent water just south of St. George's, claims (one of at least 10,000) to be the most beautiful beach in the world. In this case, the claim is not without foundation. The hotels are also open to visitors. The view of St. George's from Grand Anse is one more argument in favor of scenic Grenada.

Grand Etang Lake is a marvelous glasslike sheet (13 acres) of cobalt water 1800 feet high in the crater of an extinct volcano. The drive to the lake is through magnificent tropical jungle and giant tree ferns. The lake is in the midst of a bird sanctuary and forest reserve. Take a sweater or light wrap; it's cool up there.

Annandale Falls, a mountain stream cascading from a height of 50 feet into a pool, surrounded by liana vines, elephant ears, and other exotic tropical flora, is a wonderful place for picnicking and swimming in clear fresh water. But to really explore this island, head for Concord Falls, a real extravaganza north of St. George's and not far from Gouyave. You'll have to hike up and around the rugged terrain for at least two miles to reach the falls, but it's worth it to meet the people who live and work in the foothills. As you traverse the winding road, see the Grenadians tending their lush gardens and don't pass up their offer to "bathe," which means a refreshing dip in one of the freshwater mountain pools.

Gouyave, a colorful market town on the coastal road north of St. George's, is one of the centers of nutmeg industry. There's a factory where the nutmeg and mace are processed, which you can tour. But you'll get a better idea of the manufacture at Grenville (see below).

Sauteurs, at the northernmost tip of the country, is Grenada's third largest town, with the great cliff from which the Caribs leapt rather than be captured by the French. A church and cemetery nearby seem entirely appropriate in this dramatically morbid setting. Looking down from the forbidding height of Le Morne des Sauteurs, you can imagine the ferocity of the French to whose tender mercies the Indians preferred death on the jagged rocks below.

Grenville, the second city of Grenada, is on the east coast. There is a waterfront fish market. The fruit and vegetable market (Sat. mornings), a block inland from the bay, is full of local color and animation. The nutmeg factory welcomes visitors; you can watch the whole processing of nutmeg and mace. If you're used to nutmeg in small cans of or sprinkled on top of eggnog, you'll be impressed by the huge sacks and crates of shredded mace and nutmeg here.

The nutmeg itself *(Mysterica fragrans)* grows on trees in shady groves. You can see it on the tree or being sorted by colorfully dressed native women at the lovely spice farm at St. David's. On such a farm you can sense the economic heartbeat of the Spice Island. On the cocoa plantations, with their trays of chocolate-colored pods drying in the sun, you can watch men polishing the cocoa by treading on it in vats with their bare feet.

A DAY ON YOUR OWN

Rent a car, chart your course, pack a bathing suit, towel, and picnic lunch and plan to make a day of it on the "Isle of Spice Drive." Leaving St. George's, the capital city, the drive proceeds along the island's western coast with its tremendous scenic appeal. The approach to the tiny picturesque fishing village of Gouyave is an unforgettable sight. Stop enroute at the Dougaldston Estate and see most of the island's spices in their natural form. Then continue on to the Spice Factory five minutes away and see the processing of some of the scented spices which you buy on the shelves of your supermarket. Continue north to the historical "Carib Leap" at Sauteurs, then round the island bend to Levera Beach for your picnic and afternoon in the sun. This beach is an idyll of sand, water, palm trees, and sea grapes at the island's corner, where the Atlantic meets the Caribbean and the Grenadines start curving north to St. Vincent.

PRACTICAL INFORMATION FOR GRENADA

HOW TO GET THERE. By air. *LIAT* operates out of Barbados and Trinidad (check those chapters for service to those islands) and with island-hopping service from St. Vincent. *Inter-Island Air Service* has scheduled flights to the island of Carriacou.

BY SEA. The island is visited by those cruise ships that dip far into the area. Among them are the ships of the *Chandris; Costa; Cunard* and *Sitmar Lines.*

To reach the satellites of Carriacou, Petit Martinique, and Isle de Ronde, inter-island schooners provide sea service. Check the Tourist Office for departure times and fares (which are modest).

FURTHER INFORMATION. The *Grenada Tourist Department* in St. George's, Grenada, has all the facts and is courteous and prompt with replies. For on-the-spot information in New York, contact the *Grenada Informa-*

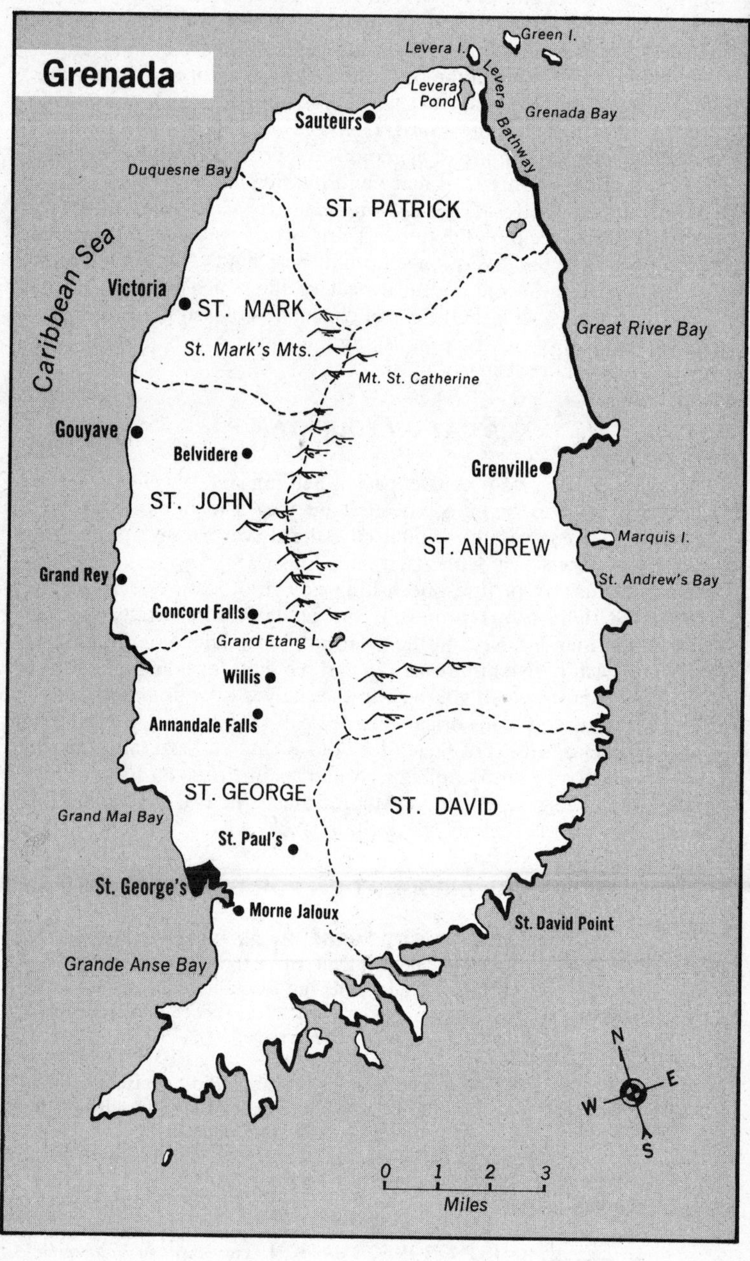

Grenada
Green I.
Levera I.
Levera Bathway
Levera Pond
Grenada Bay
Sauteurs
Duquesne Bay
ST. PATRICK
Caribbean Sea
Victoria
ST. MARK
Great River Bay
St. Mark's Mts.
Mt. St. Catherine
Gouyave
Belvidere
Grenville
ST. JOHN
Marquis I.
ST. ANDREW
Grand Rey
St. Andrew's Bay
Concord Falls
Grand Etang L.
Willis
Annandale Falls
ST. GEORGE
ST. DAVID
Grand Mal Bay
St. Paul's
St. George's
Morne Jaloux
St. David Point
Grande Anse Bay
N
E
W
S
0
1
2
3
Miles

tion Office, 141 East 44th St., New York, N.Y. 10017. Sources of information in other cities are *The Grenada High Commission,* 280 Albert St., Ottawa, Ontario K1P 5G8, Canada, or the *Grenada Consulate of Trade and Tourism,* 143 Yonge St., Toronto, Ontario M5C 1W7, Canada; or the *Grenada High Commission,* 102–105 Grand Buildings, Trafalgar Square, London SC 2, England.

PASSPORTS, VISAS. Proof of citizenship and a return air ticket are all that's required for entry into Grenada. Your passport, even if expired, is the best proof of citizenship.

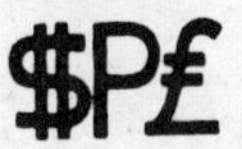

MONEY. Eastern Caribbean currency is used in Grenada. $2.70 EC = $1 US; $6 EC = 1£. All prices referred to herein are in $ U.S. unless otherwise noted, but be sure to ask which dollars are referred to when you make purchases and business transactions in Grenada. They usually talk E.C., except in places intended for U.S. visitors.

TAXES AND OTHER CHARGES. There is a 7½% government tax on hotel rooms, plus a 10% service charge. The airport departure tax is $5 EC per person.

HOW TO GET ABOUT. Local buses are cheap, but more picturesque than comfortable. Plank seats. Take a taxi. Fares are fixed: from Horse Shoe Bay to St. George is $5 US, for example. Fare from the airport to most hotels (an hour's drive, by the way) is about $20 US per taxi or about $5 US per seat in a car. Rental cars range from $20 to $25 US. There are a number of reliable companies on the island: *Avis* (GITS), *David's, McIntyre Bros., Maitlands, Royston's,* and *Hertz* (GICO). All firms can arrange for your car to be at the airport when you arrive. Remember driving is on the left. Your hotel can arrange round-the-island trips for $60 US or an hourly rate of $15 US. An interesting excursion, particularly popular with cruise passengers, is the boat trip at St. George's Harbour and surrounding area, and runs $13 US per person.

EVENTS AND HOLIDAYS. The National Festival on Grenada is its week-long celebration of Carnival in August. It's all here, the parades, pageants, steel-band competitions, and the crowning of the Carnival Queen. In addition, Grenada celebrates New Year's Day, Independence Day (Feb. 7), Labor Day (May 1), Whit Monday, the Emancipation Holidays (first Mon. and Tues. in Aug.), Remembrance Day (2nd Sun. in Nov.), Christmas Day, and Boxing Day.

WHAT WILL IT COST?

The accommodations are so varied on this island that depending upon your choice, you can figure anywhere from $100–200 per day for *two* persons during the winter season. This includes all three meals and car rental for one day.

STAYING IN GRENADA

HOTELS. Considering its limited number of hotel rooms, Grenada offers more variety than almost any other Caribbean island. Accommodations range from the sparsely rustic guest houses to beach-side hotels both intimate and luxurious, to hillside retreats that have all the extras—even two huge, antique mahogany four-posters and a sea view. A few places are in town, some are on the more remote bays, but most of Grenada's accommodations hover on and around Grand Anse Beach, a glorious stretch of sand where the "action" is.

Blue Horizons Cottage Hotel. 18 fully equipped one-bedroom suites, all with air-conditioning and kitchenettes, set around the swimming pool on their three acres overlooking Grand Anse beach. Their *La Belle Creole* restaurant on yet another hilltop is a West Indian gourmet's delight. $65–75 double EP in winter; $45–55 double off-season.

The Calabash. At L'Ance aux Epines beach, bowered in tropical foliage. 22 cottage suites in a garden setting. Secluded, sheltered beach. Boats for charter, yacht anchorage nearby, tennis, billiard room. Popular gathering place for repeat visitors and some residents. Food has a well-deserved reputation. Rates are high, because of repeat visitors and word-of-mouth renown. $160 double in winter; $87 double off-season including two meals.

Cinnamon Hill and Beach Club. To date, the island's only condominium hotel. Its 20 suites, which offer one bedroom or two, run a jagged pattern up the hillside and give you the feeling that you're in a Mediterranean village. Just a short walk down to the beach. Dine poolside at their *Hacienda Restaurant,* or arrange to have breakfast cooked and served in your suite. One-bedroom suites run $92 double in winter; $60 double off-season.

Horse Shoe Bay. This place is spectacular, parading down a hillside to the beach and sea. 12 elegant rooms and a popular dining area in the main building, overlooking the pool which is several feet below. The 2-bedroom cottage suites are 2 to a building; ideal for 2 couples or a family. Balconies and some with kitchen units and dining areas. Snack bar at beach. Restaurant has a strong local following of people who know good food and like it well served. $145 double in winter, $85 double off-season, including breakfast and dinner.

Ross Point Inn. The first of the group to make a big thing of local foods; the West Indian food is still among the best on the island. A pleasant small hotel on the water overlooking the sea and small beach. Atmosphere informal and friendly. All rooms are air-conditioned and have private baths. $95 double in winter, $55 double off-season, including breakfast and dinner. Atmosphere is very West Indian casual.

Secret Harbour. 20 suites at L'Anse aux Epines on Mount Hartman Bay that are bigger than some people's apartments, all furnished with huge four-posters—2 per room, some antiques. The hillside suites curve around the slope so that everyone has a sea view (and privacy). Room service. Spectacular pool, with private beach and beach bar below. Watersports options include boating, fishing, and snorkeling. One tennis court; excellent food served on its terrace restaurant. $175 double in winter, $115 off-season, including two meals.

Spice Island Inn. A rare combination of a resort that tries to please everybody and almost does it. 10 pool suites, each with private garden and swimming pool, were added to the original 20 beach suites, for a total of 30 rooms with access to 1200 feet of Grand Anse beach. There are nice touches everywhere—original art in the bedrooms and lobby, no breakfast rules, and ingeniously designed suites with a veranda overlooking the beach and a private garden between the bed-sitting room and bath. Try the green turtle soup, Grenada lobster, or soursop ice cream. Their elaborate Wednesday-night buffet and their Friday-night beachside barbeques (complete with a steel band) draw local people and visitors from all over the island. Accommodations run from $150–186 double in winter; from $96–116 double off-season, including breakfast and dinner. (The higher rates are for suites with private pools.)

HOTELS ON CARRIACOU

Camp Carriacou. A small cottage colony on the southern end of the island. Rustic tropical living by the sea, and a chance to meet the people on this seven-mile-long hideaway. Dinners at their *Big Drum* restaurant feature local seafood dishes. There is an EP plan, but on this small island, where restaurants are few, you're better off with MAP, which runs $51 double in winter; $36 double off-season.

Silver Beach Cottages. Duplex apartments provide 8 rooms on Beausejour Bay. Accommodations can be rented hotel style or from $75 weekly.

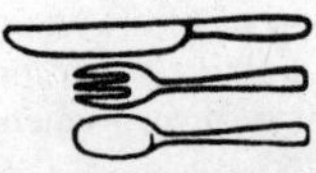

RESTAURANTS ON GRENADA. There's a lot of small truck farming in Grenada with the happy result that this island has more fresh fruit and vegetables than its neighbors. Bananas, mangoes, oranges, grapefruits, mandarines, tangerines, sapodillas, guavas, papaws, watermelon, sugar apples, sweet potatoes, breadfruit, yams, cushcush, tannia, avocado pears, peas, plantain; the list is endless. There are lots of good fish in the sea, too; rock lobster, conch, sea eggs (sea urchins), turtle, whelks, oysters, and all the finny tribe.

Note: Most hotels here feature local foods in their menus: try *Spice Island Inn, Ross Point Inn, Horse Shoe Bay* and *La Belle Creole.*

Grenadian rum punches, made with lime juice, syrup, Angostura bitters, grated nutmeg, and either Barbados or local rum, are among the delights of the island. Gin and coconut water is another popular local mix.

There are only a few restaurants in the heart of St. George's. *The Nutmeg* on the Carenage is a rendezvous for yachtsmen and a favorite with everyone else for fine lobster thermidor, chicken, steaks, and fish 'n chips. The open bar and second dining room (the main one is inside and air-conditioned) have a wonderful harbor view.

The *Turtle Back* Restaurant and Bar at the entrance of St. George's Harbour specializes in local delicacies, while the *Red Crab Pub* on the l'Anse aux Epines Road serves a drink, snack, or dinner. Pub food (fish and chips and a stein of beer) is featured. New restaurants appear from season to season, but some of the more established places are *Rudolf's* and the *Bird's Nest* (Chinese food).

For a true West Indian dining delight call ahead and make reservations at *Betty Marascol's Great House,* which is located near Sauteurs at the northern end of the island. The former plantation home is replete with antiques and history, and the special lunches are truly memorable. They are served in the elegant dining room and include such buffet selections as fresh crab in lobster sauce, avocado salad with fresh carrots, pumpkin with sweet potatoes and onions, all accompanied by Betty's special "pepper pot," which is a thick stew made with pork and ox tail. Open for lunch only, at one of the most reasonable prices we've found for authentic Caribbean fare—$10 US per person, including a rum punch for a starter.

SHOPPING. The special souvenir here is the spice basket, hand-woven panniers of palm leaf or straw, filled with cinnamon, nutmeg, ginger, vanilla, bayleaf, cloves, and all the pungent aromatic spices for which the isle is famous. Even the humble airport shop, in the building across the road from the modest terminal, has its share of spice baskets and homemade guava jelly for those last-minute gifts for friends at home. Grenada also has its share of the straw, sisal and khuskhus mats, baskets, rugs, hats, etc. For the most part, items made here are a step or two above some of the other items, but the best buys are not necessarily in the most commercial shops. There's more interesting craft in the villages, if you can seek out someone who learned from an older person.

Right in the heart of the hotel area in Grand Anse is a splendid new shopping and banking area. The *Shopping Plaza,* on Melville St., in St. George's, is a center for handicrafts and locally-designed tropical wear. Don't fail to visit *Glencraft, Noah's Arcade,* and the *Government Handicraft Centre.* You'll find these along with other straw goods at the *Straw Mart.*

Shops shut very early for lunch, at 11:45, reopening from 1 until 3:45. On Thurs. afternoon most remain closed.

There are many imported English woolens and other British goods at fair prices. Try *Granby Stores* or *Charles of Grenada.* These should take care of all your needs in the textile, jewelry, perfume, and cosmetic lines.

Dinah's Originals on the Esplanade, has the best selection of resort wear—shifts, Liberty of London dresses, calypso print shirts and skirts, swimsuits, bikinis. Dinah will also whip up anything made to your own measurements and whim and mail it to you at home, all very reasonably too.

The Yellow Poui, Granby St., an art center, offers a fine collection of paintings, sculpture, graphics.

Spice Island Perfume Ltd., on the Carenage, will make you heady with its scents and herbs.

Buy Rite Supermarket carries a good assortment of supplies for the fisherman or skindiver, as does *Spice Island Charters.*

The *Sea Change Book & Gift Shop* is a delightful place for browsing among paperbacks and sniffing the spice baskets. The shop also sells handbags, turtleshell jewelry, paintings and mahogany items, coins and postage stamps from the islands.

SPORTS AND OTHER ACTIVITIES. *Swimming* is just about perfect at Grand Anse, a long white sand beach with crystal water, and at other beaches around the island.

Spear-fishing is popular among the coral reefs and along the rocky coastline. Check at your hotel desk for details. *Grenada Water Sports,* on Grand Anse Beach, has all equipment, regularly takes trips.

Scuba diving. Exciting reef discovered off Molinere Pt. (50 feet down). The cost is $22 US for 1½ hours, including equipment.

Deep-sea fishing is excellent. There's an international tournament every Jan. U-Drive boats may be chartered for $25 a day (food and drink not included). Rods, reels, and lures can be rented, but tackle on charter boats is definitely limited. You can buy or rent tackle and diving equipment at the *Buy Rite Supermarket* in St. George's or at *Spice Island Charters.*

Grenada Yacht Services Ltd. (Box 183), located on the inner lagoon at St.

George's, provides complete services for yachtsmen as well as a marine supply store. *Spice Island Charters* have a marina and chandlery at L'Anse aux Epines. *Yacht Cruises* along western and southern coasts of Grenada are a delight; your local hotel can arrange them, but better plan to make it a full day's outing. The *Annual Yachting Regatta* at Easter is an exciting inter-island affair, as is the *Carriacou Regatta,* which begins with a race to Carriacou, the Sat. of an Aug. weekend.

The annual *Round-Grenada Yacht Race* in Jan. and the annual *Game Fishing Tournament* in mid-Jan. are increasingly popular events.

If you want to play *tennis,* you will find two concrete courts at the Richmond Hill Tennis Club, floodlit for night playing. Contact the secretary. The Tanteen Tennis Club, on the way into St. George's, has courts on which guests may play, but with all this you'll probably play at one of the hotel courts. Secret Harbour and the Calabash have courts.

Golf. The Grenada Club has a nine-hole course where you can play for a fortnightly greens fee of $10 US.

Spectator sports include cricket (from Jan. to May), football (from July to Dec.), and horse racing. There are annual race meetings, each meeting being a 2-day affair. The Easter and Aug. meetings are at Queen's Park, St. George's. The New Year's and Whitsuntide meetings are at Seamoon, St. Andrews. Not as colorful and exciting as Barbados, but fun all the same.

Grenada's *Carnival* takes place each year in August, with pageants, steel band processions, floats, beautiful girls, coronations, street parades, and the like. Climax is the mass band parade, at which time the local frenzy is at its height.

GUADELOUPE

A French Creole Potpourri

Guadeloupe is actually two islands, separated by a narrow, shallow channel of the Caribbean called Rivière Salée. The northeastern section, flat and covered with waving sugar cane, is called Grande-Terre. Pointe-à-Pitre, a city of 82,530, is here, right on the Rivière Salée. Across a drawbridge is the other island, called Basse-Terre (Low Land), despite the fact that it is crowned by towering volcanic mountains: La Soufrière (4812 feet), Sans Toucher, and other peaks whose cascading mountain torrents feed half a dozen rivers on Guadeloupe.

This low land-high land confusion refers not to the height of the land, but to the location of the "wings" in relation to the trade winds. Grande-Terre faces the highest winds; Basse-Terre, with its mountains, is the lee, where the winds are "lower." The town of Basse-Terre on the southwestern coast of Basse-Terre is the capital of Guadeloupe. Its population is 38,396, and the town is the neat, clean administrative center of Guadeloupe. Its hillside suburb of St. Claude is the elegant residential community for the old society of the island. The drive from Pointe-à-Pitre and Raizet airport to Basse-Terre through the Natural Park and along the western coast is the "compulsory excursion" of Guadeloupe, through some of the most spectacular scenery in the Caribbean.

History

It was on November 4, 1493, that Columbus discovered Guadeloupe. On the preceding Sunday, he had sighted Dominica, which he named in honor of the day. The luxuriant and majestic island which appeared shortly afterward on the port side was Guadeloupe. He went ashore at Ste. Marie, a point near Capesterre on Basse-Terre, now marked with a monument and a sign in Latin. In giving this name to a tropical island, Columbus kept a promise made to the monks of the monastery of Guadelupe in Estremadura, Spain. He proclaimed it and the whole archipelago to be the property of their Catholic Majesties, Ferdinand and Isabella. It was on his second voyage, in 1496, that he went ashore at Marie-Galante, naming it for his flagship, the *Maria Galanda.*

Thus began the attention from the Spanish conquistadors. Ponce de León and other Spanish soldiers of fortune could not subdue the pugnacious Caribs and never succeeded in colonizing the island. The Spaniards abandoned it in 1604. The French moved in in 1635, when Charles Leynard de l'Olive and Jean du Plessis d'Ossonville took possession under authority of Cardinal Richelieu's Compagnie des Isles d'Amérique. In 1759, after several skirmishes, the British took control of Guadeloupe for a four-year period ending in the transfer of the French West Indies to the French in exchange for their rights in Canada. It was during this time that influences from the British and their African slaves became mingled with the vital influences from the French African slaves. One short period of British occupation (from April to June of 1794) was the only other time that the island did not fly the French tricolor. The Treaty of Paris in 1815 permanently restored Guadeloupe and Martinique to France. Slavery was abolished and universal suffrage established in 1848. It has been a full-fledged *département* of France since 1946.

EXPLORING GUADELOUPE

Grande-Terre, flatter and less interesting than Basse-Terre, is a mass of green and silver sugar cane. The roads are good; the beaches wonderful. Driving east from Pointe-à-Pitre, a jaunt of a few miles will take you to the Fort Fleur d'Epée. Only some of the walls and a small chapel are left above ground; the real fascination is the circle of dungeons and passageways below. The view from the fort overlooking the sea is spectacular! From Bas du Fort, you can see the resort area to the right, and well-established Gosier, bubbling with new properties, to the left.

Gosier is the town that has become the heart of Guadeloupe's vacation life. Bistros, discotheques, and small hotels are hidden down side streets. Big hotels rise on or near the beach. Ten miles east on the same road is Ste. Anne, a little sugar town, neat and prosperous, with a stretch of magnificent beach that is enjoyed by visitors and fishermen alike. The Club Méditerranée's luxury resort, the former Caravelle Hotel, is at one end of this strand. The route continues, shaded by flowering pepper trees, to St. François, where the Méridien and Hamak hotels hold forth (it was here that former President Carter met with the French, British and German heads of state at the 1979 summit conference), and on to the Pointe des Châteaux at the extreme eastern point of the island. Lonely and unspoiled, here is a place to remember. The sea flings itself against huge rocks, which seem to have been thrown down by some giant hand. The jagged cliffs suggest the majestic headlands of Brittany. On one of them stands an impressive cross, dominating this spectacular scene; it is the only sign of man's handiwork here. It's not far from here, at Pointe Tarare, that the naturists have staked out their claim for one of the beaches.

Six miles offshore from Pointe des Châteaux is the isle of Désirade, which Air Guadeloupe services with several flights daily. This former leper colony has become a picturesque place well worth a day's excursion; the isles of Petite-Terre are on your right, to the southeast.

Le Moule, a short drive from the Pointe heading northwest along the coast, is another superb beach developed as a vacation area. The horseshoe beach is one of the island's best. Despite its peaceful aspect, it has been a battleground. Carib warriors and French and English soldiers fought here, and an old cemetery nearby commemorates their ancient conflict with petrified skulls, unearthed by the final victor, the sea.

Allow a full day for the 86-mile journey from Pointe-à-Pitre to Basse-Terre and La Soufrière. If you are coming in by cruise ship, you may be aboard one which leaves you in Basse-Terre and picks you up in Pointe-à-Pitre after your bus ride along the coast. The terrain of Basse-Terre is far more interesting than that of Grande-Terre. There's a spectacularly engineered road cutting across the spine of Basse-Terre. Called La Traversée, the road winds through the island's newest tourist attraction, the 74,100-acre Natural Park, the only preserve of its kind in the French islands. Walking and hiking paths lead to beautiful sites, impressive waterfalls, picnic areas, lakes and rivers. The tourist office in Pointe-à-Pitre can supply you with a complimentary map.

If you take the coastal road, you will drive through Goyave after crossing the drawbridge over Rivière Salée, the only river connecting the Caribbean and the Atlantic. Look back from Goyave to the view of Pointe-à-Pitre with its prominent "skyscrapers" standing as monuments to the French island's prosperity.

The road surface is good around Ste. Marie, where Columbus landed in a flurry of Carib arrows. The East Indians who live in this vicinity are the descendants of the laborers who were brought in to work the sugar plantations, replacing the black slaves who revolted, were freed in 1848, and subsequently given the right to vote. Inland in this area lives a community of about 300 albinos, a group so unique that they have kept to themselves for generations, living according to their customs, shunning visitors (and particularly cameras), and marrying relatives, which has insured their unusual appearance.

Past Capesterre, the fishing village of Bananier gives a Mediterranean feeling with a cluster of small houses sloping down to the sea. Trois Rivières is the jumping-off place for a fascinating excursion to the Iles des Saintes (see below). Nearby you can visit the Parc Archéologique des Roches Gravées, where sculptured rocks, heavily incised with Indian engravings are among the few relics left by the Arawaks who once dominated the Caribbean.

After Trois Rivières, the road cuts inland, past Dolé-les-Bains with its well-known thermal baths. Shortly after you pass through Dolé, you'll see the village of Gourbeyre and, beyond, the silhouette of Fort Saint-Charles guarding the approaches to Basse-Terre. Basse-Terre is a postcard capital, with well-laid-out parks, handsome administrative buildings, a 17th-century cathedral, all tucked into a niche between towering Mt. Soufrière and the sea. The steep and narrow road inland leads to St. Claude, a suburb four miles up from Basse-Terre. Here, amid the lushest of tropical trees and gardens, live the wealthy owners of the banana plantations and, more modestly, the higher echelon of that army of *fonctionnaires,* the civil servants of France. This is the place for lunch, at Relais de la Grande Soufrière (see Hotels) and, since they only serve between noon and 2 P.M., it's advisable to make reservations. At St. Claude, you are already on your way up the slopes of the majestic Soufrière, which has never blown its top with the force of its neighbor to the south, infamous Mt. Pelée in Martinique.

From La Soufrière, you can drive past Rivière Noire and Rivière Rouge to Matouba, an East Indian village where ancient rites, including the sacrifice of animals, are still practiced by survivors of this transplanted people. The black sands of the western shore of Basse-Terre are speckled with fishing villages, the most promising being that of Bouillante, where Brigitte Bardot is a sometime resident. It's at Pigeon Island, off these shores, that Jacques Cousteau has found some of his most interesting Caribbean specimens.

A DAY ON YOUR OWN

Basse-Terre and Grande-Terre, the two main islands that make up Guadeloupe, offer several days worth of sightseeing. If you only want to spend one day away from the beach, you'll probably be pleased with an excursion that takes you through the heart of Basse-Terre's 74,100-acre Natural Park.

Rent a car, take along a bathing suit and an English-French dictionary (if you think you'll need assistance), obtain a brochure and map from your hotel or from the Tourist Office in Pointe-à-Pitre and head west across the bridge from Grande-Terre to Basse-Terre.

Follow the "Route de la Traversee" into the Park and stop for hiking, swimming and sightseeing at spots indicated by signs set up by the Park Service. When you join the coastal road at Mahaut, turn south toward Basse-Terre, the tiny capital city. You'll pass Vieux-Habitants, with its church that dates back to 1650.

Basse-Terre, at the foot of La Soufriere Volcano, is a charming city with colonial-style government buildings, a colorful marketplace and a central park. Stop for a planter's punch at any one of the little restaurants along the way, but plan lunch at the *Relais de la Grande Soufriere* up the mountainside in Basse-Terre's suburb of St. Claude. The *Relais* is a hotel-school that functions as a hotel, with a supervised student staff. Reservations are recommended for the daily *prix fixe* lunch.

After lunch, drive beyond St. Claude to the *Savane à Mulets* parking lot near the crater of La Soufriere. If it's clear, you'll have a breathtaking view of Dominica, Les Saintes, Basse-Terre and the sea.

On the return to Pointe-à-Pitre, visit the Archaeological Park at Trois-Rivieres, with its Arawak Indian rock carvings set in a lovely park. Historical information about the rocks is available on the spot, as is a botanical guidebook.

Then follow the coastal road through Capesterre, with its East Indian population and Hindu Temple of Changy; Ste. Marie, where Columbus landed; the beach at Viard; and the villages of Goyave and Petit-Bourg, before recrossing the bridge back to Pointe-a-Pitre.

If time permits, consider off-island trips to Guadeloupe's satellites, *Iles des Saintes* and *Marie-Galante.*

ILES DES SAINTES

Les Saintes are a cluster of eight islands off the southern coast of Guadeloupe, accessible by boats that depart once a day from either Basse-Terre or Trois Rivières. If you're planning to go, allow at least an hour for the drive from Pointe-à-Pitre to Trois Rivières. The trip, apt to be rough, takes about an hour each way. There is also scheduled small plane service by Air Guadeloupe; some of the hotels arrange day charter trips. The trip is well worth an effort. Not only has Jacques Cousteau spent time in the waters around these remote islands, but the naturists have claimed a beach for their third nudist retreat in Guadeloupe. The eight islands by name are Terre-de-Haut, Terre-de-Bas, Ilet Cabrit, Grand Ilet, La Coche, Les Augustins, Le Pâté, and La Redonde. The two main Saintes, Terre-de-Haute and Terre-de-Bas, attract many Guadeloupians fleeing the commerce of the big islands on weekends. Terre-de-Haut, the most interesting to visit, has about 1500 inhabitants, of whom some 300 are descendants of Breton and Norman sailors. They look like a group of blue-eyed Vikings, with those apple cheeks that come from salt air, *calvados* (apple brandy), and cider. Many of these whites have preferred inbreeding to intermarriage. Les Saintois, as they are called, and the Sabans from the Dutch island to the north are said to be the best seamen in the West Indies. Certainly they are the most picturesque; they still wear the wide-brimmed curved straw hats, the *salacos,* that are often likened to inverted saucers.

The chief settlement of Terre-de-Haut is Bourg, a single paved street following the curve of the fishing harbor. The white houses lining the street are painted with blue and red trim and occasionally sport a carved balcony or some other touch of Victorian gingerbread. Bourg has one or two bistros and cafés, and timeless primitive charm. Donkeys are the local beasts of burden; fishnets are drying all over the island, strung from poles; children play on the beaches–and everywhere else.

There is a ruin, Fort Napoléon, a reminder of the 18th century

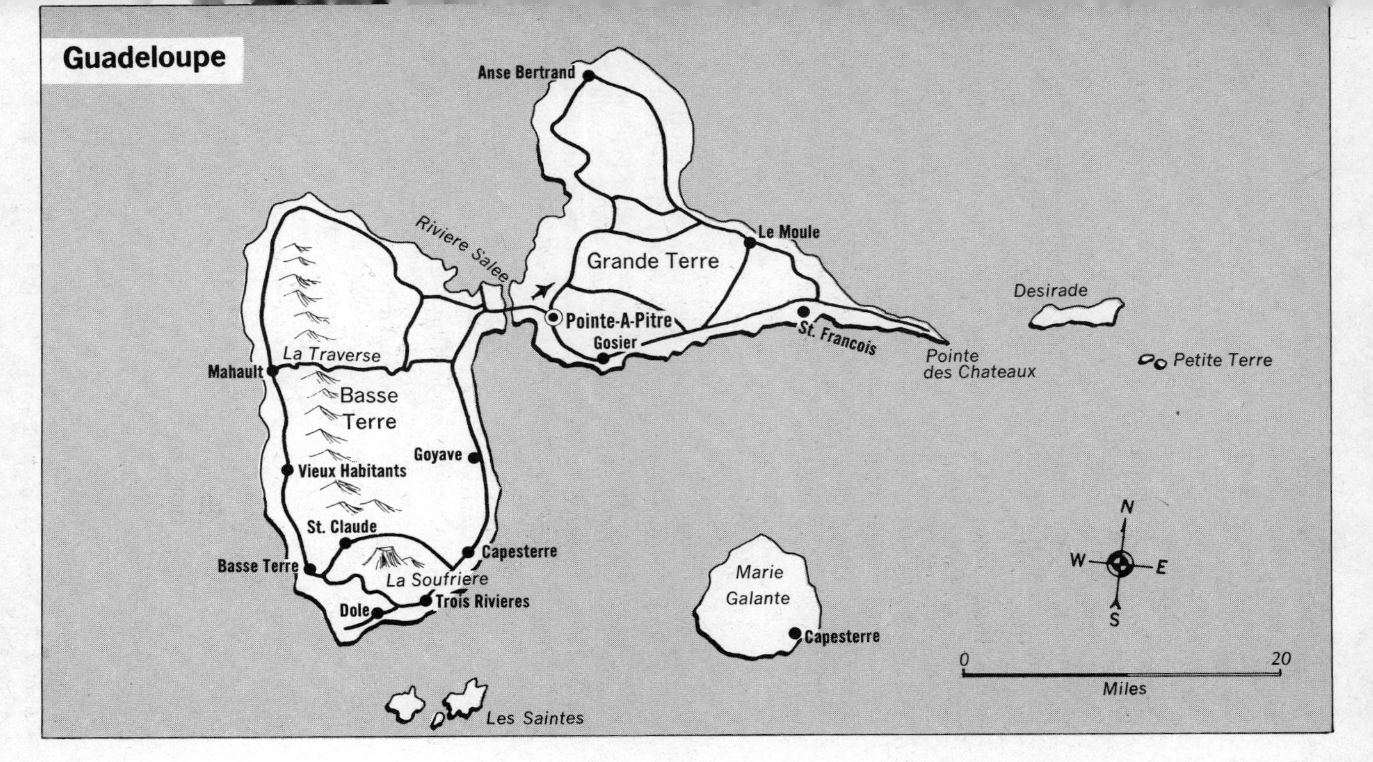
Guadeloupe
Anse Bertrand
Riviere Salee
Le Moule
Grande Terre
Desirade
Pointe-A-Pitre
Gosier
St. Francois
Pointe
des Chateaux
Petite Terre
La Traverse
Mahault
Basse
Terre
Goyave
Vieux Habitants
St. Claude
Capesterre
Basse Terre
La Soufriere
Trois Rivieres
Dole
Marie
Galante
Capesterre
N
W
E
S
0
20
Miles
Les Saintes

battles between Admirals Rodney and De Grasse, to explore. But all of Terre-de-Haut was made for exploring, swimming, and sunbathing on the lovely beaches.

These hardy island sailors, Les Saintois, could not be more friendly when it comes to renting rooms to strangers. Far from the toot of most cruise ship whistles, Terre-de-Haut does have electricity, running water, a small airstrip, a radio station, and a couple of jeeps and cars. It has also recently become a port of call for some of the windjammers that cruise this part of the Caribbean. Otherwise, the clock has stopped here.

For real exploring, rent a boat to go to the third Sainte, Ilet Cabris, to walk around the remains of Fort Josephine, constructed in 1780.

On Terre-de-Haut, *Le Bois Joli* in the western part of the island overlooks a nice beach, has 20 rooms and a pleasant dining room. It's relaxing, quiet, and very informal.

Three other possibile overnight spots on the Iles de Saintes are the five 3-bedroom bungalows of *La Colline,* with lower rates than *Le Bois Joli,* the 9-room *Kanaoa,* a large waterfront villa with good food, and *La Saintoise,* with 10 rooms and modest rates. None of these places offers any gala night life, but that's not why you came here in the first place.

MARIE-GALANTE

Twenty-five miles and two hours by launch from Basse-Terre or by small airplane flights out of Raizet Airport via Air Guadeloupe or charter from the small airport at the Méridien and Hamak hotels near St. François, this is a cotton and sugar island with a population of some 30,000. To see colorful *foulard et madras* costumes, come here on a Sunday. The women still dress in their turbans and long dresses, although there is an increase these days in the skirt-and-blouse or shift attire that fills the streets of Pointe-à-Pitre.

The capital is Grand Bourg, with a population of about 8000 and a protected beach. Along the shore, there is a handful of spots where you can get an inexpensive lunch or dinner, usually freshly caught seafood in Creole sauce. If you want to stay overnight, plan ahead for a room at *Le Salut* (there are 15 rooms) or *Solédad* (18 rooms). These are the only places, unless the 200-year-old Château Murat finally opens its doors as a hotel. This has been rumored for some time, but as of this writing, the Château is still an impressive, unoccupied building recalling Marie-Galante's bygone prosperity.

PRACTICAL INFORMATION FOR GUADELOUPE

HOW TO GET THERE. By air. Pointe-à-Pitre is two miles from Guadeloupe's modern Raizet International Airport, linking the city with flights from the U.S., Canada, Europe, and several Caribbean islands. *American Airlines* flies in non-stop from New York; *Eastern* serves several U.S. gateways via Miami and St. Croix. *Air Canada* flies non-stop from Montreal; direct from Toronto. *Air France* has non-stop service from Paris, and direct service from Miami and San Juan.

Inter-island carriers include *LIAT, Prinair, Windward Islands Airways,* and *Air Guadeloupe.* The latter, along with small *Air France* planes, link the islands of the French West Indies together. In addition to Raizet airport, there is a small airport at St. François, near the Meridien and Hamak Hotels and another at Baillif on Basse-Terre.

By sea. Several cruise lines use Guadeloupe as a port of call during the winter season. Among them are: *Carnival Cruise Lines; Chandris; Costa Line; Cunard Line; Home Line; Norwegian American Line; Paquet Line; Princess Cruises; Royal Caribbean; Sitmar;* and *Sun Line.*

FURTHER INFORMATION. For information in New York, contact the *French West Indies Tourist Board,* 610 Fifth Avenue, N.Y. 10020. In other U.S. cities, contact the *French Government Tourist Office:* 645 No. Michigan Ave., Chicago, Ill. 60611; 9401 Wilshire Blvd., Beverly Hills, CA 90212; 2050 Stemmons Freeway, Dallas, Texas 75258. In Canada: 1840 West Sherbrooke, Montreal, P.Q. H3H 1E4; or at 372 Bay Street, Toronto, Ont. M5H 2W9. In London: 178 Piccadilly, London W1V OAL. For on-island information, visit *L'Office du Tourisme,* 5 Square de la Banque, 9718 Pointe-à-Pitre.

ISLAND MEDIA. An invaluable source for current facts while you visit is *Bonjour Guadeloupe,* an informative booklet, which is available in English and in French. Your hotel will have copies.

AUTHORIZED TOUR OPERATORS: Adventure Tours; Butler Travels; Caribbean Holidays; Cavalcade Tours; Club Mediterranee, Inc.; Flyfaire; GoGo Tours; Playtime Vacations; Red & Blue Tours; Travel Center Tours; in the U.S. From Canada: Sunflight Holidays; Tours Mont Royal; Holiday House; Skylark; Unitour; Wayfarer. From London: James Vence Travel.

PASSPORTS, VISAS. U.S. & Canadian citizens may stay up to 21 days without a passport, but proof of citizenship is required. A valid passport is required for longer stays. Regulations are subject to change, so be sure to check ahead with the nearest French consulate. Citizens of the United Kingdom need passports, but no visas. All visitors must have a return or ongoing ticket.

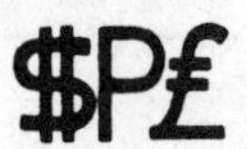

MONEY. The French franc is legal tender here. Figure approximately six francs to $1 U.S., making the franc worth about 16¢. Nine francs = 1£. The best exchange rate is given at the banks; a hotel's rate may be slightly less. *NOTE:* Travelers should be aware that French francs can be reconverted only at the *banks* where the original conversion took place, and only when the receipt for same is presented. You cannot reconvert your money at the hotels. There is no limit to the amount of money you can bring in, and U.S. and Canadian dollars are accepted in many places. However, for meals and incidental expenses, you'll fare better if you use local currency.

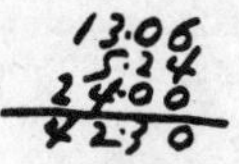

TAXES AND OTHER CHARGES. There is no government tax on hotel rooms, but in most places there is a 10% service charge. Nor is there an airport departure tax, except for charter flights.

HOW TO GET ABOUT. Taxis are readily available at the airport, the major hotels and in Pointe-à-Pitre. Fares are government regulated, and are reasonable enough in daytime, but will be about 30% higher at night. The bus transportation is modern, efficient, and inexpensive. There are inter-island systems, as well as inter-city service in Pointe-à-Pitre.

Car rentals are available at Raizet Airport, Basse Terre, Pointe-a-Pitre, and through most hotels. They run between 70–250 francs per day. *Avis, Hertz,* and *National* are here, along with local firms. Bicycles and motorcycles can be rented through ERICK on Rue de la Republique in Pointe-à-Pitre.

EVENTS AND HOLIDAYS. The highlight of Guadeloupe's year is its pre-Lenten Carnival, a colorful frenzy of celebrations that last for weeks. Masked revelers, costumed dancers and parades in the streets, follow elaborate floats; there are street parties and dancing all over the island, all of it coming to a close on Ash Wednesday with a torch-light parade and the burning of "King Carnival." Another special time is early August when the Fête des Cuisinières or Cooks' Festival heralds another parade and celebration. Women done up in colorful Creole costumes and carrying exotic island specialties in mouth-watering splendor, parade together toward the Cathedral in Pointe-à-Pitre. Following a High Mass, they all join together for a five-hour feast, complete with singing and dancing. Visitors are always welcome.

Public and religious holidays are New Year's Day; Easter Monday; Ascension Thursday; Pentecost Monday; Bastille Day; Schoelcher Day (July 21); Assumption Day (Aug. 15); All Saint's Day (Nov. 1); Armistice Day (Nov. 11), and Christmas Day.

WHAT WILL IT COST?

A typical day on Guadeloupe for *two* persons during the winter season will run:

	US$	£
Hotel accommodations (average rate), including Continental breakfast	75	41
Luncheon at a moderate restaurant	20	11
Dinner at hotel or in-town	40	22
Tips and hotel service charge	10	5
Car rental for one day	20	11
	$165	£90

STAYING IN GUADELOUPE

HOTELS. Guadeloupe hotels have a French atmosphere everywhere, and although hotel personnel do speak some English, many of the maids and bellboys do not. But, no matter, since they're willing, pleasant, and always smiling.

Auberge de la Vieille Tour. From its sugar tower beginning (the name means inn of the old tower), this inn has the advantage of being in the heart of the hotel area at Gosier, within walking distance of night life, good restaurants, and a 10-minute drive from Pointe-à-Pitre. On a 15-acre estate, the 82 rooms have small private terraces. There's a freshwater swimming pool, beach, 3 floodlit tennis courts; fine restaurant in the main building; bar; snack; and *L'Ajoupa,* a thatched outdoor bar/restaurant. One of the islands most popular hotels. $95 double EP in winter; $62 double off-season.

Auberge du Grand Large. At Ste. Anne Beach, up one of the side streets, these 10 rooms are air-conditioned beach villas. The atmosphere is very informal, with a Mediterranean look. The beautiful beach of the fishing village of Ste. Anne is a short walk away. Dependably good French-Creole cuisine served on the terrace restaurant; colorful bar. $65 double in winter; $50 double off-season, breakfast and dinner included.

Le Bougainvillee. In the heart of Pointe-à-Pitre, the island's bustling commercial center, this 32-room hotel on the corner of Rue Frébault and Rue Delgrès caters primarily to businessmen and visitors who prefer to stay in town. All rooms are air-conditioned and have balconies, but not all have full bath. Excellent 7th floor roof-top terrace dining spot overlooks the bay. $50 EP double in winter; $35–42 EP double off-season.

Callinago Beach Hotel and Village. The two-story, 41-room Callinago Hotel is part of a lovely complex on the beach at Gosier. The hotel itself is a charmer, with all rooms air-conditioned, with private bath, balcony, and telephone. French and Creole cuisine served in the dining room overlooking the sea, or on the pool terrace. The village, which opened in 1979, consists of 7 two- and three-level buildings, with 96 studios and 22 duplex apartments, stretched across the hilltop above the hotel's swimming pool. All studios have balconies, complete kitchens, full baths, and combined living room/bedroom accommodations. The duplex units are two studios in one, connected by a spiral staircase. Small commissary on the premises. Shares hotel swimming pool next door. Rates at the hotel run $86 double in winter; $50 double off-season, including Continental breakfast. The studio apartments are $68 double per day in winter; $40 double per day off-season.

Club Mediterranee Caravelle. This spectacular Club Med, located at Ste. Anne, about 12 miles from Pointe-à-Pitre, doesn't sprawl cottage type as their other properties do. Instead, the Caravelle is a 3-unit complex, with two buildings (one 3-story; one 6-story) that fan out from the main. All 275 rooms are twin-bedded and air-conditioned. All have private bath; some have balconies. In the main wing, bathrooms have twin wash basins and special theatre-style make-up lights.

The entire complex is shaded by hundreds of coconut palms that give way to one mile of sparkling white sand beach. The emphasis at this Club is its beach, which is ideal for swimming, sailing, windsurfing, or simply for strolling to chat with the local fishermen.

The usual Club Med style of using beads instead of cash and a full schedule of activities, with never a dull moment unless you want one. Swimming pool; 6 floodlit tennis courts; open dining terrace; nightly cabaret-style entertainment; discotheque. The all-inclusive rates run $475–580 per week, per person off-season; $680–740 during the winter.

Club Mediterranee Fort Royal. This settlement on Guadeloupe's northwestern tip is set on a rocky promontory, bridging two magnificent beaches near the port of Deshaies. The Club added 75 white-washed cottages to what was the Fort Royal Hotel for a total of 150 rooms. All are air-conditioned, with twin beds and private bath.

Outdoor dining area with authentic French and West Indian cuisine; nightly entertainment. Olympic-size free-form swimming pool; 4 tennis courts; and two beaches (one for swimmers; the other for surfers).

Snorkelers and scuba divers head for the Club's watersports center at nearby Pigeon Bay where free instruction is offered for novices, as well as deep dives for those who are certified. Buffet lunches are served here as well, and there is roundtrip shuttle service provided throughout the day.

One of the highlights at this Club is "The Mini Club," especially designed for children from 4 to 12 years of age. Counselors are on hand to offer the youngsters a full program of activities from 9 a.m. until 6 p.m. Sports, arts and crafts, swimming in a mini-pool, picnics, special excursions, and entertainment at an outdoor mini-theater, are all part of the full day. No extra charge, and ideal for parents looking for a day on their own.

The Club package price includes accommodations, transfers, meals (with unlimited table wine), tips, and free use of all sports equipment. $475–580 per week, per person off-season; $680–740 in winter. At this club children receive a 50% reduction the year round.

Ecotel-Guadeloupe. A handsome hotel near Gosier, with 44 tastefully decorated rooms in white stucco units surrounded by a stone wall. Small bar; swimming pool; poolside snack bar; fine *Le Galion* gourmet restaurant. Beach privileges at nearby *Ajoupa* Club on the grounds of the *Auberge de la Vieille Tour.* Built by Gilbert Corbin, who designed Guadeloupe's impressive Raizet Airport. Part of a hotel school concept where the staff learns while you vacation. $63 double in winter; $40 double off-season, with Continental breakfast included.

Frantel. 200 rooms in 7 two- and three-story units, with first-class facilities. Studio style rooms, tile floors, wood trim on white walls, and a sitting area plus balcony. Rattan furniture throughout. Nice restaurant; *Le Fou-Fou* popular discotheque. Tennis, swimming pool, and beach at Bas du Fort. $86 double EP in winter; $60 double off-season.

Hamak Hotel. This 56-room property in St. François is convenient to the small air strip; 18-hole Robert Trent Jones golf course; marina and one of the island's two gambling casinos. Accommodations are in villas, which are between the beach and golf course. Tennis, water sports, windsurfing, restaurant, bar and hammocks (for which the hotel is named). Villas run $200, with Continental breakfast and golf greens fees included, in winter; $100, villa only, off-season.

Holiday Inn. Located on the beach at Gosier, this 156-room property has all the HI amenities you'd expect. Two restaurants, two tennis courts, discotheque. Two beaches, one facing Gosier for swimming; the other facing Bas du Fort for water skiing and other sports. Most rooms have a sea view; some are equipped for the handicapped, a convenience many Holiday Inns are now offering. $94 double in winter; $56 off-season, including breakfast.

Meridien-Guadeloupe. A 272-room resort complex that covers 150 acres fronting on a beautiful stretch of white sand beach near the fishing village of St. François. About 23 miles from Raizet Airport. Facilities include a supper club; formal and informal dining rooms; Le Bet-à-Feu disco; 3 tennis courts; freshwater pool; all water sports. Small airport here for direct flights to and from Guadeloupe's satellite islands. $89–100 double EP in winter; $69–76 double off-season.

Novotel-Fleur D'Epée. Within walking distance of the *Frantel,* at Bas du Fort, west of Gosier. 190 rooms, most with balconies; some with terraces, in a Y-shaped building that occupies most of a peninsula. Open and airy lobby, with garden and a circular stairway. Two restaurants; bar; entertainment. Freshwater pool; 2 tennis courts; beach; water sports. $100 double in winter; $60 double off-season, including full breakfast.

PLM Arawak. On a white sand beach outside the town of Gosier, this hotel is a 10-minute drive from Pointe-à-Pitre. 112 rooms and 6 suites have private terraces and sea view. The new wing, at a lower price, has 40 rooms without terraces. Main dining room; luncheon restaurant; two bars; and the *Tchappe* discotheque which is popular for non-hotel guests as well. Swimming pool; two tennis courts. Water sports available. Location makes it easy to get around Gosier, the heart of the vacation action. Rates range anywhere from $74–100 double in winter; from $50–64 double off-season, full breakfast included.

PLM Sun Village Hotel. Bright and new, with 105 studio and duplex suites stretched out on a hilltop overlooking Bas du Fort. Kitchenettes in all units; large attractive pool. *Le Boucanier* French restaurant and mini-supermarket on premises. Daily shuttle to Arawak Beach. Ideal for families. Studios run $49–64 double in winter; $38–44 double off-season.

Relais de la Grande Soufriere. At St. Claude, on the slopes of Mt. Soufrière. Elegant, government-sponsored hostelry, and hotel school. 20 air-conditioned, attractive rooms. Excellent food, service, because the students are doing their best to please. The Relais is a popular luncheon spot while touring Basse-Terre and is also frequented by the capital's businessmen, since it is just up the mountain from the city. Enjoyed mostly by people who really want to be "in the country" and don't need all the modern luxuries. $54 double in winter; $39 double off-season.

Salako. A contemporary 7-story resort hotel, with 120 air-conditioned rooms with sea view. Dining room; open air bar/restaurant and rotisserie; music for dancing nightly. 2 lighted tennis courts, freshwater swimming pool. Rooms are average size, but the balcony makes the difference. $70 double in winter; $57 double off-season, with full breakfast included.

HOME RENTALS. Apartments, villas, and weekend houses are available—some in villages; some close to the sea. Rates vary considerably according to location. Contact the Guadeloupe Tourist Office, #5 Square de la Banque, 97181 Pointe-à-Pitre for full particulars.

Or for deluxe villa accommodations, write directly to *Residence Du Lagon,* B.P. 992, Pointe-à-Poitre. They have 20 spacious two-bedroom villas in St. François. Each is on the beach; has 2 air-conditioned bedrooms; 2 kitchenettes; garden and patio. Weekly rates range from $380 US off-season to $600 US in winter.

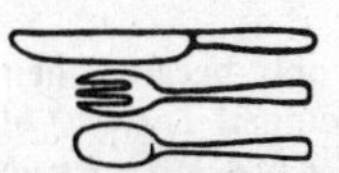

RESTAURANTS. Food is expensive, as are most things in these islands, but French imagination and taste are happily apparent throughout the island cuisine. The sea supplies wonderful raw material: lobster, red fish, conch, and that Caribbean specialty the sea urchin, known here as *oursin.* So does the land. Among the island specialties are stuffed crab, stewed conch, roast wild goat, jugged rabbit. Broiled local dove is a delicacy as highly regarded here as in France. In addition, there are dozens of Creole dishes, complete with their fiery spices. To show off their cuisine all at once, and in every variety, the women of Guadeloupe show off in August, when they celebrate the annual *Fête des Cuisinières* (Festival of Cooks), an all-day event of feasting, singing and dancing.

To complement the cuisine, there is a great supply of French wines, champagne, and liqueurs, plus the excellent local rum. Their punch, which is a brew of rum, lime juice and syrup, is pleasant, but potent. The big hotels rely heavily on imported meats and other items, which are sometimes well prepared, sometimes not. You'll find the best dining in the small restaurants and smaller hotels.

Restaurants we think you might enjoy and their locations are: In Pointe-a-Pitre: *Le Grenier* for French fare; and *L'Oasis,* where grilled meats and French dishes share the limelight, and the new *La Canne à Sucre* for Guadeloupean Creole cuisine at its finest.

At Raizet Airport, you'll find *Oiseau de Iles* outstanding, not only for its superb hors d'oeuvres, but for its Creole and French specialties.

In the Gosier and Bas du Fort area, where most of the hotels are, *Chez Rosette* is a Creole restaurant and its menu lists a wealth of taste tests. Try the *Omelette Rosette* or the *Crabes farcis* as an appetizer, and follow it with *Colombo de poisson,* a curried fish dish accompanied by rice. The restaurant seats about 120 people in two dining rooms, served by Guadeloupean dressed in *madras et foulard. La Chaubette* on Ste. Anne road, and *La Créole-Chez Violetta,* at the end of the village of Gosier, are well-known for their Creole cooking. Try *Le Baoulé* for French food, and the outdoor restaurant *Le Sud Américain,* for barbecued meats done South American style.

In the village of Petit-Havre, don't miss *Le Bistrot,* for open-air dining on French fare in a lovely seaside setting. At St. François, try *La Langouste,* which serves lobster plucked fresh from the Caribbean, which is at your feet. Nearby, try the waterfront restaurant *La Pecherie;* and near the marina, the elegant *Prunier-Hamak* for French food in all its glory.

Chez Paul in Matouba, the Indian town not far from Soufrière, serves Indian and Creole cuisine, and is especially known for its curry dishes. And for excellent seafood, try *Le Karacoli* on Grand Anse beach in Deshaies.

For in-hotel dining, you'll enjoy the Meridien hotel's *St. Charles,* an elegant (and expensive) dining room with music for dancing, and at *Auberge de la Vieille Tour,* where the menu features island foods which are served by hotel-school-trained waitresses. One of the most unique dining experiences on Guadeloupe is often connected with a tour of Basse-Terre and La Soufrière. *Relais de la Grande Soufrière,* the island's hotel school, serves luncheon and dinner. The food is prepared under the tutelage of the chef-teacher, who is from Paris. Their earnest efforts are delicious and properly served. Reservations are recommended.

NIGHTLIFE. Most of the nightlife outside the hotels is casual, in discotheques. Names change, but some that have survived a few seasons are *Boukarou, Les Chatagners,* and *Club 97-1* in Gosier; *Datcha* on the village side of Vieille Tour, and the separate disco part of *La Créole,* mentioned above for its food.

Hotel night clubs usually require more formal dress, if only because their main patrons are the hotel guests, who enjoy dressing for dinner. The best of the lot is the *Meridien,* followed by the *Tchappe* at the PLM Arawak, *Le Rhum Keg* at the Vieille Tour, and *La Grappe Blanche* at the Salako.

The *Casino* at St. François, near the Meridien and Hamak Hotels, was for years the only one on the island. It is now joined by a second casino, which is located on the grounds of the PLM Arawak in the Gosier Area, just 15 minutes from Pointe-à-Pitre.

Here, as in Martinique, a special entertainment is the Folkloric Group, which performs local dances in costume. Check with your hotel to find out where they are performing during your stay. Scheduled performances are sometimes held on cruise ships while in port, but it may be easier to get to the show at one of the tourist hotels.

SHOPPING. Rue Frébault, Rue de Nozières, and Rue Schoelcher in Point-à-Pitre are the shopping centers. It's not Paris, but the shops have French imports, including perfumes at prices lower than in metropolitan France. In addition to this, there is a selection of wines, liqueurs, canned gourmet foods, and kitchen utensils. Good native rum is inexpensive, but don't leave your buying until the airport if you want local items. The free-port shop there carries only imported liqueurs, Lalique crystal, and a small selection of ties and scarfs. Native objects of straw and wood can be found in the back streets of Pointe-à-Pitre. These include the *salacos,* or bamboo hats, worn by the fishing folk of Iles des Saintes. Native *doudou* dolls, baskets and objects of aromatic vetiver roots are good souvenirs.

In some tourist shops a discount of 20% is offered if you pay with travelers' checks. Ask. Remember you are in a *département* of France; the stores close for a long lunch from noon until 2:30. They also close on Saturday afternoons and Sundays, unless there's a cruise ship in port.

SPORTS AND OTHER ACTIVITIES. *Swimming* is good at light sand beaches along the south coast of Grande-Terre. The east coast is rugged. The naturist beach (nudist) is near Pointe des Châteaux and is open to all, you're encouraged to conform. There's another naturist beach not far from the Club Med at Deshaies, near the northern tip of Basse-Terre. A third in this category is on Les Iles des Saintes.

Water skiing, windsurfing, sunfish sailing, and other water sports are available at most hotels. For information on *sailing,* contact *L'Office du Tourisme* in town or *Guadeloupe Chartaire* or *Guadeloupe Yachting* on the outskirts of Pointe-à-Pitre. Day sails can be arranged through some of the hotels.

The best beaches are at Ste. Anne and at Gosier, where you can rent a dressing room, shower, beach chairs, and other equipment. Le Moule, on the northeast coast of Grande-Terre, is a splendid strand of sand, and on the west coast, at Grand Cul de Sac Marin, are the beautiful Anse-Bertrand and Port Louis beaches, both excellent for *snorkeling* and *spear-fishing. Scuba diving* is coming into its own here. Formerly offered only at the Club Med, and only for their guests, there is now a new center that serves guests at all the hotels. It's called the Pirate Scuba Club and is based at the Callinago Beach Hotel. Instructors are on hand to teach in English, French and Spanish; complete diving equipment is available for rent. Another good scuba club, *Gama,* is based at the Frantel and serves the Bas du Fort hotels as well as the Auberge de la Vieille Tour. The small *Club Beethoven* at the Holiday Inn can arrange guided scuba excursions to nearby islets.

Play *golf* at the Robert Trent Jones 18-hole championship course in St. François (greens fees fluctuate so check at your hotel desk); play *tennis* at any one of 30 hotel courts. The largest is the Caravelle-Club Med, which has 6 floodlit courts. For non-Club members, the Meridien is next with 3 courts lighted for nightplay.

Hiking and *mountain climbing* activities are worthwhile. Starting from Basse-Terre, you can reach the spectacular Chutes du Carbet (Carbet Waterfalls). For the trip to La Citerne, near the summit of La Soufriere, the best starting point is St. Claude or at the end of the drive up the volcano. Paths are marked; no guide is needed, but one will be able to impart added information. If you're on your own, keep a sharp eye for shifting hot lava bogs. Check with the tourist office in Pointe-à-Pitre for the informative booklet on climbing and hiking.

HAITI

Blue Waters and Majestic Mountains

Of all the countries of the Caribbean, Haiti exerts the strongest fascination with its exotic flavor and its strange harmony of contrasts. Its people come from Senegal, from the Sudan, the Gold Coast, Dahomey–and from France.

On the map, Haiti has been compared to the yawning mouth of a crocodile, its upper lip in the Atlantic, its lower jaw in the Caribbean, snapping at Cuba about fifty miles to the west. It occupies the western third of the land which Columbus discovered in 1492 and named La Isla Espanola, or Hispaniola, "The Spanish Island." The native Arawaks called their island *Hayti,* "the mountainous country." This is more accurate; four-fifths of Haiti is mountainous, with peaks soaring as high as 9,000 feet.

History

The folkways of half the tribes of Africa have been transplanted to a tropical island along with the culture of Europe's most civilized country. In the 18th century Haiti knew the mincing tempo of the minuet, the classic cadences of Corneille, the brilliance and wit of salon conversation, the luxury of Paris fashion. Life, for the upper classes at least, was as gay and glittering as a ball in the Faubourg St. Germain, if anything more sensuous, thanks to the combination of slave-supported indolence and the climate of the tropics. In the background was the beat of voodoo drums, drums of the kidnapped Quimas, the Bambaras, the vigorous Mandingues, the melancholy, homesick Ibos, who were to rise in revenge against their masters and forge a new destiny from the broken chains of slavery. The violent, dramatic story of that rebellion, ending in 1804 with the establishment of the first and only Black Republic in the New World, is the history of Haiti.

The Arawaks, who referred to themselves as *Tainos,* "the good people," made the mistake of greeting Columbus with gifts of gold. Subsequent Spanish colonists "fell upon their knees, then fell upon the natives," exploiting, enslaving, and slaughtering them in their frantic search for gold, so that within fifty years all but a few hundred of the original million Arawaks were dead. The importation of African slaves began. French buccaneers got into the act in the 17th century, moving from their settlement on Tortuga, from which they were being pushed by the English. The French established the city of Cap Français (now Cap-Haïtien) in 1670. The 1697 Treaty of Ryswick gave them Haiti and left the eastern two-thirds of the island, now the Dominican Republic, under Spanish control.

The one-time rulers of Haiti were the mulatto aristocracy known as Creoles. These descendants of French colonials and African slaves had a privileged position in plantation days; they, too, had slaves. They are almost without exception very good looking, combining African warmth with a Gallic refinement. Many Creoles are Paris-educated and have the intellectual complexity and vivacity of the French. Their manner in general is polished, worldly, cultivated, and suave.

The French of the educated Haitian is very articulate, but the mass of people speak the Creole patois, which has some striking similarities. If you speak French to the man on the street, he will try very hard to understand, even though he naturally speaks in Creole dialect. If he does not understand, he may dissolve into a clatter of giggles or say *"oui"* (yes), turn away, and forget about you. *"Pa conay,"* Creole for "I don't know" is obviously derived from *"Je ne connais pas,"* and *"pa capab,"* which means "No can do" comes from *"pas capable."* Although Creole is being taught in adult schools, French remains the official language of Haiti. Your hotel manager and anyone else who usually works with visitors will also speak English, but don't count on it outside the major cities.

Four National Heroes

In order to understand the national consciousness of the first Black Republic, you must share the Haitian's awareness of his country's four great national heroes: Toussaint l'Ouverture, Henri Christophe, Jean Jacques Dessalines, and Alexandre Pétion.

In 1791, the voodoo drums beat out a tattoo of freedom and revenge. The black slaves, inflamed by the libertarian ideals of the French Revolution and enraged at the cruelty of their masters, rose in revolt against the French planters. With plantation houses going up in flames, their occupants massacred, the slaves running amok, and the Spanish and English moving in to occupy Saint-Domingue, the

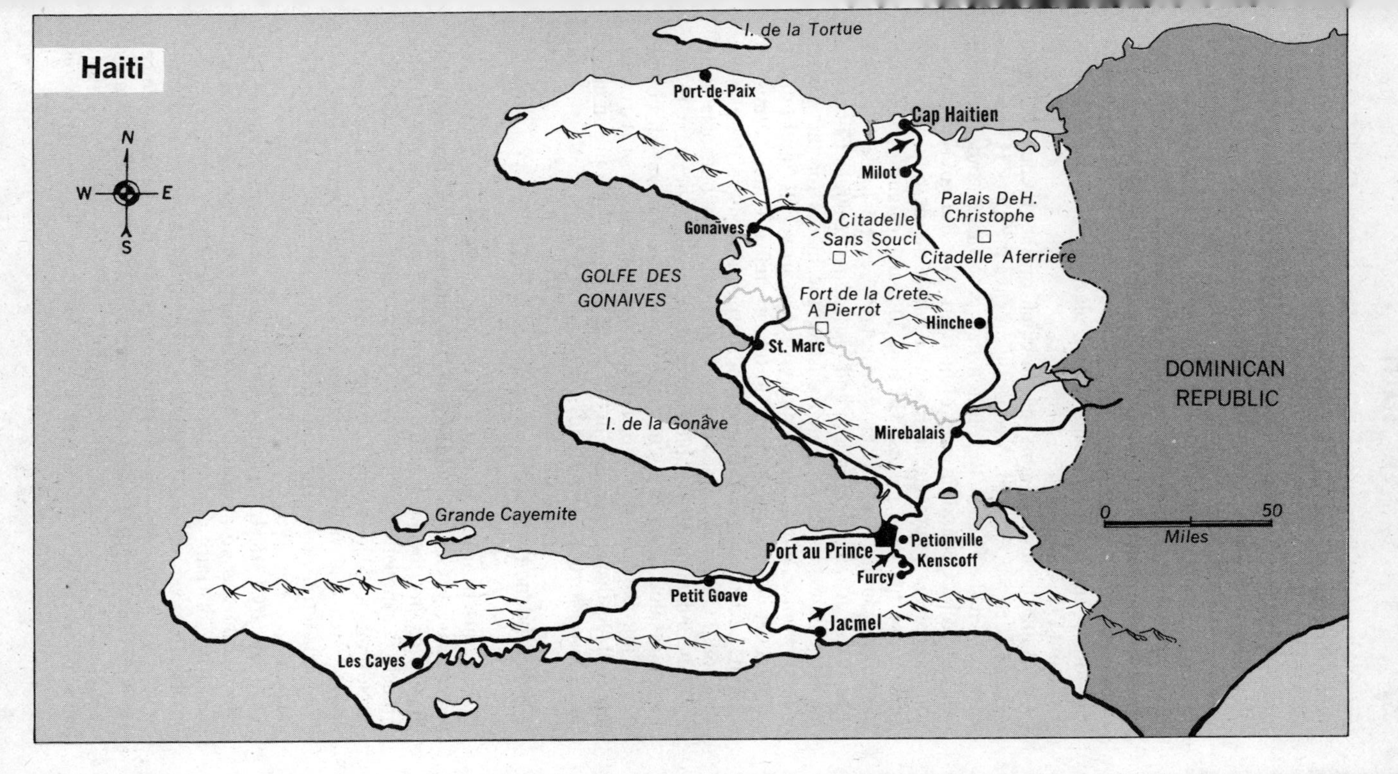

Haiti
N
W
E
S
I. de la Tortue
Port-de-Paix
Cap Haitien
Milot
Palais DeH. Christophe
Citadelle Sans Souci
Citadelle Aferriere
Gonaïves
GOLFE DES GONAIVES
Fort de la Crete A Pierrot
Hinche
St. Marc
DOMINICAN REPUBLIC
I. de la Gonâve
Mirebalais
Grande Cayemite
0
50
Miles
Petionville
Port au Prince
Kenscoff
Furcy
Petit Goave
Jacmel
Les Cayes

French were juggling a hornet's nest. The French Civil Commissioner, Sonthonax, seeking to win over the rampaging blacks, proclaimed the slaves of the north free in 1793. French General Laveaux then summoned an ex-slave, François Toussaint, a leader of his people, to restore order. Toussaint arrived and a small black army quickly formed, drove out the Spanish and English and liberated Laveaux himself, who had been held prisoner by the British at Cap Français. So swift and maneuverable was Toussaint on the battlefield that a French general remarked, *"cet homme fait ouvertures partout"* (This man makes openings everywhere.) The name stuck. Henceforth and forever in history, the "first of the blacks" was to be known as Toussaint l'Ouverture.

Toussaint became commander-in-chief of the French Colonial Army. Order was restored. A constitution gave the black Haitians the rights which the French Revolution had proclaimed, and Toussaint was Governor General, in control of Haiti. This did not set too well with Napoleon Bonaparte, into whose hands the destiny of France and Europe had now passed. He sent 70 warships and 45,000 men under the command of his brother-in-law General Leclerc to seize "this gilded African," bring him and his leading generals, Christophe and Dessalines, to Paris, then reenslave the blacks for the greater glory of France. When Leclerc and his forces arrived at Cap Français, General Christophe, in command of the city, refused them permission to land. Leclerc attacked. Christophe burned the city to the ground. Toussaint l'Ouverture came close to winning the war, but some of his generals, including Christophe, surrendered. When he went to the French headquarters to discuss an armistice, he was seized, bound, thrown into the hold of a ship, and sent to France to die of starvation and cold less than a year later in the glacial dungeon of a prison in the Jura (now a part of Switzerland).

Independence

With this treachery and the disclosure of Napoleon's intent to restore slavery, Generals Christophe, Dessalines, and Pétion resumed the war against the French. It was now a war of independence. The French, decimated by yellow fever, which killed Leclerc, capitulated in November 1803. France had lost her richest colony and a crucial staging area for Napoleon's designs on North America. The vast Louisiana territory was subsequently sold to the United States for $15 million.

On January 1, 1804, the second Declaration of Independence in the New World was promulgated. Saint-Dominigue resumed its old Indian name of Haiti; the first Black Republic had been born.

Dessalines was crowned Emperor of Haiti as Jacques I in a ceremony rivaling Napoleon's coronation in pomp, if not circumstance. He didn't last long. He was assassinated in 1806, and Haiti became a republic with Henri Christophe as its first president. A power struggle ensued between Christophe and French-educated Alexandre Pétion, whom the southern mulattoes preferred as a ruler. The ensuing civil war ended in a stalemate. Pétion, a quiet, cultured statesman, ruled in the southwest of the island. A pioneer of Pan-Americanism, he supplied Simon Bolívar with funds and arms for his heroic struggle on the Spanish Main leading to the independence of Venezuela and Bolivia. Pétion also founded the first high school in Haiti, which still bears his name, the Lycée Pétion in Port-au-Prince.

Henry Christophe, proclaiming himself King of the North, the Northwest, and the Artibonite, surrounded himself with a self-appointed nobility, and embarked on a building career that constructed 8 châteaux and 9 royal palaces in less than 14 years. More than 200,000 men performed the labors of Hercules in erecting Sans-Souci Palace and the fabulous Citadelle Laferrière in the north, the eighth wonder of the world. (See below: Exploring Haiti.) King Henry I, growing more and more tyrannical, less and less popular with his subjects, committed suicide in 1820—with a gold bullet, say legend and Eugene O'Neill. He was buried in the Citadelle, and the bizarre days of Haitian royalty were over.

Voodoo

Voodooism, a black African religion, is still found in Haiti, existing side by side with the Catholic Church, the official religion. Contrary to popular belief, it is not "black magic," but more a true folk religion, with its liturgy established in a series of complex ritual drawings, songs and dances, accompanied by the frenzied rhythms of sacred drums. The *vêvê,* a geometric design traced on the ground, is an essential element of the voodoo ceremonial rites. The emblem of the divinity one wishes to summon is drawn on the ground with cornflower. It is believed that Haitian painting originated from the *vêvê.* But even on non-voodoo practitioners, the drums make their impact felt. It is not difficult to be carried away by the relentless accelerating tempo, whether you hear them distantly in the hills, on location, or at the special performances for visitors in the hotel night clubs.

Voodoo is conducted by a *hougan* (priest) or *mambo* (priestess) in a charm-trimmed *hounfor,* or neighborhood voodoo temple, decorated with primitive symbols representing various voodoo gods or *loa.* One, *Damballa Wedo,* a rain god important to any peasant, is symbolized by a snake. The snake motif has led some people to believe that voodooism is "snake worship." It's not. There will be all sorts of charms, trinkets, gourds, colored paper, bottles, and other objects hanging from the ceiling of the temple. There will be a pole, like a painted maypole, in the center of the temple, and there will be *rada,* the sacred voodoo drums.

When the Haitian drummers start in on these; when the initiated come in singing; above all when the dancers start whirling about the center pole, you'll be caught up irresistibly in a furious percussive rhythm. Participants in the voodoo ceremony dance with an abandon which often reaches a climax with the dancer going into a trance. This means the dancer is "possessed" by the *loa;* the god has actually entered into his body and soul.

(Saturday night is voodoo night in Haiti. See Night Life below.) The version you will see at the tourist spots is no less exhausting to the first-time viewer than the real thing is to the experienced practitioner. Voodoo is at once cult and diversion. It is certainly the most lively witness of the survival of African past in Haiti.

Haitian Painting and Folk Art

The celebrated renaissance in Haitian painting began in 1944, when an American artist and schoolteacher, DeWitt Peters, opened *Le Centre d'Art* in Port-au-Prince. Three years later, Haitian painting caused a sensation at the UNESCO international exhibition in Paris. In 1948-49, Haitian "primitives" were shown and bought in New York and all over America. The same year, the American poet and art critic, Selden Rodman, launched the mural movement in painting. Thirteen tempera murals were painted by native Haitian artists the following year in the Episcopal Cathedral of the Holy Trinity (see Exploring Haiti), and the walls of hotels, airport, and exposition buildings began to glow with the rich colors of these self-taught primitive artists. Many of the painters are now widely known wherever pictures are exhibited and bought: the late Hector Hyppolite, who was a voodoo priest; Wilson Bigaud, the first Haitian to exhibit at the Carnegie International; Philomé Obin and Enguerrand Gourgue whose pictures are in the permanent collection of New York's Museum of Modern Art.

In recent years, the movement has grown more diverse and may have lost some of its original spontaneity in the process. *Le Centre d'Art* continues to support the work of primitive painters. The rival *Foyer des Arts Plastiques,* originated by Max Pinchinat, who studied abroad on a fellowship and became a friend of Picasso, emphasizes the less parochial, more international work of New York and Paris-trained artists of the contemporary school. Another splinter group was the La Brochette Group, which struck out under the leadership of Paris-trained Luckner Lazare to establish a contemporary style of national Haitian art. The work of many Haitian painters is still colorful, original, and imaginative, although not always inexpensive. Among the scores of artists to look for are Rigaud Benoit, Wilson Bigaud, Luce Turnier, Antonio Joseph, Toussaint Auguste, Adam Léontus, Préfète Duffault, Dieudonné Cedor, Jasmin Joseph, René Exumé, Max Arnoux, Daniel and Emile Lafontant, André Pierre, André Normil, Gerard Valcin, Casimir Laurent, St. Pierre. Other artists of significance include Jacques Gabriel, Herve Telemaque, Henri Jacques who paints as *Arijac,* Patrick Villaire, Tiga, Frido, Alberoi Bazile, Fernand Pierre, and Felix Jean. Haiti's sculptors of importance are Jasmin Joseph, Odilon Duperrier, André Dimanche, François Sañon, Georges Liautaud, and Hilaire Mollenthiel.

Places to look for and at works of art are the *Galerie Monnin* on

Blvd. Jean Jacques Dessalines in town or its Thomassaint branch on the Kenscoff Road or at the *Museum of Haitian Art* at Place des Héros, where some of the best early primitives may be seen. The museum was opened in May 1972 to house the works preserved by Bishop Voegeli of the Episcopal Church and by DeWitt Peters. It was built on a shoestring, primarily with money from *Le Centre d'Art* and a few friends, including a gift of $10,000 from the discretionary fund of U.S. Ambassador Knox. Technically, it is owned by the Episcopal Church, which has directed the Museum's Conseil d'Administration to maintain it as the *Museum of Haitian Art.* During its first year, the museum held five special exhibitions heavily attended by students who seem to identify with the traditional arts of Haiti.

EXPLORING HAITI

Port-au-Prince, with a population of 850,000, is the capital of Haiti, full of color and full of incongruities. Among the city's landmarks is the National Palace: the gleaming white residence of the President of the Black Republic.

Place des Héros de l'Indépendence, popularly known as the Champ de Mars, spreads out before the palace. This handsomely landscaped park contains monumental statues of Jean Jacques Dessalines, father of his country, Henri Christophe, and Alexandre Pétion. Adjoining the Champ de Mars is the Place Toussaint l'Ouverture in whose center stands a statue of the hero, executed by Haitian sculptor Normil Ulysse Charles. Government buildings surround the Champ de Mars: the Dessalines Barracks, the General Hospital, Headquarters of the Haiti National Guard, a U.S. embassy building located on the Exposition Grounds, a number of hotels and restaurants. The National Museum occupies the former residential palace of ex-President Magloire in Turgeau. There you will find interesting exhibits of Haitian history including one most impressive relic: the anchor of Columbus' flagship, the *Santa Maria,* which broke up on a reef in Haiti and furnished salvage for the construction of the island's first white settlement. On one side of the National Palace in Pétíon Square, Dessalines and Pétion lie in a dignified mausoleum, closer together in eternal death than they ever were in life. On another side, the twin-towered, pink and white Catholic Cathedral rises against the tropic sky, its Romanesque cupolas recalling those of Sacré Coeur in Paris, though there is no central dome. The rosace, highly regarded, will not overwhelm you if you've seen the cathedrals of Europe. Finished in 1915, this is the official religious center of Haiti, just as the Champ de Mars is the official center of Port-au-Prince. Less grand, but architecturally more appealing, is the Old Church, built in 1720 and recently restored. One of the few genuine relics of French colonial days, it lies just northwest of the cathedral.

Of more general tourist interest is the Episcopal Cathedral of the Holy Trinity (Sainte Trinité) a couple of blocks north of the Champ de Mars. The apse of this church, with its celebrated murals, constitutes the most important single monument of that Haitian primitive art renaissance which took the art world by storm in 1947. The depiction of Biblical events in the brilliant colors of contemporary Haiti never fails to touch the visitor with its naive, direct charm. These murals are your best introduction to Haitian painting. If you like it, you must visit the Centre d'Art where it all first came to public attention and where you can see not only a dazzling collection of paintings, but the students and teachers of this fecund movement at work. Other galleries are mentioned below under Shopping.

A visit to the old Iron Market is practically obligatory. Its two iron warehouses, linked by a gate with two vaguely Moroccan-looking minarets, is one of the landmarks of Port-au-Prince. There are hundreds of stalls clustered about; it's a sort of cross between the Caledonian Market, the Paris Marché aux Puces, and an Oriental bazaar. Bargaining and haggling are the order of the day in this miniature city of barter, teeming with humanity and local color.

One of the many sharp contrasts so characteristic of Port-au-Prince is provided about 100 yards west of this native bazaar by the International Exposition Grounds, centuries removed in atmosphere and architecture from the Iron Market. The Exposition Grounds are on the waterfront, bordered by Truman Boulevard, a wide thoroughfare built in the best spirit of Western city planning. The buildings of Haiti's Bicentennial International Exposition, modern in design but a bit seedy after years of desultory upkeep, are now used as shops, government buildings, theaters. The charming illuminated fountain provides a focal point for the Exhibition Grounds, and there are a number of sidewalk cafés and restaurants in the immediate vicinity. Also important: the annex of the Théâtre de Verdure, which presents a folkloric dance troup twice weekly; in dramatic contrast, the circular Gaguère cockpit. At night, with the fountain illuminated and people strolling through the landscaped plaza of the Exposition Grounds, the place still has the atmosphere of a World's Fair.

Up to the Flowering Alps

The attractions of Port-au-Prince are debatable; some tourists go so far as to say that they like the capital more the farther they are away from it. But there is unanimous agreement on the charms of Pétionville, the mountain village resort 2000 feet above the capital; Kenscoff, 4000 feet higher, with its open native market; Furcy, still higher at an altitude of 7000 feet. The road winds through forests and trees supporting vines of crimson blossoms, past modern villas, vintage Victorian mansions, humble thatched *cailles,* or peasant huts, each form emphasized by contrast with the other. Always and always one passes the seemingly endless line of strong, graceful women making their way to market with their headbaskets full of the fruits and vegetables from their gardens, Pétionville, with its hotels, inns and restaurants, is the uphill heart of Haiti's tourism. Once the home and playground of the Creole elite, many of the former residences are now available for visitors' dining pleasures.

The road continues to wind up the mountains to Kenscoff, where the farmers and native women display their colorful wares on the mountain slopes, bartering and haggling to make sales. This is the Châlet des Fleurs, with its acres and acres of sweet peas and other flowers grown for air shipment to the U.S. market. In its spectacular green mountain setting, this floral display surpasses anything we've seen on the French Riviera.

The road, narrow, twisting, and full of switchbacks beyond Kenscoff, ends 1000 feet farther up at Furcy. That majestic peak you see from here is La Selle (the Saddle), Haiti's highest, soaring to nearly 9000 feet, and robed in a mantle of dark green pines. This unique pine forest, in whose density escaping slaves once took refuge, can be reached by a long trek from Port-au-Prince. The road is terrible, but the exotic spell of the virgin forest and the crocodile-filled waters of Etang Saumâtre on the border of the Dominican Republic more than compensates hunters and explorers for their spine-shattering ordeal.

On the southern extremity of Haiti's lower jaw, Jacmel is an unspoiled little hill town overlooking the bay of the same name. It has excellent examples of 19th century architecture reminiscent of New Orleans. The colonial flavor of this town, about a 2-hour drive over a new highway from Port-au-Prince's airport, puts it worlds away in ambiance. Its Iron Market, built almost 70 years ago, was an effort to outdo the one in Port-au-Prince. (It falls somewhat short, but not much. It lacks only the tourists.) Ten miles east is Raymond-les-Bains, with the most beautiful white sand beach in Haiti, the obvious answer to that line of rocks and shale euphemistically described as "beach" in Port-au-Prince.

The old port of Saint-Marc; the romantic buccaneer island of Gonâve, home of primitive fishermen and the giant iguana; Jéremie, with another unspoiled beach; Gonaives, where Dessalines proclaimed his country free—these are a few of the places off the beaten track that will appeal to those who want something different. Getting to any of these places has all the adventure of uncharted tourism. We don't recommend the jaunt for those who need all the comforts of a guided tour, but back-packers and the hardy will enjoy the challenge.

Climax of Haitian Tourism

Cap-Haïtien, with its twin wonders of Sans Souci and La Citadelle La Ferrière, called Le Cap by residents, is Haiti's most historic town. Once known as the Paris of Saint-Domingue, it was the richest capital in the world.

The city itself, with its multicolored houses trimmed with Victorian gingerbread, exhales an aura of history, palpable as a scent. This in spite of the fact that only a few of Le Cap's colonial monuments have survived the fires of revolution, civil war, and earthquake. The Centennial Cathedral still stands, the Justinien Hospital, sections of the historic bulwarks, and some lovely old French fountains. In the suburb of Carenage you can visit the ruins of the palace where Napoleon's sister, Pauline Bonaparte, held court.

In 1951, Cap Haitien underwent an $8 million renovation program.

Such improvements as the waterfront boulevard, paved streets, a water system, underground sewers, and an enlarged airport were effected without sacrificing any part of the old city's French-Creole charm. Accessible by a 40-minute air trip or a 4-hour drive over the new highway from Port-au-Prince, Cap Haitien is slowly developing beach and hotel facilities.

A DAY ON YOUR OWN

This will be a memorable day, but a long one, especially if you drive up from Port-au-Prince. In that case, eliminate Sans Souci and head straight for the Citadelle, the "eighth wonder of the world."

To reach Sans Souci and the great Citadelle of Henry Christophe, you drive to the village of Milot, which the Black Emperor intended to develop as a kind of New World Versailles, though his royal palace was to be an imitation of King Frederick's Sans Souci at Potsdam. It is startling to see "the most regal structure ever raised in the New World" rising in ruined splendor against the deep green of tropical mountains. The superb double staircase, like a dramatic stage against the façade of time-worn brick, sets the proportion of this incongruous palace. You walk through the reception rooms, the ballrooms, the banquet halls, roofless now and bare, exposed to the tropic sky. You will see the remains of the conduits which brought the waters of a mountain stream under the main floor to cool the palace, and the private quarters of the royal family, the waiting rooms where courtiers, with such absurd names as the Duke of Marmalade, danced attendance on the resplendent despot. Try to imagine it as it was, panelled with mahogany, hung with imported Gobelin tapestries, ablaze with crystal chandeliers.

If this was vanity, wait until you see the Citadelle. You approach this "eighth wonder of the world" with the indispensable assistance of horse or mule and guide, all of which are for rent at Milot. The ascent used to take about two hours up a steep trail through mahogany and palm groves, banana and pomegranate trees, past native *cailles,* redolent of good strong Haitian coffee. Now you can jiggle and jog by car up to about half an hour's mule ride from the top. If you tire of the journey, solace yourself with the thought that you are not on foot and dragging the tons of masonry, cannon, and iron that were brought up this tortuous trail to build the Citadelle. Two hundred thousand former slaves were conscripted by Henry Christophe for the work; 20,000 of them lost their lives in the belief that the Citadelle had to be finished as an impregnable defense against any future invasion by the hated French. In 1817, after 13 years, the last stone was fitted into place.

On the final lap of the trail, you are 3000 feet high in the shadow of the Citadelle, soaring upward from its rocky base like the prow of a great stone ship. The walls, 140 feet high, are 12 feet thick at the base, 6 at the parapet. More than a masterpiece of architectural engineering, they are a symbol of unconquerable human will.

You enter the precincts of the Citadelle through an iron-studded gate, and find yourself, as though back in the Middle Ages, in a world of battlements and terraced stonework. The lower reaches of the fortress are a labyrinth of storehouses, cisterns, dungeons, built on a scale to accommodate a garrison of 15,000 men. Christophe actually stocked the place with enough provisions to enable such a garrison to withstand a year's siege. A stone staircase will lead you to the gallery of the cannon, a vast esplanade 30 feet wide and 150 feet long, bristling with cannon, 365 of them cast in England, France, and Spain, each one dragged up here by Christophe's men. There are four such cannon galleries, each with round ports for firing on the invader that never came.

The guide will show you the suite of 40 rooms which King Christophe modestly assigned himself, and the royal billiard room with an open fireplace worthy of a feudal lord. Climax of the Citadelle is the upper court, open to the sun and the trade winds, providing an unsurpassed panoramic view of mountains, valleys, and the sea. It was on these rarified heights that Christophe is said to have given the order to a troop of soldiers to march off the parapet into space in a demonstration of loyalty for the benefit of an English visitor. Whether this is apocryphal or not, it must have been similar excesses of cruelty and vanity which provoked the revolt of Christophe's own palace guard in 1820.

After that, the final mad touch of vanity, a gold bullet in the brain, and Henry Christophe's body was brought here to the upper court and buried in quicklime to save it from the fury of the mob.

PRACTICAL INFORMATION FOR HAITI

HOW TO GET THERE. By Air. *American Airlines* has nonstop flights from New York. From Miami, *Air France* stops at Port-au-Prince, continuing east to San Juan before heading south to Guadeloupe and Martinique. *Eastern* goes to Haiti via Miami and San Juan. *Air Florida* has daily nonstop service from Miami to Port-au-Prince.

BY SEA. Haiti has come into its own as a cruise stop, partly because of its own attractions (Cap Haitien and the Citadelle and the excitement of Port-au-Prince), but also because it is close enough to the U.S. mainland to fit into the energy-crisis-shortened cruises. Ships of the *Norwegian Caribbean Line, Home Lines, Holland America, Royal Caribbean, Sitmar,* and *Norwegian American Lines* often call at Cap Haïtien or Port-au-Prince.

FURTHER INFORMATION. The *Haitian Government Tourist Office* maintains facilities at Rockefeller Center, 1270 Avenue of the Americas, New York, N.Y. 10020; 150 S.E. 2nd Avenue, Miami, Fla. 33131; 919 N. Michigan Ave., Chicago, Ill. 60611; 1930 Post Oak South Blvd., Houston, Tex. 77056. In Canada, contact them at 44 Fundy/Floor F, Place Bonaventure, Montreal, H5A 1A9; or 920 Yonge Street, Toronto, M4W 3C7. The main office is *Office National du Tourisme, Ave. Marie Jeanne,* Port-au-Prince, Haiti.

ISLAND MEDIA. The *News of Haiti* is the only English-language newspaper. You'll find it at your hotel.

AUTHORIZED TOUR OPERATORS: Adventure Tours; Butler Travels; Caribbean Holidays; Cavalcade; Flyfaire; GoGo Tours; and Sojourn Tours from the U.S. From Canada: Fairway Tours; Holiday House; Sunflight Holidays; and UTL Tours.

PASSPORTS, VISAS. All visitors are required to have proof of citizenship and ongoing or return tickets.

MONEY. The unit of Haitian money is the *gourde,* divided into 100 centimes. The gourde is worth 20¢ in U.S. money, and is issued in notes of 1, 2, 5, 10, 20, 50, 100, 500 and 1,000. There are 5, 10, 20, and 50 centime coins. American money is acceptable throughout Haiti at even exchange value, as are travelers' checks. You can bring in any amount of foreign currency.

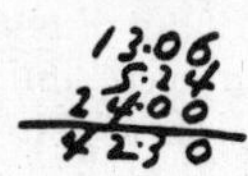

TAXES AND OTHER CHARGES. Hotels levy a 5% Government tax on accommodations, in addition to a 10% service charge. There is a $5 US departure tax per person, whether you leave by cruise ship or by plane.

HOW TO GET ABOUT. There's no place in the Caribbean where the transportation system is more chaotic than in Haiti. Taxis are not metered, but the price from the airport to a hotel in Port-au-Prince is fixed at $10; $11 to Pétionville up the hillside; $11 to Habitation Leclerc and Royal Haitian, $12 to International, $40 to Taino Beach. Fares are per car. A taxi ride from the center of Port-au-Prince to the outskirts runs from $1 to $3. You can beat this by hailing a public car *(publique),* in which you and any other passengers the driver can fit in each pay 20¢ inside the city limits. Make sure that you are left outside the grounds of your hotel; if the car goes inside it, it becomes a taxi with taxi rates.

Tour drivers are available through your hotel for about $5 per hour, $30 per 8 hour day, but discuss the price before you start out. Bargaining is in order if you're up to it. Hundreds of young children will happily (and often successfully) offer to be your guide. Sometimes it's worth hiring one just to keep the others away; their information and assistance are usually well worth the few dollars (usually about $2 per hour). Rental cars are $18 per day plus 14¢ per mile. Contact *Hertz, Avis, Budget* or *National* for rental.

Camionettes (station wagons) make the run up and down the hill from Port-au-Prince to Pétionville. Fare can be as little as 20¢. All rates double after 7 P.M.

A new highway has replaced the old back-breaker road between Port-au-Prince and Cap-Haitien, reducing driving time to about four hours for the 190-mile trip. Daily flights also connect these two principal cities.

Since one of the prime attractions in the Caribbean is beaching, and the Port-au-Prince and Pétionville hotels offer little in that line because of their in-town and hillside locations, you'll want to make a trip to Ibo Beach. It will cost $25 per person, lunch and drink included.

Weekend sailing trips can be arranged out of Port-au-Prince to Kyona Beach. Check with your hotel.

EVENTS AND HOLIDAYS. Highlights on Haiti are the combination Independence Day/New Year's Day celebrations, and Carnival on the Sunday, Monday, and Tuesday before Ash Wednesday, replete with the usual parades, floats, kings, queens, disguises, and prizes. *RaRa* is another carnival, held from Ash Wednesday to Easter in Leogane, twenty-two miles from Port-au-Prince. Features African dancing, along with Afro additions to the Christian story. Other holidays are Good Friday, Pan American Day (Apr. 14), Labor Day (May 1), Presidency-for-Life-Day (June 22), U.N. Day (Oct. 24), All Saints' Day (Nov. 1), Discovery Day (Dec. 5), and Christmas Day.

WHAT WILL IT COST?

A typical day in Haiti in season for *two* persons will run:

	US $	£
Hotel accommodations at a moderate hotel, including breakfast and dinner	70	38
Luncheon at an in-town restaurant	15	8
Tip or service charge at restaurant; hotel tax and service charge	15	8
One-day tour via taxi or rental car	25	14
	$125	£68

STAYING IN HAITI

HOTELS. Accommodations in Haiti are limited in number, but varied in offerings. They range from modest small inns and guest houses to palatial retreats for the sybarites. Port-au-Prince is the heart of the matter, with hotels on levels that wind up to Petionville. Those who have done it simply have been the most successful. Swimming pools and air-conditioning are essential for downtown hotels, where the heat can reach exhausting heights. The beach hotels are north of Port-au-Prince on the road to St. Marc, or west toward Petit Gonave.

ARCHAIE BEACH AREA

Cacique Island Ibo Beach Resort. Off shore on sand blown across from the island of Gonave, there are 100 units here, simple A-frame bungalows and apartments, all with private bath. Very informal island living; dining is alfresco; meals are charcoal-broiled, with lobster and fresh fish the highlights. 3-tiered swimming pool; 3 tennis courts; 18-hole miniature golf course; all water sports. $65–75 double all year, breakfast included.

Kaliko Beach Club. 50 sunny, large, comfortable rooms in circular-design bungalows with terraces and air-conditioning. Set in a tropical garden on 15 acres of Pointe Paturon with 2,000 feet of beachfront. Two restaurants: *Le Triton* for informal dining on the beach and *Kaye Paille* for more formal dining after dark. Tennis, freshwater swimming pool, snorkeling, scuba diving, fishing, sailing, and trips to nearby islands. $50–70 double in winter with breakfast and dinner included.

Kyona Beach Club. 10 rooms in thatched units on the beach, this club is fast beginning to emerge as a scuba diver's inn. Gear and lessons available; other water sports. Outdoor dining for seafood and Creole specialties. $46–56 double, including breakfast.

Ouanga Bay Beach Club. 40 beachfront rooms "next door" to the weekend house of the "President-for-Life." The food is fabulous at the *al fresco* restaurant. Life is beach-casual. $44–60 double EP all year.

CAP HAITIEN

Mont Joli. 45 air-conditioned double rooms, some with a beautiful view from the hillside setting, which is just 10 minutes from the airport. Swimming pool; beach for sailing, snorkeling, and water skiing, 15 minutes away. Restaurant and bar. Special activities include arrangements for Citadelle and Sans Souci visits, and coffee plantation tour. $65–70 double, breakfast and dinner included.

Roi Christophe Hotel. Completely refurbished, this pleasant little 18-room hotel has attractive grounds and lots of history. Once the Governor's mansion, and later a prison for Henri Christophe. Freshwater swimming pool. Colonial dining room features Creole food. $55–66 double, including two meals, all year.

DELUGE

Xaragua Hotel. 42 air-conditioned, oceanfront rooms, a graceful combination of Caribbean tradition and modern construction. Freshwater swimming pool, tennis courts, gift shop. Restaurant and bar. $50–70 double in winter with breakfast and dinner included.

GRAND GOAVE

Taino Beach. 44 rooms in 2-story thatched chalets done in Haitian style, on the beach in a lovely area. You can go by car, but the best bet is an hour's boat trip from Port-au-Prince across smooth waters that are protected by Gonava Island. A charming beach resort, with a French restaurant; freshwater pool; all water sports. $90–110 double, breakfast and dinner included.

MONTROUIS

Club Mediterranee. This latest addition to the Club Med villages lies 50 miles north of Port-au-Prince. There are accommodations for 700 in two- and three-story clusters of bungalows stretched along a deserted white sand beach. Three separate dining areas; 14 tennis courts; fresh-water swimming pool; windsurfing; water sports. From $450–530 per person for a full week, everything included.

PETIONVILLE

El Rancho. Expanded from a private home, this hotel now has 115 air-conditioned, well-furnished rooms. Its location in the mountains of Petionville, offers a great view of the valley. The food is good, entertainment usually excellent. 2 lighted tennis courts; 2 swimming pools. Rates run from $60–125 double, with breakfast only included.

Ibo Lele Hotel. Haitian works of art are incorporated in the decor of the 70 rooms; some suites. Located in the hillside breezes, with swimming pool and patio; restaurant which features French fare; and the *Shango* nightclub with a voodoo show that draws visitors and residents alike. The added plus here is their beach club on Cacique Island, a 20-mile drive away and then a 5-minute boat trip. Airport and beach transportation included in the hotel rate. $65–90 double, including breakfast.

Villa Creole. A former Haitian home that stretches out over the hillside, with 80 air-conditioned rooms. Breakfast is served poolside; the dining area rambles around the edges of the pool; mostly undercover. Fine food, with many local specialties; dancing and entertainment. You can walk to *El Rancho* from here and, if you're up to it, almost everywhere else uphill in the heart of Petionville for shopping. (Taxis are available if you prefer.) $65–90 double, including breakfast.

PORT-AU-PRINCE

Castel Haiti. The only high-rise hotel in Haiti, this 100-room property pierces the Port-au-Prince skyline from a slight hill just outside the hubbub of town. The rooms are air-conditioned with private bath and large balconies. Swimming pool, nice restaurant, nightclub with entertainment. Popular with tour groups. Anywhere from $41–65 double EP.

Grand Hotel Oloffson. A tropical oasis with rattan furniture and 25 rooms scattered in the main house and other small buildings that cling barnacle-like to the fringes. French cuisine in the dining room; lively conversation in the bar; entertainment in season. Spring-fed swimming pool; informal and unique atmosphere. From $70 double MAP all year.

Habitation LeClerc Resort and Casino. Built on an estate once owned by Napoleon's sister, Pauline, these 15 palatial acres house 44 fabulous villas (with a private pool for every two), 8 suites, and 27 other units around one of the two large swimming pools. This place was designed for "groovy people," presumably very rich ones. Food and drinks are served anywhere on the estate. A new, plush and exclusive casino recently opened. Other facilities include an elegant dining area, bar, game room, pool with sunken bar, and 2 tennis courts. Arrangements can be made for golf at the not-too-exciting 9-hole course nearby; or for fishing, water sports and horseback riding, a short drive away. $120–170 double EP; from $96 double off-season.

Holiday Inn Le Plaza. The first of the chain's properties on the island, opened in 1980. Formerly the Plaza Hotel, it has undergone a complete renovation. 80 rooms in two stories overlooking the city's main plaza. $53–65 double EP all year.

Royal Haitian Hotel & Casino. On the bayfront of Port-au-Prince, this attractive property has 80 modern, air-conditioned rooms set within 15 acres of tropical gardens. 2 swimming pools; 2 tennis courts; dining room with excellent chef; poolside bar; and elaborate casino. $70–90 double in winter; $56–66 double, off-season with full breakfast included.

Sans Souci. A colonial West Indian home with 24 large, air-conditioned rooms. Good food; outdoor barbecues a feature; dancing; entertainment. Swimming pool. $60 double, breakfast included.

Splendid. Started life as a private mansion; the 40 rooms for guests have the variety you'd expect in an old home. 7 are in the main building; the others in two buildings, all furnished as is the rest of the hotel, with Haitian-made furniture. Old-fashioned atmosphere is typical of many Haitian properties. Swimming pool on premises; all other activities can be arranged. $50–55 all year double EP.

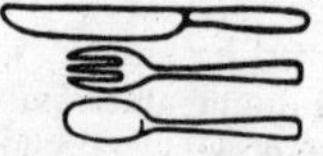

RESTAURANTS. This is the island you'll remember for its food—the French cuisine is authentic; the Creole specialties, combining French, tropical, and African elements, are delicious. Some of the special dishes worth tasting are: guinea hen with sour orange sauce; *tassot de dinde* (dried turkey); *grillot* (fried island pork); *diri et djondjon* (rice and black mushrooms); *riz et pois* (rice and kidney beans).

Langouste flambé is flaming local lobster; *ti malice,* a delicious sauce of onions and herbs; *piment oiseau,* a hot sauce that will make you feel like a fire-breathing dragon. A local favorite is *grillot et banane pese* (pork chops and bananas). If you have a sweeth tooth, you'll love *pain patate,* the famous sweet potato pudding, and mango pie. The *haute cuisine francaise* has most of the specialties: onion soup, *escargots,* and a superb *bouillon de crabe.* Fresh coconut ice cream is an island specialty; cashew nuts are another, and there's a full array of avocados, mangoes, and other tropical vegetables and fruits.

You'll find French wine and champagne in the better restaurants, but the island drink is rum, and the best is probably *Jane Barbancourt,* made by a branch of Haiti's oldest family of rum and brandy distillers.

While hotel food is usually good and sometimes excellent, there are a handful of elegant restaurants where the atmosphere is almost as fine as the food. They are expensive, but if you plan a night out, try one of the following: *La Lanterne* in Petionville is deluxe. Superb dining in a lovely restored family home, with dozens of different dishes, all beautifully served by candlelight at poolside. Fine wines, along with special *flambe* entrees. *Chez Gerard,* a few paces off the main square in Petionville, has a delightful setting in a garden around another restored home. They specialize in French and Haitian cooking.

In Port-au-Prince, try *Place Vendome* on Harry Truman Blvd. French and Creole specialties; all served in 18th century surroundings. *La Select,* on the road to Pétionville, serves authentic Haitian dishes in an informal atmosphere. *Le Rond Point,* on the Exposition Grounds, is an old favorite for Haitian cooking. Fresh seafood specialties are featured, such as lobster marinated in local rum and served *en flambé.*

NIGHTLIFE. There is plenty to do after dark in Haiti—some of it to the beat of the drums; some of it to the sounds of jackpots ringing from the one-armed bandits at the casinos. There is something going on at at least one major hotel every evening, with the highlight the folkloric groups who put you right into the swing of things Haitian.

The *Casino International,* on Harry Truman Blvd. in the center of the city, offers gala floor shows in addition to the games of chance. The other casinos are at the *Hotel Roi Christophe* in Cap Haitien, the *Royal Haitian Hotel* and at *Habitation Le Clerc.*

There are voodoo performances at some of the hotels, but your chances of seeing the "real thing" are slim. Remember that voodoo is a religion and onlookers are not encouraged. Similar to voodoo in dance pattern, but without the religious significance, is *bambouche,* a peasant celebration of sorts. Saturday night is usually the night this takes place in one of the open-air community dance halls. Check with your hotel to find out where, and to make arrangements for a visit.

SHOPPING. Bargaining is the order of the day at Haiti's Iron Market, a teeming mass of people and produce with some good (and some terrible) carved wood items and paintings "buried" amid chickens, vegetables, and people. Go with someone who's experienced in dealing with this bubbling cauldron of humanity, unless you're impervious to noise and hawkers.

Shopping centers are conveniently located in the Exposition Grounds and around the dock, but you'll find good shops and boutiques scattered all around the city, from the sea wall to the residential section and up to the surrounding mountain spots in Petionville.

Haitian paintings have become world-famous and this is the place to search or at least browse through the galleries. The selections range from $25 well into the thousands. The best places to look in Port-au-Prince are *Issa's,* which has the most expensive collection of Haitian art and sculpture; and *Nader's* which is one of the country's largest galleries and the best known. The *Red Carpet,* facing the El Rancho Hotel in Petionville, was the first art gallery to promote Haitian painting. It also has a wide range of mahogany, sisal goods, and original sculptures.

SPORTS. Although Haiti is not famous for its beaches, they are being developed, and the emphasis is more and more on water sports. A scuba diving center is emerging at the Kyona Beach Club; while several "in-city" hotels are arranging to make beaches accessible for their guests. Ibo Beach on Cacique Island, which is just about a half-hour from Port-au-Prince, can be reached in 5 minutes by motor launch.

There are glass-bottom boat trips to Sand Cay Reef from Port-au-Prince's International Casino pier daily for a spectacular look at marine life. You transfer to an inflated tube, wear a mask, and are taken over the marine gardens, where the fish will eat out of your hand. The cruise lasts three hours.

Windsurfing has become a fast-growing sport at most of the beach hotels.

Tennis may be played at the Petionville Club, or on the courts at the El Rancho; Ibo Beach; Ibo Lele; Kalon Beach, and Royal Haitian hotels, and at Habitation LeClerc.

There is only one 9-hole *golf* course, which is at the Petionville Club.

Hunting is a notable all-year-round Haitian diversion, but the best season is from October to April, especially for duck shooting. The most important lakes for this are located in central Haiti, in the south, and in the west. All can easily be reached by car from the capital city. The season for hunting pigeon, guinea fowl and quail is from August to January. You'll need special permission to bring guns and ammunition into Haiti: contact ABC Tours, 156 Rue D. Destouches, Port-au-Prince, at least 8 days in advance, listing weapon brand, caliber and serial number.

Soccer is a very popular spectator sport, but *cock fighting* is the national passion. There are fights every Saturday and Sunday in the circular *Gaguere,* the open-walled cockfight stadium on the Exposition Grounds in Port-au-Prince.

JAMAICA

Flower of the Indies

An independent nation for twenty years, Jamaica seems to have weathered all storms (natural and political), and has again emerged as a paradise island and major tourist attraction. Its rental villas are spectacular; its hotels bordering on luxurious; and its restaurants superior. Combine all that with long sandy beaches, a rugged and lush terrain, and a restoration of many of its historic landmarks, and you have Jamaica today.

The country lies 600 air miles southeast of Florida; 90 miles south of Cuba. Its bubbling capital, Kingston, with more than 1,000,000 people, is the largest English-speaking city south of Miami. Behind it lie the folded mountains, with four of the island's peaks rising to heights of more than 6,000 feet. Blue Mountain, the highest, soars to 7,400 feet. This, within the confines of a country no longer than 144 miles, no wider than 49, gives the island the grandeur of a continent.

There are continental variations in the climate too. On the sun-drenched, palm-shaded beaches, you are most definitely in the tropics. But climb 1,000 feet or so to one of the typical "hill stations," and you'll find the evenings breezy and cool. Another 1,000 feet, and you'll be reaching for a sweater or sitting happily by a fire. While daytime, sea-level temperatures, even in the dead of winter, will be balmy and sunny, the evenings can be cool enough for sweaters or jackets, particularly now that air-conditioning has invaded the hotels.

There's no question that Jamaica is one of the most exotic of the Caribbean islands. Its lush and green vegetation is laced by hundreds of cascades, spilling down from the well-watered mountain heights and rushing to the coast in a series of arrowy rivers. At the mouths of these rivers lie the tranquil harbors of Jamaica, with beach after splendid beach sweeping along the coast.

It's the north coast beaches that have gotten most of the attention in recent years, as resort development spread from its once elegant focus–Montego Bay–east through Falmouth, Runaway Bay, and St. Anns, to places in Oracabessa, Ocho Rios and Port Maria, where Ian Fleming of James Bond fame used to live. West of Montego Bay, there are the lush developments at Round Hill and Tryall, and the newly-developed seven-mile stretch at Negril. The routes to the coasts, good roads though narrow, lead through the tropical rain forest, deep gorges, and lush planted valleys of this interior; you won't see more spectacular scenery in all the West Indies.

And, for added enjoyment, the Jamaica Tourist Board, has organized an effective *"Meet the People"* program, which introduces visitors to like-minded Jamaicans.

History

The island's history is the familiar Caribbean story of human adventure and greed. Colonized by Columbus' son Diego as a kind of private fief under the Spanish crown, the island suffered the usual horrors of Spanish inefficiency and cruelty. When the Spaniards built their first settlement, New Seville, in 1509, there were about 60,000 native Arawaks on the island. In 1655, when the English seized Jamaica, there were none of these gentle Indians left.

Under British rule, Jamaica became the greatest base for pirate fleets roving the Caribbean. Leader of the pirates was that famous British buccaneer, Henry Morgan. He had excellent connections; one of his good friends was the Governor of Jamaica, and the free-booters operated under the official protection of His Majesty's Government. They made their headquarters a town called Port Royal on a spit of land across from present-day Kingston. This place became a bazaar, where British merchants could buy pirate loot at bargain prices. The waterfront was like a giant flea market, teeming with pirates and their wealthy customers. With the contempt of the glutted, the buccaneers lost fortunes in gambling. Rum flowed freely. Prostitution flourished. Port Royal was the "Babylon of the West," "a Hades where Mammon holds sway," in short, "the wickedest city in Christendom."

Less than thirty years old, Henry Morgan was the cock of this gilded walk. When tried on charges of piracy, he contended that he was not a pirate at all, but a respectable privateer, since England had been at war with Spain during most of his career. The jury agreed. He was acquitted, knighted, and appointed Lieutenant Governor of Jamaica! Sir Henry Morgan died in bed in 1688 and had a state funeral in Port Royal. Four years later, on June 7, 1692, an earthquake tilted two thirds of the city into the sea. Two thousand citizens perished; 6000 houses collapsed, all the shops crumbled and sank with £1 million sterling worth of pirate treasure into mud. A tidal wave finished the job, and it took until the 20th century—a few years ago in fact—for persevering divers to get through the murky waters of the harbor arca to search for—and find—some of the treasure.

Sugar, with its attendant prosperity and misery, dominated island life throughout the 18th century, with close to a million slaves passing through the slave market of Jamaica Bay. By 1785, the island population numbered 250,000 black slaves, 25 for every white inhabitant. In addition, there were 10,000 vari-colored freedmen, most of them the offspring tf white masters and black slaves. While many Jamaicans can trace their ancestry to either, or usually both, there were also large influxes of Portuguese Jews, East Indians, Chinese, Lebanese, as well as other Europeans. Most of them settled in the coastal towns and went into business; you'll see strong evidence of this when you compare the faces in Kingston with those of the tiny hill villages. The Jamaica slave trade was abolished in 1807; slavery itself in 1838. The country's ties with Great Britain remained for more than a century and beyond. In 1958 Jamaica achieved self government; and on August 6, 1962, full independence.

EXPLORING JAMAICA

Kingston

The tourist possibilities of Kingston are soon exhausted, and so is the tourist, especially if he hits the capital during a humid spell, in which case his one thought will probably be to escape to the cool uplands or the beaches of the north coast. The Crafts Market is certainly one of the sights of this busy town, a kind of bright pendant to the somewhat tarnished chain of shops which is King Street.

Art collecting has become an increasingly important attraction for visitors. There are more than 20 galleries in the Kingston orbit alone! Many Jamaican artists have private studios (the Tourist Board can put you on to a few), and the National Gallery of Art in Devon House is well worth a visit.

Try escaping into the past by visiting Port Royal at the tip of the Palisadoes. The harbor itself, seventh largest in the world, has all the attractions of a bustling, present-day port. Water taxis leave twice daily from No. 2 Pier.

Port Royal has a special fascination. Once the richest and bawdiest city of the New World, the village is now humble and quiet. The thriving old city tumbled into the Caribbean in the earthquake of 1692. A few oldsters claim that when the wind and tide are right you can still hear the bells of an engulfed church, tolling in the fathoms of the sea.

Outstanding among the sights of Port Royal is Fort Charles, on the site of a fort the English erected in 1656 to guard the entrance to Kingston Harbour just in case the disgruntled Spaniards should take it into their heads to reclaim their stolen property.

Enough of Port Royal has survived tremors and fires to keep the place historically alive. You will enjoy walking down the narrow

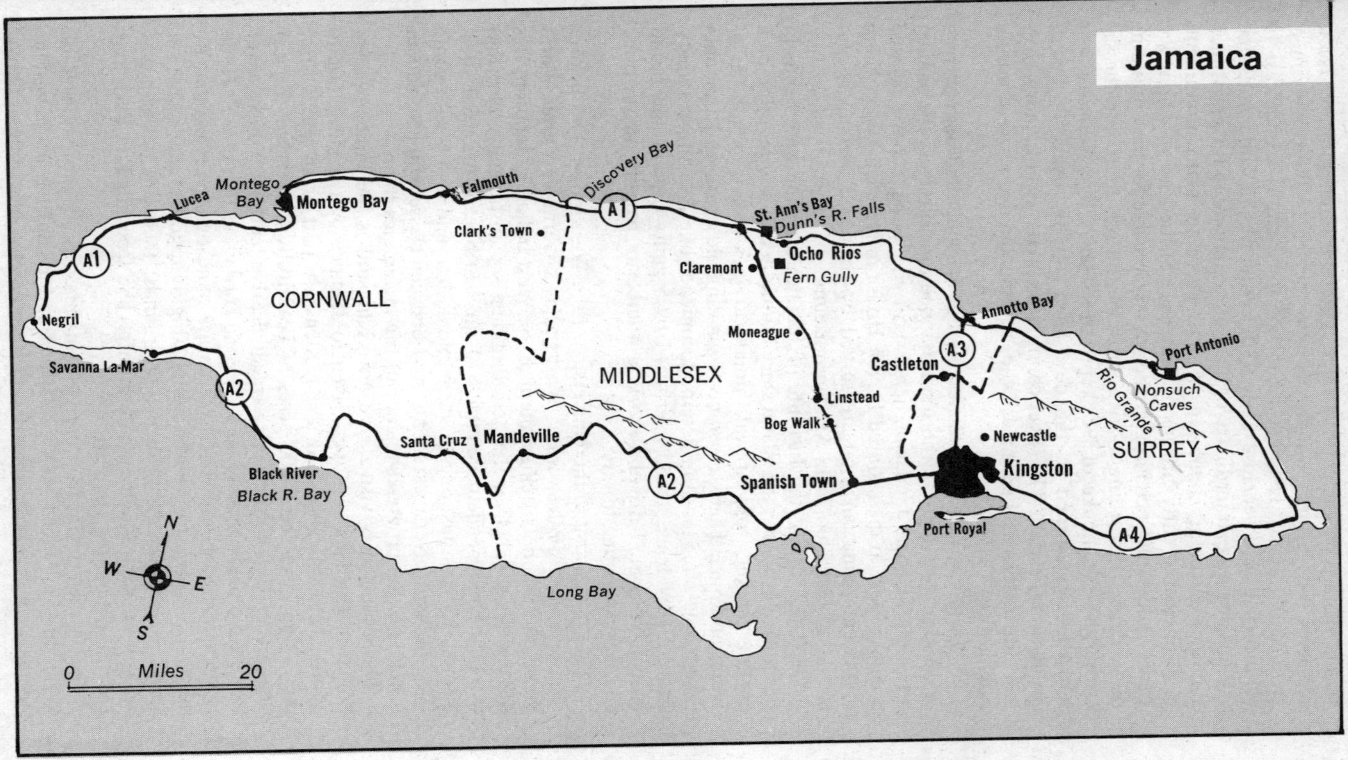

Jamaica

Montego Bay
Lucea
Montego Bay
Falmouth
Discovery Bay
A1
St. Ann's Bay
Dunn's R. Falls
Ocho Rios
Fern Gully
Clark's Town
Claremont
A1
Negril
CORNWALL
Annotto Bay
Moneague
Port Antonio
A3
Savanna La-Mar
Castleton
MIDDLESEX
Rio Grande
Nonsuch Caves
A2
Linstead
Bog Walk
Newcastle
Santa Cruz
Mandeville
SURREY
Kingston
Black River
Black R. Bay
A2
Spanish Town
Port Royal
A4
N
W
E
S
Long Bay
0
Miles
20

streets, flanked by ancient houses. St. Peter's Church, built in 1725 to replace Christ Church, which slid into the sea in the cataclysm of 1692, and recently restored, is one of the famous landmarks. Its sunbleached walls enclose early 18th century candelabra and altar railings and an extraordinary organ loft, testimony to the craftsmanship of 18th century Jamaican artisans. There are many monuments to distinguished early citizens of Jamaica, not the least of whom was Lewis Galdy, a French emigré who was responsible for the rebuilding of St. Peter's. According to his tombstone, he was flung into the sea during the earthquake of '92, kept himself alive by swimming, was rescued and returned to the devastated city by boat. St. Peter's proudest possession? The silver communion plate, gift of Henry Morgan, the notorious buccaneer who became lieutenant governor of Jamaica.

Excavation has been conducted both in the water and on land by a series of archaeologists, who have mapped and surveyed the sunken ruins. For typical Jamaican items, visit the Grog Shoppe (closed Sundays) next to the restored Devon House in New Kingston, where drinks and Jamaican food are served by costumed bartenders and barmaids. Here, too, is an African museum.

Don't fail to visit the Institute of Jamaica near the waterfront. In this museum-library, the island story is unfolded in a series of graphic exhibits ranging from Arawak Indian carvings to living examples of Jamaican fauna. There are some fascinating old charts and almanacs here; some stranger-than-fiction documents like the Shark Papers, damaging evidence tossed overboard by a guilty captain and found years later in the belly of a shark; a number of paintings and prints; and an outstanding library.

Don't miss a visit to the University of the West Indies. This institution, organized by the various West Indian governments after World War II, is a symbolic achievement of the West Indian Federation. It is the cradle for much of the new thinking, socialistic and other, that marks the independent countries of the Caribbean. A casual stroll through the campus, once a sugar plantation, and a talk with some West Indian University students in or between classes will give you an insight into the progressive tenor of life in Jamaica today.

The most widely visited site near Kingston is the famous Royal Botanical Gardens at Hope. Given to Jamaica by the Hope family after slavery was abolished, the gardens are part of an agricultural center and have about 200 acres of beautifully landscaped tropical trees, plants, and flowers. They are all clearly identified. You've never seen such orchids, unless you've been to Hawaii, as those in the Hope Gardens orchid house. The gardens are handsomely maintained by the Jamaica Ministry of Agriculture; highly qualified guides are on hand to escort visitors through the grounds; there are free concerts here on the first Sunday of the month. The Coconut Fun Park and Zoo will delight the children.

The Castleton Gardens are also maintained by the Minister of Agriculture, at the height of 2000 feet and 19 miles from Kingston. Here in a cool uplands you will find an impressive ensemble of native trees and plants along with various shrubs, flowers, and other plants that have been imported into Jamaica and have flourished in this soil. Excellent guides are also available here, and the charms of the visit are further enhanced by picnic facilities and invitations to swim in a refreshing mountain stream near the gardens.

Port Antonio

Following Route A3 from Castleton, turn right (east) at Annotto Bay and follow A4 thirty-one miles along the coast to Port Antonio. This northeast coastal corner is the cradle of Jamaican tourism, for here, near the turn of the century, the United Fruit Company came in, built a hotel, and started that migration to the north beaches. Port Antonio was the holiday capital of Jamaica before Montego Bay and Ocho Rios were generally heard of, and it still holds its own. In the hills overlooking Port Antonio are luxury villas owned by some of the world's richest, some of them for rent through JAVA (see Hotels).

Port Antonio is the chief banana port of Jamaica, and the land-locked bay behind which rise the majestic Blue Mountains. This whole area is popular for swimming and skin diving. The harbor is just about perfect for sailing, and all the necessities are immediately at hand, including an almost constant breeze. You can even watch the local artists and craftsmen at work at Dragon Plaza.

Nearby, in the hills, the Nonsuch Caves and coconut plantation on the "Seven Hills of Athenry" is a major tourist attraction on the site of old United Fruit Company lands. The view of the coastline from here is unrivaled. Also the Somerset Falls, west of the Rio Grande, are now competing with Dunn's River for beauty and tourist popularity.

Port Antonio is especially noted as a Caribbean center for deep-sea fishing. Some anglers pronounce it the best in the West Indies. The 100-fathom line is just half a mile from shore, so there is no long trip to the fishing area. Marlin, tuna, kingfish, wahoo, yellow-tail, and bonefish swim these waters. Even nearer at hand are tarpon and snook. Port Antonio bills itself as the place where "the big ones don't get away," and visitors have been known to pull in twice their weight in dolphins (the local fish, not the mammal) in the course of an hour's fishing, an achievement any fisherman should be satisfied with.

Port Antonio's picture-book charm is accentuated by Folly, the romantic ruins of a palatial mansion, whose crumbling walls and yawning windows produce a surrealist effect.

Port Antonio is headquarters for rafting on the Rio Grande, a unique Jamaican pleasure, which you ought to enjoy while here. The Rio Grande is one of those swift Jamaican rivers fed by the torrents and cascades of the John Crow Mountains and becoming navigable only as they approach the sea. Your trip will be made from a rafting base on the river near Berrydale downstream to the port of Burlington, where the river flows into the Caribbean at St. Margaret's Bay. The rafts, made of bamboo, are 25 to 30 feet long, 4 feet wide, and accommodate 3 passengers and a skilled raftsman, who stands amidships or near the bow to guide this craft with a long pole. It is a pleasant 3-hour ride, mostly a glide through tropical scenery, occasionally accelerated by "mini rapids." The pleasures of rafting can be varied by fishing and bathing from the raft when it pauses in some tranquil pool, and you can take a picnic lunch and eat it on the raft or river bank. At all events, the trip, through a jungle of ferns, palms, and feathery bamboos, is a delightful experience. At Rafter's Rest you will find a group of rondavels–completely equipped cottages with a cocktail lounge and a swimming pool. For a look at one of nature's wonders, don't miss a visit to Peach Falls, just east of Port Antonio. They are spectacular, and a tour, which can be arranged through the Jamaica Hill Hotel, can be one of the highlights of your visit to the island.

Ocho Rios

This center of another of Jamaica's resort areas can be reached in a number of ways. You can continue on Route A3, following it as it turns northwest at Annotto Bay. Most tourists coming from Kingston take A1 west through Spanish Town, through the spectacular gorge of Bog Walk (a grunting Anglo-Saxon rendering of the original Spanish Boca de Agua), over Mt. Diablo, turning right at Moneague and proceeding on A3 by way of Fern Gully, a beautiful gorge shaded by giant tropical ferns, to Ocho Rios. The delightful Fern Gully itself is a travel experience: three miles "meandering in a mazy motion" of green shade and dappled light in a deep defile at the base of fern-clad cliffs, twisting and turning through an eroded stone pass until the deep blue of Ocho Rios Bay bursts on the vision with stunning impact.

Lovers of flora should visit the Upton Country Club Botanical Gardens and the Shaw Park gardens with a fine collection and charming waterfalls.

The 60-mile stretch between Discovery Bay and Annotto Bay, included in the area of Ocho Rios, is one of the coastal areas most touched by the tides of New World history. At Discovery Bay, you can tread where Columbus trod when he landed here in 1494. Columbus Park, a 2.75-acre historic area near Discovery Bay, and Mystery House, with a handful of Jamaican relics, are among the favored attractions along the north coast road. Both are located on the Kaiser Bauxite Company area and are the result of community efforts by Kaiser employees. Adjacent to the Mystery House is the Kaiser lagoon with a geyser and plenty of fish, put in regularly to be fished out by the public.

Sixteen miles east, at St. Ann's Bay, you will be standing on that part of Jamaican soil first settled by the white man. Nearby is the site of Sevilla Nueva, which the Spaniards founded in 1509, its last vestiges now marked by a sign amidst the shimmering plumes of sugar cane and a monument dedicated to Christopher Columbus' memory.

About four miles east of St. Ann's Bay, a *must* for every visitor is

Dunn's River Falls and beach. At this point, the clear waters of a mountain stream, rushing down through a wooded gorge, suddenly widen and fall in a transparent film over a natural stone stairway before meeting the warm Caribbean. The cascades and pools of Dunn's River can be explored from a trail that flanks the stream, but the best thing by far is to put on trunks or bikini and get into the swim. It's a challenging climb to the top–some 600 feet–and your best bet is to go with a guide, who will not only lead the way, but carry your camera and photograph you as you tumble and tread your way.

At least part of your exploring of the Ocho Rios area should be done underwater or with benefit of a glass-bottom boat.

This area has become so built up in recent seasons that the main lure now is its shopping centers. You'll find them at various locales, with such names as Coconut Grove, Ocean Village, Little Pub and Pineapple Place.

There are at least three weekly outdoor events held in natural surroundings. In the evening, a feast is held at Dunn's River Falls, with music, night climbs up the Falls, torches, a band, and dancing. A spectacular event is a night on the White River, featuring a torchlight canoe ride to a clearing along the bank for dinner and local show. You may even get a rebate for the missed supper at your own hotel. Borne by hand-hewn silk-cottonwood canoes, you are rowed up the river toward the waterfalls. On disembarking, a Jamaican upcountry-style picnic is held, with music, country dancing, and drink. In a thatched hut beside a cascade of waterfalls you can buy some rural Jamaican treats, sold by torchlight.

Montego Bay

Usually called Mo' Bay by anybody who's been in Jamaica more than 24 hours, Montego Bay is, to put it conservatively, the greatest and most, both in clutter and action. The Montego Bay area stretches twenty miles from Rose Hall around the curve of the bay west to Round Hill and Tryall Golf and Beach Club. It has its own international airport, and there are innumerable gilded beachcombers of the International Set who have never set foot in any other part of Jamaica.

It all began back at the turn of the century. People didn't swim in those days; they bathed. And only a few hardy souls did that. Men wore bathing costumes to the knee; women were encased from head to foot and from wrist to wrist in what looked like mourning weeds. They also wore hats and shoes. Thus protected from sun and surf, bathing was said by certain advanced thinkers to have a certain therapeutic value, providing of course that it wasn't overdone. One of these innovators was Doctor McCatty, a physician of Jamaica, who indulged in bathing with other daring medical spirits at a beach he happened to own in Montego Bay, a shining, white, unpopulated strand which was entered through a cave. Residents who saw these physicians carrying on in this odd way called the beach "The Doctor's Cave." In 1906, Dr. McCatty and his friends, convinced of the tonic effect of bathing on the nervous system, decided to form a club. Dr. McCatty donated the beach, and The Doctor's Cave Bathing Club was established. The rest is resort history, and the blaring radios, bouncing beachballs, and cauldron of humanity that now covers small Doctor's Cave Beach is a far cry from the elite of those early days. *Everyone* goes to Doctor's Cave Beach these days. Less crowded is Cornwall Beach, next door (this is the site of the Cornwall Beach Party). There is also a new public beach, the Walter Fletcher, located west of Doctor's Cave.

Land of Look Behind

The Cockpit Country with its strange pitfalls and potholes carved by some primitive geological force into limestone is one of the most primitive sections of the whole West Indies. It was here that fugitive slaves of the Spanish took refuge from the conquering English in 1665. From hideouts in these impregnable hills they waged such relentless guerrilla warfare against the new invaders that the English called for a ceasefire in 1735, on the ex-slaves' terms. The descendants of these unsubdued slaves, the Maroons, live to this day in the Cockpit, free of taxation and other government interference in their affairs, their rights guaranteed by treaty. Only in the event of a capital crime can they be called to account by the government (and we've been told there "hasn't been one in 200 years"). Just 15 miles from Montego Bay, this is the historic "Land of Look Behind," where British colonials rode back to back on a single horse to avoid being ambushed by these fierce fighters for freedom. The Maroons–there are about 5000 of them–are ruled by one of their number known as "the colonel," and you should send word ahead before entering their country. The country can be explored on horseback (or gazed upon from a helicopter), and some adventurous tourists have been known to do it from Good Hope. Ask the Jamaica Tourist Board about minibus tours from Montego Bay to Accompong.

For less strenuous sightseeing, drive 10 miles east of Montego Bay along the coast road to the restored Great House, Rose Hall–and a great house it was indeed–with more than 50 doors, 365 windows, a dozen stairways, perhaps the grandest 18th century plantation house in the whole West Indies. The second mistress of Rose Hall was Annie Palmer, reputed to be a sort of female Bluebeard. She is credited by local history with murdering her three husbands and a plantation overseer who was her lover. She herself was done in by an unknown assailant. Her amours have been recorded in two novels, one called *The White Witch of Rose Hall,* the other *Jamaica White.* You can tour the property and be guided through the Great House. There is also a small restaurant and pub.

Another of Jamaica's picturesque harbors is Falmouth, 12 miles east of Rose Hall on an estuary looking out to sea and back inland to the Cockpit Country. Many of the scenes depicting Georgian architecture in the movie *Papillon* (with Dustin Hoffman and Steve McQueen) were filmed in Falmouth's main street. Note the courthouse. It's a faithful copy of the original early 19th century structure destroyed by fire in 1926.

For rafting on the Martha Brae, you will start from Rafters Village, 3 miles from Falmouth, and float to the sea at Rock. The village has a restaurant, picnic facilities, swimming pool, and handicraft shop.

One of the interesting day excursions for Montego Bay visitors is the trip up and out in the Governor's Coach, a train ride into the interior of Jamaica with stops at Ipswich Caves and Catadupa, where townspeople take your measurements and your choice of fabrics on your way up and sell you a finished dress or shirt on your return trip. Lunch is provided at the side of a river, and a band accompanies the group to keep spirits high. The Appleton Rum Factory at Maggotty is also included.

You can fly from Montego Bay to Kingston and enjoy a graphic geology lesson looking down on Jamaica from the air. You can take the long and magnificent drive around the eastern end of the island, one of the scenic splendors of the world. Or you can take a train. The third is the cheapest, and in many ways the most interesting, way. You'll be pulled by a small diesel, and slowly. It will take you 4½ hours to cover the 100 miles between Montego Bay and the capital. There will be stops and station waits, long enough for you to get out, stretch your legs, and look over the local scene. In the course of this leisurely ride, you will pass rivers, mountains, valleys, virgin forests, coffee and banana plantations, mahogany groves, sugar cane, huts, men tilling their fields, women pounding corn, tending pigs, suckling babies. In short, you will pass through the heart of Jamaica.

Mandeville

This cool "summer capital" of Jamaica is sixty-five miles west of Kingston. Take Route A1 to Spanish Town, once the Spanish capital. Don't expect any touches of old Castile, however; the place is as English as Trafalgar Square. But Admiral Rodney, not Lord Nelson, stands in Government Square to greet you, flanked by two cannons he captured from the French in 1782. Note the old House of Assembly, and the nearby Cathedral of St. James, oldest Anglican church in the West Indies. King's House, now being excavated by archaeologists, was built by the Spanish. Be sure to visit the fascinating Jamaican People's Museum, the Old Kings House next door and a new Folk Museum. The impression of Englishness grows as you drive west to Old Harbour, where a slight detour will take you to Colbeck Castle. This, you will discover, is a monumental ruin with four square towers which was built in the 17th century by Colonel John Colbeck of His Majesty's Army. Its main façade, over 100 feet in length, and its symmetrical proportions will remind you of the great country houses of England. The fortress-like construction of the towers, 40 feet high with walls nearly 3 feet thick, shows that Colbeck Castle was more than a residence; it was a sentinel and bastion against the fierce Maroons.

If you're in the mood for exploring, you can turn south at Freetown onto secondary road B12 and make a big loop to Alley, an important sugar town where the big Monymusk Refinery, one of the most modern in the world, will show how the raw cane is processed into sugar. The village of Alley itself is charming, with its little English church of St. Peter's surveying the cane fields. This is a corner of Jamaica seldom seen by tourists.

The main road north to Mandeville follows the Milk River a good part of the way. As you approach you may be reminded of the rolling hills and valleys of Devonshire. The illusion is quickly spiked by the sharp, fanlike outlines of palm fronds, and, if the season is right, the red flame of poinciana blossoms, the orange and grapefruit in the citrus groves. Mandeville itself has its village green, its Georgian courthouse, its neat cottages and gardens, and above all its parish church, whose tall steeple would be perfectly at home in the Midlands. The climate is crisper here.

This could be called the garden capital of Jamaica. There are private gardens, and each summer there is an exhibit by the Jamaica Horticultural Society. This is the center of the island's citrus industry; in season, the colorful market in the busy town square overflows with the fruits and flowers of the tropic soil.

Less "touristed" and therefore much less expensive than the better known Jamaican resorts, Mandeville has hill country "isolation" and back country village charm. Horseback riding, cycling, croquet, hiking, tennis, and golf are the diversions here, and you feel more like engaging in them in the cool climate. If you want something more active, descend to the coast for deep-sea fishing. Headquarters is the Blue Water Fishing Club at Whitehouse. Prize catches of marlin, tarpon, kingfish, and wahoo have been made here in these waters which rival those off Port Antonio for game fish.

Center for the once-popular crocodile hunting (now prohibited) is Black River, the town at the mouth of its namesake stream, the largest navigable river in Jamaica, where there is excellent fresh-water fishing. The marshy banks of Black River are home for what the people and even the tourist office call alligators, but their snouts are longer and narrower than an alligator's and their lower teeth clamp shut into marginal notches as do those of a crocodile (not into pits as alligators' do).

The drive from Mandeville to Black River passes through one of the great scenic wonders of Jamaica. Just west of West Lacovia, the road enters a grove of giant bamboos which meet overhead. This is the famous Bamboo Avenue, a cool, airy Gothic nave of light and shade extending for a mile and a half.

Negril

This area grew so slowly that for years it was "Jamaica's best kept secret," but now that it has become a water-sports haven, and a respite for the very casual, even "hedonistic" life, it has come into its own. Located on the western tip of the island, its accommodations are similar to those the Club Meds offer, with activities planned around the clock. Negril is the place to lead an unfettered, beachside life on a seven-mile stretch of glorious sands.

Natural foods and a naturist beach are all part of the scheme of things at Negril today. Scuba diving, snorkeling, sailing, windsurfing, parasailing and swimming are the daytime activities; while tossing a caftan or shirt over your bikini is the proper attire for dining and dancing after sundown.

A DAY ON YOUR OWN

One of the loveliest attractions in Jamaica is Dunn's River Falls. Plan to make a day of it—pack a picnic lunch, a bathing suit, a towel, and don't forget your camera—this spot is a real beauty. No matter where you're staying, you can, and should, make a trip to the Falls an all-day excursion. As an example, a day-trip from Kingston follows:

Leave the city and its hubbub, drive through the quiet suburbs, then over Stony Hill to the Castleton Botanic Gardens. Plan to stop here for at least a half hour. Then head northward, skirting the banana and sugar plantations to emerge at Port Maria, on the island's north coast. Watch for the "Firefly" sign and turn off for a brief look at the home Noel Coward chose as his winter retreat. Continue on through Ocho Rios, past Reynold's bauxite pier, where *Dr. No* was filmed, and on to Dunn's River Falls. Swim, climb the falls, and enjoy a picnic at the perfect spot.

To see even more of the countryside, return to Kingston by an entirely different route. Head out through Fern Gully, a 4-mile long lush forest trail, then through the Moneague plains, Mount Diablo, and Linstead, to make a short stop at Spanish Town, the former capital of Jamaica, before returning to the capital city.

PRACTICAL INFORMATION FOR JAMAICA

HOW TO GET THERE. By Air. Visitors staying in Ocho Rios and Runaway Bay area hotels, in addition to those at Montego Bay or in the Round Hill-Tryall area and even Negril, will find Montego Bay's International Airport the most convenient. Visitors to Port Antonio and Kingston will find Kingston's Norman Manley Airport the most convenient. When you arrive at either airport, you can take the "shuttle" service of *Trans Jamaica Airlines.*

From New York, *American Airlines, Air Jamaica* and *Pan American* fly non-stop. *Air Florida, Air Jamaica, Pan Am* and *Eastern* come in from Miami; *BWIA* from San Juan. *Air Jamaica,* the country's national carrier, provides the most frequent service between U.S. cities and the island. They also fly from Toronto; *Air Canada* from Montreal and Toronto. *British Airways* and *Air Jamaica* come across from London.

By Sea. Over 200 cruise-ship calls are made in Jamaica, mainly by ships out of Miami, Tampa or Port Everglades on a regular weekly or fortnightly basis. There are ships that leave out of other ports but not on regular schedule. Cruise ships come in to Montego Bay, Kingston, Ocho Rios and Port Antonio. Many of the cruises offer land packages before and after cruise and some excellent tours-ashore programs are offered at each port. Among the ships that call are those of Carnival Line, Holland American, Costa Line, Norweigian Caribbean, Paquet, Princess Cruises, Royal Caribbean Line, Royal Viking and Sun Line.

FURTHER INFORMATION. The *Jamaica Tourist Board* has offices at 866 Second Ave., New York, N.Y. 10017; 36 S. Wabash Ave., Chicago, Ill. 60603; 1320 So. Dixie Highway, Coral Gables, Fla. 33146; or at 3440 Wilshire Blvd., Los Angeles, Ca. 90010. In Canada, contact them at 2221 Yonge St., Suite 507, Toronto, Ont. M4S 2B4; In London: Jamaica House, 50 St. James St., London SW1A 1JT.

On the island, the JTB's head office is at 77–83 Knutsford Blvd. in Kingston. They also have regional offices at Cornwall Beach in Montego Bay; and at the Ocean Village Shopping Centre in Ocho Rios.

ISLAND MEDIA. *The Visitor* is a weekly vacation guide published for tourists and distributed free. Local newspapers are *The Daily Gleaner* and the *Daily News.*

AUTHORIZED TOUR OPERATORS: Adventure Tours; Alken Tours; Butler Travels; Caribbean Holidays; Caribbean Vacation Center; Cavalcade Tours; Flyfaire; Butler Travels; Jamaica Travel Center; Lib/Go; Red & Blue; Sojourn Group Tours, Sunburst Holidays and Thompson Vacations from the U.S. From Canada: Fairway Tours; and Holiday House. From London: ALTA Holidays; Kuoni Travel; Rankin-Kuhn; Sovereign Holidays; Thomas Cook; and James Vence Travel.

PASSPORTS, VISAS. None is required of citizens of Canada or the U.S. entering Jamaica as tourists for any period up to 6 months. However, some proof of citizenship is required, and you must have sufficient funds to maintain yourself on the island, and on onward ticket. Passports are required of British subjects. All will be given a tourist card on arrival, which should be presented to the Immigration Office at that time, and returned to them on departure. *NOTE:* Jamaica is very strict about drugs–possession of *ganja* (marijuana) may get you a jail cell, and you'll certainly be deported. Above all, don't try to smuggle it out of the country. The authorities are on to all the tricks.

MONEY. Jamaica currency is used here. $1 Jamaican is equivalent to about 56¢ U.S. Or, $1.75 J = $1 U.S.; $3.96 J = 1£. There are several restrictions concerning money here: it is an offence for visitors to bring in or take out Jamaican currency. Exchange money only at commercial banks, the bureaus at the airports, or your hotel and make sure you obtain a receipt, so that reconversion can be handled easily at the end of your stay. *SPECIAL NOTE:* All hotel bills, in-bond purchases, and car rentals must be paid in foreign currency; all other transactions in Jamaican currency.

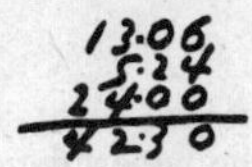

TAXES AND OTHER CHARGES. There is a 5% government tax on hotel rooms; plus a per night room occupancy tax of anywhere from $2–6 U.S., depending upon hotel category and season of the year. Some hotels add a 10-15% service charge. The airport departure tax is $10 Jamaican.

HOW TO GET ABOUT. Taxis are best for short hops; tours or seat-in-car travel for the longer trips around Jamaica. The taxis are metered, but still establish the price with the driver ahead of time. When you travel from your hotel, check with the desk about prices and make arrangements for your driver to wait or to come back at a specified hour to pick you up–it's not always easy to hail a taxi, particularly if your're in some out-of-the-way spot. Trips taken between the hours of midnight and 5 A.M. have a 25% surcharge on the metered rate. Rates are figured per-car, not per-passenger.

There are more than 40 car-rental agencies across Jamaica. Among them are *Avis, Budget, Hertz, Martin's Jamaica,* and *National.* Rates run from $30 U.S. per day.

Local bus service is good in Kingston and Montego Bay, but not recommended for the rest of the island, where service is sparse. The Kingston bus terminal is Victoria Park at the top of King Street. There is twice-daily ferry service to Port Royal from Victoria Pier in downtown Kingston.

A diesel train service runs between Montego Bay and Kingston and Port Antonio every day. The Kingston-Montego Bay train trip is a 4½-hour kaleidoscope of life and scenery of the Jamaican interior; from Kingston to Port Antonio, the trip takes 3½ hours.

Trans Jamaican Airlines, the island's domestic airline, has greatly expanded its services, operating daily shuttle flights between each of the island's main resorts–Kingston, Montego Bay, Port Antonio, Mandeville, Ocho Rios and Negril. During the winter season, these resort areas are linked to one another by 2 to 6 roundtrip flights each day. Fewer flights during the summer months.

EVENTS AND HOLIDAYS. The highlight of the yearly celebrations here occurs on the first Monday in August, Independence day. Other public holidays are New Year's Day; Ash Wednesday; Good Friday; Easter Monday; Labour Day (May 23); National Heroes Day (Oct.16); Christmas Day; and Boxing Day (Dec. 26).

WHAT WILL IT COST?

A typical day in Jamaica for *two* persons during the winter season will run

	US$	£
Hotel accommodations in one of the resort areas	70	38
Breakfast at the hotel	7	4
Luncheon at a moderate restaurant	13	7
Dinner at the hotel or "in-town"	30	16
Taxes, tips & service charges	15	8
Car rental for one day	30	16
	$165	£89

STAYING IN JAMAICA

HOTELS. You can find just about what you want in Jamaica, where the Tourist Board and the government have worked together in very successful attempts to become the all-inclusive resort. For general guidance, the plushest hotels are on the North Shore, at least a half hour from Montego Bay, and around the Ocho Rios area. Port Antonio is a bit more remote, at the eastern end of the island; while Negril, at the westernmost point, is the latest development, not only for its beautiful beaches, but for its "carefree" life style. Mandeville, in the hills, is real country living, while Kingston offers city life, usually attracting businessmen.

FALMOUTH

Trelawny Beach Club. 350 rooms, all with private balcony, soaring up 7 stories over 4 miles of white sand beach. 4 tennis courts, swimming pool, a choice of restaurants, and the *Rum Keg* nightclub. The focus here is on *"Ecstacism"* (in Negril, it's *"hedonism")* which they describe as, "the seventh sense . . . an appreciation of all the joys of nature . . . the feeling of golden, sun-drenched lazy days . . . black velvet tropic nights . . . the languid sea caressing your body!" A different life-style, but becoming more and more popular, with special week-long package plans the keynote. Also a saving on air fare if you buy the package. Without the air portion, rates run from $556–706 per person, per week, based on double accommodations, depending upon the time of year. The rate includes all three meals, unlimited use of sports equipment and facilities, entertainment, taxes, service charges and tips.

KINGSTON

Inter-Continental Kingston Hotel. Another high-rise commercial property in the capital city area, the Inter-Continental has 390 rooms overlooking the harbor. Caters to conventions, with several dining rooms available for groups of every size. Cocktail lounge, shops, swimming pool. $66–74 double EP all year.

Jamaica Pegasus. 350 rooms, all air-conditioned, in a 17-story complex near the New Kingston Hotel. The emphasis here is to make it the special convention center for Kingston, and it now offers meeting rooms that can accommodate 1,000 people. Audio-visual services are here, along with a variety of restaurants and cocktail bars, shops, and a discotheque. Two swimming pools, and a special tour desk to make arrangements for tennis, golf, and on-island touring. $90 double EP in winter.

Mayfair Hotel. 28 rooms, some with air-conditioning, some with private bath, on West King's House Close, near historic Devon House. A quiet, informal guest house, which was a former great house within tropical gardens. $35 double EP all year.

New Kingston Hotel. This property has 196 rooms, all air-conditioned, and a half-dozen suites, that rise 17 stories in the heart of Kingston's downtown area. Especially popular with convention groups, since it offers almost everything on the premises. 2 tennis courts, swimming pool, poolside bar, restaurants, lounges, and theatre-style rooms for special convention presentations. Whether you're with a group or not, don't miss the hotel's rooftop restaurant high in the sky, and the "Jonkanoo Lounge," which swings until the early hours. $69–78 double EP all year.

Terra Nova Hotel. 35 air-conditioned rooms set within beautiful grounds. A special gathering spot for the Kingston government officials at luncheon. The main part of the hotel was once a private home. Two wings were added to give it a motel-motif. Swimming pool, restaurant, cocktail lounge, nightclub. A pleasant place to stay in the Kingston orbit. $55 double EP all year.

MANDEVILLE

Hotel Astra. 25 rooms in modest, but pleasant surroundings, in the cool Jamaican hills. Rustic mountain atmosphere, with swimming pool and tennis. Comfortable restaurant and pub. $45–55 double all year, including two meals.

Mandeville Hotel. Victorian England set down in a spacious tropical garden. This venerable resort hotel has been completely renovated and its 19th century charm is only enhanced by the addition of a contemporary restaurant and cocktail lounge. 60 rooms; country club privileges at the nearby Manchester Club. $45 double EP all year round.

MONTEGO BAY

Carlyle Beach Hotel. 50 delightful rooms with balconies facing the sea, opposite a tiny beach. Beach privileges. Swimming pool, popular restaurant and pub, calypso entertainment. $65 double EP in winter; $45 double EP off-season.

Casa Montego. Striking 9-story building whose terraces and perforated walls give it the look of a filigreed ivory cube. Opposite Cornwall Beach. 125 rooms with private baths and terrace. Open-air bar, dining room, lounge, shopping arcade. Large salt-water pool; piano bar; *Ipso Facto* Disco. Rates range from $67–79 double all year.

Doctor's Cave Beach Hotel. 75 air-conditioned rooms with bath on a pretty garden acreage opposite Doctor's Cave Beach. Freshwater swimming pool; secluded dining with good food and service. $55–70 double EP in winter; $40–45 double EP off-season.

Half Moon. 190 rooms on a white sand beach, 7 miles east of Montego Bay. Dining room, bar, buffet lunches served daily on the terrace. "Get acquainted" cocktail parties, beach bonfire picnics. 13 tennis courts (4 lighted for night play); 4 new squash courts; 18-hole championship golf course with attractive club house, where you can dine by special reservation. Evening cocktail and buffet scene is "typical Caribbean." Beautiful grounds; freshwater pool; sauna and massage facilities. We like the location, lively atmosphere, the beach, and the golf set-up. Rates run from $189 double in winter; from $129 double off-season, including breakfast and dinner.

Holiday Inn. Beach front. Full convention facilities in this 520-room complex. Fresh water pool, water sports, 4 tennis courts, restaurant, nightclub. Appeals to convention groups. $70–95 double EP in winter; $57–65 double EP off-season.

Jack Tar Montego Beach. This 130-room hotel, which is right on the water on the outskirts of town, has a terrace restaurant, beach-side bar and snackery, and informal living within. Taken over by the Jack Tar group in Spring '82, we'll have to wait to see whether this will become one of their typical villages which offer all-inclusive packages based on a seven-day stay. Meanwhile, rates run $68–74 double EP in winter; $45–65 double off-season.

Montego Bay Club Resort. A 14-story property that rises nicely over Doctor's Cave Beach. Rooms are in studios or suites, with each one offering kitchenettes and private balconies. *Bamboo Room Restaurant;* poolside buffets; tennis; watersports; small shopping arcade. $70–90 double EP in winter; $50–65 double off-season.

Montego Bay Racquet Club. Cottage-type hillside hotel, with 38 air-conditioned rooms. Club-like atmosphere. Swimming pool; 7 floodlit tennis courts, air-conditioned club house; locker rooms; poolside dining. Planned for tennis and the place the pros go. $70–90 double EP in winter.

Rose Hall Inter-Continental. Double hotel complex, each one seven stories high. 508 air-conditioned rooms, each with private bath and balcony. On the beach. Gourmet dining room, coffee shop, nightclub and disco. Swimming pool; 18-hole golf course; 6 tennis courts; all water sports. Something for everyone here. $96–111 double EP in winter; $60–74 double EP off-season.

Round Hill. A long-time favorite with international society, this resort is on a 98-acre peninsula that juts out into the Caribbean, 8 miles west of Montego Bay. Surrounded by gardens, the hotel overlooks its own private beach and a view of the north shore of Jamaica. You can have your choice of a hotel suite or a villa (more expensive) on the hill with private pool. Water sports run the gamut, from sailing to water skiing. Calypso music at night and dining by candlelight. 112 units. Horseback riding, tennis, and everything for the good life. From $225 double in winter, with breakfast and dinner included.

Royal Caribbean. 168 rooms on the Caribbean at Mahoe Bay. Jamaican colonial architecture with 12 buildings in a semi-circle. Free-form pool; private beach. Complimentary tennis, croquet, putting green; chaise lounges, and mats. Fishing trips and golf can be arranged. $92–114 double EP in winter; $65 double EP off-season.

Tryall Golf & Beach Club. 12 miles west of town and another world in atmosphere. On its own bay (perfect swimming), with manicured grounds, most of which are the island's best golf course. Private homes, some available as part of the hotel room count. 36 rooms at the hilltop mainhouse. Terrace for fine dining and sunset watching. In-pool bar. This place has its own following so plan ahead. $180–200 double, including breakfast and dinner.

Upper Deck. Unique setting high above Montego Bay. 109 rooms on three floors, all with full kitchens or kitchenettes. A powder house used by Admiral Nelson in 1782 serves as the commissary. The *Admiral's Inn Grill Room and Bar* faces the bay and offers splendid sunsets with meals and drinks. Pool. $72–75 double EP in winter, $36–38 double off-season.

Verney House. 30 rooms with balconies, on a hillside overlooking the bay. Spacious gardens; nice dining room; swimming pool with bar. Like living with a family, which, naturally, is not for everyone. $35–40 double EP in winter.

NEGRIL

Coconut Cove. On 7 miles of white sand beach, these 44 units at Rutland Point make for a good, lively, and informal vacation. The units are 1- and 2-bedroom for housekeeping. Restaurant and pool on premises, along with other sports facilities. $130–140 double EP in winter; $60–70 double EP off-season.

Hedonism II. Formerly the Negril Beach Village, this fine property is being totally refurbished and will emerge anew in the '82–83 winter season. At Rutland Point, on the west end of Jamaica, the 250-room resort is Club Med style, with informality and action the keys. Sharks teeth are currency. Activities include tennis, scuba, sailing, water skiing, backgammon, volleyball, bicycling, horseback riding and just about anything you can think of. Open-air dining room with stage and dance floor next door; disco; pool with whirlpool; shopping arcade. The rooms are in 2-story buildings around the grounds. "Hedonism" is the keynote here! Weekly package rates are reasonable and vary according to time of year.

Sundowner. The traditional favorite for this area focuses on the water. *Aquaworld, Ltd.* can take 20 divers out at once. They operate the water sports concession. 28 rooms on 7-mile arc of Long Bay Beach. A great get-a-way place if you don't demand all the luxuries. $115–125 double in winter; $95–105 double off-season, including breakfast and dinner.

OCHO RIOS

Americana Ocho Rios. A towering 335-room hotel that soars up 11 stories over a white-sand beach. An interesting choice for dining, with five different restaurants; nightly entertainment. Two swimming pools, two tennis courts; watersports. Golf and horseback riding nearby. From $90–105 double EP all year.

Couples. Halfway between Ocho Rios and Oracabessa, Couples Resort is a complete, self-contained property on a private, palm-lined beach. It offers everything you could imagine or want. All 141 rooms have private bath, balcony, or patio with view of the mountains or the sea. It's run "Club Med" style, but it's for couples only! 5 tennis courts, swimming pool, all water sports, including deep-sea fishing at modest extra rates. Otherwise, the weekly rate takes care of all meals, drinks, and even cigarettes. The food is superb and seemingly never-ending; there is nightly dancing under the stars; native floorshows; and calypso entertainment. The friendly and accommodating staff adds to it all to make this a real "couples holiday." $1,290–1,560 per couple per week, depending upon the time of year.

Jamaica Hilton. 265 rooms on 22 landscaped acres. The wing with the seaview has its own dining room and bar. Nice patio rooms. This is a truly luxurious property with a commanding beachfront, just 5 miles west of Ocho Rios. Choice of swimming from the private white-sand beach or in the free-form freshwater swimming pool. Sailing, fishing, boating, and floodlit tennis courts. The *Aquatic Club* gives scuba lessons. Fine dining; dancing nightly on the open-air patio or in the air-conditioned nightclub, which also offers entertainment. $93–114 double EP in winter; lower off-season.

Jamaica Inn. The Jamaica Inn overlooks its own beautiful, palm-studded beach just 1½ miles east of Ocho Rios. This intimate inn has 50 airy rooms, each with private bath and patio facing the beach. A long, single-story, gallery-like structure, it has a plantation house atmosphere and repeat clientele who claim that there isn't any other hotel in Jamaica! In addition to swimming, skin diving, and fishing, the hotel can make arrangements for you to play golf, tennis, or ride horseback. $180–215 double during the season, including breakfast, lunch and dinner.

Plantation Inn. A delightful resort estate next door to the Jamaica Inn, and providing similar tranquil atmosphere. The plantation house is at street level; the beach is a steep climb below; all of it giving you a dramatic perspective of the sea from your balcony. There are 65 rooms, 17 of them with private bath and balcony. Lovely beach, tennis, golf privileges. Dancing and dining by candlelight on the veranda. From $155 double in winter; from $115 double off-season, with breakfast and dinner included.

Sheraton. 385 high-rise rooms next to the Americana Ocho Rios. There are 40 cabanas that stretch alongside. Ballroom; meeting rooms; full convention facilities; plus shopping arcade. Sightseeing and car rental desks. *Pimento Room* coffee shop; *Hugo's Bar* and *Hugo's Rotisserie; Garden Terrace* and patio. Swimming pools, tennis courts, beach, health club. Rates run anywhere from $80–100 double EP depending upon accommodations and the time of year.

Turtle Beach Towers. A condominium apartment complex with a crescent-shaped beach. 1-, 2-, and 3-bedroom units available in one of the 4 twelve-storied towers. 120 apartments in all, with views of the sea and the mountains. Maid service provided. Cooks and Nannies available at additional cost. Grocery store next door. Coffee shop/bar by the pool. $74–117 double EP in winter, $53–80 double off-season.

PORT ANTONIO

Bonnie View. On top of a 600-foot hill, a half mile from Port Antonio, this hotel looks north over the Caribbean, and south to the Blue Mountains. Most of the 30 rooms have private verandas, but are not for fussy travelers. Large swimming pool and sundeck; cocktail terrace, calypso music, and proximity to rafting on the Rio Grande. $28–34 double EP in winter; $24 double EP off-season.

Dragon Bay. On 40 acres, seven miles east of Port Antonio, with 100 rooms in cottages facing a beautiful bay. Ideal for families. Combination cook/maid service and Nannies available. Excellent hilltop restaurant; separate pagoda-style bar on peninsula hill. A favorite with sports fishermen. $100–130 double EP in winter; $56 double EP off-season.

Jamaica Hill. Delightful, luxurious cottage-style hotel on 11 acres overlooking the San San Bay. 1-bedroom suites; 2-bedroom villas, all in the garden. Tennis; new *Tree-House Bar;* swimming pool. Haute cuisine. From $200 for a one-bedroom in winter; from $150 off-season, including two meals.

Trident Villas. This hotel was rebuilt in 1981 and is more luxurious and beautiful than the original. On a point overlooking the sea, with 30 studios and 1-bedroom villas. The reconstructed main house with dining and bar facilities overlooks pool and water. Tennis, horse-back riding, sailing and snorkeling included in rate. $234–274 MAP in winter; $194–234 MAP off-season.

RUNAWAY BAY

Club Caribbean. 116 rooms in rondavels along a 1000-foot private beach. English pub, beachfront bar, discotheque. Fresh water pool; 2 tennis courts. Caters to young groups. $80–90 double EP all year.

Eaton Hall. This spot has a lot to offer if you want elegance out of the ordinary. Its 17th and 18th century core has been restored, and the 10 individual villas around the grounds harmonize with the old look. Interiors of the original house are Jamaican hardwoods; suites are furnished with antiques and Jamaican reproductions. 2 swimming pools, tennis, excellent French and Jamaican cuisine. In addition to the villas, there are 36 rooms in two garden wings. Rates range from $70–100 double EP all year.

Runaway Bay Hotel & Golf Club. This modern resort complex has 152 nicely-furnished rooms on one of the best beaches on the north coast. 18-hole championship golf course, plus an executive course, and Club House. Two swimming pools; tennis courts. Terrace dining; dancing and entertainment nightly. Although Runaway Bay caters to groups and conventions, it's ideal for families. Check on the special package plans available. Otherwise, rates run $80–95 double EP in winter; $50–60 double off-season.

HOME RENTALS. Hundreds of apartments, homes and villas are available in Jamaica. The best contacts are *Villas and Apartments Abroad* at 19 East 49th St., New York, N.Y. 10017, and JAVA *(Jamaica Association of Villas and Apartments)* at 200 Park Avenue, New York, N.Y. 10017. Rates run anywhere from $400 per week for a two-bedroom cottage to $3,000 per week for a six-bedroom villa. The *Jamaica Tourist Board* has full-color brochures and rate sheets available.

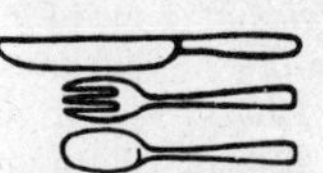

RESTAURANTS. Jamaican food is like Jamaican life—full of fire and spice! The Jamaicans, like other residents of the tropics, have always made liberal use of pungent spices and peppers. The national dish is *Ackee and Saltfish,* which is made of codfish and the cooked fruit of the ackee, an exotic vegetable that grows on one of the trees that was brought here by the infamous Captain Bligh. Other typical Jamaican dishes are *peas and rice,* a tasty concoction that really has no peas at all. They use kidney beans, white rice, coconut milk, scallions, and coconut oil, and the end result is terrific. Don't be put off if you see *Sea Roaches* on the menu—they are actually baby lobsters. Jamaican curries are hot and good; curried goat and rice is an island favorite. Mackerel and bananas combines the leading island fruit with imported salt fish. *Pepperpot soup,* another island specialty, is made of salt pork, salt beef, okra, and Indian kale, which emerges as a dish called *Callalou.* It's greener than the sea and a million times as thick.

Patties are what they call Jamaica's staple snack. They can be found everywhere, but vary according to filling and price. Basically, they are pastries filled with ground beef and a breadcrumb additive. For another on-island treat, try their *chicken fricassee,* which is quite different from anything you've ever prepared at home. It's a thick and rich chicken stew, with carrots, scallions, yams, onions, tomatoes, and peppers, all prepared in unrefined coconut oil.

One of the highlights in Jamaican dining is roast suckling pig. Not easy to find; but when you see it on the menu, try it. It's boned, stuffed with rice, peppers, diced yam, and thyme, then mixed together with shredded coconut and corn meal, before it's roasted to a crisp golden brown.

Jamaican fruits are exotic and delicious, expecially the mango. But also try the passion fruit and rose apples, custard apples, pineapple, and, of course, the bananas. Another scan of the menu may list *Matrimony,* which is really a marriage of slices of orange and star apples in a unique fruit salad. Another island specialty to consider is an exotic dessert which combines mangoes with dry champagne.

With all its native dishes, as well as its Continental fare served at most of the hotels, Jamaica also holds its own as far as "quenchers" are concerned. *Tia Maria* is world famous as one of the most popular coffee liqueurs; *Rumona* is their rum cordial; and their rums, *Myers* and *Appleton* are among the best to come out of the Caribbean.

Some of the best dining here can be found in the smalller hotels and guest houses, but there are a few specialty spots that are very popular in the major resort areas. Restaurants we think you might enjoy, and their locations follow.

In **Kingston,** the top spot is *Terra Nova,* the gourmet restaurant in the hotel. It has long been the favorite of government officials, and more recently for tourists who like the leisurely and excellent dining, and the orchestra for dancing the night away. The *Swiss Chalet,* on Holborn Rd., is outstanding and serves both local and Continental food; for Chinese fare, which is very popular here and encompasses every Oriental delight, try *Wong-Kai* on East Street, which is expensive but worth it; *Dynasty* at the Mall on Constant Spring Road; or *Meemee* on Northside Drive, which is interesting and inexpensive.

Don't miss the *Grog Shop* at historic Devon House for excellent Jamaican dishes. Or travel out of the city to the *Blue Mountain Inn,* a charming manor house with memorable food, served by candlelight.

For dining out in the **Montego Bay** area, the *Club House Grill,* at the Half Moon/Rose Hall Golf Club, is well-known for its well-prepared food, especially the prime ribs, which are carved at your table. The *Diplomat* is one of the most expensive and elegant in this area, with the specialties of the house revolving around lobster and crab dishes. Try the *House of Lords Restaurant* for seafood specialties or *the Front Porch* for excellent local dishes. Both are moderately priced. Or dine out expensively and sample "Jamaican haute cuisine" at the *Calabash Restaurant* on Queen's Drive, or *The Brigadoon* nearby.

The *Town House* restaurant, in a restored Georgian building on Church Street, is one of the most popular in the area. It's elegant, expensive, but offers such delectable seafood specialties that it's worth the tariff. For casual dining, a great way to meet other vacationers is the JTB-sponsored *Cornwall Beach Party,* held at Cornwall Beach on Fridays. Check for the time, but be assured that the prices are right.

In **Ocho Rios,** dining out is a pleasure. Find fine seafood entrées at the *Seagull* at the Mallards Beach Americana, at *Chez Robert* in the Coconut Grove Shopping Center, and at the *Almond Tree* restaurant on Main Street. The San Souci's *Casanova Restaurant* serves Venetian cuisine in an elegant setting; or find intimate, lagoon-side dining at *Moxon's of Boscobel,* a seven-mile drive out of town. They are all expensive; all still require jackets and reservations; but all worth the price.

NIGHTLIFE. *Reggae* is the rhythm here—easy to learn and lots of fun. There are dozens of "in-town" discos, but for a look at the real Jamaica, check your hotel bulletin board—they usually schedule calypso bands and folkloric groups, as well as beach picnics and barbecues. The JTB has added to the options by arranging evenings on White River and Great River, and barbecues at Dunn's River Falls.

SHOPPING. Shopping Jamaica goes two ways: things Jamaican and things imported. The former are made with style and skill; the latter are duty-free bargains.

Jamaican crafts take the form of resortwear, hand-loomed fabrics, embroidery, silk-screening, wood carvings, oil paintings and fine arts in other media, and rum. Visitors to Kingston can stop at the *In-Craft* workshop and store to buy small woven straw items, sandals, order custom-made rugs, and choose from reproductions of pewter and china recovered from the ruins of submerged ancient Port Royal.

The fashion scene is organized under the Jamaica Fashion Guild banner, and its member companies have current fashion ideas, but others who are not members also offer independent and attractive designs. For sophisticated designs, look in at *Ruth Clarage, Ltd.* Lively and popular patterns; available at Pineapple Place in Ocho Rios; at several hotels and at the City Centre in Montego Bay.

At Highgate, a mountain village on the junction road about an hour from Ocho Rios, near the Brimmer Hall Plantation, the Quakers run a workshop specializing in wicker and wood furniture, floor mats, and other tropical furnishings. They welcome custom orders. Highgate is a pretty village. Worth the trip in conjunction with a visit to Brimmer Hall as a day's excursion from Ocho Rios.

Wood carvings seen on the road, especially around Falmouth, are made of native mahogany or *lignum vitae,* a local blond hardwood. For some time during the slow periods in the sugar fields, sugar workers in the area would try their hands at wood carving, selling their work on the road. In response to complaints from tourists who'd bought the carvings and found the pieces falling apart or in poor condition, the Jamaica Tourist Board set up wood carving workshops in conjunction with the Jamaica School of Art. Carving instructors voluntarily gave the local craftsmen advice on curing the wood properly and advanced the art of the Falmouth carvers. The program was so successful it has been taken to Ocho Rios and Montego Bay. It's still supplementary income to sugar field workers.

Jamaican rum is a great take-home gift, too. The Rumona liqueur is the world's only rum liqueur and is hard to find outside the island. Tia Maria is Jamaica's coffee liqueur.

In-bond shopping used to mean that you selected an item in the store and it was delivered to your flight or boat at a much lower price than if you'd taken it with you. Problems resulted, and visitors can now take purchases directly from in-bond stores–providing you can prove you are a visitor. (Liquor and cigarettes must still be picked up at point of embarkation.) To be sure you are getting the bargain you think you are, plan ahead. Check the stores at home on recording equipment, Swiss watches, cameras, French perfumes, British woolens, crystal, jewelry, and china. Jamaican shopkeepers claim a saving up to 40% off U.S. prices. Be familiar with U.S. Customs regulations. Don't expect to find every style and pattern. *NOTE:* You *must* pay for purchases in U.S. or Canadian dollars (to shore up the country's foreign exchange reserve). This means, from our experience, that you pay "tourist prices," but if the item is something you really want, maybe that doesn't matter.

In addition to the shops in the large hotels, stores tend to be clustered in shopping plazas at major tourist areas.

Flamouth: By far the most unique shopping opportunities are those offered by Muriel and Keith Chandler, who feature batik fabrics that they make in volume and sell under the name *Caribatik Ltd.* Their studio/workshop is on the coast road. Should you choose to bring your own patterns, they'll make them to order.

Kingston: *Swiss Stores,* on the corner of Harbour and Church Streets, specializes in famous brand watches at duty-free prices; there are also several shopping plazas to explore in this busy capital. Visit the *Kingston Crafts Market* on the waterfront for straw and wood, and the *Devon House* for paintings and local craft.

Montego Bay: in town along Gloucester Avenue, the coast road; at the *Casa Montego Arcade; Beachview Arcade* opposite Doctor's Cave Beach; *City Center Building; Montego Freeport; Holiday Village,* opposite the Holiday Inn.

Ocho Rios: *Pineapple Place* and *Coconut Grove,* not far from the area's best hotels (Jamaica Inn, Plantation Inn, etc.), are two shopping areas with branches of some of the Jamaica Fashion Guild shops (colorful resortwear) and the imported crystal, china, etc. that come at free-port prices.

Gemcutters Jamaica, Ltd., 7 Bravo St., St. Ann's Bay, not far from the Barclay's Bank branch, offers jewelry made from polished and honed semi-precious stones. Bracelets are in the $10-25 range, as are cuff links; rings, pins, etc. all available.

Around the Little Pub, there are several small boutiques; *Design Concept* is located in the Little Pub and carries jewelry. The newest of the Ocho Rios Shopping Centers is *Ocean Village,* with a branch of the Tourist Board, next to Mallards Beach.

Port Antonio: *Dragon Plaza* has about a dozen shops featuring crafts and resortwear, plus a supermarket for villa and apartment residents.

Before supermarkets became popular, Jamaica depended on open markets for the exchange of goods. Each town still has its market days—Sat. plus one other. Even in Montego Bay. Farmers bring their produce (and their gossip) to trade. Tourists are welcome as long as they keep in mind that this is a serious market place and not a show of local color put on for their behalf. If you wish to photograph the shoppers, ask their permission first and be prepared to pay them a quarter or two (in Jamaican currency). Country people don't know about candid photography and associate pictures with formal occasions. They may not want to be photographed, since they are not dressed in their best clothes. It's a matter of pride. Some won't allow their photos to be taken under any circumstances, and their privacy should be respected.

SPORTS AND OTHER ACTIVITIES. *Swimming and snorkeling* are year-round activities. *Scuba diving, skin diving, waterskiing,* and *sailing* are next in line, with most available from the hotel beaches. In the Discovery/Runaway Bar area, you'll find all facilities at Berkely Beach, the Club Caribbean or the Runaway Bay Hotel. Scuba runs $20 US per dive; waterskiing $10 for 6 circles; Sunfish rental $6 per hour. They can also arrange one-hour glass-bottom tours for $5 per person.

In Montego Bay, *Water Whirl, Ltd.* operates from Cornwall Beach and several hotels. All sports here, including windsurfing at $8 per hour.

Check with *Aqua Sports, Ltd.* at Negril for week-long diving plans, or try para-sailing (25 minutes for $15). And, in Ocho Rios, contact *Ruddy Watersports* for everything from deep-sea fishing charters (from $150 half-day for 1-4 persons to $400 for a full day for up to 5 people) to yacht cruises throughout the day and sunset cruises in the early evening.

Fishing is especially good in Port Antonio. Licenses are not required. Deep-sea fishing for sailfish, marlin, bluefin, tuna, and yellowfin can be arranged through the hotel. For full details on arrangements and fishing trips to the California Bank, contact the Eastern Jamaica Angler's Association, P.O. Box 140, Port Antonio, Jamaica, W.I.

For *surfing,* head straight for the eastern coast of Portland Parish, to Boston Bay, where long combers roll into a white sand beach. The bay is not too far from Port Antonio.

Golf is a year-round activity in Jamaica. In Kingston are *Caymanas* and *Constant Spring,* 18 holes. Mandeville has the *Manchester Club,* 9 holes. In Montego Bay are *Eden Golf and Country Club, Half Moon-Rose Hall,* and *Tryall,* all 18-holes. Ocho Rios has *Runway Bay* and *Upton*, 18 holes.

Tennis is becoming increasingly popular, with hotels adding courts, resurfacing courts, and night-lighting them. Tennis is generally free to guests; fee for nonguests. Devoted tennis players will want to investigate the Montego Bay Racquet Club, which is a hotel as well as club for local tennis buffs. Instruction and tournaments are arranged.

Horseback riding is excellent in Montego Bay. Good Hope Plantation is a superb hotel for riders, and the place for day rides as well. It has marked trails. good horses, and tourist facilities.

MARTINIQUE

A Tropical Beguine

"Pearl of the Antilles," Martinique is the largest and northernmost of the Windward Islands. It is 50 miles long, 22 wide, and has a population of approximately 325,000. When Columbus landed at Carbet on the western coast in 1502, he got such a hot and arrowy reception from the Caribs that he left before he could think of a name. The Carib name, Madinina, meaning Island of the Flowers, remained, eventually to be Gallicized as Martinique. It could not be more appropriate. The island is a bower of hibiscus, anthurium, bougainvillea, wild orchids, and other tropical flowers, best seen during the summer months, when they are at their peak. A lush land of year-round summer, this island's average temperature varies between 75° and 80°, but make allowances for the mountain peaks, where evenings are cool. There's a cool and dry season from November to April, but that doesn't mean "no showers." In the rain forest, torrents are frequent and even at the beach the clouds can give you a quick "refresher." The warm, dry season is April to July; from September to November, the weather is warm (the trade winds are not at full force at this time) and sometimes rainy.

The terrain ranges from salt fields and barren rock in the arid south to the verdure-clad slopes and luxuriant rain forest of the north. Fort-de-France, with a population of more than 100,000, is the capital of Martinique and a popular port of call for cruise ships. It is a city well worth a wander and almost impossible to "tour." The main square, a beautifully landscaped park called La Savane, is the gathering place for spontaneous athletes who pick up a quick game of soccer or for sitting and watching the world go by. Snack trucks line one side and seem to have an endless stream of patrons. The side streets of town, flecked with shops selling some tourist items but mostly goods for daily use, are balconied with intricate wrought iron. The Cathedral and the Library are the two main buildings to note.

Across the bay is the village of Trois Ilets, which is the birthplace of Marie Josèphe Rose Tascher de la Pagerie, who was to captivate Napoleon Bonaparte (who renamed her Joséphine) and reign for five years as Empress of the French. Something in the soil or air of Martinique seems to have produced women of irresistible fascination. Mme. de Maintenon, first the mistress and finally the morganatic wife of Louis XIV, was raised in Martinique.

The verdant northland of Martinique is grove upon grove of banana, pineapple, coconut, even tomatoes, and other more familiar vegetables. Other crops include cane, vanilla, coffee, cocoa, cinnamon, and mahogany. The greatest of these is rum. It comes in a variety of colors, and its special flavor has the quality of good cognac. There is "Vieux Acajou" (Old Mahogany) and "Jeune Acajou" (Young Mahogany), another, more poetic way of saying dark and light. Punch, that drinking staple that brews sugar, water, lime juice, and rum into a potion poured from a carafe, is offered at most cafés and bistros.

Carnival Capers

The hottest thing in Martinique, however, is neither rum nor sun. It's the *biguine.* Contrary to popular superstition, Cole Porter did not begin it. He patterned his great song after Martinique's dance. The *biguine* is more than a dance, it's a way of life.

A session at this uninhibited dance will give you a taste of what Carnival, or "Vaval," is like in Martinique. It's the event of the year and, while it may have lost some of its naïveté in recent years, it's still the emotional upheaval of the year. Masquerades and singing and dancing in the streets are the normal order of weekend events beginning right after the new year begins and carrying on until the final explosion on the Monday and Tuesday before Lent. There is a great ball on Mardi Gras night, but the best is yet to come.

On Ash Wednesday, when the exhausted celebrants of more effete lands are having their fevered foreheads blackened with cinders, nearly 3,000 masked Martiniquais jam the streets of Fort-de-France. These are *les diablesses* (literally, the female devils, but both sexes participate *à la Martiniquaise).* All are grotesquely masked and costumed. Anything goes as long as one principal rule is adhered to: The costumes must be in two colors only, black and white. Clarinets and trumpets announce the fête; the chachas start the rhythm. The parades of this protracted wake in honor of Vaval, king of the carnival, and of Bois Bois, another major character whose part in the whole affair has not exactly been defined (although he *may* be the devil), start early in the morning. By noon, much rum has gone down the hatch, and many a *diablesse* is drunk. Luncheon has a sobering and strengthening effect, fortifying the devils for the really strenuous work of the afternoon and evening. By afternoon, Vaval's funeral cortege is jumping. The whole town is like some wild ballet. The funeral pyre of Vaval is built on the waterfront across from *La Savane,* the central park of Fort-de-France. When dusk falls, the pyre is lighted. The *diablesses* dance around it in a frenzy. All the hysteria of mock grief greets the effigy of Vaval, which goes up in flames. The frenzy is at its apogee; the *diablesses* are possessed, wild, grotesque shadows dancing in the flickering flames. *"Au 'voir Bois Bois, adieu Vaval!"* Soon Vaval is consumed. The flames subside. Think it's over? Man, it's only 9 o'clock! This is Martinique! There'll be dancing until midnight in every hotel and ballroom of Fort-de-France, then the final funeral cortege as Vaval's coffin is buried at last with everyone weeping, singing, waving torches. Carnival is over until next year.

So much for La Fête de la Diablesse, a rare spectacle, in fact unique.

The *biguine* and the *diablesses* indicate only one facet of the character of Martinique. There is the grace and charm of the mazurka, reminiscent of Josephine's day, with the lovely Creole girls in Empire gowns stepping and gliding in a dance which ends as they fall limply into their partners' arms. There are the vigorous folklore dances of the sugar cane harvest, done to the rhythm of swinging machete and beating drum. There are country dances as old as Africa or Auvergne. Above all, there is the sweet side, the sentimental aspect of Martinique, best expressed in the famous song, *Adieu Foulard, Adieu Madras,* retelling the simple story of a Creole beauty's hopeless love for her *"Doudou,"* her naval officer lover whom orders compel to sail with the tide. The song is woven into the regular repertoire of the *Grand Ballet de la Martinique,* the 30-member group (20 dancers, 6 musicians, choreographers, directors and costumers) who have been performing the traditional dances on the island and in Europe and the United States since their start in 1961. Be sure to catch one of the group's performances either at one of the tourist hotels or aboard a cruise ship when it's in port.

History

French colonization of Martinique dates from 1635. From that time on, this mountainous island shared the turbulent history of the mother country, knowing revolts, insurrections, foreign occupation, and all the hazards of colonial competition. However, since 1946 it has been an Overseas Department of France, sharing with Guadeloupe and the rest of France all the benefits of the social security system of the country.

EXPLORING MARTINIQUE

Fort-de-France, capital of Martinique, is a bustling port of 100,000 people, many of whom fit Lafcadio Hearn's description of a population of "straight as palms, supple and tall, colored women and men

[who] impress one powerfully by their dignified carriage and easy elegance of movement." If you see them on Saturday night, possessed by the *biguine,* or the latest disco, you may not recognize them as they go to mass on Sunday morning. There are still a few of the country people who wear the traditional costume to the Sunday services—the bright-colored dresses, foulards, and intricately tied madras head-dresses. On Sundays, the favorite people-watching places are outside the Cathedral in downtown Fort-de-France, and in the Savane, the centrally located park, which serves as a promenade and playground for the capital. Be sure to see Vital Debray's realistic white marble effigy of the Empress Joséphine in the high-waisted flowing robe of the First Empire. A 30-minute trip by cab or car will take you to the village of Trois Ilets around the bay, Joséphine's birthplace, where there's a small museum called La Pagerie. If you're staying at the Méridien, Bakoua, Frantel, the PLM Marina-Pagerie, or any nearby hotel, you can stop at La Pagerie on your way to the airport. Allow at least half an hour. Mementoes of Marie Josèphe Rose, her first marriage to Beauharnais and her second to the Emperor Napoleon fill the small museum on the grounds of her childhood home. The two-room museum is housed in a charming little stone building that was once the kitchen of the old estate. A few yards away is a newer building, the private home of Dr. Robert Rose-Rosette, an expert on Joséphine, who put together, owns, and maintains the museum. The grounds are peaceful, dramatically shaded by two huge African tulip trees and sequestered down a long dirt road that only the taxi drivers know for sure. There's a small entrance charge on the grounds. La Pagerie Museum is closed on Mondays.

If Napoleon's empress is the national heroine of Martinique, the hero is a more democratic type. He is Victor Schoelcher, Alsatian deputy and leading French abolitionist, whose efforts were instrumental in freeing the slaves of the French West Indies in 1848. On the Savane, the Schoelcher Library honors his memory—and some honor it is! There's no more elaborate façade on a library anywhere in the West Indies; the pastel mosaics flow into an aura of brick red, ochre, and pale blues that stays in the memory (and in the photographs) long after the image has passed. Students and other scholars seem to hover around the library steps all day, every day. (The library, which was transported to Martinique from the International Exhibition in Paris of 1889, is at the northwest corner of the Savane.) A statue of Schoelcher, who lived from 1804 to 1893, stands, his arm benevolently around a young slave, in front of the Cour de Justice building. One of the shopping streets is named after him, and so is the first west coast suburb you come to after driving out of Fort-de-France.

Fort-de-France reminds many American visitors of New Orleans, and there is a vintage resemblance, especially in the houses, with their French iron grille work. Be sure to visit the island's Musée Départemental de la Martinique, bordering the Savane, on Rue de la Liberté, not far from the new Hotel Lafayette. It's open daily except Saturday afternoon and Sunday. You can wander through a few rooms of relics from the first and second Arawak periods, the first having been set at

A.D. 180 to 460. Teeth, beads, and a partial Arawak skeleton were unearthed in excavations on the coast of Martinique in March 1972. Lectures are presented here, check with the tourist office on the waterfront for dates and times.

Once you have explored the Savane and the side streets and taken in the waterfront with the view of the Bay of Fort-de-France (best seen from one of the boats that ply the bay between L'Anse Mitan and/or Pointe du Bout; the trip is 20 minutes to the other shore; you will be ready for those untrammeled views of nature which led Paul Gauguin to greater heights of enthusiasm than even Tahiti could evoke. As you drive up the coast you'll pass through the village of Le Carbet. Nearby is where Gauguin lived in 1887, and the small Carbet Gauguin Museum is worth a visit.

There are 175 miles of well-surfaced roads on Martinique, but don't expect to get around in a hurry on this mountainous island. Although the local drivers zig and zag in their driving version of the *biguine,* you'll be happier closing your eyes and leaving the driving to them or driving slowly and cautiously, sticking to your side of the road. If you want to explore the island thoroughly, buy the excellent *Carte Routière et Touristique,* which shows every nook, cranny, and knoll.

You can rent yourself a car at a dozen different agencies. If your French is good enough for you to get along in Creole, you can also take one of the local buses, almost all of them modern Mercedes models.

If you want to climb to Mt. Pelée, the 4656-foot volcano which obliterated the city of St. Pierre in 1902, be sure to hire a guide. You can do so at Morne Rouge, the nearby town that is a popular vacation spot for Martiniquais. The ascent involves a two-hour hike, often tricky because tropical growth has hidden deep crevices and other hazards which your guide will know. There's no danger from the volcano at the moment; fire-breathing Mt. Pelée apparently let off enough steam in 1902 to keep her quiet for a while.

The coastal drive from Fort-de-France to St. Pierre is the classic tourist promenade of Martinique, a magnificent drive which can be, and usually is, included in day trips offered on cruise ships. The whole circuit can be made in a healthy half-day, but it's far more pleasant if you make reservations for lunch at Leyritz Plantation and return through the tropical forest after you've enjoyed a leisurely meal in the Plantation surroundings.

Exploring the ruins of St. Pierre is at once a fascinating and sobering experience. The city, gay, prosperous, and cultivated, was once known as the "little Paris of the West Indies." Its 30,000 citizens were puzzled but not unduly alarmed early in May 1902 when the volcano spread a dark cloud of smoke over the sky and scattered ashes and soot about. It was election time on the island, and local politicians felt the necessity to keep the constituents close to the polls. With his primary interest on reelection, the mayor was reassuring about the state of the volcano, and on the morning of May 8, his confidence seemed justified in the dawn of a brilliant sunny day which dispelled clouds, smoke, and ashes like some golden broom sweeping the sky clean. The citizens sighed with relief to see the sun. Normalcy had returned, and they went about their business in the normal way. Suddenly there were two explosions that literally rocked the island. One whole side of Mt. Pelée burst apart in a gigantic convulsion. Less than a minute later, St. Pierre was buried under an avalanche of fire and lava. Only one man survived, the sole prisoner in an underground jail cell. More than 30,000 people were dead. The incredible news was flashed to every corner of the civilized world: The city of St. Pierre exists no more.

Volcanologists have now realized that volcanoes tilt in one direction and that lava, therefore, pours out only one side. For that reason, our Guadeloupian colleagues assured us, the town of Basse-Terre on the side of their Soufrière is not likely to be swept into the sea by molten lava, regardless of what the volcano does. It's on the "safe" side.

No longer Paris, but Pompeii, St. Pierre will give you an eerie feeling as you explore its ruins, its broken statues toppled from the villa gardens, its boulevards vanishing beneath a tangle of tropical growth. Some new houses have risen from the ashes of the old; some streets have grown back like pale ghosts rising from the grave. But St. Pierre has never recovered and probably never will. For a graphic documentation of the disaster, visit the Musée Volcanologique, which is open from 9 to 12 and from 3 to 5 daily. Pictures of the ruined city and relics dug from the debris complete the story of St. Pierre, indelibly fixed in the mind as a nightmare passage from the Book of Revelations.

Less spectacular, less overpowering both scenically and philosophically, but certainly gayer is the excursion south of Fort-de-France to Le Diamant and the Rocher du Diamant, known to the English as HMS Diamond Rock. This rock, off the southern coast, was actually commissioned as a sloop of war in the British Navy. A British garrison of 120 manned it in 1804, and held it for 18 months in the face of the most devastating bombardment by French coastal artillery. HMS Diamond Rock seemed to be as impregnable as it was unsinkable. The French thought up a Gallic ruse, a 19th century version of the Trojan horse. Aware of a certain British weakness, they sent rum-laden galleys drifting against the Rocher du Diamant. When the ships broke down upon the shore, the floating rum barrels were eagerly collected by the thirsty men of HMS Diamond Rock, who promptly rolled them "aboard ship." History does not record how many Englishmen were sober when the French finally took over Diamond Rock a short time later. France had won another skirmish in the long struggle for Martinique.

A DAY ON YOUR OWN

Allow at least a full day to explore Martinique at your own pace, although two or three days would be better. Take along an English-French phrase book if your French is rusty, and don't forget your bathing suit and camera. Martinique is a photographer's paradise. If lunch at a beautifully restored eighteenth-century manor house appeals to you, make reservations in advance at *Leyritz Plantation Inn,* located way up north at Basse-Pointe.

The coastal drive north from Fort-de-France to St. Pierre is one of the prettiest and most popular sightseeing routes. Curiosities abound, and just past the suburb of Schoelcher on the beach at Fond Lahaye, you'll see a rare *cocotier a deux tetes,* or two-headed coconut palm. If you can't spot it, a friendly Martiniquais will help out.

Leaving Fond Lahaye, the road climbs steeply, offering sweeping views of the Caribbean, and then descends to picture-postcard villages like Case-Pilote and Bellefontaine. *Gommiers* (colorful native fishing boats carved from gum trees) line the shore. Further north is Carbet, where Columbus landed in 1502 and where Gauguin lived and painted in 1887.

At St. Pierre, the "Paris of the West Indies" that was destroyed when Mt. Pelee erupted in 1902, plan to visit the small but fascinating museum (open 9 A.M.–noon; 3–5 P.M.) detailing the disaster. Around the town, discover the ruins of what was once a magnificent city, complete with theater and cathedral.

You can stop for a Creole lunch at a beach restaurant at St. Pierre or inland at Morne Rouge. If you've made arrangements beforehand, head further north to Leyritz, located in the middle of a banana plantation. At the Inn you can take a refreshing dip in the pool and have a leisurely lunch in the open-air restaurant which was formerly the granary.

Return to Fort-de-France via La Trace, which zigzags through the lovely rain forest, or take the coastal road.

PRACTICAL INFORMATION FOR MARTINIQUE

HOW TO GET THERE. By Air. Martinique's Lamentin Airport is 4½ miles from Fort-de-France, connecting the city with flights from the U.S., Canada, Europe, and several Caribbean islands. *American Airlines* flies non-stop from New York; *Eastern* comes in from Miami via St. Croix. *Air Canada* has non-stop flights from Montreal; direct flights from Toronto. *Air France* flies in from Paris; also from Miami and San Juan.

Inter-Caribbean carriers are *Air Martinique* and *LIAT. Air France* flies its smaller planes between Martinique and Guadeloupe several times daily.

By Sea. Several cruise ships call at Fort-de-France. Among the lines are *Chandris; Costa Line; Cunard Line; Holland America; Home Line; Norwegian American Line; Paquet Line; Princess Cruises; Royal Caribbean Lines* and *Sitmar Cruises.*

FURTHER INFORMATION. For information in New York, contact the *French West Indies Tourist Board,* 610 Fifth Avenue, New York, N.Y. 10020. In other U.S. cities, contact the *French Government Tourist Office;* 645 No. Michigan Ave., Chicago, Ill. 60611; 9401 Wilshire Blvd., Beverly Hills, CA 90212; 2050 Stemmons Freeway, Dallas, Texas 75258. In Canada: 1840 West

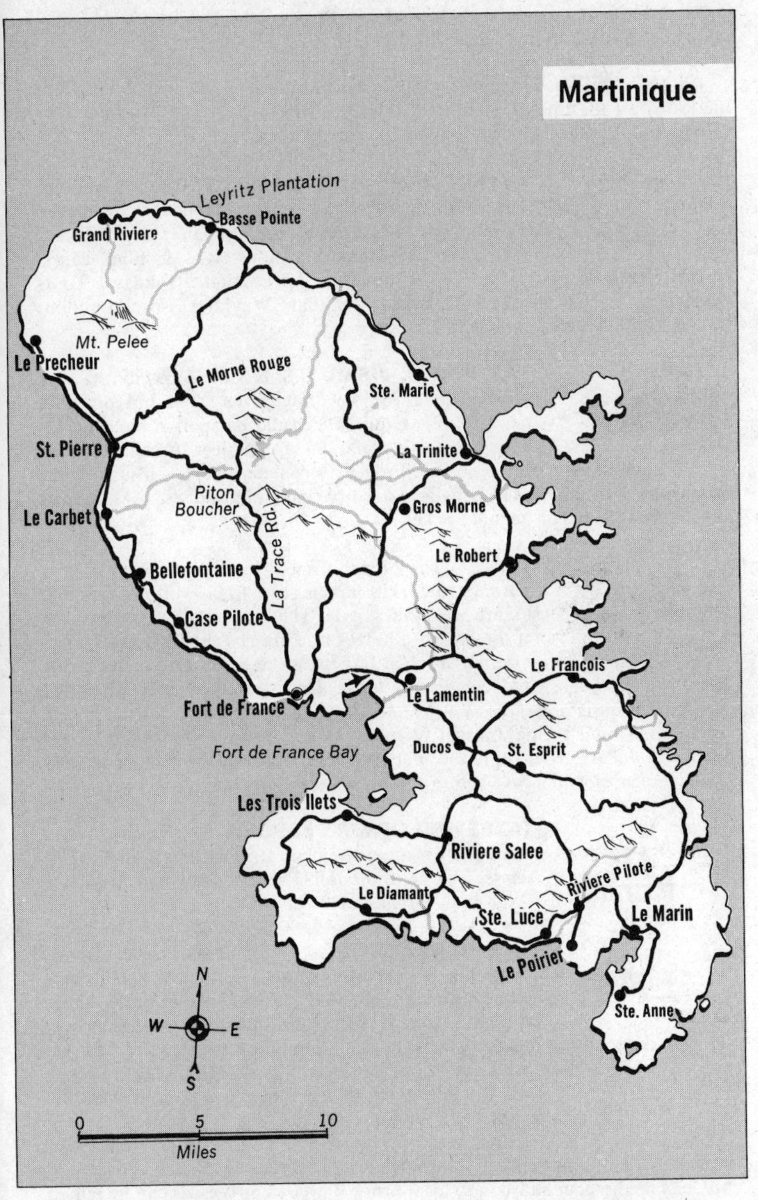
Martinique
Leyritz Plantation
Basse Pointe
Grand Riviere
Mt. Pelee
Le Precheur
Le Morne Rouge
Ste. Marie
St. Pierre
La Trinite
Piton
Boucher
Gros Morne
Le Carbet
La Trace Rd.
Le Robert
Bellefontaine
Case Pilote
Le Francois
Fort de France
Le Lamentin
Fort de France Bay
Ducos
St. Esprit
Les Trois Ilets
Riviere Salee
Riviere Pilote
Le Diamant
Le Marin
Ste. Luce
Le Poirier
Ste. Anne
N
W
E
S
0
5
10
Miles

Sherbrooke, Montreal, P.Q. H3H 1E4; or at 372 Bay Street, Toronto, Ont. M5H 2W9. In London, the FGTO office is at 178 Piccadilly, London W1V OAL. For on-island information, visit *L'Office du Tourisme,* which is located along the waterfront in Fort-de-France.

ISLAND MEDIA. For details on current happenings, ask your hotel front desk or visit the tourist office for copies of *Choubouloute, Ici Martinique* or *Zoom Amtille,* all of which are available free of charge.

AUTHORIZED TOUR OPERATORS: Adventure Tours; Butler Travels; Caribbean Holidays; Cavalcade Tours; Club Mediterranee, Inc.; Flyfaire; GoGo Tours; Hill Tours; Playtime Vacations; Red & Blue Tours; Travel Center Tours; in the U.S. From Canada: Sunflight Holidays; Tours Mont Royal; Holiday House; Skylark; Unitour; Wayfarer. From London: James Vence Travel.

PASSPORTS, VISAS. U.S. & Canadian citizens may stay up to 21 days without a passport, but proof of citizenship is required. A valid passport is required for longer stays. Regulations are subject to change, however. Please check with the nearest French Consulate before you make your trip. Citizens of the United Kingdom need passports, but no visas. All visitors must have a return or ongoing ticket.

MONEY. The French franc is legal tender here. Figure 5 francs to $1 US, making the franc worth about 16¢. Figure 3.96 francs = 1£. The best exchange rate is given at the banks; a hotel's rate may be slightly less. *NOTE:* Travelers should be aware that French francs can be reconverted only at the *banks* where the original conversion took place, and then only when the original receipt is presented. You cannot reconvert your money at the hotels. There is no limit to the amount of money you can bring in, and U.S. and Canadian dollars are accepted in many places. However, for meals and incidental expenses, you'll fare better if you use local currency.

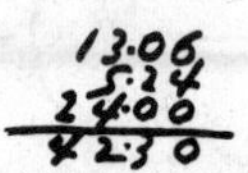

TAXES AND OTHER CHARGES. There is no government tax on hotel rooms, but most hotels add a 10% service charge to the bill. There is no airport departure tax, except for charter flights.

HOW TO GET ABOUT. You'll find taxis at the airport, at the hotels, and in downtown Fort-de-France. Fares are government regulated and will be about 30% higher at night. *Taxis Collectifs* are much less expensive and run bus-like routes to points all over the island, but they are crowded and you may have a long wait. Between Pointe du Bout, L'Anse Mitan, and Fort-de-France, there are frequent (at least every hour) ferries; you pay 5 francs one way; 9 francs round-trip for the 20-minute trip.

Cars are available for rental at the airport, in Fort-de-France, and at some of the hotels. They run between 70–250 francs per day. *Avis, Budget, Hertz* and *National* are here, in addition to local firms. Bicycles and Vespas can be rented at the Pointe du Bout Marina, or through *Vespa Martinique,* at 3 rue Jules Monnerot in Fort-de-France.

EVENTS AND HOLIDAYS. The event of the year in Martinique is Carnival, the pre-Lenten celebration that include parades, masquerades and dancing and singing in the streets. It goes on for a good six weeks and ends on Ash Wednesday with the building of a funeral pyre that will "consume" King Carnival. Another special event is *Fête Nautique de Robert,* a festival of the sea, that takes place in the village of Robert on the Atlantic Coast in September. It's held in the evening and is dramatic as boats with lights appear in parade form.

Public and religious holidays are New Year's Day; Easter Monday; Ascension Thursday; Pentecost Monday; Bastille Day; Schoelcher Day (July 21); Assumption Day (Aug.15); All Saint's Day (Nov. 1); Armistice Day (Nov. 11), and Christmas Day.

WHAT WILL IT COST?

A typical day in Martinique for *two* persons during the winter season will run:

	US$	£
Hotel accommodations at an "on-the-beach" resort property (including Continental breakfast)	80*	44*
Luncheon at a moderate restaurant	20	11
Dinner at hotel or "in-town" restaurant	40	22
Tips and hotel service charge	15	8
Car rental for one day	20	11
	$175	£96

* for country inns and Fort-de-France hotels deduct $40 US (£22).

STAYING IN MARTINIQUE

HOTELS. The choice of accommodations on Martinique is vast, not because of the number, but because of the variety. They range from country inns with 12 rooms to a Club Med property with 300. The hotels are clustered at Pointe du Bout, L'Anse Mitan, and the beaches on that point of land that forms the "other" side of the bay of Fort-de-France. Other hotels string up the Caribbean coast (west) and into the mountains, with a few properties located on the south shore.

Auberge de l'Anse Mitan. Four miles (20 minutes by hourly launch) across the bay from the capital, L'Anse Mitan is a weekend-and-longer retreat for residents of the capital and for others. The location is good. This 3-story French inn has 20 rooms with bath, simply furnished, and 2 one-bedroom private cottages, all right on the water, just a short walk from the beach. Meals are served for guests; informality is the keynote. $35 double in winter; $27 double off-season, Continental breakfast included.

Bakoua. At Pointe du Bout, next door to the Meridien and reached by hourly launch from the capital (20 minutes), this hotel is named after fishermen's hats made of "bakoua" straw. It has 98 air-conditioned, twin-bedded rooms; *Le Châteaubriand* restaurant, snack bar, floor show weekly, dancing nightly. Activities include tennis, sailing, water skiing, boating in the hotel's dugout canoe, fishing, snorkeling, horseback riding, shuffleboard, volley ball, table tennis, and swimming in the hotel pool or on the beach. $140–184 double in winter; $75–94 double off-season, including full breakfast.

Bambou. Just a short walk up the beach from l'Anse Mitan, this small hotel is great for a casual French holiday. Also superior for beachside lunches, such as local lobster, a delicious *soupe de poisson,* and wine. The 46 rooms are cottage style, behind the beach-front bar/restaurant. A popular Sunday gathering spot for Martiniquais families. Strictly informal, Mediterranean beach-style resort. $45 double in winter; $28 double off-season, including Continental breakfast.

Bristol. One of the *Relais de la Martinique,* this 10-room spot is in a former private home, right in the heart of the city. The management does all possible to put you into the life of the island people. $33 double all-year, Continental breakfast included.

Calalou. A 30-room inn on the beach at Anse a l'Ane, with open-air dining on Creole specialties. Reached by launch from Fort-de-France in about 20 minutes. $65 double in winter; $43 double off-season, including breakfast and dinner.

Caraibe Auberge. A small inn for French-speaking visitors. 12 rooms, 6 overlooking Anse Mitan beach, next to the Bambou Hotel. Air-conditioned, immaculate, simple, but very pleasant atmosphere. $40 double in winter; $27 double off-season. Continental breakfast included in the rate.

Caritan Beach Village. This 96-room beachfront property in the south of the island near Ste. Anne is one of Martinique's newest hotels. Located on a very pretty beach, the *Caritan* has simply furnished rooms with three beds, full kitchenette and sea-view balconies. An attractive swimming pool, restaurant/bar, and boutique are in the center of the village. Special to the *Caritan* is its mini-club for children. Parents can entrust their children aged 2 to 12 to the professional counselors of the mini-club during the day in winter season and peak holiday times. Rates at the Caritan are $64 for a double EP in winter, $48 double EP in off-season.

Club Mediterranee Buccaneer's Creek. A long way out of town in the southeast quarter of the island, this Club Med is just about 30 miles from the airport. The 600-bed capacity (300-room) hotel is built on 48 acres in the style of a small Creole village. There are plazas, avenues, cafes, restaurants, boutiques and a small marina. Pastel-colored cottages designed for double occupancy with twin beds, air-conditioning, private bath with shower. The property edges the sea and all water sports are available. Also 6 tennis courts, 4 of them lighted for night play. As with all Club Meds, it offers a complete weekly holiday for one price–no extras, no tips, aside from personal purchases and drinks at the bar. $680–740 in winter; $490–595 per person per week off-season.

Diamant-Novotel. The island's newest luxury hotel, with 180 rooms. Located in the south, near the fishing village of Ste. Anne, it offers a fine restaurant, nightclub, swimming pool, tennis courts and watersports. $84 double in winter; $63 double off-season. Full breakfast included in rate.

Frantel. 210 rooms in 3-story units, set as a pastel colored village in Pointe du

Bout, on a peninsula across the marina from the Meridien. Swimming pool, beach (on opposite side from marina), restaurants such as *Le Boucaut* and a popular disco called *Vesou.* $85 double in winter; $59 double off-season.

Imperatrice. On the Place de la Savane in the heart of the town, a 24-room hostelry with private baths. The Library and Museum are on the same street. If you have a room in the front, it can be noisy, but the activity you can watch from the windows overlooking the Savane makes it all worth it. If you want to be in the capital, this is not bad. Restaurant serves French food; also cocktail lounge. $35–38 double all year, including Continental breakfast.

Lafayette. At this 20-room hotel on the Rue de la Liberté in Fort-de-France, visitors have all the restaurants, shops, and nightspots of the city virtually at their doorstep. Formerly called the *Europe,* the *Lafayette* was entirely refurbished by its owner, Carl de Pompignan (son-in-law of Martinique's hotelier, Guy de la Houssaye of the *Bakoua).* The rooms are all individually air-conditioned with private bath. The *Lafayette's* restaurant is attractively decorated, with green walls, ice-cream-parlor chairs, and lovely views overlooking Fort-de-France's town park, La Savane. Rates at the Lafayette are $33–38 double EP in winter, $35–40 double EP in summer.

Latitude-Martinique. At Carbet, this hotel is near the spot Columbus landed. It's on the main road from Fort-de-France to Saint-Pierre and the volcano. A 90-room vacation village that is announced at the roadside with flags flying. The beachside complex of bungalows is designed for privacy and is set in tropical foliage. All rooms are air-conditioned with private bath and terrace. Facilities include two restaurants serving Continental and Creole food, a bar, nightclub, boutique and swimming pool. Water skiing, sailing, scuba school. $150 double in winter; from $125 double off-season, with all three meals included.

Leyritz Plantation. The pride of Martinique, this 200-year-old manor house has been painstakingly restored and opened as a hotel with 24 rooms. It is situated at Basse-Pointe in the north of Martinique, has a lovely restaurant, open-air cocktail bar, tennis court, and beautiful swimming pool. There is a private beach about 20 minutes away and an interesting doll museum on the grounds; horseback riding also available. Some rooms are in the restored main house, others in former slave cottages, some restored, some rebuilt along traditional lines. Roofs covered with bamboo to add to the flavor. About a 1½ hour drive from the airport. If you're specific about arrival time, they'll meet you. $75 double in winter; $43 double off-season, Continental breakfast included.

Madinina. Using the old Indian name for the island of Martinique, this small, 15-room inn overlooks the marina at Pointe du Bout. Reknowned for its *Chez Sidonie* restaurant, you pay almost as much for a meal as you do for a room. Accommodations are plain, but functional and clean. $40 double in winter; $25 double off-season.

Meridien-Martinique. Part of the French chain of hotels that now touches the French islands, this 303-room resort is modern in every way. At Pointe du Bout, across the bay from Fort-de-France (20 minutes) you're away from it all, but certainly not "out of it." On the beach, with the emphasis on water sports, especially on their scuba diving school. Two tennis courts, swimming pool, charters from the marina for fishing and sailing. Elegant *L'Anthurium* room for dinner and dancing; coffee shop; *Vonvon* discotheque; gambling casino; and special weekly entertainment by the Folkloric Group. $90–110 double in winter; $69–81 double off-season.

PLM La Bateliere Hotel & Casino. 215 modern rooms overlooking the sea from a promontory one mile from Fort-de-France. 6 tennis courts; large freshwater swimming pool; small man-made beach. Sunfish sailboats, pedal boats, snorkeling equipment and wind-surfing all available at no extra charge. Scuba school on premises. *Laffitte* dining room for dinner and dancing; terrace restaurant; *"Club 21"* disco and the Casino for evening entertainment. $110–125 double in winter; $50–78 double off-season, including full breakfast.

PLM Manoir de Beauregard. A manor house-turned inn, with 30 air-conditioned rooms. Located in Ste. Anne, 30 miles south of Fort-de-France; one mile from Salines beach. Antique furnishings in the rooms, both in the main house, and in those in the small, adjacent units. Restaurant that serves good French and Creole food; freshwater swimming pool; informal. $75 double in winter; $43 double off-season. Full breakfast included.

PLM Marina-Pagerie. Started for condominiums, 240 studios and apartments operate as a hotel with all conveniences. The Meridien and Bakoua are across the road, with Anse Mitan about a 10 minute leisurely walk to and along the beach. No beach here, but the bargain rates and the compact kitchens in all units make reasonable holidays a feature. 3-room suites can comfortably sleep 5. Studios and suites are small, but cheerful, and most of them high enough to offer a good view of the water. Restaurant; swimming pool; and poolside snack bar. Studios run $69–80 in winter; $40 off-season.

St. Aubin. A gingerbread manor house transformed into a 15-room hotel, located in a beautiful verdant country setting near Trinité, on the northeast coast not far from the Presqu'île de la Caravelle Nature Preserve. Ideal for vacationers seeking the peace and quiet of a total idyllic retreat, the *St. Aubin* has individually air-conditioned rooms, lounge, and an excellent restaurant presided over by owner/chef Guy Foret. Transportation to beaches and a sports center on the Presqu'île can be easily arranged by the hotel. $43 double in winter; $36 double off season, Continental breakfast included.

RENTALS. While the rental situation is not as extensive here as on other Caribbean islands, there are many private homes and villas which are rented to off-island visitors. The Tourist Office *Villa Rental Service* is your best source for information. Rates can run as low as $100 per week for 1-bedroom houses and stretch up to $600 per week and higher for a house for 6 with maid service.

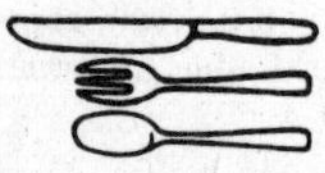

RESTAURANTS. Most Caribbean islands have more hotels than restaurants; you'll know you're in France when you see the situation reversed here. You'll find everything from spicy Creole dishes to French fare *en flambé*. Among the island specialties are *colombo,* an Indian stew of seeds and beef or pork cooked with rice. The stuffed crabs are delicious, and the French cooks do wonderful things with the local fresh-water crayfish *(écrevisses),* which incidentally are bigger than the ones in France. Try *calalou,* a subtle and savory French-Creole herb soup. Other local dishes are heart-of-palm salad, roast wild goat, raccoon, tortoise, and a great variety of seafood. The local cellars are filled with excellent French wines, but the island favorite in the drink department is *Le Punch Martinique,* a concoction of white rum, sugar syrup, lime and ice.

Among the Martinique restaurants we think you'll enjoy, and their locations follow.

In **Fort-de France:** *La Grand' Voile* (Big Sail) has taken over the top dining honors for the capital city. Located at the Yacht Club, just a short walk from the Tourist Office on the waterfront. The prices are high, but so are the standards, the quality, and the French cuisine. Good wine list. Small bar with nautical theme is a popular gathering spot. Reservations recommended.

Other "in-city" places to try are *Le D'Esnambuc,* a stylish, and expensive second-story seafood and French restaurant overlooking the harbor near La Savane, the city's central park; *L'Escalier,* one flight up on Rue de la Republique, this downtown spot serves Creole specialties, such as *crabes farcis* (stuffed land crabs) and *blaff,* a spicy fish stew; *El Raco,* offers the Spanish touch, not only in food, but in decor; *Le Tiffany* is the place for classic French fare, elegantly and expensively served in an attractive Creole-style house on the outskirts of Fort-de-France; and *Typic Bellevue,* a tiny and terrific place on the Bd. de la Marne, serves Creole specialties at reasonable prices.

At **Pointe du Bout:** *Chez Sidonie,* overlooking the marina, is justly renowned for its Creole food; while *Le Cantonnais,* nestled among the large hotels, serves island-famous Cantonese dishes.

On **Anse Mitan** beach, stop at *Le Bambou,* the seaside inn, for *crabes farci, soupe de poisson,* and lobster; or at *Verais,* where you'll dine on the veranda and enjoy special Creole entrées. *Le Matador* is one of the top Creole restaurants on the island.

In the picturesque village of **Ste. Anne,** there are 3 very pleasant choices: The small Creole inn *La Dunette* for local dishes; *Les Filets Bleus,* one of the top seafood inns here; and *PLM Manoir de Beauregard,* for excellent French and Creole dishes served in an 18th century manor house.

At **Schoelcher,** just up the coast from Fort-de-France, dine at *Le Foulard,* a very popular restaurant in a private home, for memorable Creole and French food.

Outside Fort-de-France, heading north toward St. Pierre and the volcano, *La Paillotte* is a good shore-side restaurant, casual, at Le Carbet, not far from the Latitude Hotel. Near St. Pierre is the delightful beach and restaurant of *La Guinguette,* where you can swim or watch the fishermen offshore.

Farther north and inland at Morne Rouge is *Mont Auberge,* with classic French cuisine and a view of Mt. Pelee. One of the best places for a special meal, but losing something by its necessary catering to tour groups, is *Leyritz Plantation.* Hope that you get here on a day when a cruise group is not (unless you're part of one), and relax and enjoy the foods, which are prepared by a team of chefs. The dishes are local and good—especially the *colombo.*

And, at Morne des Esses, don't miss *Le Colibri* (the name means hummingbird) for a fine old-fashioned Creole meal in a private home. Among the specialties are sea urchin tarts, lobster omelettes and stuffed pigeons.

NIGHTLIFE. With all the *joie de vivre* of Martinique, it is essential to ask locally for suggestions as to current spots. They change—and the Tourist Office or your hotel concierge can give you the latest information. Don't rely on the taxi drivers, who have been known to take visitors to the place of a friend for watered-down drinks and a sky-high tariff. If you have any questions about your bill, take your complaint directly to the Tourist Office. Remember, though, that Scotch and U.S. drinks are expensive; the rum and good *biere Lorraine* are more reasonable.

There are plenty of cafés and bars in Fort-de-France, and dancing many evenings at the Meridien's *Le Vonvon* and Frantel's *Vesou* disco. If you want to head out of town (or are staying there), the PLM La Bateliere has the "Club 21," which is this island's answer to New York's "Xenon." Other spots to try are the *Rive Gauche; Club Bernard* and *Sweety,* all in town.

Gambling casinos are in the Hotel Meridien and the PLM La Bateliere. No slot machines here, and proper dress required. Proof of identity, such as a passport or ID with photo required, as well as an entrance fee of 35 francs at the Meridien and 40 francs at the PLM La Batelière.

If you want to hear the old songs and see the old dances of Martinique, by all means try to catch one of the performances of the *Grand Ballet de la Martinique.* It's sponsored partly by the Tourist Office, originated by Roger Albert, who has done more than any other single individual to revive and perpetuate the colorful folklore of the island. There are regularly scheduled performances at the large hotels and onboard visiting cruise ships. Inquire at the Tourist Office to find out just when and where.

SHOPPING. Fort-de-France is the place to buy French luxury imports. The chief shopping avenues are Rue St. Louis, Rue Victor Hugo, and Rue Schoelcher. If you buy perfumes, china, crystal, designer imports, and other luxury items, pay with travelers' checks—you'll get a 20% discount. As with many of the luxury items for sale in the Caribbean, prices have skyrocketed in recent years, so be sure you know your hometown prices before you buy.

The leading shop in Fort de-France is *Roger Albert* on Rue Victor Hugo. He carries perfumes, watches, Lalique, china, silver, crystal, name scarves and ties. *Folie Foloi, Chantilly* and *St. Trop II* are all good boutiques on side streets off the Savane. Paris imports at hefty prices. *Cadet Daniel* and *Thomas de Rogatis* have gold jewelry with good design. *L'Or et L'Argent* has similar selections. There is also a duty-free shop at the airport for last-minute purchases.

Very special attention should be paid to the Caribbean Art Center *(Metiers d'Art)* on the waterfront facing the Tourist Office. This is not only a shop, but a good place to eyewitness the kinds of crafts available in Martinique. The cloth collages are the most interesting and different purchases. They are adapted by women in various communities from an artist's original design and are worked in sections from different colors and textures of cloth. The wall hangings range in price from about $20 to $125, depending on size and intricacy of design. Shops are open weekdays from 9 A.M. until 12:30 P.M. Then, after at least a two-hour luncheon break, they re-open until 6 p.m. Closed Saturday afternoons and Sundays, unless there is a cruise ship in port.

SPORTS AND OTHER ACTIVITIES. If it's beautiful beaches you're after, Martinique cannot compare with those on other islands, but the island does have its share along the south coast. Therefore, for *swimming,* we recommend that you hire a car and explore the entire area. Among the loveliest stretches here are at Le Diamant and at Salines, near Ste. Anne. To reach the beaches closer to town, take one of the boats that leave regularly for L'Anse Mitan or Pointe du Bout (5 francs one way; 9 francs round trip) and have lunch at a beach-side bistro or hotel (the Bakoua, Bambou, Madinina, Meridien, and PLM Marina-Pagerie are all here) and then a swim.

Sailing can be arranged from the *Fort-de-France Yacht Club* or *Martinique Charter & Services,* Box 777, Fort-de-France (fishing and day cruises) or through your hotel, particularly if you're staying at the Pointe du Bout hotels, where a catamaran and small sloops anchor offshore.

Tennis is available at the Club Med; the Tennis Club of Fort-de-France; and at the Frantel, Leyritz, Latitude, Meridien, PLM La Batelière, Bakoua and Diamant-Novotel hotels. Play golf at *"Golf de l'Esperance,"* the 18-hole championship Robert Trent Jones course at Pointe du Bout, that stretches inland from the Baie de Fort de France.

Scuba divers will be in their glory here, where there are now scuba diving schools at the Latitude, Meridien, Frantel, Diamant-Novotel and PLM La Batelière hotels. *Mountain climbing* and *hiking* are popular, particularly in the peaking north, but hire a guide, especially for Mt. Pelee. The verdant growth completely camouflages deep crevises, and some who have climbed without guides have gone down faster than they climbed up.

MONTSERRAT

The Caribbean's Emerald Isle

The island of Montserrat is a people place. From your arrival at the small airport, where you sweep in from Antigua like a bird on the wing, banking sharply to avoid the impressive hillside, until the time you visit Plymouth on market day, your Montserrat experience will be "indigenous tourism" at its best. There are few tourists, and few places to stay.

Montserrat, the "saw-toothed mountain," was named by Columbus in honor of the famed mountain near Barcelona, Spain. This Montserrat is twenty-seven miles southwest of Antigua and has thirty-nine square miles of lush, rolling scenery that puts it in competition with Dominica for honors with the botanists.

There are two volcanoes–the one known as Galway Soufrière can be climbed by the hardy folk–and an intermittent fringe of licorice beaches. For those who haven't tried a volcanic sand beach, this is an experience. The sand is just as powdery as the lighter variety, but just as black as night. Your reason for coming here will probably be peace and quiet, a bit of hiking, or perhaps some golf at the emerald-green Belham River Valley nine-hole course.

History

Even though Columbus named it, Oliver Cromwell gets the credit for turning Montserrat into the Ireland of the Caribbean. His policies sent the first shipload of Irishmen to St. Kitts, where they found the English Protestants stifling. They headed for Montserrat in 1623 to settle their own colony. The French moved in in 1664 for the traditional seesaw of power with the English, who finally gained full control in 1783.

Today there are still traces of Ireland, in the lilting brogue spoken by the islanders, in their surnames (Maloney, Ryan, O'Reilly, Kennedy, and the like), in place names such as Galway Soufrière—not to mention the acres of green with lime-colored mountains rising behind them.

EXPLORING MONTSERRAT

For one day at least, put yourself in the hands of one of the taxi drivers. They are not only friendly and informative, but give an excellent and thorough island tour at a reasonable price. Take another day to go off on your own exploration (see the section A Day On Your Own).

On the road from the airport across to the west coast and Plymouth, the capital city, you'll pass through Harris's Village. The Anglican Church there, which was built in 1900, was blown asunder by the hurricane of 1928 and shaken to its foundations by an earthquake in the 1930s. Today it stands rebuilt and impressive. You'll see Chances Peak, waiting to be climbed, and mangoes, papayas, coconut palms, banana plants, signs of the fruit and vegetable wealth of Montserrat.

Other sights include the capital city itself, with its population of 12,500 people. Wander around at your own pace, visiting at least four of the churches. And don't miss Plymouth's Saturday market, when produce comes in from all over the island. On market day, this is a West Indian town at its most unique.

Plymouth's main street, fringed with Georgian houses built from ballast rock from Dorset, is a beehive, alive with hawkers of tropical produce and hand-made items. Boats tie up at the waterfront across from the marketplace, their owners come to trade their goods and their gossip.

St. Anthony's Church on the outskirts of Plymouth was built and rebuilt. The first consecration was sometime between 1623 and 1666, and the rebuilding, after one of the several French-English skirmishes, was in 1730. Freed slaves donated the two silver chalices after emancipation in the 1880s.

Carr's Bay, a thirty-five minute drive along the north coast, is the place to go for swimming and sunbathing. It is the most popular bathing beach on the island, and one of the few that is "regular sand."

The Great Alps Waterfall is an excursion for the hardy. Although the drive is only fifteen minutes from Plymouth, the hour-or-more climb requires sturdy shoes and constitution—and a guide, since the growth covers the infrequently trodden path. The rewards are water plunging seventy feet into a mountain pool and the chance for a chilling swim.

There are other places to see, such as Runaway Ghaut (or Gut), a precipitious valley where the English and French squabbled two centuries ago, and the agricultural station, not far from the airport. The water sprinkling merrily over the experimental station is a sign of Montserrat's many underground springs.

A DAY ON YOUR OWN

Plan a full day's excursion to the volcano Galway Soufrière. Rent a car or a Mini-Moke and begin your day with a light breakfast, while arranging for the large picnic lunch you'll take with you. Take suntan lotion, a long-sleeved shirt, and wear comfortable shoes.

Drive south from Plymouth along the verdant mountain road. Be prepared to hike. It is an up and down experience once the road peters out to an overgrown "path" taking you through giant tree ferns, rain forest growth, and an occasional stream. The reward is a boiling crater pouring yellow sulphur over its edges, one of the Caribbean's stunning natural wonders.

PRACTICAL INFORMATION FOR MONTSERRAT

HOW TO GET THERE. By air. Antigua is the gateway. *BWIA* and *Eastern* fly there from New York and Miami; *Air Canada* and *BWIA* from Toronto; and *British Airways* from London. All flights connect with *Leeward Islands Air Transport (LIAT)* for the ongoing fifteen-minute flight to Montserrat.

FURTHER INFORMATION. For information directly from the island, contact the Montserrat Tourist Board, Box 7, Plymouth Montserrat, W.I. For sources closer to home, turn to the Eastern Caribbean Tourist Association, 220 East 42nd St., New York, N.Y. 10017, or the Caribbean Tourism Association, 20 East 46th St., New York, N.Y. 10017.

In Canada, contact Mr. D. W. Currie, Montserrat Government Representative in Canada, Station "A", Toronto M5W 1E4, Canada. In London, the ECTA office is at 200 Buckingham Palace Road, London SW1W 9TJ, England.

PASSPORTS, VISAS. You will be asked for some proof of citizenship, and a passport (even an expired one) is best. Voter's registration card or birth certificate will do, but a driver's license is not enough. No visas required.

MONEY. Eastern Caribbean currency (EC$) is used, but U.S. dollars are readily accepted at hotels and banks. The exchange is $2.70 EC = $1 U.S.; $6 EC = 1 £.

TAXES AND OTHER CHARGES. There is a 7% government room tax, in addition to a 10% service charge at hotels. The airport departure tax is $5 US.

HOW TO GET ABOUT. There are 130 miles of road. Rental cars are available from $22–30 per day. The driver's license is $5 US and can be obtained from the local police station. All that's required is your hometown license. Taxis are plentiful, as you will note at the airport, and be assured

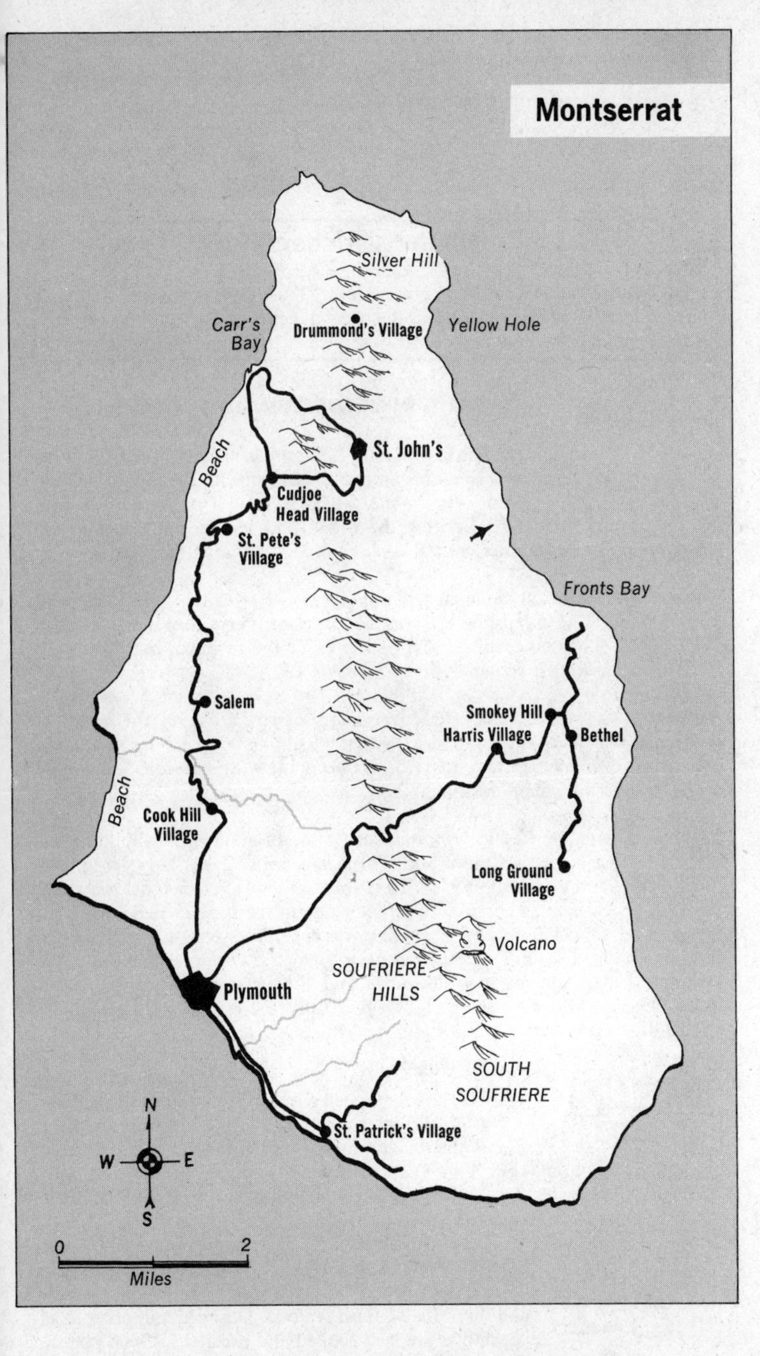

Montserrat
Silver Hill
Carr's Bay
Drummond's Village
Yellow Hole
St. John's
Beach
Cudjoe Head Village
St. Pete's Village
Fronts Bay
Salem
Smokey Hill
Harris Village
Bethel
Beach
Cook Hill Village
Long Ground Village
Volcano
SOUFRIERE HILLS
Plymouth
SOUTH SOUFRIERE
St. Patrick's Village
N
W
E
S
0
2
Miles

that your hotel can contact one at any time. Driving in Montserrat, as in most of the Caribbean islands, is on the LEFT! Be careful.

EVENTS AND HOLIDAYS. Other than the cricket matches and the annual Carnival, there is nothing special here. During the rest of the year Montserratians celebrate the Queen's Birthday with some fervor, and all the religious holidays that are observed in the Western Hemisphere.

WHAT WILL IT COST?

On Montserrat, $90 for two persons during the winter season will more than do it. This rate, which can fluctuate depending on your choice of accommodations, includes all meals, service charges, and an island tour.

STAYING IN MONTSERRAT

HOTELS. The entire island has no more than 100 hotel rooms in inns and guest houses, with the top of the crop being *Vue Pointe,* which is located on a secluded hillside. Because the island and the accommodations are small, breakfast and dinner are always included in the hotel rate.

Coconut Hill Hotel. A renovated plantation house with ten rooms, all with private baths. The atmosphere is casual, pleasant, very informal. Delicious West Indian food served in the dining room. You're in town, but a distance from the usual tourist activities. $60–65 double EP.

Montserrat Springs. Sixteen attractively furnished rooms over the beach at Richmond Hill. West Indian food served on the dining terrace. Nice swimming pool. Some evening entertainment (local) during the winter season. $80 double in winter; $55 double off-season.

Vue Pointe. Run by Cedric Osborne, son of the original owner-builder, this property is the largest on the island. The octagonal cottages have large bedroom, bath, great view and privacy. They spill to the black beach below, where there's a beach bar. Swimming pool, main dining room (with delicious West Indian food served family-style so that you can have seconds), and lounge areas at the top of the hill with the reception area. The Osbornes make you feel at home. Entertainment most evenings and the best touring advice. Golf course nearby; also possibilities for fishing trips. $95–130 double in winter; $50–80 double off-season.

HOME RENTALS. There are several private homes available for rent when the owners are not in residence. A cluster of homes covers the hillside not far from the Vue Pointe Hotel, making all the hotel facilities accessible for the "night out." For home rental, contact Montserrat Estates, Ltd., Box 221; Ryan Enterprises, Ltd., Box 425; or Neville Bradshaw Agencies Ltd., P.O. Box 270; all at Plymouth, Montserrat.

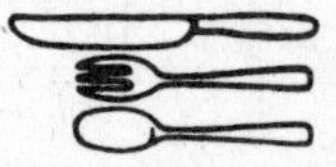

RESTAURANTS/NIGHTLIFE. The island specialty is "mountain chicken," as the local frogs' legs are called, and there is also fresh seafood. Dasheen and other local vegetables are well cooked and excellent. If you plan to dine outside your own hotel, make reservations beforehand. One place for in-

Photo by V. Puzo

Hibiscus, bougainvillea and frangipani are colorful competition for the towering palms and sea grape trees of the Caribbean. Interspersed are the old mills, such as this one on Barbados, left over from the bygone era when sugar was king.

Photo by V. Puzo

Courtesy of Caribbean Tourism Association

The lively beat of the Caribbean makes the islands an ongoing festival. Folkloric groups, such as those in Curaçao, perform all year, while the pre-Lenten Carnival in Aruba is an annual event.

Courtesy of Aruba Tourist Bureau

Courtesy of Caribbean Tourism Association

The smaller islands, such as St. Vincent, offer all the peace and serenity one could hope for. Others, such as St. Kitts, add historic fortresses to the scene.

Courtesy of Caribbean Tourism Association

Courtesy of Caribbean Tourism Association

Locally made straw goods are always an attraction, especially the hats, which offer shade from the Caribbean sun. At sunset, the views are spectacular. Charlotte Amalie, on St. Thomas, is one of the most impressive.

Courtesy of Caribbean Tourism Association

town dining is the *Yacht Club,* at Wapping, which serves fine food and paralyzing rum punches. For intimate dining on international cuisine, try the *Belham Valley Restaurant.* As far as nightlife on Montserrat, you'll only find some entertainment at the hotels and even that ends early.

SHOPPING. Other than *Perks Punch,* the local rum punch liquer, and a few souvenirs at *Dutchers,* there's very little to buy here. For island-made items, visit the *Craft Center,* where you'll find a selection of hand-woven sea-island cotton and 100% woolen sweaters, which are made locally.

SPORTS AND OTHER ACTIVITIES. It's *golf* at the nine-hole Belham River Valley course, and *hiking* to such places as Galway Soufrière, that are the main attractions. But, if you bring you own equipment, you can *snorkel* and *scuba* dive to your heart's content. *Tennis* is at the Vue Pointe Hotel; *fishing* and *horseback riding* can be arranged through your hotel. For spectator sports, *cricket* is king, and matches are played from February through June. *Snorkeling* equipment is available at the Vue Pointe Hotel. They will also arrange yacht cruises to Rendezvous Bay and Redonda. *Bird watching* at the Foxes' Bay Bird Sanctuary is a highlight here.

NEVIS

Alexander Hamilton and Other Gentry

Capped by clouds, Nevis is a dramatic thirty-five-mile-square island that lies two miles south of St. Kitts. Its forest-clad slopes rise almost straight up from the sea to Nevis Peak, the island's center, which soars 3,500 feet into the sky. This mountain is joined by a saddle to two lesser peaks, Hurricane Hill (1,192 feet) in the north and Saddle Hill (1,432 feet) in the south.

Long beaches, with white and with black sand, and off-shore coral reefs surround the island. Some beaches are edged with rocky promontories, others with long rows of towering palms. Inland, estate houses and plantations will give you an idea of how Nevis flourished during its heyday centuries ago. But all is quiet today, so quiet in fact that a dozen tourists on the beach will seem like a crowd. Nevis is an island that offers solitude and history for the traveller in search of one, the other, or both.

History

History has it that when Columbus came in 1493, he focused on the mammoth clouds over the island's tallest peak and was reminded of a snow-covered range in the Pyrenees. He then christened the island *Nieves,* which in Spanish means "snow." The name held, although the spelling changed over the years.

The next seafarers to arrive were Captain John Smith and his English crew in 1607. They were enroute to Virginia to settle the Jamestown colony, but stayed in Nevis long enough for the Captain to note, "here we found a great poole, wherein bathing ourselves we found much ease." Permanent colonization took place in 1628 when English Captain Anthony Hilton arrived with eighty planters on board his ship. And so a small colony began, one that would expand with vast sugar plantations and elegant estate houses.

Alexander Hamilton was born here in 1755, and the ruins of that estate can still be seen in Charlestown, the island's capital. Admiral Lord Nelson, Captain of His Majesty's Ship *Boreas*, was headquartered in Antigua but discovered Nevis as a fresh-water stop and returned often enough to court and eventually marry Frances Nisbet, who lived on a sixty-four-acre plantation on the north shore. Their best man was the Duke of Clarence, who was later to become King William IV of England. Their wedding took place at Montpelier Estate, now the site of a 19-room hotel. The marriage is recorded at historic St. John's Church in Fig Tree Village.

The "great poole" that Captain John Smith recorded was to become famous for its hot springs and curative waters. The Bath Hotel, an imposing place on a hilltop, was built during the eighteenth century. The word spread, and it eventually became the most important health spa in the British West Indies. It is in ruins today, high above Charlestown, but there is continued talk of a complete restoration.

Even though the sugar plantations are long gone, you'll still find canefields, impressive sugar mills, and ruins of plantation homes all over the island. Some of the estate houses of that era, such as Montpelier, have been restored and are now hotels giving visitors the feeling of nineteenth-century luxury living.

Nevis, along with St. Kitts, became an Associated State of Great Britain in 1967, and even though there has been talk of independence, their status has not changed.

EXPLORING NEVIS

With its beaches for strolling, its great houses for fine accommodations, and its historic sites, Nevis has more than enough to offer the visitor on tour. The city of Charlestown, once the hub of activity, is quiet today. Most of the excitement occurs when the thrice-daily ferry arrives from St. Kitts, bringing day visitors and a new supply of necessary produce.

Two blocks away, the remains of the estate where Alexander Hamilton was born are fenced off and surrounded by overgrown palms and colorful bougainvillea. Only the steps to the entrance are left, but the small museum next door will make history come alive.

Among the sites to see are St. John's Church in Fig Tree Village, just a few miles from town. A charming Anglo-Gallic church, pure in style, it looks as though it had been transported from a Cornish village. Beneath its memorial plaque you'll find the tattered register and an entry that reads: "Horatio Nelson, Esquire, to Frances Nisbet, Widow, on March 11, 1787." A walk through the small graveyard around the church adds to one's sense of history.

It's tricky, but you can drive inland and then up toward the sky and Nevis Peak. You'll wind and weave your way, and with each bend in the road will find another spectacular view of the island, its beaches and coves.

A DAY ON YOUR OWN

Although you can make a circular tour of the island, including stops at historic sites, in about four hours, allow a full day. Have the hotel prepare a picnic lunch, or mix and match your own from the tiny grocery stores on Main Street in Charlestown. Start early so that you'll be able to enjoy the beaches when the sun is at its height. There are no changing facilities, so wear a bathing suit with a cover-up and bring a towel.

After your walking tour of Charlestown, drive a few blocks to the outskirts of the city and up a winding hill to the ruins of The Bath Hotel. Enough remains to give you some idea of what it was like in its golden years, and what compelled the gentry from as far away as England to sail across and bathe in its thermal waters.

Return to the main road and head toward Zion Hill, making a stop enroute at St. John's Church at Fig Tree. Then continue on until you see the sign on your right indicating the Montpelier Hotel. Head toward the sea for a look at what was once a renowned plantation. It has been nicely renovated–a swimming pool sits right next to an ancient sugar mill–and is a delightful place to stay.

Return to the coastal road and head north. You'll see cattle grazing below and wind-swept palm trees in thick rows. Small farms that are sectioned off, and with the surf rolling in, are reminiscent of Scotland. As you round the top of the island you'll pass through Newcastle, once second in importance to Charlestown, now a quiet village that you could easily miss because it looks like a ghost town.

Then round the top of the island, head south and stop at the black-sand beach on the way to Charlestown. This is one of the island's most beautiful beaches, not only on its shore side, but opposite, where there is a lagoon that looks like a setting from "South Pacific." Take it all in, collect a few shells, and then retreat to the terrace at Pinney's Beach Hotel at the edge of town for a cool drink and to watch the sunset darken St. Kitts across the way.

PRACTICAL INFORMATION FOR NEVIS

HOW TO GET THERE. By air. St. Kitts is the gateway to Nevis, her sister island. *BWIA* flies non-stop from New York to St. Kitts; *BWIA* and *SunJet* fly in from Miami. *LIAT* takes over from there, with a 10-minute flight to Nevis.

By sea. There is ferry service from St. Kitts three times a day except on Thursday and Sunday. The crossing ($6 US) takes about an hour.

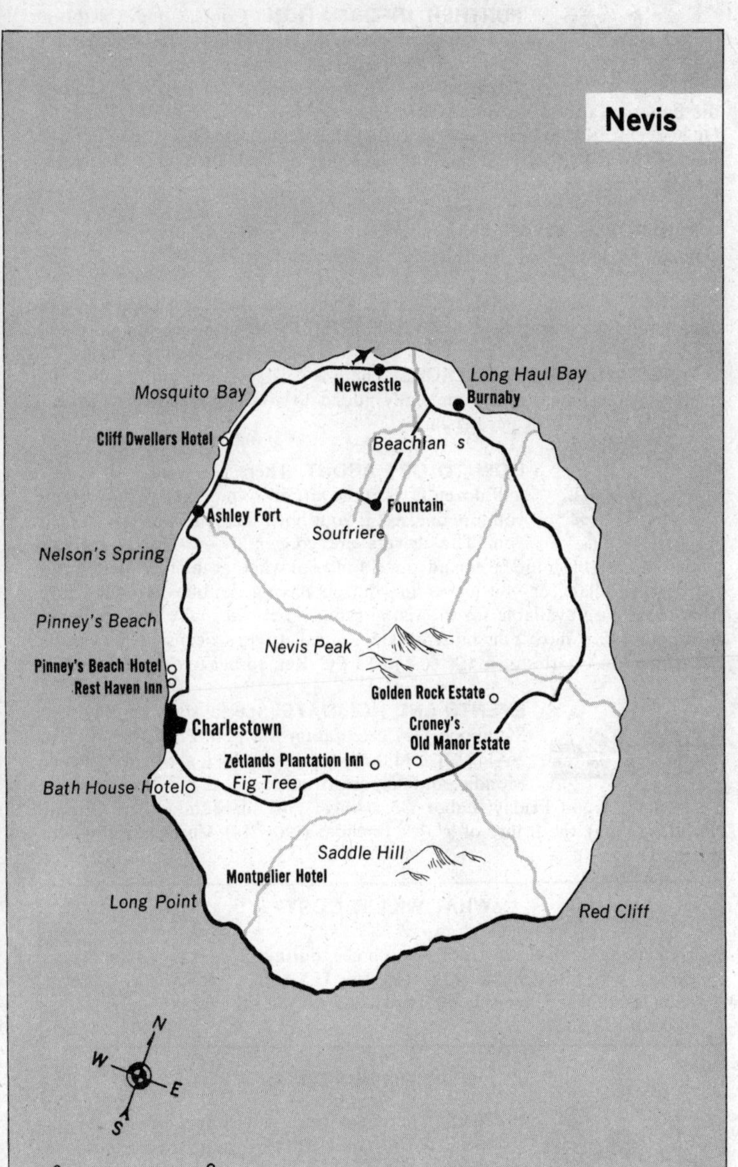

Nevis
Long Haul Bay
Newcastle
Burnaby
Mosquito Bay
Cliff Dwellers Hotel
Beachlan s
Ashley Fort
Fountain
Soufriere
Nelson's Spring
Pinney's Beach
Nevis Peak
Pinney's Beach Hotel
Rest Haven Inn
Golden Rock Estate
Charlestown
Croney's
Old Manor Estate
Zetlands Plantation Inn
Bath House Hotel
Fig Tree
Saddle Hill
Montpelier Hotel
Long Point
Red Cliff
N
W
E
S
0
2
Miles

FURTHER INFORMATION. Contact the Caribbean Tourism Association, 20 East 46th St., New York, N.Y. 10017; or the Eastern Caribbean Tourist Association, 220 East 42nd St., New York, N.Y. 10017. In Canada: the Eastern Caribbean Commission, Place de Ville, Suite 1701, 112 Kent St., Ottawa, Ont. K1P5P2; in London at 200 Buckingham Palace Road, London, Eng. SW1W9SP. There is a small tourist office in Nevis, on Chapel Street, just off Main Street in Charlestown.

PASSPORTS, VISAS. Proof of citizenship is required (a passport, even an expired one, is the best proof) as well as a valid return ticket.

MONEY. Eastern Caribbean dollars (EC) are used here, but US and Canadian dollars are accepted. $1 US = 2.70 EC; 6 EC = 1£.

TAXES AND OTHER CHARGES. There is a 5% government tax and 10% service charge which is automatically added to your hotel bill. The airport departure tax is $4 US per person.

HOW TO GET ABOUT. There are usually at least a half dozen taxis at the airport to meet the flights. Before you hire one, ask if your hotel has sent someone to meet you. The drivers are congenial and also good tour guides, but establish the fare in advance. Find out whether the rate quoted is in EC or US dollars, or you may find yourself paying double the actual fare. Mini-mokes are available for the rental (your hotel can make arrangements) for about $20 a day. You must obtain a local driver's license at the traffic department in Charlestown at a cost of $4 EC. Remember to drive on the left.

EVENTS AND HOLIDAYS. Special days on Nevis are Statehood Day celebrations on Feb. 27, Carnival (Dec. 26–Jan. 2), and the horse races which are held on Easter Monday and August Monday. Other holidays are: New Year's Day, Good Friday, Labor Day (May 1), Whit Monday, the Queen's Birthday (June), the Prince of Wales' Birthday (Nov. 14), Christmas Day, and Boxing Day.

WHAT WILL IT COST?

Depending upon the hotel of your choice, during the winter season *two* people will spend an average of $160 U.S. for a typical day. This includes all three meals, hotel service charges, and the rental of a Minimoke for the day.

STAYING IN NEVIS

HOTELS. There are fewer than a dozen places to stay on Nevis, but for an island this small, the accommodations are excellent. They run from motel-type units on the beach to beautifully refurbished estate great houses. There is very little in the way of planned entertainment, and since there are no restaurants outside the hotel orbit, **rates quoted are MAP (breakfast and dinner included).**

Cliffdwellers. This lovely hilltop property has fourteen Polynesian-style cottages perched on a cliff at Tamarind Bay. The rooms are large, each with a balcony and sea view, and are stretched across the property's seventeen acres. Tennis court, swimming pool, restaurant for high dining. Snorkeling on the beach below. Deep-sea fishing and horseback riding can be arranged. $150 double in winter; $100 double off-season.

Croney's Old Manor Estate. Twelve rooms–three large doubles in the main house, the others in surrounding West Indian–type cottages. The freshwater pool with sundeck adds a modern touch. Fine dining, free open bar. Croney's still operates as a plantation farm, and boasts a restored sugar mill. The hotel is in Gingerland, about forty minutes from the airport. $115 double in winter; $85 double off-season.

Golden Rock Estate. Ten attractive rooms, all with private bath and porch. This place was developed with typical American ingenuity from an old reconditioned sugar estate. The present managers, originally from the U.S., made Nevis their home while they tanned and cured goatskins to start a handbag industry. Related to thc original plantation owner, they put all their island know-how into keeping things moving. There's a tennis court, swimming pool, and transportation to two island beaches. $130 double in winter, $100 double off-season.

Montpelier Hotel. The main house is West Indian–style, set in the gardens on the site of historic sugar works. Nineteen rooms nicely decorated with terraces. Tennis court, freshwater pool and pool bar. Very attractive dining room. Free transportation to the beach, which is fifteen minutes away. $125 double in winter, $85 double off-season.

Nisbet Plantation Inn. This is another lovely island restoration, with twenty-five rooms, most in cottages but some in the plantation house itself. It is situated on a beautiful beach close to Newcastle on the windward coast. Repeat clientele fill most of the rooms at the height of the season. Not for those who demand a lot of action, but ideal for anyone who wants to settle in and enjoy plantation life and a casual house-party atmosphere. $150 double in winter, $100 off-season.

Pinney's Beach Hotel. A nice beachfront property, with fifty rooms in cottages, just a few minutes from Charlestown. The restaurant is high-domed indoors, terraced outdoors. Some entertainment in the evening. Swimming on its long beach is the highlight. $70 double in winter, $60 double off-season.

Rest Haven Inn. The only place with a modern motel look, Rest Haven has thirty-one rooms, most with sea views, many with efficiency units. Restaurant, lounge, small freshwater pool. Near Pinney's Beach, just a short walk from town. $55–90 MAP all year round.

Zetlands Plantation. Twenty-two rooms. Efficiency plantation suites, converted sugar mill, chalet and main building. Dining room, lounge. Freshwater pool, tennis, transportation to beach. Located on the mountain slopes, about four miles from town. $125 double in winter, $60 double off-season.

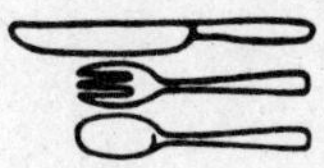

RESTAURANTS/NIGHTLIFE. The terrace at Pinney's Beach Hotel is great for lunch. Otherwise, dine at your hotel or make arrangements beforehand for meals at some of the others. As far as entertainment is concerned, it's what you make it. The movie theatre in Charlestown is managed by Calvin Ward, who is also a knowledgeable taxi driver/tour guide. He told us the theatre opens and closes depending upon the arrival of films by ferry from St. Kitts.

SHOPPING. If you search carefully you can find pottery sold privately from homes in Newcastle. In Charlestown you'll find the headquarters for Caribbee clothes, which are fashioned of good materials, with interesting tropical designs but prices that are way out of line. There are souvenirs at the Island Gift Shop and the Handicraft Society. But our favorite search was through grocery stores to find the famous Nevis hot sauce, which is very popular and not easy to find.

SPORTS AND OTHER ACTIVITIES. You'll find at least one tennis court at most of the hotels, but swimming and sunbathing are what it's all about on Nevis. Horseback riding and deep-sea fishing can be arranged through your hotel.

PUERTO RICO

Ponce de León's Gateway

Today's visitors head for this landfall, not necessarily in search of the Fountain of Youth that led Ponce de León through the island in the sixteenth century, but in search of a vacation paradise that offers something for everyone. Among the attractions are long white sand beaches, towering palm trees, a thick and lush rain forest, and mountains that soar into the Caribbean sky. Tiny tree frogs called *coquís* chirp through the quiet nights, while casinos, cabarets, and flamenco dancers offer excitement until dawn.

Add luxury resorts along the sea; country *paradores*; all watersports; museums; historic restorations; Taino Indian sites; and even a racetrack–Puerto Rico has it all. The name means "rich port," and, although all that glitters here is not gold, there's more than enough to go around on this island which measures 100 miles long by 35 miles wide.

For centuries, Puerto Rico had developed artists, musicians, writers whose work had transcended coastlines and brought them international acclaim. The work of painter Francisco Oller hangs in the Louvre. Puerto Rican writers offer a continuing enrichment to Spanish-language literature. Followers of fine music will recognize the names of pianist Jesús María Sanromá and basso Justino Diaz. The faces of José Ferrer, Rita Moreno, Chita Rivera, and José Feliciano are familiar to moviegoers and devotees of the more popular side of music.

To acquaint the world with the arts and culture of Puerto Rico, "Operation Serenity," was established in 1955. It created a climate in which talent could grow and flourish. The Puerto Rico Symphony Orchestra, a conservatory, and a music school were soon part of the plan. The late Pablo Casals, the famed cellist who adopted Puerto Rico (the birthplace of his mother) as his permanent home, is credited with having sparked this musical renaissance. For many years he was the star of the annual Casals' Festival—an ongoing delight and special attraction each year.

"Serenity" also prompted the establishment of the Institute of Puerto Rican Culture, which successfully effected a renaissance of appreciation of the island's creations in folklore, music, sculpture, painting, theater—the last through an annual theater festival. The Institute is bringing back the past—refurbishing old churches, historic landmarks, building museums, and supervising the restoration of Old San Juan's lovely Spanish buildings. At least a dozen professional galleries are now open in the old city, and a dozen or more are dotted in communities around the Puerto Rican countryside. The Areyto Folkloric dancers have been encouraged to learn and perform (in costume) the old dances of Puerto Rico in the *Le Lo Lai* Festival, a weekly program of folklore, printed in the monthly *Que Pasa.* At the performances, you'll see the *"cafetal"* (coffee plantation) dances and the dance performed by the Taino Indians at the death of a child. The group does an interesting imitation of the popular cockfights as well as other typically Puerto Rican events.

History

The Spanish culture dates to 1508, when Juan Ponce de León (whose remains are entombed in the San Juan Cathedral) established the first settlement. For three centuries thereafter, an international rivalry flared for possession of the island. Sir Francis Drake tried for it in 1595, but was whomped. Peace reigned in the 19th century. Luis Muñoz Rivera, the George Washington of Puerto Rico, won from Spain in 1897 the Charter of Autonomy which gave the island dominion status. But the autonomy was short-lived. The Spanish-American War erupted, and U.S. forces landed on the south coast July 25, 1898. Under the Treaty of Paris, proclaimed April 11, 1899, Puerto Rico passed from Spanish to U.S. sovereignty.

Military government prevailed until the Foraker Act of 1900 was passed, reestablishing civil government, but a colonial one under the thumb of Washington. The islanders were Puerto Rican citizens, ruled by a foreign power, until 1917 when the U.S. Congress made them American citizens and gave them some autonomy.

In 1926, under the sugar barons, cane cutters were getting ten cents an hour and eagerly selling their vote for $2 to elect company lawyers to the island legislature. Needlewomen, for hemming a dozen handkerchiefs, earned three cents.

Luis Muñoz Marín, at that time agitating for independence, described his island in 1929 as "a land of beggars and millionaires, of flattering statistics and distressing realities. More and more, it becomes a factory worked by peons, fought over by lawyers, bossed by absent industrialists, and clerked by politicians. . . ."

However, by 1938, Muñoz had satisfied himself that independence was not feasible. In groping for something more practical, he formed the Popular Democratic Party and promised land reform and labor laws instead of independence. He was elected to the island Senate. The Popular Party set in motion a plan to industrialize the island and "Operation Bootstrap" was underway.

EXPLORING PUERTO RICO

Part of Puerto Rico's special charm is the juxtaposition of old and new. Nowhere is this more apparent than in Old San Juan, where the moss-covered bastions of El Morro and precincts of the now-restored old city sit cheek by jowl with modern office buildings and high-rises.

Old San Juan was founded in 1521, but centuries have layered their patterns on the buildings in town. Spanish buildings nestle against more modern architecture in this area, still partially encircled by its walls, begun in 1630. The ambitious restoration preserves the atmosphere of 16th and 17th century Spain, as it came to the New World in the minds of the immigrants.

Plaza Colón, the starting point for a walking or minibus tour of Old San Juan, is dominated by a statue of Columbus, erected in the Plaza in 1893 to commemorate the 400th anniversary of his discovery of Puerto Rico.

The chief tourist attraction of Old San Juan is El Morro, the great fortress which the Spanish constructed at the northwest tip of the city from 1539 to 1586. Covering more than 200 acres, rising 145 feet above the Atlantic, this great bastion of colonial Spain remained impregnable from the sea even when attacked in 1595 by such doughty foes as Drake and Hawkins. It was taken by the English from the land side and held briefly in 1598. The Spanish continued to improve the fortifications, and it wasn't until 1776 that El Morro was completed. The National Park Service retains the castle and part of the grounds, giving conducted tours daily. There's a splendid view from the ramparts, and the labyrinthine tunnels are fascinating. If you look over the seawall you'll see the old San Juan Cemetery and its elaborate circular chapel.

A Gem of Medieval Architecture

Near the main entrance of El Morro is San José Church, the oldest Christian place of worship still in use in the Western Hemisphere. Started by the Dominicans in 1523, the church preserves its vaulted Gothic ceilings, a rare survival of authentic medieval architecture in the New World. Ponce de León lay buried here for three and a half centuries before his mortal remains were transferred to the Cathedral. His family coat of arms still hangs beneath the ceiling of the main altar. Outside on the plaza Ponce himself stands in brazen glory, his

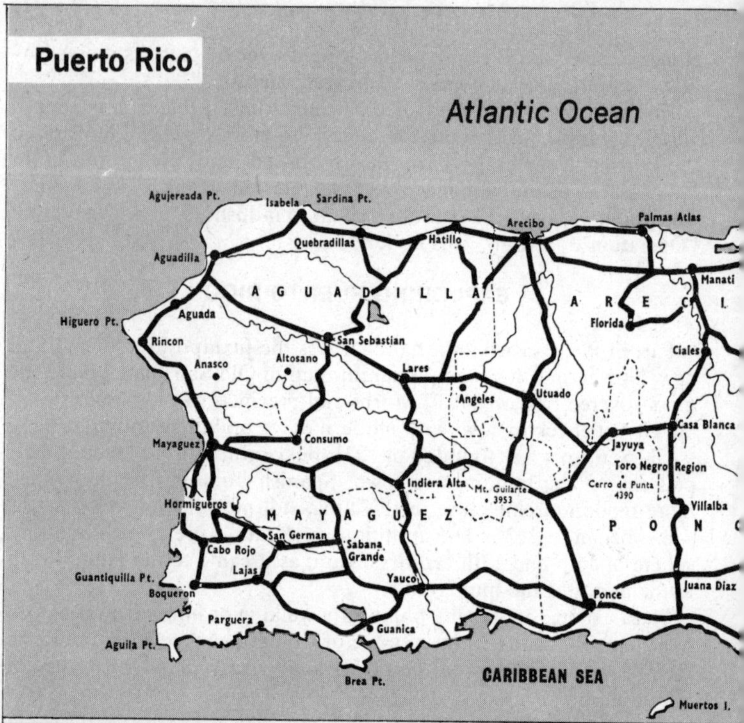

Puerto Rico

Atlantic Ocean

Agujereada Pt.
Isabela
Sardina Pt.
Quebradillas
Hatillo
Arecibo
Palmas Atlas
Aguadilla
Manati
A G U A D I L L A
A R E C I
Higuero Pt.
Aguada
Florida
Rincon
San Sebastian
Ciales
Anasco
Altosano
Lares
Angeles
Utuado
Casa Blanca
Mayaguez
Consumo
Jayuya
Toro Negro Region
Indiera Alta
Mt. Guilarte
3953
Cerro de Punta
4390
Hormigueros
Villalba
M A Y A G U E Z
P O N C
San German
Sabana Grande
Cabo Rojo
Lajas
Yauco
Juana Diaz
Guantiquilla Pt.
Boqueron
Ponce
Parguera
Guanica
Aguila Pt.
Brea Pt.
CARIBBEAN SEA
Muertos I.

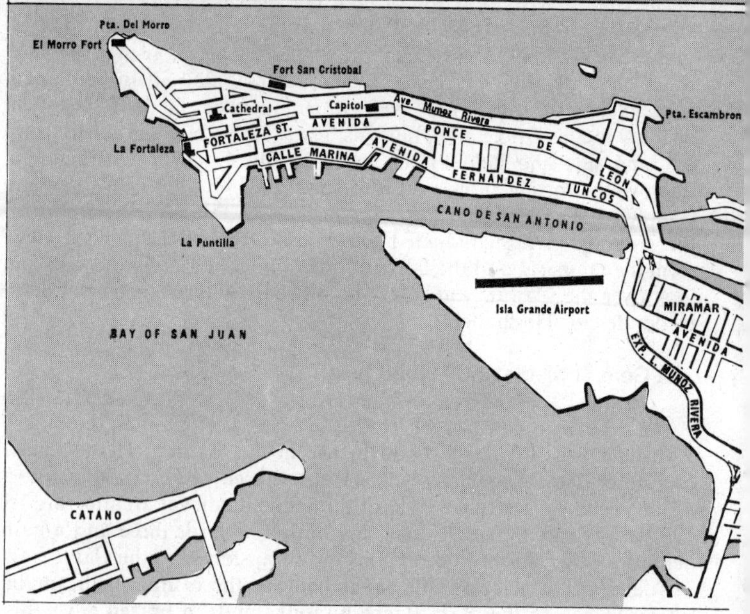

Pta. Del Morro
El Morro Fort
Fort San Cristobal
Capitol
Cathedral
Ave. Munoz Rivera
AVENIDA
Pta. Escambron
FORTALEZA ST.
PONCE DE LEON
La Fortaleza
CALLE MARINA
AVENIDA
FERNANDEZ JUNCOS
CANO DE SAN ANTONIO
La Puntilla
Isla Grande Airport
MIRAMAR
AVENIDA
EXP. L. MUNOZ RIVERA
BAY OF SAN JUAN
CATANO

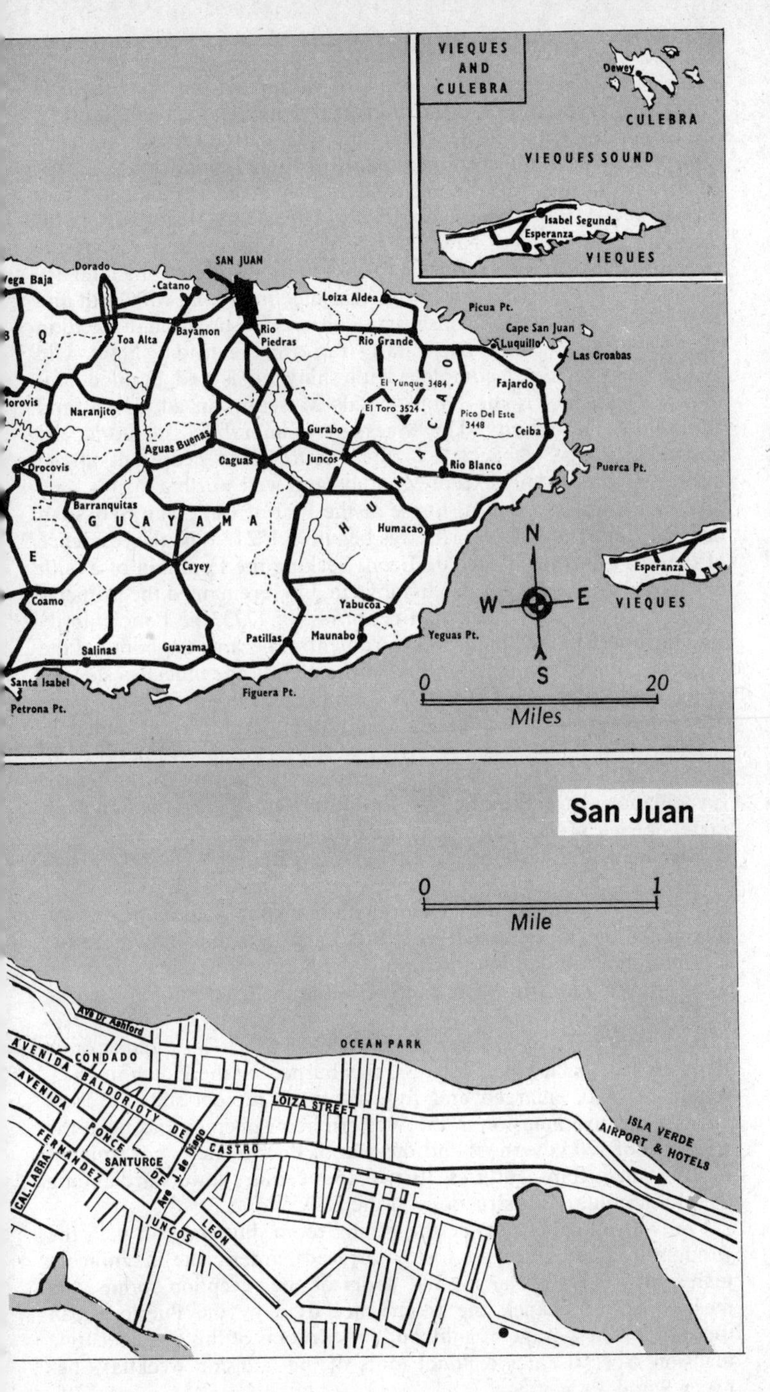
VIEQUES AND CULEBRA
Dewey
CULEBRA
VIEQUES SOUND
Isabel Segunda
Esperanza
VIEQUES
SAN JUAN
Dorado
Vega Baja
Catano
Loiza Aldea
Picua Pt.
Cape San Juan
Luquillo
Las Croabas
Toa Alta
Bayamon
Rio Piedras
Rio Grande
Fajardo
Morovis
Naranjito
El Yunque 3484
El Toro 3524
Pico Del Este 3448
Ceiba
Gurabo
Aguas Buenas
Caguas
Juncos
Rio Blanco
Puerca Pt.
Orocovis
Barranquitas
G U A Y A M A
H U M A C A O
Humacao
Cayey
Esperanza
VIEQUES
N
W
E
S
Coamo
Yabucoa
Salinas
Guayama
Patillas
Maunabo
Yeguas Pt.
Santa Isabel
Figuera Pt.
Petrona Pt.
0
20
Miles
San Juan
0
1
Mile
Ave Dr Ashford
AVENIDA
CONDADO
OCEAN PARK
AVENIDA BALDORIOTY DE CASTRO
LOIZA STREET
ISLA VERDE AIRPORT & HOTELS
FERNANDEZ JUNCOS
PONCE DE LEON
SANTURCE
Ave J. de Diego
CAL. LABRA

statue fashioned from bronze cannons captured from the British in 1797. Next to the church is the old Santo Domingo Convent, built by the Dominican Friars at the same time as San José Church. A handsome example of 16th century Spanish colonial architecture, it was taken over by the government in 1810, when the Dominican order was dissolved. For many years, this was the Army Headquarters for the Antilles Command. Now it has been exquisitely restored by the Institute of Puerto Rican Culture for use as a showplace for island art. Most recently restored are a library and meeting room, with 16th and 17th century books and furnishings. Concerts are occasionally held in the vast arcaded patio (particularly fun are the Friday night, Old World band concerts, complete with shiny tubas and braided uniforms). Here, too, is the Pablo Casals Museum, an added cultural addition to the old city. The Maestro's memorabilia, including the famous cellos, which he left to the Puerto Rican people, is all on display. It's open daily except Monday, and well worth a visit.

Casa Blanca, a beautiful house at the foot of Calle San Sebastian near the ramparts of El Morro, was begun in 1521, to be the residence of the first governor, Ponce de León. Seeking the Fountain of Youth in Florida, Ponce did not live to move in, but it remained the property of his family for two and a half centuries. In 1773, the Ponce family sold the house to the Spanish Government. It became the home of the Spanish military commander, and subsequently the official residence of the U.S. Army's top brass. Now Commonwealth government property, it has been restored for use as a museum and cultural center.

La Fortaleza, the official residence of the Governor of Puerto Rico, is open to the public. It's just a short two-block walk to the left of Casa Blanca as you face the bay. En route you will pass the San Juan Gate, opened in 1635, and once the main entrance to the walled city of San Juan. The view of the bay, of Casa Blanca, and the massive ramparts of the town is most impressive from here. Just up the street is a small plaza, donated to the city in honor of its 450th anniversary, dominated by an impressive sculpture, La Rogativa, commemorating a legend that the flaming torches of a religious procession *(rogativa)* were what caused British troops to abandon their siege of San Juan in 1797.

Begun in 1533 as a fort, La Fortaleza, which is a remarkable building, half-palace, half-fortress, was burned by the Dutch in 1625, rebuilt in 1640, enlarged and restored to its present state in 1846. Oldest executive mansion in the Western hemisphere, it has been the residence of 170 governors and the seat of Puerto Rico's government for more than four centuries. Its two 16th century towers are among the oldest military constructions in the New World.

You will probably not see the dining room, but you can pass the wrought-iron gates, see the lovely terraced gardens, the magnificent mahogany stairway, the marble floors of the reception rooms, the mosaic-studded chapel, the room once used by the Puerto Rican treasury for the storage of gold, and other rooms of this fine executive mansion. Special aides conduct tours of the mansion weekdays between 9 and 4 P.M.

Catholic Shrine

Walk down Calle del Cristo with its blue ballast stones, past the Cathedral to Cristo Chapel, which was built to mark the spot where a horse and rider in 1753 leaped over the 70-foot bluff on which it is built. (Legend had it that the young rider survived, but unfortunately his death was later substantiated by researchers.) Next to the Cristo chapel is the cool little Parque de las Palomas, with benches and an unobstructed view of the harbor. From the old city wall you'll see the courtyard of La Princesa Prison, at the end of what was once a landscaped promenade. Bastión de la Palma, another pleasant park, is at the harbor end of San José Street. Go back up Calle del Cristo to the corner of Calle Luna and the great Catholic shrine of Puerto Rico, the Cathedral of San Juan Bautista. Begun as early as 1521, the Cathedral has risen several times like a phoenix from its ashes. The present building dates from 1802 but conserves Gothic details dating from 1540. In it you will find the tomb of Juan Ponce de León; numerous mementos of *los reyes Católicos,* Ferdinand and Isabella; in a glass case opposite Ponce's tomb, the remains of a converted, martyred Roman centurion, St. Pio, once buried in the catacombs of Rome, now seen in the light of the New World. Ask to see the Renaissance madonna and the 16th century chalices.

Following the streets of Old San Juan as they wind up and down hills is good for the ankles and the stomach muscles. Halfway between the Cathedral and San Juan Gate, you will find one of the original staircase streets which has not succumbed to cars. This is the Callejón de Las Monjas, and if you climb it to the next street, you'll see another, the Caleta del Hospital, rising another steep block.

Visit the Museum of Colonial Architecture, La Casa del Callejón, at 319 Fortaleza Street, a restored 18th century building, which has displays of four centuries of Puerto Rico's Spanish colonial architecture. There are scale models of some of the important structures you will have already visited, and a collection of antique tiles. Upstairs is the Museum of the Puerto Rican Family, furnished in the manner of a typical 19th century urban household. In the first floor courtyard and small rooms, a restaurant features traditional Puerto Rican food and drink. You'll be ready, by this time, for one or both.

At 101 San Sebastian, adjacent to San José Plaza, is the Casa de los Contrafuertes, or Buttress House, built in the early 18th century—one of the oldest colonial buildings still standing in San Juan. It has been restored by the Institute of Culture, and houses the Museum of Puerto Rican Santos, with fine examples of the small religious figures carved from wood, some 200 years old, and the Pharmacy Museum. Upstairs is a graphic arts museum.

La Casa del Libro at 255 Cristo Street is a superb museum of rare books in an 18th century house, beautifully restored and furnished, open to the public from 11 A.M. to 5 P.M. Monday through Friday. Next to La Casa del Libro is the Institute of Culture's Museum of Puerto Rican Art with a permanent exhibition of works by old masters and modernists. The façade of the City Hall, *La Alcaldia,* on the north side of the Plaza de Armas, is an exact copy of the municipal building in Madrid, built here in the 17th century. It houses a small museum of San Juan's history.

Casa Don Q. on Cristo, is an 18th century Spanish colonial town house, meticulously restored by the rum-producing Serrales family as an oasis for visitors. The upstairs veranda houses a bar, replica of one in La Mancha where complimentary rum drinks are offered.

If you are an addict of military architecture, you will want to visit the Fort San Cristóbal, begun in the 17th century to protect San Juan from any land attack from the east. It is very much larger than the El Morro fort, though with fewer levels. There are magnificent views from its ramparts and gun emplacements. The National Park Service conducts daily tours. South of the Plaza de Colón are the harbor piers and the colorful waterfront of Old San Juan. From here you can take a ferry ride (10 cents) to Cataño across the bay, an excursion whose chief rewards are refreshing breezes and a splendid view of the Old City. On Sundays and holidays there are special 1½-hour cruises around the Bay, departing at 2:30 and 4:30 from the ferry terminal (adults, $1.50; children under 12, $1.00).

Facing the Plaza Colón on the south side is the municipal Tapia Theatre, built about 1832 and remodeled in 1949, and named after the 19th century playwright Alejandro Tapia y Rivera. Plays and ballets are often staged here. Behind the theater is the old stone public baths building, restored for use as a small museum of pre-Colombian art.

East of Plaza de Colón the island becomes an isthmus. Two major thoroughfares, Avenida Ponce de León and Avenida Fernandez Juncos, lead out of Old San Juan to the booming business and tourist sections of Santurce.

Once east of Plaza de Colón, distances are too great and sights too decentralized to warrant further exploration afoot. You can go by bus, taxi or *público* to places of interest along Ponce de León Avenue. They include El Capitolio, Puerto Rico's imposing white Georgia marble capitol. Although construction on the neo-Renaissance building was begun in 1925, the impressive rotunda was not completed until a few years ago. A booklet is available from the House secretariat on the second floor describing the extensive mosaics and marble friezes executed in Italy from sketches by Puerto Rican artists. The two modern buildings flanking the Capitolio house are the Senate and the House of Representatives. On the sea side of El Capitolio is a cliff-top observation plaza with a bird's-eye view of the surf and, to the east, of the tourist towers of the Condado. Steps lead from the plaza down to the popular surfing beach below.

There's no doubt that while exploring this coastal area, you'll want to visit and photograph old Fort San Jerónimo, whose crumbling, sun-mellowed texture provides such a striking contrast with the spit-and-polish façade of the Caribe Hilton Hotel immediately to the west. Built in 1788, San Jerónimo staved off a major English attack in 1797. It has been restored and now houses a museum of Spanish military armor and weapons.

Well frequented by travelers is Boca de Cangrejos, a rocky point of land east of booming Santurce near the International Airport. On lagoon and sea, it is a good place for fishing and snorkeling; the reef is above water at low tide so walk far out to the best places for sighting the coral caves through which swim schools of brilliant tropical fish. Center of activity in Boca is the Cangrejos Yacht Club whose members keep power boats moored in the lagoon near the club house. La Paseadora, a 30 passenger launch, tours the tranquil lagoon and goes out into the Atlantic for a brief view of the hotels along the beach. The one-hour excursions begin at 11 A.M. daily except Monday (adults, $2.50; children up to 10 years, $1.50).

Fashionable Santurce and Busy Rio Piedras

If you're looking for those technicolor local markets, shining with all the rich produce of the tropics, you'll find two in Santurce and Río Piedras. The first district, with its shiny shops and office buildings, you will already have passed through, driving down the main drag, Avenida Ponce de León. Santurce's "progress" from tranquil suburb to booming metropolis is the story of 20th century San Juan. Away from the traffic of Ponce de León Avenue, you'll still find a few old Spanish estates, vestiges of a quieter day, but most of them have been subdivided. Smart modern houses are the mark of residential Santurce today.

Heading south toward Rio Piedras from Santurce you pass through what has become the city's new hub–Hato Rey. Once a no man's land, it is now marked by a towering concentration of handsome office buildings that house almost all the major banks, corporations, and professionals.

Rio Piedras, once a quiet town, is now a southern suburb of San Juan. The University of Puerto Rico is here. Its campus is a landscaped beauty and the site of the annual Casals Festival, as well as concerts and theatrical productions held throughout the year. Visit their Museum of Anthropology, Art and History, which has a small but intriguing collection of artifacts. The highlight here, however, is the vast Botanical Garden, with a network of paths that cut through a thick forest, past a lotus lagoon, and through a bamboo promenade to reach their spectacular orchid garden.

Before extending your explorations "out on the island," as the Puerto Ricans say, perhaps you will want to see another industrial process in action, the distillation of rum. If you are planning to go to Arecibo or Ponce, you can save this experience for the Ron Rico or Don Q Rum distilleries, which operate respectively in those two towns. Otherwise drive to the little town of Palo Seco on the southwestern shore of the Bay of San Juan, where the Bacardí people will show you how sugar is transformed into rum and ply you with copious draughts of same, after which the view across the bay to El Morro and San Juan seems even more romantic than usual! A 50¢ bus ride will carry you between the distilleries and the Cataño-San Juan ferry dock.

Out on the Island

Puerto Rico has about 4000 miles of good roads, and you could spend weeks exploring the island. The short tour below you can drive yourself, arrange through one of the agencies indicated in the monthly *Que Pasa,* or take your own group in a *público.* (See the section A Day on Your Own for a sample island tour by rental car.)

Rum and Pineapple Route

Our short tour, an all-day affair, could be termed the rum and pineapple route, since it will permit you to visit a distillery and tour the pineapple country. Take Route 2 west out of San Juan through Bayamón, Vega Baja, and Manatí. Branch right on Route 681 beyond Manatí and follow the coastal road to Arecibo. Settled in 1556, Arecibo is one of Puerto Rico's oldest towns. Four miles east of the town you can visit an Indian cave, used as a place of worship before the Spaniards came, its walls decorated with pre-Columbian drawings and carvings in low relief. Arecibo is a center for deep-sea fishermen. Information can be obtained at the Club de Caza y Pesca. Freshwater fishermen also like to try their luck near here in the lakes made by Dos Bocas and Caonillas dams.

The Public Works Department operates a free launch service to points around man-made Dos Bocas Lake. Launches leave from the Embarcadero (Route 10, Km. 63) for two-hour roundtrips at 7 and 10 A.M. and 2 and 5 P.M., and for a one-hour trip at 12:30 P.M. Near Dos Bocas is the teak-filled, 5800-acre Río Abajo State Forest, with a ranger's office, sawmill, and brookside picnic area. A small swimming pool is open weekends.

There are also dozens of mountain caves and ruined sugar mills to explore and the world's largest radar-radio telescope, open Sundays from 2-4:30 P.M.

The Ron Rico rum distillery at Arecibo welcomes visitors. Have lunch, visit the sugar mills; then take Route 2 back to Manati, heart of the pineapple country. If you turn left here on Route 685 you come to grotto-like Mar Chiquita Beach, where the sea plunges in through an opening in the rock cliffs to a lovely crescent beach.

Heading back to San Juan on Route 2, a short detour on Route 165 will take you past Catano to the Bacardí distillery and to the causeway leading to Cabras Island, a popular picnic area with snack bar and thatched huts, a 17th century Spanish fort, El Canuelo, in picturesque ruins, lovely views of the bay and the Old City.

Scenic Stretches

If it's just simply fabulous scenery you crave, you should include any (or all) of the following *particularly scenic stretches* of road to be found in Puerto Rico: in the western half of the island, (1) Route 149 from Villalbra to Ciales; (2) Route 143 from Barranquitas through the Toro Negro forest to Route 10; (3) Route 105 from Mayagüez to

Maricao, south on Route 120 through the Maricao State Forest to Sabana Grande; (4) Route 10 from Arecibo to Utuado, right on 111 to Aquadilla. In the eastern half of the island (in addition to El Yunque; see above) you can travel: (1) the completed segments of the long-awaited Panoramic Route, eventually to stretch all the way from Yabucao in the southeast corner to Mayagüez on the west coast, by taking Route 1 to Caguas, Route 30 to Humacao, south on 901 to Maunabo and circling back north again on Route 3; (2) Route 181 from Trujillo Alto to Gurabo; (3) Route 181 from Trujillo Alto to left turn on 858, then right on 852, then follow signs on small unnumbered roads to 853, where you turn right then left on 185, then right on 186 to Río Grande; (4) Route 1 south from Caguas, left on 765, then right on 763 until it merges with 184, south on 184 to Patillas; (5) Route 15 from Cayey to Guayama, another section of the Panoramic Route, passing Jajome, the Governor's summer residence.

Most spectacular of all is the San Juan-Ponce toll road, which cuts a wide and wonderful swathe through the rugged mountains of the Cordillera Central making driving time between the two cities an hour and a half.

When organizing your trips, here are some places of more than ordinary tourist interest to include: *Aguada and Aguadilla.* On the northwest coast, Aguada, settled in 1590, claims to be the place where Columbus first set foot on Puerto Rican soil and marks the spot, at the end of Calle Colón, where the Admiral's foot presumably stepped. Aguadilla, a few miles to the north, disputes the foregoing claim and has its own monument. Aguadilla is a center of the island's straw hat industry. The former Ramey Air Force Base is a few miles north of town and, as Borinquen Field, is open to civilian air traffic. Now operated as a resort complex, Punta Borinquen, the former officers homes (solid 3-bedroom houses) are rented to vacationers for a modest $60 per day. Las Playuelas beach is nearby.

Aguas Buenas. Half an hour from San Juan up into the cool mountains. The towering antennae that mark the town from afar belong to the government-operated radio and television stations, WIPR. A pleasant, typical town built around a plaza.

Barranquitas. A charming mountain town almost in the center of Puerto Rico and between San Juan and Ponce, this is a popular year-round resort because of its cool climate. Birth and burial place of the great statesman Luis Muñoz Rivera (1859-1916), father of the former governor, whose home is a library and museum, open to public. One Sunday in mid-July, the Institute of Culture sponsors a craft show in the town plaza. Artisans come from all over the island to commemorate Muñoz Rivera's birthday.

Boquerón. Beautiful public beach on the west coast rivaling Luquillo.

Cabo Rojo, once the lair of the pirate Roberto Cofresí, is a quiet town on the dry southwestern coast, known by the Puerto Ricans as the "desert" country. About 8 miles south of Cabo Rojo are the marine salt beds with a commercial production of some 12,000 tons of salt annually. At the southwesternmost tip of the island is Faro de

Punta Jaguey, a lighthouse standing sentinel over the rugged cliffs. En route, at El Combate, there is a ramshackle fishing village set at one end of a long beach of incredible tranquility and beauty, and fresh fish and lobster are prepared in the one or two small cafés by the pier.

Camuy, west of Arecibo, is the site of an extensive cave system, hailed by the National Speleological Society as unique and awe inspiring.

Caparra, on Route 2, a few minutes south of San Juan, is historically interesting as the site of the first settlement in Puerto Rico. You can still see the foundations of Ponce de León's first house, built in 1508. Excavated and restored by the Institute of Culture, they stand in a small park. A small museum contains Indian relics, charts, and ornaments uncovered during excavation.

Dorado Beach, 20 miles west of San Juan, is the locale of the Caribbean project started by Laurence Rockefeller interests. Visitors can stop for lunch, a swim, tennis or golf at secluded *Dorado Beach* or the 503-room Cerromar Beach Hotel. The town of Dorado is small, rural Puerto Rican and, except for those residents who work at the hotels, little affected by tourism.

A few minutes past the entrance to Dorado Beach is the seaside village of *Cerro Gordo,* where many Sanjuaneros weekend. The beach here is one of the area's best, and the small inn in the heart of the weekend community serves Puerto Rican specialties.

Fajardo. On the northeast coast of the island, this fishing and sailing center changed hands three times during the Spanish-American War. The Isleta Marina yachting center is nearby, but in Fajardo itself, you'll find Las Croabas with its array of fishing boats; the Puerto Chico marina, and the Villa Marina Yacht Harbor. The beautiful uninhabited island called *Icacos* is not far offshore. You can negotiate with one of the fishermen to take you over for a swim, or make a full day of it by signing aboard the *Spread Eagle* catamaran for a quiet sail that includes snorkeling the reef, swimming, sunbathing, and a buffet lunch for $25 per person. Ferries also leave from Fajardo for the offshore islands of *Culebra* and *Vieques* ($2.25 one-way). Culebra has its white-sand crescent beaches, its reefs to explore, and a few small inns. Vieques is similar, with a fine beach on Sun Bay, which has lockers, showers, a snack bar, and the small inn, *La Casa del Frances.*

Guánica was the site of the American landing on the south coast in 1898. The Copamarina Hotel is here, near an inviting beach, and there's a picturesque old Spanish lighthouse. Nearby, the strange scrub-and cactus landscape of the Guánica State Forest extends to the edge of the sea. Special attraction here is the population of Puerto Rican whippoorwills, believed to be extinct but rediscovered in 1961.

Hormigueros. A southwestern village a few miles south of Mayagüez, it is famous for its Shrine of Our Lady of Monserrat, who, in the 17th century, responded to a peasant's call for help and saved him from the charge of a mad bull. An annual pilgrimage takes place every September 8.

Humacao is a bustling industrial town on the eastern coast of the island, producing tons of sugar in the most up-to-date refineries, and providing a dramatic contrast to sleepier, undeveloped neighboring villages. There's a magnificent public beach north of town, with lockers, changing facilities, restaurants.

Just to the south of Humacao, in an area of extraordinary beauty, is 2800-acre Palmas del Mar resort and leisure community which includes residential, resort, and commercial facilities as well as botanical gardens, marinas, beaches, restaurants, villages for golf or tennis, a special inn, and a brand-new hotel in the center of it all.

Jájome, the attractive summer residence of the Governor of Puerto Rico, is located right on Highway 15 between Cayey and Guayama, an old south coast Puerto Rican city, founded in 1790. Now enlarged, the main stone structure was originally built by the Spaniards to house *camineros* (highway maintenance men). Cordillera Central, in superbly graded serpentine style, is admired by engineers, and the scenery makes it a top flight favorite. Near the Governor's residence is a replica of the Grotto of Lourdes.

Mayagüez, with a population well over 100,000, is the third city of Puerto Rico, smack in the center of the western coast. Long the needlework center of the island, it is still a good place to pick up lovely embroidery and drawn-thread work. Just north of the city is the Mayagüez Institute of Tropical Agriculture with splendidly landscaped grounds replete with exotic trees: cacao, ilang ilang, cinnamon, and bamboo. And don't miss a trip to the zoo nearby, where more than 500 birds and animals, both indigenous and imported, roam 45 acres.

Parguera is a fishing village on the southwestern coast, popular with visitors, but still "unspoiled." You can rent fishing boats and tackle here, fill your scuba tanks, eat seafood at the Villa Parguera Hotel or in a number of unpretentious local restaurants where they know how to grill lobster and fry *pescado.* The great attraction, though, is Phosphorescent Bay. Draw your arm through the water and you describe an arc of darting quick silver flame. Impressive on any night, the phosphorescent effects are most striking during the dark of the moon. You can arrange for a motor boat tour of the bay at the Villa Parguera.

Forever Spain

Ponce, the "Pearl of the South," is the second city of Puerto Rico, but is still little known to most visitors to the island. It is just a one-and-a-half-hour drive from San Juan and, with a population close to 150,000, hopes to become an important port and tourist center. Take the time to walk through this charming provincial capital and to enjoy its main plaza where fountains play and gardens flourish in front of Our Lady of Guadalupe Cathedral, which dominates the square. The Parque de Bombas, Ponce's ancient firehouse, is the single-most-photographed object in Puerto Rico. It's painted in a riot of colors, including red, green, and black, and its trucks are painted a bright yellow. Walk on and note the *rejas,* balconies and other wrought-iron details on the old Spanish houses. The local market and waterfront are exceptionally colorful. El Tuque Beach, two miles southwest of Ponce, is a first-rate beach and recreational area. There are picnic tables, lockers, swimming pool, coffee shop. It's closed on Mondays. If you still haven't seen the process which turns sugar cane into demon rum, here's another chance, at Ponce's Don Q Rum Distillery.

The Ponce museum, designed by Edward Durell Stone, is across from the Catholic University on Las Americas Avenida. It has hexagonal art galleries, a circular pool, and graceful, curving stairways leading to the second floor. Works on view in this Museo de Arte de Ponce include paintings from major European schools from the 14th to 20th centuries as well as Puerto Rican artists.

Las Americas Expressway, known as route 52 and opened officially in late '75, makes it possible to race from San Juan to Ponce in an hour and a half. The 63-mile road weaves around some of Puerto Rico's highest mountain peaks, once you've mastered the traffic and confusion of Rio Piedras in the San Juan orbit. Explore Ponce, have lunch in town or at the Holiday Inn pool, and drive back, or fly *Prinair* to San Juan (20 minutes) from the Ponce Airport.

San Germán, in the southwest sector of the island, is one of the most attractive towns in Puerto Rico and in the West Indies. Founded on its present site in 1573, it keeps the look of a little Spanish town, the special ambience of Mediterranean civilization. Although its population is under 20,000, San Germán was once the rival of San Juan. Until the second half of the 17th century, San Juan and San Germán were the only two towns on the island; the rest were merely hamlets.

But today, while San Juan is exploding, San Germán remains relatively untouched by the innovations of a newer time, in spite of being headquarters for the 8000-student Inter-American University. This only tends to give a more cultural air to this charming town.

The Porta Coeli (Gate of Heaven) Church takes you back to the dawn of the Renaissance. Built in 1606, it is the oldest church under the U.S. flag to remain intact. Its altar, its carved wooden pillars, its heavy entrance doors are just as they were nearly five centuries ago. It houses a colonial religious art collection.

Vieques is one of Puerto Rico's three island "possessions" (the other two are its neighbor *Culebra,* notable for its crescent beaches and underwater sea life on its reefs, and *Mona,* a barren plateau off the eastern coast). Vieques is easily reached by ferry from Fajardo. Horses can be rented at La Casa del Francês, a lovely old plantation house, now a guest house. There are several gorgeous beaches. Another, even brighter, phosphorescent bay has been discovered here and is expected to add greatly to the island's tourist potential.

A DAY ON YOUR OWN

Pack a bathing suit and picnic lunch, wear rubber-soled shoes and plan to spend a full day. Your destinations are El Yunque, the lush inland rain forest, and Luquillo Beach, a real beauty on the island's northeastern shore.

Head first for El Yunque, "The Anvil," the only tropical forest under the jurisdiction of the U.S. National Park Service. It's an easy drive, taking Route 3 to Palmer, then turning right on Route 191. As you approach, you ascend into a cool, magical world of giant ferns, exotic trees, wild orchids, green vines, brilliantly colored parrots, and splashing mountain waterfalls. You are in the Caribbean National Forest, one of the most luxuriant in the world, thanks to 200 inches of rainfall per year. When you look down from the observation tower on the sea and palmy plains of Puerto Rico, you'll be astonished that two such different worlds can exist within so small an area. There is a restaurant here, and its terrace affords a splendid panorama. There is also a picnic area, where shelters are provided for the times when it rains in the rain forest–but don't worry, it won't last long. So plan to spread out. There are lots of tables, benches and barbecue pits, and a swimming pool formed by the damming of an icy mountain stream.

Use your eyes and ears and you might spot the nearly extinct Puerto Rican parrot or hear the call of the *coqui,* the tiny tree frog that sings out his own name.

Hiking enthusiasts can choose from trails leading to the area's three peaks: El Yunque (round-trip 2½ hours), Mt. Britton (1½ hours), and El Toro (a full day). Information is available at the National Park Service's Visitors' Center.

Return to Route 3, turn right to Luquillo, and swim at one of the most beautiful beaches in Puerto Rico. Luquillo Beach is a palm-shaded, gently sloping, sweeping crescent of sand. There are changing facilities, lockers, and a small snack bar for your comfort.

From Luquillo, the scenic way back to San Juan is Route 187. Turn onto it at Rio Grande, and it will take you to Loiza Aldea, a small colonial village whose church of St. Patrick was the first in the Western Hemisphere to be dedicated to Ireland's patron saint. Loiza Aldea's annual fiesta, the last week in July, is a colorful festival you will enjoy attending. Here, too, you can dig for amulets and pottery fragments in middens left by early Indian tribes.

Take the old ferry across the Loiza River and then follow the coastal road. The spectacular ocean views and rural communities make this a delightful, although bumpy, drive–but be sure to check beforehand to make sure the road is open and the ferry operating.

Then return to San Juan, content with the pleasures of the forest and the island's sun-swept sands.

PRACTICAL INFORMATION FOR PUERTO RICO

HOW TO GET THERE. By air. Puerto Rico's San Juan International airport is a gigantic web of activity that serves as the gateway to the Caribbean. There are dozens of flights from major U.S. cities via *American Airlines, Capitol Airways, Delta, Eastern* and *Pan American; Iberia, Lufthansa,*

and *Pan American* fly in from Europe; and *Avianca, Mexicana,* and *Viasa* connect Puerto Rico to the larger cities in Mexico and South America.

Puerto Rico is the northern terminal, as Barbados/Trinidad is the southern, for inter-island flights. Several recognized lines fan out of Puerto Rico to the islands. *Prinair,* the "national" airline of Puerto Rico, leads the pack with a colorful confetti of planes–DeHavilland Herons and Convairs–linking the islands between Puerto Rico and Guadeloupe. Their services are supplemented by an expanding network of small charter planes. It is possible to get to all islands, even the smallest, out of Puerto Rico and often at the height of the season. This is the best way to get south.

By Sea. There is no passenger service direct from New York to San Juan, although most cruise lines do stop here on their journeys through the Caribbean. In recent seasons, San Juan has become homeport for several ships that set out from here on journeys farther south. *Cunard, Chandris, Costa, Princess Cruises, Sitmar Cruises* and *Sun Line* operate more than a dozen ships from San Juan's harbor.

FURTHER INFORMATION. The development of the island's tourism program is the responsibility of the *Puerto Rico Tourism Company,* a quasi-public corporation. The head office is in Puerto Rico on Calle San Justo in Old San Juan, but regional offices are at 1290 Avenue of the Americas, New York, N.Y. 10019; 11 East Adams St., Chicago, Ill. 60603; 150 Second Ave., S.E., Miami, Fla. 33131; 10100 Santa Monica Blvd., Los Angeles, Calif. 90067; in Canada, at 10 King St., E., Toronto 210, Ont.

Elsewhere on the island, the Tourism Company has offices at the Tourism Pier in Old San Juan and at the airport in the lower lobby.

ISLAND MEDIA. The best regional guide for the visitor is *Que Pasa,* a thick booklet that is chock full of information about the island. Write for one ahead of time, or pick one up at the tourist office on your arrival. The *San Juan Star,* which is published daily, will keep you abreast of what's going on on the island.

AUTHORIZED TOUR OPERATORS: Adventure Tours; Butler Travels; Caribbean Holidays; Cavalcade Tours; Flyfaire; GoGo Tours; Playtime Vacations; Red and Blue Tours; and Travel Center Tours in the U.S. From Canada: Holiday House; Mirabelle Tours; Skylark Holidays, Ltd.; Sun Quest Tours; and Sunflight Holidays.

PASSPORTS, VISAS. None needed for U.S. citizens. Canadian citizens need proof (a passport is best); British citizens need a passport and visitor's visa.

MONEY. U.S. dollars. $1.85 = £1.

TAXES AND OTHER CHARGES. There is a 5% government tax on hotel rooms. Some of the hotels add a service charge on top of that, but most do not.

HOW TO GET ABOUT. All taxis authorized by the Commonwealth Public Service Commission are metered. You'll probably take a taxi from the airport to your hotel, unless you are heading for Dorado Beach or Palmas del Mar, in which case you have a choice of the limousine services authorized by those hotels or Crownair's small airplanes that make the trip in 10 minutes. Special tourism buses operate at 45 minute intervals, more or less, between the major hotels along the San Juan strip and the area's tourist attractions.

Transportation by buses or *guaguas* in San Juan and vicinity is quite good. Buses operate on wrong-way exclusive lanes on the main thoroughfares. In Old San Juan, blue and white minibuses run from 7 A.M. to 7 P.M. every day except Sunday. For public transportation outside of San Juan, it's the famous *públicos.* They are 5-passenger cars of current vintages, and they run on more-or-less scheduled runs. If you want to see the island cheaply as the Puerto Ricans see it, take a *público.* You'll find them along the waterfront in Old San Juan and at various other spots such as the airport. Or call 722-0234 to have a *público* pick you up at your hotel. The Department of Tourism has a list of reliable companies. Don't expect to get much of a guided tour unless you speak Spanish. The Puerto Rico Motor Coach Co. has daily scheduled service in fast air-conditioned coaches between San Juan and Mayagüez, with stops at Arecibo, and Aguadilla.

Stateside driving licenses are honored in Puerto Rico for 120 days. You can rent cars from *Avis, Atlantic, Budget, Hertz,* and *National.* Several have offices at the airport and in hotel lobbies.

There are a number of sightseeing tour operators who cover the chief sights of the islands in comfortable buses or limousines. Try *Borinquen Tours, Normandie Tours,* or *Turismo International.* Many independent drivers are authorized as tourist guides by the Tourism Department and display a special shield on their vehicles. Half-day excursions include Old and New San Juan, El Comandante Race Track, a cockfight, and a rum distillery. There is an evening tour of night clubs; a day excursion across the island, to Ponce; a 2-day tour around the island, half-day tours to El Yunque Rain Forest and Luquillo Beach, and to Dorado, Pineapple Country, and a rum distillery; a half-day tour of the country including a cockfight and a tour to El Comandante Race Track for half a day.

The 400-passenger ferries of the Puerto Rico Ports Authority leave Fajardo twice daily for Vieques and Culebra.

In addition to the many small planes for charter, the following airlines offer flights within Puerto Rico and/or to nearby islands: *Crownair* to Dorado, Palmas del Mar, St. Thomas, Tortola and Virgin Gorda; *Vieques Air-Link* to Vieques, Culebra.

Prinair, the best of the lot for frequency and service (although there's not much in the way of in-the-air service on these short, small plane flights), darts to Ponce, and Mayagüez in Puerto Rico; to Antigua; the Dominican Republic; Guadeloupe; Haiti; St. Kitts; St. Maarten; St. Croix and St. Thomas in the U.S. Virgin Islands; and Tortola in the British Virgins.

EVENTS AND HOLIDAYS. Puerto Rico has more than its share of special events and holidays, and celebrates each one with gusto. Their *LeLoLai* festival started out on a small scale, but is now a year-round party that includes something different every night. There are concerts, folkloric dances, beach parties, special fiestas, all designed to acquaint the visitor with the folkways of Puerto Rico. The highlight of Spring is the Casals' Festival which runs for two weeks in early June, with concerts featuring soloists and conductors from all over the world to honor the man who chose Puerto Rico as his home. In addition to U.S. holidays, Puerto Rico also celebrates its Constitution Day (July 25) and Discovery Day (Nov. 19). On the religious side, Saint's days, such as San Juan Bautista (June 24) are observed in towns and villages across the island.

WHAT WILL IT COST?

A typical day in winter for *two* persons in San Juan will run:

	US$	£
Accommodations in the Condado/Isla Verde area (overall average)	85	46
Breakfast at the hotel coffee shop	10	5
Luncheon at a moderate restaurant	15	8
Dinner at an "in-town" restaurant	30	16
Taxes, tips, and service charges	15	8
Car rental or one-day sightseeing	25	14
	$180	£97

STAYING IN PUERTO RICO

HOTELS. Puerto Rico is one of the few islands that offers something for everyone and some place to suit every pocketbook. The accommodations range from lavish, high-rise, casino-oriented deluxe hotels on the "San Juan strip" to charming, tiny *paradores* that are country inns. There are also lush resort complexes outside of San Juan: *Dorado* and *Cerromar* on the northern shore, the *Mayagüez Hilton* on the west coast; and Palmas Del Mar, a real extravaganza, on the southeastern side of the island.

The *Paradores Puertoriquennos* are a chain of government-sponsored inns that are located across the island. They all subscribe to standards of excellence; are inexpensive; offer a completely different outlook and atmosphere; and are designed to give you a feeling of the country life, which they have done very successfully.

SAN JUAN AND AREA

(CONDADO/ISLA VERDE/OLD SAN JUAN)

Almedro By the Sea Guest House. 7 air-conditioned rooms at Punta Las Marias. Very attractive setting in a garden on the beach. Kitchen facilities available; just a few minutes from the airport. $40 double EP in winter; $25 double EP off-season.

Best Western Pierre Hotel. 184 delightful, air-conditioned rooms with private baths, located in central Santurce. The *Swiss Chalet* restaurant adjoins the *Bar Ticino* which is in the hotel itself. Swimming pool, drugstore, shopping arcades, beauty parlor, and complete sight-seeing service. Continental atmosphere. Especially popular with business travelers who must be in the downtown area during the day. $62–68 double EP in winter; $45–52 double EP off-season.

Caribe Hilton. This 707-room hotel rises 20 stories high into the Caribbean sky. It has everything, including an overlook to old Fort San Geronimo, and a location that is between Old San Juan and the "in" area. There are 2 fresh-water swimming pools; 4 tennis courts lighted for nightplay; a putting green; health club; shops; casino, the works. Fine dining at their *La Rotisserie* gourmet restaurant; dining, dancing and entertainment at their *Club Caribe;* and late-night fun at *Juliana's* disco.

Carib-Inn. On 6 acres close to the beach in the Isla Verde section, this hotel was built for the tennis set. There are cork-turf courts, some with night lights; a tennis shop, and a pro. Even the swimming pool was designed in the shape of a racquet. 225 rooms and suites with an ocean or a mountain view. *Tudor Room* for Continental dining; *Cousin Ho's* for Szechuan, Hunan, and Cantonese food at its best; the *Trophy Lounge* for dancing. The Disco and casino keep things going until the early hours. $75–85 double EP in winter; $57–66 double off season.

Condado Beach/La Concha Hotels & Convention Center. Once separate entities, these hotels are now joined together into an expansive property with Puerto Rican culture a feature of food and shops. Dining and dancing at the water's edge under a spaceage roof which simulates a conch shell. There are several restaurants and bars; a rooftop lounge magnifies views of sea and city. Nightclubs with name entertainment. Two swimming pools, tennis courts, beach, all water sports, and a shopping arcade. Rates at Condado Beach run $132 double EP in winter; $76–106 double EP off season. At La Concha: $140 double EP in winter; $80–116 double EP off season. But check the special package plan rates for savings.

Condado Holiday Inn. On the beach along San Juan's plush hotel row, this is now the city's second largest hotel. 580 air-conditioned rooms; 3 pools; 2 tennis courts; 4 restaurants and lounges. Beach with all water sports. The Lagoon Wing has a disco and a complete kosher kitchen; casino is island's largest. $160 double EP in winter; $86–122 double EP off season.

Da Vinci. 91 rooms here, some with kitchenettes, in a decor which is a mixture of European and Mexican styles. Within walking distance of the Convention Center and San Juan's nightlife, this hotel offers convenience and a bit of resort life. There is a swimming pool, a nice restaurant, and a patio café. $60–72 double EP in winter; $34 double EP off season.

DuPont Plaza San Juan. Formerly the Sheraton, this refurbished property has 450 rooms on 21 floors on Condado Beach. Impressive layout. Rooftop *Penthouse* and *Lounge,* plus the *Zanzibar Lounge* for music, dancing and entertainment. $95–120 double EP in winter; $60–90 double EP off-season.

Dutch Inn and Towers. 144 air-conditioned rooms and apartment suites here, including those in the 10-story tower in the Condado section. Freshwater swimming pool; excellent *Greenhouse* restaurant; sidewalk cafe; nightclub. $70–90 double EP in winter; $62–80 double EP off season.

El Convento. The only large hotel in Old San Juan, this is a rebuilt and restored Carmelite convent on the Little Plaza of the Nuns across from the Cathedral. More than 300 years old, this lovely hostelry is now one of San Juan's showplaces. The heavy, carved furniture and rich rugs and tapestries are treasures to enjoy. All through the hotel you'll find tiled floors, white limestone walls, ceiling beams, Spanish paintings and 100 rooms, arranged around a galleried, open courtyard, which in itself is a gem. A decoratively shaped swimming pool with umbrellas to provide the shade while you breakfast, lunch, or sip cocktails. In the evening lights play on the galleries, fountain and plants, while you dine divinely, and then enjoy the special flamenco show. $80 double EP in winter; $60 double EP off season.

El San Juan Hotel & Towers/Palace Hotel. Another San Juan extravaganza, that is now called the El San Juan Resort Center, has scooped up the ever-vibrant El San Juan, its towers, and what was formerly the Americana Hotel. This complex stretches across some 20 acres and has a room count of 1,200. Here again, you must sift and sort, but here again, you have every option. The only difference seems to be the height of the buildings and the architecture. An endless choice of dining facilities, discos, games of chance, and water sports on the oceanfront. Rates run anywhere from $100–145 double EP in winter, depending upon your choice, but this complex is geared to 3 night/4 day visitors and offer all-inclusive rates you can't beat. The 7 night/8 day plans at the El San Juan Resort Center are even more attractive.

Howard Johnson's Nabori Lodge. On Ashford Avenue across from the Dupont Plaza. Near, but not on the beach, so guests in the 150 air-conditioned rooms and suites enjoy the rooftop pool solarium, restaurants, cocktail lounge, and ice cream area with the expected 28 flavors and the familiar U.S. surroundings with a Puerto Rican touch. From $89 double EP in winter; from $53 double EP off-season.

Isla Verde Beach Resort. Its several stories seem low by comparison to the high-rise hotels in the neighborhood. 395 rooms, all air-conditioned; on the beach with all water sports available. Swimming pool; 3 tennis courts; the usual HI accoutrements and dining and entertainment choices. $80–110 double EP in winter; $53–85 double EP off season.

HOTELS AROUND THE ISLAND

AGUADILLA

Parador Montemar. The most modern and spacious of the *paradores,* this property has 40 air-conditioned rooms, two restaurants, a cocktail lounge, and entertainment on weekends. Well-known for the "Crash Boat Beach" nearby, where fishing is easy and bountiful. Small swimming pool on the premises; buffets and barbeques weekly events. $53 double EP all year.

CABO ROJO

Boquemar Hotel. A completely unpretentious 20-room hotel in the heart of the fishing village of Boqueron, at the southwest corner of Puerto Rico. Restaurant features freshly caught fish. Swimming and boating. One of the best buys on the island, but definitely not for the fussy. $27–32 double EP all year round.

COAMO

Parador Baños de Coamo. Opened in 1977 as another in the chain of Paradores. Baños was one of the island's first hotels—before people started focusing vacations on the sea. In the mountains, about a two-hour drive from San Juan and northeast of Ponce. The main house of the former spa has been refurbished with 48 modern rooms, with bath and balcony around a center courtyard. Swimming pool, restaurant and bar. A quiet mountain spot with emphasis on the thermal baths. $45 double EP all year round.

DORADO

Cerromar Hotel. The 508-room, 8-story hotel is 2 miles along the shore near Dorado Beach, but on a sandy crescent of its own. There's a pool, beach bar (with the best *piña coladas* around), two 18-hole Robert Trent Jones golf courses, which abut the two from the Dorado Beach Hotel. Jitney service connects the two resorts. The 13 courts here, and 7 at next-door Dorado have special tennis programs. The Club Cerromar has elegant dinners, with dancing and show; Surf Room is the large dining room; the Garden Terrace for lunch, breakfast and early suppers. Banner Bar, across the hall from the Casino in the entertainment and convention room wing of the hotel. All rooms have luxury appointments, well maintained; balconies overlook the sea and beach. From $145 double EP in winter; $75 double off-season.

Dorado Beach Hotel. On a private 1,000 acre estate with beach, two pools, a wading pool, and full recreation/sports facilities. Two 18-hole Robert Trent Jones golf courses; 300 air-conditioned rooms and suites, most on the beach, and all tucked in and around beautifully planted areas. Meals are lavish in the regular dining room, and there is also *Su Casa,* a Spanish restaurant in the original plantation house. Small casino. The rates are high, but quality, which food and standards also tend to be. From $195 double in winter; $130 double off-season, including breakfast and dinner.

FAJARDO

Delicias Hotel. Modern hostelry located pier-side in the beach section of Fajardo. 20 air-conditioned rooms, good bar, and restaurant. This place used to be the only place to stay out at this end of the island and still has a strong following. It is a casual, informal, sportsman's kind of place. $26 double EP all year.

HUMACAO

Palmas Del Mar. A gorgeous property set on 2,700 acres, with 542 rooms in one-, two- and three-bedroom villas; in deluxe junior suites at the Palmas Inn; and in luxurious rooms at the brand new Candelero Hotel. Just a 45-minute drive from San Juan, this resort complex hugs Puerto Rico's southeastern shore. Swimming in any of 4 pools, or along its 3 miles of beach; golf on their 18-hole championship course designed by Gary Player; 20 tennis courts (4 lighted for night play); all water sports; horseback riding through miles of trails; and bicycle riding for yet another look at the landscape. For wining, dining, and entertainment, there are several choices: *El Jumacao* for dining and dancing, and *La Galeria* piano bar for impromptu sing-a-longs at the Palmas Inn; *Las Garzas* for open-air dining at the Candelero Hotel; and the *Sun Fun Hut,* poolside for informal meals three times a day. The *Gibraltar Pub* in the Monte Sol Tennis Village is famous for its chili; and the *Cafe de la Place* for its elaborate buffets. Rates at the Palmas Inn run $190 double EP in winter ($110 double off-season); at the Candelero Hotel $120–165 double EP in winter ($75–100 double off-season); Villas: one-bedroom $104–180; two-bedroom $169–290; three-bedroom $234–390 depending upon the time of the year.

JAYUYA

Parador Hacienda Gripinas. Of all the *paradores,* this is our favorite. It's just perfect as a country inn hideaway, with 19 rooms set on a former coffee plantation. Hosts Milagros and Edgardo Dedós, and their pre-school daughter Lymari, capture you as "family" on arrival. A casual and comfortable place to stay, with superb food, a large swimming pool, and a poolside Sunday buffet, which draws close to 100 people from as far away as San Juan. No air-conditioning, but you don't need it–the mountain air and breezes are wonderful, and the sounds of the *coquís* in the trees provide a special evening lullaby. The all-year-round rate is $30 double EP, and the meals, which are terrific and moderately priced, an added bonus.

LA PARGUERA

Villa Parguera. Hard by Phosphorescent Bay in the little fishing village of La Parguera. Puerto Rican-American cuisine. There are 45 rooms with private or semi-private bath; most are air-conditioned. Saltwater swimming pool, boats, deep-sea fishing. $42 double EP all year round.

MARICAO

Parador Hacienda Juanita. 21 rooms almost hidden in the foliage of a traditional coffee plantation that has been in operation since the 19th century. Swimming pool, tennis courts, large restaurant for indoor or terrace dining. $30 double EP all year.

MAYAGÜEZ

Mayagüez Hilton. On the west coast, perched on 25 acres overlooking the sea. Guests in the 150 air-conditioned rooms have the choice of shops, pool, tennis courts. Transportation can be arranged to nearby beaches, some with good surf. Plenty of unusual sightseeing in this area, including a country taste of the Puerto Rican life. Noteworthy restaurant and cocktail lounge. $63–79 double EP all year round.

PONCE

Holiday Inn. 120 air-conditioned, two-double-bedded rooms, with a panoramic view of the city, and all the expected Holiday Inn accoutrements, including TV in the rooms. Restaurant, lounge, large swimming pool, tennis courts lit for night play. Babysitting service and special children's rates. From $85 double EP in winter; $64 double off-season.

Melia Hotel. On Ponce's main plaza. All 80 rooms have baths and are air-conditioned. Patio restaurant and bar. Popular with businessmen. $45 double EP all year.

QUEBRADILLAS

Parador El Guajataca. 38 attractive, air-conditioned rooms are right on the shore, facing the sea and the beach. Family-run, the first of the paradores, and completely renovated. The food is Puerto Rican country food, hearty and tasty. Swimming pool, bar, access to golf course which is about a half-hour away. On the northwest coast, just about a two-hour drive from San Juan. $45 double EP all year round.

RINCON

Villa Cofresi. On the beach and the best known place to stay in this casual surfers' mecca. The 55 rooms are simple, attractive. A family hotel. Swimming pool; restaurant. $34–40 double EP in winter; $30–34 off-season.

RIO GRANDE

Rio Mar. At the northeast corner of the island, near Luquillo Beach. The 110 rooms in villas cluster near the shore on a 523-acre site that includes 13 tennis courts, a swimming pool, beach, and 18-hole golf course. Built in Mediterranean style, the complex has terra cotta roofs, white stucco walls and terraces with a view. Choice of restaurants; commissary. $99–112 double EP in winter; $51–68 double EP off-season.

ISLANDS OFF-SHORE

CULEBRA

Punta Aloe. The 9 separate units with kitchens here can accommodate up to six people. Informal and pleasant. $60 daily; $315 per week all year.

VIEQUES

La Casa Del Frances. Once the home of a French plantation owner, this 12-room inn is on the southern shore of the island, near the fishing village of Esperanza. Swimming pool; outdoor dining terrace. There are 3 good beaches not far from the hotel. Activities include scuba diving, hunting for doves and ducks in season, and horseback riding. $34–44 double EP all year.

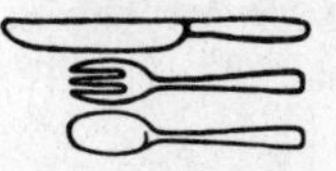

RESTAURANTS. The local cuisine, as might be expected, has a strong Spanish accent. The most basic dish is simply rice and beans, and the citizenry would surely perish if there were no *arroz y habichuelas* (rice and beans). Rising above simple fare, the most popular dish is *arroz con pollo,* chicken and rice, a distant, far less complicated relative of the great Spanish dish *paella*—which now abounds in Puerto Rico, too, at better restaurants. It includes shrimp, mussels, lobster, perhaps other seafood, and Spanish sausages called *chorizos,* in addition to chicken, and the rice is yellow with saffron. There are also now many fine Cuban specialties—notably their magnificent black bean soup being taken to Puerto Rican hearts. For local specialties, try *asopao,* a rice dish with chicken or seafood, wetter than *arroz con pollo* but not wet enough to be a soup. Or try *tostones;* they're the big island plantains (bananas) fried in deep fat. *Lechòn asado* is suckling pig roasted on a spit. You'll find this crisp and succulent specialty at *lechoneras* all over the island, although chicken barbecue joints are gradually replacing them. Such creations as *hallacas* and *pasteles* will remind you of *tamales,* but they're not half as fiery as their counterparts north of the border up Mexico way. *Pescado* simply means any fish caught, but if you get it fresh out of the Caribbean in the little fishing village of Parquera on the south coast, you'll ask the cook for more.

Jueyes are delicious land crabs, but eat them only in good restaurants or a place recommended by local friends. Puerto Rican coffee is strong, black, and wonderful. It tastes almost best of all at some tiny roadside stand in the mountains, accompanied by freshly-baked *pan de agua,* the coarse native bread that is quite like the very best French bread. The national drink of Puerto Rico is rum, and it is available in a staggering variety of combinations. Some excellent island rums–*Barrilito,* for one–are made in such small quantities that they never reach the mainland.

The big hotels have more restaurants than some small Caribbean islands. Reservations are essential at the supper clubs and better restaurants; the coffee shops are always open.

For up-to-the-minute dining guides, pick up a copy of *Que Pasa* and/or the pamphlet *Puerto Rico Guide to Dining and Night Life,* both available from the tourist offices in the United States and Canada, as well as on the island.

We call $16 and above *expensive;* $7–15 *moderate;* anything below that, *inexpensive.*

Bull's Eye. Juicy steaks and succulent lobster served, along with dozens of choices from their terrific salad bar. The décor is Spanish and splendid. Located in the El Caribe Building opposite the Hilton. Moderate.

El Convento. This hotel's Ponce de Leon room is the place to choose for international dishes, served elegantly in a restored 17th-century chapel. A flamenço show follows the dinner hour. Expensive.

El Cid. Pleasant dining spot facing the Condado Lagoon. Spanish and International specialties; nightly music. Moderate.

El Meson Vasco. Basque food served in the old building at the top of Cristo Street across from the San Jose Plaza. Open for lunch and dinner. Moderate.

El Patio De Sam. In Old San Juan, with a big, cool patio that is a gathering place for local artists. Hamburgers, steaks, and seafood are offered at moderate prices.

El Zipperle. On Roosevelt Ave. in Hato Rey, a comfortable, modern, air-conditioned restaurant with mostly Spanish, but some German specialties. Moderate.

Gran Segovia. This is one of the best restaurants in Puerto Rico. Soft lighting, superior Continental cuisine, and extensive wine list. Reservations a must here on Ashford Ave. in Condado. Expensive.

Greenhouse. This enclosed café at the Dutch Inn gives the feeling of dining in a tropical park. Lush flowers and plants throughout. Nice selection of international dishes. Moderate.

Heidelberg Haus. In Santurce, this is the place for good German fare and lively music nightly. Moderate.

King Neptune. One of the newest seafood restaurants in San Juan, the King Neptune in the Palace Hotel offers "all the shrimp you can eat" from their seafood bar; fresh fish, lobster, as well as Puerto Rican specialties. Moderate.

La Chaumiere. Fine French cuisine served here at 367 Tetuan, in Old San Juan. Dinner only and expensive.

La Danza. Puerto Rican food and atmosphere here, at the corner of Cristo and Fortaleza in old San Juan. Piano and guitar music nightly. Moderate.

La Gallega. This is a charming place, with local color, that offers good Spanish dishes. Try *Fabada Asturiana,* a tasty mixture of white beans, sausage, and ham, in a spicy sauce. Located at 309 Fortaleza in Old San Juan. Moderate.

La Gondola. One of the most popular places in Old San Juan for hearty Italian fare. This building was a bank in the Spanish colonial days, and its old vault is now the wine cellar. Moderate.

La Mallorquina. Typical Spanish and Puerto Rican dishes served in a Spanish colonial atmosphere in Old San Juan's oldest restaurant. Their *asapao* is among the best in Puerto Rico. *Calamares en su tinta* (squid in its own ink) a specialty. Open for lunch and dinner. Moderate.

La Rotisserie. Elegant and delightful restaurant on the second floor of the Caribe Hilton. Each dish is specially prepared and beautifully served. One of the few places where jackets and ties are still required, adding to the pleasures of exclusive dining. Expensive.

La Vista. In the International Airport. Very comfortable with striking decor, and a dramatic view of the runway. The food is attractively prepared and served. Spacious, congenial bar adjacent. Moderate.

La Zaragozana. One of the town's most exclusive eateries, in an historic Old San Juan colonial home. Spanish, Puerto Rican, and Cuban cuisine. Music nightly. Expensive.

Los Chaveles. Spanish specialties, nicely served here, on Roosevelt Ave. in the Hato Rey area. Inexpensive.

Mago's. An old favorite beefeater's paradise in Old San Juan. Businessmen fill the place at lunch; nights are very quiet. Good value here. Moderate.

Russian Tea House. Home-cooked Stroganoff and other exotic dishes, served in exotic surroundings in 1025 Ashford Ave. in Condado. Also known as Countess Gypsy Markoff Amaya's, so don't be surprised when the fortune teller appears. Dinner reservations required. Moderate.

Scotch 'n Sirloin. Across the street from the Russian Tea House, this is a very popular steak and seafood place, especially during the lunch hour. Moderate.

Swiss Chalet. A favorite spot of ours, which seems to have been transported directly from The Alps. All the Swiss tradition and history, and the chalet motif. All the Swiss specialties, but an extensive variety of other excellent dishes. Prices are moderate at luncheon; expensive in the evenings when there is music for dancing.

NIGHTLIFE. When the sun goes down, the bright lights go up in the huge hotels, and out comes the brightest galaxy of stars this side of the Great White Way. The casinos are in full swing; the Las Vegas-spectacular cabaret revues lively and glittering; and the local folkloric shows an added bonus.

Outstanding among the nightclubs are the *Club Caribe* at the Caribe Hilton,

El Tropicoro in the El San Juan, and *Ponce de Leon* at El Convento. You'll also find nightly shows and entertainment at the *Caribar* at the Caribe Hilton, the *Club Gitano* at the Condado Holiday Inn, and the *Zanzibar* at the Dupont Plaza. Dancing can be enjoyed at *Mano-A-Mano* in the El San Juan Towers; the *El Chico* at the El San Juan; and the *Penthouse Lounge* at the Dupont Plaza.

Disco the night away at *Juliana's;* the *Flying Saucer* or *The Warehouse.* Or gamble it away at the *Caribe Hilton;* the *Carib-Inn;* the *Condado Holiday Inn;* the *El San Juan;* the *Holiday Inn Isla Verde;* the *Dupont Plaza; La Concha;* the *Palace;* or out of the San Juan orbit, at the *Cerromar* and *Dorado Beach* Hotels.

SHOPPING. If you are looking for bargains in imported perfumes, porcelain, glassware, watches, and the like, you should go to St. Croix or St. Thomas (half an hour by air). Puerto Rico is not a free port, although there is a shop at the Tourist Pier where cruise ship passengers departing from San Juan to a foreign port may purchase cigarettes, perfumes, jewelry, and porcelains at prices equal to, and occasionally lower than, those in the free-port islands. But the fun of shopping in Puerto Rico is in looking for unusual buys in local handicrafts: the small carved religious figures called *santos,* cigars rolled to your order, stringed musical instruments, hammocks, devil's masks imaginatively fashioned from coconut husks, tortoise-shell jewelry, embroidered clothing, woven straw, silk-screened fabrics, papier maché fruits and vegetables, and ceramics. Painting and sculpture in Puerto Rico are generally highly original and are attracting increased attention from the sophisticated art world. New galleries have sprouted everywhere, especially in Old San Juan. The hotel districts are full of boutiques, ranging from the very elegant to the latest "in" styles.

Don't miss the *Artisans Market* for handicraft at its best. It's held every weekend from noon until 5 P.M. at the Condado Convention Center in association with the Institute of Puerto Rican Culture. In Old San Juan there are dozens of galleries, but our favorite is *Galería Botello,* which houses the work of Angel Botello. Part of the gallery is set aside for exhibitions of works by other island arts and his own extraordinary collection of santos. For fun, stop in at *The Gentle Swing* on Calle Cristo and watch artisans weave hammocks and then offer them for sale. And don't miss a visit to *The Butterfly People,* which is in a restored mansion on Fortaleza Street. The butterflies aren't free, but some of the colorful and intricate works are inexpensive enough to take home. There's a small *crêperie* here for a quiet lunch while browsing.

But, for a real day-long spree, head for *Plaza las Americas,* Puerto Rico's newest and largest shopping mall, which is just a few miles south of the Condado area. Lots of restaurants *(Sweeney's* is tops!), and dozens of shops to enjoy and explore. Among them are the *Bell, Book and Candle;* the *Clock Shop; Fiorucci's* and *Giusti* for designer fashions; *La Fragrance* for perfumes; and *Magritte Chocolatier* for all the sweets you can savor. There's also a branch of *Galería Botello* here.

SPORTS AND OTHER ATTRACTIONS. *Swimming* at island beaches and in hotel pools. Luquillo Beach is one of the most beautiful and is equipped with picnic tables and parking lots.

Closer to town, Isla Verde public beach has all amenities for day visitors plus plenty of privacy for those who desire it.

Next comes *deep-sea fishing,* which has undergone a boom in Puerto Rico as the waters off Florida have been almost depleted. You can make arrangements to fish for marlin, albacore, bonito, tarpon, sailfish, and others through your hotel or through Captain Mike Benitez at the San Juan Yacht Club. He has boats for charter, fully equipped for as low as $150 per day, and he will give lessons to neophytes at no increase in charge. For deep-sea fishing off the northeast coast, call the El Conquistador Hotel. At Palmas del Mar, $300 is the daily rate for 6 on a 44-foot boat. On the southwestern coast, see Capt. Jaime Pagan for renting sailboats, motorboats, waterskiing, snorkeling, etc. Prices from $15 up.

Fresh-water fishing is also popular in the well-stocked mountain streams and lakes. Blackmouth bass, bluegill, and catfish abound.

Boating and sailing activities have their headquarters in the yacht clubs of San Juan, Ponce, and Mayagüez. Jack Becker day-sails his 36-ft. Catamaran to the clear waters of Icacos Island from Sardinera, near Fajardo; $25 per person includes picnic lunch, snorkel gear. Accommodation for 20 passengers; exclusive charters may be arranged. Isleta Marina, on a small island just offshore Fajardo, has roofed docking space for 35 boats and open slips for 70; offers complete yachting service, fuel, marine supplies, provisions.

Skin diving and *snorkeling* can usually be arranged through your hotel. Most major resorts have Water Sports Directors who give scuba diving instruction. For diving on the south coast, air fills are usually available at La Parguera, but it's a good idea to bring your own equipment.

Surfing is popular near the Isla Verde Beach Resort but the best surfing beach is at Punta Higuero between Aguadilla and Rincón.

Tennis may be played at hotel and club courts and on the courts of the Univ. of Puerto Rico in Rio Piedras.

For *golf,* there are courses at Dorado del Mar, Palmas del Mar and the Berwind Country Club; each has 18 holes. Among the most beautiful in the world are the four 18-hole courses shared by the Dorado Beach Hotel and its sister hotel, the Cerromar. Guest privileges are extended. Guests at west end resort (at Mayagüez, Rincón, Aguadilla, Quebradillas, etc.) can play golf at the Ramey Air Force base course, now known as Borinquen Golf Course.

Spectator sports include *horse racing* all year round on Wed, Fri., Sun., and holidays at El Comandante in Rio Piedras. This is one of the hemisphere's most beautiful and modern tracks, and special trips leave San Juan on all racing days. Arrange through your hotel or call El Comandante. *Bird watchers* and *marine life* enthusiasts can secure free information from the Natural History Society of Puerto Rico, P.O. Box 1393, Hato Rey, Puerto Rico 00919. For a very small fee you can join the society and be eligible for field trips.

Cockfighting from Nov. 1 through Aug. 31 in the many *galleras* (cockpits) throughout the island. Tourists can get a good introduction to this unusual sport at the new air-conditioned Coliseo Gallistico, opposite the Holiday Inn. Its luxuries extend to a restaurant and cocktail lounge, and a ring carpeted in artificial grass. Fights on Fri. evenings; Sat. and Sun. afternoons.

Second most popular sport is *baseball.* The Puerto Ricans are wild for it. Games are played in stadiums in six cities, and the rivalry between San Juan, Santurce, Ponce, Caguas, Arecibo, and Mayagüez is fiercer than anything in the U.S.A. The season starts in Oct. and lasts five months, at the end of which the Puerto Rican pennant winner plays in a Caribbean world series. Many of the players are island-born Big Leaguers.

SABA

Straight Up to "The Bottom"

When you're at "The Bottom" on this tiny Dutch island, you're not walking on the ocean floor, but strolling through the capital city. It's small, but you couldn't expect anything else–Saba is just five square miles. A cone-shaped island that seems to have sprung up from the sea, it is a lush land devoid of beaches but resplendent in green hills.

The license plates here read "Saba, N.A. Unspoiled Queen," and Saba is still that. It has few shops, even fewer hotels, and just about 1,000 residents, all of them terribly proud of their island and eager to show it off to visitors.

A hand-laid stone road skirts the island, winding like a long snake through and over the hills. The Bottom, interestingly enough, is at the top, reached via a series of hairpin turns on Saba's only road.

There are only four villages, and until the arrival of the first jeep thirty-five years ago, islanders made their way on foot–and sturdy leg, we imagine, because before the road there were merely hundreds of steps which had been chiseled out of the volcanic rock.

"Once upon a fairy tale island there were Hansel and Gretel houses, a vertical highway built by hand, and The Bottom was always up!" So begins the blurb of the Saba Tourist Bureau, a two-person hierarchy that touts this island's treasures with obvious enthusiasm. This is one tropical island that has adapted to the day tourist who dips over from Sint Maarten and to the occasional overnighter, but it will always maintain its unique identity. Its terrain makes it impossible to do otherwise, Topographically, the island is the most unusual in the entire Caribbean. The whole place is an extinct volcano, rising abruptly from the sea without a single beach. It lies 150 miles east of Puerto Rico, 28 miles south of Sint Maarten, 7 miles northwest of Statia. When you approach this dot from the air, as most of us do these days, you wing into a minute airstrip pasted like a Band-Aid on one of the few level stretches, Flat Point. Fortunately, STOL (Short Takeoff and Landing) planes are built for just this kind of place—with its 1300-foot airstrip!

To approach by sea, as the occasional cruise ship passengers do, you swing up to the area of the 250-foot pier, dedicated in November 1972 at Fort Bay. Prior to that time, you took your chances with the seas and the Saba boatmen through churning surf to shore. If the sea had been acting up at Fort Bay and it was too rough to land, you would be taken to Ladder Bay to climb "The Ladder," 524 steps up to reach The Bottom. Roads have replaced part of that trek, but 135 steps remain to remind us of what used to be. Today, small boats can tie up at the Fort Bay pier, but cruise passengers adapt to the familiar lighter runs and come in by sea from an anchorage offshore.

History

Columbus first saw Saba in 1493, but the Dutch settlers did not arrive until almost 150 years later. In 1690, these intrepid islanders turned back a French invading force with stones, by piling boulders on planks laid across poles, then pulling away the poles to send the avalanche of stones thundering down the steps on the enemy below. The settlers founded an agricultural economy which endured until 1850, when sugar and indigo declined in world importance. Then the Saba men took to the sea, and the women took up their intricate needlework.

As a member of the Netherlands Antilles, the islanders by tradition looked to Holland for education and technology. But it was Josephus Lambert Hassell who decided that Saba had to have a road. He took a correspondence course to build one. Dutch advisors had pooh-poohed the Saban's roadbuilding desires, because they considered the terrain much too steep, but Mr. Hassell was determined. He'd been a carpenter and was a practical man. With a team of 10 to 20 men, he built a well-graded concrete road wiggling from village to village. It took him 20 years!

About 45% of Saba's population is white, said to have descended from Caribbean seafarers, who may have found in The Bottom the snug harbor of their dreams. Native-born Sabans are found in the navies and merchant fleet of half the world's nations.

EXPLORING SABA

Exploring Saba is a delight and, although highlights can be covered on the day tour, really worth more time than most people give it. Bottom, not a crater but a bowl-shaped valley, is the principal village. It has the never-failing, unexpected charm of a Dutch village, with gabled roofs, chimneys, gardens, and all, plunked down on a plateau in the midst of tropic seas.

From The Bottom, your trusty jeep will take you to even tinier villages; St. John, Windwardside, Hell's Gate. You could easily imagine them under a Christmas tree, especially Windwardside, with its red-roofed white houses. At 1900 feet, Windwardside is 1100 feet higher up than Bottom. It clings to the crest of the volcano, cooled by the never-failing trades, on top of the world, and with a vertiginous view of the Caribbean. From Zion Hill to Hell's Gate, you can look over a sheer drop to the sea, the kind of view that has you holding your breath. You can explore the precipitous terrain on horseback, burro-back, or your own two feet.

A tour around the island with stops for picture-taking is $20 per carful. Lunch may be reserved (your driver will arrange it) at any guest house or hotel for $5-$8.

PRACTICAL INFORMATION FOR SABA

HOW TO GET THERE. *Windward Island Airways* links Saba with St. Maarten and St. Eustatius.

FURTHER INFORMATION. In the U.S., contact the Saba Tourist Information Office at 25 West 39th Street, New York, N.Y., 10018. in Canada, you'll find them at 243 Ellerslie Ave., Willowdale, Toronto, M2N 1Y5. On the island itself, Mr. Glen Holm operates the Tourist Bureau, which is located in Windwardside.

ISLAND MEDIA. Some information on Saba can be found in the orange sheet entitled *St. Maarten Holiday;* the rest, which is mainly local news, appears in a mimeographed compilation called the *Saba Herald.*

PASSPORTS, VISAS. Some proof of citizenship is required—valid or outdated passport, birth certificate, voter's registration card, etc. No visa needed.

MONEY. The official currency here is the Netherlands Antilles florin (or guilder). The exchange fluctuates slightly, but the generally accepted rate is 1.77 NAf = $1 US; 3.96 NAf = 1£.

TAXES AND OTHER CHARGES. The hotels and restaurants usually add a 10% service charge to your bill. There is also a 5% Government Room Tax.

HOW TO GET ABOUT. Other than walking (remember those steep steps!) or hitchhiking, the best way is by taxi—fares are low and even an all-day exploration of the island won't run more than $20 (not per person, but the Jeep-ful!). There are five cars available for rental at $20 per day. Contact the Tourist Bureau to make arrangements.

EVENTS AND HOLIDAYS. Every day is a special event on this friendly island when the tourists come. In addition, island-wide holidays are New Year's Day, Good Friday, Easter Monday, the Queen's Birthday (April 30), Labor Day (May 1), Ascension Day, Whit Monday, Kingdom Day (Dec. 15), Christmas Day, and Boxing Day (Dec. 26).

WHAT WILL IT COST?

A typical day on Saba in season for *two* persons will run:

	US$	£
Hotel accommodations, including all three meals, varies according to the inn selected. The over-all average is	60	32
Tips/service charges at hotels and restaurants	15	8
Full-day sightseeing by taxi or rental car	20	11
	$95	£51

STAYING IN SABA

Saba's hotels are tiny, with not one of the three having more than ten rooms.

Captain's Quarters. A sheer joy, with just ten rooms, a nice swimming pool on the bluff, and a "do-what-you-will" atmosphere that makes it difficult to leave. Rooms have private bath and balcony, all meals are included in the rate, and "Bessie's Cottage" has two double rooms, one single, two baths, and a sitting room, just in case you prefer "a house of your own." Meals are served on fine china, and good wine is quaffed from crystal goblets. $70 MAP double all year.

Caribe Guest House. A small, somewhat spartan five-room cottage located at The Bottom. Radio and TV optional extras. Nice dining, and the year-round rate of $40 double includes two meals.

Cranston's Antique Inn. Eight rooms, three with private bath, in an eighteenth-century home at The Bottom. This was formerly the government guesthouse, and as such, features four-poster beds in every room, one of which (# 1) was used by Queen Juliana of the Netherlands during an official visit. The $42 double year-round rate includes all three meals.

HOME RENTALS. There are a few homes for rent, as well as accommodations available in private homes. Contact Mr. Glen Holm, the Director of Tourism, Windwardside, Saba, N.A. for full details.

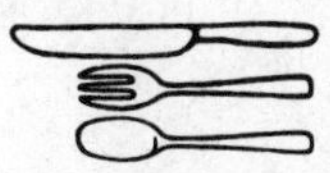

RESTAURANTS/NIGHTLIFE. We haven't heard of a tourist yet who wanted to retreat to Saba for its gourmet cuisine or its all-night discos. Those who come, and there are many, discover just what keeps it such an unspoiled landfall. The food is certainly adequate, with seafood the highlight, at the small hotels, and the late-night scene is totally absent. That is really what a vacation on Saba is all about.

SHOPPING. There isn't much to buy, but what there is is indigenous to the island. Local shopping articles, fabric and clothing with island designs, are sold by Saba Artisans Foundation. Visit the "Green Shutters" or "Around the Bend" for hand-made lace crafts, delicately fashioned by the Saban women. *Saba Spice,* a local liqueur brewed by the islanders, is a special, low-priced treat.

SPORTS AND OTHER ACTIVITIES. Hiking and mountain climbing are

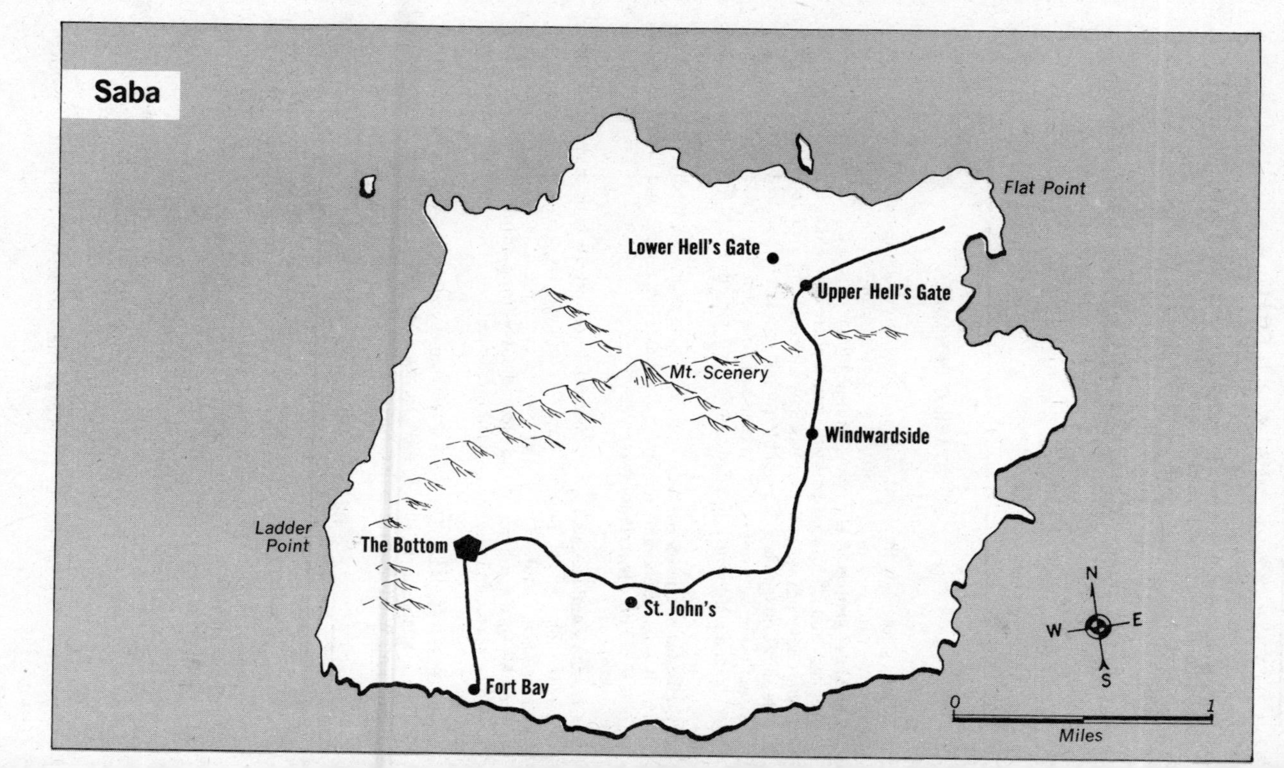
Saba
Flat Point
Lower Hell's Gate
Upper Hell's Gate
Mt. Scenery
Windwardside
Ladder Point
The Bottom
St. John's
Fort Bay
N
W
E
S
0
1
Miles

naturals here, and now scuba diving has taken hold. The waters have a visibility of up to 200 feet for divers to explore. *Saba Deep,* which has its headquarters at Captain's Quarters, has the equipment for rent and can arrange diving trips either on the spot or beforehand.

ST. BARTHELEMY

The Normandy of the Indies

Many people on this tiny island in the French West Indies still speak a Norman dialect, and many women still wear white starched bonnets, a tradition since the island was colonized by Normandy fishermen in the seventeenth century.

St. Barts, as it is fondly called, is just eight square miles of beaches, mountains and rocky coves, but it has all it needs to enchant. Seemingly, and practically, it is away from it all—125 miles northwest of Guadeloupe and fifteen miles southeast of St. Martin, but still French to the nth degree and, oddly enough, easily accessible.

Surprisingly, too, St. Barts has managed to tuck a number of fine hotels and restaurants into its curving, volcanic confines. It is still one of the few remaining "true get-away" islands in the Caribbean.

History

Columbus came first, but he did little more than claim the island for Spain and name it for his brother Bartholemew. Spanish settlers weren't terribly interested, and in 1645 St. Barthelemy was settled by Frenchmen from nearby St. Kitts. In 1674, the island was resettled by Frenchmen from Normandy and Brittany. The island was ceded to the Swedes in 1784 in exchange for trading rights at the port of Gothenburg in Sweden, and the capital city was dubbed Gustavia in honor of the king. It was almost 100 years before the French returned, and all has been quiet ever since, although the capital city retains its Swedish name. Today St. Barthelemy is one of the satellites of

Guadeloupe and, as such, is part of an Overseas Department of France.

EXPLORING ST. BARTS

Exploring means the two-fold pleasure of seeing the island and meeting its people. As you drive notice how the water seems to change color at every bend in the road; the hills are alive with century plants in bloom; the narrow streets are shadowed by brilliant bougainvillea; and sun-washed beaches are edged with palm trees. Gustavia, the capital, is tiny, but more than seventy-five percent of the St. Bartians live here. In the village of Corossol, you'll find the spot where time stopped two centuries ago. (See the section A Day on Your Own.)

The people of St. Barts speak old Norman French, and customs from that part of France remain. In the old days a man worked hard to buy a home before he married, and illegitimacy was practically unknown.

Some of the older generation still wear the costumes of their youth, with ladies garbed in long dresses, their heads covered with *quichenottes,* white bonnets in the Norman French tradition. The men, descendants of a long line of seamen, still wear their navy blue caps at a jaunty angle. They're a very friendly people and will make you feel right at home.

Other reasons for settling into St. Barts are sunshine, peace and quiet, and remarkable French food cooked at the beach over an oil-drum grill, in a small kitchen at one of the village bistros, or at your hotel.

A DAY ON YOUR OWN

For your day on St. Barts, rent a VW Beetle or Mini-Moke and be sure to take along a bathing suit for an afternoon swim at one of the island's 22 attractive public beaches.

Begin the day with a morning stroll through the little streets of Gustavia. Shops feature French perfume, crystal, gold jewelry and other luxury items at duty-free prices, although the selections are limited. Also check locally made fashions at Jean-Yves Froment and La Caleche boutiques.

Include a visit to the Yacht Club's small museum of island history and culture and note the mementos of St. Barts' Swedish past. Before leaving Gustavia, stop for a mid-morning coffee and croissant at one of the harborside cafes and enjoy the picturesque view.

From Gustavia, follow the road north to Corossol, a little fishing village where the older women still wear the *quichenottes.* Please ask before you rush out to photograph them. The women sell handmade straw goods such as handbags, baskets, hats, and delicate single strands of tiny birds.

Next, head for one of the island's beaches. Crescent-shaped St. Jean beach, easily reached by following the road past the airport, is one of the most popular swimming spots. Afterward relax over a lobster lunch at the St. Jean Beach Club or Le Pelican Beach Grill, informal spots right on the beach.

Later continue along the road past St. Jean Bay. At Lorient the road makes a grand loop of the eastern part of the island, past the villages of Marigot, Grand Cul de Sac, and Grand Fond, where the rocky coastline and stone fences are reminiscent of Normandy. At Grand Fond you'll leave the coast and turn inland, traveling over the hills back to Lorient and then to Gustavia.

If a drink at sunset is in order, drive up to the mountaintop Castelets Hotel by following the road behind Gustavia harbor. The hotel's driveway is steep, but the view from the panoramic bar is well worth the trip. You might stay to enjoy the classic French cuisine, or choose from at least a dozen other fine island restaurants with a Gallic flair.

PRACTICAL INFORMATION FOR ST. BARTHELEMY

HOW TO GET THERE. By air. From St. Martin/Sint Maarten: *Windward Islands Airways* makes the ten-minute hop from Juliana Airport on the Dutch side; *Air Guadeloupe* takes off from Esperance Airport on the French side. There are also direct, one-hour flights to St. Barts from Guadeloupe aboard *Air Guadeloupe* and from St. Thomas aboard *Virgin Air.*

FURTHER INFORMATION. Contact the French West Indies Tourist Board, 610 Fifth Ave., New York, N.Y. 10020. In Canada: The French Government Tourist Office at 1840 West Sherbrooke, Montreal, Quebec H3H 1E4; or at 372 Bay Street, Suite 610, Toronto, Ontario M5H 2W9. In England, the FGTO is located at 178 Piccadilly, London W1V OAL. You can also obtain information about St. Barts on the spot at the new Office Municipale du Tourisme, in the Mairie (City Hall) on the rue August Nyman in Gustavia.

PASSPORTS, VISAS. Some proof of citizenship (valid passport preferably) is required for stays up to twenty-one days. After that, you must have a valid passport. All visitors must also have a return ticket. Regulations are subject to change, however. Please check with the nearest French Consulate for latest details.

MONEY. The French franc is legal tender. It is worth about 16¢ US. Figure 6 francs to $1 US; 9 francs to £1.

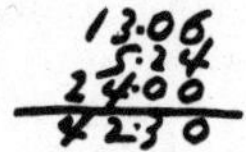

TAXES AND OTHER CHARGES. There is no government tax on accommodations, but hotels do add a 10% service charge. There is no airport departure tax.

HOW TO GET ABOUT. Taxis are available at the airport and cost $2–$5 US, depending on the location of your hotel. You can rent VW Beetles, jeeps and Mini-Mokes for $25 per day, including unlimited mileage, a full tank of gas, and free delivery and pick up. On-island rental operators are

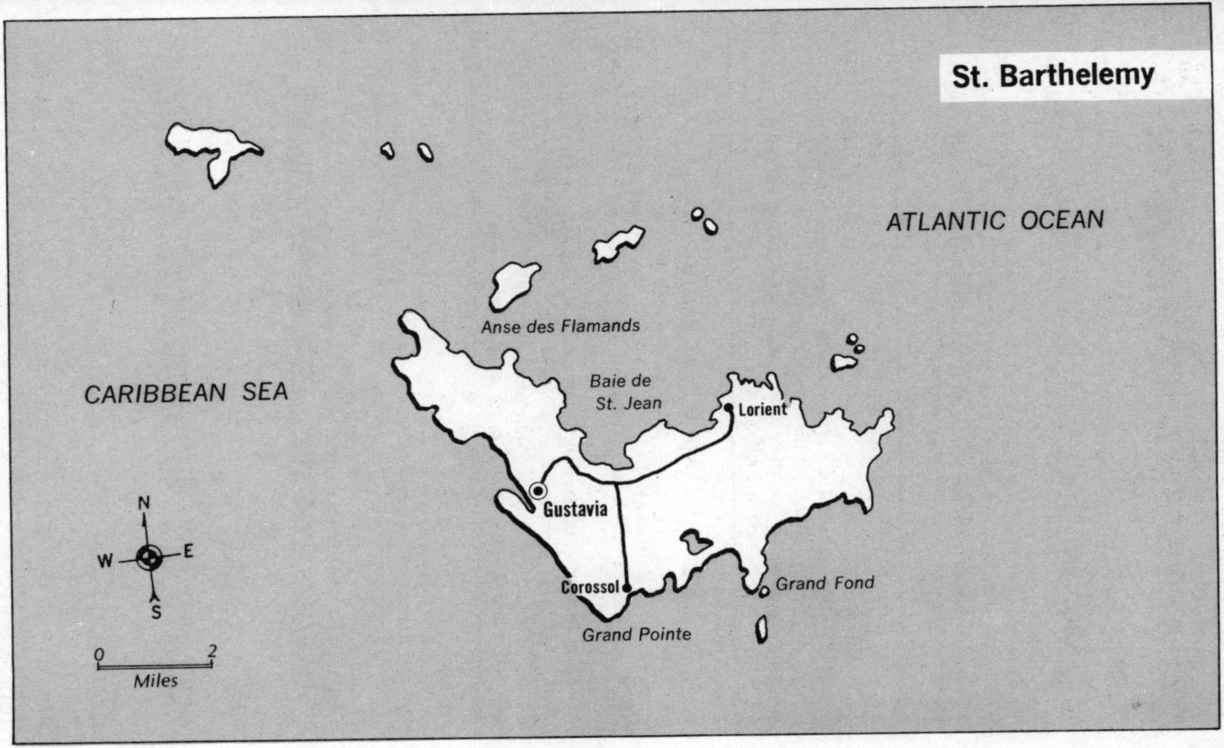

St. Barthelemy

ATLANTIC OCEAN

Anse des Flamands

Baie de
St. Jean

Lorient

CARIBBEAN SEA

Gustavia

Corossol

Grand Fond

Grand Pointe

N
W
E
S

0
2
Miles

Constant Gumbs, Charles Greaux and Henry Greaux, all in Gustavia. At the airport there is Hippolyte Ledée.

Tours are available by mini-bus for a half or full day. Contact St. Barts Tour in Gustavia for possibilities.

EVENTS AND HOLIDAYS. The highlight is the three-day celebration at the end of August to honor St. Barthelemy, the island's patron saint. It has all the makings of a French country fair. In recent years, the St. Barts Regatta in late February has become a prestigious and popular event. In addition, there are Carnival festivals and Bastille Day fireworks. Public holidays include: New Year's Day, Easter Monday, Ascension Day, Pentecost Monday, Schoelcher Day (July 21), Assumption Day (Aug. 15), All Saints Day (Nov. 1), Armistice Day (Nov. 11), and Christmas Day.

WHAT WILL IT COST?

On St. Barts, figure $150 per day for *two* persons, which will include hotel accommodations, all three meals, and a VW Beetle for the day. Prices can be less if you choose to do your own cooking, or more if you choose a life of ease in a villa.

STAYING IN ST. BARTS

HOTELS. St. Barts has just 15 hotels, but they run the gamut from a homey guesthouse with five rooms to a resort property with fifty.

Autour du Rocher. This five-room hotel at Lorient has had a complete facelift, along with a group of new owners, including musician Jimmy Buffett, and now features a restaurant serving Continental food and traditional island dishes. The accommodations are simple, the atmosphere casual. We've always enjoyed this place. $74–95 double in winter, $40 double off-season, breakfast included.

Baie Des Flamands. Twenty-four rooms in a two-story block, with dining room and terrace bar overlooking the sea. Located on a beautiful beach, at Anse des Flamands, there's also a seawater pool. Mostly French-Canadian holiday-seekers here. For just plain beach, this is the best on the island. Spartan accommodations, but neat and clean. $80 double EP in winter, $44 double EP off-season.

Castelets. A spectacular spot, unique construction and a plan for providing all luxuries. An out-of-the-way but exclusive chic chalet village. The mountaintop dining is gourmet, with fine French fare served to the strains of Bach and Brahms. $90–220 double in winter, $65–155 double off-season, with Continental breakfast included for the club rooms. Private villas available.

Eden Rock. For several years the only place to stay on St. Barts, this private home of the island's former mayor Remy de Haenen holds a handful of guests in six rooms in the main house and puts others up in a coordinated place down at the beach. All furnishings are antiques from the area; family prints and massive four-posters (with mosquito netting) fill the bedrooms. Informal atmosphere. $60 double in winter, $45 double off-season, Continental breakfast included.

Emeraude Plage. Fourteen cottages with kitchenettes, on the beach below the Eden Rock. Guests can climb to the Eden Rock terrace for cocktail hour. Restaurants are within walking distance. Take bug repellent for sand flies. A half mile from the airport. $80 double EP in winter; $54–66 double EP off-season.

Filao Beach. Named for a local tree that resembles a sea pine, the 30-room hotel is actually a cluster of bungalows grouped in semicircle fashion around a small swimming pool. Each bungalow has a terrace with sea view and is decorated in a smart contemporary style. With an enviable location directly on St. Jean Bay beach, the Filao has its own white-sand beach. Two minutes away is the superb new *Le Pelican,* which Filao management and guests have come to consider their hotel restaurant. Winter rates here are $112–120 double, while in off-season doubles are $56–60, with full American breakfast included.

Hibiscus Hotel. Gustavia. The nine rooms and six-person duplex of this new hotel on a small hill overlooking Gustavia Harbor are decorated in soft ochre and old rose tones. Each comes equipped with a kitchenette. There is a small pool and a restaurant called *Au Vieux Clocher,* which has become quite popular with the visiting yachtsmen set. Gustavia's public beach is within walking distance and busier beaches with watersports are easily accessible by car. Rates are $82 double EP in winter and $72 duble EP during off-season.

PLM Jean Bart. This PLM resort property has fifty rooms, thirty with kitchenette, in cottages terraced up the hillside from St. Jean Bay. It is the first fully serviced resort on St. Barts. Freshwater swimming pool, snack bar, restaurant overlooking the bay; disco and evening entertainment. The beautiful St. Jean beach is within walking distance. $120 double EP in winter; $46–64 double EP off-season.

Presqu'ile. The twelve rooms are right on the harbor in the heart of Gustavia. Restaurant/bar. You'll want a car if you plan to do more than wander around the small town. $35 double, breakfast included, all year.

Sereno Beach Hotel. A lovely new 20-room property on a beautiful white-sand beach at Grand Cul de Sac. Excellent French-Creole restaurant, tropical garden bar and pool. $130 double EP in winter; $65 double EP off-season.

St. Barths Beach Hotel & Tennis Club. Covering "all" coasts, ownership of Baie des Flamands has built a second property, on a quiet cove beyond Autour du Rocher and Eden Rock. Coral reef offshore makes snorkeling interesting, as well as keeping things relatively calm for comfortable sailfish/sunfish sailors. Tennis; even windsurfing. Thirty-six rooms in two-story wings with sea view. Quiet, do-what-you-like French holiday spot. $90 double EP in winter, $45 double off-season.

Tropical Hotel. Just 50 yards from St. Jean Bay, the recently opened *Hotel Tropical* has 20 twin-bedded, air-conditioned rooms arranged in a U-shape around a cloister-like garden. Just beyond lies a reception bungalow containing the hotel's music and reading rooms. Breakfast is served on the terrace which girds the Tropical's small pool. The restaurants and shops of St. Jean are all within easy reach. Rates here are $90 double EP in winter, $50 double EP off-season.

Village St. Jean. This retreat is perched on a hillside above St. Jean Bay. The

Village is made up of twenty-five rooms in several buildings, each with a kitchen unit and separate bedrooms, perfect for families or two compatible couples. If you plan to do your own cooking, it's advisable to bring some frozen foods and beef packed in dry ice from your hometown market. There's plenty of fresh fish and lobster on location. Restaurant and bar at the village's beach club down the hill. From $72 double EP in winter, from $32 double off-season.

HOME RENTALS. There is a long list of possibilities for home rentals, chalets, and villas on St. Barts. Contact Sibarth Rental and Real Estate, B.P. 55, Gustavia; Les Bougainvillees, B.P. 10, Gustavia; or Les Trois Chalets, St. Jean.

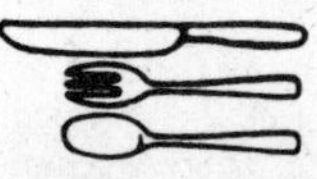

RESTAURANTS/NIGHTLIFE. Dining in St. Barts is a joy—there are more than twice as many restaurants as hotels on the island, and most combine a French flambé flair with West Indian cookery. Reservations are in order almost everywhere, since the cooking is often done to the exact number of expected guests. Move around the island and try those we have enjoyed in Gustavia, at Lorient, Morne Lurien, and St. Jean.

In *Gustavia: La Crémaillère* is special and its classic French cuisine even more so. Its Parisian chef serves up everything from the surrounding sea and does it beautifully. Expensive, but worth it, not only for the food, but for the atmosphere, which can be in an open-air garden or a provincial indoor dining room. *Auberge du Fort Oscar,* a wonderful boîte in a private home, calls its menu "creole cuisine à la Martiniquaise," which really means a selection of French soufflés, local fish sautéed with spices, and even plantains flambéed in rum. The prices are moderate and the camararderie an added bonus. *Le Sapotillier* on the quay is small and intimate, specializing in grilled steaks and fish at moderate prices.

At *Lorient: Autour du Rocher* offers hilltop dining and imaginative seafood entrees at moderate rates.

At *Morne Lurin: Castelets* is an elegant and expensive spot dramatically set atop a mountain peak. Class French cuisine and memorable service.

At *St. Jean Bay: Chez Francine* is a beachside café where lobster is the specialty; the *St. Jean Beach Club* is a delightful thatched restaurant on the beach for simple fare at breakfast and lunch. For French-Creole dishes, try the open-air dining room at *Eden Rock.*

For entertainment on the island, leisurely dining is the most popular choice. There are no casinos and nightclubbing is limited. Check with hotels on the current spots. *L'Ananas* and *Bar de l'Oubli* in Gustavia bring together a nice crowd for after-dinner nightcaps.

SHOPPING. There isn't much to buy, but what there is is in Gustavia. You'll find a small selection of jewelry, crystal, perfume, and watches at duty-free prices. Also look for island straw work and locally made fashions. Le Caleche and Jean-Yves Froment boutiques are worth a visit. La Case, at the east end of Gustavia Harbor, has some interesting island crafts. In addition, you can shop right from your car at Corossol. The starched white Norman bonnets are sold by the local ladies, who surround your car as soon as it comes to a stop.

SPORTS AND OTHER ACTIVITIES. If a full array of organized sports is your preference, St. Barts is not the answer. You come here for swimming on its beaches and sailing or windsurfing off its shores. In the past two years watersports have grown. Snorkeling and deep-sea fishing can be found at Loulou's Marina in Gustavia, windsurfing rental and instruction at St. Barts Beach Hotel, and scuba through St. Barts Water Sports based in Gustavia.

ST. EUSTATIUS

A Silent Shell of Former Glory

It's peaceful, quiet, full of history and friendship. St. Eustatius, or Statia, as she is more commonly called, measures just eight square miles and has a total population of 1500. Viewed from Saba, its Netherlands Windwards sister island, Statia looks like two barren cones. It is actually two extinct volcanoes connected by a valley. Oranjestad, the capital, overlooks the sea from a hilltop perch where it was built following the eighteenth-century bombardment of the harbor town. Statia's principal activity today is agricultural, primarily yams and sweet potatoes, which are exported to the larger Dutch islands. Once known as the "Golden Rock" of the Caribbean for its prominent role in international commerce, Statia today is a silent shell of her former glory.

This is an island with only four guest houses. They are small and suit the island mood. Exploring the ruins on Statia is the highlight—either on foot or by donkey, which seems to suit the leisurely pace of life here.

History

Discovered by Columbus in 1493, but not really colonized until the Dutch arrived in 1636, as frequently happened in the Caribbean, Statia changed hands between the Dutch, English and French several times until the Treaty of Utrecht awarded it to Holland in 1733. Such has been its status ever since.

A neutral island in the eighteenth century, Statia was a bustling

Dutch port for the trans-shipment of arms, food and clothing to the beleaguered American revolutionaries, fighting England's colonial blockade. As many as 200 ships crowded into Statia's harbor on a single day in those momentous times. Behind the harbor, sugar, tobacco, and other crops flourished on the island's fertile soil.

Historically, Statia was the first foreign power to recognize the new American flag–on November 16, 1776, when the *Andrew Doria,* a brig-of-war under the command of Captain Isaiah Robinson of the Continental Navy, sailed into port. But it wasn't long before the wrath of England, long irritated by this nettle of neutrality, finally came down on Statia. On February 3, 1781, Admiral Rodney commanded an English fleet to surround the island, shattering its buildings and pillaging its wealth while pelting the thriving harbor of Oranjestad with shot from ships offshore.

Today you can walk through the ruins and restorations and see four centuries of history come to life within a few hours.

EXPLORING ST. EUSTATIUS

Exploring Sint Eustatius begins at the airport, where your arrival is entered in a threadbare ledger. If you are asked what time you plan to leave, it is so that they can find you wherever you are on the island to let you know if your plane will be late! The island's taxi drivers will secure luncheon reservations for you if you're not staying the night.

Fort Oranje is usually the first site in town, and the most historic. Its monument reads:

> In Commemoration of the Salute to the Flag of the United States fired in this fort on 16 November 1776, By order of Johannes de Graaff, Governor of St. Eustatius, In reply to a National Gun-Salute Fired by the United States Brig-of-War Andrew Doria under Captain Isaiah Robinson of the Continental Navy.

From the edge of the Fort you can look down to the sea and, if the water is not ruffled, see a wall of the old city that was blown apart by the English. All the government offices, plus a host of post office boxes, are inside the Fort. There's also "the jail, which we never use"!

Statia's real pleasures are mostly natural–a few beaches, mountain peaks to climb, and a somnolent aspect. The favorite pastime for visitors is digging for "bluebeards," beads that were made in Holland and used for buying slaves. Some believe that these were the currency used to purchase Manhattan from the Indians.

One interesting way to "take the island" is by donkey. You can explore Statia from its Atlantic to its Caribbean side for just $13 per day to rent the donkey (unlimited mileage!!), and you'll find him a fine tour guide. He can amble you through the ruins of Lower Town, Oranjestad, or up the steep Bay-Path to Upper Town and Fort Oranje. Then, as he nibbles on hibiscus, browse among the tombstones of the second oldest Jewish cemetery in the Western Hemisphere, or in the ancient ruins of the Dutch Reformed Church, which is now being restored.

Your next stop might be "Miss Teenie's Behind," a somewhat irreverent name for the old plantation that was originally called "Miss Teenie's Land Behind the Mountain." Legend has it that Miss Teenie's ghost walks to the sea at dawn, so keep that in mind when planning your day. This spot, which is on the slopes of the extinct volcano called The Quill, is one the donkeys know well!

A DAY ON YOUR OWN

We recommend a walking tour, so you can watch centuries slip away as you wander. This tour, which was organized by a small but active local Historical Foundation, includes dozens of examples of seventeenth- , eighteenth- , and nineteenth-century architecture. Some of the buildings are still in use, others are in varying stages of romantic decay. The visitor who follows the well-designed tour map, which is available without charge, will discover examples of ecclesiastical, commercial, domestic, civic and military architecture all nestled together.

The tour begins amid the ruins of what was at one time the busiest port in the Caribbean, Oranjestad's so-called "Lower Town." Here at the water's edge Foundation members have planted palms and flowering shrubs and installed benches in the shade of a towering almond tree.

In the mid-1700s the town stretched for two miles along the Bay and was aswarm with merchants and sailors from all over the world. Today the warehouses and taverns which once were piled high with fine European imports simply store equipment for the island fishermen. But the restoration of an eighteenth-century cotton gin is impressive. It is the Mooshay Bay Publick House—be sure to stop in.

Leaving "Lower Town" you'll climb the steep, stone-paved dogleg of the Fort Road. At its crest lies the major portion of the town, perched like one of the island's seabirds atop the cliffs. It was here that the gentry lived.

The oldest and most historically important structure on the island is Fort Oranje, visible from the head of Fort Road across *Claes Gut.* Built in 1636 on the site of an even earlier fortification, this one has been restored recently and is well worth a visit.

A few steps away, a cluster of buildings called "Three Widows' Corner" surrounds a quiet courtyard. An exterior staircase built of yellow ballast brick ascends to the upper floor of an eighteenth-century townhouse. Beside it you'll find a typical nineteenth-century Victorian "gingerbread" dwelling.

A short distance away there are two houses of worship to visit. The Dutch Reformed Church, which is reached by turning west from "Three Widows' Corner" onto Kerweg, rises at the edge of the cliff. *Honen Dalim,* one of the most venerable synagogues in the Western Hemisphere, was begun in 1740, severely damaged over the years and finally left in disuse, but is on the list of historic spots to be restored.

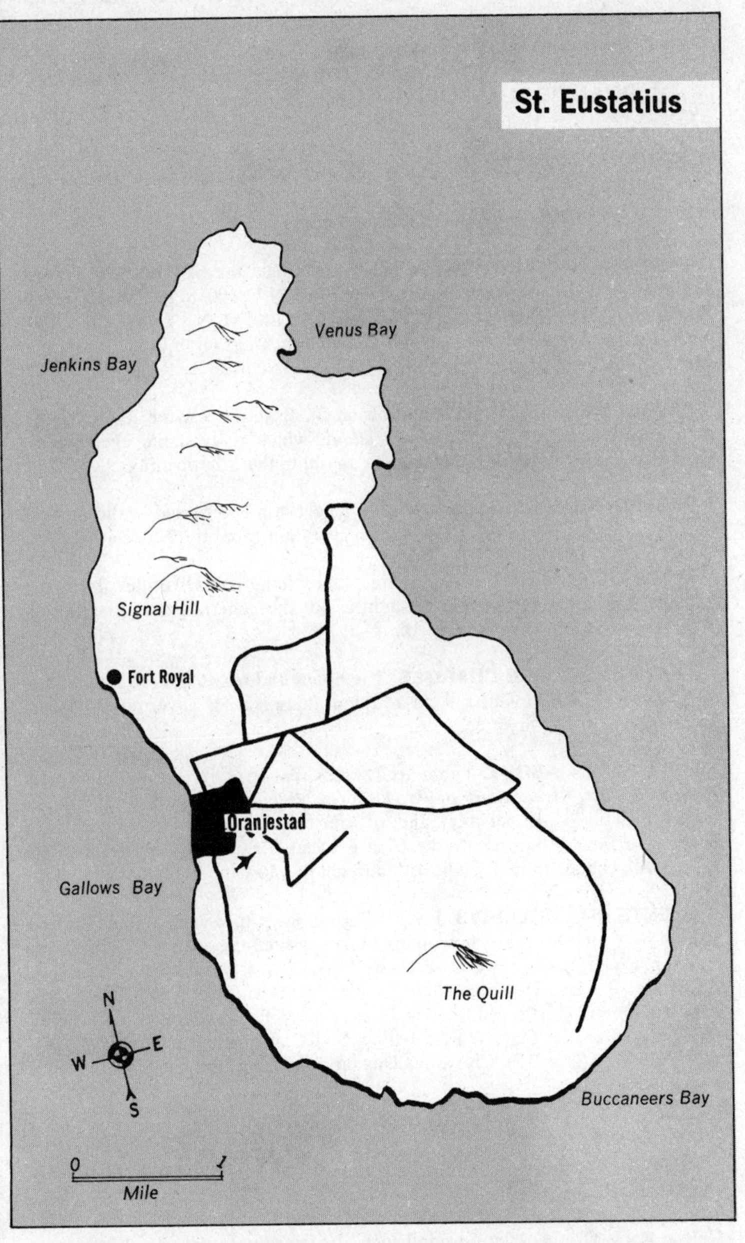
St. Eustatius
Venus Bay
Jenkins Bay
Signal Hill
Fort Royal
Oranjestad
Gallows Bay
The Quill
Buccaneers Bay
N
E
W
S
0
1
Mile

Your walking tour won't take more than two or three hours. Then leave the driving to someone else and spend the afternoon letting the donkey do the work! (see Exploring).

PRACTICAL INFORMATION FOR ST. EUSTATIUS

HOW TO GET THERE. By air. *Windward Island Airways* flies in from Saba, St. Kitts and St. Maarten. The flight from St. Maarten is the longest (twenty minutes) and runs $40 round-trip.

FURTHER INFORMATION. In the U.S., contact the St. Eustatius Tourist Information Office, 25 West 39th St., New York, N.Y. 10018; in Canada, you'll find them at 243 Ellerslie Ave., Willowdale, Toronto, M2N 1Y5. On the island itself, James Maduro, director of the Tourist Bureau at Oranjestad, knows, or can find out, everything.

ISLAND MEDIA. Some information on St. Eustatius can be found in the orange sheet entitled *St. Maarten Holiday,* which is available everywhere. Otherwise, rely on the tourist offices for anything that's happening.

PASSPORTS, VISAS. Some proof of citizenship is required–valid or outdated passport, birth certificate, voter's registration card, etc. No visa needed.

MONEY. The official currency here is the Netherlands Antilles florin (or guilder). The exchange fluctuates slightly, but the generally accepted rate is 1.77 NAf = $1 US; 3.96 NAf = 1£.

TAXES AND OTHER CHARGES. The hotels and restaurants usually add a 10% service charge to your bill. In addition, there is a 5% government tax on accommodations at the inns.

HOW TO GET ABOUT. There are cars for rent here, through *Glover's Car Rental; Rivers; Richardson;* or *Maduro Car Rentals* (about $20 per day), motorcycles (at $12.50 per day), and, of course, the donkeys (at $13 per day), but if your time is limited, the best bet is to take taxis. Not only reasonable rates, but a chance to really talk with and get to know the Statians.

EVENTS AND HOLIDAYS. It has been set down that when one of Statia's elderly residents was asked how many tourists visited the island, his reply was, "we don't have tourists; we have *guests!*" And that is what special events on Statia are all about. However, there are also island-wide holidays: New Year's Day, the Queen's Birthday (Jan. 31), Good Friday, Easter Monday, Labor Day (May 1), Ascension Day, Whit Monday, Statia and America Day (Nov. 16), Kingdom Day (Dec. 15), Christmas Day, and Boxing Day (Dec. 26).

STAYING IN ST. EUSTATIUS

HOTELS. There are only three inns in Statia, all small and quiet, but each with a special look.

Golden Rock. On the Atlantic-side beach, the ten rooms are in small cottages, with two rooms per unit. Swimming pool, outdoor dining terrace, indoor dining room and cocktail lounge. About a ten-minute drive from town, this

WHAT WILL IT COST?

A typical day on St. Eustatius in season for *two* persons will run:

	US$	£
Accommodations, including breakfast and dinner	100	54
Luncheon at one of the hotels	10	5
Tip/service charge/hotel gvt. tax	15	8
One-day sightseeing	20	11
	$145	£78

spot has a nice sea view along with the tropical breezes. $100 double in winter; $80 double off-season, with breakfast and dinner included.

Mooshay Bay Publick House. Fourteen modern rooms in a restored cotton gin across the road from its sister inn, The Old Gin House. Very attractively done, with pub-like tavern for dining, and a nice swimming pool, in the old town area at the water's edge. $130 double in winter; $115 double off-season, two meals included.

The Old Gin House. This restored tavern began life as a restaurant at the water's edge in the old town. It now has nine rooms for guests who want a special place within the sound of the surf. Scenic, and the hub of the island's social life. The rooms are all with a sea view and all furnished with antiques, most of them brought down by the Connecticut owners. A perfect, isolated, getaway spot with nice comforts. $130 double in winter; $115 off-season, including breakfast and dinner.

RESTAURANTS/NIGHTLIFE. There are just a half dozen or so on the island. Among them are: **The Old Gin House:** Long famous for its Antillean and Continental specialties served nicely on a covered terrace overlooking the sea. *Expensive.*

Mooshay Bay Publick House. Good food served in their tavern, which has an authentic Old World pub atmosphere. *Expensive.*

Golden Rock: Excellent local lobster and fresh-caught fish carefully prepared and nicely served. *Moderate.*

L'Étoile. In-town spot offering a selection of West Indian specialties that are superb. *Moderate.*

Talk of the Town. Small and cozy, with just six tables and a tiny bar. Famous for their pepper steak. *Inexpensive.*

There is little in the way of nightlife other than conversation with other guests or Statians at your hotel.

SHOPPING. The only place for shopping is a combination grocery-gift shop called *Mazinga,* which is behind the Deputy's Office on Fort Oranje Street.

SPORTS AND OTHER ACTIVITIES. *Swimming, snorkeling, sunbathing* and *hiking* have been the major attractions here until this year, when "Statia" set its cap for divers. The new *Happy Hooker Watersport Center* in Oranjestad is the island's first diving operation. The certification course, including equipment, is $150. Dive packages are available at $120, which includes equipment, 6 guided reef trips and 6 air-fills.

ST. KITTS

Columbus's Namesake

St. Kitts, with its proper name, St. Christopher, on its postage stamp and government documents, contains about 35,000 people on its sixty-five miles. The island is shaped like a cricket bat and is dotted with plantations bordered by mountains and sea and by ravines or rows of palms. The center of the island is almost unpenetrated by roads, particularly in the north. It is left to cultivation and the long-time Kittians who flouted government efforts to move them nearer public transportation. St. Kitts is reached from Puerto Rico or the U.S. Virgin Islands in under an hour and from St. Martin or Antigua in half an hour. The island has a pleasant white sand beach in an area known as Frigate Bay, which is destined for big things as the heart of the island's tourism industry. The literal high point of all is Mt. Misery, which soars some 4,000 feet into the tropical sky. St. Kitts is a quiet island, and chances are will remain so. The only real noise today comes from the slot machines at the Royal St. Kitts Hotel; otherwise, all you'll hear is the rustle of cane as trade winds sweep across the sugar fields.

History

Columbus discovered the island in 1493, naming it St. Christopher after himself. The English Anglicized that almost as soon as they arrived, "determined to found a little bit of England overseas," which they most emphatically did on January 28, 1623, when Sir Thomas Warner landed for the second time–this time with his wife and fourteen men—near a coconut grove by Sandy Point. He was reportedly looking for fresh water, but stayed to begin the colonizing of St. Kitts.

Oldest of the British West Indian settlements, St. Kitts is proud of its title, "Mother Colony of the West Indies," which it earned by sending out colonizing parties to other islands, most notably to Antigua. Other parties went out to colonize Barbuda, Tortuga, and Montserrat, while the French under the leadership of their governor general, De Poincy, sailed off to claim Guadeloupe, Desirade, Les Saintes, Martinique, St. Barthelemy, St. Martin, and St. Croix.

The French and English battled here as they did in the rest of the islands, and ultimately reached an agreement which gave the French the north and south portions while the English held the middle. This explains the capital's name of Basseterre (low land). Another relic of the Anglo-French era is in the lovely village of Half-Way Tree, where a big tamarind tree marked the approximate half-way point in English territory on the south side of the island. The English got full title to the island by the 1783 Treaty of Versailles and have guided it since then, up and through the step to Associated State in 1967.

This is the island where the Count De Poincy cultivated his cherished poinciana, sending it out from here around the Caribbean.

EXPLORING ST. KITTS

The harbor of Basseterre, the capital, has the look of an old print. The pier is where inter-island boats come in, and their produce is sold right on the dock. The "Circus" with its gingerbread clock tower is the hub of in-town activities. Government House is a good example of the colonial style, as is the Old Court House on Pall Mall Square, which often has interesting exhibits in the second-floor library.

Around the island's perimeter are a few other coves, but nothing spectacular compared to its fellow islands. The area at Black Rocks, where the Guy Fawkes' day picnic is held each year, is dramatic and worth a stop when you drive around the island. The jagged volcanic rocks have been worn to fanciful shapes by pounding Atlantic surf.

At the northern point, the fishing village of Dieppe Bay is worth a stop. A good road follows the coast, almost girdling the island. On any tour, you'll see Brimstone Hill, "The Gibraltar of the West Indies," ten miles from Basseterre. This is one of the most important and impressive historical monuments in the West Indies. The bastion, with its formidable, frowning ramparts, took a century to build, positioned as it is, 700 feet atop the Gibraltar-like rock. The view encompasses the Dutch islands of St. Eustatius and Saba, St. Martin, and French St. Barts on the west, and Nevis to the southeast. It is the high point of an island tour. The area is dotted with places of historic interest: Old Road Village, where Thomas Warner and his intrepid colonists first stepped ashore in 1623; Sandy Point, their first settlement; Middle Island Village, with St. Thomas Church and the tomb of Sir Thomas Warner, who "gave forth large narratives of military worth written with his sword's poynt."

Many ruined forts and battlegrounds bear mute testimony to the ancient enmity between England and France. Bloody Point marks the spot where they combined forces in 1629 to repel with great slaughter a mass attack by the original owners of the island, the Carib Indians. If you or your driver has gotten permission, visit Fountain Estate, long ago the seat of the governors of the French section of St. Kitts.

A DAY ON YOUR OWN

Make your day on St. Kitts an historic one. Brimstone Hill makes an ideal goal for a picnic lunch. Head for it from Basseterre and drive the ten miles leisurely. Despite its look of impregnability from the ocean, you can drive up to the fortress easily from the coastal road that circles the island and passes it. From here you'll have an excellent view of where Admirals Hood and DeGrasse engaged in one of the most famous naval battles in history.

Take the time to wander the ramparts and visit the restoration, most notably the bastion officially opened on June 1, 1973, by His Royal Highness the Prince of Wales and named for him. At that time the British Government presented the Society for the Restoration of Brimstone Hill with ten oak plaques bearing the crests of ten of the regiments–including the West Indian Regiment–which served at the Fortress. The Prince of Wales Bastion is the Visitor's Center, with an office, souvenir shop, restaurant, and plans for the bastion as it was from 1783 to 1794. Conjure up thoughts of those heydays as you spread your luncheon picnic on the hilltop and drink in the view of the surrounding islands and sea.

PRACTICAL INFORMATION FOR ST. KITTS

HOW TO GET THERE. By air. Direct service from the U.S. via *BWIA* out of New York; *BWIA* and *Sun Jet* from Miami. St. Kitts is also served by *American* or *Eastern* airlines to San Juan, the U.S. Virgin Islands, Antigua and St. Martin with connections on *Prinair, LIAT* and *Windward Islands Airways*.

By sea. Three daily round-trips ($6 US) offered to sister-island Nevis. A new deep-water port is expected to greatly increase cruise ship calls.

FURTHER INFORMATION. Contact the Caribbean Tourism Association, 20 East 46th St., New York, N.Y. 10017; or the Eastern Caribbean Tourist Association, 220 East 42nd St., New York, N.Y. 10017. In Canada: the Eastern Caribbean Commission, Place de Ville, Suite 1701, 112 Kent St., Ottawa, Ont. K1P5P2; in London at 200 Buckingham Palace Road, London, Eng. SW1W9SP. The tourist office on St. Kitts is located at Treasury Pier in Basseterre.

PASSPORTS, VISAS. Proof of citizenship (a passport, even expired, will do) and a valid return ticket are required.

MONEY. Eastern Caribbean dollars (EC) are used here, but U.S. and Canadian dollars accepted. $1 US = 2.70 EC; $6 EC = £1.

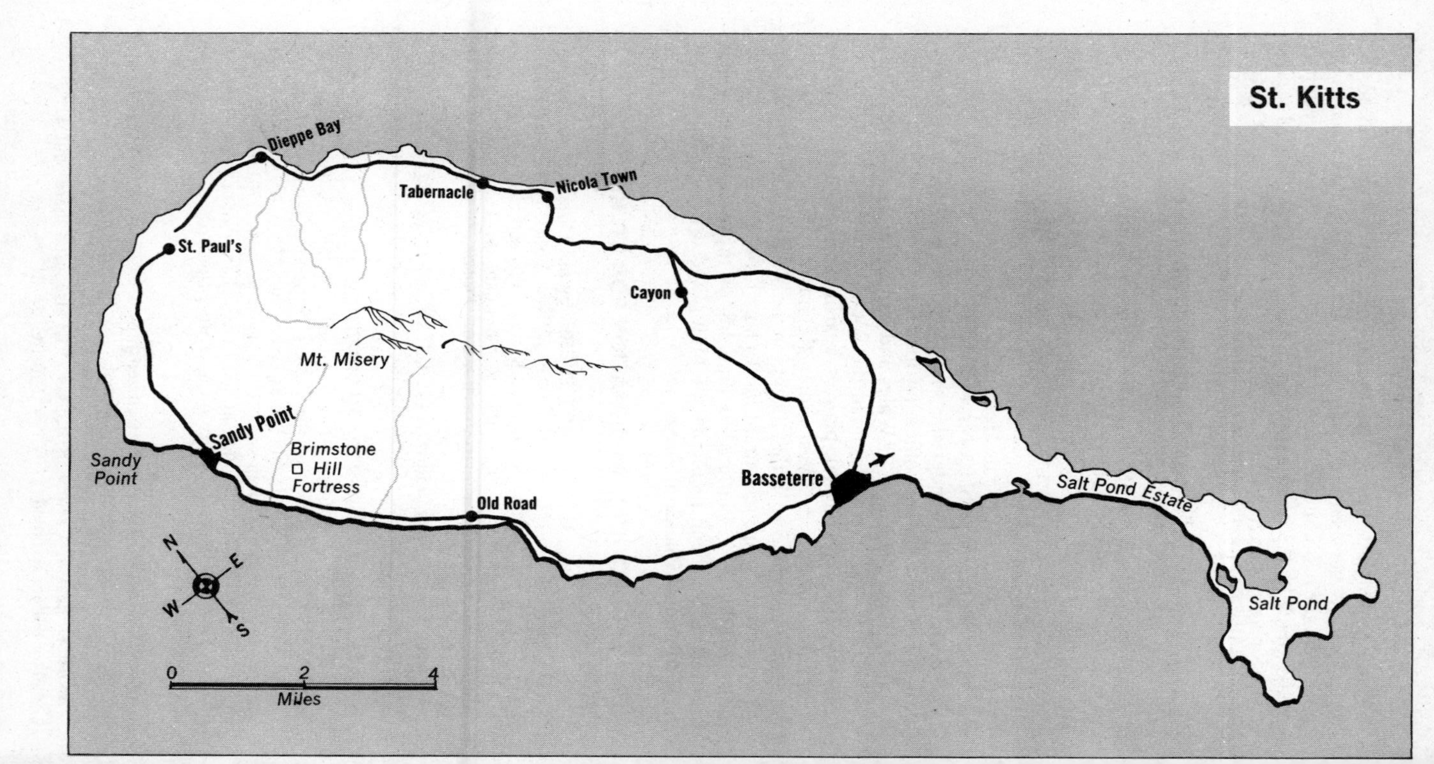
St. Kitts
Dieppe Bay
Tabernacle
Nicola Town
St. Paul's
Cayon
Mt. Misery
Sandy Point
Brimstone
Hill
Fortress
Sandy
Point
Old Road
Basseterre
Salt Pond Estate
Salt Pond
N
E
W
S
0
2
4
Miles

TAXES AND OTHER CHARGES. Hotels add a 10% service charge and 5% government tax to your bill. There is an airport departure tax of $4 US per person.

HOW TO GET ABOUT. Taxis are readily available at the airport and in town, but establish the rate and currency in advance. If you assume you're paying in US dollars and the quoted fare is in EC dollars, you'll be paying double. Cars can be rented either through the hotels or at Buckley's or Caine's in Basseterre, from $25–35 per day. You will need a local driver's license, which can be obtained at the Police Station in Basseterre for $4 EC. Remember to drive on the left.

EVENTS AND HOLIDAYS. Special days on St. Kitts are Statehood Day (Feb. 27) and Carnival Week (Dec. 26–Jan. 2.) Other holidays are New Year's Day, Good Friday, Easter Monday, Labor Day (May 1), Whit Monday, the Queen's Birthday (June), August Monday, the Prince of Wales' Birthday (Nov. 14), Christmas Day, and Boxing Day.

WHAT WILL IT COST?

On St. Kitts, a typical day for *two* during the winter season will run about $150 U.S., which includes room, hotel service charges, all three meals, and car rental for one day.

STAYING IN ST. KITTS

HOTELS. If you're a Caribbean addict, the inns on St. Kitts will intrigue you. There's "one of each" of the old-time West Indian inns, Modernized to cope with today's demands but miraculously retaining the charm that is fast disappearing elsewhere in the Caribbean. There are two unique inns in the north and two in the south, where there are better beaches. The most luxurious is the Royal St. Kitts Hotel and Casino with 138 rooms at Frigate Bay.

Banana Bay Beach. On the south shore. Take the boat from Basseterre, which you reach by taxi from the airport. (This beachside inn is actually closer to the Nevis airport, but the 1,000-foot channel is apt to be rough.) A totally relaxed, informal atmosphere. Ten rooms in one-story modern buildings. Entertainment is beach oriented. Management assists with boat trips to Nevis and elsewhere to explore or snorkel. Local lobster and fresh fish and fruits are on the menu. $175 double in winter, $135 double off-season, with all three meals included.

Cockleshell. At Cockleshell Bay, next door to Banana Bay on the south coast. About forty-five minutes by boat along the coast south of Basseterre. Management meets you if you let them know when you're coming. Ten spacious rooms, each with veranda. Beach at your feet; congenial atmosphere in the main house. Fishing, snorkeling, and boat-sightseeing easily arranged. The hotel draws a list of repeaters who like being unreachable. Ideal for those in search of sun-and-read time. $130 double in winter; $100 double off-season, breakfast and dinner included.

Fairview Inn. An eighteenth-century great house in the country, about ten minutes' drive from Basseterre. There's a small mountain in the "backyard" for climbing. Thirty rooms, a few upstairs in the main house but most in separate out-buildings behind. Freshwater swimming pool. Casual, comfortable Kittian atmosphere. Dining room serves local food, which is delicious. $70–80 double EP in winter; $50–56 double EP off-season.

Fort Thomas Hotel. On the outskirts of Basseterre, at the water's edge, this sixty-four room hotel is modern and attractive, with a huge pool and lovely view. Dining room, lounge, some evening entertainment. $126 double EP in winter; $80 double EP off-season.

Golden Lemon. In the north at Dieppe Bay, a simple fishing village with happy people, many of whom are employed at Golden Lemon. Guests are encouraged to enter into the community if they wish. Decor includes local antiques and some stateside trimmings. Four-poster beds. Meals are an occasion and open to outsiders if reservations are made in advance. $160–195 double in winter, $100–145 double off-season, with two meals included.

Leeward Cove Condominimum Hotel. New air-conditioned apartments consisting of one- and two-bedroom suites. Set in the hills of the Frigate Bay area on a lovely five-acre tract of land between the Atlantic Ocean and the Caribbean Sea. Watersports, tennis, fishing. From $50–100 double.

Ocean Terrace Inn. Known as OTI by those "in the know" and with a strong following of repeat visitors, most of the thirty double rooms are big, air-conditioned, and have a view overlooking Basseterre. Creole and continental dishes served in the restaurant. The OTI's "Bitter End" is *the* night spot on the island and is open Fridays, Saturdays, and at other times if business warrants. A popular halting place for folks who have errands in town. Swimming pool and pool bar. $65–160 double EP in winter; $45–86 double EP off-season.

Rawlin's Plantation. Formerly an operating plantation, the property now offers six double rooms in and around seventeenth-century buildings. On the hillside, with beach at Dieppe Bay a short drive away. No planned entertainment, but peaceful and pleasant. One two-bedroom villa with own kitchen also available on premises. The only places we know that are comparable to this Kittian plantation are those on nearby Nevis. $160 double in winter, $90 double off-season, including two meals.

Royal St. Kitts. A long time in the making, this 138-room property is the first large resort on St. Kitts. An eighteen-hole championship golf course surrounds it. There are swimming pool, two beaches, tennis courts, restaurant, snack bar—and the island's only casino. Rooms are modern, in Mediterranean-style villas. $174–220 double in winter; $115–160 double off-season, including two meals.

HOME RENTALS. For cottages and informal housekeeping efficiencies, we suggest Conareef Cottages, which have twin-bedded rooms, living room, kitchenette, patio, and are at a beach. Daily, weekly, and longer rates can be arranged, and are all very reasonable. Mr. D.K. Stott carries the listing for these and other small beach cottages. Contact him at P.O. Box 432, Basseterre, St. Kitts, W.I.

SHOPPING. The shops on St. Kitts are all in the main section of Basseterre, from the Circus up Front Street and on the main side streets, with such English names as Liverpool Row, Bank Street, Princes Street, and the like. There isn't much to buy here. You'll find the best selection of native and local articles at the Curio Shop, the Tourist Bureau, and The Lotus. There is a very small (mostly liquor) duty-free shop located at the airport.

SPORTS AND OTHER ACTIVITIES. The best beaches on St. Kitts are at Cockleshell Bay, Frigate Bay, and White House Bay on the Caribbean side. The first overlooks the two-mile-wide strait that separates St. Kitts from Nevis. The view of Nevis from here at sunset has been called "one of the most unforgettably beautiful sights in the world."

Scuba diving, fishing charters and other watersports can be arranged through your hotel. Horseback riding is also available on a limited basis. Hunting of migratory birds is popular between June and September, pigeon shooting between October and December. You can play tennis at Royal St. Kitts Hotel and at the St. Kitts/Tennis and Olympic Club; golf at the eighteen-hole Frigate Bay course. Finally, the volcanic topography invites hiking and mountain climbing, especially to the top of Mt. Misery, the island's pride.

ST. LUCIA

Where Mountains Rise in Majesty

The island of St. Lucia (pronounced Loo-sha) is twenty-one miles south of Martinique, twenty-six miles north of St. Vincent, and on a clear day you can see both islands as you sail off the coast. New York is about 2,015 miles to the north, and San Juan about 460 miles northwest. The island stretches its bumpy twenty-seven-by-fourteen-mile frame in the Caribbean, a tropical quilt of coconut palms, bananas, and exotic tropical blooms covering it from head to toe. There are 120,000 St. Lucians, with 45,000 of them living around the capital of Castries, on the northwestern shore, while the others inhabit villages along the west coast, in the mountains, and on the rugged Atlantic shore.

Mountainous St. Lucia, with deep valleys brilliantly accented with hibiscus, oleander, bougainvillea, flamboyant trees, orchids, roses and lilies, has twin peaks as dramatic as exclamation points. Rising majestically in the southern quarter near the west coast town of Soufrière, the Petit Piton is 2,461 feet, and Gros Piton reaches 2,619 feet. Boy scouts lead the way for climbers who set out to scale the peaks.

History

Columbus is said to have discovered the island on June 15, 1502, during his fourth voyage, but some say the first visitors were unknown Spaniards in 1605. When the English established a colony in 1639, the Caribs murdered every one of them. The French, who claimed St. Lucia in 1642, also had a hard time with the original owners, and were finally compelled to make a treaty of peace with them in 1660. For the next century and a half, the English and French battled over the island, which changed hands no less than fourteen times.

Although St. Lucia had been British since the Treaty of Amiens in 1802, the Lucians were very attached to their French heritage in the form of *patois*, the language of the countryside. The celebration of French holidays interlock with the British ones to create a year-round celebration.

St. Lucia became an Associated State of the British Commonwealth, along with its British "cousins" in the Caribbean, in March 1967. It took another dozen years before the island achieved the independence it desired. The Duchess of Kent represented the Crown at the island-wide celebration on February 22, 1979.

EXPLORING ST. LUCIA

Visitors arriving by cruise ship in Castries come directly into the harbor. There's usually a steel band to greet you on the wharf, and there are more than 200 cars available for sightseeing. (If you're not on a cruise ship, this is a good day to avoid town.)

Castries is not one of the most colorful Caribbean towns, but it is interesting, with an active, landlocked harbor. Destroyed by fire twice within a generation, it doesn't have the Georgian or Victorian colonial look that is the hallmark of many West Indian towns, though Columbus Square is edged with some interesting restored buildings.

The town is alive with the commerce of this Caribbean island, and a few minutes wandering around Columbus Square, through the Catholic Cathedral that rims one side, with a halt for a cool drink by an upstairs window of the famous restaurant *Rain* on another side, gives a definite West Indian feeling.

You'll see many St. Lucian women wearing banana fibre rings, or colta, on their heads to balance baskets, around the market place at the waterfront. The madras and foulard, borrowed from their island neighbors on Martinique and Guadeloupe, are not often seen in town, but are worn by some of the celebrants at unique island festivals in the countryside.

Castries' modern look results in part from rebuilding along the sides of ruined structures instead of on top of them. Two hills, Morne Fortune and Vigie, rise behind the town and its protected harbor. Drive to the top of the former to see Fort Charlotte, an example of the eighteenth-century fortifications which figured in the 150-year tug of war between France and England for this pretty prize. It was the Duke of Kent, Queen Victoria's father, who captured it for the British in 1794. The military buildings are well preserved. The Morne is now the set for an educational complex, as well as a place for local cricket matches and activities. The view is one of the thrills of the island, especially in that brief tropical sunset that turns the deep blue harbor the color of wine.

St. Lucia's fuming Soufrière is a "must" on any island tour. It's been called the only drive-in volcano in the world. You can drive to the lip of the smoldering crater and watch your guide (or someone else's) boil an egg in the stream.

More traditional island attractions are the golf course that meanders over the northern tip of the island; the Saturday market in Castries (where everything comes from the mountain villages, including chairs, baskets, and produce); and Marigot Bay, a south-shore cove that has been a popular natural harbor for large yachts and was the site of the beaching of the pink snail for the Rex Harrison movie "Doctor Dolittle."

In addition, there are three classic excursions: one to Pigeon Island; another to the active volcanic caldera in the south of Soufrière; and the tour that takes you to the tropical-looking south shore and along the wild Atlantic coast, winding through plantations of banana, copra, and other crops.

Getting to Pigeon Island is a simple matter now that it is joined to the main island by a dredged strip of land.

Thanks to the land that links Gros Islet to Pigeon Island, making it "Pigeon Point," it is possible to drive to the Arawak relics and other ruins in a matter of minutes. The St. Lucia National Trust is holding Pigeon Island as a National Park, preserving its tropical trees and shrubs, and marking its Arawak remnants, its lookouts, gun batteries, and barracks. Plan ahead—"Pigeon Point" is the perfect place for a picnic prowl.

A DAY ON YOUR OWN

St. Lucia's major attraction, the volcano of Soufrière, is a rewarding day trip. There are three ways of reaching it—two by land, one by sea. Choose one, then pack a picnic lunch, bathing suit and towel.

Soufrière is about twelve miles south of Castries as the crow flies, and twenty-nine miles by the West Coast Road, which passes through the valleys of Cul-de-Sac and Roseau, the villages of Anse-la-Raye and Canaries, and on to Soufrière. It is fascinating, bumpy, and scenic, and the drive takes 1½ hours.

Soufrière can also be reached by the East Coast Road. Scenically it's magnificent, with a rain forest, the Atlantic dashing against the cliffs, sprawling plantations—but don't count on making this trip in a hurry.

Going by sea is shorter and easier, but be sure to check the schedules carefully or you may find yourself stranded in Soufrière for the night. Two huge brigantine schooners make day excursions down the coast ($30 US per person), docking at the beautiful little town of Soufrière, right at the base of those two celebrated Pitons. The town itself is a picture postcard of pastel houses, golden beach, limpid water, fishermen going out in dugout canoes, and children basking in the sun and plunging into the sea.

You can't walk more than a few steps without bumping into a guide whose business and pleasure is to escort you to the volcano. There are plenty of cars for rent, and your boat excursion includes an open-air island-style bus tour. The ascent presents no problem at all.

The sensation of walking over the lip and down into the caldera is like a descent into the nether regions. You are actually inside the volcano, surrounded by jets of sulphurous steam. These jets are what keep the uncontainable pressure from building up.

After you have explored this boiling cauldron, ask the guide to show you the nearby sulphur baths. They have been in use since 1785, when Louis XVI had the water channeled for the benefit of his colonial troops. There are pools where you can bathe. The water may look dirty, but it isn't at all.

PRACTICAL INFORMATION FOR ST. LUCIA

HOW TO GET THERE. By air. *BWIA* (British West Indian Airways) has service from New York and Miami. *Eastern Airlines* flies direct to St. Lucia. *LIAT* flies in from Antigua and Barbados. *British Airways* flies in from London.

By sea. Cruise ships realize the attractions of St. Lucia, and those that dip far into the Caribbean stop in Castries. Among them are the liners of Costa Cruises, Cunard Lines, and Holland America Cruises. Hundreds of yachts come into Castries for safe anchorage and fresh supplies. Marigot Bay, scene of many French-English sea skirmishes, is also a favored harbor, with no shopping available here, but great boat charter activity. The Rodney Bay Development, north of Castries, is island port for Stevens Yacht Charters.

FURTHER INFORMATION. Contact the St. Lucia Tourist Board at 41 East 42nd St., New York, N.Y. 10017. In Canada: St. Lucia Tourist Board, 151 Bloor St., W., Toronto, Ont. M5S1P7. In London: The Eastern Caribbean Tourist Association at 200 Buckingham Palace Rd., London SW1W 9TJ, England. The head office is the St. Lucia Tourist Board, Box 221, Castries, St. Lucia, W.I. Their head office is located on Fisherman's Drive; their in-town Information Office is located at the Northern Wharf.

ISLAND MEDIA. You'll find a lot of local news and some international coverage in the island's newspaper, *The Voice of St. Lucia.*

AUTHORIZED TOUR OPERATORS. Adventure Tours; Butler Travels; Caribbean Holidays; Cavalcade Tours; Flyfaire, Inc.; and Lib/Go from the U.S. From Canada: Fairway Tours; Holiday House; and Sunburst Holidays. From the U.K.: Alta Holidays; Kuoni Travel, Ltd.; Pegasus Holidays; Rankin Kuhn & Co.; and Sovereign Holidays.

PASSPORTS, VISAS. Proof of citizenship (your birth certificate, passport—even if expired—will do) and a return or ongoing ticket.

MONEY. The Eastern Caribbean dollar (EC) is the local currency, figured at \$2.70 EC = \$1 US; \$6 EC = 1 £. Be sure which exchange is being used—most places quote in EC dollars.

TAXES AND OTHER CHARGES. There is a 7% government tax on hotel rooms. In addition, a 10% service charge is added to your bill. The airport departure tax is \$4 US per person.

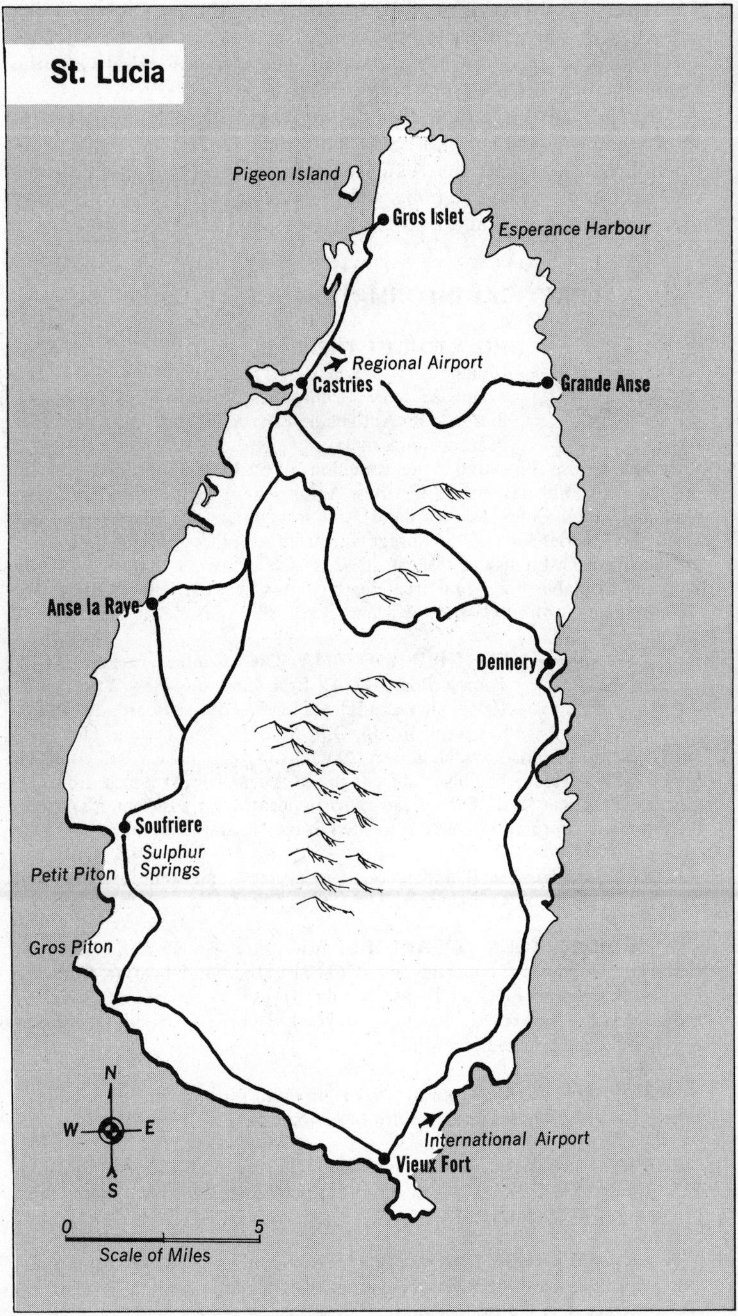

St. Lucia

Pigeon Island
Gros Islet
Esperance Harbour
Regional Airport
Castries
Grande Anse
Anse la Raye
Dennery
Soufriere
Sulphur Springs
Petit Piton
Gros Piton
N
W
E
S
International Airport
Vieux Fort
0
5
Scale of Miles

HOW TO GET ABOUT. There is adequate taxi service. A car-and-driver all-day tour should be negotiated with the driver beforehand. Make sure that the rate quoted is either in EC or US dollars, otherwise you may be paying double. Figure $60 US per car for a complete island tour. There are several car rental firms, both local, and Avis, Hertz and National representatives. Rates run $23–30 US per day, plus mileage, and gas.

EVENTS AND HOLIDAYS. The biggest celebration of all is Independence Day, February 22. In May there are the Carnival festivities, which makes that month the highlight of the year. Other holidays are: New Year's Day, Good Friday, Easter Monday, the Queen's Birthday (June), Emancipation Day, Thanksgiving Day, Christmas Day, and Boxing Day.

WHAT WILL IT COST?

A typical day on St. Lucia in winter for *two* persons will run:

	US $	£
Hotel accommodations, including breakfast and dinner	135	73
Luncheon at a moderate restaurant	15	8
Hotel tax; service charge; tips	20	11
One-day car rental	25	14
	$195	£106

STAYING IN ST. LUCIA

HOTELS. There are a dozen resort properties, giving you the opportunity to choose exactly what's right for you. Options run from 18 rooms in a lovely West Indian home to 250 rooms in a busy and very active hotel.

Anse Chastanet. Comfortable cottages made special by their location—scampering up from beach to hilltop (the climb is not for the faint of heart), with several providing a bird's-eye view of the Pitons. In the Soufrière area, out of the mainstream, on the southwest shore of the island. Nice beach with active, attractive bar and restaurant, West Indian food. Fourteen bungalows plus two villas with four bedrooms; one one-bedroom and two two-bedroom suites. A real West Indian Eden, with botanic gardens nearby and plenty of area for nature walks, plus beach for good snorkeling. $160 double in bungalows, $180 double in suites in winter, including two meals.

Cariblue Hotel. 102 rooms on 1,500 acres at Anse de Cap, the northern tip of the island, within walking distance of the nine-hole golf course at Cap Estate. The hotel attracts Europeans, and has tennis courts and a beach good for sunworshippers or as a source for snorkeling, waterskiing or Sunfish rental. There's a pool, open-air restaurant, nightly entertainment. From $180 double in winter, $105–149 double off-season, including breakfast and dinner.

Dasheene. Planned as a condominium resort of two- and three-bedroom villas and apartments. All units are open, airy, with spectacular view of the bay below and the Pitons set at "eye level." Attractively furnished. Small pool; transportation to Anse Chastanet beach. One-bedroom apartments run $75 double EP in winter, $55 off-season. Two-bedroom villas are $95 in winter, $70 off-season.

East Winds. A unique spot on the beach off the main road between Castries and Cap Estate. The units are built for do-it-yourself holidays, but the congenial management make it as easy as possible, assisting with commissary provisions and providing good meals at the beachside informal gathering spot (with bar and nautical-style reading nook). Guests love this informal spot that has ten doubles in five duplex cottages. The day-to-day diversions include sailing on a Sunfish, snorkeling, beaching, visits from children from the farm next door, and chirps from their aviary of budgerigars. $60 double EP in winter; $42 double EP off-season.

Halcyon Beach Club. On Choc Bay, about a fifteen-minute drive north of Castries, this hotel is action-packed, as are its sister hotels, Halcyon Days and Halcyon Sands. The ninety-eight large air-conditioned rooms all have private patios. A pier complex called Fisherman's Wharf sits over the sea—for those who like al fresco dining with the sea beneath their feet. The hotel also has a pool, discotheque, tennis courts, and shops. $128–140 double in winter; $102–126 double off-season, breakfast and dinner included.

Halcyon Days. Close to the airport at Vieux Fort, on an eighty-three-acre shore-side coconut grove where the wind blows steady and strong. The 250 rooms are minute but efficiently furnished. The entire atmosphere is geared to keeping you active and out of doors. Day excursions, fishing, sightseeing, picnic outings, pool, tennis, scuba, shops. Dining room has a cozy look at nighttime. Horseback riding can be arranged. The emphasis is on casual holidays. $134 double in winter, including breakfast and dinner.

La Toc. Cunard Trafalgar complex, about a ten-minute drive from Castries. Located on a beach cove, this 100-acre resort includes a 150-room hotel, and fifty villas privately owned and rented as a whole or in sections. The lively decor in the pool-level informal dining spot gives an almost Mexican feeling. The action on the beach includes Sunfish, snorkeling, etc. Championship tennis courts are lighted for night play. Nine-hole golf course around the premises. $30 million has been put into making this resort luxurious. Two pools, one at the hotel and a more exclusive one for villa renters. Bar and restaurant service. Hotel rooms run $150–190 double in winter, $89–109 double EP off-season. Villas run $175–220 double EP in winter, $105–170 off-season.

Malabar Beach. Comfortable cottage colony at the end of Vigie runway, on the beach. Sixty-eight rooms in one area, eighteen cottages along the shore. Swimming pool. The formal restaurant with candlelight is water-side; cocktail terrace is so much "on the water" that it is sometimes in it. Stands at one end of Vigie Beach (The Red Lion Beach Inn at the other). $110–130 double EP in winter; $160–175 double off-season, including all three meals.

Red Lion Beach Inn. This pleasant property was formerly the Halcyon Sands Hotel. Just 57 rooms set in three acres of gardens on Vigie Beach. New Tudor-style pub; nice restaurant; evening entertainment; swimming pool; water-sports. Rates run $60–80 double EP in winter; $55–75 double off-season.

The St. Lucian Hotel. Formerly the Holiday Inn, with 185 air-conditioned rooms with balconies in a two-story complex. Still all the usual HI comforts, with coffee shop and restaurants, dancing, entertainment, tennis, and all water-sports. $128–140 double EP in winter; lower rates off-season.

Villa Hotel. West Indian home turned inn, with eighteen rooms, some of them air-conditioned. On the road up the Morne, overlooking Castries. Open-air dining room, comfortable bar area. Typically West Indian, in the old style. $65 double EP in winter; $36 double off-season.

HOME RENTALS. For information about furnished homes for rent, write to *Rent-a-Home,* Box 337, Castries, St. Lucia, or to *Happy Homes,* Box 12, also in Castries. *La Toc Village* is the largest apartment operation, with daily rates for two at $120 during the winter season. In Canada, *World Wide Villa Vacations,* 44 King St., West, Toronto M5H 1G8 lists them and plans week-long packages. In the U.S., contact *Caribbean Home Rentals,* P.O. Box 710, Palm Beach, Fla. 33480. *Villa Beach Apartments* have 5 self-contained units. *Morne Fortune Apartments* have 1-bedroom units as well as 1- and 2-bedroom units suitable for 4 people.

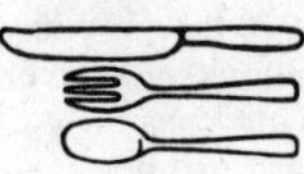

RESTAURANTS. The resort hotels serve, of the local foods: *langouste* (local lobster) cooked any way you can get it, and *lambi* (conch), fresh fish, breadfruit, and other local vegetables. There's a Creole touch to the local cooking. We call $7–14 *Moderate,* $15 and up *Expensive.*

The Coal Pot, on Vielle Ville Bay, a curve in Castries harbor reached by a road down the side of the Vigie runway, is an attractive, expensive dining spot. Reservations are essential. The place seats 28 and is a source of information about yachting and a second home for visiting yachtsmen. Good for lunch, cocktails, and candlelight dinner. (Expensive.) Onion and *calaloo* soups are featured at lunch; lobster and flying fish for dinner.

Green Parrot, on Red Tape Lane a 20-minute wiggly drive up to Morne Fortune, serves good local food and steak. (Expensive.) The *Calabash* restaurant, in new quarters, takes special care in preparing interesting dishes and charges about $2.75 E.C. for lunch. *Rain* is the most popular in-town eatery, with a Somerset Maugham South Seas atmosphere in its Kelly green-trimmed white building on one side of the main Columbus Square. This place serves an assortment of sandwiches and local foods at moderate prices. *Le Boucan* restaurant, a new in-town spot, has a sidewalk café and offers good food at moderate prices.

The Still, attractive setting on the outskirts of Soufriere, is a popular lunch stop for groups from boat trips or hotels. Reservations are essential for dinner since the place does not open if there are not more than 10 people coming. Note the turtles in the water tank by the parking lot, and the spice drying racks (still used). (Moderate.) The *Ruins* at Soufrière, built around a backyard fig tree, trimmed with conch shells and serving mouth-watering West Indian specialties, is worth the trip to the south. "Pepper Pot" and fried plantain are two local items worth trying.

NIGHT LIFE. Centers mostly on hotels, with the *Halcyon* spots and the *St. Lucian Hotel* vying for action honors. The pace slows considerably during summer months, but winter is resort-festive. For disco fans, *Lucifer's* is the most popular spot on the island. The other, which also swings until the early hours is at the Vale Country Club. Ask for the names of the current in-town action spots if you want a local evening; otherwise go to bed and make the days count.

SHOPPING. Specialties for St. Lucia include the unique silkscreen designs at *Bagshaw's.* We're not impressed by the styling and recommend buying the shift-kits and taking it to your hometown dressmaker or whipping it up yourself. Men's sport shirts are good buys. Linen table mats in tropical flower and bird designs make nice gifts, as do cocktail napkins, shopping bags, and other items. The studio is well posted, en route from Castries to La Toc.

The resort hotels have boutiques, namely *La Toc, Cariblue, Halcyon, St. Lucian,* with some preselected tropical items of interest to visitors.

In Castries, shops are mostly for the St. Lucians, and the special items of interest to visitors are mingled with the home-owners' stock, making quick shopping difficult. Crystal and china are available at *Danish House* on Mongiraud St., a step or two from Micoud St., and *DeLima* on Wm. Peter Blvd.

The Shipwreck Store, one of the franchise chain that speckles the Caribbean, says it carries "things made only in St. Lucia and the West Indies. We have nothing in our shop from Brooklyn, Japan, Hong Kong, Hoboken, or Denmark (not that we have anything against the Danes)." Bowls and beads vie for shelf space with books and other items. Warri boards for that Caribbean seed game are available here; so are tables of local woods.

The *Home Industries* shop on Jeremie Street has the best prices for straw hats, bags, sandals, sisal rugs, and the now popular flour-sack shirts. They can make to order if you give them enough (two days) warning.

Noah's Arkade has straw items, wood work, some simple caftans and other clothes, and a great selection of English import books for beach reading.

If you drive up the Morne, make the effort to find *Design St. Lucia.* Prices were high, we thought, but some of the designs are interesting enough to warrant them, even though the tailoring is not.

SPORTS AND OTHER ACTIVITIES. St. Lucia is coming into its own as a *yachting* harbor. Always popular Marigot Bay has now been joined by two other harbors, that at Rodney Bay in the north and additional facilities at Castries.

There are *golf* courses at Cap Estate, the northern tip of the island, with a club house and greens fees of $5. Golf is also available at La Toc. (9-holes). $7.50 greens fees.

Tennis is available at hotels as noted and through the St. Lucia Tennis Club. Your hotel can make the arrangements for the club.

Fishing for barracuda, mackerel, kingfish, etc. is possible by day or longer. 23-foot speedboats for 6 people are about $12 per hour; deep-sea fishing is $125 full day; $75 half-day.

There's a *Trekking Centre* at Cariblue. Your hotel can make arrangements.

Of course, there's *swimming* at all the west coast beaches, with rugged surf on the east coast (Atlantic), not recommended for anyone but a pro who is smart enough to go with an experienced companion.

The mid-portion of St. Lucia has plenty of trails to *walk-hike,* and *climbers* will want to tackle the Pitons.

ST. MARTIN/SINT MAARTEN

Wooden Shoes and Blue Berets

St. Martin/Sint Maarten, which measures just thirty-seven square miles, is a dual international pleasure island that is half Dutch and half French—the smallest territory in the world that is shared by two sovereign states. In addition to its dozens of beaches, it offers the "Dutch touch" which sparkles in town and at the gambling casinos, and the French flair which dominates the cuisine even at the tiniest bistro.

History

Columbus supposedly discovered the island on St. Martin's Day in 1493. He called it San Martin and sailed on to other islands, having had a taste of Carib reception committees elsewhere. The French and Dutch began small settlements from 1631 to 1633, and French pirates made their mark on the island community in 1638. The Spanish dropped by briefly in 1640, the same year that the Dutch were digging into permanent settlements on San Martin under the leadership of Peter Stuyvesant, who lost his leg during the skirmish.

In 1648, according to local legend, French and Dutch prisoners of war, brought to the island to destroy the Spanish fort and buildings, came from their hiding places after the Spaniards had been routed from the island and realized that they had an island to share. They agreed to divide the island by peaceable means and registered their plan with the Dutch colony that was then in authority on nearby Statia and with the French government of Guadeloupe. The oft-told story goes that the frontier was defined by a walking contest. A Frenchman and a Dutchman, starting at the same spot, walked around the island in opposite directions. It was agreed that the boundary line would be drawn straight across the island where they met. The Frenchman walked faster, but the Dutch portion, though smaller, turned out to be more valuable, thanks to the important salt ponds. Local legend has it that the Frenchman's stroll was supplemented with potions of wine and that the Dutchman was slowed because of his own Dutch gin. No matter what the reasons were for the division, in 1948 the islanders unveiled a ceremonial plaque at the border, commemorating 300 years of harmonious coexistence. There are no barriers, no customs inspectors, no formalities–simply a hand-painted sign, "Bienvenue Partie Française," as you head into the French portion on either of the two roads that thread the border crossing. Nowhere else in the world do two countries maintain their entirely different local customs (and holidays) on an area as small as this one.

EXPLORING ST. MARTIN/SINT MAARTEN

The Dutch portion of the island is the southern segment, overlooking the peak that is Saba and the island of St. Barts. What was once a big, beautiful, landlocked bay in the western portion of the island, Simson Bay Lagoon, has now been opened to the sea on both the Dutch and French sides, turning the lagoon into a favored harbor and a pleasant (and protected) day sailing area. Sailors who plan to make this lagoon a landfall should be sure to make arrangements to get in. The drawbridges on both sides are opened irregularly, if at all, and usually only on the French side. Nevertheless, the metamorphosis of the lagoon finds it now a water-sports haven.

Just over 13,000 people inhabit the 16 square miles on the Dutch side. The island, indented by several superb bays, has a hilly heartland, with Sentry Hill rising to a peak of 1200 feet. Philipsburg, the diminutive capital, is one of the most oddly situated towns in the area. It's strung out on a sandbar like a string of coral beads between Great Bay (the main harbor) and Great Salt Pond, part of which has now been reclaimed for expansion of the town. A desalinization plant, to provide much-needed fresh water, was completed in 1970, and today's modern hotels have potable water from the tap.

The French side of the island is 21 square miles and has a population of 12,000. You can drive along good roads from one capital to the other in 20 minutes and will find it amazing in this two-country island that the customs of each native land have remained entirely separate but equal. They share only each other's holidays–which means that many shops are closed most of the time!

There is excellent food on the French side, in bistros reminiscent of the Mediterranean shore. Fresh fish is plucked from the sea and served in style, with wine (which is expensive).

As for touring the French side, the roads are not as good when you leave the "beaten path," but they do bump and jolt along to some spectacular seaside coves and beaches. There are places where you will find small fishing villages, untouched thus far by the tourism that is tramping rapidly over the Dutch side of the island. At the fishing villages on the east shore, you can bargain for a small boat, with boatman, to take you to places such as offshore Ilet Pinel, with palm-fringed beach, for a picnic lunch you've had packed by your hotel. Be sure, however, to keep your boatman on call; it's a long swim home!

For the less adventuresome, a tour through the village of *Grand Case,* where a handsome new beach club resort and about 15 restaurants and bistros dot the shore, will lead eventually to *Marigot,* the small capital city.

One of the most noteworthy sights of the French side is the modern "ghost town" that was the resort dream of Claude Phillipe, erstwhile maitre d' at the Waldorf and other swanky New York spots. He was building the resort par excellence in the Caribbean more than 15 years ago. Several sieges of bankruptcy and legal tangles created the sight of a group of half-finished Mediterranean-style units that sit, unoccupied, awaiting their fate.

A DAY ON YOUR OWN

Motoring is one of the delights of uncrowded, lightly trafficked, relaxed St. Martin. Plan to spend an entire day poking into and around the constantly changing scenery.

You'll probably want to stop for a swim and a picnic, so head out early, and watch the tiny island come to life. Westward, the road begins a steep, winding ascent and sweeping views of the sea appear. From the overlook between Cay Bay and Cole Bay you'll see Saba, St. Eustatius and Anguilla rising in the distance.

Cay Bay Beach is little changed since Peter Stuyvesant lost his limb to a cannonball in 1644 during an unsuccessful landing to take St. Martin from the Spanish.

Begin your tour at the ruins of seventeenth-century Fort Amsterdam, built by the Dutch to protect their turf from the Spanish and the French. After that the road winds into the valley of Cul de Sac, where sugar, tobacco and indigo plantations flourished in the eighteenth and nineteenth centuries. Further along is the island's oldest cemetery.

An invisible border between Dutch Sint Maarten and French St. Martin runs through the middle of Simson Bay Lagoon. Sailors and water skiers crisscross its calm waters, heedless of sovereignty. Beyond is the French capital, Marigot, and the island's famous ghostly complex, the uncompleted resort of La Belle Creole, still compelling in the grandeur of its builder's dream.

Then the road drops to the lowlands, where a swing bridge opens to admit yachts to the lagoon. Five minutes away are Mullet and Maho Bays, two of the island's best beaches. Stop at either one for a leisurely swim.

Note the obelisk marking the border between the Dutch and

French sides of the island. To the left is the sign "Welcome to Sint Maarten," on the right "Bienvenue Partie Francaise" (Welcome to the French side). There are no customs officials, only cows grazing in the meadows.

On past the stone ruins of an old plantation house is Marigot, where West Indian gingerbread houses with wrought iron balconies line the street. There are bistros all along the shore, and the waterfront is the site of a colorful Saturday morning market.

Several steep hills separate Marigot from Grand Case, a tiny fishing village with a fine beach and about 15 restaurants serving French or Creole food. Or, if you have the time, stop at French Cul de Sac, where a fisherman will take you over to uninhabited Pinel Key for a swim and a picnic.

The only indication of crossing back to the Dutch side is a small marker. (Here another optional side tour leads over a roller coaster road to the posh Oyster Pond Hotel and the new Dawn Beach complex.) The main road through Middle Region and Prince's Quarter looks down on the dikes of Great Salt Pond, no longer mined but once a source of wealth to the Dutch.

End your tour in Philipsburg, with its brightly colored Antillean houses and its modern boutiques overflowing with imported goods. Exploring Philipsburg is best done on foot and should be a separate day's outing.

PRACTICAL INFORMATION FOR ST. MARTIN/SINT MAARTEN

HOW TO GET THERE. By air: 707s and DC8s can slide into the Dutch side's Queen Juliana airport, joining the many small planes which have used the field for years. *American Airlines* has non-stop service between New York and St. Maarten. *American* also has a new daily flight: San Francisco–Dallas/Ft. Worth–San Juan–St. Maarten. *Eastern Airlines* flies in from Miami. Out of Puerto Rico, *Prinair,* and an assortment of small charter or infrequently scheduled services are operated. The flight time is about 1 hour from Puerto Rico. *LIAT* flies up from Antigua. *ALM* flies north from Aruba and Curaçao. *Winair* is the local carrier, based on St. Maarten and making scheduled flights to Saba, St. Eustatius and St. Barts. *Air Guadeloupe* flies several times daily from Juliana Airport to Pointe-à-Pitre, Guadeloupe, and several times daily from the small Grand Case Airport to St. Barts.

By sea. Cruise ships make St. Maarten a regular stop for shopping. They anchor in the harbor, coming in by tender to the main street of Philipsburg on the Dutch side. Among them are ships of the *Chandris, Costa, Cunard, Holland America, Home Lines* and *Royal Viking* lines.

FURTHER INFORMATION. Apply to the St. Maarten Tourist Information Office at 25 West 39th St., New York, N.Y. 10018; in Canada at 243 Ellerslie Ave., Willowdale, Toronto, M2N 1Y5. Or contact the French West Indies Tourist Board at 610 Fifth Ave., New York, N.Y. 10020. On St. Maarten, the Tourist Office is located on De Ruyterplein in the heart of Philipsburg.

ISLAND MEDIA. The most valuable information sheet for visitors is the *St. Maarten Holiday,* a 28-page orange-colored publication which lists all shops,

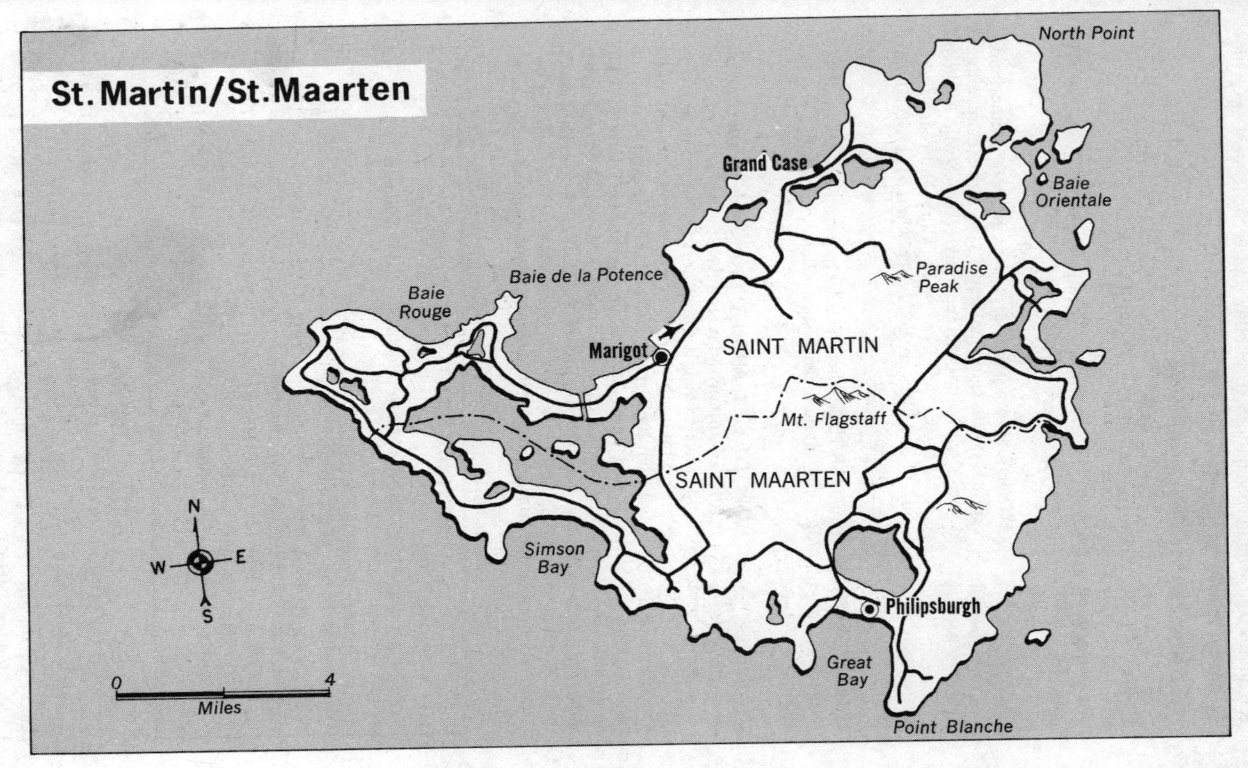
St. Martin/St. Maarten
North Point
Grand Case
Baie Orientale
Paradise Peak
Baie de la Potence
Baie Rouge
Marigot
SAINT MARTIN
Mt. Flagstaff
SAINT MAARTEN
Simson Bay
Philipsburgh
Great Bay
Point Blanche
N
W
E
S
0
4
Miles

restaurants and events. It's published monthly and is available free at the airport at any tourist office or at the hotels.

AUTHORIZED TOUR OPERATORS. Caribbean Holidays; Cavalcade Tours; Flyfaire; GoGo Tours; Butler Travels; Playtime Vacations; Travel Center Tours and Tour Tree International from the U.S.

PASSPORTS, VISAS. Some proof of citizenship is required—valid or outdated passport, birth certificate, voter's registration card. No visa needed.

MONEY. Most prices are given in both Netherlands Antilles florins (guilders) and $ U.S. The exchange fluctuates slightly, but the generally accepted rate is about 1.77 NAf to $1. 3.96 NAf = 1£. Although French francs are used on the French side, U.S. dollars are good everywhere. The U.S. dollar is worth about 6 francs.

TAXES AND OTHER CHARGES. There is a 5% government tax on hotel rooms on the Dutch side, a few on the French side. All visitors pay a $5 Juliana airport departure tax.

HOW TO GET ABOUT. Taxi service is government regulated: authorized taxis have St. Maarten Taxi Association stickers visible. Fares are 25% higher between 10 P.M. and midnight; 50% higher between midnight and 6 A.M. Car rentals can be booked at the airport, and picked up at your hotel. You can leave the car at the airport on departure. This is an easy island to drive around, but there's not much to see after you've checked out the French town of Marigot, driven through Grand Case, and browsed through the Philipsburg shops. A 1-day circle tour should take care of sightseeing.

One-day plane excursions to the nearby islands (Saba, Anguilla, Statia, St. Kitts and St. Barts) are easy.

WHAT WILL IT COST?

A typical day on St. Martin for *two* persons in season will run:

	US$	£
Accommodations at a beachfront hotel	120	65
Breakfast at the hotel	10	5
Lunch at a moderate in-town restaurant	15	8
Dinner at a moderate restaurant	30	16
Tips/service charges/hotel tax	15	8
One-day sightseeing by rental car	20	11
	$210	£113

EVENTS AND HOLIDAYS. The biggest celebrations here are St. Martin's Day on Nov. 11, Kingdom Day on December 15 and the Queen's Birthday on April 30. But don't forget Bastille Day (July 14), which is a dual celebration on this island. Other holidays are New Year's Day, Good Friday, Easter Monday, Labor Day (May 1), Ascension Day, Whit Monday, All Saint's Day (Nov. 1), Concordia Day (Nov. 11), Kingdom Day (Dec. 15), Christmas Day, and Boxing Day (Dec. 26).

STAYING IN ST. MARTIN/SINT MAARTEN

HOTELS. There are excellent accommodations all over the island. Francophiles will enjoy the Mediterranean-style facilities on the French side (St. Martin). The Dutch side (Sint Maarten) offers more of an American flair, which of course includes the casinos. We have divided them here, listing the Dutch side first.

HOTELS ON SINT MAARTEN

Belair Beach Hotel at Little Bay. Attractive property with 72 suites. Each has a master bedroom, smaller guestroom, two baths, kitchenette, and terrace or balcony. Spectacular dining around its indoor swimming pool. Friendly bar and small shopping arcade. Rates for the suites run $190–210 double EP in winter; $115–130 double off-season.

Caravanserai Hotel. Situated on a peninsula at Maho Bay, this resort inn has eighteen rooms in the "old" wing, plus thirty-two apartments in two-story units near the pool. Dining is on the terrace, evenings by candlelight, sometimes with musical entertainment. This place has grown, but still offers a lot for those who love the good life. There are two swimming pools, tennis court and beach. The only problem is that it's so close to the airport that the jet noises can sometimes be deafening. $150 double EP in winter; $90 double EP off-season.

Cupecoy Beach Club & Hotel. A beautiful new property with 165 rooms in one- and two-bedroom suites, many with a lovely sea view. Large freshwater swimming pool has a swim-up bar; two restaurants; cocktail lounge with piano bar; beautiful beach. Rates for rooms run from $125; one-bedroom suites from $165; two-bedroom suites are $400. Slightly less during the off-season.

Dawn Beach Hotel & Villas. There are 95 one-story villas here at Oyster Pond. Each has a living/bedroom, kitchenette, and private terrace. Long white-sand beach; swimming pool; open-air restaurant and bar. Tennis courts; watersports; and all the facilities of its sister hotel, Oyster Pond, nearby. $115 double EP in winter; $60 double off-season.

Holland House. 42 studios, all air-conditioned, with balconies and kitchenettes. Convenient location in the center of Philipsburg. $105–120 double EP in winter; $55–65 double EP off-season.

Little Bay Beach Hotel. On its own 1,000-foot beach, this 120-room property offers all the traditional Caribbean vacation pleasures including a gambling casino. Beachfront rooms are supplemented with other accommodations around the pool. Dining is indoors or on the terrace; steel band entertainment and beachside barbecues. Three tennis courts lighted for nightplay; freshwater swimming pool. Just one mile from Philipsburg. $130–160 double EP in winter; $75–95 double off-season.

Maho Reef and Beach Resort. Their 112 rooms and 35 lanai suites overlook the beach. Guests can dine outdoors pool-side, or indoors in the lavish, air-conditioned dining room. Entertainment includes swimming pool, beach, tennis courts, gambling casino, and nightly dancing and floor shows. In winter the MAP plan is mandatory here. Rates run $175 double with breakfast and dinner included. During the off-season, rates range from $56–80 double EP.

Mullet Bay Beach Hotel. 610 condominium units operated as a hotel, clustered around a beautiful eighteen-hole golf course. The best rooms, we feel, are those in two-story buildings 1 through 4 because they are near the restaurant, pool and casino. The beach is a seaside boardwalk away. There's a feeling of isolation from the other units, partly because they are spread over 170 acres and partly because the roving jitney takes its own time to make the circuit.

You'll walk miles here. In addition to the fine golf, there are eighteen tennis courts and arrangements for all watersports. Several restaurants to suit your dining choices, plus a commissary where you can buy your own snacks. $130 double EP in winter; $75 double EP off-season. One-bedroom suites run $170 in winter; $100 off-season.

Oyster Pond Hotel. A deluxe twenty-room resort where class is the image. Remarkable architecture, Moorish-style white stucco. All rooms have balconies, perfect for watching the pelicans dive. The club overlooks the Oyster Pond Lagoon and the sea. Peaceful interior courtyard, excellent restaurant, two tennis courts, and a long white sand beach. Watersports and marina facilities. $125–170 double EP in winter; $66–76 double EP off-season.

Pasanggrahan. A special inn right in Philipsburg, this guest house has held onto its simple charms while never forgetting that the government once set it aside for visiting royalty. Twenty-five double rooms with private bath in two pavillions along the beach. $96 double in winter, including two meals.

Sint Maarten Beach Club Hotel & Casino. New, luxurious property with 78 apartments all in the heart of Philipsburg. Most are one-bedroom suites ($140–160 for two); also two-bedroom suites available for four at $250–300 per day. Their own beach and gambling casino.

Summit Hotel. On a bluff overlooking Simson Beach, this informal resort sits like a Monopoly-house cluster on a hill. Simple construction, A units on first floor, B on second, and all seventy units connected by a boardwalk. Good view from the pool and dining area. The beach is nearby, but not that easily accessible. $84–94 double EP in winter; $40–50 double EP off-season.

HOME RENTALS. There are thirty or more private homes and villas with one to five bedrooms available on or close to the beaches. Contact Caribbean Home Rentals, P.O. Box 710, Palm Beach, Fla. 33480. For a full listing of guest houses and apartments, contact the Sint Maarten Tourist Information Office at 25 West 39th St., New York, N.Y. 10018.

HOTELS ON ST. MARTIN

Beausejour Hotel. In Marigot, and owned by the same people who manage La Calanque Restaurant one block away. Ten air-conditioned rooms with shower and refrigerator. Breakfast is served on the outdoor terrace. From $35–45 double all year, including Continental breakfast.

Coralita Beach Hotel. On Baie Lucas, this fifty-room charmer has its own secluded bay, two restaurants which feature French and Creole cuisine, a swimming pool with sundeck, and a floodlit tennis court. Down at the beach guests have free beach chairs and umbrellas and can also rent snorkeling equipment. $68 double EP in winter; $40 double EP off-season.

Grand Case Beach Club. Brand new resort located on a secluded beach. 48 air-conditioned units, which include studios, one-bedroom apartments and two-bedroom townhouses, all with kitchenettes. Tennis court, watersports, car rental. Rates in high season run $95 for studios; $135–165 for apartments; $190–220 for a townhouse.

Le Galion Beach Hotel. Just over the border, this forty-five-room resort has not one beach, but two (the second is the only one on the island where "bathing in the buff" is permitted). The rooms are large; the main dining area is modern and open to the sea breezes. Small swimming pool, watersports, including scuba, tennis court, and a disco for late-night entertainment. $110–150 double EP in winter; $60–85 off-season.

Le Pirate Hotel. An inn that's been "in" for years, entirely refurbished a short time ago. The guests like the casual, independent atmosphere, and being right on the water, on the outskirts of Marigot. The restaurant here is very special, with the cuisine definitely fabulous-French. $110 double MAP in winter; $40 double EP off-season.

La Samanna. Exquisite, expensive, and a perfect hideaway for those who want peace and quiet in an elegant Mediterranean-style resort. The main building has fourteen twin-bedded rooms. The villas have suites—sixteen two-bedroom units, and six villas with two bedrooms each. This is a beautiful and well-kept property, with a long and secluded beach. The pool has all the lounge chairs and the proper umbrellas for shading and dining that you would expect. The dining room offers the best Gallic fare and a terrace with a view. Two tennis courts, watersports. Rooms, apartments and villas run anywhere from $180–825, depending upon choice of accommodation. Many of the villas have three bedrooms, which house six people.

PLM St. Tropez Beach Hotel. A large, white stucco building with 130 rooms done to give an airy, cosmopolitan, and Mediterranean feeling. Each room has a balcony. The dining room is shoreside, the Byblos disco behind it is congenial. The swimming pool is properly set in the center of it all. There is a tennis court with lights for nightplay, but the *Marigot Nautic Sports* watersports center on the beach is more of a highlight. $72–117 double EP in winter; $37–52 double off-season.

HOME RENTALS. For apartments, homes or villas, contact Mrs. Janet Nichols, at St. Martin Real Estate, Marigot, St. Martin, F.W.I., or St. Maarten Rentals, Pelican House, Beacon Hill, St. Maarten, Netherlands Antilles. In the U.S. check with St. Martin Assistance Service Homes, 1995 New York Ave., Huntington Station, N.Y. 11746 or AT HOME ABROAD, 405 East 56th St., New York, N.Y. 10022.

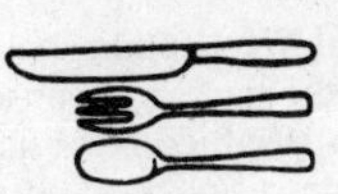

RESTAURANTS. An added bonus to staying on an island that is half-Dutch and half-French is the wide selection of restaurants and the variety of fare. Everything from Dutch rijsttafel to French bouillabaisse is available, along with Creole and seafood dishes. We call $12 and under *Inexpensive;* $13–24 *Moderate;* $25 and above per person *Expensive.*

On the Dutch Side

Antoine's. Fine dining in the heart of Philipsburg in a special spot facing the harbor. Excellent French fare served in an elegant setting. *Expensive.*

Bali Hai. One of the island's newest, this restaurant is set in a restored 250-year-old plantation house. Terrace dining with traditional *rijsttafel* the specialty. *Moderate.*

Bilboquet. Well worth the trip to Pointe Blanche. A nice variety with ever-changing menus offering Continental, International and Caribbean specialties. *Moderate.*

Caravanserai. Located on Maho Bay, dining here is ideal. Famous for their *rijsttafel* on Wednesdays and their Champagne Brunch on Sundays. *Expensive.*

Chesterfield's. Excellent seafood, served on an indoor/outdoor pierside terrace overlooking Great Bay. *Moderate.*

Deli. Just what the name implies, with lox and bagels, thick pastrami and hot corned beef sandwiches. Located at the Mullet Bay Beach Hotel. *Inexpensive.*

Dragon Phoenix. They call this the place where "East meets West at the head of town." On Back St. in Philipsburg. Full Chinese cuisine, local seafood, and U.S. prime steaks. *Moderate.*

L'Escargot. In a townhouse on Front St., with roast duckling, sweetbreads, crêpes, omelets and snails as part of its fine French cuisine. *Expensive.*

Garden Cafe. Great luncheon spot in the tropical garden at the edge of the beach behind the Pasanggrahan Hotel. *Inexpensive.*

La Grenouille. So French, but located in the Dutchman's Walk in Philipsburg. Everything is truly French, from the imported oysters and wines to the homemade pastries. *Expensive.*

Le Pavillon. A tiny and intimate restaurant on the beach in Simson Bay village. French and Creole specialties. *Moderate.*

The Rusty Pelican. In-town, casual place for fresh fish or chili served in a nautical atmosphere. *Inexpensive.*

West Indian Tavern. Pub-like atmosphere and garden on the inland side of Front Street. Local lobster is the highlight here. *Moderate.*

On the French Side

Chez Lolotte. Traditional dishes representing both French and Creole schools of cooking are the attractions of this enclosed tropical garden restaurant in the heart of Marigot. Reservations recommended. *Expensive*

Chez Rene. Casual dining for 20 guests on a beachside terrace, and formal dining for about 40 more in the smartly done interior. Bouillabaisse is a specialty, as are rack of lamb, turtle steak, plus fish prepared in a variety of ways. *Expensive.*

La Calanque. Superior restaurant on the wharf in Marigot, with excellent French cuisine. *Expensive.*

L'Aventure. A lovely place for dining on the open-air balcony overlooking the harbor, or indoors in a candlelit atmosphere. *Expensive.*

La Vie En Rose. Second-floor restaurant that is reminiscent of Paris as it was in the Twenties. Creative and varied French menu. *Expensive.*

Le Santal. A luxurious, elegant seaside setting with fine crystal and stylish pink-and-white table décor. Superbly prepared classic French cuisine. Reservations suggested. *Expensive.*

Maison Sur le Port. This special restaurant in a typical West Indian home has a spacious terrace, perfect for cocktails overlooking the harbor at sunset. Varied menu, with huge salads and guacamole the house specialties. *Moderate.*

Chez Max. A rôtisserie on the rue Felix Eboué. The decor looks eccentric and a bit thrown together, but the cuisine is pure island Creole. A bowl of spicy hot Bello pepper is on every table. *Inexpensive.*

Other "over the beach" seaside dining spots include *Le Fish Pot,* where bouillabaisse is featured, along with excellent seafood dishes *(Moderate);* and the *Rainbow Cafe,* for seaside dining at the edge of Grand Case Bay *(Moderate).*

NIGHTLIFE. Most of what there is in the evening centers on the casinos and supper clubs at the Sint Maarten Beach Club; the Maho Reef & Beach Resort; and the Little Bay-Belair, Great Bay, and Mullet Bay hotels. There are also discos for late-nighters, such as the *Le Byblos* in the PLM St. Tropez; the *Admiral's Club* on Front St. at the head of town in Philipsburg; *The Last Dance,* next door to the L'Escargot Restaurant; and the *Hillside Disco Club* at Mullet Bay.

SHOPPING. The island is a treasureland for shoppers, where they'll find an excellent selection of duty-free items, as well as interesting locally made handicraft. Find lovely old Dutch silver, Delftware, crystal, cameras and perfumes at much less than U.S. prices.

In Philipsburg, you'll find branches of well-known Curaçao shops such as *Spritzer* and *Fuhrmann, Yellow House, Penha* and *Kan,* each with wide selections and special values. Fine imports in the fashion category can be found at *St. Trop' Boutique, Windward Islanders, La Romana Boutique,* and *Sylvia's Fashion Habit.* Fabrics by the yard, luggage, and even Scandinavian furniture is available at Continental. Fine jewelry set with genuine gemstones, watches, and other less expensive jewelry are specialties at *The Beehive. Julio's Smoke-'n-Booze* lets you sample liquor before buying and also carries an impressive array of cigars. And, for something useful that will also serve as a conversation piece, don't miss the *Batik Caribe.* There you'll find (and become acquainted with) the "pareu," a length of fabric that can be twisted and turned in at least a dozen ways to become a beach wrap, a flowing skirt, or an evening ensemble, all in a minute or two. For other selections, try *Albert's Store* for fine linens, or *Around the Bend,* for those made locally. *Boolchand's, Gulhomar's, Taj Mahal* and *Kohinoor* are Indian shops carrying a variety of articles, including hand-drawn and embroidered table linens.

On the French side, at Marigot, the shops are legion–small and fully stocked, especially with a perfume selection that seems endless. Visit the *Handmade Boutique* for local items, and, at Grand Case, don't miss *Pierre Lapin,* a superior boutique. Also at Grand Case is *L'Atelier,* an interesting shop for handmade ceramics and straw goods, cane furniture. A potter's wheel is available.

SPORTS AND OTHER ACTIVITIES. There is a fine eighteen-hole *golf* course at Mullet Bay, but *tennis* is special here, with dozens of courts across the island, and many of them lighted for nightplay. Most of the hotels offer *snorkeling* equipment and *scuba* lessons with equipment, and can also arrange *deep-sea fishing* trips in search of wahoo, marlin, bonito and dolphin. Check with *Maho Water Sports,* which has its headquarters at the Mullet Bay Beach Hotel, or with *Water Sports Unlimited* at the Holland House or Sint Maarten Beach Club on the Dutch side. For water sports on the French side, check with *Marigot Nautic Sports* at the PLM St. Tropez or the scuba and watersports center at *Le Galion Hotel.* They all offer a selection of water sports activities at reasonable prices.

Cruising to nearby islands is also ideal. One option is to take the 36-foot trimaran *Tryst* over to St. Barts for a full-day trip at $35 per person, including open bar. From Philipsburg, the 57-foot *Maison Maru* provides an idyllic way to see the entire island from the sun deck. During the cruise, the boat stops in Marigot for shopping; at a private beach for swimming; and anchors offshore for a buffet luncheon. $30 per person.

ST. VINCENT AND THE GRENADINES

The Breadfruit Isle and Its Sun-kissed Satellites

This area is one of the "finds" in the Caribbean. St. Vincent and its Grenadines offer some of the best sailing, swimming, and snorkeling, some of the most interesting flora and fauna, a volcano to climb, whaling villages where the pursuit is carried on as it has been for centuries–from long boats sent out when the school is running–and comfortable inns with personality, good food, and pleasant staff.

St. Vincent is eighteen miles long by eleven miles wide, and has a population of about 100,000, some of whom, descendants of the original Caribs, live in the north on the sides of the volcano. It lies twenty-one miles south of St. Lucia, which you can see clearly from the northern part of the island, and ninety-five miles due west of Barbados, which most likely will be your junction for getting there. The "tail" of the comet of St. Vincent is a string of islands and cays that splays south from Bequia, Petit Nevis, Isle Quatre, and Pigeon Island to Battowia, Balliceaux, Mustique, Canouan, Mayero (with its Tobago Cays), Palm Island, Petit St. Vincent and Union Island. Below that lie the other Grenadines, those that are linked to Grenada. The entire sparkling collection of them are havens for sailors and those in search of the barefoot life.

Sometimes called the "Breadfruit Isle," because Captain Bligh first introduced the tree here from Tahiti, St. Vincent produces this along with coconut and arrowroot, bananas, sea island cotton, and an array of other tropical fruits and vegetables best seen in the market place in Kingstown, or where they grow on the slopes of Mesopotamia Valley. Even though it is the most English of the British Windward Islands,

St. Vincent maintains a strong thread of French influence. You need only glance at your map—Chateaubelair, Grand Bonhomme, Petit Bonhomme—to see that the island has a dual personality. They too have a Mt. Soufrière. So many volcanic mountains in the West Indies have the name Soufrière that some travelers have been misled into believing that this is the French word for volcano. (Actually, it means sulphur mine.)

St. Vincent's Soufrière has behaved badly. On May 6, 1902, it put the island on the map by killing 2,000 inhabitants in a major eruption. All was quiet for the next seventy years, and Soufrière was classified as "semi-dormant," even though rumblings in late 1971 bubbled up a new island in the middle of the crater lake. Now we're not sure of its classification, since a major eruption in April 1979 put the island back on page one.

History

Discovered by Columbus on St. Vincent's Day in 1498, the island remained the undisputed possession of the Carib Indians until 1627. The fierce, war-loving Caribs had been here for several generations before Columbus, having arrived from the South American mainland and exterminated the gentle Arawaks. The Caribs fought off all would-be colonists with such fury that St. Vincent was declared a neutral island by French and British agreement in 1748. Ceded to the British in 1763, it was captured by the French in 1779, restored to the British by the Treaty of Versailles in 1783. On October 27, 1979, St. Vincent and the Grenadines gained full independence from Great Britain.

EXPLORING ST. VINCENT

Kingstown, the island's capital, has a vivid and vibrant Saturday market that sprawls in and around the area at the end of town. The array of fruits and vegetables, a technicolor panorama, is enhanced by the weekly loading of the banana boats.

On a day-to-day basis, Kingstown's Botanic Gardens, which were founded in 1765, are its main attraction. Its chief topic of conversation is a breadfruit tree grown from the original seed brought from Tahiti by Captain Bligh of "Mutiny on the Bounty" fame. The Gardens have other magnificent and unusual trees, such as the Cannon Ball and the Sealing Wax Palm. Kingstown itself is as English in character and spirit as its name. Some of the nineteenth-century houses are reminiscent of those seen in the quiet streets of London's Mayfair or Chelsea.

St. George's Cathedral and the Methodist Church are symbols of Anglican England, transported bell, book and candle to the tropics. St. Mary's Roman Catholic Church is a strange and wonderful example of eclectic ecclesiastical architecture, with Romanesque arches, Gothic spires, and delicate embellishments that are somewhat Moorish in design. The result is a fascinating, somewhat eerie maze of balconies, battlements, turrets and courtyards that can be explored with the permission of the Canadian priests in charge. The original church was built in 1823, enlarged in 1877, again in 1891, then renovated in 1935. It is one of the highlights of the capital city.

Don't miss the view from Fort Charlotte, 600 feet above the city. You can see Kingstown, the harbor, and the Grenadines lacing through the gentle Caribbean sea.

At the opposite end of Kingstown, on the road to the airport, the St. Vincent Craftsmen Government Handicraft Centre operates in one of the island's most picturesque buildings, the cotton ginnery. This project has centers in villages around the island, where the local people perfect their native handicrafts to sell in today's residential and tourist market.

Of St. Vincent's 400 miles of road, only about 200 are paved, and these stick to the edge of the island. A trip north of Kingstown up the leeward coast is notable for splendid scenery and lovely little fishing ports like Layou and Barrouallie. The former has one of the Carib Stones, huge sacrificial altars with carved heads; the latter is the headquarters for local whaling.

Be sure to visit the Falls of Baleine, at the northern end of the island, to admire its beautiful sixty-foot cascade, or drive through the Mesopotamia Valley to the agricultural heart of St. Vincent, which takes in twenty-eight miles of rural beauty. Actually, the official name for this lovely stretch is the Marriaqua Valley, and Mesopotamia is only one of its villages. What you're looking for is the lush valley, and different maps chart it differently.

A DAY ON YOUR OWN

There are several choices. You can boat over to one of the islands in the Grenadines. For the explorer, climbing and hiking is the "in" thing to do. Don't bother with a bathing suit, but pack a picnic lunch and be sure you're outfitted in a sturdy, cool, hiking costume. You'll find the view as spread out and spectacular as your picnic.

There are three popular St. Vincent rendezvous for those who like to climb. The easiest is Dorsetshire Hill, about three miles from Kingstown, with a sweeping scope of the capital and its harbor. Mount St. Andrew, on the outskirts of the city, involves a pleasant climb on a well-marked trail through a rain forest. Mt. Soufrière is for the young in heart if not in body, but the view, with all St. Vincent and the Caribbean at your feet, is worth the effort of the climb. The trip begins by car along the windward coast, crosses the famed Rabacca dry river and continues on to the Bamboo Forest. From there you'll have to hoof it uphill for about two hours. The summit is 4,048 feet, or 3/4 of a mile, straight up.

The Grenadines

There are almost 100 islands, some no more than specks on the map, almost all of them perfect for picnics, snorkeling, scuba diving,

St. Vincent
CARIBBEAN SEA
Fancy
Falls of Baleine
Crater Lake
Chateaubelair
Georgetown
Barrouallie
Layou
Biabou
Mesopotamia
Ft. Charlotte
Kingstown
Stubbs
Young I.
Calliaqua
N
W
E
S
0
5
Miles

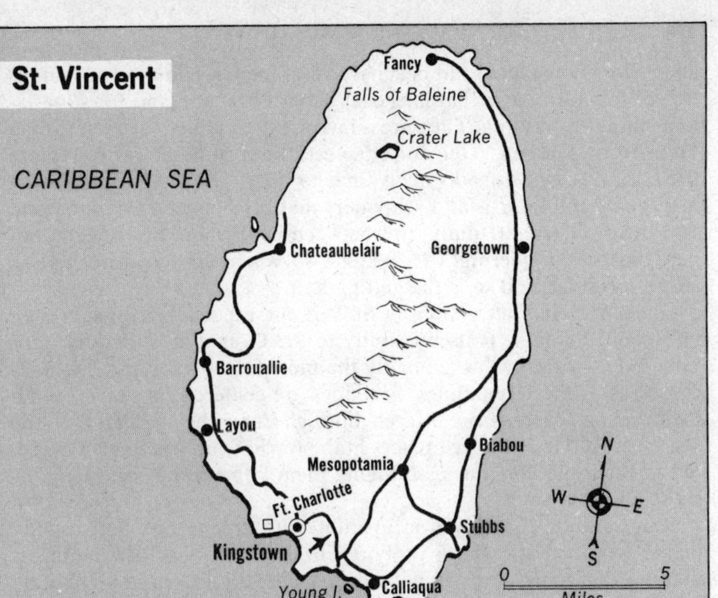

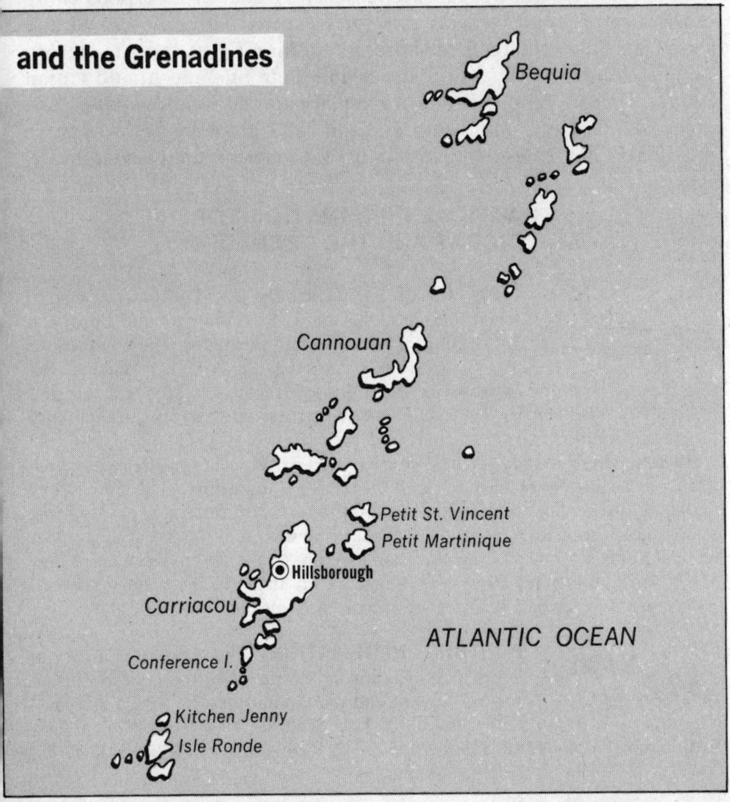

and the Grenadines
Bequia
Cannouan
Petit St. Vincent
Petit Martinique
Hillsborough
Carriacou
ATLANTIC OCEAN
Conference I.
Kitchen Jenny
Isle Ronde

and sunning on white sand beaches. All of the Grenadines are famous for crystal-clear water that laps over superb beaches, and for superlative sailing and fishing. They are a favorite haunt of yachtsmen sailing south from Antigua. You don't have to be a millionaire to explore these islands, but you do need time to adapt your schedule to the mail-boats and inter-island schooners that ply between Grenada and St. Vincent. There are daily trips between Bequia and St. Vincent, but most boats stay overnight in Bequia, so you must too. Life here is island informal, and so is the getting here.

One of the chief attractions of St. Vincent, especially for yachtsmen and island hoppers, is its proximity to the Grenadines. Bequia, pronounced "Beck-way," is probably the most famous and most tourist-conscious of the Grenadines. Activities are centered on the sea, with the whaling season from March through June the highlight of the year. This is one of the last places in the world from which whalers set out to catch the "big ones," bringing them home to be sectioned offshore on Petit Nevis.

Boat building is a major occupation, with at least one hull usually in the works at the shore of Port Elizabeth. A boat christening is unique—don't miss it if you have the chance. It's a far more elaborate ceremony than that for a new child, and the revelry lasts until dawn.

Princess Margaret Beach, reached only by boat or a perilous climb down a rutted road, is a favorite for escapists. Three's a crowd and snorkelers enjoy the reefs offshore. In addition to the spots to stay on Bequia, there are resorts on Palm Island, Petit St. Vincent and Union Island. There is also a noteworthy place to stay on Mustique. The other islands have small, informal inns and guest houses which we mention in the section "Staying in St. Vincent and the Grenadines."

PRACTICAL INFORMATION FOR ST. VINCENT AND THE GRENADINES

HOW TO GET THERE. By air. The easiest way to reach these islands from U.S., Canadian, and European gateways is via Antigua and Barbados. The connections are via *LIAT* (Leeward Islands Air Transport). *LIAT* also flies to Mustique and Union Island in the Grenadines. *Mustique Airways* has daily flights from St. Vincent. There are private airstrips on Canouan and on Union Island which serve small planes.

By sea. There is daily ferry service between St. Vincent and Bequia, which takes just a little over an hour and costs $6 EC roundtrip. The *Seimstrand* mailboat also services the Grenadines from St. Vincent once a week, stopping at Bequia, Canouan, Carriacou, Mustique and Union Island. *Geest Lines* banana boats stop to pick up the island's crop, and a few passengers. A few cruise ships stop here, along with rugged craft that ply the waters between Kingstown and Barbados, and continue on through the Grenadines.

FURTHER INFORMATION. The Eastern Caribbean Tourist Association is the main source of information for St. Vincent and the Grenadines. In New York, contact them at 220 East 42nd St., New York, N.Y. 10017; in Canada, Place de Ville, Suite 1701, 112 Kent St., Ottawa, Ont. K1P5P2,

Canada; in Britain, at 200 Buckingham Palace Rd., London SW1W 9SP. On the island, visit the St. Vincent Tourist Board in Kingstown.

PASSPORTS, VISAS. U.S. and Canadian citizens require proof of identity; British citizens require a valid passport; all visitors must have a return or ongoing ticket.

MONEY. The Eastern Caribbean dollar (EC) is the local currency. $1 US = $2.70 EC; $6 EC = 1£.

TAXES AND OTHER CHARGES. All hotels add the 5% government tax; some add a service charge to your bill (10–15%). The airport departure tax is $10 EC per person.

HOW TO GET ABOUT. A few rental cars are available at approximately $20 US per day, but taxis suffice for most travel. If you don't have an International Driver's License, you'll need a temporary driver's license, which costs $5 EC. Remember to drive on the left. Taxi rates run from $25–30 EC per hour.

To get to and through the Grenadines, the best way is by charter yacht at your own speed. Caribbean Sailing Yachts has a "sail 'n learn" program and a fleet of specially built forty-four foot yachts ready for bare-boat or skippered charters out of St. Vincent. Also from St. Vincent are the home-built island schooners, which make the 1½-hour crossing to Bequia for $5 each way daily.

EVENTS AND HOLIDAYS. Independence Day on Oct. 27 and Carnival Tuesday, the first Tuesday in July, are the highlights. Other holidays are New Year's Day, Discovery Day (Jan.22), Good Friday, Easter Monday, Labor Day (May 1), Whit Monday, August Monday, Christmas Day, and Boxing Day.

WHAT WILL IT COST?

With the exception of the hotel on Young Island, $100 per day for *two* persons in winter will more than do it on St. Vincent. This includes all three meals and a rental car or full-day sightseeing by taxi for one day. As you've noted, the islands of the Grenadines can easily double that figure.

STAYING IN ST. VINCENT AND THE GRENADINES

HOTELS. St. Vincent is a gem if you're looking for the traditional West Indian island. Though the heights of luxury that exist on nearby islands have thus far eluded St. Vincent, so have the hordes of tourists. You can still enjoy the Caribbean life-style here, with good local food and clean, comfortable places to stay. On the Grenadines, you can find a cluster of unique personality inns that have no match other than those scattered throughout the British Virgin Islands.

HOTELS ON ST. VINCENT

Cobblestone Inn. In Kingstown, on the main street. Hard work (and lots of money) transformed this former sugar warehouse into an attractive inn, popular with overnighters who are heading into or out of the Grenadines, and for those who like to be at the center of things. The lobby is through a courtyard and up stairs, as are all twenty air-conditioned rooms. The first-floor dining room is a gathering place for visiting yachtsmen, etc. The cocktail area atop the three floors is a great place to sit and watch the sun go down, or to have lunch if there's food service there when you visit. $50 double all year, breakfast included.

Coconut Beach. On the beach, down the road from Grand View and Villa Lodge, this place offers ten rooms with a sea view. The decor in the rooms is blue and green, the atmosphere is beachside casual. Popular with Americans and Canadians who want informality in the sun. $60 double all year, breakfast and dinner included.

Grand View. Perched on a point about twenty minutes from Kingstown, this former home has eleven doubles and one single, all immaculate, always freshly painted, and with typical West Indian hospitality. Excellent food. The beach is down the hill. $69 double EP in winter; lower rates off-season.

Haddon. This place is adequate, the management is friendly, but the location on a hillside on the road to Kingstown leaves something to be desired. Fifteen rooms, simply furnished. The Tennis Club, with two asphalt courts, is across the street. Transportation is provided to nearby beaches. $46–50 double all year, two meals included.

Heron. One of the all-time greats insofar as West Indian guest-house life is concerned. There's nothing fancy. Overhead fans cool the Planter's Porch, where you can watch the activity of the Geest banana boat pier. The fifteen rooms are spartan, clean and neat, and most have a private bath. $46–50 double in winter, breakfast and dinner included.

Indian Bay Beach. Twelve units, with kitchens in most rooms. Popular with vacationing Canadians and others who seek the freedom apartment life offers. Right on the beach. Watersports available. $35 double EP in winter; $25 double EP off-season.

Mariner's Inn. Twenty rooms on Villa Beach, with a beach bar that is the congregating point not only for guests but for yachtsmen anchored in the harbor. This is a West Indian house, with rooms replete with antique four-posters and other typical touches. Popular with those who want barefoot informality. The food is good. A steel band plays during the week, and there's other nightly entertainment as well. $70–80 double in winter, $60–70 double off-season, breakfast and dinner included.

Ra-Wa-Cou. The ten cottage-style apartments all have fully equipped kitchens. Maid service is included, and cooks are available if you like. The open-sided dining room overlooks the swimming pool and a lovely, black-sand beach with rolling surf. Another highlight here is horseback riding. Locale is out of town, and a rental car is a good idea if you want to travel. $99 double in winter, $86 double off-season, two meals included.

Sunset Shores. Part of an ambitious plan for a resort complex that proved to be a bit ahead of its time for St. Vincent, the core now in existence is possibly the most hotel-like facility on the island. Twenty air-conditioned rooms with private patios. On the beach, with beach bar and view down the Grenadines, looking first at Young Island. $79 double in winter, $58 double off-season, breakfast and dinner included.

Villa Lodge. At the gate of the road to Grand View and down to Indian Bay Beach, this former home is a casual holiday spot. Eighteen air-conditioned rooms and a pleasant atmosphere. $70 double in winter, $50 double off-season, including two meals.

Young Island. On its own island, 600 feet offshore (constant boat service). The twenty-four cottages are tucked into the foliage and meander up the hillside. Each cottage has a living room/bedroom/bath, and an outdoor shower which is discreetly bambooed from view on the patio. The beach-side area has Sailfish and snorkel equipment. There's a pool in the foliage and tennis a good walk up the hill. Dining room with evening entertainment. The view, overlooking the jagged Vincentian skyline and the yachts at anchor in the harbor, is hard to beat. Informal and very congenial atmosphere. $205–235 double in winter, $125–145 double off-season, including breakfast and dinner.

Yvonette Beach Apartments. At Indian Bay, these twelve housekeeping apartments are linked in one meandering building. All have kitchen units, and all overlook Young Island. Two miles from Kingstown. $46 double EP in winter; from $20 double EP off-season.

HOTELS ON THE GRENADINES

BEQUIA

Frangipani. The family homestead of the former premier of St. Vincent and the Grenadines has six rooms in the main house, with bathrooms down the hall. Four modern rooms with private bath are in a separate building up the hill, for those who like a bit of luxury. A comfortable, casual inn. $70 double in winter, $50 double off-season, including breakfast and dinner.

Friendship Bay. Thirty rooms, the best of them at waterside, about a fifteen-minute drive out of town. Dining room overlooking the bay, which is a beauty; entertainment most evenings; tennis court; watersports. From $120 double in winter, from $80 double off-season, including two meals.

MUSTIQUE

Cotton House Hotel. The only place to stay on this island, but it is perfection. Several small houses hold the eleven twin-bedded rooms, which are clustered around the eighteenth-century main building. There is a cottage at l'Anescoy Bay, 1/4 mile from here, which has two bedrooms, bath, kitchen, sitting room and porch. Maid service. Ideal for a family. Swimming pool, tennis court, sailing, riding, snorkeling–a self-sufficient island inn. $250 double in winter, $150 off-season, breakfast and dinner included.

PALM ISLAND

Palm Island Beach Club. Cottages of island stone and open-air dining room put you into the Grenadine frame of mind. Twenty rooms with bath, but no hot water. The beach is fringed with coconuts which were planted by the owner as part of his personal reforestation program. Watersports include fishing, boating, snorkeling, and scuba at nearby Tobago Cays as well as offshore. One tennis court, for those who want to leave their "rustic" hideaway. $190 double in winter, $100 double off-season, with all three meals included.

PETIT ST. VINCENT

Petit St. Vincent Resort. Twenty-two private cottages, each with two queen-sized beds, private patio, and choice of beach or hillside location that stretches across 113 acres. Roving jeep for room service summoned by a yellow flag (no telephones). This is a hideaway with untarnished informality. The food is good, and the Thanksgiving Day buffet is a legend with yachtsmen. Tennis, badminton, croquet, horseshoes, Sunfish and other small sail boats available. The place is barefoot casual. $190 double in winter, $130 double off-season, including breakfast, lunch and dinner.

UNION ISLAND

Sunny Grenadines. With just seven rooms, this is a very casual, no-fuss kind of place where beachcombers and those who love to look at sunsets and the sea settle in happily. $60 double in winter, two meals included.

HOME RENTALS. *Caribbean Home Rentals,* P.O. Box 710, Palm Beach, Fla. 33480, carries listings in St. Vincent and the Grenadines, plus exclusive home listings on Mustique. Rates for Mustique are tops, at $850 per week for a luxurious villa. They also have two- and three-bedroom homes on Bequia that range from $200–300.

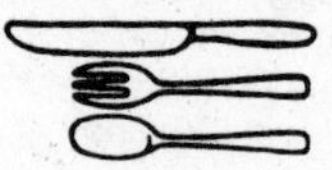

RESTAURANTS ON ST. VINCENT. This is an island on which to stay put. The best of the fine West Indian cuisine comes out of the hotel kitchens, so try everything on the menu–local fish, thick soups, island vegetables. You'll know just how fresh everything is if you make a trip into Kingstown and see the Saturday market in action. But even though your hotel food is good, make reservations ahead of time and sample the fare at the other hotels, especially the *Cobblestone* and *Heron.*

NIGHTLIFE. *The Aquatic Club* is the only real nightclub, and it's liveliest during the winter season. Some hotels have steel bands and sporadic entertainment, but these islands are for retiring early and greeting the sun in the morning.

SHOPPING. *Batik Caribe,* the name of the Stevenson's screen designs on sea island cotton, has an attractive shop next to the Shipwreck Shop on Kingstown's main street. Be sure to inquire about having clothes made–they can be ready in two or three days–at *Dan-Dans* a few doors down. Crystal, china and the like can be found at Stretchers, but they aren't a big item on this island. Handicrafts are, and all varieties of straw-made items are available at the *St. Vincent Craftsmen Shop.* You can see some of them being made. For grass rugs (be sure to measure your area at home first) try *Trotman's. The Shipwreck Shop* that has appeared all over the Caribbean is here too, with island-made items of various quality. In the Grenadines, browse at

The Crab Hole on Bequia, where you'll find flour-sack shirts and pants, shirts and wall hangings with island motifs, all of good design and high quality.

SPORTS AND OTHER ACTIVITIES. *Sailing* is the big thing, followed by all kinds of watersports. Various craft head south regularly through the Grenadines. Caribbean Sailing Yachts (CSY) (see our *Facts at Your Fingertips* section on Yacht Charters) offer "Sail-'n-Learn" programs. For other activities, play *tennis* at the Kingstown Tennis Club; play *golf* at the Aquaduct Golf Club; be a spectator at the cricket and soccer matches; or simply swim and snorkel to your heart's content.

TRINIDAD AND TOBAGO

Tranquility and Torrid Rhythm

Most southerly of the West Indies, these two islands became independent in August 1962. Trinidad is the seat of the government, while Tobago is its weekend resort. They could hardly be less alike. Trinidad is the teeming world in microcosm; Tobago is Crusoe's desert island. Trinidad is the Tower of Babel; Tobago is a tree house.

TRINIDAD

Once a part of the Spanish Main, Trinidad has the rough rectangular outline of a jigsaw puzzle piece; you can almost see where it should fit into Venezuela just a dozen miles away. The flora and fauna are not insular, but continental, thriving in complete indifference to the ageless caprices of the Orinoco. Nor is there anything insular about the people who live there. There is a rendezvous of races in Trinidad. In Port of Spain, the lively capital, East Indians throng the streets, rubbing elbows with Syrians and Lebanese, Chinese and Bengalese, half the races of the Near East and the Far. The thousand and one races of Trinidad include the English, Spanish, French, Dutch, Portuguese, Parsees, Madrassis, Americans, and Venezuelans, at peace after centuries of fighting for this rich island prize. You'll still find the last of the original Amerindian inhabitants, descendants of the Arawak and Carib Indians. And above all, the descendants of African slaves, now the creative force in politics and art. Their inherent sense of rhythm, which the planters tried to suppress by forbidding slaves to have drums, now expresses itself in three musical phenomena that have conquered the Caribbean and the civilized world: calypso, limbo, and steel bands. You will hear them all here at their best during the pre-Lenten Carnival.

The intermingling of racial strains has left a physical mark on Trinidad and given a richness to its national life which few other islands can match. You will see every known costume and fabric worn in the streets of Port of Spain. The architecture of the city mingles the latest in flat slab and column construction with Victorian fantasies and the domes and minarets of Arabia. There are Muslim mosques and Jewish synagogues, Hindu temples, the steepled churches and cathedrals of English and Roman Catholicism, a Benedictine monastery, and just about every house of worship you can think of. The island is home to Jew and Gentile, Hindu and Muslim, the followers of Zoroaster and Mary Baker Eddy.

This diversity is reflected in island place names. Port of Spain replaces Puerto de España. Towns with Hindustani names like Fyzabad are next door to English St. Mary's, Spanish San Fernando, Carib Siparia, pre-Carib Rampanalgas, French Plaisance, and Roussillac. You drive from Point-à-Pierre to Waterloo by way of Claxton Bay and California.

Even more important than the diversity of Trinidad is its unity. As time passes, the children of many races and colors who make up the polyglot population of this island feel more and more Trinidadian. They seem to have two things in common: pride in their island and confidence in their future. In recent years, the young people who have turned to the United States, Canada, and Great Britian have returned to their homeland with all the advanced and aggressive ideals of metropolitan life. Their disillusionment over deals with the transfer of the naval base at Chaguaramas and impatience with the tedious process of growing up to the role of major power had forged a firm link with South American politics as performed in Guyana.

History

Trinidad's independent course is based partly on the fact that it is not dependent on tourism revenues. Approximately 36% of island income comes from the production of crude oil; the rest from asphalt, agriculture, one of the largest sugar mills in the British Commonwealth, and Angostura Bitters, whose secret formula is a Trinidad invention. The people are industrious. In addition, Port of Spain is a commercial hub without peer in the Caribbean.

Columbus arrived at the island on his third voyage, in 1498, and named it La Trinidad for the three hills around the bay where he anchored, which symbolized the Holy Trinity to his pious mind. It was almost a century before the Spanish settled it. Two early English tourists were Sir Robert Dudley and Sir Walter Raleigh. En route to the Orinoco and his ill-starred search for El Dorado, Raleigh stopped just long enough to burn the Spanish colony to the ground and discover the strange viscous lake of pitch which now enriches Trinidad by contributing to the world's production of asphalt. The Span-

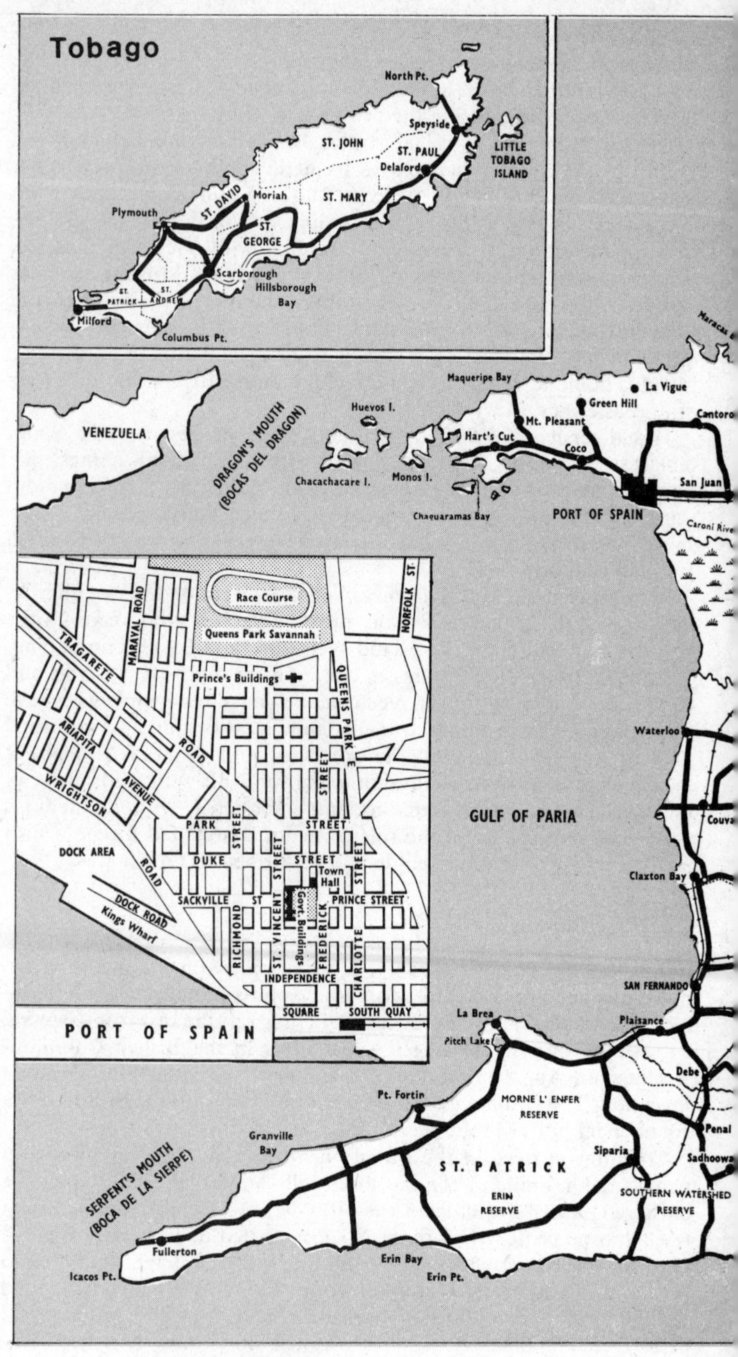

Tobago
North Pt.
Speyside
LITTLE TOBAGO ISLAND
ST. JOHN
ST. PAUL
Delaford
ST. DAVID
Moriah
ST. MARY
Plymouth
ST. GEORGE
Scarborough
Hillsborough Bay
ST. PATRICK
ST. ANDREW
Milford
Columbus Pt.
Maqueripe Bay
La Vigue
Green Hill
Mt. Pleasant
Cantoro
Hart's Cut
Coco
San Juan
Huevos I.
VENEZUELA
DRAGON'S MOUTH (BOCAS DEL DRAGON)
Chacachacare I.
Monos I.
Chaguaramas Bay
PORT OF SPAIN
Caroni River
Race Course
Queens Park Savannah
NORFOLK ST.
MARAVAL ROAD
TRAGARETE ROAD
Prince's Buildings
QUEENS PARK E
ARIAPITA AVENUE
WRIGHTSON ROAD
STREET
PARK STREET
DOCK AREA
DUKE STREET
Town Hall
SACKVILLE ST
PRINCE STREET
DOCK ROAD
Kings Wharf
Govt. Buildings
RICHMOND STREET
ST. VINCENT STREET
FREDERICK STREET
CHARLOTTE STREET
INDEPENDENCE SQUARE
SOUTH QUAY
PORT OF SPAIN
Waterloo
GULF OF PARIA
Couva
Claxton Bay
SAN FERNANDO
La Brea
Plaisance
Pitch Lake
Debe
Pt. Fortin
MORNE L' ENFER RESERVE
Penal
Granville Bay
Siparia
Sadhoowa
SERPENT'S MOUTH (BOCA DE LA SIERPE)
ST. PATRICK
ERIN RESERVE
SOUTHERN WATERSHED RESERVE
Fullerton
Icacos Pt.
Erin Bay
Erin Pt.

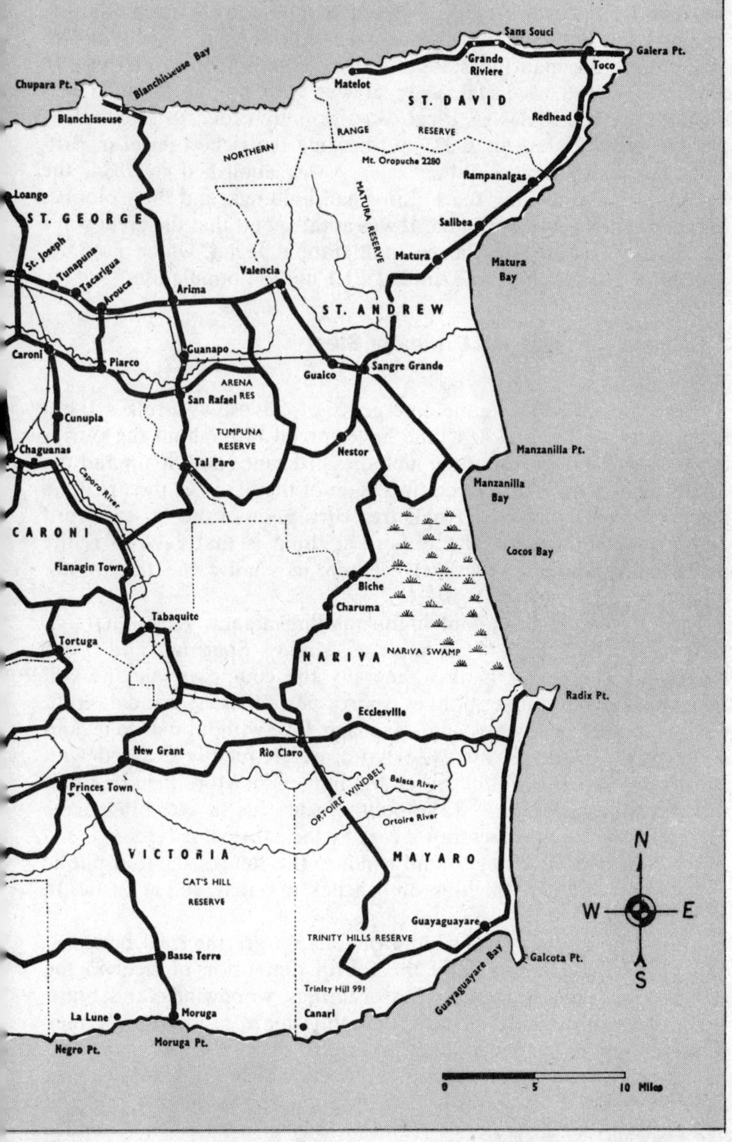
Trinidad
Caribbean Sea
Sans Souci
Galera Pt.
Grando Riviere
Toco
Matelot
ST. DAVID
Redhead
RANGE
RESERVE
NORTHERN
Mt. Oropuche 2280
Rampanalgas
MATURA RESERVE
Salibea
Matura
Matura Bay
Chupara Pt.
Blanchisseuse Bay
Blanchisseuse
Loango
ST. GEORGE
St. Joseph
Tunapuna
Tacarigua
Arouca
Valencia
Arima
ST. ANDREW
Caroni
Guanapo
Piarco
ARENA RES
Guaico
Sangre Grande
San Rafael
Cunupia
TUMPUNA RESERVE
Nestor
Chaguanas
Tal Paro
Manzanilla Pt.
Caparo River
Manzanilla Bay
CARONI
Cocos Bay
Flanagin Town
Biche
Charuma
Tabaquite
Tortuga
NARIVA
NARIVA SWAMP
Radix Pt.
Ecclesville
New Grant
Rio Claro
Balaca River
Princes Town
ORTOIRE WINDBELT
Ortoire River
N
VICTORIA
MAYARO
CAT'S HILL RESERVE
W
E
Guayaguayare
TRINITY HILLS RESERVE
Guayaguayare Bay
Galcota Pt.
Basse Terre
S
Trinity Hill 991
La Lune
Moruga
Canari
Negro Pt.
Moruga Pt.
0
5
10 Miles

ish rebuilt their settlement, imported African slaves, and began to cultivate the fertile soil. The thriving colony was raided by the Dutch in 1640, by the French in 1677 and 1690. In 1783, a royal proclamation from Madrid offered inducements to foreigners of all nations to settle in Trinidad, the sole condition being that immigrants must be Roman Catholic. The result of this initial Caribbean crash program was a big influx of settlers, augmented by many French families coming from Haiti and other places where the French Revolution was giving the black man ideas about liberty, equality, and fraternity. In 1797, the British, as usual, were at war with Spain. Trinidad was captured by His Majesty's Fleet, was formally ceded to England by the Treaty of Amiens in 1802, and became the richest jewel in Britain's Caribbean crown. When slavery was abolished in 1834, the blacks began cultivating the soil in small holdings, and the Colonists brought in laborers from India. It was at this point that the great wave of Hindu, Moslem and Parsee immigration began, which now accounts for nearly a half of Trinidad's 1.1 million population.

Calypso Carnival and Drums of Steel

It is impossible to date the emergence of calypso as a folk art, but its melodies in 2/4 and 4/4 time have spread throughout the Caribbean. Its wellsprings are in the melodies of France and Spain and the tribal rhythms of Africa. Even the origin of the name is obscure. One theory is that calypso is an Anglicized corruption of the African word *kai-so,* meaning bravo. The important thing is that calypso is the living expression of a very lively people; its vitality and rhythm are the essence of Trinidad.

The calypso singers adopt high-sounding names: King Pharaoh, Attila the Hun, Lord Nelson, The Mighty Sparrow, and Lord Kitchener. The singer is also generally the composer, and he will improvise on any theme: politics, sports, personalities, scandal, graft, the high cost of living, love and marriage, love without marriage, and every event of human life. The lyrics are frequently charged with coruscating sarcasm, double entendre, innuendo. More than one politician has been defeated at the polls because his shortcomings have been dinned into the electorate's ears by the satire of calypso.

You'll hear calypso singers and bands in the "tents," the four public halls of Port of Spain, in clubs, on beaches, in hotels, and at parties in private homes.

No less ubiquitous in the Land of Calypso are the steel bands. It took the Trinidadians to add the fourth dimension of steel to the conventional orchestral categories of strings, woodwinds, and brass. With an intuitive skill and taste that still amaze musicologists, they contrived new instruments out of oil drums, gas tanks, pots, pans, and biscuit tins. The vibrant percussive effects which Trinidadians coax from these steel instruments have been compared to "melted gold and molten lava, the cross between the melody of a harpsichord and a clarion, an organ and a Hawaiian guitar." The steel bands have their origins in the Shango drums of slaves from the Yoruba and Mandingo tribes of Africa, drums whose music was forbidden by the planters. As always in the rich cultural melting pot of Trinidad, there were other influences in the development of this musical phenomenon, notably the percussion instruments brought in by East Indian immigrants.

Whatever its ancestry, the steel band as we know it today became public on V-E Day, 1945, when the population of Trinidad grabbed garbage pail lids, empty cans, and anything they could lay their hands on to beat out a victory march in the streets of Port of Spain. It wasn't long before the resonance of metal containers was being controlled by marking their surfaces into segments that would produce the notes of the scale. An uncanny sense of rhythm and tone guided the "untutored" ears of the steel band tuners. Within a year, there were ensembles of "ping pongs," "piano pans," "second pans," "tenor kittles," and "tune booms." Within a decade, steel bands had carried a new and fascinating musical art to the United States and Europe. With calypso, steel bands have become a symbol of the irrepressible vitality of Trinidad. You'll hear a broad spectrum of music ranging from the traditional calypso to concert arrangements of Bach, Rossini, etc. The best time is after New Year, when all the island musicians tune up for the greatest Carnival of the West Indies.

For color, rhythm, fabulous costumes, and sheer, unrepressed spirit, it is unsurpassed. The excitement really starts right after New Year's Eve in Port of Spain, with the calypso bands rehearsing songs nightly before huge audiences in the "tents." One of the songs will be chosen by popular vote as the "road march" of the Carnival, the greatest honor that composer, band, and singer can hope to attain. Meanwhile, leaders of various costume groups are deciding on carnival themes, designing and sewing their elaborate costumes in secret. These preparations begin as soon as carnival is over and carry through a full year of mounting enthusiasm. For those who have an urge to join in the romp, places in various bands can be purchased for fees graded to the prestige of the group and the intricacy of the costumes.

In spite of all the professionalism, Carnival has a completely spontaneous air. The town bubbles over with excitement, and all work stops for the several days before culmination of Carnival, and the eve of Ash Wednesday. The top calypsonian is proclaimed King, and the Queen and King of the bands "preside" as well. Carnival opens at dawn on Monday with *"Jour Ouvert,"* which the Trinidadians have gaily corrupted to *"Joo-Vay."* The whole place starts "jumping up," literally leaping into the air to the compelling rhythms of the steel bands. The celebration progresses from mere abandon on Monday to overmastering rapture on Tuesday morning and reaches throbbing, ecstatic climax on Tuesday night. Pandemonium reigns, a wild tumult in the streets. Everybody is jumping. Suddenly it's midnight, and Ash Wednesday. Carnival collapses like a punctured balloon. In the morning, Trinidad goes back to the worries of a work-a-day world. If you plan to visit during Carnival, make your reservations far in advance; it draws a repeat crowd from the United States, Canada, and the other islands.

EXPLORING TRINIDAD

Port of Spain is best explored on foot (see the section A Day on Your Own). It is a big city, set between high hills and the curving shoreline of the Gulf of Paria. The view from the hills embraces a checkerboard of red and white roofs, one of the busiest harbors in the Caribbean, and the shore of the Spanish Main, clearly visible across the Bocas or the Dragon's Mouth. At night, from some vantage points, you can see the lights of Venezuela. During the day, Port of Spain hums with the activity of an international capital. Its 100,000 citizens, scurrying about their business, seem like the United Nations on parade.

Those interested in Caribbean flora and fauna will be enchanted with the Asa Wright Nature Centre, about 40 minutes' drive from Piarco Airport and about an hour's drive from downtown Port of Spain.

The Spring Hill Centre is about seven miles north of the town of Arima, at about 1200 feet in the northern mountain range of Trinidad. Formerly a private estate, the property was purchased from the family in 1967, when it was set up under a trust administration by the Royal Bank Trust Company. The Centre was a coffee-cocoa-citrus plantation and, since its previous owners shared an interest in nature with the public, the area has long been a favorite with those interested in seeing Tufted Coquettes, Squirrel Cukoos, Toucans, and other birds in their natural habitat.

Those planning to stay a few days at the Centre should have slacks and long-sleeved shirts and good outdoor shoes for plodding along the paths of the reservation. The driest season is from Jan. until May and in the late fall but, even during rainy months, the sudden showers bring the reward of flourishing growth. It's advisable to bring some lightweight rainwear and your favorite insect repellant.

Thanks to Pitch Lake and its inexhaustible supply of asphalt, Trinidad has 4,600 miles of the best roads in the Caribbean. They traverse mountains, plains, green valleys, sugar, cocoa, and coconut plantations–every possible variation of tropic scenery. The island is large enough for all-day drives, small enough so that you can become acquainted with it in a short time. The following tours, with time duration suggested, can be taken either on your own or under the auspices of one of the Port of Spain sightseeing tour operators listed under How to Get About. All mileage indications are for roundtrip from Port of Spain.

Laventille Hills. An eight-mile run to the east of Port of Spain by way of Belmont and Laventille, returning by the Eastern Main Road. High point of the trip is visit to the shrine of Our Lady of Laventille. At the top of this church stands an immense statue of Our Lady which is one of the landmarks of Port of Spain. It is illuminated at night on the 13th day of each month about between May and Oct. and can be seen from almost any part of the city. On those dates there are special services in the chapel commemorating three apparitions of the Virgin to the children of Fatima, Portugal. The panoramic view from this shrine is second to none. Nearby is Fort Chacon (Spanish built) and Fort Picton (built by the English and called Picton's Folly). Allow about an hour for this trip.

Fort George. Built by Governor Hislop in 1605, this fort is on a peak 1,100 feet above Port of Spain and offers a series of uninterrupted views in all directions. The one to the west, overlooking the Boca Grande and the mountains of Venezuela is especially impressive.

Caroni Bird Sanctuary. This 437-acre sanctuary is seven miles from Port of Spain. There are about 6000 Scarlet Ibis in this area, and a special "hide" has been constructed for watching.

Best time to go is in late afternoon before sunset, when the birds return in a blaze of color to their nests. The surroundings are fascinating, with lakes full of blue, mauve, and white lilies, alligators resting on the mudbanks, oysters growing on underwater trees. Tours by flat-bottomed boats may be taken if they are in the vicinity. Otherwise, wait in midlake in your boat to see them.

Morne Coco Road. A clockwise tour starting on the Western Main Road, via Four Roads to Petit Valley, over the Morne Coco Road to Maraval Village, and back to Port of Spain by the Saddle Road. Beautiful scenery. Allow two hours for this 15-mile jaunt.

The Saddle. Another circular run, encompassing the beauties of the northern part of the island (18-mile radius). The Saddle is a pass through the ridge, which separates the valleys of Santa Cruz and Maraval. Luxuriant vegetation and splendid views of the Santa Cruz Valley characterize this trip. After descending from the Saddle, the road runs under vaulted arches of giant bamboo. Tour operators do this trip in two hours; it can be done more quickly.

The North Coast Road or "Skyline Highway." This tour–34 miles–is the most popular shore excursion with Caribbean cruise passengers. You go over the Saddle, then wind for 12 miles through the Northern Range to Las Cuevas Bay. Continue on through the rain forest to Blanchisseuse, a small and colorful French Creole village on the north coast. You'll find tiny Victorian cottages laden with gingerbread trim; a little wooden church that features primitive religious painting; and a wooden bridge spanning the river where village inhabitants fish and often bathe. Driving about 1000 feet up, you have one splendid view after another, the grand climax being the 100-mile east-west sweep from Tobago to Venezuela. Take your swim gear. Mountain-hemmed Maracas Beach is white sand, limpid water, and coconut palms. There are changing facilities for a nominal fee. If you have time for only one Trinidad excursion, this Skyline Highway tour should be it. Pack a picnic lunch; there is one small restaurant and bar at Maracas Beach.

Blue Basin. This is the sort of idyllic dell where you expect to hear the horns of elfland. It's at the head of the Diego Martin Valley, reached via the Western Main Road, Four Roads, Diego Martin, and the River Estate (maintained by the University of the West Indies for experiments with cacao), with its sixteen miles of hibiscus hedge lining the road.

A cool cascade tumbles into the pool of Blue Basin, and the swimming is divine. You have to walk half a mile from the car park at the end of the road to reach this enchanted spot. Wear comfortable shoes. The footpath is on the steep side, but the destination warrants the exertion. You can do this 20-mile roundtrip including the trail scramble in a couple of hours, but the best idea is to take a picnic lunch and make a real excursion.

Pitch Lake is 105 acres of thick, hot, viscous grey pitch, which the Trinidad and Tobago Tourist Board has likened to "a magnified elephant skin." Walk on this tough hide if you want to; the experience may remind you of your childhood when you couldn't resist taking a few gumshoe steps in fresh hot tar. The lake, which is 285 feet deep at the center, has, according to the Tourist Board, supplied 15 million tons of asphalt to the world over the past 70 years and has paved the streets of the world from Lake Shore Drive to the Champs Elysées.

The 130-mile round trip to Pitch Lake from Port of Spain will take you on Princess Margaret Highway through Chaguanas, the home of East Indian hand-made jewelry; Pointe-à-Pierre with its great oil refinery; and San Fernando with its large East Indian population, the second city of Trinidad. Two short detours are interesting. The first, north of San Fernando, will take you to Brechin Castle, largest sugar refinery in British territories. The second is south of Oropouche to the Fyzabad oil wells and Siparia. Here in the church of La Divina Pastora is the celebrated Black Virgin of Siparia, clad in leather, surrounded by tokens of recognition from grateful former invalids who have been healed by her intercession. A fête and procession are held in honor of the Black Virgin in April of each year.

This tour, the eighth of our suggested itineraries, can't be done comfortably in less than a full day, say 10 hours at the minimum. These excursions, especially the Pitch Lake and Skyline Highway outings, should give even the short-term visitor a memorable idea of the great scenic variety as well as the economic importance of Trinidad.

Anyone staying longer than a few days in Trinidad will certainly want to explore the exhilarating east coast of the island, with the Atlantic rushing in on firm sand beaches fringed with coconut palms. At low tide, these beaches become a thoroughfare, a "superhighway" stretching from Manzanilla Point south to Guayaguayare Bay. North of Manzanilla Point is the half-mile crescent of Balandra Beach. On the northern coast, in the Toco district, there is a series of lovely beaches and secluded coves, linked by rugged headlands plunging down to blue waters. This is certainly the "other side" of Trinidad.

A DAY ON YOUR OWN

The logical starting point for your walking tour of Port of Spain is Queen's Wharf, not far from where the cruise passengers land. Walk one block north to Independence Square, which is no square at all but a street, and wander along Frederick Street, a perfect place for window shopping, people-watching, and a visit to the Tourist Board at No. 56.

A block to the north is Queen Street and beyond that Woodford Square. The big neo-Renaissance building facing you from St. Vincent Street is known as Red House. Built in 1906, it is the seat of the Government of Trinidad and Tobago. The Anglican Cathedral of the Holy Trinity dominates Woodford Square on the south side and the building looks as Gothic as any of the well-known churches of England. Pay special note to the carvings on the altar and choir stalls inside.

The Roman Catholic Cathedral of the Immaculate Conception, which dates from 1816, is just a few blocks away, and the Jama Masjid Mosque, an impressive structure, is within walking distance. Both the cathedral and the mosque have outlets that lead to the Central Market. You'll find the market stalls a colorful display that seems never ending, with green, red, and yellow peppers—both the hot and sweet variety—gourds, pumpkins, gingerroot, cassave, huge milk-white dasheen, purple eggplant, green and blushing mangoes, bananas, plantains, lettuce, spinach, figs—in fact, all the variety of spices and vegetables that go into the unique cuisine of Trinidad.

Just three blocks east of Woodford Square is a landmark of Port of Spain, the Angostura Bitters Factory. Established in 1875, Angostura Bitters is known all over the world, and every drop of it is made in Trinidad. The secret formula is closely guarded.

Seven blocks up Frederick Street is what tradition calls the fashionable promenade of Port of Spain, the Queen's Park Savannah. This 200-acre lawn with its race course and cricket fields is Trinidad's tropical version of St. James's Park, Green Park, and The Mall rolled into one. The Trinidad Hilton is on the east, but head for the south side, which is confusingly called Queen's Park West. The venerable Queen's Park Hotel is here (why not stop for a cool drink?), as is its staid contemporary, the National Museum and Art Gallery. This small museum is guarded by Spanish cannon which date from England's capture of the island in 1797. Near the entrance is the anchor Columbus lost in Trinidad; it was dredged up 400 years later at Point Icacos off the southwest coast. The Savannah is a wonderful place to watch the world of Trinidad. It's also the best vantage point from which to explore the architectural diversity of the city. And you're close enough, and probably ready, for lunch at the Trinidad Hotel, where you'll have one more sweeping view of the area.

North of the Savannah on Circular Road are the Royal Botanic Gardens which are well worth some time. They cover some sixty-five acres and have been developing since 1820. There are licensed guides to take you around. You'll find them (or they'll find you) at the entrance and, even if you think you know a lot about plants and do not like "routine patter" tours, you'll find them indispensable. The variety of trees and flowers includes lotus lilies sacred to the Egyptians, the holy fig tree of the Buddhists, the bleeding "raw beef" tree, monkey pods, monkey puzzles, Indian and Chinese banyans, Ceylon willows, and an orchid house, fernery, and nutmeg ravine, plus punctuation marks of the spectacular tropical blooms that have never failed to please.

Finally, visit the Emperor Valley Zoo nearby, which is an added attraction to the fauna of Trinidad. Now that it has been enlarged, lions, tigers, and American bison have joined the Trinidadian wildlife.

By then, footsore and possibly weary, you'll have discovered Port of Spain by day, so head for your hotel and a short rest. The city by night is a spectacular on its own and you won't want to miss it.

TOBAGO

Twenty-two miles northeast of Trinidad is the enchanting island of Tobago, sedate sister of bustling Trinidad. Twenty-six miles long by 7 wide, the island has verdant mountains, beautiful white beaches, resort hotels, sparkling blue bays, and almost all the exotic flowers and trees that can grow in the tropics, plus more exotic birds per acre than any other West Indian island.

History

Plowing south from Grenada to Trinidad, Columbus should have sighted this fish-shaped island lying to port on his third voyage, in 1498. He missed it, however; there is no mention of the island in his log. Even more remarkable, he failed to give the place a name. Subsequent Spanish colonists called it Tobago from the Indian word, *tobaco,* meaning the Y-shaped pipe with which the natives smoked tobacco.

In the 18th century, when sugar was King of the Caribbean, Tobago raised cane with the best of them, producing as much as half a million gallons of rum in 1793. This helps to explain why four nations and assorted buccaneers battled for more than a century over this rich little prize. The Spanish, Dutch, French, Swedes, and the English all laid hands on Tobago at one time or another, but the English were the most tenacious. Although the French took possession under the terms of the Treaty of Amiens in 1802, the English seized it the following year. In 1814, England became the rightful owner under the Congress of Vienna treaties. Tobago today is the vacation portion of the Dominion of Trinidad and Tobago, an independent country within the British Commonwealth since August 31, 1962.

Tobagonians are fond of telling the world that their land is Robinson Crusoe's island. Since Daniel Defoe never set foot on any isle but England, and since Alexander Selkirk, the flesh-and-blood prototype of Crusoe was actually marooned on the Pacific island of Juan Fernández, Tobago's claim would seem to be grounded more in the realms of gold than in the swamps of science. But do not underestimate the power of poetic truth. You will see Crusoe's cave on Tobago, and you will agree that this isle is a more suitable place for Crusoe and his Man Friday than Juan Fernández. There can be no doubts when it comes to those other explorers, The Swiss Family Robinson. Their tree house was right here on Tobago.

Swiss Family Robinson, Robinson Crusoe: both names evoke a mental image of the tropics just discovered, still unspoiled. Tobago is about as close as one can come to a realization of that romantic picture. This is perhaps the secret of its charm for the traveler. The climate, averaging between 80 and 84° is cooler and less humid than that of Trinidad. Another attraction is the economic factor. Off the sea lanes of the big cruise ships, this little sea-girt paradise was until recently one of the least expensive of West Indian resorts. Today it is the ideal holiday resort for Trinidadians and others and now attracts international hoteliers. While rates have increased, they are still below those of most of the more popular islands, and there are an 18-hole golf course and tennis courts for those who want more action than the beautiful beaches offer.

EXPLORING TOBAGO

Scarborough, a town of 17,000, is one of the quietest places under the sun. Its official sights are few. There is a native market with its usual air of color, heat, and sound, open every day, but buzzing a little louder on Wednesdays and Saturdays. You can drive up the hill to Old Fort King George. From this height, 430 feet, you will have a view of town, bay, and countryside and the great sweep of the Atlantic stretching 21 miles southwest to Trinidad, clearly visible like a ship on the horizon. Nothing remains of the old French fort, but you can see the ruins of the old barracks and an old mortar near the lighthouse, a silent reminder of Tobago's days of violence. The impression of past history is deepened as you descend the hill past a row of silent cannon trained toward the sea and enemies long forgotten. Below the General Hospital you will see another relic of the past, the old prison. Here, in 1801, after a revolt of the slaves, the ringleader and 38 of his associates were imprisoned. To terrorize the blacks into submission, the governor pretended to hang all 39 of the prisoners from a gibbet on the prison walls. The townspeople watched 39 hangings; the slaves were terrified into submission, the planters appalled at such reckless destruction of their property. But only one man, the ringleader, was really executed, his body being strung up again and again from the gallows.

A DAY ON YOUR OWN

Using Scarborough as a starting point, excursions can be made to all parts of the island. Allow a full day for the trip to Charlotteville and Man o'War Bay on the northern coast. This run will take you on the Windward Road along the Atlantic Coast, through lovely valleys, up steep hills, through groves of coconut and cocoa, and along mountain ridges affording matchless views over the beaches, bays and reefs until you come to Speyside. This is a delightful fishing village, set on the crescent of Speyside Bay. Behind it, the green profile of Pigeon Peak rises 1800 feet, Tobago's highest mountain, dominating the northern end of the island.

Speyside is the jumping-off place for a star-shaped island with three names: Little Tobago, Ingram Island, and Bird-of-Paradise. The last is the least official and the most firmly established. It was here that Sir William Ingram brought those gold-plumed Greater Birds of Paradise from New Guinea in 1909, and it's here alone that you can see them in the Western Hemisphere. The island is now a 450-acre bird sanctuary reached by a boat from Speyside. Guides will meet you on the island and conduct small groups along the trails where you are most likely to see these extraordinary cockerels flashing about with their great sprays of golden plumage. Silence is also golden in these precincts. The birds are timid, and to get a glimpse of them, use the stealthy Indian approach. Many other exotic birds may be seen here. Hawks and other birds of prey are shot on sight. Admission to the sanctuary is free. Go in the early morning or late afternoon.

From Speyside, drive uphill northwest across a narrows to Charlotteville and Man o'War Bay, one of the finest natural harbors in the Caribbean. Forty fathoms deep at the mouth, 10 fathoms just offshore, it could accommodate any number of cruise ships. The south side of the bay is a long sandy beach. Above it on the hillside, the white houses of Charlotteville nestle like pigeons come home to roost. Pigeon Peak rises grandly behind the whole scene, verdant, majestic, silent. A Government Rest House is situated on the palm-fringed beach at Man o'War Bay—a perfect setting for a swim and a picnic.

Store Bay is the base for a difficult mile-and-a-half hike to "Robinson Crusoe's Cave." It can be reached only on foot. "A local descendant will take you there," writes Commander Alford, author of *The Island of Tobago,* "but it is only fair to warn you that there is not very much to see!" This advice, coming from a staunch exponent of the theory that Robinson Crusoe slept here, was enough to discourage us. Instead of slogging off to the Robinson Crusoe Cave, head instead in the direction of the Robinson Crusoe Hotel and a king-size planter's punch.

PRACTICAL INFORMATION FOR TRINIDAD

HOW TO GET THERE. By air. From New York you can fly *American Airlines* or *BWIA* (British West Indian Airways) direct. *Eastern Airlines* funnels its U.S. flights through New York and Miami to San Juan for *Eastern* continuing flights to Trinidad. *Air France* flies via Martinique or Guadeloupe.

From Miami, *BWIA* flies direct or via intermediate islands.

From Canada, *BWIA* and *Air Canada* fly from Toronto; from Montreal, *Air Canada.*

From London, *British Airways, BWIA.*

Within the West Indies, regular and frequent service is provided by *LIAT, BWIA, Eastern,* and a number of small airlines. *Trinidad and Tobago Air Services (TTAS)* make the 15-minute flight between islands several times daily.

By sea. Some cruise lines, such as *Holland America* and *Sunline,* include Trinidad as a port of call.

FURTHER INFORMATION. In New York, the *Trinidad and Tobago Tourist Board* maintains offices at 400 Madison Ave., Suite 712-714, New York, N.Y. 10017, *Trinidad and Tobago Tourism and Trade Center,* 200 Southeast First St., Suite 702, Miami, Fla. 33131; in Canada, the *Trinidad and*

Tobago Tourism & Trade Center, 145 King Street West, Second Floor, Toronto, Ontario M5H, 1J8; In England, *Trinidad and Tobago Tourism & Trade Center,* 20 Lower Regent St., London, SW1Y, 4PH. The local office in Trinidad is 56 Frederick Street in Port of Spain.

ISLAND MEDIA. For information of local events, as well as international news, read any of Trinidad's three newspapers: *The Express, The Guardian,* or the *Evening News.*

AUTHORIZED TOUR OPERATORS. *Butler Travels; Caribbean Holidays; Cavalcade; Flyfaire;* and *GoGo Tours* in the U.S.; *Sunburst Holidays* in Canada.

PASSPORTS, VISAS. Passports are required for all visitors. Visas are required for U.S. citizens who stay more than two months. Non-U.S. citizens arriving from the U.S. and planning to return there must produce a U.S. Certificate of Income Tax Compliance and U.S. entry permit for reentry to U.S. Airport tax $1. Although you do not need a smallpox vaccination if you come from the U.S. directly, it is required if you have stopped at other islands en route. Check your specific itinerary with the officials or, to be on the safe side, keep the smallpox vaccination effective.

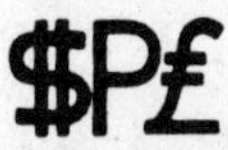

MONEY. Trinidad and Tobago use TT dollars, which equal 42¢ US; 38¢ Canadian. A U.S. dollar today = $2.40 TT; $4.80 TT = £1. It is advisable to exchange money for local currency since purchases will cost you less in local currency. Banks give the best rate.

TAXES AND OTHER CHARGES. There is a 3% Government Tax on accommodations, as well as a 10% Service Charge. The airport departure tax is $5 TT.

HOW TO GET ABOUT. There are about 4,600 miles of good roads around Trinidad and good roads also on most of Tobago. Remember to drive on the left, even though your car is a right-hand drive. U.S. license is valid. For car rental, *Hub Travel Ltd.* at 44 New Street in Port of Spain is the *Hertz* licensee. Hub also has a number of branch offices, in the Hilton, Holiday Inn, Piarco Airport and, in Tobago, at Radisson Crown and Mt. Irvine. Rates for a wide choice of cars run $40–45 per day, which is the highest rate anywhere in the Caribbean. Although unlimited mileage is included in the rate, gasoline is extra. It is better to take a taxi.

Piarco Airport is about 45 minutes from town. Several tour operators provide roundtrip transfers for $9.50. There are plenty of taxis at about $20 TT. If you are going somewhere for dinner or the evening, it's wise to negotiate for your driver to wait or pick you up; sometimes it's difficult to find a cab late at night.

Sightseeing tour operators in Port of Spain are *Hub Travel Ltd.,* the *St. Christopher Taxi Co-op Society Ltd.,* and *Baachus Taxi and Car Rental.* Hub Travel charges $5.50 for a 2-hour city tour and $6 for a 4-hour trip to Maracas Bay for swimming. The 6-hour La Brea Pitch Lake Tour costs about $12 per person, and the 7-hour island circle tour, including a welcome drink, is $20. A 5-hour cruise in Port of Spain Bay costs $13.50 per person and includes transfer from your hotel, refreshments and snacks, and swimming facilities at Monos Island.

EVENTS AND HOLIDAYS. *Carnival* is the biggest event of all, with the *Festival of Hosein* (a week after Moslem New Year), and *Dewaii,* or the Festival of Lights, which takes place in the Fall. In addition to the *Tropical Flower Festival* held in Queen's Park Savannah in May, there are arts and music festivals scheduled throughout the year. In addition, public holidays are: *New Year's Day, Good Friday, Easter Monday, Whit Monday, May Day* (May 1), *Discovery Day* (July 31), *Independence Day* (Aug. 31), *Christmas Day,* and *Boxing Day.*

WHAT WILL IT COST?

A typical day on Trinidad in season for *two* persons will run:

	US$	£
Hotel accommodations in Port of Spain	65	35
Breakfast at hotel	10	5
Luncheon at an in-town restaurant	15	8
Dinner at a moderate in-town spot	20	11
Tips or service charges at the restaurants; taxes and service charge at hotels	15	8
Car rental for one full day	40	22
	$165	£89

STAYING IN TRINIDAD

HOTELS. The hotel industry has received a boost from the Government's enthusiasm for increased tourism. But you'll find that while Trinidad concentrates on hotels with pools and entertainment, the resort hotels are better on Tobago's beaches.

Chaconia Inn. Located a few miles north of Port of Spain, this fifty-room property has nicely furnished, air-conditioned rooms, some efficiencies. Swimming pool, disco, and open-air restaurant. $65–75 double EP all year round.

Holiday Inn. Their 253 rooms include some suites with private balconies. The amenities are what you would expect of a Holiday Inn, but one special feature is the revolving rooftop restaurant with good food and a fine city view. Swimming pool, wading pool, shopping arcade, cocktail lounge with nightly entertainment. $80–100 double EP in winter, with rates running much higher during Carnival and somewhat lower off-season.

Kapok Hotel. One of the best in-town bargains for highrise convenience (at the fringe of the Grand Savannah; a short walk from the Royal Botanic Gardens). Eighty pleasant air-conditioned rooms, small pool behind the hotel, but the highlight here is its *Tiki Village Restaurant* on the roof. From $42–50 double EP all year.

Trinidad Hilton. The twelfth floor is at ground level, and taxis swirl into the *portecochere* at the lobby on the top of the hotel. Interesting "upside-down" idea which we still find appealing. Guests in any of the 442 rooms can enjoy the ultimate in facilities, which include swimming pool with sunken bar, tennis courts, snack bar, on-premises shops and *Le Boucan,* the finest supper-club restaurant on the island. In addition, some of Trinidad's best native entertainers perform here throughout the week. $75–85 double EP all year.

HOME RENTALS. While there are a few homes and apartments for rent in Trinidad, most visitors prefer the hotels. Self-sufficient types might be interested in the rustic facilities at the *Asa Wright Nature Center,* a former coffee estate, which is in the middle of a fascinating wildlife preserve. Just fourteen rooms in simple accommodations, about a forty-minute drive from the airport. Rates run $96 double, including all three meals.

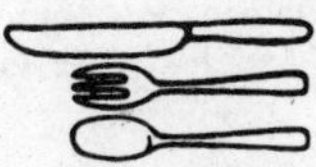

RESTAURANTS. Trinidad is famous for its international specialties. You'll find good Chinese, Indian, Indonesian, and West Indian restaurants in Port of Spain and environs. Typical of West Indian fare are "the King and Queen of Creole soups," *sans coche* and *calaloo.* The former is a fabulous ragout of fat pork, salted beef, pig tail, a couple of pounds of meat, onions, chives, split peas, butter, yams, dasheen, cush-cush (couscous), cassava, sweet potato, Irish potato, green plantain, coconut milk, and green pepper—topped with dumplings. All *calaloo* requires is three bunches of dasheen leaves, a spinach-like leaf, two crabs, twelve okras, two onions, a bunch of chives, a clove of garlic, and a couple of ounces of fat pork and salt beef. Try peppery pigeon pea soup if you see it on a menu; it's also a local specialty.

For main courses, local specialties are *tatoo,* or fried iguanas, *manicou,* or possum stew, pork *souse,* green salad, and *tum-tum,* or mashed green plantains. Pork *souse* is a spicy Creole dish garnished with cucumber, lime, and onions, seasoned with hot pepper. Served cold, it's a great picnic favorite on many islands; it calls for a rum punch. In addition to armadillo (whose tender, succulent meat bears no resemblance to its armored plate exterior), the Trinidadians are fond of venison, wild duck, quenk (the local word for wild pig), and lappe, or island rabbit.

Try the *pastelles,* a Spanish-island concoction of meat folded into cornmeal and wrapped in a banana leaf. Crab *matete* is crabmeat and farina. Crab backs and crab meat taken from the shell, highly seasoned, then put back in the crab shell.

Among the Indian contributions are red hot curries and something called *roti,* which is like a king-sized *crêpe,* rolled around a filling of chicken, fish, or meat and seasoned to the palate-burning point. You'll see roti carts all around Port of Spain, particularly along Frederick Street. Or at night they are sold from stalls and vans in Independence Square.

Delicious bean-sized oysters are one of the specialties of the local seas and have far more flavor than their big brothers. They grow in the mangrove roots. There is also *chip-chip,* a tiny shellfish that tastes a bit like a clam. From fresh water streams comes the *casadou* or *cascadura,* a fish that is especially good when stuffed.

Rum is the national drink of Trinidad, as it is of most West Indian countries. The joys of rum and Coca Cola and gin and coconut water have been recorded in calypso verses. Since Trinidad is the home of Angostura Bitters, you can count on a generous portion of the red liquid in all mixed drinks. A kindred bitters, *Carypton,* is used to make the Trinidad specialty known as the "green swizzle."

We call $6 and under *Inexpensive;* $7–15 *Moderate;* $16 and above *Expensive.*

Le Boucan. The atmosphere and the food are the drawing cards. The presentation of Island fare and French dishes *en flambe* is the reason that the Trinidad Hilton can continue to claim this restaurant as the island's most popular spot. *Expensive.*

Le Cocrico. Fine dining in an old Victorian home on Henry St. Enjoy drinks in the parlor and then an elaborate dinner in the antique dining room. The menu is French-Creole and imaginative, with roast duckling in ginger sauce one of the specialties. *Expensive.*

Luciano's. In a rural setting, fountains splashing near the dining area add to the already romantic atmosphere. Serves good international cuisine and some of the Italian dishes that made Luciano famous when he had his place in downtown Port of Spain. *Moderate.*

Mangal's Indo-Chinese Restaurant. Located at 15 Queen's Park East, this spot specializes in Trinidadian-style Indian dishes, as well as Chinese entrees. But the emphasis is on the curry, and the hotter the better. Waitresses wear kimonos in the Peacock dining room and saris in the Maharajah. *Moderate.*

Peppermill. At the Pelican Inn. An intimate little bistro with a pub-type atmosphere. Features include a fine salad bar and fresh, well-prepared Creole specialties. *Inexpensive.*

Rinaldo's Bistro. Located at 6A Warner St., you'll find an extensive variety of Italian fare served up in an atmosphere that is unique–it's an old rum house complete with authentic brick walls and hand-hewn ceilings. *Expensive.*

The Outhouse. A strange name for the old Victorian cottage on Woodford St., but a delight for its fresh seafood, hot and cold vegetarian dishes, and home-made ginger ice cream. *Moderate.*

Tiki Village. Atop the Kapok Hotel, the *Tiki* is convenient to all in-town hotels. It's very different, with its Polynesian atmosphere and food, and very popular with residents, which adds to the enjoyment. *Moderate.*

Veni Mange. The place for local Creole dishes, and the best callaloo on the island. Only open for lunch. *Moderate.*

NIGHTLIFE. Conservative visitors focus only on the hotel entertainment available at the *Hilton,* the *Holiday Inn,* and a few other places, with a late night stop at the *Pelican.* For those who want it, Trinidad has everything. *Jaybee's Disco,* in the Valpark Shopping Plaza just outside the city, is one of the hottest spots in town, and swings until the early hours.

Evenings in Trinidad begin when most people are ready to go to bed. Remember that this has been a sailors' town for generations. Night clubs throb with calypso and pulsating bands; ask around for the current favorite.

SHOPPING. Port of Spain is one of the big bazaars of the West Indies, with all the expected items from India, the Orient, Europe, and other West Indian locales. In all but the top shops, you can bargain–and should if you want a reasonable price. Be very sure you are buying what you think you are; all that glitters is not gold here. Many shops offer the "in-bond" system, whereby you pick out and pay for your purchases which are then delivered to the airport or pier for you to pick up just prior to leaving the country.

Among the duty-free airport shops are *Stecher's* for perfume, tobacco, and some luxury items; and *De Lima* for cameras, local jewelry, and watches.

Kacal's at the Hilton is a showplace for the fine arts and crafts of Trinidad and Tobago.

Stecher's, mentioned above for its airport shop, has its main branch at Independence Square. Watches, china, crystal, jewelry, perfumes, silver, handbags, etc. are displayed more attractively than in most island shops. There are smaller branches at the Hilton and on Tobago.

There is a wide selection of the usual items in Port of Spain's well stocked department stores; *Stephens,* at 8 Frederick St., and *J. T. Johnson, Ltd.,* at number 13. *Stephens* is strong on English china (Minton, Wedgwood, Spode, and Royal Doulton). They've also got some Limoges porcelain, Lalique glassware from Paris, and handcut English crystal. Good selection of local souvenirs. *Johnson's* has Dent's doeskin gloves, an outstanding buy here, and the selection of dolls, ties, and scarves is among the best of the Trinidad souvenirs.

You'll have a grand time looking over the glittering crop of intricately-made East Indian filigree jewelry in Trinidad's shops. The celebrated cascadura bracelet and cunningly-contrived jewel boxes are among the most popular items in this island specialty. *Lakhan's Bazaar,* on Western Main Road, St. James, has Oriental wood carvings, brass and copper ware, saris and silk handkerchiefs, scarves and stoles as well as good silver jewelry, ivory figurines, and the like. But you haven't really cased the local jewelry situation until you've browsed through *Trinidad Jewelry Ltd.* at 17 Frederick St. They have a wide selection of filigree jewelry in 9 kt. gold as well as in sterling silver. *Y. De Lima,* three doors away at No. 23, also has East Indian jewelry that makes such a lasting souvenir of Trinidad and a fine selection of watches, perfumes, cameras, binoculars, china, etc.

Check the work at the *Blind Institute* at the corner of Duke and Edward St. Things to look for are those wonderful palm fiber tote bags, cleverly waterproofed in a manner invented by the Caribs. These are handsome and perfect for all the excess baggage you pick up in the shops.

Among the island souvenirs that will delight both child and adult are the many dolls which reflect Trinidad's cosmopolitan culture. Steel band players, native limbo dancers, calypso characters like *Minnie of Trinidad,* sari-draped Hindu beauties, Moslem Hosein dolls: these are just a few of the colorful miniature personalities that you can take with you.

SPORTS AND OTHER ACTIVITIES IN TRINIDAD. The best *swimming* beaches are on the north and east coasts of the island, a day's excursion from the Port of Spain hotels. Also Maracas Bay, 14 miles from the capital, has excellent swimming and good *surfing,* particularly in the windier winter months. The long continuous swells are just right for surfing between November and March. Bring your own board and a picnic lunch. There is a very informal snack spot, but hotels will pack picnics, which you'll probably prefer. Other beaches are at Las Cuevas, Manzanilla, Mayaro, Balandra, and Toco, but facilities are limited. If you want *pool swimming,* most of the social activity is at the Hilton or the Holiday Inn. Both have changing rooms and a small charge for pool chairs and towels.

Tennis is available at the Trinidad Hilton and Trinidad Country Club.

The *golf* course at Moka a few miles outside Port of Spain, has championship 18-hole status.

Fishing is popular throughout the year. June through Oct. is the best time for trolling for king fish and Spanish mackerel along the north coast, in the Gulf of Paria, and in Serpent's Mouth, one of the straits that separate Trinidad from Venezuela. Wahoo, bonito, skipjack, red fish, barracuda, marlin, yellowfin tuna, dolphin, and tarpon are some that haunt these waters. You'll enjoy fly fishing, bait casting, and spinning for mountain mullet and giant gobies in the streams along the north coast of Trinidad. Fishing trips can be arranged through your hotel or tour operators.

Hunting offers exceptional thrills in Trinidad because of the wide variety of quarry. Oct. 1 to March 31 is the season for the armadillo (tatoo), lappe, and the peccary or wild hog, which Trinidadians call quenk. Hunting license is obtainable from any warden's office for a fee of $2.50 U.S.

Spectator sports include *cricket,* which Trinidadians follow with a passion. This island has contributed some of the great batsmen and bowlers of the century, so good that they have inspired epic calypsos. Season is Jan.–June. *Horse racing,* with at least 28 days of racing scheduled each year, is colorful. The big meets at Queen's Park Savannah in Port of Spain are held after Christmas and in June.

PRACTICAL INFORMATION FOR TOBAGO

(Other than that listed below, the *Practical Information* for this island is the same as for Trinidad.)

HOW TO GET THERE. By air. *Trinidad & Tobago Air Services* (TTAS) makes several flights daily for the 15-minute hop between Trinidad and Tobago's Crown Point Airport. Airfare is included in excursion fares to Trinidad. There are also small charter planes stationed at Trinidad's Piarco.

By sea. There are three government coastal steamers linking Trinidad and Tobago several times weekly. The trip takes about 7 hours. Roundtrip fare is $8. The overnight trip can be rough and uncomfortable. But the newest and most luxurious way to go is aboard the *Gelting,* a 305-foot, 1,000-passenger ferry that makes the crossing in 4½ hours. It cruises, as a cruise ship would, in order to give passengers a special view of both islands. Dining rooms and bar, along with space for automobiles, should you choose to bring your rental car from Port-of-Spain. Rates run $9 roundtrip for cabin class; $6 for tourist class.

HOW TO GET ABOUT. Public buses, surprisingly modern and very cheap, make several daily trips from one end of the island to the other, with stops in everyone's "backyard." We don't recommend this for expediency, but for an interesting excursion at a very low fare. Sightseeing tours are arranged by your hotel. Figure $80 for a 3-hour tour for up to 4 persons. Hotels will also arrange for self-drive cars. There are 220 miles of good roads. Driving is to the left. Your own driver's license is valid. Bicycles may be rented, but are practical only to ride around the hotel grounds. Horses can be rented by the hour or half-day.

WHAT WILL IT COST?

Two people can enjoy this island fully for $120–150 per day during the winter season. That includes all meals, and options for golf, deep-sea fishing or island touring.

STAYING IN TOBAGO

HOTELS. Hotel development on Tobago has been toward small, tastefully designed retreats, none of them high-rise, and all nestled into the coves that brought the visitors and the developers in the first place. All hotels are beach-oriented; most convey an intimate, homey atmosphere.

Arnos Vale Hotel. On the north coast, about one mile from Plymouth and not far from Fort James, this hotel is a traditional favorite. It's one of the oldest hotels on the island, but refurbished and awakened to keep up with the best. Twenty-eight rooms in garden setting with great beach views. Red tile roofs, stucco, and natural stone give it a Mediterranean air. Freshwater pool, tennis court, beach house with bar and luncheon facilities. Barbecue nights. $140–170 double in winter; $100–120 double off-season, including breakfast and dinner.

Crown Point. Seventy-seven condominium units, with rooms-with-kitchenette, and some more spacious cottages. On the beach at Store Bay, it has a pool, tennis court, and restaurant which features Continental food. In winter the rates run $70–80 double EP; $44–66 double off-season.

Crown Reef. Scheduled to reopen in the late fall of 1982, after completing a multi-million-dollar renovation of the exterior, all public areas and guest rooms. The lobby will include a new bar and boutiques. Nightly entertainment and dancing in the *Shipwreck* bar; fine dining featuring international and island Creole specialties. Rooftop sundeck, tennis courts and swimming pool. Rates on request.

Kariwak Village. Twenty attractive suites in octagonal cottages that surround the swimming pool at this new property. Bar and restaurant on the premises; the beach is just a five-minute walk away. $85 double in winter including breakfast and dinner; $50 double EP off-season.

Mount Irvine Bay. On the grounds of the eighteen-hole championship golf course, this modern resort hotel has 110 rooms, and is part of a big (but controlled) plan for a resort community. Twenty minutes from the airport, on Mt. Irvine Bay. Rooms have outdoor patio perfect for breakfast. Small, private beach just across the road from the hotel and several others within easy walks. Swimming pool, two restaurants, Cellar Pub for nightly entertainment. Very attractive spot which draws the golfing crowd. $160–194 double in winter; $100–130 off-season, with breakfast and dinner included.

Turtle Beach. A spray of rooms along one of Tobago's many beautiful beaches. Two-story units with fifty-two modern, sea-view rooms. Shuffleboard, swimming pool, bicycles, and just plain lounging are the main activities when you finish snorkeling, scuba diving, swimming and water skiing. Not too far from the golf course, on a spectacular long curve of beach, which is indeed breathtaking at sunset when a fishing fleet lands near the hotel's shoreside bar to provide twilight entertainment. $140 double including meals in winter; $48 double EP off-season.

HOME RENTALS. One of the best opportunities for unique vacations on Tobago is a "cottage" which can be anything from a spacious house equipped for luxury resort living to an old Caribbean homestead rented out for part of the year. The Tobago Cottage Owners Association (cable address is TO-

BACOA TOBAGO) has a listing of 20 properties scattered around the island, with the greatest concentration near the Mt. Irvine Hotel and the golf course. Some places are on the beach, many are near villages and on plantations; all offer an opportunity to enjoy a tropical vacation in "your own" home at a reasonable cost. Maid service and cooks and gardeners are often included in the rate, which can run from $10 per person per day for a small place to $300 per week for 4 people and on up to places that go for $150 per day (for 10 people) in the winter season. All rentals are less in summer months.

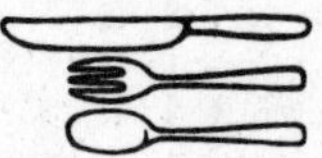

RESTAURANTS. The cuisine (similar to Trinidad's) is British, American, and Creole, plus some notable seafood specialties: lobster, conch, and jackfish. Rum is the "comfortable waters" of Tobago. The Sunday beach luncheon at the *Arnos Vale* is a super-picnic: 5 courses, hot and cold. It's open to the general public, for a fee, of course.

NIGHTLIFE. Wholesome and healthy centered probably at your hotel. *Crown Reef* has steel band music, and limbo dancers at their barbecue suppers as does *Mt. Irvine.* There is one small night club, *La Tropicale,* which is the best place to meet the local population.

SHOPPING. You won't find the myriad shops of Trinidad, but latter-day Crusoes can fill their requirements and their bags, too, in Scarborough's stores. Merchandise for sale is similar to that found in Trinidad shops, but the choice is likely to be much narrower. Prices, on the other hand, tend to be lower. East Indian fabrics and jewelry are outstanding buys.

For native goods and handicrafts, you have a choice between *Blackman's* and the *Tobago Tourist Bureau Shop;* both are on Main St. and Market Square.

For rum, bitters, and other "ardent spirits," it's *Youngs' Grocery* on Burnett St.

SPORTS AND OTHER ACTIVITIES. The beaches and bays which ring this island are a standing invitation to *swim, sunbathe,* and *picnic.* You'll find coves so solitary that you really will feel like Crusoe. In addition there are the excellent hotel beaches and beautiful stretches of sand and clear water at Man o'War Bay, Courland, and others.

Snorkeling is the outstanding specialty of Tobago, especially over the celebrated Buccoo Reef, an underwater wonderland that has few equals. Your hotel will arrange for you to visit the reef, which must be timed to coincide with low tide. A boat takes you out to the reef in Buccoo Bay, and you can explore the submarine gardens through the boat's glass-bottom or with snorkel or diving mask, supplied by the boatmen along with canvas shoes. Even nonswimmers can enjoy this experience, wading knee deep in water of incredible clarity. You become so absorbed in gazing at these exotic coral gardens and their schools of many-colored striped and spotted fish that you forget about time and the problems of the world above the surface. The great danger, even for the already tanned, is overexposure to the blazing tropic sun, whose power is amplified here by reflection. It is imperative to wear an old shirt and pants on this expedition as well as a broad-brimmed hat. There's no other shade; once you're off the boat you have to supply your own. You must also wear sneakers or other canvas shoes to protect your feet from the razor-sharp coral.

When it comes to *reef fishing, spear fishing, lobstering,* and *deep-sea fishing,* your hostelry will advise you on guides and boats as well as about the necessity of renting or buying tackle.

Tennis is not a major attraction here, but there are courts at the *Arnos Vale, Crown Point,* and *Mount Irvine* hotels.

The *Tobago Golf Club* at Mt. Irvine Bay offers a par 72, 18-hole championship course 6780 yards long, with watered greens and fairways. Greens fees run $8.50 off-season; $12 during the winter for Mount Irvine Hotel guests. Non-hotel guests are welcome to play for greens fees of $15 off-season or $18.50 during the high season.

Horseback riding is one of the pleasures of Tobago. Good mounts can be hired through your hotel. Northwest Tobago is ideal for hiking and horseback riding, but take a guide. You'd be surprised how easy it is to get lost on a small island.

Go to your hotel manager or the Revenue office in Scarborough for all information on *hunting* (duck, waterfowl, heron, etc.).

Chief spectator sport is *horse racing* at the Tobago Turf Club. There are two annual meets, in March and in Nov., with people and horses coming over from Trinidad to compete with the local products. Feeling, color, excitement, just about everything is sky-high at these two-day meets. Check with Tobago Tourist Bureau for precise dates, and come if you want to see the high jinks.

Goat racing, a one-day-only event in Tobago, takes place at Buccoo Point on Easter Tues. (the fourth day following Good Friday). Here, too, on this day, there's *crab racing*—a funny, but interesting sight.

TURKS AND CAICOS ISLANDS

Caribbean Castaways

For too many years, the 8,000 people of the Turks and Caicos Islands were the only ones who had ever heard of these specks in the Atlantic Ocean, eight main islands and about 30 smaller cays, stretching over an area about 75 miles wide by 50 miles north to south, southeast from the Bahamas. Today, however, those in search of quiet, peaceful, sandy shores head to the few new inns and resorts of the Turks and Caicos for sea- and sun-oriented holidays.

The two groups of islands, separated by the Turks Island Passage, a 22-mile deep-water channel, were officially sighted by Ponce de Leon in 1515. Some historians believe that it would have been impossible for the ubiquitous Christopher Columbus to have sailed from San Salvador in the Bahamas to Cuba, even with stronger-than-usual winds over the stern of the *Santa Maria,* without touching near Jacksonville on East Caicos. There's no official record of his visit, however, and the name game he played on all the other islands was not played here. These islands–at least the Turks Islands–got their name, according to one local legend, from the scarlet blossoms on the local cactus, which reminded some early settler of the Turkish fez! As for the Caicos Islands, the name probably is a derivative of the word *cayos,* Spanish for cays or small islands.

History

The English were the first (and about the only) people to bother with the Turks and Caicos Islands in the early years. Bermudians moved south to rake salt from the flats as early as 1678, spending

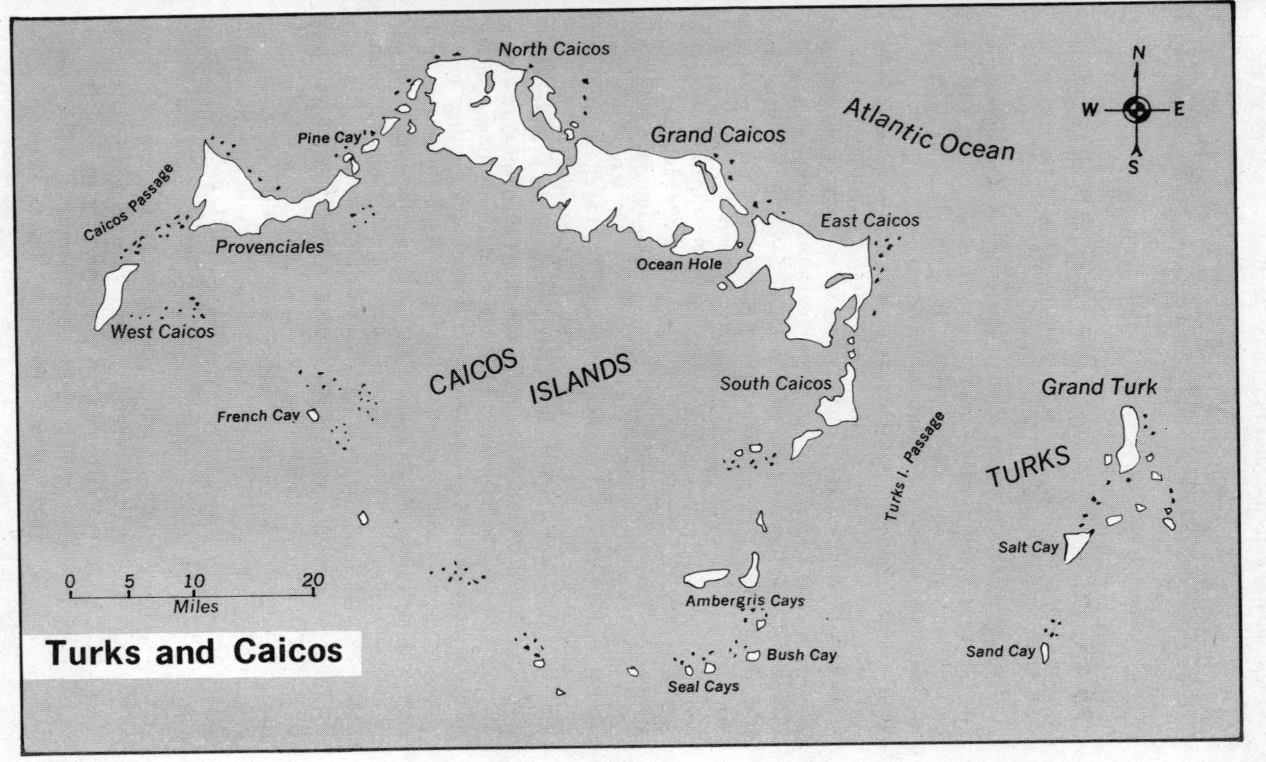
North Caicos
Atlantic Ocean
N
W
E
S
Pine Cay
Grand Caicos
Caicos Passage
Provenciales
East Caicos
Ocean Hole
West Caicos
CAICOS
ISLANDS
South Caicos
Grand Turk
French Cay
Turks I. Passage
TURKS
Salt Cay
0
5
10
20
Miles
Ambergris Cays
Bush Cay
Sand Cay
Seal Cays
Turks and Caicos

several months here and returning to the Bermuda islands to sell their crop. In 1766, one Andrew Symmers settled here to hold the islands for Her Majesty the Queen of England. Loyalists from Georgia, fleeing the oppression in the late 1700s, obtained land grants in the Caicos Islands and began plantation life, with imported slaves.

The vagaries of Caribbean living and the seesaw of power that saw islands farther south switch allegiances with staggering rapidity saw the Turks and Caicos governed by the Bahamas for a time after 1799, and, following the dissolution of that charter in 1848, under the watchful eye of the government of Jamaica.

The Turks and Caicos today are a British Crown Colony, with a governor appointed by the Queen.

Shankland Cox and the Natural Environment

When tourism was first touted as a means for increasing the standard of living in the islands—and creating some source of income for the islanders—the Turks and Caicos Islands subscribed to a long-term development plan designed by Shankland Cox, an English firm brought to the islands to complete a development survey. The complete report presented a program for development that is being followed today, allowing for residential and hotel properties, all low profile and most with few rooms and focus on the sea for entertainment. In tandem with the Shankland Cox program, the officials worked with a team from the United States to prepare a report on the ecology of the islands, with particular emphasis on the effect development would have on the natural environment. One of the recommendations in the report is that "it would be a great mistake to undertake development imitative of the large projects elsewhere in the American tropics. This is especially true of dredge-and-fill operations which destroy lowlands in order to create land for massive housing: lowlands, especially mangroves, are at the base of inshore marine nutrition. Lowlands must be conserved." The report further suggests that "canals and marinas should not become sumps for eutrophy and pollution" and that "there is a unique opportunity to develop these islands in a special way . . . these fragile islands should [not] be wasted in a rush for short-term gain."

Most of the population of the islands is centered on Grand Turk (the center of government), South Caicos, and North Caicos, with some settlements on Grand Caicos, Providenciales, and Salt Cay. Their rudimentary economy is largely based on tourism, but many of the islands still await the first footfall on freshly washed beaches and provide unique away-from-it-all havens.

PRACTICAL INFORMATION FOR THE TURKS AND CAICOS

HOW TO GET THERE. By Air. *Air Florida* flies to Grand Turk daily from Miami. *Bahamasair* to South Caicos via Nassau. *Turks & Caicos National Airline* (TCNA) connects all the major islands.

By sea. Charter boats cruise around the islands and an occasional cruise ship anchors off one of the sandy bays for a "day at the beach," but the islands are definitely off the beaten path for the usual cruises.

FURTHER INFORMATION. *The Turks and Caicos Tourist Board* has its main office on Grand Turk, W.I. In the U.S., contact the Turks and Caicos Tourist Board, 4470 Northwest 79th Ave., Miami, Fla. 33166. They also have representatives at 111 Queen St. E., Toronto, Ont. M5C 1F2, Canada; West India Committee, 18 Grosvenor St., London W1X OHP, Eng. The islands are members of the Caribbean Travel Association at 20 E. 46th St., New York 10017. Most hotels are very helpful with full information about what's available on and around the islands and the Tourist Board distributes one of the area's most complete, easy to read, information-packed booklets on request. It has maps with hotel locations noted, plus informative comments on the several islands and their specific characteristics.

PASSPORTS & VISAS. Some proof of citizenship is required. As we mention elsewhere, a passport—even if it's expired—is the best proof; your driver's license is not sufficient.

MONEY. U.S. dollars are legal tender. $1.85 U.S. = 1£.

TAXES AND OTHER CHARGES. Hotels charge a tax of $1 per person per night, along with a 10% service charge. The airport departure tax is $5 per person.

HOW TO GET ABOUT. Boat is best, if you're planning any exploring from island to island. Small planes spring from airport to airport and private planes bring many of the island's vacationers. Walking is the best way to wander; there's not a lot to see and many of the islands are little more than sandy spits, but the water is just about perfect and the bays are conducive to swimming, snorkeling, even scuba and some fishing. Driving from place to place is a last resort, but necessary for some of the hotel-town/airport links.

On Grand Turk you can rent a bicycle for $5, a Moped for $10, or a car for $25 daily.

EVENTS AND HOLIDAYS. Highlights here are the Commonwealth Day celebration in May, which opens with the South Caicos Regatta; the Queen's Birthday celebration is June; and Carnival, which takes place at the end of August. Other holidays are New Year's Day, Good Friday, Easter Monday, Constitution Day (June 12), Emancipation Day (Aug. 7), Peacemaker's Day (Nov. 9), Christmas Day, and Boxing Day.

STAYING IN TURKS AND CAICOS ISLANDS

HOTELS. In less than ten years, tourism has become the main source of income (and the main industry) for the Turks and Caicos Islands. A comprehensive plan, and careful controls, will keep inns small and manageable, with owner/manager personality a prominent factor. Over $5 million has been invested in hotel facilities thus far and that amount or more will come into the area in the near future. Fewer than 300 beds are now available.

Hotels are spotted on the islands of Grand Turk (Turks Head Inn, Salt Raker Inn, and the Hotel Kittina), Pine Cay (Meridian Club), Providenciales (Third Turtle Inn), North Caicos (The Prospect of Whitby) and South Caicos (Admiral's Arms Hotel), with a new hotel proposed for Salt Cay. Additional hotels and hotel/condominiums are planned for Grand Caicos and North Caicos.

GRAND TURK

Hotel Kittina. On "hotel row" with Salt Raker and Turks Head Inn, all small, congenial, and pleasant. The twenty-three rooms and apartments are comfortable, not lavish, with the newest rooms in the recent addition being around an inner court with the dining room off to the side. New emphasis here is on three- and seven-day dive packages. $65–70 double EP in winter; $30–38 double EP off-season.

Salt Raker Inn. Has ten rooms in a nicely renovated building that dates from 1835. A congenial mix of guests with varying interests. The obvious attraction of the area for scuba and snorkel enthusiasts assures one or two of those. The beach is across the road; diving arrangements are usually worked through Pepcor. The "blazing bougainvillea garden" is an attraction on this parched island, as are the four stools at the bar. $65 double EP in winter; $25–35 off-season.

Turks Head Inn. Nine rooms and one cottage along the beach that is the center of town. The "more than 100-year-old" house is Bermuda style, with an inner court, thatch-roofed bar and a publike atmosphere at lunch that attracts the residents. Rooms run $35–50 double EP in winter, $27 off-season. The cottage for two rents for $40–60 double in winter, $30 off-season.

NORTH CAICOS

The Prospect of Whitby Hotel. Named for the famous Thames-side pub in London and hoping "to emulate the traditional English atmosphere of friendliness and hospitality . . ." The hotel has twenty-five air-conditioned rooms, all overlooking the beach. There is a tennis court, but the emphasis is on watersports, with two dive masters, a scuba program, sailboats, water skiing, deep-sea fishing, and beach cruise picnics. $150–200 double in winter, $85 double off-season, with two meals included.

PINE CAY

Meridian Club. Started as one of the area's most ambitious projects, this property is part of a development for private homes. The accommodations at the Club take care of seventy-five guests in beach suites, private cottages and apartments. Freshwater pool, tennis, watersports. $115 double EP in winter; $80 double off-season.

PROVIDENCIALES

Third Turtle Inn. Out-of-the-way relaxation at this twenty-four-unit spot overlooking Sellars Pond Marina. Ideal for the self-sufficient. Watersports are high on the list of activities. $155 double all year, with three meals included.

SOUTH CAICOS

Admiral's Arms. This small inn has thirteen rooms set in an informal seaside (not beachside) location. The pool carved out of the sandy-rocky shoreline is a gathering place for guests, most of whom enjoy prowling around Cockburn Harbour or heading out to sea on scuba and snorkeling expeditions. Early breakfasts can be arranged for fishermen. The meals are hearty and feature fish and whatever can be grown locally. $50 double EP in winter; $30–40 double EP off-season.

WHAT WILL IT COST?

$100 for two persons per day in winter is the average for these islands. This includes meals. Rates for special watersports are extra, with charges varying from island to island.

RESTAURANTS/NIGHTLIFE. Dining is still at the hotels on the islands. Other than evening conversations with fellow guests, there is no nightlife—everything is geared to early rising for the watersports activities.

SHOPPING. Little to buy here other than native straw- and shell-work, but it's nicely done, especially the conch jewelry.

SPORTS. *Watersports* are "it" for the Turks and Caicos. Boats can be rented for the day from many hotels, especially the Third Turtle Inn on Providenciales and the Admiral's Arms at South Caicos. The *sport fishing* is excellent off Grand Turk, Salt Cay, South Caicos, and Providenciales. A 334-lb. blue marlin was caught off Providenciales, and an unweighed sailfish impressed the folks when it was caught off Salt Cay.

The charter rates on Providenciales for a day of sport fishing run about $60 per day for an Aquasport or a 17-ft. Boston Whaler and $20 for a day aboard a Sportfisherman. A Diving Barge charters for about $110. On South Caicos, 17-ft. boats charter for about $10 per hour and at Grand Turk a 21-ft. fibre glass boat for skin diving was about $50. A sailing sloop rented for about $30.

For *scuba divers* who are coming to this area in ever increasing numbers, prompted by "the word" from the experts. *Pepcor Ltd.* and *Underwater Research Ltd.* have dive shops on Grand Turk. Equipment is available, including tanks. *West Indies Divers Ltd.* operate through the Admirals Arms Hotel on South Caicos and Art Pickering provides complete diving service for Providenciales. Diving equipment is also available on Pine Cay.

Cricket and other local sports center on South Caicos and Grand Turk.

The plans for *golf* courses for Pine Cay and Providenciales are still only conversation. *Tennis* courts are available at *The Prospect of Whitby Hotel* on North Caicos; the *Meridian Club* on Pine Cay; and *The Third Turtle Inn* on Providenciales. There is also a public court on South Caicos.

THE U.S. VIRGIN ISLANDS

America's Tranquil Trio

Picture pastel-colored, Old World Danish towns rising incongruously from blue Caribbean bays, streamlined modern buildings gleaming against the bougainvillea and hibiscus, and a quiet tropical wilderness, most of it a National Park, and you have the three major landfalls of the U.S. Virgin Islands.

They lie about 40 miles east of Puerto Rico, in an inverted triangle, with St. Croix at a point 40 miles south of St. Thomas and the British Virgins off to the right–all of them jewels that rest on the hilt of the Antillean scimitar that curves southward to the Spanish Main.

What makes these islands a special place for travelers is that each is different–St. Thomas, the most gregarious and lively; St. Croix, slower-paced with a quiet charm; and St. John, the lush, sleepy little brother of the trio. Another factor is that all three can be visited easily and inexpensively by seaplane or ferry.

History

Columbus first sighted St. Croix in 1493, christened it "Santa Cruz," and then sailed north to discover the other sand-fringed isles and cays, which he named in memory of St. Ursula's 11,000 virgins who died in an epic defense of their chastity. A less pious admiral, Sir Francis Drake, rebaptized the islands a century later in honor of a more worldly virgin, Elizabeth I of England.

The largest of the islands, St. Croix was to fly under seven flags–Dutch, French, Danish and Knights of Malta among them–before the U.S. purchased the entire chain from Denmark in 1917.

St. Thomas was settled by the Danes in 1666. Once on shore, they divided it up into plantations of 125 acres each. It was determined that the rent to be paid by the landowners would be one turkey per year, which was to be delivered to the Governor. Eventually shipping and commerce replaced agriculture on the island, and Charlotte Amalie, the capital, became an official free port in 1724.

Historically, St. John followed the path of its larger fellow-Virgins. It has known the tread of Dutch, English, Spanish, French and Danish adventurers. The Danes didn't settle St. John until 1717, and by 1726 all available land had been taken over by plantations and sugar was king.

The slaves, ill-treated by their Danish masters, revolted in 1733, at which time many of the planters took refuge at Caneel Bay Plantation. It took French soldiers imported from Martinique to quell the rebellion. Some slaves are said to have leaped off the cliff at Mary's Point in preference to capture and its consequences. The islanders insist that the ghosts of these ancestors still haunt this lofty promontory.

The abolition of slavery in 1848 dealt a death blow to the sugar economy of St. John. The planters left; the tropical jungle took over; and the island returned to bush—a bush that was to become a tropical paradise for visitors a century later.

EXPLORING ST. CROIX

St. Croix is 40 miles south of St. Thomas, just 20 minutes away by the amphibian planes that sweep into and out of Charlotte Amalie and Christiansted several times daily.

The island is pronounced "Saint Croy" by the local people and everyone else "in the know" (no one uses the French form) and is the largest of the U.S. Virgin Islands: 28 miles long, up to seven miles wide, encompassing 84 square miles of rolling land that used to be covered with waving carpets of sugar cane. The ruins of great plantation houses recall the days when St. Croix rivaled Barbados as the greatest producer of sugar in the West Indies.

Those days are long gone, but the island's heritage still prevails. Its capital, Christiansted, is a beautifully restored old Danish port on a coral-bound bay on the northeastern shore. The red-roofed, 18th century buildings are pale yellow, pink and ochre, resplendent with bright blazes of bougainvillea and hibiscus to add to the tropical technicolor. The buildings are solid stone, with thick walls that are still able to perform the miracles of 18th century air-conditioning. Arcades transform cobblestone sidewalks into shaded collonades, adding a European touch that makes shopping and sightseeing a real pleasure.

A DAY ON YOUR OWN

The best place to begin your exploration of St. Croix is in *Christiansted.* Its town square and waterfront area at the foot of King Street

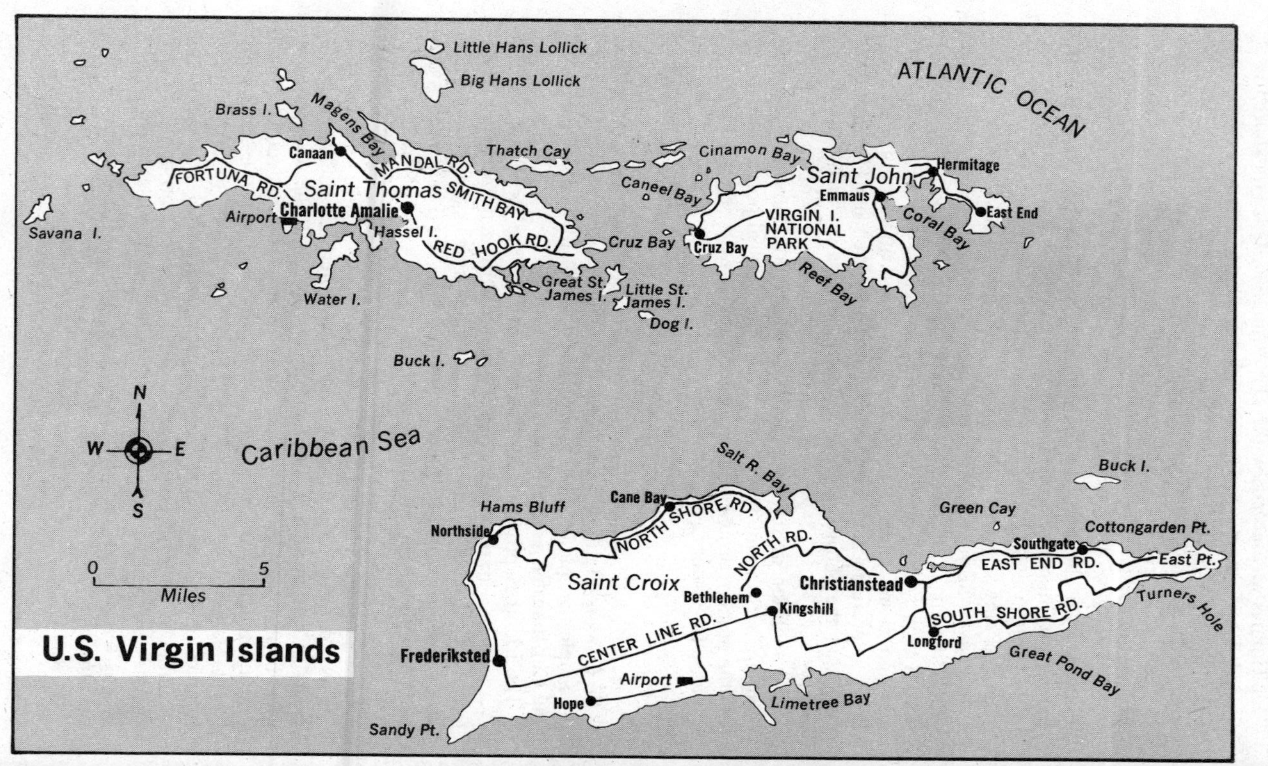
U.S. Virgin Islands
ATLANTIC OCEAN
Caribbean Sea
Little Hans Lollick
Big Hans Lollick
Brass I.
Magens Bay
Canaan
Thatch Cay
MANDAL RD.
FORTUNA RD.
Saint Thomas
SMITH BAY
Charlotte Amalie
Airport
Savana I.
Hassel I.
RED HOOK RD.
Water I.
Great St. James I.
Little St. James I.
Dog I.
Cruz Bay
Caneel Bay
Cinamon Bay
Saint John
Hermitage
Emmaus
East End
Coral Bay
VIRGIN I. NATIONAL PARK
Reef Bay
Buck I.
N
W
E
S
0
5
Miles
Salt R. Bay
Hams Bluff
Cane Bay
NORTH SHORE RD.
Northside
NORTH RD.
Saint Croix
Bethlehem
Kingshill
Christiansted
CENTER LINE RD.
Frederiksted
Airport
Hope
Sandy Pt.
Limetree Bay
Green Cay
Buck I.
Cottongarden Pt.
Southgate
EAST END RD.
East Pt.
Turners Hole
SOUTH SHORE RD.
Longford
Great Pond Bay

have, for the past 30 years, been officially classified as a National Historic Site. Outstanding here are the 17th century Dutch Fort, Christiansvaern; the Danish Post Office; the original Customs House; the old church known as the Steeple Building; and the splendid and imposing Government House.

Visit the Steeple Building, which houses the St. Croix Museum (not the big, exhausting type, but a fine collection of pre-Columbian artifacts, plus a number of historically interesting relics of Danish plantation days). You will be able to obtain self-guiding leaflets at the National Park Service office in the Fort.

Explore Government House, which was the original seat of government for the nearby Danish West Indies. Its ballroom is decorated with replicas of the original Danish furnishings, a gift from Denmark to the U.S. The celebrated hardware store across the street, where Alexander Hamilton worked at the age of thirteen, burned down after being in continuous operation since that time. It has been rebuilt, with the same name, but with a new interior inside the "old" facade.

The Christiansted shopping center is cheek-by-jowl with the National Historic Site. Centering on Company Street and King Street, it's smaller than the one at Charlotte Amalie, St. Thomas, but has the same free-port advantages and offers similar temptations.

Frederiksted, St. Croix's "other town" lies 17 miles to the west. In between are the old sugar plantations, some in picturesque ruins; one or two are still in use and have been restored as guest houses. Their names are haunting: Anna's Hope, Peter's Rest, Upper Love, Jealousy, Lower Love, Sally's Fancy. They are fascinating with their round sugar mills, their noble double stairways, their mute and melancholy testimony to past grandeur.

Palatial Judith's Fancy was once the residence of the Governor of the Knights of Malta. It is a romantic ruin set in the midst of an estate of several hundred scenic acres, long since developed as a residential community. No one with a feeling for history can remain insensible to the experience of seeing where Columbus anchored at Salt River in 1493. He called it El Cabo de las Flechas, or Cape of the Arrows, in memory of the reception he got! You'll get a fine view of it from the hill beyond Judith's Fancy.

Don't miss a stop at Whim Greathouse, which is one of the island's great showplaces. This house has been converted to a museum and personifies the high life of the sugar planters in the late 1700s at the peak of St. Croix's prosperity. Its great windmill has been rebuilt, and is one of the most photographed sites on the island.

One mile east of Whim, visit St. George's Botanical Gardens, which are set on 16 verdant acres of land that was once an Indian settlement. An arcade of royal palms marks the entryway, then leads to the rare and exotic plantings which have been developed around the ruins of the old village homes and work buildings. There's also a tropical garden with papaya, avocado, limes, grapefruit and tangerines growing in color and profusion, along with such brilliant tropical plants as frangipani, bougainvillea, poinsettia and hibiscus.

Frederiksted itself, which harbors assorted ships and a population of some 3,500, was ravaged by a fire in 1878. When the houses were rebuilt, Victorian architecture was the rage, so you have the pastel-colored Danish-type houses plus lacy galleries of iron and wood, cupolas, curlicues and enough gingerbread details to illustrate all the fairy tales of Hans Christian Andersen.

The old and famous Fort Frederik, at the harbor's edge, has been completely restored and stands as it did when the Danes built it in 1760. Visit the cells, the non-commissioned officer's quarters, the canteen and the arsenal on the ground floor and the Commandant's Quarters upstairs. There is also a small museum with changing exhibits; a restored Customs House next door; and a few duty-free shops housed in old Victorian homes.

EXPLORING ST. JOHN

About 30 minutes by ferry, three miles east of St. Thomas across Pillsbury Sound from Red Hook, St. Thomas, St. John comes close to realizing that travel folder dream, "an unspoiled tropical paradise." Two-thirds of St. John's 21 square miles officially became the Virgin Islands National Park in 1956, the 29th American area to receive this guarantee of national protection. For campers, the park has ample facilities. St. John's restrained and tasteful development to date and its presentation to the American people are the work of Laurance S. Rockefeller, who has contributed largely to Caneel Bay Plantation, a most attractive resort.

Beautiful and seemingly undisturbed, St. John is covered with tropical vegetation, including a bay-tree forest which once supplied St. Thomas with the raw material of its fragrant bay rum. Clean, gleaming white sand beaches fringe the many bays that are scalloped out along the northern shore, and the iridescent water is just about perfect for swimming, fishing, snorkeling, and underwater photography. At Trunk Bay, one of the loveliest of all, there is an Underwater Trail with flora and coral formations signposted along the way, and just off the Cinnamon Bay camping area is a small undisturbed islet with an extraordinary marine population.

Today, there are only about 3,000 permanent residents on St. John, most of them native Virgin Islanders. The continentals are in the tourist business or are permanent residents who've chosen the island for retirement. Cruz Bay, the administrative capital, is still a small West Indian village, even with the advent of the National Park Service (with its demonstration building) and two small shopping arcades. *Mongoose Junction,* a mini-mall, has 8 intriguing shops, with the emphasis on local crafts, a restaurant, and a great "deli" for eat-in and take-out. *Lemon Tree Mall* nearby is new and fun for browsing. While the boutique at *Caneel Bay* is the only place with real resort wear, don't miss a visit to *Islandia* in town for a cool drink and a look at their Finnish fashions.

St. John is for the traveler who wants to escape from the pressures of 20th century life for a day, a week, perhaps forever. Sightseeing is done by jeep which, with or without a driver/guide, can be hired on the island. Guides are useful, sometimes indispensable in exploring the scenic mountain trails and the sobering bush-covered ruins of old forts and palatial plantation houses. At Annaberg Mill, the vast estate has been well cleared and partially restored, with a Forest Service pamphlet available at the site explaining the workings of the old sugar plantation and pointing out ruins of particular interest. You can take a trail from Cruz to Coral Bay once used by the Indians long before Columbus stumbled on these islands. Another trail will lead you to ancient, still undeciphered Indian inscriptions on the rocks above Reef Bay. The warlike Caribs were here and the peaceful Arawaks, whose language survives them in two of our adopted words, a reflection of amenities bequeathed to the white man: tobacco, hammock. Both tribes are gone. The land remains, the beaches, the forests, the mountains, the lagoons, and the ambient sea.

A DAY ON YOUR OWN

Rent a jeep, start out early in the morning in Cruz Bay, the island's capital, and stop first at a wonderful "deli" called *The Moveable Feast* to put your picnic lunch together. Pack a bathing suit, a towel, a camera, and then head for the hills.

Start your climb from Cruz Bay along the spine of the island, reach Centerline Road, and at the peak, you'll have one of the most beautiful views of the Virgin Islands and offshore cays. Just beyond this lookout point, the road will slope downward toward the north shore. Plan at least a one-hour stop at *Annaberg Mill* and explore the ruins of this 200-year-old sugar plantation. Then backtrack to the shore road and head for Maho Bay, with its beautiful beach and tranquil waters. You might want to take a quick swim here, but save your picnic for *Hawk's Nest,* where you can enjoy two beaches, both of them less crowded than those you'll find enroute.

You'll pass more ruins along the way, and if you haven't seen the *Cinnamon Bay Campgrounds,* stop and take a look. Really superb for campers and well run by the National Park Service. Continue on to *Trunk Bay,* and if you snorkel, this is *the* spot . . . the underwater trail is a fine one, with markers posted along the trail. The next stop will be *Hawks' Nest,* and this is your swimming and picnic spot. Take the time to relax here and enjoy the beauty that is St. John.

If you're not staying at Caneel Bay, plan to visit the plantation for a late afternoon drink at their restored sugar mill. If you're just visiting St. John for the day, you'll still have time to catch the last evening ferry back to St. Thomas.

EXPLORING ST. THOMAS

Thirteen miles long, less than 3 miles wide, the island of St. Thomas rises abruptly from the sea to an altitude of 1500 feet. Roads festoon the hillsides like Christmas tinsel, bending and weaving their narrow paths to new residential villages. The Atlantic cuts its sprawling shores on the north, the Caribbean indents it on the south into a series of jagged, spectacular bays. One of these forms the deep-water harbor of the Virgin Islands' superbly situated capital, Charlotte Amalie.

This historic port, more commonly known as St. Thomas harbor, was the nearest thing to home port for such cutthroats as Captain Kidd and Edward Teach (Blackbeard the Pirate). From this lair, Sir Francis Drake launched his attacks on Spanish galleons laden with New World gold, lumbering through the Anegada passage on their way home to Spain.

Today the harbor bustles with yachts, ships, and the constant buzzing of the Virgin Islands Seaplane Shuttle's amphibians that provide commuter service between the Virgins. Container ships and a few island sloops bring meat, vegetables, and fish to markets of St. Thomas, but the prize product today is tourists. At the height of the season, you will see as many as six major cruise lines tied up in a row at the West India Company pier, while three more ride at anchor outside the harbor.

Charlotte Amalie climbs as high as it can up the hillside without the benefit of terraces. Its only similarity to the town the pirates knew is the three hills which sailors still compare to the foretop, main, and mizzenmast of a ship.

The Danes, who moved quietly into St. Thomas in the 17th century amidst the colonial squabbles of England, Spain, and France, built this town and named it after the consort of King Christian V. The governor divided the islands into "states" and soon there were over 170 thriving sugar plantations–and a slave trade that supplied the plantations of America and made St. Thomas the biggest slave market in the world.

Charlotte Amalie, already famous as a free port and a protected harbor, welcomed all comers: New England sea captains, Civil War blockade runners, religious refugees from Europe, even pirates who came to buy supplies and sell their loot in this busy trading post with no holds barred, no questions asked. On two occasions, the pirates actually captured the place. On two others, the British seized St. Thomas in protest against the toleration of so much illegal piracy. St. Thomas, accustomed to receiving visitors of every stamp, took everything in its stride. The visitors in their turn stamped the port of Charlotte Amalie indelibly with all the color and excitement of a busy waterfront town.

The color and excitement are still there. And, despite the ravages of time, the city, with its narrow streets, ancient warehouses, and old walls, recalls its past.

A DAY ON YOUR OWN

Charlotte Amalie is a town to be explored by walking. But should you start your tour at the top of the island, you'll find the vista from Skyline Drive, overlooking the town and harbor, one of the most memorable views of the Caribbean. Beginning at the bottom, you can (and most will) dart into and out of the warehouses that once housed pirate treasure and now store the imports that tourists gather to the full $600 duty-free quota and more.

In the heart of the shopping center, most visitors are surprised to learn that the great impressionist painter Camille Pissaro was born here, and that his parents are buried in the Jewish Cemetery of St. Thomas.

While supermarkets have taken over most of the shopping baskets from the local markets, it is still possible to catch an island schooner at the waterfront with its pile of coconuts or fish from nearby sources, or the local ladies selling produce at the open market on the far end of the main street.

Over half the buildings of St. Thomas are more than a century old–something of a record for an American community. Most venerable of all is Old Fort Christian, built by the first Danish settlers more than 300 years ago and named for King Christian V. A striking example of 17th century military architecture, this fort served as jail, church, vicarage, courthouse, and governor's residence all rolled into one massive pile of masonry. Numerous pirates were hanged at Fort Christian. It is still used as a jail and police station, but several cells have been set aside for a small collection of Arawak and Carib relics and remnants of the early Danish settlements.

Also dating from the 17th century are the Nisky Moravian Mission, rebuilt in 1969 after being gutted by fire, and the tower of Bluebeard's Castle, now part of a hotel. Two old churches are worth a visit: the Dutch Reformed Church, one of the first of this faith in the New World outside of New Amsterdam-New York, and the 18th century Lutheran Church, second oldest in the Western Hemisphere and still using its two-centuries-old ecclesiastical silver.

The Jewish Synagogue, the second oldest in the Caribbean, long thought to be the first, is the only one on American soil to maintain the old tradition of keeping clean sand on its floor to commemorate the flight of the Jews from Egypt through the desert. This place of worship and the interesting Jewish cemetery are another reminder of the rich cultural heritage and the tradition of tolerance which have shaped the Virgin Islands.

Charlotte Amalie's Grand Hotel, which opened in 1841, is a fascinating relic of 19th century luxury. Its original third story was blown off in a hurricane, and the rest of it was destroyed by fire years ago. Now fully restored, but not as a hotel, the Grand houses several shops on the main floor and the pleasant *Grand Gallery Restaurant* upstairs. Swing around the corner to the "Project St. Thomas" office for full information on the island, and for one of the 28-flavor selections of ice cream cones at Howard Johnson's.

Other buildings of more than usual interest include the handsome Government House, built in 1867 for meetings of the Danish Colonial Council and now the center of political life and the official residence of the Governor. Nearby is one of the few remaining stair-streets of the old town, this one called the "Ninety-Nine Steps" although there are not 99 steps today. Two centuries-old Crown House, the former residence of early Danish officials, is in this area and open to the public. Atop the Ninety-Nine Steps on Government Hill, it's a fine example of how the rich lived here in the early 18th century. Hotel 1829, built as Lavalette House by a French sea captain, opens onto a Spanish-style courtyard draped with colorful bougainvillea. Also to note are the Lutheran Parsonage and the Danish Consulate, dominating the whole bay from Denmark Hill, both typical of 19th century Danish architecture; and "Quarters B," once the German consulate, now a government office building famous for its unusual staircase, transplanted from a ship. The character of the whole municipal area is protected by a watchful government commission which is supposed to check all construction plans before issuing building permits.

If you have prowled around the waterfront and the shopping district, climbed the Ninety-Nine Steps, and seen more than one of these historic buildings, you will be ready for some refreshment. Take a cab up to the Mountain Top Restaurant, which is world-famous for its banana daiquiris and spectacular view. Stay for lunch and enjoy tropical salads, sandwiches from the grill, or local specialties.

There is still the post office with murals painted by Stephen Dohanos under WPA auspices; the College of the Virgin Islands, near the airport, is a fine example of contemporary Caribbean architecture; and the Virgin Islands Museum at Fort Christian has enough mementos of island history to warrant a visit.

A View from the North Side

Having explored Charlotte Amalie, it is time to cross the mountain range that cuts St. Thomas in two and visit the north side of the island, far more beautiful, the northsiders will tell you, than anything on the Caribbean side. Here are the splendid panoramic views over the Atlantic. Magens Bay, which many call the most beautiful beach in the world, and the whole eastern sweep of American and British Virgins, green in the opalescent sea. The north side has more rain, lusher vegetation, more tranquility, better beaches.

Of special interest in this area are: Drake's Seat, where that old sea dog surely never sat, but from which you will have a grand view of the waters in which he operated and which are now named in his honor; Venus Pillar, the astronomical obelisk on Magnolia Hill; or Mafolie, the quaint French refugee settlement with its pretty little church.

Finally, end your day on your own at fantastic *Coral World,* a $2.5-million underwater observatory and marine park, which is located at Coki Point, one of the best snorkling beaches on St. Thomas. The attraction features a marine garden with 21 aquarium tanks of natural seascapes, a crafts bazaar, restaurant and bar. The 3-story tower stands 100 feet offshore and is topped by a geodesic dome from which St. John may be seen. A circular reef tank–a 360-degree glass tank, surrounds the viewer. The reef tank contains sharks, barracudas, sting rays and other large ocean fish. On the sea floor–14 feet below the waterline–visitors get a close-up view of a coral reef through 24 picture windows. Stay on for a lobster dinner by candlelight at *The Ancient Mariner* restaurant.

PRACTICAL INFORMATION FOR THE U.S. VIRGIN ISLANDS

St. Thomas and St. John

HOW TO GET THERE. By Air. *American* leads the way, via St. Croix while airport work prevents big jet landings at St. Thomas. *Eastern* flies from Miami to St. Croix and St. Thomas. Out of San Juan, the half-hour flight to St. Thomas is made by *Prinair, Aero Virgin Islands* and *Ocean Air. Virgin Islands Seaplane Shuttle* makes what has become a several times daily commuter run between St. Thomas and St. Croix.

BY SEA. St. Thomas has been the number one cruise port for the past several seasons, some days seeing as many as nine large ships in Charlotte Amalie harbor at a time! More than 21 cruise lines include St. Thomas as a port, sailing out of New York, Norfolk, Virginia, and Florida (Port Everglades and Miami), as well as out of other East Coast ports and from the West Coast. In addition, the cruises that start in Puerto Rico stop in St. Thomas and sometimes in St. Croix.

Boat service to St. John is out of St. Thomas, from East End's Red Hook Landing. *Caneel Bay* operates its own boat for its guests; there is also the government boat to Cruz Bay.

There is regular boat service, leaving from the St. Thomas waterfront, to the British Virgin Islands, stopping at West End and Road Town, Tortola.

FURTHER INFORMATION. *The Virgin Islands Department of Commerce* operates tourist information offices at 1270 Avenue of the Americas, New York, N.Y. 10020; in Chicago at 343 South Dearborn St., Chicago, Ill. 60604; in Los Angeles at 3450 Wilshire Blvd., Los Angeles, CA 90010; in Dallas at 3300 W. Mockingbird Lane, Dallas, TX 75235; in Miami at 7270 N.W. 12th St., Miami, FLA 33126; in Seattle at 1402 Third Avenue, Seattle, WA 98101; and in Washington, D.C. at 1050 17th Street, N.W. There are island offices at Christiansted and Frederiksted, St. Croix, and in Charlotte Amalie, St. Thomas.

ISLAND MEDIA. The *St. Thomas Daily News* provides local and international coverage. For visitors, two fine sources of information are *This Week* (printed in different colors for each island) and *Here's How,* both filled with facts on shopping and touring.

AUTHORIZED TOUR OPERATORS. Adventure Tours; Butler Travels; Caribbean Holidays; Cavalcade Tours; Flyfaire; GoGo Tours; Playtime Vacations; Red & Blue Tours; and Travel Center Tours from the U.S. From Canada, Fairway Tours and Holiday House.

HOW TO GET ABOUT. They drive on the left-hand side in the Virgin Islands. *Avis, Hertz, National* and many local agencies are found in St. Thomas *(Hertz* and *Avis* at the airport as well as in town). Or rent a scooter from *Honda Rental, Ltd.* (advisable only if you know the roads well). Taxis are available everywhere. In St. Thomas, the rates are for one person; additional passengers pay extra. Most drivers are courteous and qualified to act as guides.

On St. John, transportation is by jeep, Volkswagen, mini-moke or Taxi. A bus makes scheduled stops at Cruz, Caneel, Trunk and Cinnamon Bays. The *Red Hook Ferry* plies regularly between St. Thomas and Cruz Bay on St. John. The *Caneel Bay Plantation Ferry* serves the hotel from the National Park Dock near Red Hook with four roundtrips daily.

PASSPORTS, VISAS. None required for U.S. citizens. Reentry regulations must be complied with by those coming from foreign ports. Non-U.S. citizens must have passports and clear Immigration when coming from their own country or from the U.S.

MONEY. These are U.S. islands, and the dollar is good everywhere. $1.85 U.S. = 1£.

TAXES AND OTHER CHARGES. All room rates are subject to a 5% Government tax. Some hotels add a 10% service charge. Be sure to check in advance. There is no airport departure tax from these islands.

EVENTS AND HOLIDAYS. Carnival festivities, West Indian-style, are the highlight each year, especially on St. Thomas. However, the U.S. Virgin Islands celebrate all the U.S. mainland holidays, along with several of their own. Among them are *Three Kings Day* (Jan. 6); *Transfer Day* (3rd Monday in March); *Organic Act Day* (3rd Monday in June); *Emancipation Day* (July 3); *Hurricane Supplication Day* (4th Monday in July); *Columbus/Puerto Rico Friendship Day* (2nd Monday in October); *Hurricane Thanksgiving Day* (3rd Monday in October); and *Liberty Day* (Nov. 1).

WHAT WILL IT COST?

A typical day in the U.S. Virgin Islands for *two* persons during the winter season will run:

	US$	£
Hotel accommodations (overall average)	95	51
Full breakfast at the hotel	8	4
Lunch at a moderate restaurant	12	6
Dinner at one of the top restaurants	30	16
Tips, taxes, and service charges	20	11
One-day sightseeing by rental car or taxi	25	14
	$190	£102

STAYING IN THE U.S. VIRGIN ISLANDS

HOTELS ON ST. THOMAS. The Virgin Islands win the numbers game. They have more hotels per square inch than any other area in the Caribbean. The concentration is at Charlotte Amalie, St. Thomas, and Christiansted, St. Croix, but almost every beach has its hotel as well. The government rate sheet, published twice yearly (for low summer and high winter rates) lists about 100 choices, with 50 on St. Thomas, 40 on St. Croix, and 10 on St. John. Places range from luxury hotels (the chains have not come in here with their traditional style, although there is a *Holiday Inn* on St. Thomas) to small guest houses and includes apartments, cottages, private homes, villas and campsites.

St. Thomas leads in the guest house field, with more personality inns than any other island in the Caribbean; St. Croix has beach resorts and places scattered around the countryside to bring the "good life" to the vacationer; St. John has Caneel Bay, in a class by itself for elegance and comfort in peace and quiet, and the campsites at the 29th U.S. National Park.

Bluebeard's Castle. This prime property is a long-time favorite for its 100 neat and modern rooms. There's the terrace for dining with a spectacular view of Charlotte Amalie, a more formal indoor dining area and the *Pirate's Parlour* nightclub with professional entertainment. Saltwater swimming pool, 2 lighted tennis courts, all in a verdant tropical setting around the 300-year-old Bluebeard's Tower. The hotel provides transportation to the beach at Magens Bay at modest charge. $115–145 double EP in winter, $79–105 double EP off-season.

Bolongo Bay. This tranquil hotel has 36 air-conditioned, self-contained apartments on a private beach 10 minutes from town. Beachside bar–breakfast and lunch; all water sports. Freshwater swimming pool, 4 tennis courts. All units have full kitchen facilities and daily maid service. $120 double in winter, $85 double off-season, including Continental breakfast.

Carib Beach Hotel. 92 air-conditioned rooms in a garden setting on the beach, 2 miles from town. Rooms in the new section are preferable; minimum-rate rooms are small. Cocktail lounge, piano bar, nightly entertainment, restaurant. Snorkeling equipment available. Unusual Mermaid Walk over edge of Lindbergh Bay. Freshwater pool. Can be noisy because of its proximity to the airport. $78–118 double EP in winter, $60–81 double EP off-season.

Cowpet Bay Villas. A Chinese wall of condominiums rented as hotel rooms and/or apartments when the owners are not in residence, this place is on one of the island's prettiest bays. It looks mammoth from the water, but has a cosy, pleasant atmosphere. 105 rooms, 42 larger units, some with as many as 4 bedrooms. Located on the east end, about a 20-minute drive from town (but there's no real need to go there; everything's here). Fully equipped units, maid service, private tennis club. St. Thomas Yacht Club is not far away, but some boats anchor right at this bay. Dining places on premises and nearby. Winter rates run: $175–245; off-season rates $110–160, depending upon number of bedrooms, which ranges from one to four.

Frenchman's Reef. 410 air-conditioned rooms, all with phone and TV, on the best hotel site in St. Thomas–an eastern point overlooking the mouth of the harbor. Huge dining room, 3 cocktail lounges, freshwater swimming pool, 4 lighted tennis courts, shopping arcade with 24 duty-free shops. Activities center in the *Top of the Reef* Supper Club, *La Terraza Lounge* or the *Lighthouse* bar. This is a vast *Holiday Inn*-affiliated complex, which also has full convention facilities. $138–188 double EP in winter, $88–128 double EP off-season.

Harbor View. Best known for its cuisine and dinnertime ambience, this restored Danish manor house has 10 air-conditioned rooms that are simply but attractively furnished. You're in the hills of town, not far from Main St. as the crow flies, but a wiggly, narrow-road drive up and down. Freshwater pool, elegant dining room with superior food, cocktail lounge with pianist. $80 double all year, including Continental breakfast.

Hotel 1829. Historic hotel, once a private home, now restored and flower-bowered for guests who like atmosphere. It's on Government Hill, a short walk up from the post office in town. The 18 rooms are not fancy, but do offer a traditional West Indian town-house ambience. Freshwater pool, backgammon tables, pleasant bar area is a popular gathering place. It's a 15-minute drive to the nearest beach. $55–155 double EP in winter; from $65 double EP off-season.

Inn at Mandahl. 8 studio-type living-bedrooms located next to the Mahogany Run golf course. A quiet hilltop retreat. Freshwater pool, great view, exceptional restaurant. $100 double in winter; $58 double off-season, including Continental breakfast.

Island Beachcomber. 50 air-conditioned rooms with bath on a white sandy beach on Lindbergh Bay. All rooms have refrigerators and patios. Popular with a casual crowd who like the informality, the snorkeling, the sailing and the boating. On-the-beach bar for cocktails. Dinner by candlelight at beach-side restaurant. Convenient to airport. $70–80 double EP in winter, $65–75 double EP off-season.

Limetree Beach. On palm-shaded beach at Frenchman's Bay, about 15 minutes' drive from town. Luxurious three-level cottage units with 84 rooms, the "superior" accommodations particularly lovely. Bar, restaurant in hilltop estate have fine food, view, dancing. Nice luncheons served in beach restaurant and bar. Good sports facilities (freshwater pool, scuba instruction, sailing, 2 tennis courts). $110–125 double EP in winter, $88–108 double EP off-season.

Mafolie. An apartment hotel 800 feet above St. Thomas Harbor on Mafolie Hill, with pool. Excellent restaurant, breathtaking views. 23 rooms, some with kitchenettes. Sundeck, free transportation to Magenss Bay. Unless you just like to sit and read by the pool, you'll want a car for a day or two of touring. $58–62 double in winter, $46–50 double off-season, including continental breakfast.

Magens Point Hotel. Out of the hubbub, but an easy drive up and over the mountain to Charlotte Amalie. 28 large rooms with 2 double beds, hillside view of the sea, pool and bistro-style restaurant on premises. Free transportation to Magens Bay Beach, just down the hill. *Lobster Pot* gourmet restaurant is one of the island's favorites. Congenial atmosphere. $109 double EP in winter, $73 double EP off-season.

Mahogany Run. New and spectacular 315-acre resort which features the island's first 18-hole championship golf course. Accommodations are in one- and two-bedroom villas, all with fully-equipped kitchens, some with private swimming pools. $215–230 double EP in winter; from $110–180 EP off-season.

Morningstar Beach Resort. 24 units on the beach, just below *Frenchman's Reef Hotel.* About 10-minute drive from town. Once one of the famous, this beach is still one of the most beautiful although crowded with day visitors since it is the closest to town. The food in the restaurant is average but expensive; water sports available. $70–80 double EP in winter, $60–65 double EP off-season.

Pavilions and Pools. A lovely and secluded spot at the east end, overlooking the sea and St. John. Each room has its own private pool, and the concept became so popular that the "hotel" has now curled along the road and down a lane, with 25 units. Pavilions sleep 4 with living room, kitchen, bedroom, bath, garden, full maid service. $128–138 double in winter, $95–105 double off-season, including Continental breakfast.

Pineapple Beach Resort. 132 rooms in cottage units or condominiums on a sprawling property, 4 miles from town. Several restaurants, some beachside; nightly entertainment. This resort tries to be all things to all people, with water sports, swimming pools and tennis courts. $102–129 double EP in winter, $78–98 double EP off-season. Check on their variety of special package plans.

Point Pleasant. 85 lovely units stretched across 15 acres, 140 feet above sea level, on the island's northeastern shore. The view alone (St. John and the British Virgin Islands) is worth the stay. You'll find happiness and comfort in any of the units, which now include villas, studios and efficiencies. Each has a complete kitchen and a private balcony or patio. All are air-conditioned but also have two-speed paddle fans for those who would combine a light ceiling breeze with the Trade Winds. Pleasant terrace lounge and restaurant; "swimming pool on the beach" rivals its counterpart with a large redwood deck high over the sea. Also included in the daily (or weekly) rate are the free use of cars, Sunfish sailboats, and snorkel gear. Villa rates run $182–242 double in winter ($126–174 off-season), studios $146–186 double in winter ($95–131 off-season), and efficiencies $120 double in winter ($85 off-season).

St. Thomas Hotel & Marina. 223 rooms in studios and suites, all with kitchenettes, overlooking the harbor. Nice accommodations even for non-yachting types who come to anchor at the 200 slips. The indoor restaurant is good; the one on the terrace special because of its spectacular harbor view. Also a coffee shop, a cocktail lounge with nightly entertainment and a large freshwater swimming pool. $80–112 double in winter, $58–75 double off-season.

St. Thomas Diving Club. A historic spot that was once the Russian Consulate, this 16-room property now places its emphasis on scuba and snorkeling excursions. Saltwater pool, beach, tennis facilities, pleasant seaside gallery where meals are served. $52–65 double EP all year. Be sure to check on special scuba-diving package plans here.

Secret Harbour. On a magnificent beach 5 miles east of Charlotte Amalie, this property's 85 beautiful air-conditioned studios, one- and two-bedroom apartments have fully equipped kitchens and maid service. Meals served on seaside terrace or on your own gallery. All water sports; 3 tennis courts on premises. Near all the "East-End" action, but removed from it by its location and ambience. $125–165 double EP in winter; $75–95 double EP off-season.

Shibui. As Japanese in motif as it sounds, with 20 individual cottages overlooking the sea on Contant Hill, 10 minutes from town. Each has full kitchen, living room, bedroom, luxurious bathroom with sunken tub. Ceiling-high screens and windows slide aside to let in the breeze. Some small efficiencies are available. Maid service. Freshwater swimming pool; beach privileges down the mountain at *Island Beachcomber Hotel.* Its teahouse restaurant is popular for drinks, dinner and nightly entertainment. $110 double EP in winter, $75 double off-season, including Continental breakfast.

Sugar Bird Beach & Tennis Club. 99 rooms in a resort hideaway on Water

Island, off by itself on a landfall in Charlotte Amalie's harbor. Free launch operates between 7 A.M. and midnight. Expensive "get-away-from-it-all" atmosphere, with swimming pool, tennis courts, terrace restaurant and nightly entertainment. $110–145 double EP in winter; $70–95 double EP off-season. Add $25 per person per day for breakfast and dinner.

The Virgin Isle Hotel and Beach Club. This very attractive hilltop hotel property has 225 rooms, a large freshwater swimming pool, tennis courts, and a special view-top restaurant. Also has *Lindy's Deli,* which, true to its name, has everything from hot pastrami to creamy cheesecake. Their Beach Club and restaurant are a short ride away and are perfectly set up on a mile-long stretch of white sand. From $95 double EP in winter; $63 double EP off-season.

HOTELS ON ST. JOHN. There's only one resort here. The others are inns, cottages, or campsites for the self-sufficient.

Caneel Bay Plantation is in a class by itself on this or any other island. Adjoining the 29th U.S. National Park, it's service, luxury, and peace and quiet personified. This is where the famous come to regroup and the rest of us are so busy enjoying our vacation that we don't care that they're there. The 156 rooms are graded in two categories, superior and deluxe, and are scattered about the 170-acre peninsula in low-profile buildings. A shuttle bus loop connects the room areas and three dining locations. Reservations are a must for the special fare at Turtle Bay Estate House. Also popular at night is the steak barbecue at the Sugar Mill. Hammocks are tied to palms at appropriate sites; scuba, snorkeling and sailing are superb. 7 tennis courts available to guests at no charge. Limited entertainment in evenings. Bring lots of books. The Caneel cruiser meets guests at the dock on the east end of St. Thomas. Day excursions are arranged to islands nearby. Summer package vacations tie a few days here with a few at *Little Dix* on B.V.I.'s Virgin Gorda. Winter rates run $216–320 double; $160–235 double off-season, with breakfast, lunch, and dinner included.

Cinnamon Bay Campsites, listed through the National Park Service, are often rented a year in advance. Write to the National Park Service, Box 4930, St. Thomas, Virgin Islands for details. Campsite rentals for the 40 concrete cabins rent at $36 per day; tents at $28 per day for four people. Equipment for cooking is included. Bare tent sites are $4. If you have favorite camping equipment, bring it, but write for a reservation anyway.

Holiday Homes of St. John is a fine rental firm which lists 10 private homes around the island available for rental on a weekly or longer basis. All houses are well maintained; some are quite luxurious. You'll do well to bring favorite food-stuffs, packed in dry ice, and canned goods from home. You can get some things in Cruz Bay (and fresh fish by catching it yourself), but prices are high for bought items. Rates begin at $85 double EP in winter; $75 double EP off-season.

Maho Bay Camps Inc. 96 units, tucked in and around the foliage on 14-acres that rise from the sea (and a gorgeous curve of white sand beach) not far from Trunk Bay and the National Park headquarters. Informality for nature lovers is featured, with boardwalks threading the area so that you will not walk on the plants. Herb garden and small commissary are among the facilities; water-sports (scuba, snorkel) are a common interest. Units are comfortable 2-room bungalows with refrigerator unit, grill and terrace for al fresco dining. $45 double EP in winter; $35 double EP off-season.

Serendip Condos. 10 suites, each with twin bedroom, living room, kitchen, and bath. Up the hill out of Cruz Bay overlooking the Bay and Pillsbury Sound. There's a bar-lounge for conversation with other guests; otherwise it's you and your own pals. $75 double EP in winter; $50 double EP off-season.

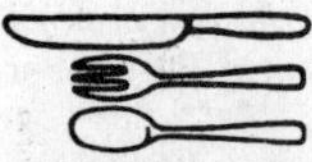

ST. THOMAS RESTAURANTS. It used to be almost impossible to find West Indian cooking in St. Thomas, but that's changed now, with such places as *Daddy's* near the lagoon marina offering a nice variety, and the *Fish Market* at Scott Beach down the road serving special seafood dishes *al fresco.* The selection of other restaurants runs from steak and lobster places to French, Mexican and Polynesian. In most places dining is casual but neat. Winter vacationers dress up more, especially at places like *Bluebeard's Castle, Frenchman's Reef* and *Harbor View.* Almost all hotels in our listing have restaurants, and when they are exceptional we have so noted. A few of them are featured again in our restaurant roster. We call $8 and below *Inexpensive,* $9–14 *Moderate,* and $15 and above *Expensive.*

Ancient Mariner at Coral World. Breakfast, lunch and dinner by candlelight (lobster is their specialty), just a few steps away from the underwater observatory. *Moderate.*

Cafe Normandie. On Rue de St. Bartholomew in Frenchtown, the ideal setting for this tiny, intimate Parisian restaurant. The candlelight adds to the elegance and the extensive menu does the rest. *Escargots,* Beluga caviar or oysters on the half-shell for starters; then a vast choice of entrées, with pheasant, squab, duckling and lobster the highlights. The home-baked cheese bread and the delectable desserts are memorable. Reservations are a must. *Expensive,* but well worth it.

Daddy's. Located at Red Hook out at the island's East End, this spot is very popular for its West Indian dishes. Try the local fish, which is simmered in a spicy Creole sauce, or Daddy's special seafood casserole. Lots more to choose from and to enjoy. *Moderate.*

Drake's Inn. Dark and air-conditioned spot, tucked into Drake's Passage in the heart of town. Lively and friendly place, especially at lunchtime. *Inexpensive.*

Drunken Shrimp. For a bit of the South Seas in the Caribbean. The decor is Polynesian and the menu follows suit. Located at the East End on a peaceful lagoon. Lots of sweet-and-sour dishes, all good, along with specialties from the grill. Piano bar every night except Sunday, when the whole place turns into a Polynesian luau. *Moderate.*

El Papagayo. All that's missing here are the mariachis to make music as the Mexican food is prepared. Great setting in a tropical garden at Estate Tutu, complete with garden bar and fountains. Endless decisions to make, but the special combination dinners *(enchilada, taco & chile relleno; chile colorado & stuffed quesadilla,* etc.) make it easier. Ideal for a quick lunch or a pleasant and unhurried dinner. *Moderate.*

Fisherman's Wharf. At Compass Point, near Red Hook, at the East End. A favorite place for dining on an anchored barge in the lagoon—it's as nautical as it should be, the food is as seaworthy as it should be, and the atmosphere is perfect for all. The smoked marlin appetizer is a great beginning; entrées include everything from red snapper to broiled lobster tails for the fish folk, and as an added attraction a "Texan barbecue" of ribs, steaks and sausage. *Expensive,* but worth it for food and ambience.

Harbor View. *The* place to live the good 19th-century Danish life when the planters reigned supreme. Restored and lovely, with elegant china and tableware and food to match. Cocktails on the gallery overlooking the harbor, dinner in the parlor, Irish coffee later on around the piano. Make this your special evening. *Expensive,* but you won't be disappointed. Reservations essential; jackets for men, long dresses for women the norm.

Kum Wah. Extensive Cantonese and Shanghai specialties nicely served here, in St. Thomas Gardens, next door to the Orchidarium. *Inexpensive.*

L'Escargot. Two choices here for authentic French food. The country-style restaurant is out at the Sub Base, the in-town version at Creque's Alley near the Royal Dane Mall. Extensive menu "out in the country"; fewer choices but just as good downtown. *Expensive.*

Lobster Pot. A great spot with a great view out on the north shore at the Magen's Point Hotel. Lobster is the feature, with salads at lunch and broiled one- and two+-pounders at dinner. Lots of other selections as well, along with entertainment most evenings. *Moderate* for lunch, *expensive* for dinner.

Mountain Top. Justly famous for its view down Drake's Passage toward the British Virgin Islands, for its banana daiquiris and more recently for its luncheon, which features a different West Indian specialty each day. A favorite spot for visiting cruise ship passengers. *Moderate.*

Parkside. Just a dozen or so tables in this old town house on Norre Gade, facing Roosevelt Park. Lunch and dinner served indoors or on the open-air porch. Excellent food and service, with French, Swiss, and West Indian fare the highlights. If you can't make it for lunch or dinner, stop by for their 4–6 P.M. Happy Hour. *Moderate.*

Sebastian's. Very popular spot on the waterfront serving breakfast, lunch, dinner and late-night snacks. Good seafood; thick and juicy hamburgers. *Inexpensive to Moderate.*

Sparky's Waterfront Saloon. Informal and fun anytime of day or night. Well-known for their *pina coladas* and their Sunday brunch. *Inexpensive.*

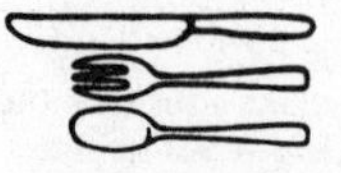

RESTAURANTS ON ST. JOHN. *Caneel Bay Plantation* is the only dress-up place, and they insist on reservations and proper decorum. Otherwise, dining out on St. John is as casual as the island is, but there are a few special spots that are good and inexpensive. Try *The Lobster Hut* for just that, as well as burgers and conch fritters; or *The Moveable Feast,* a deli-restaurant for eat-in or take-out.

At *Cinnamon Bay Camp,* the cafeteria is open until about 7 P.M.; there's a bar here, too, but the other places have more atmosphere.

ENTERTAINMENT. The entertainment varies here, but there is enough of it to run the gamut from steel and scratch bands to supper club shows. *Frenchman's Reef's* "Top of the Reef" has shows nightly; there is a disco at *Jelly's Seafood House;* guitar music at *The Lobster Pot;* and usually impromptu entertainment at *Sparky's Waterfront Saloon.* Bluebeard's Castle has music in its *Pirate's Parlour* and a piano player in its *Rogue's Galley* on the terrace below; the Virgin Isle Hotel has *Le Disco,* offering a light-and-sound show five nights a week.

The big hotels usually try to have some entertainment during season. Check the yellow sheet, *St. Thomas This Week,* while you're in town.

You can visit cruise ships when they are in port. Inquire at the Visitors' Bureau office on the waterfront in town, or go to the West India Company dock east of town just beyond Yacht Haven.

The winter season of St. Thomas winds up with a bang in the last week of April with a Carnival originally founded to celebrate the spring sugar harvest. The streets of Charlotte Amalie are a riot of color. Pennants, streamers, palm fronds flutter in the tropic breeze. The early days of Carnival are marked by the coronation of the Queen, surrounded by her ladies in waiting. There are boat races, calypso contests, and the opening of Carnival Village, with rows of decorated booths selling a whole gamut of home-cooked delicacies. The highlight of Carnival is the parade presided over by a character called Mocko Jumbi on 10-foot stilts.

BOAT HIRE AND CHARTER. For settler and tourist alike, one of the prime attractions of the Virgin Islands is the unrivaled opportunity for sailing and other water sports. Among the many large and small islands, one can cruise for days in a small boat under idyllic circumstances, seldom venturing into the open sea, enjoying beaches you can reach only by boat. Many of the islands and cays, unchanged since Columbus first saw them, are virgin in fact as well as name, and they beckon irresistibly to certain 20th century explorers. It is possible to charter various craft for cruising in St. Thomas, from a 100-ft. schooner on down. Most are sailboats; the emphasis here is *not* on power boats of which there are only a few for charter. For cruises of 4 days or more contact *Caribbean Discovery Charters* or *Virgin Island Water Safaris,* both based at the St. Thomas Hotel and Marina. For full information on the more than 200 crewed charter boats in the V.I., contact: *The Virgin Islands Charter-boat League,* St. Thomas, U.S. Virgin Islands 00801.

On St. Thomas, if it's day sailing you're interested in, try *The Watersports Center* at Sapphire Beach. For Sunfish and Sailfish, it's Lindbergh, Sapphire, Secret Harbour, Limetree or any of the hotel beaches. The *Ho-Tei,* 50-ft catamaran berthed at the Coast Guard Dock, goes out for group day sails at $20 per person.

ST. THOMAS SPORTS. *Swimming* at Carib Beach Hotel, Lindbergh Bay (public) and at Island Beachcomber, Coki Point, Limetree Hotel, Morningstar Beach, Magen's Bay, Sapphire Bay. Water Island on St. Thomas. St. John's beaches are lovely crescents of white powder sand rimming the bays; Caneel Bay Plantation has eight!

Scuba diving on St. Thomas. The Watersports Center at Sapphire Bay (tel. 775-0755) offers aqua-lung instruction, underwater guide service, and underwater photography instruction. One of the great attractions of the area for scuba divers and underwater photographers is exploring the wreckage of the British steam vessel *Rhône,* which sank 100 yards west of Salt Island 100 years ago in a hurricane. Scuba gear and instruction on St. Thomas are also offered by Joe Vogel. His office is "under" Sebastians on the waterfront. Aqua-Action at Lindberg Bay, Cowpet Bay and Secret Harbour. On St. John, the National Park Service rents snorkel gear at Cinnamon Bay.

Deep-sea, net, seine, line, spear-fishing, and even catching lobsters with a gloved hand. Equipment, boats at Yacht Haven, Charlotte Amalie, or American Yacht Harbor at Red Hook for fishing arrangements. Incidentally, an 845-lb. blue marlin caught in V.I. waters in July 1968 broke the IGFA world records. For the most up-to-date information on all the foregoing for the U.S. islands, consult the Office of Fishing and Water Sports, Dept. of Commerce, St. Thomas.

Golf has finally come to St. Thomas with a new 18-hole championship course at Mahogany Run. Tee off here in an ideal setting, which is part of a 315-acre golf and tennis condominium complex.

Tennis is coming into its own as well, with courts at almost all the major hotels, many of them lighted for nightplay.

SPORTS AND OTHER ACTIVITIES ON ST. JOHN. The St. John Safari, for $30 from your St. Thomas hotel to and around St. John and back to your hotel, is the quick-and-easy way to cover St. John. Sports revolve around the water and the National Park. *Scuba trips* depart twice daily from Cruz Bay dock. 10 A.M. and 2 P.M. All equipment is provided; instruction from professional instructors. *Snorkeling, wreck diving,* and *underwater photography.* Spear fishing is forbidden in the National Park area. For *sailing,* visit *Trade Winds Charters,* near Islandia across from the National Park offices. The day rates for sail-yourself charters are very reasonable.

For *National Park Tours,* contact the Park Service Ranger at the main building in Cruz Bay. It's at the dock; you can't miss it—and shouldn't miss a tour with a qualified guide. Then you can wander on your own.

ST. THOMAS SHOPPING. Bring all your keen shopping experience to the fore to spot the bargains. Liquor is one, foreign designer fashions, exotic and rare imports are others. Remember that U.S. residents may take back $600 worth of purchases duty free. These purchases may be carried home with you or declared and shipped ahead. In addition, you may mail home each day a "gift under $40" to any friend or relative, as long as neither one is sent more than one gift per day.

Once again, we refer you to *Here's How* and *This Week in St. Thomas* for suggestions, but here are some of our favorite shops.

The *Continental,* at the town square near the Fort and away from the hubbub, but just by a few steps, has *everything.* Quality merchandise: men's and women's clothing including cashmeres, Liberty prints, LaCoste, Blyle, French sport imports, etc. Also crystal, china, Danish silver and porcelain, Scandinavian housewares, and fabric by the yard.

A. H. Riise, in spectacularly restored private warehouses, with old bricks sandblasted to warm hues, has a variety of counter-boutiques in its gift shops, and endless lines of interesting bottles in its liquor store a few doors down Main Street, as Dronningen's Gade is now called. At the gift shop counters, you'll find perfumes and cosmetics, sweaters and blouses, neckties and some menswear; watches, jewelry, china and crystal—in fact, a little bit of everything, most of it high quality merchandise. Be sure to saunter to the back and up a few steps to the Art Gallery where local artists are often featured.

Boutique Riviera sells terrific designer fashions, Louis Vuitton luggage and quality name jewelry. They're located in town and have a small branch at Frenchman's Reef Hotel.

Tropicana Perfume Shoppes is so vast that there are three stores on Main St. Best buys are on the French imports, although they have a full line of fragrances from Estee Lauder, Elizabeth Arden and Revlon.

For watches, check *Boolchand's, Accuracy, Inc.* and *Sparky's;* for interestingly-displayed island-made items, browse through the new shopping area on Mountain Top.

Courreges and *Gucci* have their own boutiques in town, with each offering a nice variety at good prices. One of the largest selections of dinnerware, such as Limoge, Spode, Royal Worcester, etc., can be found at *The English Shop.*

Even if you don't buy, enjoy the glitter of the finest jewelry at *Cardow; Colombian Emeralds; H. Stern;* or at *Irmela's Jewel Studio.* Irmela Neumann not only sells gold and precious stones from her small shop in Drake's Passage, but will design jewelry to your liking as well.

Little Switzerland, one of the first of the luxury stores (cameras, jewelry, watches, gift items, crystal, china) where success resulted in boutique after boutique along the Main Street. All shops were consolidated into one splendiferous emporium, at No. 5 Dronningen Gade (as Main Street is officially called.) The camera and hi-fi store is still No. 1.

St. Croix

HOW TO GET THERE. *By Air. American* flies to St. Croix, from New York, with connecting service to St. Thomas while work on that airstrip prevents big plane landings. *Eastern* flies in from Miami twice a day. *Virgin Islands Seaplane Shuttle* flies "constantly" between St. Thomas and St. Croix.

Prinair makes the 45-minute flight from San Juan several times daily, as do *Aero Virgin Islands, Coral Air* and *Oceanair.*

From Europe, flights reaching Antigua or Puerto Rico allow for connections to St. Croix.

By sea: Frederiksted, the smaller of the two towns on St. Croix, has a deepwater pier that is touched by some of the short cruises out of San Juan and Miami. Although the same customs exemption applies for St. Croix ($600 duty free for U.S. citizens) and there are many excellent shops, this island has never been able to draw the cruise ships the way St. Thomas has.

For AUTHORIZED TOUR OPERATORS; FURTHER INFORMATION; EVENTS AND HOLIDAYS; WHAT WILL IT COST; and TAXES AND OTHER CHARGES, see listings under St. Thomas and St. John.

HOW TO GET ABOUT. Remember to drive on the left if you rent a car (which is the best way to get around). *Olympic, Hertz, Avis* and *Budget* are the car rental leaders. Airport pick-up and delivery is no problem, with prior notification of your flight.

Taxi rates are posted on a panel near your luggage pick-up at the airport. Look before you leap into a cab, and be sure of the fare. Rates are usually per person, even if you are a family of four. It's advisable to negotiate with a cab driver if you are going to want island tours and a lot of transportation. These days, he'll probably give you a good rate.

Buses do travel main routes on the island, the 17 miles between Christiansted and Frederiksted and the 22-mile length of the island. Rates are inexpensive; stops are frequent.

To reach Buck Island, nonsailors prefer the *Reef Queen,* with a glass panel that permits seeing the marine gardens without leaving the boat. Swimmers can dive off and snorkel with guide. Rate for a full day (bring a picnic; drinks can be purchased aboard) is $25. The *Queen* leaves from the Fort in Christiansted. Sailors can charter a boat for the day. Sloops, catamarans, etc., take 6 passengers. Departures from town, from Buccaneer Hotel and from Grapetree Beach. The yacht costs $25 per person for a full day.

PASSPORTS, VISAS. None for U.S. citizens. Same as for U.S. mainland for all others.

MONEY. U.S. currency. $1.85 = 1£.

HOTELS ON ST. CROIX. The general statements on island hotels, made at the beginning of the section referring to St. Thomas, apply to St. Croix as well.

Anchor Inn. 30 air-conditioned rooms in a space you would not believe could hold even 10. The rooms are attractive, if short on sunlight, and right in the middle of town, overlooking the harbor, with balconies in most rooms. Small pool, restaurant concession on the premises (and plenty of places to eat within walking distance). $75–82 double EP in winter; $60 double EP off-season.

Arawak Cottages are on the grounds of Sprat Hall, north of Frederiksted, in a secluded, grassy setting. There are 1-bedroom duplex housekeeping units, some with air-conditioning, and 2-bedroom cottages that are fine and reasonable for families. All are brightly furnished in rattan, have louvered porches ideal for lounging. Swimming just down the road at Arawak Beach; scuba diving excursions and horseback riding available. $95–110 double EP in winter; $70 double EP off-season.

Buccaneer Hotel. St. Croix's top resort. On a grand tropical setting, with hilltop, hillside and beach-front rooms. All 146 of them are neatly arranged and spread out in mini-complexes to avoid making the property seem overpowering. 18-hole golf course; several excellent tennis courts; 3 restaurants; all watersports; and a long and lovely powdery white-sand beach. This was formerly the enclave of the Knights of Malta in 1653, and, although they have long since given up their island rule, the royal treatment you'll receive still fits. $110–180 double EP in winter; $70–100 double off-season.

Cane Bay Plantation offers 16 apartments with balconies overlooking the beach, plus 5 completely furnished housekeeping cottages with private baths on the north shore drive between Christiansted and Frederiksted about 40 minutes' drive from each. Beach, pool, 2 restaurants. Excellent view of Bay, Ham's Bluffs. The cottages (actually they are old slave quarters, charmingly restored) are set in a 26-acre estate. Informal island-style place not too far from Fountain Valley Golf Course. You'll want a rental car to get anywhere. The brunches and some of the other specialty meals have become a Cruzan tradition. Reservations for meals, if you're not staying here, are essential. $135–170 double in winter; breakfast and dinner included; lower rates, off-season.

Carvavelle Hotel. On the waterfront in Christiansted, 46 air-conditioned rooms with bath and dressing room, most overlooking the harbor. Nice location; small swimming pool; excellent restaurant called *The Binnacle* on premises for indoor and outdoor dining. Rates run $66–84 EP in winter, $53–69 EP off-season.

Club Comanche. A long-time favorite with its share of atmosphere. One of the first hotels on the island, it's grown, expanded, burned, and been rebuilt. Some great antiques in the "old" building. The 42-room hotel appeals to repeaters, commercial visitors, and those who have friends in the islands and want to be in the heart of the boating life of Christiansted. The old-timers gather at Dick Boehm's excellent *Comanche* restaurant on premises. Water sports, sailing excursions, and offbeat entertainment readily available. No beach. Pool. Two steps from all the shops. Rates run $50–70 double, breakfast included.

Frederiksted Hotel. 38 pleasant efficiency rooms, each with two double beds and balconies, surrounding a large swimming pool. Close to the waterfront in Frederiksted, with complimentary transportation to a beach nearby. Local entertainment some evenings; breakfast served on poolside patio. Rates run about $56–82 double EP in winter; $38–43 double off-season.

Gentle Winds Beach Villas. 50 beautifully decorated one-, two- and three-bedroom suites in condominium units that spiral down to a long private beach. All have fully-equipped kitchens, maid service, lanai and terrace. Swimming pool and tennis courts add to their plan to make this property a do-it-yourself resort unto itself. $220–280 EP in winter; $120–160 EP off-season.

Grapetree Beach Hotel. Almost secluded, at the "East End" of the island, the aim is to offer enough to avoid your going back and forth to Christiansted, 10 miles away. Boutiques, large pool and two restaurants, all a few steps from this broad beach. All watersports, in addition to sailboats that head out for half- and full-day sails to Buck Island across the way. $100–160 double EP in winter; $75–90 double EP off-season.

Holger Danske. Right in the heart of town, not too far from the seaplane ramp, 3 stories of 44 efficiency units, small and hermetically sealed to the Caribbean view. Most popular with young-at-heart who want reasonable-to-low prices and aren't demanding of a lot of fancy service. Convenient to shops and other restaurants. Small pool. $74–82 double EP in winter, $55–65 off-season.

Hotel on the Cay. 55 air-conditioned rooms in a modern stucco building which sits on its own island in Christiansted harbor. Hilltop restaurant, beach snack bar. Beach barbeques and entertainment on special nights each week. New all-weather tennis courts; Olympic-size pool. Just a few minutes to town by small boat, which is "on-the-run" constantly from early morning until midnight. $139–149 double EP in winter; $67–84 double EP off-season.

King Christian Hotel. 40 air-conditioned rooms with private bath and balcony, in a completely rebuilt and redecorated old Danish building on the waterfront. Small swimming pool, sun deck. Shops nearby. *Chart House Restaurant* has adjoined lounge, with indoor and outdoor dining on the waterfront and nightly entertainment. All balconies overlook the harbor. $45–84 double EP in winter; $35–55 double EP off-season.

King Frederik. 11 air-conditioned units, each with kitchen facilities, tastefully furnished and sedate, on a small but beautiful beach near Frederiksted, at opposite end of island from livelier Christiansted. Some rooms have private galleries overlooking tropical gardens. Pool, bar, patio. $36–64 double EP in winter; $29–48 off-season.

King's Alley Hotel. A modern hotel right at the water's edge in Christiansted with a view of the harbor and Hotel on the Cay. All 22 rooms are air-conditioned, nicely furnished, and have baths and sliding glass doors opening on private balconies. In a tropical garden. Continental breakfast and drinks on terrace. Swimming pool; evening entertainment poolside; several fine restaurants nearby. $60–80 double EP in the winter; $45–55 double EP off-season.

The Lodge. 17 simple rooms wih private bath on Queen Cross St. in the heart of Christiansted. Casual and comfortable. Swimming pool privileges at the nearby Caravelle Hotel. $55–60 double in winter; $45–52 double off-season, including Continental breakfast.

Mill Harbour is a condominium-hotel on a good white sand beach 5 minutes' drive out of Christiansted. There's a choice of good-looking tropical or Spanish decor in the fully-equipped 2- and 3-bedroom apartments, a fresh-water swimming pool, tennis, poolside bar for lunch, drinks. Maid service. A 2-bedroom apartment in winter runs $170–195 daily for 4. Rates, when divided per person, are *moderate,* and this condominium concept is better than many we've seen.

Queen's Quarter Hotel. Small, comfortable and private place on a bluff in the center of St. Croix's hills. Their 50 rooms, in studios, villas and suites, all have kitchen facilities and maid service. Lovely setting within their acres of blazing tropical foliage. Tennis courts, pool and outstanding *Queen's Court* restaurant. From $110 double EP in winter; from $65 double EP off-season, depending upon accommodations.

Tamarind Reef Hotel. 16 one- and two-bedroom suites on the beach on the island's north shore. As private as you'd like it to be, since there is no restaurant here, but there are kitchenettes in each suite. Large saltwater swimming pool and sun deck; all watersports available on the beach. Ideal for families. $75–110 double EP in winter; $58–78 double off-season.

Waves at Cane Bay. Ten nice efficiencies here, which are large and offer separate kitchens. Not air-conditioned, but ceiling fans and the Trade Winds are guaranteed to cool you. Seaside pool. Convenient to Fountain Valley Golf Course; arrangements for snorkeling and scuba diving at Cane Bay Beach. $60 double EP in winter; $35 double EP off-season.

HOME RENTALS: There are dozens of beautiful homes available for rental all over the island throughout the year. Most have private swimming pools and/or beach facilities; all are fully-equipped and many offer maid service as well. Those who have discovered how ideal these properties are for families book well in advance. Write well ahead of time to any of the following: *American Rentals,* Hamilton Mews, Christiansted, St. Croix, U.S. Virgin Islands 00820; *Elaine Bidelspacher Rentals,* Grapetree Bay, Star Route, St. Croix, U.S.V.I. 00864; *Cram St. Croix Rentals,* c/o 725 Stone House Road, Moorestown, New Jersey 08057; or *Caribbean Home Rentals,* P.O. Box 710, Palm Beach, Fla. 33480.

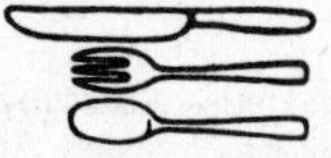

ST. CROIX RESTAURANTS. You can't go wrong on this island, with more than 40 restaurants serving up everything from asapao to zucchini. Make it your own international gourmet safari and find menus and prices to suit every palate and budget. We surely can't list them all, but our special favorites follow.

We call $8 and below *Inexpensive,* $9–14 *Moderatae,* and $15 and above *Expensive.*

In Christiansted

The Binnacle. Waterside dining, either indoors or on the patio at the Caravelle Hotel. House specialties include saltimbocca, done to a proper Italian turn, and shrimp tempura, as delicately done as it is in Japan. Stay on later and enjoy festivities at their piano bar. *Moderate.*

Captain Weekes Ten Grand. For the best West Indian fare, such as kallalou, johnnycakes and goat stew, served generously in a humble setting adjacent to Fort Christianvaern. *Inexpensive.*

Chart House. On the corner of King's Wharf, where all the sailboats anchor, and appropriately designed in a nautical theme. Their salad bar seems endless, and their entrees, such as beef kabob and Alaskan King crab are delectable. *Expensive,* but also included, in addition to as many turn-arounds of salad as you'd like, is an appetizer and a choice of baked potato or rice.

Comanche Restaurant. Dick Boehm's place here in King's Alley has been a tried and true favorite of ours for years. With fans spinning overhead, a huge outrigger canoe suspended from the ceiling, and oversized fan chairs commanding the tables, you know you're in the tropics. Their curries are superb, and their fresh-caught fish topped with Creole sauce delectable. *Expensive.*

Donn's Anchor Inn. Open-air dining on a terrace overlooking the water. Famous for their Sunday brunch, which ranges from an avocado and bacon omelette to buttermilk pancakes done in beer, with all of it accompanied by sparkling champagne. *Moderate* prices for all meals.

Eccentric Egret. On King Street, in the heart of town, this restaurant takes its name from the snowy egret which can be found skimming the surf or strutting the island's shore. Dining in one of two rooms, both on the second floor of a restored building. Their salad Jordan is a master Caear, with such added treats as artichoke hearts, tomatoes and olives; and their house specialty, asapao aurora, is a delicious dish of fresh shrimp or lobster served with two kinds of rice, sliced pimento and a secret hot sauce. *Moderate.*

Frank's. An Italian feast here anytime—either inside in a small dining room or outdoors in the cobblestone courtyard. Extensive menu, with veal piccata with capers one of the specialties. *Moderate.*

Front Porch. In King's Alley on the second floor of the Comanche Hotel, this spot is justly famous for its breakfast menu, which is served daily. Omelettes galore, fresh papaya and all the accoutrements you can dream up. *Inexpensive.*

Golden China Inn. Authentic Chinese cuisine, featuring Szechuan, Mandarin, Cantonese and Hunan specialties. Sift and sort, sample Chinese wine and enjoy the Oriental music in the background. *Inexpensive.*

Reef Restaurant. Although it has changed hands many times, this place keeps coming back to please diners who choose good food served nicely in an open-air, on-the-beach setting on the island's East End. *Moderate.*

1742 Great House. One of the old St. Croix homes which has been renovated in the famous Apothecary Hall on Company Street. Terrace dining on its second-floor balcony, with the emphasis on fine French cuisine. Dinner only. *Expensive.*

Tivoli Gardens. Nice layout in a garden setting atop the Pan Am Pavilion. A potpourri of dining areas, along with its menu, and all of it backed by live music, which, depending upon where you're seated, can be loud. *Expensive.*

Top Hat. The only place to go for authentic Danish fare. It's run by Danish-born Hanne and Bent Rasmussen, a terrific couple who are always on hand and always aim to please. Their house specialty is frikadeller, which is served with tangy red cabbage, but their menu is not restricted to Scandinavian dishes. Among other terrific entrees are steak tartar, wiener schnitzel and roast duckling in orange sauce. After any or all of this, try to save room for Hanne's special creation: fried Camembert cheese served with a strawberry jam topping. *Expensive.*

In Frederiksted

Barbara McConnell's. Off the main stream here, but long a St. Croix institution. Her restaurant is located in a restored home that was the Anglican Vicarage in 1760. Imaginative lunches and dinner prepared by reservation only. *Expensive,* but worth it.

Swashbuckler. Pleasant and attractive spot at the end of Strand Street. They specialize in steaks, but also offer seafood and Cruzan cuisine. *Moderate.*

ENTERTAINMENT. A great deal of the night life in St. Croix is at the hotels, most of which have music, dancing, and entertainment. In Frederiksted there's dancing to steel band music, most nights, at the *Seven Flags,* also local. On St. Croix the Fesitval is at Christmastime, with three weeks of dances, parades, crowning of queens, princes and princesses, calypso shows, and music from steel bands.

In Christiansted, it's the *Moonraker Lounge* on the second floor of the Lodge Hotel on Queen Cross Street, or *The Grandstand Play.*

Certain folklore specialties of the Virgin Islands are featured at this time. Watch for Africanized quadrilles and Irish jigs, relics of plantation days, danced with tap drum and flute accompaniment. Ask at your hotel about events for visitors. We *do not* recommend walking around the Islanders' Carnival Village.

On Peppertree Hill, almost in the middle of St. Croix, is the Island Center, a cultural complex built as a result of tireless efforts on the part of many new island residents. Check with your hotel to see what plays, musicals, or other performances are taking place during your visit to St. Croix. Previous seasons have featured well-known performers from the United States and from neighboring islands as well as Virgin Islands professional groups.

EXCURSIONS FROM ST. CROIX. One off-shore aspect of St. Croix which should not be missed is Buck Island National Monument. Plan to devote a full day to this adventure, with a leisurely morning sail (cold beer provided on board, but better ask your hotel to pack a picnic lunch). Buck Island itself has a glorious border of beach, but its principal attraction is the underwater snorkeling trail. Swimmers are able to follow a sequence of labels that identify the different types of coral, underwater growth, and brightly hued tropical fish.

A late-afternoon sail back to Christiansted Harbor completes the day. See Sports, below, about chartering one of the many boats available for this short haul. Fare includes snorkel gear, instruction, and a guided underwater tour for swimmers; nonswimmers are invited to see the sights from a glass-bottom boat.

SHOPPING ON ST. CROIX. Just as much of a duty-free selection on this island as on St. Thomas, although not as many shops.

Many of St. Thomas' leading shops have branches: *Continental, Little Switzerland, Bolero, Compass Rose,* and *Patelli.* The latter is in King's Alley, where there is also: *The Gold Shop;* the *Cage of Gold;* the *Perfume Bar; Mahoney Place* for tropical fashions; and *Land of Oz,* with unusual adult games, puzzles and toys.

Longest of the Christiansted arcades is in the Caravelle Hotel, where you'll find *Betsy Cantrell's,* children's wear by Merry Mites; and *Violette Boutique,* sportswear, accessories, jewelry by Europe's leading designers. *Island Imports* represent *Maison Danoise* with their fine line of china, glass, and silver and in addition have a fine stock of English leather goods, framed old prints and maps, straw hats and bags, and unique shadow-boxes made in St. Croix.

At the Pan Am Pavilion is *Quick Pics* for stereo and camera equipment; *The Jewelry Store; Many Hands,* fine arts and handicrafts exclusively from the V.I., and *The Spanish Main,* silk-screen originals by Jim Tillett.

Copenhagen, Ltd. has everything in the decorative arts from Scandinavia, including Bing and Grondahl Xmas plates, and Arabia dinnerware. Boda and Kosta glass, plus pewter from Holland, straw rugs from Dominica, perfumes from France, cigars from Jamaica, mahogany crafts from Haiti.

Java Wraps features Balinesian fashions; fine gold, crystal and china at *Heritage House; Sonya's Corner Shop* has beautifully hand-designed gold and silver jewelry.

There are many liquor merchants—*Comanche Liquor Locker, Grog & Spirits, Tradewinds, The Conch Shell,* and *Carib Cellars.* All will pack your 5 duty-free bottles in a safe carrying carton. At Carib Cellars you can sample Cruzan liqueurs brewed from coconuts, bananas, pineapple, almonds, roses, and hibiscus!

Danish furniture is also available at the *Continental.* They'll take your order and have it delivered to the States from Denmark.

Other shops worth looking into are *The Linen Cupboard* for Madeira work, Saba drawnthread; *The Wadsworth Boutique,* on the waterfront, for straw bags, charms, fanciful jewelry, including a gold lizard pin, scarves, and other accessories.

Nini of Scandinavia has fabrics by the yard from Sweden and fashions (including the Finnish Marimekko dresses), wooden shoes, jewelry from Denmark.

At *Whim Greathouse* there's a small shop selling locally made jewelry, notepaper, jams, soaps, perfumes, etc. They'll make a Planter's Chair to order.

The *Royal Frederik,* in Frederiksted, has Ballantyne cashmeres, beaded bags and sweaters from the Continent and Hong Kong. Royal Delft china (exclusive here). *A. H. Riise's* gift shop has a branch here, too. *Raine's,* in nearby Victoria House, has a fine selection of designer sports clothes for men and women. *Island Stuff* sells hand-screened Caribbean prints and Indonesian batiks. *Gerdian's,* at #1 Strand St. on the waterfront, has watches, gold jewelry, china and crystal.

At *Fletcher Pence's* studio in the hills above Frederiksted you can purchase the artist's handsome wood sculptures.

SPORTS ON ST. CROIX. On St. Croix, there are public tennis courts in Christiansted and courts at the Buccaneer, Gentle Winds, Grapetree Beach, and Queen's Quarter hotels, and at Hotel on the Cay, just a few minutes' water ride from King's Wharf. Additionally, the Caribbean Tennis Club, close to Christiansted, has 12 courts (7 lighted for night-play) and a Pro Shop, which are open to visitors.

For *golf,* 18-hole course at Fountain Valley, St. Croix, is a championship one designed by Robert Trent Jones, created by Rockefeller. It has a pro shop, restaurant, showers and lockers, etc., and is open to the public. Buccaneer Hotel has 18 holes, pro shop, golf carts on its seaside acreage. There is also a 9-hole course at The Reef.

Watersports are really the highlight here on St. Croix. There's terrific *snorkeling* along its seven-mile reef on the south shore; its marine gardens and underwater trail to the northeast. Should you not arrive with your own mask and fins, you can rent them through most of the major hotels or at any of the island's watersports centers. A few to consider are: *Caribbean Sea Adventures,* which also specializes in *scuba diving* safaris and *sportfishing* trips. Contact *Sun Sails* for daily and sunset excursions under sail—both are headquartered on King's Wharf in Christiansted. *The Dive Shop,* which has its office aboard a houseboat in Christiansted harbor, offers rental of scuba gear and underwater photography equipment, as well as special dive charters. In Frederiksted, *West End Boating,* next to the La Grange Beach and Tennis Club, can arrange scenic cruises and sailboat rentals.

The ultimate enjoyment on this island, as we've said previously, is the marked underwater trail at Buck Island. Don't miss it!

INDEX

INDEX

GENERAL

(See also Practical Information sections in chapters for individual islands.)

GEOGRAPHICAL

(The letters H and R indicate hotel and restaurant listings.)

ANGUILLA

ANTIGUA

ARUBA

BAHAMA ISLANDS

BARBADOS

BONAIRE

BRITISH VIRGIN ISLANDS

CAYMAN ISLANDS

CURACAO

DOMINICA

DOMINICAN REPUBLIC

GRENADA

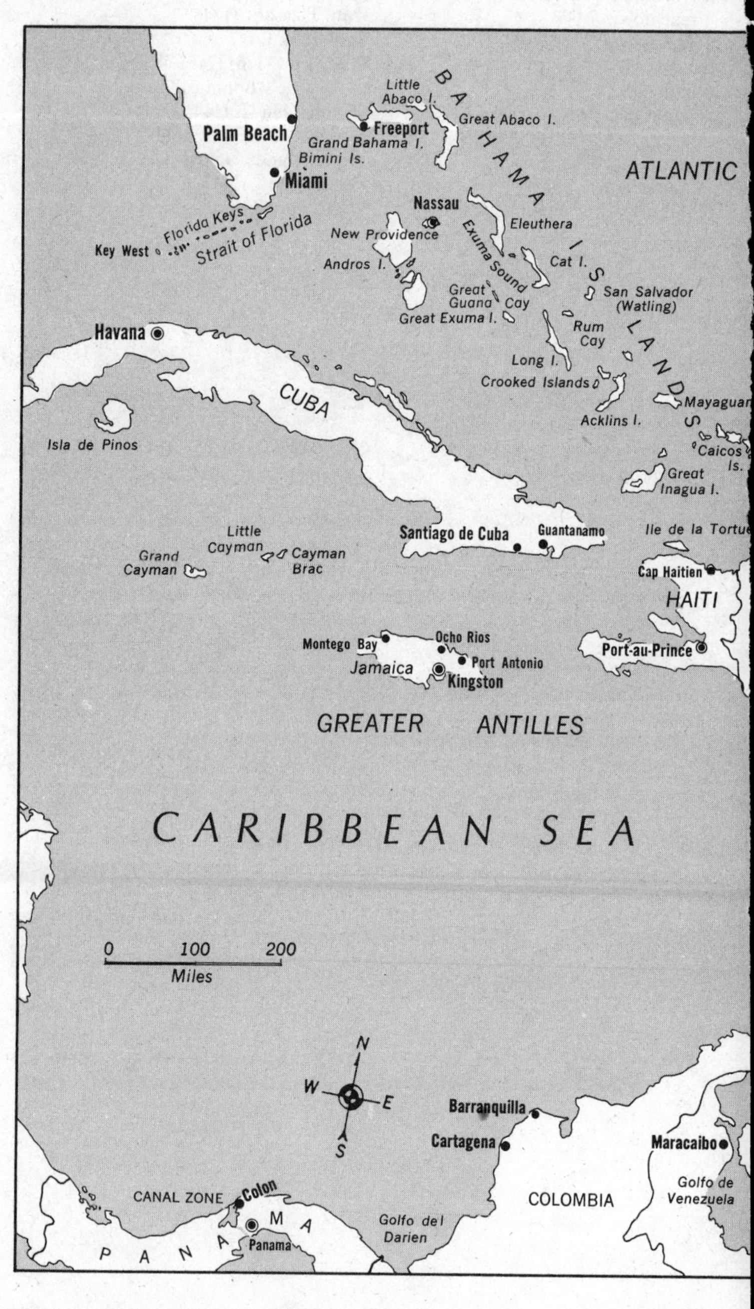

Palm Beach
Miami
Key West
Florida Keys
Strait of Florida
Little Abaco I.
Freeport
Grand Bahama I.
Bimini Is.
Great Abaco I.
BAHAMA ISLANDS
ATLANTIC
Nassau
New Providence
Andros I.
Exuma Sound
Eleuthera
Cat I.
Great Guana Cay
Great Exuma I.
San Salvador (Watling)
Rum Cay
Long I.
Crooked Islands
Acklins I.
Mayaguan
Caicos Is.
Great Inagua I.
Havana
CUBA
Isla de Pinos
Santiago de Cuba
Guantanamo
Ile de la Tortue
Little Cayman
Cayman Brac
Grand Cayman
Cap Haitien
HAITI
Port-au-Prince
Montego Bay
Ocho Rios
Port Antonio
Jamaica
Kingston
GREATER ANTILLES
CARIBBEAN SEA
0 100 200
Miles
N
W
E
S
Barranquilla
Cartagena
Maracaibo
Golfo de Venezuela
COLOMBIA
CANAL ZONE
Colon
Panama
PANAMA
Golfo del Darien

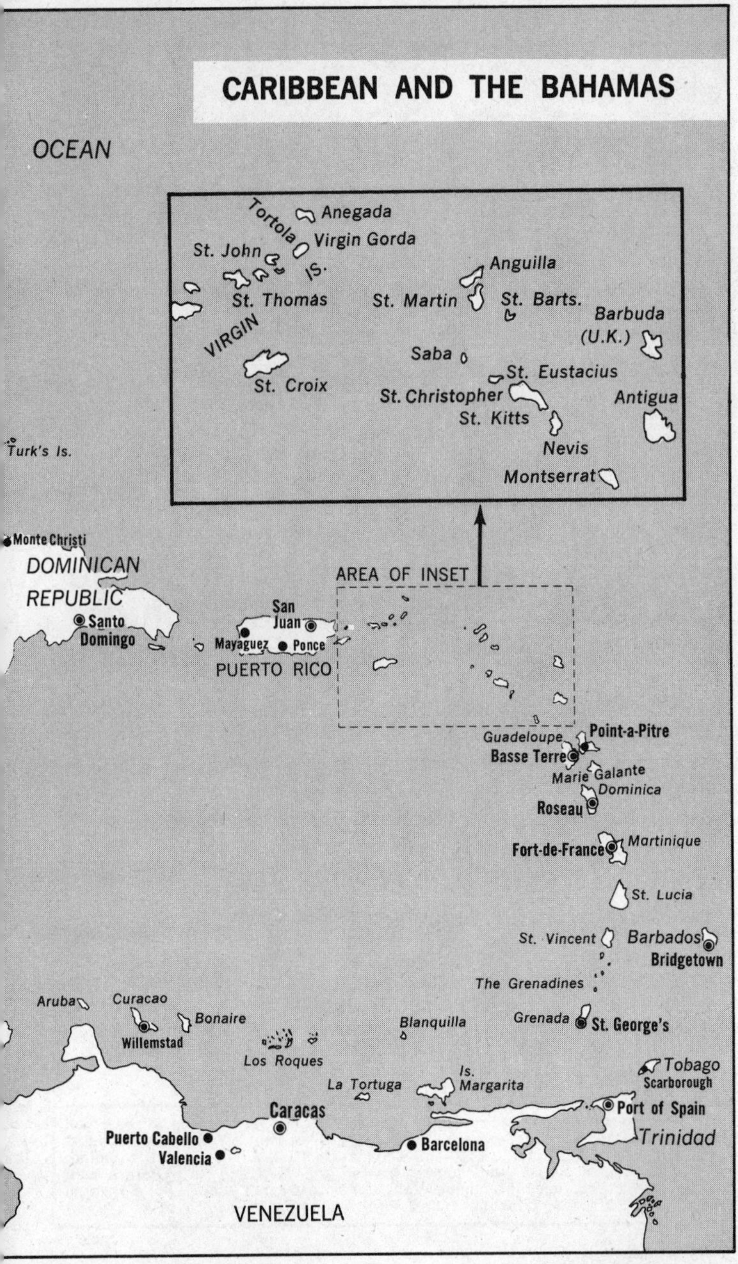

CARIBBEAN AND THE BAHAMAS
OCEAN
Tortola
Anegada
Virgin Gorda
St. John
VIRGIN IS.
St. Thomas
St. Croix
St. Martin
Anguilla
St. Barts.
Barbuda (U.K.)
Saba
St. Eustacius
St. Christopher
St. Kitts
Antigua
Nevis
Montserrat
Turk's Is.
Monte Christi
DOMINICAN REPUBLIC
Santo Domingo
San Juan
Mayaguez
Ponce
PUERTO RICO
AREA OF INSET
Guadeloupe
Point-a-Pitre
Basse Terre
Marie Galante
Dominica
Roseau
Fort-de-France
Martinique
St. Lucia
St. Vincent
Barbados
Bridgetown
The Grenadines
Grenada
St. George's
Aruba
Curacao
Willemstad
Bonaire
Los Roques
Blanquilla
La Tortuga
Is. Margarita
Tobago
Scarborough
Caracas
Port of Spain
Trinidad
Puerto Cabello
Valencia
Barcelona
VENEZUELA